Dewey Decimal Classification and Relative Index

Dewey Decimal Classification and Relative Index

Devised by Melvil Dewey

EDITION 20

Edited by

John P. Comaromi, Editor

Julianne Beall, Assistant Editor

Winton E. Matthews, Jr., Assistant Editor

Gregory R. New, Assistant Editor

VOLUME 2

Schedules 000–599

FOREST PRESS

A Division of
OCLC Online Computer Library Center, Inc.
ALBANY, NEW YORK
1989

Library of Congress Cataloging-in-Publication Data
Dewey, Melvil, 1851-1931.
Dewey decimal classification and relative index / devised by Melvil Dewey. -- Ed. 20 / edited by John P. Comaromi, Julianne Beall, Winton E. Matthews, Jr., Gregory R. New.
Contents: v. 1. Introduction. Tables -- v. 2-3. Schedules -- v.4. Relative index. Manual.
1. Classification, Dewey decimal. I. Comaromi, John P. (John Phillip), 1937- . II. Beall, Julianne, 1946- . III. Matthews, Winton E. IV. New, Gregory R. V. Forest Press. VI. Title.
Z696.D519 1989   025.4'31--dc19   88-24629

The paper used in this publication meets the minimum requirements of American National Standard for Information Science - Permanence of Paper for Printed Library Materials. ANSI Z39.48-1984.

ISBN: (set) 0-910608-37-7; v. 1 0-910608-38-5; v. 2 0-910608-39-3;
v. 3 0-910608-40-7; v. 4 0-910608-41-5

Contents

Volume 1

Publisher's Foreword — xi

Preface by the Decimal Classification Editorial Policy Committee — xiii

Acknowledgments — xvii

New Features in Edition 20 — xix

Introduction to the Dewey Decimal Classification — xxv

  About the Introduction — xxv

  Classification: What It Is and What It Does — xxv

  History and Current Use of the Dewey Decimal Classification — xxvi

  Overview of the Dewey Decimal Classification — xxvi

    Conceptual Framework — xxvi

    Notation — xxvii

    Principle of Hierarchy — xxviii

  Classifying with the DDC — xxix

    Determining the Subject of a Work — xxix

    Determining the Discipline for a Work — xxx

    More Than One Subject — xxxi

    More Than One Discipline — xxxi

    When All Else Fails — xxxii

  How DDC 20 Is Arranged — xxxiii

  Key Features of the Schedules and Tables — xxxiii

    Summaries — xxxiii

    Entries — xxxiv

    Notes — xxxv

  Number Building — xl

  Number Building: Citation and Precedence Order — xliii

    Citation Order — xliii

    Precedence Order — xliii

  The Relative Index — xliv

    How to Use the Relative Index — xlv

    Format and Arrangement of the Relative Index — xlv

    Order in Which Numbers Are Displayed — xlvi

    Interdisciplinary Numbers — xlvi

    Terms Included in the Relative Index — xlvii

    Terms Not Included in the Relative Index — xlviii

Options   xlviii

Close and Broad Classification   xlix

Book Numbers   xlix

Selected Bibliography   l

Glossary   li

Index to the Introduction and Glossary   lix

Publishing History of the Dewey Decimal Classification   lxi

Tables   1

    Use of the Tables   2

    Table 1. Standard Subdivisions   3

    Table 2. Geographic Areas, Historical Periods, Persons   25

    Table 3. Subdivisions for Individual Literatures,

       for Specific Literary Forms   389

       Table 3-A. Subdivisions for Works by or about Individual Authors   389

       Table 3-B. Subdivisions for Works by or about More than One Author   394

       Table 3-C. Notation to Be Added Where Instructed in Table 3-B

         and in 808-809   409

    Table 4. Subdivisions of Individual Languages   415

    Table 5. Racial, Ethnic, National Groups   421

    Table 6. Languages   438

    Table 7. Groups of Persons   457

Relocations and Reductions   479

Comparative Tables   496

    Music   496

    British Columbia   505

Equivalence Tables   506

    Music   506

    British Columbia   514

Contents

Volume 2

Summaries	ix
Schedules	1
Use of the Schedules	2
000 Generalities	3
100 Philosophy, parapsychology and occultism, psychology	77
200 Religion	127
300 Social Sciences	237
400 Language	692
500 Natural sciences and mathematics	718

Volume 3

Schedules	1
Use of the Schedules	2
600 Technology (Applied sciences)	3
700 The arts Fine and decorative arts	446
800 Literature (Belles-lettres) and rhetoric	643
900 Geography, history, and auxiliary disciplines	693

Volume 4

Relative Index	1
Use of the Relative Index	2
Abbreviations Used in the Index	3
A-Z	5
Manual	731
Use of the Manual	732
Notes on Table Numbers	733
Notes on Schedule Numbers	791
Appendix: Policies and Procedures of the Library of Congress Decimal Classification Division	959

Summaries

First Summary*
The Ten Main Classes

000	**Generalities**
100	**Philosophy & psychology**
200	**Religion**
300	**Social sciences**
400	**Language**
500	**Natural sciences & mathematics**
600	**Technology (Applied sciences)**
700	**The arts**
800	**Literature & rhetoric**
900	**Geography & history**

*Consult schedules for complete and exact headings

Second Summary*
The Hundred Divisions

000 Generalities
010 Bibliography
020 Library & information sciences
030 General encyclopedic works
040
050 General serials & their indexes
060 General organizations & museology
070 News media, journalism, publishing
080 General collections
090 Manuscripts & rare books

100 Philosophy & psychology
110 Metaphysics
120 Epistemology, causation, humankind
130 Paranormal phenomena
140 Specific philosophical schools
150 Psychology
160 Logic
170 Ethics (Moral philosophy)
180 Ancient, medieval, Oriental philosophy
190 Modern Western philosophy

200 Religion
210 Natural theology
220 Bible
230 Christian theology
240 Christian moral & devotional theology
250 Christian orders & local church
260 Christian social theology
270 Christian church history
280 Christian denominations & sects
290 Other & comparative religions

300 Social sciences
310 General statistics
320 Political science
330 Economics
340 Law
350 Public administration
360 Social services; association
370 Education
380 Commerce, communications, transport
390 Customs, etiquette, folklore

400 Language
410 Linguistics
420 English & Old English
430 Germanic languages   German
440 Romance languages   French
450 Italian, Romanian, Rhaeto-Romanic
460 Spanish & Portuguese languages
470 Italic languages   Latin
480 Hellenic languages   Classical Greek
490 Other languages

500 Natural sciences & mathematics
510 Mathematics
520 Astronomy & allied sciences
530 Physics
540 Chemistry & allied sciences
550 Earth sciences
560 Paleontology   Paleozoology
570 Life sciences
580 Botanical sciences
590 Zoological sciences

600 Technology (Applied sciences)
610 Medical sciences   Medicine
620 Engineering & allied operations
630 Agriculture
640 Home economics & family living
650 Management & auxiliary services
660 Chemical engineering
670 Manufacturing
680 Manufacture for specific uses
690 Buildings

700 The arts
710 Civic & landscape art
720 Architecture
730 Plastic arts   Sculpture
740 Drawing & decorative arts
750 Painting & paintings
760 Graphic arts   Printmaking & prints
770 Photography & photographs
780 Music
790 Recreational & performing arts

800 Literature & rhetoric
810 American literature in English
820 English & Old English literatures
830 Literatures of Germanic languages
840 Literatures of Romance languages
850 Italian, Romanian, Rhaeto-Romanic
860 Spanish & Portuguese literatures
870 Italic literatures   Latin
880 Hellenic literatures   Classical Greek
890 Literatures of other languages

900 Geography & history
910 Geography & travel
920 Biography, genealogy, insignia
930 History of ancient world
940 General history of Europe
950 General history of Asia   Far East
960 General history of Africa
970 General history of North America
980 General history of South America
990 General history of other areas

*Consult schedules for complete and exact headings

Third Summary*
The Thousand Sections
Generalities

000	**Generalities**		**050**	**General serials & their indexes**
001	Knowledge		051	American
002	The book		052	In English
003	Systems		053	In other Germanic languages
004	Data processing Computer science		054	In French, Provençal, Catalan
005	Computer programming, programs, data		055	In Italian, Romanian, Rhaeto-Romanic
006	Special computer methods		056	In Spanish & Portuguese
007			057	In Slavic languages
008			058	In Scandinanvian languages
009			059	In other languages
010	**Bibliography**		**060**	**General organizations & museology**
011	Bibliographies		061	In North America
012	Of individuals		062	In British Isles In England
013	Of works by specific classes of authors		063	In central Europe In Germany
014	Of anonymous and pseudonymous works		064	In France & Monaco
015	Of works from specific places		065	In Italy & adjacent territories
016	Of works on specific subjects		066	In Iberian Peninsula & adjacent islands
017	General subject catalogs		067	In eastern Europe In Soviet Union
018	Catalogs arranged by author & date		068	In other areas
019	Dictionary catalogs		069	Museology (Museum science)
020	**Library & information sciences**		**070**	**News media, journalism, publishing**
021	Library relationships		071	In North America
022	Administration of the physical plant		072	In British Isles In England
023	Personnel administration		073	In central Europe In Germany
024			074	In France & Monaco
025	Library operations		075	In Italy & adjacent territories
026	Libraries for specific subjects		076	In Iberian Peninsula & adjacent islands
027	General libraries		077	In eastern Europe In Soviet Union
028	Reading, use of other information media		078	In Scandinavia
029			079	In other areas
030	**General encyclopedic works**		**080**	**General collections**
031	American		081	American
032	In English		082	In English
033	In other Germanic languages		083	In other Germanic languages
034	In French, Provençal, Catalan		084	In French, Provençal, Catalan
035	In Italian, Romanian, Rhaeto-Romanic		085	In Italian, Romanian, Rhaeto-Romanic
036	In Spanish & Portuguese		086	In Spanish & Portuguese
037	In Slavic languages		087	In Slavic languages
038	In Scandinavian languages		088	In Scandinavian languages
039	In other languages		089	In other languages
040			**090**	**Manuscripts & rare books**
041			091	Manuscripts
042			092	Block books
043			093	Incunabula
044			094	Printed books
045			095	Books notable for bindings
046			096	Books notable for illustrations
047			097	Books notable for ownership or origin
048			098	Prohibited works, forgeries, hoaxes
049			099	Books notable for format

*Consult schedules for complete and exact headings

Philosophy and psychology

100	**Philosophy & psychology**		**150**	**Psychology**
101	Theory of philosophy		151	
102	Miscellany of philosophy		152	Perception, movement, emotions, drives
103	Dictionaries of philosophy		153	Mental processes & intelligence
104			154	Subconscious & altered states
105	Serial publications of philosophy		155	Differential & developmental psychology
106	Organizations of philosophy		156	Comparative psychology
107	Education, research in philosophy		157	
108	Kinds of persons in philosophy		158	Applied psychology
109	Historical treatment of philosophy		159	
110	**Metaphysics**		**160**	**Logic**
111	Ontology		161	Induction
112			162	Deduction
113	Cosmology (Philosophy of nature)		163	
114	Space		164	
115	Time		165	Fallacies & sources of error
116	Change		166	Syllogisms
117	Structure		167	Hypotheses
118	Force & energy		168	Argument & persuasion
119	Number & quantity		169	Analogy
120	**Epistemology, causation, humankind**		**170**	**Ethics (Moral philosophy)**
121	Epistemology (Theory of knowledge)		171	Systems & doctrines
122	Causation		172	Political ethics
123	Determinism & indeterminism		173	Ethics of family relationships
124	Teleology		174	Economic & professional ethics
125			175	Ethics of recreation & leisure
126	The self		176	Ethics of sex & reproduction
127	The unconscious & the subconscious		177	Ethics of social relations
128	Humankind		178	Ethics of consumption
129	Origin & destiny of individual souls		179	Other ethical norms
130	**Paranormal phenomena**		**180**	**Ancient, medieval, Oriental philosophy**
131	Occult methods for achieving well-being		181	Oriental philosophy
132			182	Pre-Socratic Greek philosophies
133	Parapsychology & occultism		183	Sophistic & Socratic philosophies
134			184	Platonic philosophy
135	Dreams & mysteries		185	Aristotelian philosophy
136			186	Skeptic and Neoplatonic philosophies
137	Divinatory graphology		187	Epicurean philosophy
138	Physiognomy		188	Stoic philosophy
139	Phrenology		189	Medieval Western philosophy
140	**Specific philosophical schools**		**190**	**Modern Western philosophy**
141	Idealism & related systems		191	United States & Canada
142	Critical philosophy		192	British Isles
143	Intuitionism & Bergsonism		193	Germany & Austria
144	Humanism & related systems		194	France
145	Sensationalism		195	Italy
146	Naturalism & related systems		196	Spain & Portugal
147	Pantheism & related systems		197	Soviet Union
148	Liberalism, eclecticism, traditionalism		198	Scandinavia
149	Other philosophical systems		199	Other geographical areas

Religion

200 Religion
201 Philosophy of Christianity
202 Miscellany of Christianity
203 Dictionaries of Christianity
204 Special topics
205 Serial publications of Christianity
206 Organizations of Christianity
207 Education, research in Christianity
208 Kinds of persons in Christianity
209 History & geography of Christianity

210 Natural theology
211 Concepts of God
212 Existence, attributes of God
213 Creation
214 Theodicy
215 Science & religion
216 Good & evil
217
218 Humankind
219

220 Bible
221 Old Testament
222 Historical books of Old Testament
223 Poetic books of Old Testament
224 Prophetic books of Old Testament
225 New Testament
226 Gospels & Acts
227 Epistles
228 Revelation (Apocalypse)
229 Apocrypha & pseudepigrapha

230 Christian theology
231 God
232 Jesus Christ & his family
233 Humankind
234 Salvation (Soteriology) & grace
235 Spiritual beings
236 Eschatology
237
238 Creeds & catechisms
239 Apologetics & polemics

240 Christian moral & devotional theology
241 Moral theology
242 Devotional literature
243 Evangelistic writings for individuals
244
245 Texts of hymns
246 Use of art in Christianity
247 Church furnishings & articles
248 Christian experience, practice, life
249 Christian observances in family life

250 Christian orders & local church
251 Preaching (Homiletics)
252 Texts of sermons
253 Pastoral office (Pastoral theology)
254 Parish government & administration
255 Religious congregations & orders
256
257
258
259 Activities of the local church

260 Christian social theology
261 Social theology
262 Ecclesiology
263 Times, places of religious observance
264 Public worship
265 Sacraments, other rites & acts
266 Missions
267 Associations for religious work
268 Religious education
269 Spiritual renewal

270 Christian church history
271 Religious orders in church history
272 Persecutions in church history
273 Heresies in church history
274 Christian church in Europe
275 Christian church in Asia
276 Christian church in Africa
277 Christian church in North America
278 Christian church in South America
279 Christian church in other areas

280 Christian denominations & sects
281 Early church & Eastern churches
282 Roman Catholic Church
283 Anglican churches
284 Protestants of Continental origin
285 Presbyterian, Reformed, Congregational
286 Baptist, Disciples of Christ, Adventist
287 Methodist & related churches
288
289 Other denominations & sects

290 Other & comparative religions
291 Comparative religion
292 Classical (Greek & Roman) religion
293 Germanic religion
294 Religions of Indic origin
295 Zoroastrianism (Mazdaism, Parseeism)
296 Judaism
297 Islam & religions originating in it
298
299 Other religions

Social sciences

300	**Social sciences**		**350**	**Public administration**
301	Sociology & anthropology		351	Of central governments
302	Social interaction		352	Of local governments
303	Social processes		353	Of U.S. federal & state governments
304	Factors affecting social behavior		354	Of specific central governments
305	Social groups		355	Military science
306	Culture & institutions		356	Foot forces & warfare
307	Communities		357	Mounted forces & warfare
308			358	Other specialized forces & services
309			359	Sea (Naval) forces & warfare
310	**General statistics**		**360**	**Social services; association**
311			361	General social problems & welfare
312			362	Social welfare problems & services
313			363	Other social problems & services
314	Of Europe		364	Criminology
315	Of Asia		365	Penal & related institutions
316	Of Africa		366	Association
317	Of North America		367	General clubs
318	Of South America		368	Insurance
319	Of other parts of the world		369	Miscellaneous kinds of associations
320	**Political science**		**370**	**Education**
321	Systems of governments & states		371	School management; special education
322	Relation of state to organized groups		372	Elementary education
323	Civil & political rights		373	Secondary education
324	The political process		374	Adult education
325	International migration & colonization		375	Curriculums
326	Slavery & emancipation		376	Education of women
327	International relations		377	Schools & religion
328	The legislative process		378	Higher education
329			379	Government regulation, control, support
330	**Economics**		**380**	**Commerce, communications, transport**
331	Labor economics		381	Internal commerce (Domestic trade)
332	Financial economics		382	International commerce (Foreign trade)
333	Land economics		383	Postal communication
334	Cooperatives		384	Communications Telecommunication
335	Socialism & related systems		385	Railroad transportation
336	Public finance		386	Inland waterway & ferry transportation
337	International economics		387	Water, air, space transportation
338	Production		388	Transportation Ground transportation
339	Macroeconomics & related topics		389	Metrology & standardization
340	**Law**		**390**	**Customs, etiquette, folklore**
341	International law		391	Costume & personal appearance
342	Constitutional & administrative law		392	Customs of life cycle & domestic life
343	Military, tax, trade, industrial law		393	Death customs
344	Social, labor, welfare, & related law		394	General customs
345	Criminal law		395	Etiquette (Manners)
346	Private law		396	
347	Civil procedure & courts		397	
348	Law (Statutes), regulations, cases		398	Folklore
349	Law of specific jurisdictions & areas		399	Customs of war & diplomacy

Summaries

Language

400	**Language**	**450**	**Italian, Romanian, Rhaeto-Romanic**
401	Philosophy & theory	451	Italian writing system & phonology
402	Miscellany	452	Italian etymology
403	Dictionaries & encyclopedias	453	Italian dictionaries
404	Special topics	454	
405	Serial publications	455	Italian grammar
406	Organizations & management	456	
407	Education, research, related topics	457	Italian language variations
408	With respect to kinds of persons	458	Standard Italian usage
409	Geographical & persons treatment	459	Romanian & Rhaeto-Romanic
410	**Linguistics**	**460**	**Spanish & Portuguese languages**
411	Writing systems	461	Spanish writing system & phonology
412	Etymology	462	Spanish etymology
413	Dictionaries	463	Spanish dictionaries
414	Phonology	464	
415	Structural systems (Grammar)	465	Spanish grammar
416		466	
417	Dialectology & historical linguistics	467	Spanish language variations
418	Standard usage Applied linguistics	468	Standard Spanish usage
419	Verbal language not spoken or written	469	Portuguese
420	**English & Old English**	**470**	**Italic languages Latin**
421	English writing system & phonology	471	Classical Latin writing & phonology
422	English etymology	472	Classical Latin etymology
423	English dictionaries	473	Classical Latin dictionaries
424		474	
425	English grammar	475	Classical Latin grammar
426		476	
427	English language variations	477	Old, Postclassical, Vulgar Latin
428	Standard English usage	478	Classical Latin usage
429	Old English (Anglo-Saxon)	479	Other Italic languages
430	**Germanic languages German**	**480**	**Hellenic languages Classical Greek**
431	German writing system & phonology	481	Classical Greek writing & phonology
432	German etymology	482	Classical Greek etymology
433	German dictionaries	483	Classical Greek dictionaries
434		484	
435	German grammar	485	Classical Greek grammar
436		486	
437	German language variations	487	Preclassical & postclassical Greek
438	Standard German usage	488	Classical Greek usage
439	Other Germanic languages	489	Other Hellenic languages
440	**Romance languages French**	**490**	**Other languages**
441	French writing system & phonology	491	East Indo-European & Celtic languages
442	French etymology	492	Afro-Asiatic languages Semitic
443	French dictionaries	493	Non-Semitic Afro-Asiatic languages
444		494	Ural-Altaic, Paleosiberian, Dravidian
445	French grammar	495	Languages of East & Southeast Asia
446		496	African languages
447	French language variations	497	North American native languages
448	Standard French usage	498	South American native languages
449	Provençal & Catalan	499	Miscellaneous languages

Natural sciences and mathematics

500	**Natural sciences & mathematics**	**550**	**Earth sciences**
501	Philosophy & theory	551	Geology, hydrology, meteorology
502	Miscellany	552	Petrology
503	Dictionaries & encyclopedias	553	Economic geology
504		554	Earth sciences of Europe
505	Serial publications	555	Earth sciences of Asia
506	Organizations & management	556	Earth sciences of Africa
507	Education, research, related topics	557	Earth sciences of North America
508	Natural history	558	Earth sciences of South America
509	Historical, areas, persons treatment	559	Earth sciences of other areas
510	**Mathematics**	**560**	**Paleontology Paleozoology**
511	General principles	561	Paleobotany
512	Algebra & number theory	562	Fossil invertebrates
513	Arithmetic	563	Fossil primitive phyla
514	Topology	564	Fossil Mollusca & Molluscoidea
515	Analysis	565	Other fossil invertebrates
516	Geometry	566	Fossil Vertebrata (Fossil Craniata)
517		567	Fossil cold-blooded vertebrates
518		568	Fossil Aves (Fossil birds)
519	Probabilities & applied mathematics	569	Fossil Mammalia
520	**Astronomy & allied sciences**	**570**	**Life sciences**
521	Celestial mechanics	571	
522	Techniques, equipment, materials	572	Human races
523	Specific celestial bodies & phenomena	573	Physical anthropology
524		574	Biology
525	Earth (Astronomical geography)	575	Evolution & genetics
526	Mathematical geography	576	Microbiology
527	Celestial navigation	577	General nature of life
528	Ephemerides	578	Microscopy in biology
529	Chronology	579	Collection and preservation
530	**Physics**	**580**	**Botanical sciences**
531	Classical mechanics Solid mechanics	581	Botany
532	Fluid mechanics Liquid mechanics	582	Spermatophyta (Seed-bearing plants)
533	Gas mechanics	583	Dicotyledones
534	Sound & related vibrations	584	Monocotyledones
535	Light & paraphotic phenomena	585	Gymnospermae (Pinophyta)
536	Heat	586	Cryptogamia (Seedless plants)
537	Electricity & electronics	587	Pteridophyta (Vascular cryptogams)
538	Magnetism	588	Bryophyta
539	Modern physics	589	Thallobionta & Prokaryotae
540	**Chemistry & allied sciences**	**590**	**Zoological sciences**
541	Physical & theoretical chemistry	591	Zoology
542	Techniques, equipment, materials	592	Invertebrates
543	Analytical chemistry	593	Protozoa, Echinodermata, related phyla
544	Qualitative analysis	594	Mollusca & Molluscoidea
545	Quantitative analysis	595	Other invertebrates
546	Inorganic chemistry	596	Vertebrata (Craniata, Vertebrates)
547	Organic chemistry	597	Cold-blooded vertebrates Fishes
548	Crystallography	598	Aves (Birds)
549	Mineralogy	599	Mammalia (Mammals)

Technology (Applied sciences)

600	**Technology (Applied sciences)**	**650**	**Management & auxiliary services**
601	Philosophy & theory	651	Office services
602	Miscellany	652	Processes of written communication
603	Dictionaries & encyclopedias	653	Shorthand
604	Special topics	654	
605	Serial publications	655	
606	Organizations	656	
607	Education, research, related topics	657	Accounting
608	Invention & patents	658	General management
609	Historical, areas, persons treatment	659	Advertising & public relations
610	**Medical sciences Medicine**	**660**	**Chemical engineering**
611	Human anatomy, cytology, histology	661	Industrial chemicals technology
612	Human physiology	662	Explosives, fuels technology
613	Promotion of health	663	Beverage technology
614	Incidence & prevention of disease	664	Food technology
615	Pharmacology & therapeutics	665	Industrial oils, fats, waxes, gases
616	Diseases	666	Ceramic & allied technologies
617	Surgery & related medical specialties	667	Cleaning, color, related technologies
618	Gynecology & other medical specialties	668	Technology of other organic products
619	Experimental medicine	669	Metallurgy
620	**Engineering & allied operations**	**670**	**Manufacturing**
621	Applied physics	671	Metalworking & metal products
622	Mining & related operations	672	Iron, steel, other iron alloys
623	Military & nautical engineering	673	Nonferrous metals
624	Civil engineering	674	Lumber processing, wood products, cork
625	Engineering of railroads, roads	675	Leather & fur processing
626		676	Pulp & paper technology
627	Hydraulic engineering	677	Textiles
628	Sanitary & municipal engineering	678	Elastomers & elastomer products
629	Other branches of engineering	679	Other products of specific materials
630	**Agriculture**	**680**	**Manufacture for specific uses**
631	Techniques, equipment, materials	681	Precision instruments & other devices
632	Plant injuries, diseases, pests	682	Small forge work (Blacksmithing)
633	Field & plantation crops	683	Hardware & household appliances
634	Orchards, fruits, forestry	684	Furnishings & home workshops
635	Garden crops (Horticulture)	685	Leather, fur, related products
636	Animal husbandry	686	Printing & related activities
637	Processing dairy & related products	687	Clothing
638	Insect culture	688	Other final products & packaging
639	Hunting, fishing, conservation	689	
640	**Home economics & family living**	**690**	**Buildings**
641	Food & drink	691	Building materials
642	Meals & table service	692	Auxiliary construction practices
643	Housing & household equipment	693	Specific materials & purposes
644	Household utilities	694	Wood construction Carpentry
645	Household furnishings	695	Roof covering
646	Sewing, clothing, personal living	696	Utilities
647	Management of public households	697	Heating, ventilating, air-conditioning
648	Housekeeping	698	Detail finishing
649	Child rearing & home care of sick	699	

The arts

700	**The arts**		**750**	**Painting & paintings**
701	Philosophy & theory		751	Techniques, equipment, forms
702	Miscellany		752	Color
703	Dictionaries & encyclopedias		753	Symbolism, allegory, mythology, legend
704	Special topics		754	Genre paintings
705	Serial publications		755	Religion & religious symbolism
706	Organizations & management		756	
707	Education, research, related topics		757	Human figures & their parts
708	Galleries, museums, private collections		758	Other subjects
709	Historical, areas, persons treatment		759	Historical, areas, persons treatment
710	**Civic & landscape art**		**760**	**Graphic arts Printmaking & prints**
711	Area planning (Civic art)		761	Relief processes (Block printing)
712	Landscape architecture		762	
713	Landscape architecture of trafficways		763	Lithographic (Planographic) processes
714	Water features		764	Chromolithography & serigraphy
715	Woody plants		765	Metal engraving
716	Herbaceous plants		766	Mezzotinting & related processes
717	Structures		767	Etching & drypoint
718	Landscape design of cemeteries		768	
719	Natural landscapes		769	Prints
720	**Architecture**		**770**	**Photography & photographs**
721	Architectural structure		771	Techniques, equipment, materials
722	Architecture to ca. 300		772	Metallic salt processes
723	Architecture from ca. 300 to 1399		773	Pigment processes of printing
724	Architecture from 1400		774	Holography
725	Public structures		775	
726	Buildings for religious purposes		776	
727	Buildings for education & research		777	
728	Residential & related buildings		778	Fields & kinds of photography
729	Design & decoration		779	Photographs
730	**Plastic arts Sculpture**		**780**	**Music**
731	Processes, forms, subjects of sculpture		781	General principles & musical forms
732	Sculpture to ca. 500		782	Vocal music
733	Greek, Etruscan, Roman sculpture		783	Music for single voices The voice
734	Sculpture from ca. 500 to 1399		784	Instruments & instrumental ensembles
735	Sculpture from 1400		785	Chamber music
736	Carving & carvings		786	Keyboard & other instruments
737	Numismatics & sigillography		787	Stringed instruments (Chordophones)
738	Ceramic arts		788	Wind instruments (Aerophones)
739	Art metalwork		789	
740	**Drawing & decorative arts**		**790**	**Recreational & performing arts**
741	Drawing & drawings		791	Public performances
742	Perspective		792	Stage presentations
743	Drawing & drawings by subject		793	Indoor games & amusements
744			794	Indoor games of skill
745	Decorative arts		795	Games of chance
746	Textile arts		796	Athletic & outdoor sports & games
747	Interior decoration		797	Aquatic & air sports
748	Glass		798	Equestrian sports & animal racing
749	Furniture & accessories		799	Fishing, hunting, shooting

Literature and rhetoric

800	**Literature & rhetoric**	**850**	**Italian, Romanian, Rhaeto-Romanic**
801	Philosophy & theory	851	Italian poetry
802	Miscellany	852	Italian drama
803	Dictionaries & encyclopedias	853	Italian fiction
804		854	Italian essays
805	Serial publications	855	Italian speeches
806	Organizations	856	Italian letters
807	Education, research, related topics	857	Italian satire & humor
808	Rhetoric & collections of literature	858	Italian miscellaneous writings
809	Literary history & criticism	859	Romanian & Rhaeto-Romanic
810	**American literature in English**	**860**	**Spanish & Portuguese literatures**
811	Poetry	861	Spanish poetry
812	Drama	862	Spanish drama
813	Fiction	863	Spanish fiction
814	Essays	864	Spanish essays
815	Speeches	865	Spanish speeches
816	Letters	866	Spanish letters
817	Satire & humor	867	Spanish satire & humor
818	Miscellaneous writings	868	Spanish miscellaneous writings
819		869	Portuguese
820	**English & Old English literatures**	**870**	**Italic literatures Latin**
821	English poetry	871	Latin poetry
822	English drama	872	Latin dramatic poetry & drama
823	English fiction	873	Latin epic poetry & fiction
824	English essays	874	Latin lyric poetry
825	English speeches	875	Latin speeches
826	English letters	876	Latin letters
827	English satire & humor	877	Latin satire & humor
828	English miscellaneous writings	878	Latin miscellaneous writings
829	Old English (Anglo-Saxon)	879	Literatures of other Italic languages
830	**Literatures of Germanic languages**	**880**	**Hellenic literatures Classical Greek**
831	German poetry	881	Classical Greek poetry
832	German drama	882	Classical Greek drama
833	German fiction	883	Classical Greek epic poetry & fiction
834	German essays	884	Classical Greek lyric poetry
835	German speeches	885	Classical Greek speeches
836	German letters	886	Classical Greek letters
837	German satire & humor	887	Classical Greek satire & humor
838	German miscellaneous writings	888	Classical Greek miscellaneous writings
839	Other Germanic literatures	889	Modern Greek
840	**Literatures of Romance languages**	**890**	**Literatures of other languages**
841	French poetry	891	East Indo-European & Celtic
842	French drama	892	Afro-Asiatic literatures Semitic
843	French fiction	893	Non-Semitic Afro-Asiatic literatures
844	French essays	894	Ural-Altaic, Paleosiberian, Dravidian
845	French speeches	895	Literatures of East & Southeast Asia
846	French letters	896	African literatures
847	French satire & humor	897	North American native literatures
848	French miscellaneous writings	898	South American native literatures
849	Provençal & Catalan	899	Other literatures

Geography and history

900	**Geography & history**	**950**	**General history of Asia**	**Far East**
901	Philosophy & theory	951	China & adjacent areas	
902	Miscellany	952	Japan	
903	Dictionaries & encyclopedias	953	Arabian Peninsula & adjacent areas	
904	Collected accounts of events	954	South Asia India	
905	Serial publications	955	Iran	
906	Organizations & management	956	Middle East (Near East)	
907	Education, research, related topics	957	Siberia (Asiatic Russia)	
908	With respect to kinds of persons	958	Central Asia	
909	World history	959	Southeast Asia	
910	**Geography & travel**	**960**	**General history of Africa**	
911	Historical geography	961	Tunisia & Libya	
912	Graphic representations of earth	962	Egypt & Sudan	
913	Ancient world	963	Ethiopia	
914	Europe	964	Morocco & Canary Islands	
915	Asia	965	Algeria	
916	Africa	966	West Africa & offshore islands	
917	North America	967	Central Africa & offshore islands	
918	South America	968	Southern Africa	
919	Other areas	969	South Indian Ocean islands	
920	**Biography, genealogy, insignia**	**970**	**General history of North America**	
921		971	Canada	
922		972	Middle America Mexico	
923		973	United States	
924		974	Northeastern United States	
925		975	Southeastern United States	
926		976	South central United States	
927		977	North central United States	
928		978	Western United States	
929	Genealogy, names, insignia	979	Great Basin & Pacific Slope	
930	**History of ancient world**	**980**	**General history of South America**	
931	China	981	Brazil	
932	Egypt	982	Argentina	
933	Palestine	983	Chile	
934	India	984	Bolivia	
935	Mesopotamia & Iranian Plateau	985	Peru	
936	Europe north & west of Italy	986	Colombia & Ecuador	
937	Italy & adjacent territories	987	Venezuela	
938	Greece	988	Guiana	
939	Other parts of ancient world	989	Paraguay & Uruguay	
940	**General history of Europe**	**990**	**General history of other areas**	
941	British Isles	991		
942	England & Wales	992		
943	Central Europe Germany	993	New Zealand	
944	France & Monaco	994	Australia	
945	Italian Peninsula & adjacent islands	995	Melanesia New Guinea	
946	Iberian Peninsula & adjacent islands	996	Other parts of Pacific Polynesia	
947	Eastern Europe Soviet Union	997	Atlantic Ocean islands	
948	Northern Europe Scandinavia	998	Arctic islands & Antarctica	
949	Other parts of Europe	999	Extraterrestrial worlds	

Schedules

Use of the Schedules

Full instructions on the use of the Schedules are found in the Introduction to the Dewey Decimal Classification in Volume 1.

The first three digits of a DDC number are normally found at the top of the page.

A number in square brackets [ ] is not currently in use.

A number in parentheses ( ) is an option to standard usage.

000

---

000 Generalities

See Manual at 000

SUMMARY

001	Knowledge
002	The book
003	Systems
004	Data processing Computer science
005	Computer programming, programs, data
006	Special computer methods

001 Knowledge — *use for facts — Questions & Answers* *class Facts & Records in 032-02*

General aspects: history, description, critical appraisal of intellectual activity in general; increase, modification, dissemination of information and understanding

Class here discussion of ideas from many fields

Class epistemology in 121; a compilation of knowledge in a specific form with the form, e.g., encyclopedias 030

See Manual at 500 vs. 001

SUMMARY

001.01–.09	Standard subdivisions
.1	Intellectual life
.2	Scholarship and learning
.3	Humanities
.4	Research
.9	Controversial knowledge

.01 Theory of knowledge

Class philosophy of knowledge, philosophical works on the theory of knowledge in 121

.1 Intellectual life

Nature and value

For scholarship and learning, see 001.2

See also 900 for broad description of intellectual situation and condition

[.14] Intellectual cooperation

Number discontinued; class in 001.1

.2 Scholarship and learning

Intellectual activity directed toward increase of knowledge

Class methods of study and teaching in 371.3; scholarship and learning in a specific discipline or subject with the discipline or subject, e.g., in the humanities 001.3, in history 900

For research, see 001.4

See Manual at 500 vs. 001

.3 Humanities

Including relative value of science versus the humanities

.4 Research

Class here evaluation research, works discussing what research is

Class research in a specific discipline or subject with the discipline or subject, using notation 072 from Table 1, e.g., research in linguistics 410.72; works embodying the results of research with the subject of the research, but not using notation 072 from Table 1, e.g., results of research in linguistics 410 (*not* 410.72)

See Manual at 500 vs. 001

.42 Research methods

Class here research methods not otherwise provided for [*formerly* 001.43], scientific method

Class computer modeling and simulation in 003.3

For historical, descriptive, experimental methods, see 001.43

.422 Statistical methods

See also 310 for collections of general statistical data, notation 021 from Table 1 for statistics on a specific discipline or subject

See Manual at 519.5, T1—015195 vs. 001.422, T1—072

.422 2 Collection of data

Including statistical aspects of field work and questionnaires

Class here sampling techniques

See also 001.433 for field work, questionnaires in descriptive research

.422 4 Tabulation of data

General aspects: arrangement, layout, construction of tables and series

Class tabulation of data for presentation in 001.4226

.422 5 Analysis of data

See Manual at 519.5, T1—015195 vs. 001.422, T1—072

.422 6	Presentation of data

.422 6   Presentation of data

Examples: charts, graphs, nomograms

Class tabulation of data for analysis and comprehensive works on tabulation and presentation of data in 001.4224

[.424]   Operations research

Relocated to 003

.43   Historical, descriptive, experimental methods

Research methods not otherwise provided for relocated to 001.42

.432   Historical method

Example: case studies

.433   Descriptive method

Including collecting, field work, questionnaires, surveys

See also 001.422 for statistical methods, 310.723 for methods of collecting general social statistical data

.434   Experimental method

.44   Support of and incentives for research

Examples: awards, certificates, honors, medals, prizes, endowments, fellowships, financial patronage, grants, scholarships

Class student finance in higher education in 378.3; awards granted in a specific discipline with the discipline, using notation 079 from Table 1, e.g., awards in fine and decorative arts 707.9

See also 929.81 for awards for general achievements

[.5]   Communication

Relocated to 302.2

[.53]   Cybernetics

Relocated to 003.5

[.533]   Self-organizing systems

Relocated to 003.7

[.534]   Perception theory

Perception theory relocated to 003.52, computer pattern recognition to 006.4

[.535]   Artificial intelligence

Artificial intelligence relocated to 006.3, automata theory to 511.3

[.539]   Information theory

Information theory relocated to 003.54; recall, precision, relevance, irrelevance to 025.04

[.543 6]	Cryptography
	Relocated to 652.8

[.6]   Data processing   Computer science

Relocated to 004

.9   Controversial knowledge

Example: well established phenomena for which explanations are controversial

Including the end of the world

Class here interdisciplinary works on controversial knowledge and paranormal phenomena

Class controversial knowledge concerning a specific discipline or subject with the discipline or subject, e.g., the paranormal and legendary as subjects of folklore 398.4, Piltdown man hoax 573.3, controversial medical remedies 615.856, an alleged conspiracy to assassinate John F. Kennedy 973.922

For paranormal phenomena, see 130

See Manual at 001.9 and 130

[.93]   Curiosities

Relocated to 030

.94   Mysteries

Reported phenomena not explained, not fully verified

Examples: Atlantis, Bermuda Triangle, pyramid power

Class here nonastronomical extraterrestrial influences on earth

See also 900 for Atlantis as a subject of archaeology

.942   Unidentified flying objects (UFOs, Flying saucers)

.944   Monsters and related phenomena

Examples: abominable snowman, Loch Ness monster

See also 590 for animals whose reality is not controversial

.95   Deceptions and hoaxes

Piltdown man hoax relocated to 573.3

Class hoaxes that influenced history in 900, e.g., Pseudo-Demetrius 947.045

.96   Errors, delusions, superstitions

002 The book

General aspects: history, description, critical appraisal

Class here historical bibliography, interdisciplinary works on the book

Class comprehensive works on historical and analytical bibliography in 010.42, book publishing in 070.5, social aspects of the book in 302.232, book arts in 686

For rare books, see 090

[.021 6]   Lists, inventories, catalogs

Do not use; class in 010

[.029 4]   Trade catalogs and directories

Do not use; class in 010

.074   Museums, collections, exhibits

Class catalogs and lists in 010

003 Systems

Class here operations research [*formerly* 001.424]; systems theory, analysis, design, optimization; models (simulation) applied to real-world systems

Unless other instructions are given, class complex subjects with aspects in two or more subdivisions of 003 in the one coming last, e.g., control of discrete-time linear systems 003.83 (*not* 003.5 or 003.74)

Class simulation in education in 371.397; systems in a specific subject or discipline with the subject or discipline, using notation 011 from Table 1, e.g., systems theory in the social sciences 300.11

See also 511.8 for mathematical models not applied to real-world systems, 519.7 for mathematical programming not applied to real-world systems

See Manual at 003; 003, T1—011 vs. 510, T1—0151; 004.21 vs. 003

[.028 5]   Data processing   Computer applications

Do not use; class in 003.3

.1 System identification

Determining a mathematical model for a system by observing its input-output relationships

.2 Forecasting and forecasts

Class here interdisciplinary works on forecasting

Class forecasting by parapsychological and occult means in 133.3

See Manual at 003.2

.209   Historical, geographical, persons treatment of forecasting as a discipline

Class forecasting and forecasts for specific areas in 303.491–303.499

.3   **Computer modeling and simulation**

Class here interdisciplinary works on computer modeling and simulation, data processing and computer science applied to systems, computer implementation of mathematical models of systems

Add to base number 003.3 the numbers following 00 in 004–006, e.g., computer simulation languages 003.3513

.5   **Theory of communication and control**

In living and nonliving systems

Including bionics

Class here cybernetics [*formerly* 001.53], interdisciplinary works on the control and stability of systems

Class social aspects of and interdisciplinary works on communication in systems in 302.2

For artificial intelligence, see 006.3

See Manual at 003.5 vs. 629.8

.52   Perception theory [*formerly* 001.534]

Class computer vision in 006.37, psychology of human perception in 153.7, perception in animals in 591.182

See also 006.4 for computer pattern recognition

.54   Information theory [*formerly* 001.539]

Theory concerning measurement of quantities of information; accuracy in transmission of messages subject to noise (unwanted, usually random, signals), distortion, and transmission failure; and methods of coding for efficient, accurate transmission

Class here coding theory [*formerly* 519.4]

Class coding for the purpose of limiting access to information in 652.8

See Manual at 621.3822 vs. 003.54

.56   Decision theory

See also 153.83 for decision theory in psychology, 511.65 for decision theory in combinatorial analysis, 658.40301 for decision theory in management

.7   **Kinds of systems**

Examples: self-organizing systems [*formerly* 001.533], deterministic systems, hierarchical systems, lumped-parameter systems, small-scale systems

For systems distinguished in relation to time, see 003.8

See Manual at 003.7

.71   Large-scale systems

Many general works on systems treat predominately large-scale systems. Class here only works emphasizing that the systems are large

.74	Linear systems
.75	Nonlinear systems
.76	Stochastic systems
.78	Distributed-parameter systems

.8 **Systems distinguished in relation to time**

Examples: continuous-time systems, instantaneous (zero-memory) systems, time-invariant systems, time-varying systems

.83   Discrete-time systems

.85   Dynamic systems

Systems in which response depends upon past values of excitation as well as current excitation

004   Data processing   Computer science [*formerly* 001.6]

This schedule (004−006) was separately published in 1985

Class here selection and use of computer hardware; comprehensive works on hardware and programs in electronic data processing; electronic computers; electronic digital computers; computer systems (computers, their peripheral devices, their operating systems); central processing units; computer reliability; general computer performance evaluation

Unless other instructions are given, class complex subjects with aspects in two or more subdivisions of 004 in the one coming last, e.g., external storage for microcomputers 004.56 (*not* 004.16)

Class computer modeling and simulation in 003.3; engineering of computers in 621.39; data processing and computer science applied to a specific subject or discipline with the subject or discipline, using notation 0285 from Table 1, e.g., data processing in banking 332.10285

For computer programming, programs, data, see 005; special computer methods, 006

See also 025.04 for automated information storage and retrieval; 343.0999 for computer law; 364.168 for financial and business computer crimes; 371.334 for computer-assisted instruction (CAI); 652.5 for word processing; 658.05 for data processing in management; 794.8 for computer games

See Manual at 004−006 vs. 621.39; 004 vs. 005; 510, T1—0151 vs. 004−006, T1—0285

SUMMARY

004.01−.09	Standard subdivisions
.1	General works on specific types of computers
.2	Systems analysis and design, computer architecture, performance evaluation
.3	Processing modes
.5	Storage
.6	Interfacing and communications
.7	Peripherals
.9	Nonelectronic data processing

.015 1		Mathematical principles

> Class here computer mathematics [*formerly* 519.4]

.019   Human-computer interaction

> Class here psychological principles and human factors in data processing and computer science

> Apply notation 019 from Table 1 as modified here throughout 004–006, e.g., human factors in interactive systems 004.33019

> Class ergonomic engineering of computer peripherals in 621.3984

.028   Auxiliary techniques and procedures; apparatus, equipment, materials

[.028 7]   Testing and measurement

> Do not use; class in 004.24

.1   General works on specific types of computers

> Class here specific types of processors, computer systems based on specific types of computers

> Class programmable calculators in 510.28541; specific types of computers, processors, computer systems distinguished by their processing modes in 004.3

> *See Manual at 004.1*

\>   004.11–004.16 Digital computers

> Class comprehensive works in 004

> *See Manual at 004.11–004.16*

.11   Digital supercomputers

> *See Manual at 004.11–004.16*

.12   Digital mainframe computers

> Class here large-scale digital computers

> *For supercomputers, see 004.11*

> *See Manual at 004.11–004.16*

.125   Specific digital mainframe computers

> Arrange alphabetically by name of computer or processor, e.g., IBM 360 ®

.14   Digital minicomputers

> Class comprehensive works on digital minicomputers and microcomputers in 004.16

> *See Manual at 004.11–004.16*

.145   Specific digital minicomputers

> Arrange alphabetically by name of minicomputer or processor, e.g., HP/1000®

.16 Digital microcomputers

Including pocket computers capable of manipulating alphabetic as well as numeric data

Class here personal computers, comprehensive works on minicomputers and microcomputers

See Manual at 004.11–004.16

.165 Specific digital microcomputers

Arrange alphabetically by name of microcomputer or microprocessor, e.g., Apple II®

.19 Hybrid and analog computers

For nonelectronic analog computers, see 004.9

.2 **Systems analysis and design, computer architecture, performance evaluation**

.21 Systems analysis and design

Class here analysis of a user's problem preparatory to developing a computer system to solve it

Class communications network design and architecture in 004.65

For database design and architecture, see 005.74

See also 003 for interdisciplinary works on systems analysis and design, 658.4032 for management use of systems analysis

See Manual at 004.21 vs. 003; 004.21 vs. 004.22, 621.392

.22 Computer architecture

See Manual at 004.21 vs. 004.22, 621.392

.24 Performance evaluation

Class here performance measurement and evaluation to aid in designing or improving the performance of a computer system

Class performance evaluation as a consideration in purchasing in 004, using notation 0297 from Table 1, e.g., evaluating microcomputers for purchase 004.160297

See also 004.0685 for management techniques to ensure quality control in data processing

See Manual at 004.24

.25 Systems analysis and design, computer architecture, performance evaluation of specific types of electronic computers

Add to base number 004.25 the numbers following 004.1 in 004.11–004.19, e.g., architecture of digital microcomputers 004.256

.3   **Processing modes**

> Examples: batch, offline, pipeline processing
>
> Class here computers, processors, computer systems distinguished by their processing modes; centralized processing

.32   Multiprogramming

> Class here time-sharing

.33   Real-time processing

> Class here online and interactive processing
>
> Class interactive processing in databases in 005.74, in special computer methods in 006

.35   Multiprocessing

> Examples: array processing, associative processing, dataflow computation
>
> Class here parallel processing
>
> Class comprehensive works on associative processing and memory in 004.5

.36   Distributed processing

> *See also 004.6 for computer communications networks, 005.758 for distributed databases*

.5   **Storage**

> Including comprehensive works on associative (content-addressable) memory and associative processing
>
> Class associative processing in 004.35

.53   Internal storage (Main memory)

> Examples: magnetic-core, metal-oxide-semiconductor (MOS), semiconductor bipolar, thin-film memory; random-access memory (RAM); read-only memory (ROM)
>
> Class CD-ROM (compact disk read-only memory) in 004.56
>
> *See also 005.6 for microprogramming and microprograms*

.54   Virtual memory

.56   External (Auxiliary) storage

> Examples: hard and floppy disks; CD-ROM (compact disk read-only memory); magnetic tapes, e.g., cartridges, cassettes, reel-to-reel tapes; tape and disk drives; magnetic bubble memory; optical storage devices; punch cards

.6   **Interfacing and communications**

Equipment and techniques linking computers to peripheral devices or to other computers

Standard subdivisions are added for either or both of the topics named in the heading

Class here interdisciplinary works on computer communications, on telecommunications

Class data, programs, programming in interfacing and communications in 005.7; social aspects of computer communications in 302.23; economic and related aspects of providing computer communications to the public in 384.3

See also 004.36 for distributed processing

See Manual at 004.6; 004.6 vs. 005.71; 384.3 vs. 004.6; 621.382 vs. 621.3981. 004.6

[.602 18]   Standards

Do not use; class in 004.62

.61   For specific types of electronic computers

Add to base number 004.61 the numbers following 004.1 in 004.11–004.19, e.g., interfacing and communications for microcomputers 004.616

.62   Interfacing and communications protocols (standards)

Class protocols for specific aspects of interfacing and communications with the aspect, e.g., protocols for error-correcting codes 005.72

[.620 218]   Standards

Do not use; class in 004.62

.64   Kinds of hardware

Examples: baseband and broadband equipment, modems, optical-fiber cable, peripheral control units

Class peripheral control units controlling a specific kind of peripheral with the peripheral, e.g., printer controllers 004.77

>   004.65–004.68 Computer communications networks

Class comprehensive works in 004.6

.65   Communications network architecture

Class here systems analysis, design, topology (configuration) of computer communications networks

.66   Data transmission modes and data switching methods

Examples: circuit and packet switching, multiplexing

.67   Wide-area networks

.68 Local-area networks

Examples: baseband and broadband local-area networks, high-speed local networks

.69 Specific kinds of computer communications

.692 Electronic mail

.693 Electronic bulletin boards

.7 Peripherals

Input, output, storage devices that work with a computer but are not part of its central processing unit or internal storage

Class peripheral storage in 004.56

See also 004.64 for communications devices

.71 For specific types of electronic computers

Add to base number 004.71 the numbers following 004.1 in 004.11–004.19, e.g., peripherals for microcomputers 004.716

.75 Peripherals combining input and output functions

Class here computer terminals

Class tape and disk devices in 004.56

.76 Input peripherals

Examples: card readers, keyboards

Class input devices that utilize pattern recognition methods in 006.4; special-purpose input devices with the purpose, e.g., graphics input devices 006.62, game paddles 688.748

See also 005.72 for data entry

.77 Output peripherals

Examples: computer output microform (COM) devices, monitors (video display screens), printers

Class output peripherals that utilize computer sound synthesis in 006.5, computer graphics output devices in 006.62

See also 005.43 for monitors in the sense of software control programs, 005.6 for monitors in the sense of firmware control programs

.9 Nonelectronic data processing

General aspects: automatic and nonautomatic

Example: nonelectronic punch-card data processing, e.g., pre-computer use of Hollerith cards

Including nonelectronic analog computers

Class comprehensive works on analog computers in 004.19

005 Computer programming, programs, data

Class here text processing; software reliability, compatibility, portability

Unless other instructions are given, class complex subjects with aspects in two or more subdivisions of 005 in the one coming last, e.g., designing structured FORTRAN programs 005.133 (*not* 005.113 or 005.12)

Class computer programming, programs, data for special computer methods in 006

> *See also 652.5 for word processing*

> *See Manual at 004 vs. 005; 005*

SUMMARY

005.1	Programming
.2	Programming for specific types of computers
.3	Programs
.4	Systems programming and programs
.6	Microprogramming and microprograms
.7	Data in computer systems
.8	Data security

> ## 005.1–005.6 Computer programming and programs

Class comprehensive works in 005

.1 Programming

Class here application programming, software engineering

Class a specific application of programming within computer science with the application in 005.4–006.6

> *For programming for specific types of computers, see 005.2*

> *See Manual at 005.1 vs. 005.3; 005.1 vs. 510*

.101 Philosophy and theory

Do not use notation 01 from Table 1 here or with subdivisions of 005.1 for general discussions of logic in programming

> *See also 005.131 for the symbolic (mathematical) logic of programming languages*

> *See Manual at 005.101*

.102 8 Auxiliary techniques and procedures; apparatus, equipment, materials

Class special techniques in 005.11

[.102 87] Testing and measurement

Do not use; class in 005.14

[.102 88] Maintenance and repair

Do not use; class in 005.16

.11   Special programming techniques

    See Manual at 005.11

.112   Modular programming

.113   Structured programming

.12   Program design

.120 28   Auxiliary techniques and procedures; apparatus, equipment, materials

    Example: use of flow-charting and flow charts as aids in program design

      See also 005.15028 for preparation of flow charts as program documentation

.13   Programming languages

    Example: nonprocedural languages

    Including application generators

    Class here coding of programs

    See also 005.43 for job-control languages

[.130 151]   Mathematical principles

    Do not use; class in 005.131

.131   Symbolic (Mathematical) logic

    Class here mathematical principles of programming languages, e.g., automata, formal languages, grammars, recursive functions applied to programming languages

    Class the mathematical principles of programming languages applied to the development of programming-language translators in 005.45, e.g., formal-language theory applied to development of compilers 005.453015113

      See also 005.1 for general works about logic in programming

.133   Specific programming languages

    Class here comprehensive works on programming with specific programming languages

    Arrange alphabetically by name of programming language, e.g., COBOL

    Class specific machine and assembly languages in 005.136, specific microprogramming languages in 005.6

      See also 005.45 for programming-language translators for specific programming languages

.136   Machine and assembly languages

    See Manual at 005.136

.14   Verification, testing, measurement, debugging

.15　　　Preparation of program documentation

Class here preparation of software documentation

See also 005.12 for preparation of program design specifications and other technical documentation as an aid in program design, 005.3 for program documentation itself, 808.066005 for technical writing in preparation of program documentation

See Manual at 005.15 vs. 808.066005

.16　　　Program maintenance

Class here software maintenance

.2　　　**Programming for specific types of computers**

See Manual at 005.136

.21　　　For digital supercomputers

.22　　　For digital mainframe computers

Add to base number 005.22 the numbers following 005.26 in 005.262–005.265, e.g., programming for the DECsystem-10® 005.225

.24　　　For digital minicomputers

Add to base number 005.24 the numbers following 005.26 in 005.262–005.265, e.g., programming for the IBM System 38® 005.245

.26　　　For digital microcomputers

Including programming for pocket computers capable of manipulating alphabetic as well as numeric data

Class here programming for personal computers, comprehensive works on programming for minicomputers and microcomputers

.262　　　In specific programming languages

Arrange alphabetically by name of programming language, e.g., FORTRAN

.265　　　For specific computers

Class here programming for specific processors, for computer systems based on specific computers

Arrange alphabetically by name of computer, e.g., Kaypro II®

.29　　　For hybrid computers

.3	**Programs**

Software and firmware

Collections of programs, systems of interrelated programs, individual programs having interdisciplinary applications

General aspects: history, description, critical appraisal, selection, use

Class here application programs, electronic spreadsheets, integrated programs, software documentation, comprehensive works on software and firmware

Class programs for a specific application in computer science with the application in 005–006

>*For firmware, see 005.6*
>
>*See also 005.15 for preparation of program documentation*
>
>*See Manual at 005.1 vs. 005.3; 005.3*

.302 18	Standards

>*See also 005.10218 for standards for programming, 005.150218 for standards for preparation of software documentation*
>
>*See Manual at 005.1 vs. 005.3*

.302 87	Testing and measurement

>*See also 005.14 for testing and measurement in programming*
>
>*See Manual at 005.1 vs. 005.3*

[.302 88]	Maintenance and repair

Do not use; class in 005.16

.302 96	Buyers' guides and consumer reports

>*See Manual at 011.3 vs. 011.77, 005.30296*

>	005.31–005.36 For digital computers

Class comprehensive works in 005.3

.31	**For digital supercomputers**
.32	**For digital mainframe computers**

Add to base number 005.32 the numbers following 005.36 in 005.362–005.369, e.g., programs for the Burroughs B6700® 005.325

.34	**For digital minicomputers**

Add to base number 005.34 the numbers following 005.36 in 005.362–005.369, e.g., programs for the PDP-11® 005.345

.36	For digital microcomputers
.362	In specific programming languages

Arrange alphabetically by name of programming language, e.g., BASIC

See Manual at 005.362

.365	For specific computers

Class here programs for specific processors, programs for computer systems based on specific computers

Arrange alphabetically by name of computer or processor, e.g., AT&T PC 6300®¹

.369	Specific programs

Class here specific computer software systems (organized sets of programs that work together)

Arrange alphabetically by name of program or software system, e.g., Symphony®

See Manual at 005.369

.39	For hybrid and analog computers
.4	**Systems programming and programs**

Class programming and programs for interfacing and data communications in 005.71, for management of files and databases in 005.74

.42	Systems programming

Class here programming for operating systems

Class programming for specific aspects of operating systems with the aspect, e.g., programming for communications 005.711; programming for other specific kinds of systems programs with the kind, e.g., programming for compilers 005.453

.43	Systems programs	Operating systems

Examples: programs for multiprogramming and virtual memory, utility programs

Including job-control languages

Class programming for operating systems in 005.42; a specific application of systems programs with the application, e.g., programs that aid in debugging other programs 005.14, programming-language translators 005.45

For operating systems for specific types of computers, see 005.44

See Manual at 005.43

.44	Operating systems for specific types of computers

Add to base number 005.44 the numbers following 005.3 in 005.31–005.39, e.g., operating systems for digital microcomputers 005.446

.45   Programming-language translators

Class here code generators, macro processors, parsers, translators for specific programming languages

Class translators for microprogramming languages in 005.6

See also 418.02 for programs to translate natural languages into other natural languages

.452   Interpreters

.453   Compilers

.456   Assemblers

.6   **Microprogramming and microprograms**

Including firmware viewed as microprograms, firmware development, microassembly languages, microcode

Class firmware viewed as hardware in 004

See Manual at 005.6

.7   **Data in computer systems**

For data security, see 005.8

SUMMARY

005.71	**Data communications**
.72	**Data preparation and representation, record formats**
.73	**Data structures**
.74	**Data files and databases**
.75	**Specific types of data files and databases**

.71   Data communications

Class here interfacing

See also 004.6 for hardware for interfacing and data communications

See Manual at 004 vs. 005; 004.6; 004.6 vs. 005.71

.711   Programming

For programming for specific types of computers, see 005.712

.712   Programming for specific types of computers

Add to base number 005.712 the numbers following 005.2 in 005.21–005.29, e.g., programming digital microcomputers for data communications 005.7126

.713   Programs

Add to base number 005.713 the numbers following 005.3 in 005.31–005.39, e.g., communications programs for digital microcomputers 005.7136

See Manual at 005.713

.72	Data preparation and representation, record formats

Examples: conversion to machine-readable form, data entry and validation

Including digital codes, e.g., ASCII; error-correcting codes

Class data validation in file processing in 005.74, computer input devices in 004.76

For data encryption and ciphers, see 005.82

.73	Data structures
.74	Data files and databases

Including data validation in file processing

Class here file structures (file organizations), file processing, file and database management systems, database design and architecture

Class interdisciplinary works on computer science and information science aspects of databases in 025.04; comprehensive works on data validation in 005.72; data files and databases with regard to their subject content with the subject, e.g., encyclopedic databases 030, nonbibliographic medical databases 610

For specific types of data files and databases, see 005.75

See Manual at 005.74

.740 1–.740 5	Standard subdivisions of data files, of databases
.740 6	Organizations and management of data files, of databases
.740 68	Management of data files, of databases

Class here management of organizations concerned with databases, e.g., firms that create them

Do not use notation 068 from Table 1 for file management or database management in the sense of computer programs that enable operation of files or databases; class these programs in 005.74

.740 7–.740 9	Standard subdivisions of data files, of databases
.742	Data dictionaries/directories
.746	Data compression (File compression, Data compaction)
.748	Sorting

Class here merging

.75	Specific types of data files and databases

Example: centralized files and databases

.754	Network databases

Including database management systems that conform to the standards developed by CODASYL (Conference on Data Systems Languages)

.755	Hierarchical databases

.756	Relational databases
.756 5	Specific relational database management systems

Arrange alphabetically by name of database management system, e.g., dBASE III®

.758	Distributed data files and databases

See also 004.36 for distributed processing

.8   **Data security**

Class here access control

See also 658.478 for data security in management

.82   Data encryption

Class here ciphers

Class in 652.8 comprehensive works on cryptographic techniques used to limit access to information both in and out of computer systems

006   Special computer methods

Not otherwise provided for

Example: automatic data collection

Class here programs, programming, selection and use of hardware in relation to special computer methods

Unless other instructions are given, class complex subjects with aspects in two or more subdivisions of 006 in the one coming last, e.g., natural language processing in expert systems 006.35 (*not* 006.33)

See also 004.6 for computer communications; 005.74 for file and database management; 005.8 for data security; 629.89 for special methods in automatic control engineering; 003.3 for computer modeling and simulation; notation 0113 from Table 1 for computer modeling and simulation in a specific discipline or subject

.3   **Artificial intelligence [*formerly* 001.535]**

Class here question-answering systems

See also 006.4 for pattern recognition not used as a tool of artificial intelligence

.31   Machine learning

.33   Knowledge-based systems

Class here expert systems

.35   Natural language processing

Computer processing of natural language used to allow people to communicate with computers in natural language instead of through formalized commands

See also 402.85 for computer processing of natural language as a tool in linguistics

.37   Computer vision

> *See also 006.42 for optical pattern recognition*
>
> *See Manual at 006.37 vs. 006.42, 621.367, 621.391, 621.399*

.4   **Computer pattern recognition [*formerly also* 001.534]**

Class pattern recognition as a tool of artificial intelligence in 006.3

.42   Optical pattern recognition

Example: bar-code scanning

Including perceptrons

Class here comprehensive works on optical pattern recognition and computer graphics

Class optical engineering aspects of optical pattern recognition in 621.367

> *For computer graphics, see 006.6*
>
> *See also 006.37 for computer vision*
>
> *See Manual at 006.37 vs. 006.42, 621.367, 621.391, 621.399*

.424   Optical character recognition (OCR)

.45   Acoustical pattern recognition

.454   Speech recognition

Including speaker recognition

Class here comprehensive works on speech recognition and speech synthesis

> *For speech synthesis, see 006.54*

.5   **Computer sound synthesis**

> *See also 786.76 for computer music*

.54   Speech synthesis

.6   **Computer graphics**

Class here comprehensive works on computer graphics and computer sound synthesis

> *For computer sound synthesis, see 006.5*
>
> *See also 760 for computer graphic art*

.62   Hardware

Examples: digitizer tablets, graphics terminals, plotters

Class here equipment specifically designed for computer graphics and works treating use of equipment for computer graphics even if the equipment was not specifically designed for that purpose

Class works that treat equally the use of equipment for graphics and nongraphics tasks in 004

.66	Programming

Including graphics programming languages

For programming for specific types of computers, see 006.67

.67	Programming for specific types of computers

Add to base number 006.67 the numbers following 005.2 in 005.21–005.29, e.g., graphics programming for digital microcomputers 006.676

.68	Programs

Add to base number 006.68 the numbers following 005.3 in 005.31–005.39, e.g., graphics programs for digital microcomputers 006.686

[007]　[Unassigned]

Most recently used in Edition 16

[008]　[Never assigned]

[009]　[Never assigned]

010　Bibliography

History, identification, description of printed, written, audiovisual, machine-readable records

Class catalogs and lists of art works with the subject, using notation 074 from Table 1, e.g., a catalog of the prints in the Library of Congress 769.074753

See also 028.1 for reviews

SUMMARY

010.4	Special topics
011	Bibliographies
012	Bibliographies and catalogs of individuals
013	Bibliographies and catalogs of works by specific classes of authors
014	Bibliographies and catalogs of anonymous and pseudonymous works
015	Bibliographies and catalogs of works from specific places
016	Bibliographies and catalogs of works on specific subjects or in specific disciplines
017	General subject catalogs
018	Catalogs arranged by author, main entry, date, or register number
019	Dictionary catalogs

[.28]	Auxiliary techniques and procedures; apparatus, equipment, materials

Do not use; class in 010.44

.4 **Special topics**

.42 Analytical (Descriptive) bibliography

Analysis of the structure of books and their bibliographic description

Class here comprehensive works on historical and analytical bibliography

Class descriptive cataloging in 025.32

For historical bibliography, see 002

See also 070.5 for book publishing

.44 Systematic bibliography

Preparation and compilation of bibliographies

Systematic bibliography applied to a specific kind of bibliography is classed with the kind, using notation 028 from Table 1 for basic as well as auxiliary techniques, e.g., preparation and compilation of biobibliographies 012.028

[.74] Collections, guidebooks, catalogs of exhibits

Do not use; class in 011–019

011 *Bibliographies

Class here general bibliographies (in any form) in which the items are books or other written or printed works

Bibliographies of visual and audiovisual media are classed in 011.37

Catalogs are classed in 012–019 (except for catalogs of works published in specific historical periods, which are classed in 011.09)

For bibliographies of individuals, of works by specific classes of authors, of anonymous and pseudonymous works, of works from specific places, of works on specific subjects or in specific disciplines, see 012–016

SUMMARY

011.001–.009	**Standard subdivisions**
.02–.09	**[Reference works, free materials, works published in specific historical periods]**
.1	**Universal bibliographies**
.2	**General bibliographies of works published in specific languages**
.3	**General bibliographies of works published in specific forms**
.4	**General bibliographies of works exhibiting specific bibliographic characteristics other than form**
.5	**General bibliographies of works issued by specific kinds of publishers**
.6	**General bibliographies of works for specific kinds of users and libraries**
.7	**General bibliographies of works having specific kinds of content**

.001–.007 Standard subdivisions

.008 Bibliographies with respect to groups of persons

Class bibliographies of works for specific kinds of users in 011.6

---

*Do not add notation 091–099 from Table 1 for bibliographies of works from specific places; class in 015

.009   Historical, geographical, persons treatment of bibliographies

> Class bibliographies of works published in specific historical periods in 011.09, bibliographies of works from specific places in 015

.02   *Of reference works

> Class bibliographies of general encyclopedic works in 016.03, of general collected biographies in 016.92

.03   *Of free materials

.09   General bibliographies and catalogs of works published in specific historical periods

> Add to base number 011.09 the numbers following —090 in notation 0903–0905 from Table 1, e.g., 16th century publications 011.0931
>
> Class bibliographies of incunabula in 011.42, bibliographies of works from specific places in 015

>   **011.1–011.7 General bibliographies**

> Lists of works not held in a specific collection or group of collections; not offered for sale by specific organizations or at auction; not restricted to specific subjects, to individuals or specific types of authorship, or to specific places of publication
>
> No matter how arranged
>
> Unless other instructions are given, class complex subjects with aspects in two or more subdivisions of this schedule in the number coming last in the schedule, e.g., Russian-language newspapers on microfilm 011.36 (*not* 011.29171 or 011.35)
>
> Class comprehensive works in 011; general bibliographies and catalogs of works published in specific historical periods, but without other specific restriction, in 011.09
>
> *See also 011.02 for bibliographies of reference works, 011.03 for bibliographies of free materials, 017–019 for general catalogs*

.1   ***Universal bibliographies**

.2   ***General bibliographies of works published in specific languages**

> Add to base number 011.2 notation 2–9 from Table 6, e.g., general bibliographies of Russian-language works 011.29171

*Do not add notation 091–099 from Table 1 for bibliographies of works from specific places; class in 015

.3 ***General bibliographies of works published in specific forms**

Examples: bibliographies of optical digital disks, of products of electronic publishing, of other works in machine-readable form

Use of this number for general bibliographies of books, of works in written or printed form discontinued; class in 011

Bibliographies of music scores are classed in 016.78026, of cartographic materials in 016.912

See also 011.4 for general bibliographies of works exhibiting specific bibliographic characteristics other than form, e.g.,rare books 011.44; 011.7 for bibliographies of works having specific kinds of content, e.g.,directories, textbooks, theses, dissertations, computer programs

See Manual at 011.3 vs. 011.77, 005.30296

> 011.31–011.35 In written or printed form

Class comprehensive works, general bibliographies of books in 011; microform versions of written or printed works in 011.36

.31 ***Manuscripts**

Bibliographies of works about manuscripts relocated to 016.091

.32 ***Paperbound books**

.33 ***Pamphlets**

.34 ***Serial publications**

Class here general indexes to serial publications

General bibliographies of works about serial publications relocated to 016.05

For newspapers, see 011.35

See also 011.48 for works in series

.35 ***Newspapers**

.36 ***Microforms**

Microreproductions of written and printed media

.37 ***Visual and audiovisual media**

Examples: filmslides, filmstrips, motion pictures, pictures, video disks, videotapes

Bibliographies of dramatic and entertainment motion pictures and videotapes are classed in 016.79143

Class microforms in 011.36

For sound recordings, see 011.38

See also 011.3 for bibliographies of optical digital disks

*Do not add notation 091–099 from Table 1 for bibliographies of works from specific places; class in 015

.38   *Sound recordings

    Examples: cassettes, cylinders, disks, tapes, wires; talking books for blind users; recorded radio programs

    Class sound films in 011.37, sound recordings of music in 016.780266

.4   *General bibliographies of works exhibiting specific bibliographic characteristics other than form

    See also 011.3 for works published in specific forms

.42   *Incunabula

    Bibliographies of works about incunabula relocated to 016.093

.44   *Rare books

    Bibliographies of works about rare books relocated to 016.094

    For incunabula, see 011.42

.47   *Reprints

.48   *Works in series

    See also 011.34 for serial publications

.5   *General bibliographies of works issued by specific kinds of publishers

.52   *Publications of international organizations

    Example: publications of UNESCO

.53   *Government publications

.532   *Issued by legislative bodies and their committees

.534   *Issued by executive agencies

.54   *Publications of university and college presses

.55   *Publications of private presses

    Presses printing in limited quantities or for limited distribution

.56   *Publications of underground presses

    Class here clandestinely published works

.6   *General bibliographies of works for specific kinds of users and libraries

.62   *For children and young adults

    Class here bibliographies of works for children

.624   *For specific sexes

.624 1   *Boys and young men

.624 2   *Girls and young women

*Do not add notation 091−099 from Table 1 for bibliographies of works from specific places; class in 015

.625   *For young adults

> Class works for young men in 011.6241, for young women in 011.6242

[.625 054]   For children

> Use of this number discontinued; class in 011.62

[.625 055]   For young adults

> Use of this number discontinued; class in 011.625

.63   *For handicapped users

> Examples: braille, large-type publications

> Class talking and cassette books for blind users in 011.38

.67   *For specific types of libraries

> Example: bibliographies of books for public libraries

.7   ***General bibliographies of works having specific kinds of content**

> Examples: directories, textbooks, translations

> Class reference works in 011.02, general encyclopedic works in 016.03

.73   *Best books

> Class best books for specific kinds of users and libraries in 011.6

.75   *Theses and dissertations

> General collections of abstracts of theses and dissertations are usually classed here (or in 015), but those giving substantive information are classed in 080

.77   *Computer programs

> Add to base number 011.77 the numbers following 005.3 in 005.31–005.39, e.g., bibliographies of programs for digital microcomputers 011.776

> *See Manual at 011.3 vs. 011.7, 005.30296*

*Do not add notation 091–099 from Table 1 for bibliographies of works from specific places; class in 015

> ### 012–016 Bibliographies and catalogs of individuals, of works by specific classes of authors, of anonymous and pseudonymous works, of works from specific places, of works on specific subjects or in specific disciplines

Observe the following table of precedence, e.g., scientific works published in France by Roman Catholic authors 016.5 (*not* 013.22 or 015.44)

Bibliographies and catalogs of works on specific subjects or in specific disciplines	016
Bibliographies and catalogs of individuals	012
Bibliographies and catalogs of anonymous and pseudonymous works	014
Bibliographies and catalogs of works by specific classes of authors	013
Bibliographies and catalogs of works from specific places	015

Class comprehensive works in 011

012   Bibliographies and catalogs of individuals

Works by or about persons not clearly associated with a specific subject

Class here biobibliographies

Biobibliographies of persons associated with a specific subject are classed with biographies of the subject, e.g., biobibliographies of psychologists 150.92

013   Bibliographies and catalogs of works by specific classes of authors

Works not dealing with a specific subject

For bibliographies and catalogs of individuals, see 012

.03–.87   Authors with common characteristics other than residence

Add to base number 013 notation 03–87 from Table 7, e.g., women authors 013.042

For authors occupied with geography, history, related disciplines, see 013.89

See also 011.75 for dissertations and theses

.89   Authors occupied with geography, history, related disciplines

Add to base number 013.89 the numbers following —9 in —91–99 from Table 7, e.g., archaeologists 013.893

.9   Authors resident in specific regions, continents, countries, localities

Add to base number 013.9 notation 1–9 from Table 2, e.g., authors resident in Ireland 013.9415

Class authors resident in specific regions, continents, countries, localities, but having other characteristics in common in 013.03–013.89

014   Bibliographies and catalogs of anonymous and pseudonymous works

Add to base number 014 the numbers following 03 in 031–039 (but not the 02 for books of miscellaneous facts), e.g., bibliographies and catalogs of anonymous and pseudonymous works in French 014.41

015   Bibliographies and catalogs of works from specific places

Works issued in specific regions, continents, countries, localities, or by specific publishers

Class here sales catalogs of specific college and university presses [*formerly also* 017–019], publishers' catalogs [*formerly also* 070.50294], bibliographies and catalogs of theses and dissertations for degrees awarded at specific institutions and at institutions in specific places

Add to base number 015 notation 1–9 from Table 2, e.g., works issued in Hong Kong 015.5125; then add 0* and to the result add the numbers following 011 in 011.1–011.7 e.g., bibliographies of theses for higher degrees at the university of Hong Kong 015.5125075

*Add 00 for standard subdivisions; see instructions at beginning of Table 1

016   Bibliographies and catalogs of works on specific subjects or in specific disciplines

In list or essay form

Including indexes [*formerly also* with the subject with use of notation 016 from Table 1]

Class here annotated subject bibliographies with descriptive annotations that do not give substantive information about the subject

(Option: Class with the specific discipline or subject, using notation 016 from Table 1, e.g., bibliographies of medicine 610.16)

Add to base number 016 notation 001–999, e.g., bibliographies of works about serial publications 016.05 [*formerly* 011.34], catalogs of works about serial publications 016.05 [*formerly* 017–019], bibliographies of works about manuscripts 016.091 [*formerly* 011.31], bibliographies of works about incunabula 016.093 [*formerly* 011.42], bibliographies of works about rare books 016.094 [*formerly* 011.44], bibliographies of philosophy 016.1

Bibliographies and catalogs of belles-lettres in more than one language are classed in 016.8088, e.g., novels 016.80883

Add to the various subdivisions of 016 notation 01–09 from Table 1 as required for works listed in the bibliographies and catalogs, but not for the bibliographies and catalogs being classed, e.g., bibliographies of serial publications on philosophy 016.105, but serially published bibliographies on philosophy that include monographs 016.1 (*not* 016.105)

Class biobibliographies of persons associated with a specific subject with biographies of the subject, e.g., biobibliographies of psychologists 150.92; bibliographies with abstracts giving substantive information about the subject with the subject, e.g., bibliographies with substantive abstracts about chemistry 540

See also 011 for general bibliographies arranged by subject, 011.31 for bibliographies of manuscripts, 011.34 for general bibliographies of serial publications, 011.35 for bibliographies of newspapers, 011.37 for bibliographies of visual and audiovisual media, 011.38 for bibliographies of recorded radio programs, 011.42 for bibliographies of incunabula, 011.44 for bibliographies of rare books, 017–019 for general subject catalogs and general catalogs of serial publications, 050 for general indexes of specific serial publications not limited by subject

See Manual at T1—07 vs. 016, 026

> ## 017–019 General catalogs

Lists of works held in a specific collection or group of collections, or offered for sale by specific organizations other than publishers or at auction, and not restricted to specific subjects, to individuals or specific types of authorship, or to specific places of publication

Class here general catalogs of serial publications and their indexes, union catalogs

Add to the notation for each term identified by * the numbers following 011 in 011.1–011.7 e.g., classified sales catalogs of periodicals 017.434

Sales catalogs of specific college and university presses relocated to 015, catalogs of works about serial publications relocated to 016.05

Class comprehensive works in 017, general catalogs of works published in specific historical periods in 011.09, catalogs of individuals, of works by specific classes of authors, of anonymous and pseudonymous works, of works from specific places, of works on specific subjects or in specific disciplines in 012–016

See also 011.1–011.7 for general bibliographies

017   †General subject catalogs

Class here comprehensive works on catalogs

Class catalogs on specific subjects in 016; a specific kind of nonsubject catalog with the kind of catalog, e.g., catalogs of works by specific classes of authors 013

> ### 017.1–017.4 Classified catalogs

Class comprehensive works in 017

.1   *†Classified catalogs of nonprivate libraries

.2   *†Classified catalogs of private and family libraries

.3   *†Classified auction catalogs

.4   *†Classified sales catalogs

For classified auction catalogs, see 017.3

> ### 017.5–017.8 Alphabetic catalogs

Class comprehensive works in 017

.5   *†Alphabetic subject catalogs of nonprivate libraries

.6   *†Alphabetic subject catalogs of private and family libraries

.7   *†Alphabetic subject auction catalogs

*Add as instructed under 017–019

†Do not add notation 091–099 from Table 1 for catalogs of works from specific places; class in 015

.8   *†Alphabetic subject sales catalogs

For alphabetic subject auction catalogs, see 017.7

018   †Catalogs arranged by author, main entry, date, or register number

Add to base number 018 the numbers following 017 in 017.1–017.4, e.g., author catalogs of private and family libraries 018.2

See also 012 for catalogs of individuals

019   †Dictionary catalogs

Add to base number 019 the numbers following 017 in 017.1–017.4, e.g., dictionary auction catalogs 019.3

020   Library and information sciences

The science and art utilized in the identification, collection, organization, dissemination, and use of books, other printed and written records, audiovisual and machine-readable materials, information

Class here archives and archival techniques

For bibliography, see 010

See also 003.54 for information theory, 651.5 for records management as a managerial service

See Manual at 020

SUMMARY

020.1–.9	Standard subdivisions
021	Relationships of libraries, archives, information centers
022	Administration of the physical plant
023	Personnel administration
025	Operations of libraries, archives, information centers
026	Libraries, archives, information centers devoted to specific disciplines and subjects
027	General libraries, archives, information centers
028	Reading and use of other information media

.6   Organizations and management

[.601]   International organizations

Do not use; class in 020.621

[.603–.609]   National, state, provincial, local organizations

Do not use; class in 020.622–020.624

.62   Permanent nongovernment organizations

.621   International nongovernment organizations

Example: International Federation of Library Associations and Institutions

*Add as instructed under 017–019

†Do not add notation 091–099 from Table 1 for catalogs of works from specific places; class in 015

.622 National nongovernment organizations

Add to base number 020.622 notation 3–9 from Table 2, e.g., Indian Library Association 020.62254, American Society for Information Science 020.62273

.623 Regional, state, provincial nongovernment organizations

.623 2 Regional nongovernment organizations

Add to base number 020.6232 notation 3–9 from Table 2, e.g., Southeastern Library Association 020.623275

.623 4 State and provincial nongovernment organizations

Add to base number 020.6234 notation 3–9 from Table 2, e.g., Ontario Library Association 020.6234713

.624 Local nongovernment organizations

Add to base number 020.624 notation 3–9 from Table 2, e.g., New York Library Club 020.6247471

[.68] Management

Do not use; class in 025.1

[.75] Book collecting

Do not use; class in 002.075

.9 **Historical, geographical, persons treatment**

Class here comparative librarianship, historical, geographical, persons treatment of librarianship (what librarians do, as distinct from the buildings and institutions within which they do it)

Class historical and persons treatment of libraries in 027.009, geographical treatment of libraries in 027.01–027.09

021 Relationships of libraries, archives, information centers

Including role as storage centers

Class here libraries, archives, information centers as social forces

See also 025.56 for orientation and instructional manuals for users; 027 for comprehensive works on libraries, archives, information centers

[.001–.009] Standard subdivisions

Relocated to 021.01–021.09

.01–.09 Standard subdivisions [*formerly* 021.001–021.009]

.2 **Relationships with the community**

.24 Educational role

For relationships with other educational institutions, see 021.3

.26 Cultural role

Example: sponsorship of community cultural programs

.28	Informational role

Example: clearinghouse for information on community action programs

.3 Relationships with other educational institutions

Example: relationships with museums

.6 Cooperation and networks

Example: centralization of systems

[.62] Branches

Number discontinued; class in 021.6

.64 Cooperation

Including bibliographical centers

Class cooperation in a specific activity with the activity, e.g., cooperative cataloging 025.35

For networks, see 021.65

.642 Cooperation through union catalogs

See also 017–019 for specific union catalogs

.65 Networks, systems, consortia

Class networks, systems, consortia for specific kinds of institutions in 026–027; networks, systems, consortia for specific functions with the function, e.g., interlibrary loan networks 025.62

.7 Promotion of libraries, archives, information centers

Example: friends-of-the-library organizations

Class here public relations

Class advertising in 659.1902

.8 Relationships with government

Regardless of governmental level

Examples: library-government aspects of exchanges, gifts, deposits; political pressures

See also 025.26 for acquisition through exchange, gift, deposit

.82 Commissions and governing boards

.83 Financial support

See also 025.11 for financial administration

022 Administration of the physical plant

Including reading rooms and other special rooms, bookmobiles

Class here library quarters in buildings devoted primarily to other activities, e.g., physical plant of school libraries; maintenance of physical plant

See also 025.82 for physical security of collections

.1 Location and site

.3 Buildings

Class here planning for buildings

See also 727.8 for library architecture

.309   Historical, geographical, persons treatment [*formerly* 022.33]

.31   For specific kinds of institutions

Add to base number 022.31 the numbers following 027 in 027.1–027.8, e.g., college library buildings 022.317

[.33]   Historical, geographical, persons treatment

Relocated to 022.309

.4 Stacks and shelving

See also 025.81 for closed versus open stacks

.7 Lighting

.8 Heating, ventilation, air conditioning

.9 Equipment, furniture, furnishings

For stacks and shelving, see 022.4

Class comprehensive works on computers in libraries, archives, information centers in 025.00285

See also 025.56 for signs

023 Personnel administration

023.2–023.4 Types of positions

Class here titles and job descriptions for specific types of positions

Class comprehensive works in 023

.2 Professional positions

Examples: librarians, consultants, systems analysts

Class administrative positions in 023.4

.3   **Technician positions**

Examples: library technicians and assistants, paraprofessionals, nonprofessionals, clerks, aides

Class administrative positions in 023.4

.4   **Administrative positions**

.7   **Titles and job descriptions**

Class titles and job descriptions for specific types of positions in 023.2–023.4

[.700 1–.700 9]   Standard subdivisions

Relocated to 023.701–023.709

.701–.709   Standard subdivisions [*formerly* 023.7001–023.7009]

.8   **In-service training**

Class here in-house courses and programs

Class comprehensive works on courses and programs for practicing library personnel in 020.715, using notation 0715 from Table 1; in-service training for specific types of positions in 023.2–023.4

.9   **Elements of personnel administration**

Examples: recruitment, selection, supervision, employer-employee relations, performance evaluation, wage and salary administration

Including staff manuals, rules, codes

Class elements of personnel administration applied to specific types of positions in 023.2–023.4

For in-service training, see 023.8

[024]   **[Unassigned]**

Most recently used in Edition 18

025   **Operations of libraries, archives, information centers**

Class here documentation (the systematic collection, organization, storage, retrieval, and dissemination of recorded information)

Use 025.001–025.009 for standard subdivisions

Class comprehensive works on operations in specific kinds of institutions in 026–027

SUMMARY

025.02–.06	[Technical processes, information storage and retrieval systems]
.1	Administration
.2	Collection development and acquisitions
.3	Bibliographic analysis and control
.4	Subject analysis and control
.5	Services to users
.6	Circulation services
.7	Physical preparation for storage and use
.8	Maintenance and preservation of collections

.02	Technical processes

Class here commercial and noncommercial processing centers

Class a specific technical process with the process, e.g., acquisitions 025.2

.04 Automated information storage and retrieval systems

Including recall, precision, relevance, irrelevance [*all formerly* 001.539]

Class here search and retrieval in automated information storage and retrieval systems; comprehensive works on automated storage, search, retrieval of information; interdisciplinary works on databases

Class computer science aspects of automated information storage and retrieval systems, of databases in 005.74; information storage in 025.3; a specific kind of information storage and retrieval system with the kind, e.g., online catalogs 025.3132

> *For information storage and retrieval systems devoted to specific disciplines and subjects, see 025.06*

> *See also 658.4038011 for management use of automated information storage and retrieval systems*

> *See Manual at 005.74*

.06 Automated information storage and retrieval systems devoted to specific disciplines and subjects

Class here documentation of specific disciplines and subjects

Add to base number 025.06 notation 001–999, e.g., MEDLARS (Medical Literature Analysis and Retrieval System) 025.0661

.1 Administration

Class administration of a specific function with the function, using notation 068 from Table 1, e.g., administration of cataloging 025.3068

> *For administration of the physical plant, see 022; personnel administration, 023*

.11 Finance

Including comprehensive works on user fees

Class government financial support in 021.83; user fees for a specific service with the service, using notation 0681 from Table 1, e.g., fees for automated information search and retrieval 025.040681

.12   Duplication services (Reprography)

Including administrative problems arising from copyright legislation

Class here photoduplication (photocopying) services, printing services

Publishing by libraries, archives, information centers relocated to 070.594

Class interdisciplinary works on photoduplication in 686.4

See also 346.0482 for copyright law, 686.2 for technology of printing

[.129]   Duplication services (Reprography)

Number discontinued; class in 025.12

.17   Administration of collections of special materials

Class here nonbook materials, comprehensive works on treatment of special materials

Add to base number 025.17 the numbers following 025.34 in 025.341–025.349, e.g., administration of a map collection 025.176, comprehensive treatment of serials 025.1732

Class a specific kind of treatment of special materials with the kind, e.g., collection development for and acquisition of materials in special forms 025.28

.19   Administration of specific types of institutions

Add to base number 025.19 the numbers following 02 in 026–027, e.g., administration of secondary school libraries 025.1978223

Class administration of a specific function in a specific type of institution with the function, e.g., administration of a map collection in a map library 025.176

.2   Collection development and acquisitions

.21   Collection development

Class here collection analysis, evaluation, management; cooperative collection development; selection policy and procedures

Class collection development for specific types of material in 025.27–025.29

For approval plans, see 025.233

.213   Censorship

Class here comprehensive works on library policies and practices relating to intellectual freedom

Class policies and practices relating to intellectual freedom in library operations other than collection development with the operation, e.g., circulation services 025.6

See also 098.1 for prohibited works, 306.376 for sociological studies of censorship, 323.44 for intellectual freedom as a civil right, 344.0531 for laws of censorship, 342.0853 for laws on intellectual freedom, 363.31 for interdisciplinary works on censorship

.216　　　　　Weeding

　　　　　　Including selection for transfer to storage

.218　　　　　Collection development in specific types of institutions

　　　　　　Add to base number 025.218 the numbers following 02 in 026–027, e.g., collection development in academic libraries 025.21877

　　　　　　Class censorship in a specific type of institution in 025.213, weeding in a specific type of institution in 025.216

.23　　　　　Acquisition through purchase

　　　　　　Class acquisition of specific types of material through purchase in 025.27–025.29

.233　　　　　Relations with vendors

　　　　　　Example: vendor selection

　　　　　　Including approval plans, blanket orders

.236　　　　　Clerical operations

　　　　　　Examples: order preparation, claiming, invoice processing, record keeping

　　　　　　Including forms used in clerical operations for acquisition through purchase

.26　　　　　Acquisition through exchange, gift, deposit

　　　　　　Example: copyright deposits

　　　　　　Including exchange centers and organizations, e.g., Universal Serials and Book Exchange; forms used for processing exchanges, gifts, deposits

　　　　　　Class acquisition of specific types of material through exchange, gift, deposit in 025.27–025.29

>　　　　　　025.27–025.29 Collection development for and acquisition of specific types of materials

　　　　　　Class comprehensive works in 025.2

.27　　　　　Collection development for and acquisition of materials on specific disciplines and subjects

　　　　　　Add to base number 025.27 notation 001–999, e.g., acquisition of materials in the social sciences 025.273

　　　　　　Class collection development for and acquisition of materials for area studies in 025.29

.28　　　　　Collection development for and acquisition of materials in special forms

　　　　　　Add to base number 025.28 the numbers following 025.34 in 025.341–025.349, e.g., acquisition of maps 025.286

　　　　　　Class collection development for and acquisition of materials in special forms on specific disciplines and subjects in 025.27

.29   Collection development for and acquisition of materials from geographic areas

> Class here collection development for and acquisition of foreign publications, materials for area studies

> Add to base number 025.29 notation 1–9 from Table 2, e.g., acquisition of materials from Latin America 025.298

> Class collection development for and acquisition of materials on specific disciplines and subjects from geographic areas in 025.27, of materials in special forms from geographic areas in 025.28

.3   **Bibliographic analysis and control**

> Example: cataloging in publication

> Including International Standard Book Numbers (ISBNs)

> Class here comprehensive works on cataloging and classification, on indexing, on information storage

> Class information storage using a specific system with the system, e.g., information storage through coordinate indexing 025.484

> Information search and retrieval using multiple kinds of information sources is classed in 025.524, but information search and retrieval using a specific system [*formerly* 025.524] is classed with the system, e.g., searching an online catalog 025.3132

> *For subject analysis and control, see 025.4*

> *See also 025.04 for comprehensive works on information storage and retrieval systems*

> *See Manual at 025.3*

SUMMARY

025.301–.309	**Standard subdivisions**
.31	**The catalog**
.32	**Descriptive cataloging**
.34	**Cataloging, classification, indexing of special materials**
.35	**Cooperative cataloging, classification, indexing**
.39	**Recataloging, reclassification, re-indexing**

[.302 18]   Standards

> Do not use; class in 025.3

> Do not add notation 0218 from Table 1 to any subdivision of 025.3

> *See Manual at 025.3*

.302 855 72   Applications of computer data representation, record formats, preparation

> Class machine-readable catalog record formats in 025.316, data entry, conversion to machine-readable form in 025.317

.302 855 74   Applications of computer data files and databases

> Class here comprehensive works on computer data files and databases used for cataloging and indexing

> Class computer data files and databases used for specific purposes with the purpose, e.g., online catalogs 025.3132

.302 855 748   Applications of computer sorting

> Class computer sorting of catalog records in 025.3177

.31   The catalog

.313   Form

> Examples: book, card, microform catalogs

.313 2   Online catalogs

.315   Structure

> Examples: classified, divided, unified catalogs

.316   Machine-readable catalog record formats

> Example: the Common Communication Format (CCF)

> Class here communication and internal formats for machine-readable cataloging records; Machine-Readable Cataloging (MARC); comprehensive works on machine-readable formats for catalog records, on machine-readable formats for catalog and index records

> Class display formats for catalog records in 025.313; input formats for catalog records in 025.317; formats for specific kinds of catalog records with the kind in 025.32–025.49, using notation 0285572 from Table 1, e.g., name authority formats 025.32220285572, serials formats 025.34320285572, subject authority formats 025.49000285572

.317   Conversion and maintenance

> Examples: preparing, correcting, updating manual and machine-readable catalog records

> Class retrospective conversion combined with recataloging and reclassification in 025.39

.317 3   Retrospective conversion

.317 7   Filing

> Including computer sorting of cataloging records

> Class here filing rules

.32   Descriptive cataloging

> Class here descriptive-cataloging codes, e.g., Anglo-American Cataloguing Rules

> Class descriptive cataloging of special materials in 025.34, cooperative descriptive cataloging in 025.35, recataloging in 025.393

.322	Choice of entry and form of heading

> Examples: corporate headings, personal-name headings, uniform titles
>
> Class here author-title indexing

.322 2	Name and title authority files

> Including reference structure

.324	Bibliographic description

> Class here codes for bibliographic description, e.g., International Standard Bibliographic Description (ISBD)

.34	Cataloging, classification, indexing of special materials

> Class here nonbook materials
>
> *See also 025.17 for comprehensive works on treatment of special materials*

SUMMARY

025.341	**Manuscripts, archival materials, rarities**
.342	**Clippings, broadsides, pamphlets**
.343	**Serials, government publications, report literature**
.344	**Machine-readable materials**
.346	**Maps, atlases, globes**
.347	**Pictures and materials for projection**
.348	**Sound recordings and music scores**
.349	**Other special materials**

.341	Manuscripts, archival materials, rarities
.341 2	Manuscripts
.341 4	Archival materials

> Class manuscripts in 025.3412

.341 6	Rarities

> Class rare manuscripts in 025.3412, archival materials in 025.3414

.342	Clippings, broadsides, pamphlets

> Class here contents of vertical files, printed ephemera

.343	Serials, government publications, report literature
.343 2	Serials

> Examples: CONSER (Cooperative Conversion of Serials) Project, International Serials Data Program (ISDP)
>
> Including International Standard Serial Numbers (ISSNs)

.343 4	Government publications

> Class government serials in 025.3432

.343 6   Report literature

Class serial report literature in 025.3432, government reports 025.3434

.344   Machine-readable materials [*formerly* 025.349]

Class here computer software

.346   Maps, atlases, globes

.347   Pictures and materials for projection

Class here comprehensive works on audiovisual materials

For sound recordings and music scores, see 025.348; maps, atlases, globes, 025.346; other special materials, 025.349

.347 1   Pictures and prints

.347 3   Motion pictures, filmstrips, slides, videotapes

.348   Sound recordings and music scores

.348 2   Sound recordings

Examples: cassettes, cylinders, disks, tapes, wires

Class sound films and videotapes in 025.3473

.348 8   Music scores

.349   Other special materials

Examples: large-type publications, realia

Machine-readable materials relocated to 025.344

.349 2   Publications in raised characters

Example: braille

.349 4   Microforms

.349 6   Games, models, miniatures, media kits

Including dioramas, flashcards

.35   Cooperative cataloging, classification, indexing

Example: cooperative development of name authority files

Class cooperative cataloging, classification, indexing of special materials in 025.34

.39   Recataloging, reclassification, re-indexing

Class recataloging, reclassification, re-indexing of special materials in 025.34

.393   Recataloging

General aspects: descriptive and subject

See also 025.396 for reclassification

.396	Reclassification

.4   **Subject analysis and control**

[.402 18]   Standards

> Do not use; class in 025.4

> Do not add notation 0218 from Table 1 to any subdivision of 025.4

> *See Manual at 025.3*

.402 8   Abstracting techniques; auxiliary techniques and procedures; apparatus, equipment, materials

> Class composition of abstracts in 808.062

.42   Classification and shelflisting

> Class classification of special materials in 025.34, cooperative classification in 025.35, reclassification in 025.396

> *For general classification systems, see 025.43; classification of specific disciplines and subjects, 025.46*

.428   Shelflisting

> Assigning book numbers (the symbols in a call number that distinguish an item in a collection from all other items in the same class number)

> *See also 025.3 for International Standard Book Numbers (ISBNs)*

.43   General classification systems

> Class parts of general classification systems applied to specific subjects and disciplines in 025.46, e.g., Library of Congress Classification Class L Education 025.4637

.431   Dewey Decimal Classification

.432   Universal Decimal Classification

.433   Library of Congress Classification

.434   Bliss's Bibliographic Classification

.435   Ranganathan's Colon Classification

.46   Classification of specific disciplines and subjects

> Class here thesaurofacets

> Add to base number 025.46 notation 001–999, e.g., classification of education 025.4637

.47   Subject cataloging

> Subject authority files, reference structure relocated to 025.49

> Class subject cataloging of special materials in 025.34, cooperative subject cataloging in 025.35, recataloging in 025.393

> *For controlled subject vocabularies, see 025.49*

.48 Subject indexing

Manual and mechanized indexing of individual, serial, collected records

Including citation indexing

Class indexing of special materials in 025.34, cooperative indexing in 025.35, re-indexing in 025.39

For controlled subject vocabularies, see 025.49

.482 Precoordinate indexing

Examples: chain indexing, PRECIS, relative indexing

See also 025.42 for precoordinate classification, 025.47 for precoordinate subject cataloging

.484 Coordinate and postcoordinate indexing

Examples: Uniterm indexing, optical coincidence card systems

.486 Title manipulation

Examples: catchword, KWIC (Key Word in Context), KWOC (Key Word Out of Context) indexing

.49 Controlled subject vocabularies

Class here subject authority files, reference structure [*both formerly also* 025.47], descriptors, indexing terms, subject headings, thesauri

Use 025.490001–025.490009 for standard subdivisions

Class thesaurofacets in 025.46

.490 01–.499 99 Vocabularies of specific disciplines and subjects

Add to base number 025.49 notation 001–999, e.g., subject headings in science 025.495

.5 **Services to users**

Class library services to special groups and organizations in 027.6, a specific service not provided for here with the subject, e.g., photocopying services 025.12, circulation services 025.6, storytelling for children 027.6251

.52 Reference and information services

Class here information and referral services; services that involve the use or assistance in the use of information tools but not the creation of them

Class comprehensive works on the creation and use of information storage and retrieval systems in 025.04, of specific tools for bibliographic control in 025.3; the use of books and other media as sources of information in 028.7

.523 Cooperative information services

.524   Information search and retrieval

Using multiple kinds of information sources, e.g., the library catalog, reference books, automated information storage and retrieval systems

Class here search strategy

Information search and retrieval using a specific system relocated to the system, e.g., searching an automated information storage and retrieval system devoted to medicine 025.0661, searching an online catalog 025.3132, retrieval through coordinate indexing 025.484

See also 025.04 for automated information storage and retrieval systems

.525   Selective dissemination of information (SDI)

Class here current awareness programs

.527   Reference and information services in specific types of institutions

Add to base number 025.527 the numbers following 02 in 026–027, e.g., reference and information services in college and university libraries 025.52777; however, class reference and information services to special groups and organizations in 027.6

Class specific aspects of reference and information service in specific types of institutions in 025.523–025.525

.54   Reader advisory services to individuals and groups

See also 028.8 for use of books and other media as sources of recreation and self-development

.56   Orientation and bibliographic instruction for users

Including signs, regulations for use, user manuals

Add to base number 025.56 the numbers following 02 in 026–027, e.g., orientation to public libraries 025.5674; however, class orientation and bibliographic instruction for special groups and organizations in 027.6

.58   Library use studies

Add to base number 025.58 the numbers following 02 in 026–027, e.g., use of government libraries 025.5875; however, class use studies of libraries for special groups and organizations in 027.6

Class studies of use of specific systems and services with the system or service, e.g., catalog use studies 025.313, studies of use of interlibrary loans 025.62

.6   Circulation services

Lending and renting materials, keeping records of loans and rentals

Class here document delivery

Class circulation services for special groups and organizations in 027.6

.62   Interlibrary loans

Including regulations

.7 **Physical preparation for storage and use**

Examples: binding, labeling, pocketing

Including repair and restoration

Class conservation and preservation in 025.84

.8 **Maintenance and preservation of collections**

Class repair and restoration in 025.7

.81 Physical arrangement and access to collections

Examples: closed and open stacks, integrated shelving of materials in different formats

.82 Security against theft and other hazards

Including taking of inventory

.84 Preservation

Class here conservation

For repair and restoration, see 025.7

> **026–027 Specific kinds of institutions**

Class here specific libraries, archives, information centers, and their collections; systems and networks for specific kinds of institutions; comprehensive works on operations in specific kinds of institutions

Class comprehensive works in 027

See Manual at 026–027

026 **Libraries, archives, information centers devoted to specific subjects and disciplines**

Class here information organizations and library departments and collections in specific disciplines and subjects; comprehensive works on archives, on special libraries

Class special libraries not devoted to specific disciplines and subjects in 027.6, e.g., general museum libraries 027.68, general libraries in newspaper offices 027.69

See Manual at T1—07 vs. 016, 026

.000 1–.000 5 Standard subdivisions

.000 6 Organizations and management

[.000 68] Management

Do not use; class in 025.19

.000 7–.000 9 Standard subdivisions

.001–.999 Specific subjects and disciplines

Add to base number 026 notation 001–999, e.g., medical libraries 026.61; however, do not add notation 068 from Table 1; class in 025.19

027 General libraries, archives, information centers

In the subdivisions of this number, the term *libraries* is used as a short way of saying libraries, archives, information centers, media centers

Class here comprehensive works on libraries, on information centers, on libraries and information centers devoted to special materials

For libraries, archives, information centers devoted to specific disciplines and subjects, see 026

See Manual at 027

SUMMARY

027.001–.009	Standard subdivisions
.01–.09	Geographical treatment
.1	Private and family libraries
.2	Proprietary libraries
.3	Rental libraries
.4	Public libraries
.5	Government libraries
.6	Libraries for special groups and organizations
.7	College and university libraries
.8	School libraries

.001–.005   Standard subdivisions

.006   Organizations and management

[.006 8]   Management

Do not use; class in 025.19

.007–.008   Standard subdivisions

.009   Historical and persons treatment

Class geographical treatment in 027.01–027.09

.01–.09   *Geographical treatment

Add to base number 027.0 notation 1–9 from Table 2, e.g., libraries in France 027.044

.1   *Private and family libraries

Collections not open to general use

Add to base number 027.1 notation 1–9 from Table 2, e.g., family libraries in the United Kingdom 027.141

*Do not add notation 068 from Table 1; class in 025.19

.2 ***Proprietary libraries**

Semiprivate libraries requiring subscription or membership fees for general use

Add to base number 027.2 notation 1–9 from Table 2, e.g., proprietary libraries in Leeds 027.242819

.3 ***Rental libraries**

Libraries whose materials are available for use on a commercial basis

Add to base number 027.3 notation 1–9 from Table 2, e.g., rental libraries in the United States 027.373

.4 ***Public libraries**

Institutions that provide free service to all residents of a community, district, region, usually supported in whole or in part from public funds

Class here public library branches, the use of bookmobiles (mobile libraries) in public librarianship

Class physical plant management of bookmobiles (mobile libraries) in 022, public library units devoted to specific disciplines and subjects in 026, public library units for special groups and organizations in 027.6

.409 Historical, geographical, persons treatment

Class treatment by specific continents, countries, localities in 027.43–027.49 (*not* 027.4093–027.4099)

.43–.49 *Treatment by specific continents, countries, localities

Add to base number 027.4 notation 3–9 from Table 2, e.g., public libraries in France 027.444

.5 ***Government libraries**

National, state, provincial, local

For government libraries for special groups, see 027.65

See Manual at 027.5

.509 Historical, geographical, persons treatment

Class specific institutions in 027.53–027.59 (*not* 027.5093–027.5099)

.53–.59 *Specific institutions

Add to base number 027.5 notation 3–9 from Table 2 for area served, e.g., Library of Congress 027.573

*Do not add notation 068 from Table 1; class in 025.19

.6   ***Libraries for special groups and organizations**

Class here library and information services to special groups and organizations, to the socially disadvantaged

Unless other instructions are given, class complex subjects with aspects in two or more subdivisions of 027.6 in the one coming last, e.g., libraries for children with disabilities 027.663 (*not* 027.625)

Class libraries for special groups and organizations devoted to specific disciplines and subjects in 026

For libraries for educational institutions, see 027.7–027.8

.62   *Libraries for specific age groups

.622   *For persons in late adulthood

.625   *For children

To age eleven

Including toy lending services in a library context

.625 1   Storytelling

.626   *For young adults

Ages twelve to twenty

.63   *For minority groups

.65   *Government libraries for special groups

Examples: government information agencies for foreign populaces, legislative reference bureaus

.66   *Welfare institution libraries

.662   *Hospital libraries

Class here comprehensive works on patients' and medical libraries

Class medical libraries in 026.61

.663   *Libraries for persons with disabilities

Example: libraries for persons with visual impairment

Class here mainstreaming (the provision of library and information services through regular channels to individuals with special needs)

.665   *Prison libraries

.67   *Libraries for religious organizations

.68   *Libraries for nonprofit organizations

Examples: libraries of learned societies, museum libraries, United Nations Library

For welfare institution libraries, see 027.66; libraries for religious organizations, 027.67

*Do not add notation 068 from Table 1; class in 025.19

.69   *Libraries for business and industrial organizations

             Example: reference collections in newspaper offices used in the writing or
             editing of articles

___

>   **027.7–027.8 Libraries for educational institutions**

             Class here instructional media centers

             Class comprehensive works in 027.7; libraries for educational institutions but
             devoted to specific disciplines and subjects in 026, e.g., university law libraries
             026.34

.7   ***College and university libraries**

             Class here comprehensive works on libraries for educational institutions,
             college and university library branches

             Class branches devoted to specific disciplines and subjects in 026, elementary
             and secondary school libraries in 027.8

.709   Historical, geographical, persons treatment

                 Class specific institutions in 027.73–027.79 (*not* 027.7093–027.7099)

.73–.79   *Specific institutions

                 Add to base number 027.7 notation 3–9 from Table 2, e.g., Perkins Library
                 of Duke University 027.7756563

.8   ***School libraries**

.809   Historical, geographical, persons treatment

                 Class specific libraries in 027.823–027.829 (*not* 027.8093–027.8099)

.82   Specific levels and specific libraries

                 Class libraries in church-supported schools of specific levels, in specific
                 church-supported schools in 027.83

.822   Specific levels

                 Class specific libraries of specific levels in 027.823–027.829

.822 2   *Elementary level

.822 3   *Secondary level

.823–.829   *Specific libraries

                 Add to base number 027.82 notation 3–9 from Table 2, e.g., Phillips
                 Exeter Academy Library 027.827426

.83   *Libraries in church-supported schools

___

*Do not add notation 068 from Table 1; class in 025.19

028 Reading and use of other information media

.1 Reviews

Class here general collections of book reviews

Class reviews of computer programs in 005.30296; techniques of reviewing in 808.066028; reviews of works on a specific subject or in a specific discipline with the subject or discipline, e.g., reviews of works on chemistry 540, reviews of entertainment films 791.43, critical appraisal of literature 800

.12 Of reference works

Class reviews of reference works published in specific forms in 028.13; reviews of reference works for specific kinds of users in 028.16; reviews of specific kinds of reference works with the kind, e.g., reviews of encyclopedias 030

.13 Of works published in specific forms

Add to base number 028.13 the numbers following 011.3 in 011.31–011.38, e.g., reviews of documentary, educational, and entertainment films 028.137

Class reviews of works published in specific forms for specific kinds of users in 028.16

General collections of books reviews are classed in 028.1

.16 Of works for specific kinds of users

Add to base number 028.16 the numbers following 011.6 in 011.62–011.67, e.g., reviews of works for children and young adults 028.162

.5 Reading and use of other information media by children and young adults

See also 028.162 for reviews of materials for young children and adults

.53 By specific age groups

Add to base number 028.53 the numbers following —05 in notation 054–055 from Table 7, e.g., reading and use of other information media by young adults 028.535

.55 Reading interests and habits of children and young adults

Class reading interests and habits of children and young adults of specific age groups in 028.53

.7 Use of books and other media as sources of information

Class here use of reference works

For reading and use of other information media by children and young adults, see 028.5

.8 Use of books and other media as sources of recreation and self-development

For reading and use of other information media by children and young adults, see 028.5

.9 Reading interests and habits

For reading interests and habits of children and young adults, see 028.55

[029] **[Unassigned]**

Most recently used in Edition 18

030 General encyclopedic works

Class here general works about curiosities [*formerly also* 001.93], books of miscellaneous facts (e.g., almanacs), encyclopedia yearbooks

.9 **Historical, geographical, persons treatment**

Class historical, geographical, persons treatment of encyclopedic works in specific languages and language families in 031–039

> ## 031–039 In specific languages and language families

By language in which originally written

Class here specific encyclopedias and books of miscellaneous facts, works about them

Books of unusual and curious facts are classed in the numbers for books of miscellaneous facts, e.g., American books of unusual and curious facts 031.02

(Option A: To give local emphasis and a shorter number to encyclopedias in a specific language, place them first by use of a letter or other symbol, e.g., Arabic-language encyclopedias 03A [preceding 031]. Option B is described under 031)

Class comprehensive works in 030; encyclopedic works originally written in two or more languages or language families with the preponderant language or language family; if none is preponderant, class in 030

031 American

English-language encyclopedias and books of miscellaneous facts originating in Western Hemisphere and Hawaii

(Option B: To give local emphasis and a shorter number to encyclopedias in a specific language other than English, class them in this number; in that case class American English-language encyclopedias in 032. Option A is described under 031–039)

.02 Books of miscellaneous facts

Examples: almanacs with general information, believe-it-or-not books

032 In English

For American English-language encyclopedias, see 031

.02 Books of miscellaneous facts

Example: Whitaker's *Almanack*

Use for facts & records

eg. Guinness Bks

033   In other Germanic languages

Class here comprehensive works on Germanic-language encyclopedias

Add to base number 03 notation 31–394 from Table 6, e.g., Dutch-language encyclopedias 033.931; then, for books of miscellaneous facts, add 02, e.g., Dutch-language books of miscellaneous facts 033.93102

Class English-language encyclopedias in 032, Scandinavian-language encyclopedias in 038

034   In French, Provençal, Catalan

Add to base number 03 notation 41–49 from Table 6, e.g., French-language encyclopedias 034.1; then, for books of miscellaneous facts, add 02, e.g., French-language almanacs 034.102

035   In Italian, Romanian, Rhaeto-Romanic

Add to base number 03 notation 51–59 from Table 6, e.g., Italian-language encyclopedias 035.1; then, for books of miscellaneous facts, add 02, e.g., Italian-language books of miscellaneous facts 035.102

036   In Spanish and Portuguese

Add to base number 03 notation 61–69 from Table 6, e.g., Portuguese-language encyclopedias 036.9; then, for books of miscellaneous facts, add 02, e.g., Portuguese-language books of miscellaneous facts 036.902

037   In Slavic languages

Add to notation for each term identified by * as follows:

02 Books of miscellaneous facts

.1	***Russian**
.8	**Other Slavic languages**

For Ukrainian- and Belorussian-language encyclopedias, see 037.9

.81	Bulgarian and Macedonian
.811	*Bulgarian
.819	*Macedonian
.82	*Serbo-Croatian
.84	*Slovenian
.85	*Polish
.86	*Czech
.87	*Slovak
.88	*Wendish (Sorbian, Lusatian)

*Add as instructed under 037

.9   **Ukrainian and Belorussian**

.91   *Ukrainian

.99   *Belorussian

038   In Scandinavian languages

Add to base number 038 the numbers following —39 in notation 396–398 from Table 6, e.g., Swedish-language encyclopedias 038.7; then, for books of miscellaneous facts, add 02, e.g., Swedish-language books of miscellaneous facts 038.702

039   In other languages

[.29]   In Old English (Anglo-Saxon)

Number discontinued because without use in context

.7–.9   **In Italic, Hellenic, other languages**

Add to base number 039 notation 7–9 from Table 6, e.g., Latin-language encyclopedias 039.71; then, for miscellaneous books of facts, add 02, e.g., Latin-language books of miscellaneous facts 039.7102

[040]   [Unassigned]

Most recently used in Edition 16

[041]   [Unassigned]

Most recently used in Edition 16

[042]   [Unassigned]

Most recently used in Edition 16

[043]   [Unassigned]

Most recently used in Edition 16

[044]   [Unassigned]

Most recently used in Edition 16

[045]   [Unassigned]

Most recently used in Edition 16

[046]   [Unassigned]

Most recently used in Edition 16

[047]   [Unassigned]

Most recently used in Edition 16

[048]   [Unassigned]

Most recently used in Edition 16

*Add as instructed under 037

[049]   [Unassigned]

Most recently used in Edition 16

050   General serial publications and their indexes

Class here periodicals

Class indexes that focus on a specific subject or discipline in general serial publications in 016, e.g., an index to information on medicine in general serial publications 016.61; books of miscellaneous facts (even if published annually, e.g., almanacs), encyclopedia yearbooks, in 030; administrative reports and proceedings of general organizations in 060

For newspapers, see 070

See also 011.34 for bibliographies of general serial publications, 011.7 for bibliographies of directories, 017–019 for catalogs of general serial publications

.9   Historical, geographical, persons treatment

Class historical, geographical, persons treatment of serial publications in specific languages and language families in 051–059

> ### 051–059 In specific languages and language families

By language in which originally written

Class here specific serial publications and works about them

(Option A: To give local emphasis and a shorter number to serial publications in a specific language, place them first by use of a letter or other symbol, e.g., Hindi-language serial publications 05H [preceding 051]. Option C is described under 051)

(Option B: Arrange serial publications alphabetically under 050)

Class comprehensive works in 050; serials originally written in two or more languages with the preponderant language or language family; if none is preponderant, class in 050

051   American

English-language serial publications of Western Hemisphere and Hawaii

(Option C: To give local emphasis and a shorter number to serial publications in a specific language other than English, class them in this number; in that case class American English-language serial publications in 052. Options A and B are described under 051–059)

052   In English

For American English-language serial publications, see 051

053 In other Germanic languages

Class here comprehensive works on general serial publications in Germanic languages

Add to base number 05 notation 31–394 from Table 6, e.g., Dutch-language serial publications 053.931

Class English-language serial publications in 052, Scandinavian-language serial publications in 058

054 In French, Provençal, Catalan

Add to base number 05 notation 41–49 from Table 6, e.g., French-language serial publications 054.1

055 In Italian, Romanian, Rhaeto-Romanic

Add to base number 05 notation 51–59 from Table 6, e.g., Italian-language serial publications 055.1

056 In Spanish and Portuguese

Add to base number 05 notation 61–69 from Table 6, e.g., Portuguese-language serial publications 056.9

057 In Slavic languages

Add to base number 057 the numbers following 037 in 037.1–037.9 for language only, e.g., Polish-language serial publications 057.85

058 In Scandinavian languages

Add to base number 058 the numbers following —39 in notation 396–398 from Table 6, e.g., Swedish-language serial publications 058.7

059 In other languages

[.29]   In Old English (Anglo-Saxon)

Number discontinued because without use in context

.7–.9 In Italic, Hellenic, other languages

Add to base number 059 notation 7–9 from Table 6, e.g., Chinese-language serial publications 059.951

060 General organizations and museology

General organizations: academies, associations, conferences, congresses, foundations, societies whose activity is not limited to a specific field

General aspects: history, charters, regulations, membership lists, administrative reports and proceedings

Class here interdisciplinary works on organizations; interdisciplinary works on licensing, certification, accreditation by nongovernmental organizations

(Option A: To give local emphasis and a shorter number to organizations in a specific country, place them first by use of a letter or other symbol, e.g., organizations in Pakistan 06P [preceding 061]. Option B is described under 061)

Class general organizations whose members are political states in 341, e.g., Arab League 341.2477; comprehensive works on licensing, certification, accreditation by governmental and nongovernmental bodies in 351.8; organizations devoted to a specific discipline or subject with the discipline or subject, using notation 06 from Table 1, e.g., organizations devoted to computer science 004.06

.4 **Special topics**

.42 General rules of order (Parliamentary procedure)

Example: *Robert's Rules of Order*

For rules and procedures of legislative bodies, see 328.1

See also 658.4563 for conduct of meetings of business organizations

.68 Management

Class here conduct of congresses and conferences [*formerly also* 658.4562]

.9 **Historical and persons treatment**

Class geographical treatment of general organizations in 061–068

> **061–068 General organizations**

Class comprehensive works in 060

061 General organizations in North America

(Option B: To give local emphasis and a shorter number to organizations in a specific country other than the United States and Canada, class them in this number; in that case class organizations in North America in 068.7. Option A is described under 060)

Class organizations in Middle America in 068.72

.1 **In Canada**

Add to base number 061.1 the numbers following —71 in notation 711–719 from Table 2, e.g., organizations in British Columbia 061.11

.3–.9   **In the United States**

Add to base number 061 the numbers following —7 in notation 73–79 from Table 2, e.g., general organizations in Ohio 061.71

Class organizations in Hawaii in 068.969

062   General organizations in British Isles   In England

.1–.8   **In England**

Add to base number 062 the numbers following —42 in notation 421–428 from Table 2, e.g., organizations in London 062.1

.9   **In Scotland, Ireland, Wales**

Add to base number 062.9 the numbers following —4 in notation 41–42 from Table 2, e.g., organizations in Scotland and Ireland 062.91

063   General organizations in central Europe   In Germany

Add to base number 063 the numbers following —43 in notation 431–439 from Table 2, e.g., organizations in Poland 063.8

064   General organizations in France and Monaco

Add to base number 064 the numbers following —44 in notation 441–449 from Table 2, e.g., organizations in Paris 064.36

065   General organizations in Italy and adjacent territories

Add to base number 065 the numbers following —45 in notation 451–459 from Table 2, e.g., organizations in Rome 065.632

066   General organizations in Iberian Peninsula and adjacent islands   In Spain

Add to base number 066 the numbers following —46 in notation 461–469 from Table 2, e.g., organizations in Portugal 066.9

067   General organizations in eastern Europe   In Union of Soviet Socialist Republics (Soviet Union)

Add to base number 067 the numbers following —47 in notation 472–479 from Table 2, e.g., organizations in Ukraine 067.71

068   General organizations in other geographical areas

Add to base number 068 notation 1–9 from Table 2, e.g., comprehensive works on general organizations in Europe 068.4, in Middle America 068.72

069 Museology (Museum science)

Museum activities and services limited to specific subjects or disciplines relocated to the subject or discipline with use of notation 075 from Table 1, e.g., activities and services of a clock museum 681.113075

SUMMARY

069.01–.09	Standard subdivisions
.1	Museum services to patrons
.2	Management and use of physical plant
.3	Equipment, furniture, furnishings
.4	Collecting and preparing museum objects
.5	Collections and exhibits of museum objects
.6	Personnel management, regulations for patrons, relationships with other organizations

[.068 2]   Plant management

Do not use; class in 069.2

[.068 3]   Personnel management

Do not use; class in 069.63

[.068 5]   Organization of production

Do not use; class in 069.1

[.068 7]   Management of materials

Do not use; class in 069.5

.09   Historical, geographical, persons treatment

Class here specific museums not limited to a specific discipline or subject

Class historical, geographical, persons treatment of museum buildings in 069.209; museums devoted to specific disciplines and subjects with the discipline or subject, using notation 074 from Table 1, e.g., natural history museums 508.074

.1   **Museum services to patrons**

Class here organization of production

.13   Circulation services

Lending and renting materials

See also 069.56 for lending and rental collections

.132   Museum objects

.134   Representations of museum objects and aids to their use

Examples: pictures, slides, films, projectors

.15   Instruction services

Examples: lectures, classes, field trips

.16   Recreational services

Examples: musical programs, theatrical presentations

.17	Special services to handicapped patrons
.2	**Management and use of physical plant**

For equipment, furniture, furnishings, see 069.3

.21	Location and site
.22	Planning for buildings

See also 727.6 for museum architecture

.24	Special rooms
.29	Utilities and related facilities

Examples: communication systems, lighting, plumbing, heating, ventilating, air-conditioning

.3	**Equipment, furniture, furnishings**
.31	Exhibit cases, screens, pedestals
.32	Audiovisual apparatus
.33	Furniture
.4	**Collecting and preparing museum objects**

General aspects: equipment, materials, methods

Class here management of collecting and preparing museum objects

Class comprehensive works on management of museum materials, on collecting or preparing museum objects and collections of museum objects in 069.5; collecting a specific kind of object or objects that pertain to a specific subject or discipline with the subject or discipline, using notation 075 from Table 1, e.g., collecting fossils 560.75

.5	**Collections and exhibits of museum objects**

Class here comprehensive works on management of museum materials, on collecting or preparing museum objects and collections of museum objects

For collecting and preparing museum objects, see 069.4

[.502 88]	Maintenance and repair

Do not use; class in 069.53

.502 89	Safety measures

See also 069.54 for prevention of thefts and identification of forgeries

---

> 069.51–069.54 General activities

Class comprehensive works in 069.5, general activities applied to special collections in 069.55–069.57

.51	Selection, acquisition, disposal

.52   Registration, recording, indexing

Class here museum documentation

.53   Maintenance, conservation, preservation, restoration, display, arrangement, storage, transportation

Including museum labels

Class historic preservation in 363.69

.54   Prevention of thefts and identification of forgeries

> 069.55–069.57 Special collections

General aspects: classification, arrangement, housing

Class comprehensive works in 069.5

.55   Study collections

.56   Lending and rental collections

See also 069.13 for circulation services

.57   Collections of secondary materials

Examples: brochures, films, motion pictures, photographs, pictures, prints, slides representing museum objects

.6   **Personnel management, regulations for patrons, relations with other organizations**

.62   Regulations for patrons

Examples: for members, for visitors

.63   Personnel management

Including in-service training, staff manuals

.68   Relations with other organizations

Class public relations for museums in 659.29069

[.7]   **Publishing and printing**

Publishing by museums relocated to 070.594, printing by museums to 686.2

[.9]   **Museums, collections, exhibits devoted to specific disciplines and subjects**

Relocated to the subject or discipline with use of notation 074 from Table 1, e.g., military museums 355.0074

070   Documentary media, educational media, news media; journalism; publishing

SUMMARY

070.01–.09	Standard subdivisions of documentary media, educational media, news media; journalism; publishing
.1–.9	Documentary media, educational media, news media; journalism; publishing
071	Journalism and newspapers in North America
072	Journalism and newspapers in British Isles In England
073	Journalism and newspapers in Central Europe In Germany
074	Journalism and newspapers in France and Monaco
075	Journalism and newspapers in Italy and adjacent territories
076	Journalism and newspapers in Iberian Peninsula and adjacent islands In Spain
077	Journalism and newspapers in eastern Europe In Union of Soviet Socialist Republics (Soviet Union)
078	Journalism and newspapers in Scandinavia
079	Journalism and newspapers in other geographical areas

.01–.08   Standard subdivisions of documentary media, educational media, news media; journalism; publishing

> Standard subdivisions are also added for newspapers and journalism alone

.09   Historical, geographical, persons treatment of documentary media, educational media, news media; journalism; publishing

> Class historical and persons treatment of journalism and newspapers in 070.9, geographical treatment of journalism and newspapers in 071–079

SUMMARY

070.1	Documentary media, educational media, news media
.4	Journalism
.5	Publishing
.9	Historical and persons treatment of journalism and newspapers

.1   **Documentary media, educational media, news media**

> Class here comprehensive works on journalism and production of specific kinds of educational, expository, news media

> Class interdisciplinary works on mass media in 302.23; specific journalistic activities and types of journalism in 070.4; expository writing and editorial techniques in 808.066; documentary, educational, news works themselves and discussion of them with the kind of general work or with the subject, e.g., general periodicals 050, recorded television programs on investing 332.6

.17   Print media

Class the book in 002

.172   Newspapers

Class newspaper publishing in 070.5722, specific general newspapers in 070–079

See also 011.35 for bibliographies of newspapers

[.172 09]   Historical, geographical, persons treatment

Do not use; class historical and persons treatment in 070.9, geographical treatment in 071–079

.175   Periodicals

Example: newsletters

Class specific general periodicals in 050; periodicals on a specific discipline or subject with the discipline or subject, using notation 05 from Table 1, e.g., science journals 505

.18   Motion pictures

Examples: educational films [*formerly* 791.4353]; documentary films, newsreels [*both formerly also* 791.4353]

Class interdisciplinary works on motion pictures in 302.2343; works about motion pictures that are interdisciplinary but lack treatment of sociological aspects in 384.8; photography aspects in 778.53; comprehensive works about documentary, educational, news and dramatic or entertainment films in 791.43

See also 371.33523 for use of motion pictures in teaching

.19   Broadcast media

.194   Radio

Examples: news [*formerly also* 791.445]; educational, expository programs [*both formerly* 791.445]

Class interdisciplinary works on radio in 302.2344; works on radio that are interdisciplinary but lack treatment of sociological aspects in 384.54; comprehensive works on documentary, educational, news and dramatic or entertainment radio programs in 791.44

See also 371.3331 for use of radio in teaching

.195   Television

Examples: news [*formerly also* 791.455]; educational, expository programs [*both formerly* 791.455]

Class interdisciplinary works about television in 302.2345; works that are interdisciplinary but lack treatment of sociological aspects in 384.55; comprehensive works on documentary, educational, news and dramatic or entertainment television programs in 791.45; photographic aspects in 778.59

See also 371.3358 for use of television in teaching

.4 Journalism

Collecting, writing, editing information and opinion of current interest for presentation in newspapers, periodicals, films, radio, television

Journalists whose careers span many activities are classed in 070.92. Persons in a specific type of journalism are classed with the type, e.g., editors 070.41092, foreign correspondents 070.4332092

Class comprehensive works on journalism and information media in 070, journalism of specific kinds of news media in 070.1, journalistic composition and editorial mechanics in 808.06607

See also 050 for general periodicals, 070.5722 for newspaper publishing, 071–079 for specific newspapers, 174.9097 for ethics of journalism, notation 05 from Table 1 for journals on a specific discipline or subject

SUMMARY

070.401–.409	Standard subdivisions
.41	Editing
.43	News gathering and reporting
.44	Features and special topics
.48	Journalism directed to special groups
.49	Pictorial journalism

.401–.407 Standard subdivisions

.408 Journalism with respect to groups of persons

Class journalism directed to special groups in 070.48

[.409] Historical, geographical, persons treatment

Do not use; class historical and persons treatment in 070.9, geographical treatment in 071–079

.41 Editing

Including editorial crusades, policy on editorial cartoons

Class here editorial policy (selection, presentation, display of news; advocacy of specific points of view)

Class comprehensive works on editing and news gathering or reporting in 070.4; editing with respect to features and special topics in 070.44; editorials in 070.442

See also 808.06607 for editorial mechanics, e.g.,copy editing, the UPI (United Press International) stylebook

[.412] Editorial policy

Number discontinued; class in 070.41

[.415] Editorial mechanics in journalistic writing

Relocated to 808.06607

.43   News gathering and reporting

Class comprehensive works on editorial policy and news gathering or reporting in 070.4; news gathering and reporting with respect to feature and special topics in 070.44

.431   News sources

.433   Reporting local, foreign, war news

Broad descriptions of local, foreign, war reporting as types of reporting, not limited to a specific subject or geographical area; how to do the reporting

Class reporting of specific subjects in 070.449, e.g., reporting on world-wide energy resources 070.44933379, reporting on the Vietnamese War 070.4499597043

Use of this number for reporting other specific types of news discontinued; class in 070.43

See Manual at 070.433

.433 2   Foreign news

Class here international news

Class foreign war news in 070.4333

.433 3   War news

.435   Wire services

Examples: Associated Press, Reuters

>   070.44–070.49 Specific types of journalism

Class comprehensive works in 070.4

.44   Features and special topics

General aspects: techniques and procedures for information-gathering, writing, editing for reports, criticisms, opinions

Class here newspaper columns

Class reports, criticism, opinions on specific subjects with the subject, e.g., criticisms of theatrical productions 792

.442   Interpretation and opinion

Examples: newspaper editorials, radio comment

Class editorial policy in 070.41

.444   Miscellaneous information, advice, amusement

Examples: humor, general personal advice columns

Here are classed biographies of journalists specializing in these types of features, e.g., general personal advice columnists 070.444092; however, biographies of cartoonists are classed in 741.5092, of humorous writers in 800, e.g., a contemporary British writer of humorous essays 824.914

Health columns relocated to 070.449613, recipes relocated to 070.4496415

Class journalistic handling of information, advice, humor on specific subjects in 070.449, e.g., advice on dating 070.44964677

See also 741.5 for artistic aspects of comics

.449   Specific subjects

Add to base number 070.449 notation 001–999, e.g., health columns 070.449613, recipes 070.4496415 [*both formerly* 070.444], radio sports programs 070.449796 [*formerly also* 791.445], television sports programs 070.449796 [*formerly also* 791.455], television news coverage of inflation 070.44933241

Here are classed journalists specializing in specific subjects, e.g., sports announcers 070.449796092

Class features and reports themselves with the subject, e.g., health columns 613

See also 070.433 for reporting of local, foreign, war news as general types of news; 070.444 for miscellaneous information, advice, amusements as types of journalism; 070.48 for general journalism directed to special groups

.48   Journalism directed to special groups

Class editing in journalism directed to specific groups in 070.41; news gathering and reporting in journalism directed to specific groups in 070.43; features and special topics directed to special groups in 070.44, e.g., news about religion 070.4492 (*not* 070.482); school journalism in 371.897

.482   Religious groups

.483   Groups by age and sex

.483 2   Children

.483 26   Boys

.483 27   Girls

.483 3   Young adults

.483 36   Young men

.483 37   Young women

.483 4   Adults

.483 46   Men

.483 47   Women

.484	Foreign-language and nondominant racial, ethnic, national groups
.486	Occupational and employee groups

General journalism for occupational and employee groups

Example: house organs

Class journalism on a specific subject directed to occupational and employee groups in 070.449

.49	Pictorial journalism

Class here photojournalism

.5	**Publishing**

Class here book publishing; publishers regardless of their field of activity; book clubs, e.g., Book-of-the-Month Club®; comprehensive works on publishing and printing

Works on ''desktop publishing'' that emphasize typography are classed in 686.22, e.g., microcomputer software for typesetting 686.2254436

For printing, see 686.2

.502 94	Trade catalogs and directories

Publishers' catalogs relocated to 015

.509	Historical, geographical, persons treatment

Class here comprehensive works on specific publishers, using the area number for the publisher's main office, e.g., U.S. Government Printing Office 070.509753 [*formerly also* 070.595], University of California Press 070.50979467

Class economic aspects of publishers as business organizations in 338.7610705

.51	Selection and editing of manuscripts

Class editorial techniques in 808.02

.52	Relations with authors

Including literary agents

See Manual at 808.001–808.7 vs. 070.52

.57	Kinds of publications

Class specific publishers in 070.509, selection and editing of manuscripts for specific kinds of publications in 070.51, relations with authors of specific kinds of publications in 070.52

.572	Serials

Class comprehensive works on journalism and publishing of serials in 070.17

.572 2	Newspapers

.573	Specific kinds of books

Examples: limited editions, paperbacks, subscription books

Class serials in book form in 070.572

.579	Special kinds of publications
.579 2	Braille and other raised characters
.579 3	Maps
.579 4	Music
.579 5	Microforms
.59	Kinds of publishers

Class specific publishers in 070.509, selection and editing of manuscripts by specific kinds of publishers in 070.51, relations with authors of specific kinds of publishers in 070.52, specific kinds of publications of specific kinds of publishers in 070.57

.592	Commercial publishers
.593	Private publishers

Class here self-publishing

Works on ''desktop publishing'' that emphasize typography are classed in 686.22, e.g., microcomputer software for typesetting 686.2254436

.594	Institutional publishers

Examples: church, society, university publishers

Including publishing by libraries, archives, information centers [*formerly* 025.12], by museums [*formerly* 069.7]

.595	Governmental and intergovernmental publishers

U.S. Government Printing Office relocated to 070.509753

.9	**Historical and persons treatment of journalism and newspapers**

Class geographical treatment in 071–079

.92	Persons regardless of area, region, place

> ## 071–079 Geographical treatment of journalism and newspapers

Class here specific general newspapers, indexes to them, other works about them

(Option A: To give local emphasis and a shorter number to newspapers and journalism in a specific country, place them first by use of a letter or other symbol, e.g., newspapers and journalism in New Zealand 07N [preceding 071])

(Option B: Arrange newspapers alphabetically under 070)

(Option C is described under 071)

Class comprehensive works in 070

071   Journalism and newspapers in North America

(Option C: To give local emphasis and a shorter number to journalism and newspapers in a specific country other than the United States and Canada, class them in this number; in that case class journalism and newspapers in North America in 079.7. Options A and B are described under 071–079)

Class journalism and newspapers in Middle America in 079.72

.1   Journalism and newspapers in Canada

Add to base number 071.1 the numbers following —71 in notation 711–719 from Table 2, e.g., journalism and newspapers in British Columbia 071.11

.3–.9   Journalism and newspapers in the United States

Add to base number 071 the numbers following —7 in notation 73–79 from Table 2, e.g., *New York Times* 071.471

Class journalism and newspapers in Hawaii in 079.969

072   Journalism and newspapers in British Isles   In England

.1–.8   Journalism and newspapers in England

Add to base number 072 the numbers following —42 in notation 421–428 from Table 2, e.g., *Times* of London 072.1

.9   Journalism and newspapers in Scotland, Ireland, Wales

Add to base number 072.9 the numbers following —4 in notation 41–42 from Table 2, e.g., newspapers in Scotland and Ireland 072.91

073   Journalism and newspapers in central Europe   In Germany

Add to base number 073 the numbers following —43 in notation 431–439 from Table 2, e.g., journalism and newspapers in Austria 073.6

074   Journalism and newspapers in France and Monaco

Add to base number 074 the numbers following —44 in notation 441–449 from Table 2, e.g., journalism and newspapers in Paris 074.36

075   Journalism and newspapers in Italy and adjacent territories

> Add to base number 075 the numbers following —45 in notation 451–459 from Table 2, e.g., journalism and newspapers in Rome 075.632

076   Journalism and newspapers in Iberian Peninsula and adjacent islands   In Spain

> Add to base number 076 the numbers following —46 in notation 461–469 from Table 2, e.g., journalism and newspapers in Portugal 076.9

077   Journalism and newspapers in eastern Europe   In Union of Soviet Socialist Republics (Soviet Union)

> Add to base number 077 the numbers following —47 in notation 472–479 from Table 2, e.g., journalism and newspapers in Ukraine 077.71

078   Journalism and newspapers in Scandinavia

> Add to base number 078 the numbers following —48 in notation 481–489 from Table 2, e.g., journalism and newspapers in Sweden 078.5

079   Journalism and newspapers in other geographical areas

> Add to base number 079 notation 1–9 from Table 2, e.g., comprehensive works on general newspapers in Europe 079.4, in Middle America 079.72

080   General collections

> Class here addresses, lectures, essays, interviews, graffiti, quotations
>
> Class essays as literary form, collections gathered for their literary quality in 800
>
> *See Manual at 080*

.9   Historical, geographical, persons treatment

> Class historical, geographical, persons treatment of collections in specific languages and language families in 081–089

> **081–089 In specific languages and language families**
>
> (Option A: To give local emphasis and a shorter number to collections in a specific language, place them first by use of a letter or symbol, e.g., collections in Urdu 08U [preceding 081])
>
> (Option B: Arrange collections alphabetically under 080)
>
> (Option C is described under 081)
>
> Class comprehensive works in 080
>
> *See Manual at 081–089*

081   American

English-language collections of Western Hemisphere and Hawaii

(Option C: To give local emphasis and a shorter number to collections in a specific language other than English, class them in this number; in that case class American English-language collections in 082. Options A and B are described under 081–089)

082   In English

For American English-language collections, see 081

083   In other Germanic languages

Class here comprehensive works on Germanic-language collections

Add to base number 08 notation 31–394 from Table 6, e.g., German-language collections 083.1

Class English-language collections in 082, Scandinavian-language collections in 088, Anglo-Saxon-language collections in 089

084   In French, Provençal, Catalan

Add to base number 08 notation 41–49 from Table 6, e.g., French-language collections 084.1

085   In Italian, Romanian, Rhaeto-Romanic

Add to base number 08 notation 51–59 from Table 6, e.g., Italian-language collections 085.1

086   In Spanish and Portuguese

Add to base number 08 notation 61–69 from Table 6, e.g., Portuguese-language collections 086.9

087   In Slavic languages

Add to base number 087 the numbers following 037 in 037.1–037.9 for language only, e.g., Polish-language collections 087.85

088   In Scandinavian languages

Add to base number 088 the numbers following —39 in notation 396–398 from Table 6, e.g., Swedish-language collections 088.7

089   In other languages

Including Old English (Anglo-Saxon)

[.29]   In Old English (Anglo-Saxon)

Number discontinued; class in 089

.7–.9   In Italic, Hellenic, other languages

Add to base number 089 notation 7–9 from Table 6, e.g., Chinese-language collections 089.951

090   Manuscripts, rare books, other rare printed materials

General aspects: critical appraisal, description, history

Example: rare broadsides

Class interdisciplinary works on books in 002; a manuscript or rare work with its subject, e.g., a book of hours 242; an artistic aspect with the aspect, e.g., illumination 745.67

> *See also 011.31 for bibliographies of both manuscripts and rare books, 011.44 for bibliographies of rare books only*

091   Manuscripts

> *See also 011.31 for bibliographies of manuscripts*

092   Block books

093   Incunabula

Books printed before 1501

> *See also 011.42 for bibliographies of incunabula*

094   Printed books

.2   Early printed books

To 1700

> *For block books, see 092; incunabula, 093*

.4   Special editions

Examples: first editions, limited editions, typographic masterpieces

095   Books notable for bindings

> *See also 686.3 for bookbinding*

096   Books notable for illustrations and materials

.1   For illustrations

Class illustrated manuscripts in 091

.2   For materials

Examples: leaves of vellum and silk, letters of silver and gold

097   Books notable for ownership or origin

098   Prohibited works, forgeries, hoaxes

.1   Prohibited works

.11   Prohibited by religious authorities

.12   Prohibited by civil authorities

.3   **Forgeries and hoaxes**

099   Books notable for format

Examples: books of unusual shapes, miniature editions

100

---

100   Philosophy, parapsychology and occultism, psychology

Class philosophy of a specific discipline or subject with the discipline or subject using notation 01 from Table 1, e.g., philosophy of history 901

See Manual at T1—01; 100; 100, 109 vs.190; 100 vs.200

101   Theory of philosophy

Class here works on the concept of philosophy, on the nature of the philosophical task, on the method of philosophy

Class schools of philosophical thought in 140 or 180

102   Miscellany of philosophy

103   Dictionaries, encyclopedias, concordances of philosophy

[104]   [Unassigned]

Most recently used in Edition 16

105   Serial publications of philosophy

106   Organizations and management of philosophy

107   Education, research, related topics of philosophy

108   History and description of philosophy with respect to kinds of persons

109   Historical and collected persons treatment of philosophy

Not limited by period or place

Class geographical and individual persons treatment in 180–190

Use 109.2 for collected persons treatment

See Manual at 100, 109 vs.190

[.22]   Collected persons treatment

Number discontinued; class in 109.2

110   Metaphysics

For epistemology, causation, humankind, see 120

111   Ontology

.1   **Existence, essence, substance, accidents**

.2   **Universals**

.5   **Nonbeing, nothingness**

.6   **Finite and infinite**

Including the absolute

.8   **Classical properties of being**

Class comprehensive works on truth in 121

.82   Unity

Including part-whole relationships

[.83]   Truth

Number discontinued; class in 111.8

.84   Goodness and evil

For ethics, see 170

.85   Beauty

Class here interdisciplinary works on aesthetics

Class aesthetics of a specific subject with the subject, e.g., of the arts 700.1

[112]   [Unassigned]

Most recently used in Edition 18

113   Cosmology (Philosophy of nature)

Including origin of universe (cosmogony), cosmic harmony

Class specific topics of cosmology not provided for here in 114–119; cosmology as a topic in astronomy in 523.1

.8   **Philosophy of life**

Origin and nature of life

Class origin and nature of human life in 128

114   Space

Class here relation of space and matter

Class matter in 117

115   Time

Including eternity, space and time, space-time, relation of time and motion

For space, see 114

116   Change
>   Including becoming, cycles, evolution, motion, process
>
>   Class relation of time and motion in 115

117   Structure
>   Including matter, form, order
>
>   Class relation of space and matter in 114

118   Force and energy

119   Number and quantity

120   Epistemology, causation, humankind

121   Epistemology (Theory of knowledge)
>   Class here comprehensive works on truth, e.g., coherence, correspondence theories
>
>   Class knowledge and its extension in 001, truth in logic in 160

.2   Possibility and limits of knowledge
>   Including solipsism and problem of other minds

.3   Origin, sources, means of knowledge
>   Examples: intuition, perception, reason, sensation
>
>   Class reason as a human attribute in 128.3

.4   Structure of knowledge
>   Subjective and objective components
>
>   Including concepts, ideas

.5   Doubt and denial
>   Class comprehensive works on doubt, denial, certainty, probability in 121.63

.6   Nature of inquiry
>   Including belief
>
>   Class faith in 121.7

.63   Certainty and probability
>   *For doubt and denial, see 121.5*

.65   Evidence and criteria

.68 Meaning, interpretation, hermeneutics

Including semantics, semiotics as topics in philosophy

Class interdisciplinary works on semiotics in 302.2

See also 149.94 for general semantics as a school of linguistic philosophy, 401.41 for semiotics in linguistics, 401.43 for semantics in linguistics

.7 **Faith**

Class belief in 121.6, religious faith in 200

.8 **Worth and theory of values (Axiology)**

Class ethical values in 170

122 **Causation**

Class here chance versus cause

For determinism and indeterminism, see 123; teleology, 124

123 **Determinism and indeterminism**

Including contingency

.3 **Chance**

Class chance versus cause in 122

.5 **Freedom**

Including freedom of will

.7 **Necessity**

124 **Teleology**

Design, purpose, final cause

[125] **[Unassigned]**

Most recently used in Edition 18

126 **The self**

Class here consciousness and personality

Class the unconscious and the subconscious in 127

127 **The unconscious and the subconscious**

128   Humankind

Class here philosophical anthropology; comprehensive works on philosophy of human life, on philosophy and psychology of human life

For the self, see 126; psychology, 150

See also 573 for physical anthropology

.1   Soul

For origin and destiny of individual souls, see 129

.2   Mind

Including mind-body relationship

.3   Attributes and faculties

Examples: appetite, imagination, memory, reason, will

Class reason as an instrument of knowledge in 121.3

For freedom of will, see 123.5

.4   Human action and experience

Nature, conditions, origin

.5   Human death

Use of this number for human life discontinued; class in 128

Class interdisciplinary works on death in 306.9

129   Origin and destiny of individual souls

Including incarnation, reincarnation, immortality

Class accounts of previous incarnations in 133.9013

See Manual at 133.9013 vs. 129

130   Paranormal phenomena

Class comprehensive works on controversial knowledge and paranormal phenomena in 001.9, phenomena of religious experience in 200

See Manual at 001.9 and 130; 130 vs. 133

SUMMARY

131	**Parapsychological and occult methods for achieving well-being, happiness, success**
133	**Parapsychology and occultism**
135	**Dreams and mysteries**
137	**Divinatory graphology**
138	**Physiognomy**
139	**Phrenology**

[.112]   Forecasting and forecasts

Do not use here or in any subdivision of 130; class comprehensive works in 133.3; a specific type with the type, without adding notation 0112 from Table 1, e.g., astrological methods of forecasting 133.5

131   Parapsychological and occult methods for achieving well-being, happiness, success

Class interdisciplinary works on successful living, on management of personal and family living in 646.7; comprehensive works on psychological and parapsychological or occult techniques for achievement of personal well-being, happiness, success in 158; specific methods of parapsychology and occultism for achieving well-being with the subject in 130–139, e.g., spells and charms 133.44

[132]   [Unassigned]

Most recently used in Edition 16

133   Parapsychology and occultism

Class here frauds in occultism

Standard subdivisions are added for either or both of the topics named in the heading

For cabalistic, Hermetic, Rosicrucian traditions, see 135.4

See Manual at 130 vs. 133; 133 vs. 200

SUMMARY

133.1	**Apparitions**	
.3	**Divinatory arts**	
.4	**Demonology and witchcraft**	
.5	**Astrology**	
.6	**Palmistry**	
.8	**Psychic phenomena**	
.9	**Spiritualism**	

.1   Apparitions

Class here ghosts

Class comprehensive works on discarnate spirits in 133.9, folkloristic ghost stories in 398.25, ghosts as a subject of folklore in 398.47, literary accounts of ghosts in 808.80375

See Manual at 133.129 vs. 133.109

.12   Haunted places

.122   Specific types of haunted places

Examples: haunted churches, forests, graveyards, houses

Class specific haunted places regardless of type in 133.129

.129   Specific haunted places

Add to base number 133.129 notation 3–9 from Table 2, e.g., the Tower of London 133.1294215

Class general historical and geographical treatment of ghosts in 133.109

See Manual at 133.129 vs. 133.109

.14	Specific kinds of apparitions

Examples: disembodied spirits, hobgoblins, phantasms of the living, poltergeists

Class haunted places regardless of kind of apparition in 133.12, materialization of spirits as a mediumistic phenomenon in 133.92

.3	**Divinatory arts**

Class here works on the symbolism of divinatory arts and objects, comprehensive works on occult methods of foretelling the future

Persons known chiefly for their predictions rather than their methods of predicting are classed in 133.3092, e.g., Nostradamus (Michel de Notredame)

Class use of extrasensory perception for divination in 133.82–133.86

For astrology, see 133.5; palmistry, 133.6; dream books, 135.3; divinatory graphology, 137; physiognomy, 138

See also 003.2 for interdisciplinary works on forecasting, 291.32 for divination as a religious practice, 303.49 for social forecasting

.32	Crystal gazing; radiesthesia; fortune-telling by cards, tea leaves and coffee grounds, oracles and sibyls
.322	Crystal gazing
.323	Radiesthesia

Location of living and inert substances through human sensitivity to latent radiations and use of divining rods, pendulums, other devices

---

>	133.323 2–133.323 7 Location of specific substances

Class comprehensive works in 133.323

.323 2	Location of water
.323 3	Location of metals
.323 7	Location of petroleum and gases
.323 9	Telediesthesia (Distant prospection)

Class location of specific substances by telediesthesia in 133.3232–133.3237

.324	Fortune-telling by cards, tea leaves and coffee grounds, oracles and sibyls

Use of this number for comprehensive works on fortune-telling discontinued; class in 133.3

.324 2	Fortune-telling by cards (Cartomancy)
.324 24	By tarot
[.324 29]	By other kinds of cards

Number discontinued; class in 133.3242

.324 4	Fortune-telling by tea leaves and coffee grounds
.324 8	Fortune-telling by oracles and sibyls
.33	Symbolic divination

Examples: divination with *I Ching*, with runes

For cartomancy, see 133.3242

.333	Geomancy
.334	Divinatory signs and omens
.335	Numerology
.335 4	Fortune-telling by numbers
.335 9	Symbolism of specific numbers
.4	**Demonology and witchcraft**

Class here black arts

For divinatory arts, see 133.3

See also 299.67 for voodooism

See Manual at 133 vs. 200

.42	Demonology

See also 291.216 for religious beliefs about demons

See Manual at 133 vs. 200

.422	Satanism (Devil worship)

See also 299 for Satanic cults regarded as religions by their adherents

See Manual at 133 vs. 200

.423	Evil spirits

Examples: incubi, succubi, vampires, werewolves

.425	The evil eye
.426	Demoniac possession
.427	Exorcism of demons
.43	Magic and witchcraft

Class here magicians' manuals, e.g., grimoire; witch hunting

Standard subdivisions are added for either or both of the topics named in the heading

For spells, curses, charms, see 133.44

See also 291.33 for witchcraft regarded as a religious practice

See Manual at 133 vs. 200

.430 9   Historical, geographical, persons treatment

                          Class here history of witch crazes [*formerly* 900]

                          See also 306.4 for social analysis of witch crazes

.44   Spells, curses, charms

                          Examples: amulets, talismans

                          Including mascots

.442   Love spells and charms

.443   Good luck spells and charms

.446   Therapeutic spells and charms

.5   **Astrology**

                          Class here astrological symbolism

.52   Signs of the zodiac

                          Class planets in 133.53

.53   Planets, sun, moon

                          Including rulership

                          Class here aspects, houses, positions of planets

.54   Horoscopes

.540 4   Special topics

.540 42   Daily guides and birthday books

.542   Casting horoscopes

.548   Horoscopes of individuals

                          Class horoscopes of individuals connected with specific topics in 133.58

.55   Astrological ephemerides

.56   Horary astrology

.58   Application to specific topics

                          Add to base number 133.58 notation 001–999, e.g., medical astrology 133.5861, astrological guides to personal sex life 133.5864677, astrological analysis and prediction about the United States and its leaders 133.58973

.6   **Palmistry**

[.62]   Chirognomy

                          Number discontinued; class in 133.6

[.64]   Chiromancy

                          Number discontinued; class in 133.6

.8   **Psychic phenomena**

     Including human aura, Kirlian photography of human aura

     Class here psi phenomena; comprehensive works on psychic communication; comprehensive works on psychic talents and gifts; comprehensive works on extrasensory perception (ESP), spiritualism, ghosts

     Class comprehensive works on divination in 133.3

        For ghosts, see 133.1; spiritualism, 133.9

        See also 778.3 for photographic aspects of Kirlian photography

---

\>   133.82–133.86 Extrasensory perception

     Class comprehensive works in 133.8

.82   Telepathy

.84   Clairvoyance

.85   Clairaudience

.86   Precognition

.88   Psychokinesis

.9   **Spiritualism**

     The phenomena and systems of ideas connected with belief in communication with discarnate spirits

     Including astral projection (out-of-body travel), communication with extraterrestrial spirits

     Class here necromancy, comprehensive works on discarnate spirits

        For ghosts, see 133.1

        See also 291.213 for spiritualism as a religious doctrine, 289.9 for spiritualist Christian sects, 292–299 for other spiritualist sects and religions

        See Manual at 133 vs. 200

.901   Philosophy and theory

.901 3   Personal survival, nature of spiritual world and life after death

     Including personal recollections of previous incarnations

        See Manual at 133.9013 vs. 129

.91   Mediumship

     Nature and practice

     Class here channeling, psychic experiences of individual mediums

        For specific mediumistic phenomena, see 133.92

.92   Specific mediumistic phenomena

> Examples: dematerialization, ectoplasm, levitation, rapping, spirit photography, table tipping, transportation

> *For psychic messages, see 133.93*

.93   Psychic messages

> Method and content of communications purporting to come from discarnate entities

> Examples: automatic writings and utterances, ouija board messages

> Including psychic messages on specific nonreligious topics not provided for in 130, e.g., unidentified flying objects (UFOs)

> Class psychic messages on religious subjects in 200; messages on a specific subject in paranormal phenomena with the subject, e.g., messages concerning nature of spiritual world and life after death 133.9013

[134]   [Unassigned]

> Most recently used in Edition 16

135   Dreams and mysteries

> Class mysteries of magic and witchcraft in 133.43

> *See also 001.94 for interdisciplinary works on mysteries in the sense of reported phenomena not explained, not fully verified*

.3   Dreams

> Including dream books

> Class interdisciplinary works on psychological and parapsychological aspects of dreams in 154.63

.4   Cabalistic, Hermetic, Rosicrucian traditions

> Use of this number for other mysteries, for initiation in other mysteries discontinued; class in 135

> *See also 296.16 for Cabala in Judaism*

[.42]   Mysteries of the ancient elements

> Number discontinued; class in 135

.43   Rosicrucianism

[136]   [Unassigned]

> Most recently used in Edition 16

137   Divinatory graphology

> Class interdisciplinary works on graphology and use of graphology in analyzing character in 155.282

138   Physiognomy

Class here comprehensive works on determination of character or divination from analysis of physical features

For palmistry, see 133.6; phrenology, 139

139   Phrenology

Determination of mental capacities from skull structures

140   Specific philosophical schools and viewpoints

Including the concept of ideology, of a world view, of a system of beliefs

Class comprehensive works on modern Western viewpoints in 190, on modern Western and ancient, medieval, Oriental viewpoints in 100; development, description, critical appraisal, collected writings, biographical treatment of individual philosophers regardless of viewpoint in 180–190; ancient, medieval, Oriental schools in 180; systems and schools of ethics in 171; a specific topic or branch of philosophy treated from a specific philosophical viewpoint with the topic or branch, e.g., existentialist ontology 111, realist epistemology 121; ideologies concerning a specific discipline with the discipline, e.g., political ideologies 320.5

See Manual at 140; 140 vs. 180–190

141   Idealism and related systems and doctrines

Examples: panpsychism, spiritualism, subjectivism, voluntarism

.2   **Modern Platonism and Neoplatonism**

Class ancient Platonism in 184, ancient Neoplatonism in 186.4

.3   **Transcendentalism**

.4   **Individualism**

.5   **Personalism**

.6   **Romanticism**

142   Critical philosophy

Class critical realism in 149.2

.3   **Kantianism and neo-Kantianism**

.7   **Phenomenalism and phenomenology**

.78   Existentialism

143   Intuitionism and Bergsonism

144   Humanism and related systems and doctrines

.3   **Pragmatism**

.5   **Instrumentalism**

.6   **Utilitarianism**

145   Sensationalism

Class here ideology as the system based on analysis of ideas into their sensory elements

Works that discuss ideology, not as a specific philosophical school, but as systems of beliefs in general are classed in 140

146   Naturalism and related systems and doctrines

Examples: dynamism, energism

.3   Materialism

.32   Dialectical materialism

Class philosophic foundations of Marxism in 335.4112

See Manual at 146.32 vs. 335.4112

.4   Positivism (Comtism) and related systems

Class here comprehensive works on the analytical movement

For linguistic analysis, see 149.94

.42   Logical positivism (Logical empiricism)

.44   Empiricism

.5   Atomism

Including logical atomism

.6   Mechanism and neomechanism

.7   Evolutionism and process philosophy

147   Pantheism and related systems and doctrines

Examples: animism, occasionalism, panentheism, parallelism, vitalism

.3   Monism

.4   Dualism and pluralism

148   Liberalism, eclecticism, syncretism, traditionalism, dogmatism

149   Other philosophical systems and doctrines

Examples: constructivism, deconstruction, objectivism

.1   Nominalism and conceptualism

.2   Realism, neorealism, critical realism

.3   Mysticism

Class occult mysticism in 130, religious mysticism in 200

.5   Optimism and meliorism

.6   **Pessimism**

.7   **Rationalism and related systems and doctrines**

      Examples: intellectualism, innatism, nativism

.72   Agnosticism

.73   Skepticism

.8   **Nihilism and fatalism**

      For existentialism, see 142.78

.9   **Other systems and doctrines**

.91   Neo-Aristotelianism, neo-scholasticism, neo-Thomism

      Class ancient Aristotelianism in 185; medieval scholasticism, medieval Thomism in 189.4

.94   Linguistic philosophies

      Including ordinary language philosophy

      Class here general semantics as a school of linguistic philosophy (e.g, the school of Alfred Korzybski)

      Class semantics, semiotics as philosophical topics in 121.68; comprehensive works on the analytical movement in 146.4

      See also 302.2 for interdisciplinary works on semiotics; 401 for philosophy of language

[.943]   Linguistic analysis

      Number discontinued; class in 149.94

[.946]   Semantics

      Number discontinued; class in 149.94

.96   Structuralism

150   Psychology

Unless other instructions are given, observe the following table of precedence, e.g., emotions of children 155.4124 (*not* 152.4)

Aptitude tests	153.94
Comparative psychology	156
Subconscious and altered states and processes	154
Differential and developmental psychology	155
Sensory perception, movement, emotions, physiological drives	152
Conscious mental processes and intelligence (*except* 153.94)	153
Applied psychology	158

Class social psychology in 302; psychological principles (other than the principles of aptitude testing) of a specific discipline or subject with the discipline or subject, using notation 019 from Table 1, e.g., psychological principles of advertising 659.1019

Testing for aptitude in a specific discipline or subject is classed in 153.94

See Manual at 150; 150 vs.302–307

SUMMARY

150.1–.9	**Standard subdivisions**
152	**Sensory perception, movement, emotions, physiological drives**
153	**Conscious mental processes and intelligence**
154	**Subconscious and altered states and processes**
155	**Differential and developmental psychology**
156	**Comparative psychology**
158	**Applied psychology**

.1   **Philosophy and theory**

.19   Systems, schools, viewpoints

See Manual at 150.19

.192   Existential, faculty, phenomenological, rational schools

Use of this number for other speculative systems discontinued; class in 150.19

.193   Functionalism

Including dynamic, holistic, hormic, organismic psychologies

[.193 2–.193 3]   Dynamic and purposive psychologies

Numbers discontinued; class in 150.193

.194   Reductionism

.194 3   Behaviorism

.194 32   Watsonian behaviorism

Examples: systems of Watson, Spranger, Hunter, Lashley

.194 34	Neobehaviorism (Pragmatic reductionism)
	Examples: systems of Guthrie, Hull, Skinner, Tolman
.194 4	Reflexology (Associationism)
	Examples: systems of Pavlov, Bekhterev, Thorndike
	Class associative learning in 153.1526
.195	Psychoanalytic systems
	See Manual at 150.195 vs.616.89
.195 2	Freudian system
.195 3	Adlerian system
.195 4	Jungian system
.195 7	Neopsychoanalytic systems
	Examples: systems of Horney, Fromm, Sullivan
.198	Other systems
.198 2	Gestalt psychology
.198 4	Field theory
.287	Testing and measurement
	Class comprehensive works on intelligence testing and personality testing in 153.93
	See also 174.915 for the ethics of psychological testing
.724	Experimental research
	See also 174.915 for the ethics of research in psychology

.8 **History and description with respect to kinds of persons**

Class psychology of specific kinds of persons in 155

.9 **Historical, geographical, persons treatment**

Class the national psychology of specific countries in 155.89

[151] **[Unassigned]**

Most recently used in Edition 16

152 **Sensory perception, movement, emotions, physiological drives**

Former heading: Physiological psychology

Class here comprehensive works on the psychology and neurophysiology of sensory perception, movement, emotions, physiological drives

Class the neurophysiology of sensory perception, movement, emotions, physiological drives in 612.8

See Manual at 152 vs.612.8

SUMMARY

152.1   **Sensory perception**
  .3   **Movements and motor functions**
  .4   **Emotions and feelings**
  .5   **Physiological drives**
  .8   **Quantitative threshold, discrimination, reaction-time studies**

.1   **Sensory perception**

Class here receptive processes and functions, discrimination, thresholds

Class quantitative threshold and discrimination studies in 152.82

See Manual at 152.1 vs. 153.7

.14   Visual perception

.142   Spatial perception

Class comprehensive works on spatial perception in 153.752

.142 2   Visual acuity

.142 3   Pattern perception

.142 5   Movement perception

Class comprehensive works on movement perception in 153.754

.143   Brightness perception

.145   Color perception

.148   Optical illusions, afterimages

Use of this number for other perceptual attributes discontinued; class in 152.14

.15   Auditory perception

.152   Pitch perception

.154   Volume perception

.157   Timbre perception

Tone discrimination

.158   Localization

.16   Chemical sensory perception

.166   Perception of smells

.167   Perception of tastes

.18   Other types of sensory perception

.182   Cutaneous (Tactile) perception

.182 2   Thermal perception

.182 3	Pressure perception
	Including perception of vibration [*formerly also* 152.1828]
	For tickle, see 152.1828
.182 4	Pain perception
	For itch and tickle, see 152.1828
.182 8	Itch and tickle
	Former heading: Derived sensory perception
	Perception of vibration relocated to 152.1823
.188	Proprioceptive perceptions
	Class here biofeedback
.188 2	Kinesthetic and vestibular perceptions
	Class here kinesthetic perception
.188 6	Visceral perceptions
	Examples: fatigue, hunger, thirst, well-being
.189	Synesthesia
.3	**Movements and motor functions**
	Class reaction-time studies in 152.83
.32	Involuntary movements
	Class here automatic movements
	For habits and habit formation, see 152.33
.322	Reflexes
	Class comprehensive works on reflexology as a psychological system in 150.1944
.322 3	Innate reflexes
.322 4	Conditioned reflexes
.324	Instinctive movements
	For innate reflexes, see 152.3223
.33	Habits and habit formation
	Class here comprehensive works on habits
	Class conscious mental habits in 153
.334	Motor learning
.335	Handedness and laterality
.35	Voluntary movements
.38	Special motor functions

.382	Locomotion
.384	Expressive movements

> Class meaning of movements (as in body language) in 153.69
>
> *See Manual at 152.384 vs. 153.69*

.384 2	Vocal expressions
.384 5	Graphic expressions
.385	Coordination

.4   Emotions and feelings

> Examples: embarrassment, envy, grief, guilt, humor, jealousy, shame
>
> Class here affects, attitudes, dispositions, moods, sentiments; complexes of emotions and feelings
>
> Class character traits such as bashfulness in 155.232, loneliness in 155.92, grief associated with bereavement by death in 155.937, depression in 616.8527

.41   Love and affection

> Including empathy

[.42–.45]   Types and aspects of emotions and feelings

> Numbers discontinued; class in 152.4

.46   Fear

> Including anxiety, worry

.47   Anger

> Including frustration
>
> Class here aggressive moods and feelings
>
> Class comprehensive works on psychology of aggression in 155.232

.5   Physiological drives

> Class motivation, comprehensive works on drives in 153.8

.8   Quantitative threshold, discrimination, reaction-time studies

> Use of this number for quantitative and psychophysical methods applied to other topics discontinued; class in 152

.82	Threshold and discrimination studies
.83	Reaction-time studies

153 Conscious mental processes and intelligence

Class here intellectual processes

Standard subdivisions are added for conscious mental processes

For emotions and feelings, see 152.4

See also 121 for epistemology, 128.2 for mind-body problem in philosophy

See Manual at 153.4 vs. 153

SUMMARY

153.1	**Memory and learning**
.2	**Formation and association of ideas**
.3	**Imagination and imagery**
.4	**Cognition (Knowledge)**
.6	**Communication**
.7	**Perceptual processes**
.8	**Volition (Will)**
.9	**Intelligence and aptitudes**

[.028 7]   Testing and measurement

Do not use; class in 153.93

.1   Memory and learning

.12   Memory

Class memory with respect to a specific topic with the topic, e.g., memory and dreams 154.63

For types of memory, see 153.13; mnemonics, 153.14

.122   Retention

.123   Recall and reproduction

.124   Recognition

.125   Forgetting

.13   Types of memory

.132   Visual memory

.133   Auditory memory

.134   Visual-auditory memory

[.136]   Other

Number discontinued; class in 153.13

.14   Mnemonics

.15   Learning

See Manual at 153.15 vs. 155.4–155.6; 153.15 vs. 370.15

.152   Methods of learning

.152 2   Rote learning, learning by repetition

.152 3	Learning by imitation
.152 4	Trial-and-error learning
.152 6	Associative learning

.152 6   Associative learning

      Including Pavlovian (classical) conditioning, operant conditioning

      Class comprehensive works on associationism in 150.1944

.152 8   Discrimination learning

.153   Factors in learning

.153 2   Attention and concentration

.153 3   Interest and enthusiasm

.153 4   Motivation

.154   Transfer of learning

.158   Learning curves

.2   **Formation and association of ideas**

.22   Association of ideas

.23   Concepts and concept formation

      For abstraction, see 153.24

.24   Abstraction

[.25]   Inspiration

      Number discontinued; class in 153.2

.3   **Imagination and imagery**

      Class here daydreams, fantasies, reveries considered as aspects of the imagination

      Class comprehensive works on daydreams, fantasies, reveries in 154.3

.32   Imagery

      Including visualization

.35   Creativity

      Class here interdisciplinary works on creativity

      Class creativity in a specific field with the field, using notation 019 from Table 1, e.g., creativity in the arts 700.19

.4   **Cognition (Knowledge)**

      For formation and association of ideas, see 153.2

      See Manual at 153.4 vs.153

[.402 87]   Testing and measurement

      Do not use; class in 153.93

.42   Thought and thinking

  For reasoning, see 153.43

[.422–.423]   Reflective and imageless thought

  Numbers discontinued; class in 153.42

.43   Reasoning

  Class here problem solving

  See Manual at 153.43 vs. 160

.432   Inductive reasoning

  Including inference

.433   Deductive reasoning

.44   Intuition

.45   Value

.46   Judgment

  Moral judgment relocated to 155.232

.6   Communication

  Class here individual aspects of interpersonal communication

  Class social psychology of, interdisciplinary works on communication in 302.2; sociolinguistics in 306.44; psychology of language and language processing (psycholinguistics) in 401.9; psychology of reading in 418.4019

.68   Listening

  Class speech perception in 401.9

.69   Nonverbal communication

  Class here body language

  See Manual at 152.384 vs. 153.69

.7   Perceptual processes

  Perceptual apprehension and understanding

  For extrasensory perception, see 133.82–133.86; sensory perception, 152.1

  See Manual at 152.1 vs. 153.7

.73   Basic elements

  Examples: apperception, preperception

  See also 155.2844 for thematic apperception tests

.733   Attention

  Including looking, listening

[.734–.735]	Apperception and preperception

Numbers discontinued; class in 153.73

.736	Subliminal perception
.74	Errors (Normal illusions)
.75	Types of perception

Example: perception of feelings of others

.752	Spatial perception

Class visual spatial perception in 152.142

.753	Time and rhythm perception
.754	Movement perception

Class visual perception of movement in 152.1425

.8	**Volition (Will)**

Including self-control

Class here intentionality, motivation, comprehensive works on drives

Class physiological drives in 152.5

.83	Choice and decision
.85	Modification of will

Class here behavior modification and attitude change when reference is to bending the will or changing conscious intent

See also 155.25 for modification of character and personality

.852	Persuasion
.853	Menticide (Brainwashing)
.854	Conformity
.9	**Intelligence and aptitudes**

Class factors in differential and developmental psychology that affect intelligence and aptitudes in 155

[.902 87]	Testing and measurement

Do not use; class in 153.93

[.92]	Factors affecting intelligence

Number discontinued; class in 153.9

.93   Intelligence tests

Class here comprehensive works on testing and measurement of cognition, of conscious mental processes, of intelligence and personality

Class aptitude tests in 153.94; educational tests and measurements in 371.26; tests to diagnose medical conditions in 616.80475 and related numbers, e.g., diagnosis of mental retardation 616.8588075

.932   Individual tests

Individually administered tests in which there is interaction between tester and person tested

.932 3   Verbal tests

Class comprehensive works on verbal intelligence tests in 153.9333

.932 4   Nonverbal tests

Class comprehensive works on nonverbal intelligence tests in 153.9334

.933   Group tests

Class here written tests

.933 3   Verbal tests

Class here comprehensive works on verbal intelligence tests

Class individual verbal tests in 153.9323

.933 4   Nonverbal tests

Class here comprehensive works on nonverbal intelligence tests

Class individual nonverbal tests in 153.9324

.94   Aptitude tests

Individual, group, verbal, nonverbal tests for special abilities

Class here vocational interest tests

Use 153.940001–153.940009 for standard subdivisions

Class comprehensive works on vocational interests in 158.6, use of aptitude and vocational interest tests for academic prognosis and placement in 371.264

See also 371.26 for achievement tests and measurements

See Manual at 153.94

.940 01–.949 99   Tests for aptitudes in specific fields

Add to base number 153.94 notation 001–999, e.g., tests for musical ability 153.9478

.98   Superior intelligence

154 Subconscious and altered states and processes

.2 The subconscious

.22 Id, ego, superego

.24 Activities

Including complexes, conflicts, reasoning, sublimation, transference

.3 Daydreams, fantasies, reveries

Class here secondary consciousness

Class daydreams, fantasies, reveries considered as aspects of imagination in 153.3

.4 Altered states of consciousness

Including alterations due to use of drugs

.6 Sleep phenomena

See Manual at 154.6 vs. 612.821

[.62] Sleep

Number discontinued; class in 154.6

.63 Dreams

Class here interdisciplinary works on dreams

Class parapsychological aspects of dreams in 135.3, physiological aspects of dreams in 612.821

.632 Types

.634 Analysis

.64 Somnambulism

.7 Hypnotism

Class here interdisciplinary works on hypnotism

Class hypnotism considered as a psychic power in 133.8, medical applications of hypnotism in 615.8512

.72 Animal magnetism

Use of this number for mesmerism discontinued; class in 154.7

.76 Induction of hypnosis

.77 Hypnotic phenomena

.772 Phenomena during trance

.774 Posthypnotic phenomena

155   Differential and developmental psychology

Class here the role of play in development

Unless other instructions are given, observe the following table of precedence, e.g., reactions of Afro-American schoolchildren to deaths in their families 155.937 (*not* 155.424 or 155.8496073)

Specific situations	155.93
Psychology of specific ages	155.4–.6
Ethnopsychology and national psychology	155.8
Evolutional psychology	155.7
Environmental psychology	155.9
(*except* 155.93)	
Sex psychology and psychology of the sexes	155.3
Individual psychology	155.2

See Manual at 155

SUMMARY

155.028 7	**Testing and measurement**
.2	**Individual psychology**
.3	**Sex psychology and psychology of the sexes**
.4	**Child psychology**
.5	**Psychology of young adults**
.6	**Psychology of adults**
.7	**Evolutional psychology**
.8	**Ethnopsychology and national psychology**
.9	**Environmental psychology**

.028 7   Testing and measurement [*formerly* 155.28]

.2   Individual psychology

Class here the self; character, identity, individuality, personality

Class general application of the topics of individual psychology in 158

[.202 87]   Testing and measurement

Do not use; class in 155.28

.22   Individual differences

.23   Traits and determinants of character and personality

.232   Specific traits

Examples: moral judgment [*formerly* 153.46], altruism, bashfulness, dependence, extroversion, introversion, perfectionism, workaholism

Including comprehensive works on the psychology of aggression

Class interdisciplinary works on aggression, aggressive social interactions in 302.54; aggressive emotions and feelings in 152.47; aggressive drives in 153.8; a specific aspect of a specific trait with the aspect, e.g., development of moral judgment 155.25

.234	Determinants

Class here environment versus heredity as determinants

Class environmental determinants in 155.9

.24	Adaptability

Including adjustment

.25	Development and modification of character and personality

Including maturity, development of self-control

See also 153.85 for behavior modification and attitude change when reference is to bending the will or changing conscious intent

.26	Typology
.262	Classical typology (Hippocrates' theory of temperaments)
.264	Modern typology

Examples: classification schemes of James, Jung, Kretschmer, Rorschach, Sheldon, Stern

.28	Appraisals and tests

Comprehensive works on testing and measurement in differential and developmental psychology relocated to 155.0287

Class comprehensive works on appraisals and tests for intelligence and personality in 153.93, use of personality tests to determine vocational interests in 153.94, to diagnose psychiatric disorders in 616.89075

.282	Diagnostic graphology

Class here interdisciplinary works on graphology

Class divinatory graphology in 137; handwriting analysis for the examination of evidence in 363.2565, for screening of prospective employees in 658.3112

.283	Inventories and questionnaires
.284	Projective techniques
.284 2	Rorschach tests
.284 3	Szondi tests
.284 4	Thematic apperception tests
.3	**Sex psychology and psychology of the sexes**
.31	Erogeneity and libido
.32	Sex and personality

.33	Sex differences
.332	Masculinity

Presumed distinctive characteristics of males, whether overtly sexual or not

.333	Femininity

Presumed distinctive characteristics of females, whether overtly sexual or not

.334	Bisexuality

Class here ambiguity of sexual orientation, display of behavior characteristics of both sexes (androgynous behavior)

Class bisexuality in the sense of sexual relations with the same as well as with the opposite sex in 155.34

.34	Sexual relations

Contains heterosexual, homosexual, bisexual relations

Class interdisciplinary works on and social psychology of sexual relations in 306.7

See Manual at 155.34 vs. 306.7

> **155.4–155.6 Psychology of specific ages**

Class here developmental psychology

Class comprehensive works in 155

See Manual at 153.15 vs. 155.4–155.6

.4	**Child psychology**

Through age eleven

Class interdisciplinary works on child development in 305.231

See also 649.1 for child rearing

.41	General topics

Class general topics applied to specific groupings in 155.42–155.45

.412	Sensory perception, movement, emotions, physiological drives

Add to base number 155.412 the numbers following 152 in 152.1–152.8, e.g., emotions in children 155.4124

.413	Conscious mental processes and intelligence

Add to base number 155.413 the numbers following 153 in 153.1–153.9, e.g., intelligence tests for children 155.41393 (*not* 155.4130287); however, class aptitude tests for children in 153.9400083

.418   Personal-social behavior

                Including play, stress

                Class socialization in 303.32

.418 028 7   Testing and measurement

                    Personality tests for children relocated to 155.41828

.418 2   Individual psychology

                Add to base number 155.4182 the numbers following 155.2 in 155.22–155.28, e.g., personality tests for children 155.41828 [*formerly* 155.4180287], moral development 155.41825

>   155.42–155.45 Specific groupings

            Observe the following table of precedence, e.g., preschool boys 155.423 (*not* 155.432)

Exceptional children	155.45
Children by status, type, relationships	155.44
Children in specific age groups	155.42
Children by sex	155.43

            Class comprehensive works in 155.4

.42   Children in specific age groups

.422   Infants

                From birth to age two

                Class here comprehensive works on children from birth to age 5

                Add to base number 155.422 the numbers following 155.41 in 155.412–155.418, e.g., emotions in infants 155.42224

.423   Children three to five

                Class here preschool children, comprehensive works on children aged two to six or three to seven

                Add to base number 155.423 the numbers following 155.41 in 155.412–155.418, e.g., conscious mental processes and intelligence of preschool children 155.4233

.424   Children six to eleven

                Class here comprehensive works on school-age children to age fourteen

                Add to base number 155.424 the numbers following 155.41 in 155.412–155.418, e.g., personal-social behavior of school-age children 155.4248

.43   Children by sex

                Class here sex psychology of children

.432   Boys

.433   Girls

.44   Children by status, type, relationships

Class here psychology of temporary or permanent separation from parents

.442   The only child

Class the adopted or foster only child in 155.445, the institutionalized only child in 155.446

.443   Siblings

For brothers and sisters of the same birth, see 155.444; adopted and foster children, 155.445

.444   Brothers and sisters of the same birth

.445   Adopted and foster children

.446   Institutionalized children

Including children raised in communities that serve as collective parents, e.g., kibbutz children

.45   Exceptional children

Add to base number 155.45 the numbers following 371.9 in 371.91–371.97, e.g., psychology of gifted children 155.455, of wild children ("wolf children") 155.4567

Class psychoanalytic principles derived in part from study of wild children in 150.195

.5   Psychology of young adults

Aged twelve to twenty

Class here comprehensive works on the psychology of young adults aged twelve to twenty and over twenty

Class interdisciplinary works on the development of young adults in 305.2355, vocational tests for young adults in 153.94000835, the psychology of young adults over twenty in 155.65

.51   General topics

Add to base number 155.51 the numbers following 155.41 in 155.412–155.418, e.g., personality tests for young adults 155.51828; however, class aptitude tests for young adults in 153.94000835

Subdivisions are added for young adults of specific ages, e.g., cognitive development of sixteen-year-olds 155.513

Class general topics applied to young adults by sex in 155.53

.53   By sex

Class here sex psychology of young adults

.532   Young men

.533   Young women

.6	**Psychology of adults**

See Manual at 155

.63	Adults by sex

Class adults of either sex by status, type, relationships in 155.64, adults of either sex in a specific age group in 155.65–155.67

.632	Men
.633	Women
.64	Adults by status, type, relationships

Class adults in a specific age group regardless of status, type, relationship in 155.65–155.67

.642	Single status
.642 2	Men
.642 3	Women
.643	Divorced status
.643 2	Men
.643 3	Women
.644	Widowed status
.644 2	Men
.644 3	Women
.645	Married status
.645 2	Men
.645 3	Women
.646	Parents

Class unmarried parents in 155.642, divorced parents in 155.643, widowed parents in 155.644

.646 2	Fathers
.646 3	Mothers

>	155.65–155.67 Adults in specific age groups

Class comprehensive works in 155.6

.65	Persons in early adulthood

Over twenty years of age

Class comprehensive works on the psychology of young adults, young adults aged twelve to twenty in 155.5

.66	Persons in middle adulthood

.67	Persons in late adulthood
[.671]	Mental and physical impairments
	Number discontinued; class in 155.67
.672	Adaptability
	Including psychological aspects of institutional life
	Class here psychological aspects of retirement, change in status

.7   **Evolutional psychology**

Evolution of basic human mental and psychological characteristics

Including behavioral genetics

See also 304.5 for genetic bases of social behavior

See Manual at 150 vs. 302–307

.8   **Ethnopsychology and national psychology**

Class here cross-cultural psychology

Class studies of cultural influence in 155.92

See Manual at 155

.81   Nonliterate peoples

.82   Racial and ethnic differences

Class here ethnopsychology

Class psychology of specific racial and ethnic groups in 155.84

.84   Specific racial and ethnic groups

Add to base number 155.84 notation 03–99 from Table 5, e.g., ethnopsychology of Afro-Americans 155.8496073

See Manual at 155.84 vs. 155.89

.89   National psychology

Add to base number 155.89 notation 3–9 from Table 2, e.g., Italian national psychology 155.8945

Class psychology of specific racial and ethnic groups regardless of national origin in 155.84

See Manual at 155.84 vs. 155.89

.9   **Environmental psychology**

Unless other instructions are given, observe the following table of precedence, e.g., the influence of family, friends, and work associates upon persons coping with a loss through death 155.937 (*not* 155.92)

Influence of specific situations	155.93
Influence of clothing	155.95
Influence of restrictive environments	155.96
Influence of injuries, diseases, physical disabilities, disfigurements	155.916
Influence of community and housing	155.94
Influence of social environment	155.92
Influence of physical environment and conditions (*except* 155.916)	155.91

.904   Special topics

.904 2   Stress

Class here works on how to cope with stress [*formerly also* 158.1]

Class job stress, job burnout in 158.7

.91   Influence of physical environment and conditions

.911   Influence of sensory stimuli

Add to base number 155.911 the numbers following 152.1 in 152.14–152.18, e.g., psychology of color 155.91145

Class sensory influences associated with climate in 155.915, sensory influences on persons with injuries, diseases, physical disabilities, disfigurements in 155.916

.915   Influence of climate

Class influence of climate on persons with injuries, diseases, physical disabilities, disfigurements in 155.916

.916   Influence of injuries, diseases, physical disabilities, disfigurements

.92   Influence of social environment

Including comprehensive works on loneliness

Add to base number 155.92 the numbers following 158.2 in 158.24–158.27, e.g., influence of family members, birth order 155.924

Class overcoming loneliness in 158.2

For influence of community and housing, see 155.94

See Manual at 155.92 vs. 158.2, 302–307

.93	Influence of specific situations

Class here influence of clothing in specific situations [*formerly also* 155.95]

.935	Catastrophic disasters

Including behavior patterns during bombings, earthquakes, fires, floods, hurricanes

Class catastrophic accidents in 155.936, death in catastrophic disasters in 155.937

.936	Accidents

Class death in accidents in 155.937

.937	Death and dying

Including reactions to death of others

Class interdisciplinary works on death in 306.9

.94	Influence of community and housing

> 155.942–155.944 Specific types of communities

Class comprehensive works in 155.94, housing in specific types of communities in 155.945

.942	Urban communities
.943	Suburban communities
.944	Rural communities
.945	Housing
.95	Influence of clothing

Influence of clothing in specific situations relocated to 155.93

.96	Influence of restrictive environments
.962	Prisons
.963	Submarine structures
.964	Subterranean structures

Including behavior patterns in caves, mines, tunnels, underground shelters

.965	Aircraft

Class here aviation psychology

.966	Spacecraft

Class here space psychology

156   Comparative psychology

Comparison of human psychology and the psychology of other organisms; study of other organisms to elucidate human behavior

Class behavior of nonhuman organisms in 574.5

See Manual at 156 vs. 302–307

> **156.2–156.5 Animals**

Class comprehensive works in 156, habits and behavior patterns of animals in 591.51

.2 **Comparative psychology of sensory perception, movement, emotions, physiological drives of animals**

Add to base number 156.2 the numbers following 152 in 152.1–152.8, e.g., comparative reaction-time studies 156.283

.3 **Comparative conscious mental processes and intelligence of animals**

Add to base number 156.3 the numbers following 153 in 153.1–153.9, e.g., comparative learning curves 156.3158

.4 **Comparative subconscious states and processes of animals**

.5 **Comparative differential and developmental psychology of animals**

[.7] **Comparative abnormal behavior of animals**

Relocated to 616.89

.9 **Plants**

Class plant behavior in 581.5

[157]   Abnormal and clinical psychologies

Relocated to 616.89

158   Applied psychology

Class here application of individual psychology in general; comprehensive works on psychological and parapsychological or occult techniques for achievement of personal well-being, happiness, success

Standard subdivisions are added for comprehensive works on how to better oneself and how to get along with other people

Class interdisciplinary works on successful living, on management of personal and family living in 646.7; interdisciplinary works on success in business and other public situations in 650.1; parapsychological and occult techniques for achievement of well-being, happiness, success in 131; aptitude and vocational interest tests (both general and applied to specific subjects) in 153.94; specific applications of psychology with the application, e.g., educational guidance and counseling 371.4

Application of a specific branch of psychology (other than individual psychology in general) is classed with the branch, e.g., how to be creative 153.35, use of personality tests for self-knowledge and self-improvement 155.28

.1   Personal improvement and analysis

Including personality analysis and improvement

Class here works intended to make one a better person or to stave off failure, to solve problems or to adjust to a life that does not meet one's expectations; works on specific systems and schools of applied psychology written for persons who wish to be improved or analyzed

Works on how to cope with stress relocated to 155.9042

Class works on how to get along with other people in 158.2, works on specific systems and schools of applied psychology written for advisors and counselors to help them assist others in 158.9

Comprehensive works on how to better oneself and how to get along with other people are classed in 158

.12   Through meditation

Including transcendental meditation

.2   Interpersonal relations

Relations between an individual and other people

Class here dominance, intimacy; overcoming loneliness; applications of assertiveness training, sensitivity training, transactional analysis

Class individual aspects of interpersonal communication in 153.6; comprehensive works on loneliness in 155.92; interpersonal relations in counseling and interviewing in 158.3, in leadership in 158.4, in cooperation and negotiation in 158.5; social psychology of communication in 302.2; intrarelationships of groups in 302.3

See Manual at 155.92 vs. 158.2, 302–307

.24   With family members

.25   With friends and neighbors

.26   With work associates

            See also 158.7 for psychology of work

.27   With strangers

.3   **Counseling and interviewing**

            Class here helping behavior

            Standard subdivisions are added for counseling and interviewing and for counseling alone

            Class interdisciplinary works on counseling in 361.323; helpfulness as a personality trait in 155.232; counseling in a specific discipline with the discipline, e.g., pastoral counseling 253.5

            See Manual at T1—019

.35   Group counseling

.39   Interviewing

            Class interviewing in a specific discipline with the discipline, e.g., employee selection interviewing 658.31124

.4   **Leadership**

.5   **Cooperation and negotiation**

.6   **Vocational interests**

            Class interdisciplinary works on choice of vocation in 331.702, aptitudes in 153.9

[.602 87]   Testing and measurement

                 Do not use; class in 153.94

.7   **Industrial psychology**

            Works focusing on the psychology of the individual employee in relation to work or taking a broad view that encompasses the concerns of individual employees, union leaders, management

            Including job stress, job burnout

            Class here psychology of work

            Class workaholism as a personality trait in 155.232; industrial psychology applied to a specific subject outside psychology with the subject, using notation 019 from Table 1, e.g., psychological principles of personnel management 658.30019

            See also 158.26 for psychology of interpersonal relations with work associates

.9 **Systems and schools of applied psychology**

Example: transactional analysis

Class here works on systems and schools of applied psychology written for advisors and counselors to help them assist others with personal improvement or analysis

Class works on systems and schools of applied psychology written for persons who wish to be improved or analyzed in 158.1; application of systems and schools of applied psychology with the application, e.g., application of transactional analysis to interviewing 158.39

See also 299.936 for scientology

[159] **Other aspects**

Number discontinued; class in 150

160 Logic

Science of reasoning

Including counterfactuals, negation, question, reference, truth tables

Class here modality, propositions

Class psychology of reasoning in 153.43, symbolic (mathematical) logic in 511.3

See Manual at 153.43 vs. 160

161 **Induction**

For hypotheses, see 167; analogy, 169

162 **Deduction**

For syllogisms, see 166

[163] **[Unassigned]**

Most recently used in Edition 16

[164] **[Unassigned]**

Most recently used in Edition 17

165 **Fallacies and sources of error**

Examples: contradiction, paradox, fiction

166 **Syllogisms**

167 **Hypotheses**

168 **Argument and persuasion**

169 **Analogy**

170   Ethics (Moral philosophy)

Class here ethics of specific subjects and disciplines

Class religious ethics in 291.5; ethics of a specific religion with the religion, e.g., Christian moral theology 241

See Manual at 303.372 vs. 170

SUMMARY

170.1–.9	**Standard subdivision**
171	**Systems and doctrines**
172	**Political ethics**
173	**Ethics of family relationships**
174	**Economic, professional, occupational ethics**
175	**Ethics of recreation and leisure**
176	**Ethics of sex and reproduction**
177	**Ethics of social relations**
178	**Ethics of consumption**
179	**Other ethical norms**

.2   **Miscellany**

[.202]   Normative ethics for specific groups

            Relocated to 170.8

            Do not use for synopses and outlines; class in 170.2

.4   **Special topics**

.42   Metaethics

            Class bases for specific systems in 171

.44   Normative ethics

[.440 8]   History and description with respect to kinds of persons

            Do not use; class in 170.8

.8   **History and description with respect to kinds of persons**

            Class here normative ethics for specific groups [*formerly* 170.202]

[.88]   Occupational and religious groups

            Do not use; class ethics of professional and occupational groups in 174, of religious groups in 200

171   Systems and doctrines

Regardless of time or place

Class a specific topic in ethics with the topic in 172–179 regardless of the system within which it is treated

See Manual at 171

.1   **Based on authority**

.2   **Based on intuition, moral sense, reason**

Including empiricism, existentialism, humanism, natural law, naturalism, stoicism

For systems and doctrines based on conscience, see 171.6

See also 171.7 for systems based on biology, genetics, evolution; 340.11 for natural law in legal theory

.3   **Perfectionism**

Systems and doctrines based on self-realization, fulfillment of personality

.4   **Hedonism**

Systems and doctrines based on achievement of individual pleasure or happiness

.5   **Utilitarianism and consequentialism**

Systems and doctrines based on achievement of greatest happiness of greatest number

.6   **Based on conscience**

Including casuistry, conflict of duties

.7   **Based on biology, genetics, evolution, education, social factors**

Including relativism, communist ethics, sociobiological ethics

See also 171.2 for systems based on natural law, naturalism

.8   **Based on altruism**

For utilitarianism, see 171.5

.9   **Based on egoism**

For hedonism, see 171.4

>   # 172–179 Applied ethics (Social ethics)

Ethics of specific human qualities, relationships, activities

Class comprehensive works in 170

172   Political ethics

.1   **Relation of individuals to the state**

Examples: civic and political activity, military service, obedience to law, payment of taxes, resistance, revolution, civil war

.2   **Duties of states and governments**

Duties of government toward citizens, e.g., education, freedom, personal security, welfare; duties of officeholders and officials

Class here justice

.4   **International relations**

Including conduct of foreign affairs, disarmament, espionage

.42   War and peace

Examples: conscientious objection, just war theory, pacifism, ways and means of conducting warfare

Class civil war in 172.1, occupational ethics of military personnel in 174.9355

.422   Nuclear weapons and nuclear war

173   **Ethics of family relationships**

Examples: ethics of marriage, divorce, separation, parent-child relationships, sibling relationships

Class ethics of sex and reproduction in 176

174   **Economic, professional, occupational ethics**

Class here ethics of work

.1   **Clergy**

See Manual at 174.1

.2   **Medical professions**

Class medical ethics related to human reproduction in 176

.22   Hippocratic oath

.24   Questions of life and death

Euthanasia relocated to 179.7

For abortion, see 179.76

.25   Innovative procedures

Examples: organ transplants, genetic engineering

Class comprehensive works on ethics of genetic engineering in 174.9574

.26   Economic questions

Examples: advertising, fee splitting

.28   Experimentation

Including experimentation on human subjects

For experimentation on animals, see 179.4

.3   **Legal professions**

.4   **Trade, manufacture, finance (Business ethics)**

Including industrial espionage

.6   **Gambling business and lottery management**

See also 175.5 for games of chance, 175.9 for betting

.9   **Other professions and occupations**

Add to base number 174.9 notation 09–99 from Table 7, e.g., ethics of genetic engineering 174.9574; however, class ethics of public administration and public office in 172.2

175   **Ethics of recreation and leisure**

Including ethics of hunting

Class here sportsmanship, fair play

Class occupational ethics for those involved in the recreation industry in 174.9, e.g., occupational ethics for professional athletes 174.9796

.1   **Radio, television, motion pictures, circuses**

.2   **Theater, opera, musical performances**

.3   **Dancing**

.4   **Athletics and games of skill**

Class card games in 175.5, human and animal combat in 175.6, racing in 175.7

.5   **Games of chance**

See also 174.6 for gambling business

.6   **Human and animal combat**

.7   **Racing**

Humans, animals, vehicles

.8   **Recreational reading**

Including comics

Class obscene literature in 176.8

.9   **Betting**

Class games of chance involving betting in 175.5

See also 174.6 for gambling business

176   **Ethics of sex and reproduction**

Including artificial insemination, celibacy, chastity, contraception, embryo transplant, homosexuality, premarital and extramarital relations, promiscuity, surrogate motherhood

Class abortion in 179.76

.5   **Prostitution**

.7   **Obscenity**

For obscenity in literature, see 176.8; obscenity in speech, 179.5

.8 **Obscenity in literature**

177 **Ethics of social relations**

Limited to the topics provided for below

.1 **Courtesy, politeness, hospitality**

Class etiquette in 395

.2 **Conversation, gossip**

.3 **Slander, flattery, truthfulness, lying**

.4 **Personal appearance**

Examples: exposure of person, ostentatious dress

.5 **Slavery and discriminatory practices**

.6 **Friendship and courtship**

Class sexual ethics in courtship in 176

.7 **Love**

Including benevolence, charity, kindness, liberality, philanthropy

178 **Ethics of consumption**

Examples: abstinence, gluttony, greediness, overindulgence, temperance

Class here use of natural resources, of wealth

Class environmental, ecological ethics, respect for nature in 179.1, consumption of meat in 179.3

.1 **In use of alcoholic beverages**

.7 **In use of tobacco**

.8 **In use of narcotics**

[.9] **In other forms**

Number discontinued; class in 178

179 **Other ethical norms**

Class here cruelty

Do not use standard subdivisions

.1 **Respect for life and nature**

Class here environmental, ecological ethics

For ethics of consumption, see 178; respect for human life, 179.7; treatment of animals, 179.3

.2 **Treatment of children**

For parent-child relationships, see 173

.3   **Treatment of animals**

Including vegetarianism

Class racing of animals in 175.7

For animal combat, see 175.6; experimentation on animals 179.4

.4   **Experimentation on animals**

Including vivisection

.5   **Profanity, blasphemy, obscenity in speech**

.6   **Courage and cowardice**

.7   **Respect and disrespect for human life**

Including euthanasia [*formerly* 174.24], capital punishment, dueling, genocide, homicide, suicide

Class here comprehensive works on ethics of violence, of nonviolence

Class ethics of violence, of nonviolence in political activity in 172, ethics of war in 172.42, of civil war in 172.1, medical ethics in 174.2, ethics of contraception in 176

For treatment of children, see 179.2

.76   Abortion

.8   **Vices, faults, failings**

Not otherwise provided for

Examples: anger, cheating, covetousness, envy, hatred, jealousy, pride, sloth

.9   **Virtues**

Not otherwise provided for

Examples: cheerfulness, gentleness, gratitude, honesty, humility, modesty, patience, prudence, self-reliance, self-control, toleration

> ## 180–190 Historical, geographical, persons treatment of philosophy

Class here development, description, critical appraisal, collected writings, biographical treatment of individual philosophers regardless of viewpoint

Do not add notation 09 from Table 1 to numbers that express specific areas, e.g., twentieth century British philosophy 192 (*not* 192.0904), but twentieth century Western philosophy 190.904

Do not add notation 092 from Table 1 to 180–190

Class comprehensive works on geographical treatment in 100, on historical treatment in 109, on collected persons treatment in 109.2; critical appraisal of an individual philosopher's thought on a specific topic with the topic, using notation 092 from Table 1, e.g., critical appraisal of Kant's theory of knowledge 121.092

See Manual at 140 vs. 180–190; 180–190

180   Ancient, medieval, Oriental philosophy

Use 180.01–180.09 for standard subdivisions

SUMMARY

180.1–.9	**Standard subdivisions of ancient philosophy**
181	**Oriental philosophy**
182	**Pre-Socratic Greek philosophies**
183	**Sophistic, Socratic and related Greek philosophies**
184	**Platonic philosophy**
185	**Aristotelian philosophy**
186	**Skeptic and Neoplatonic philosophies**
187	**Epicurean philosophy**
188	**Stoic philosophy**
189	**Medieval Western philosophy**

.1–.8   **Standard subdivisions of ancient philosophy**

.9   **Historical and geographical treatment of ancient philosophy**

Class treatment of specific schools in 181–188

.938   Greece

Use 180 for comprehensive works on ancient Greek philosophy

See Manual at 180.938

181   Oriental philosophy

Ancient, medieval, modern

.001–.008   Standard subdivisions

.009   Historical treatment

Class geographical treatment in 181.1–181.9

.04–.09   Based on specific religions

Add to base number 181.0 the numbers following 29 in 294–299, e.g., Jewish philosophy 181.06; however, class Hindu-Brahmanical philosophy in 181.41–181.48, Christian philosophy in 190; Confucian philosophy relocated from 181.09512 to 181.112, Taoist philosophy from 181.09514 to 181.114

See Manual at 100 vs. 200

> **181.1–181.9 Of specific places**

(Option: To give local emphasis and a shorter number to philosophy of a specific country, use one of the following:

(Option A: Place it first by use of a letter or other symbol, e.g., philosophy of Lebanon 181.L [preceding 181.1]

(Option B: Class it in 181.1; in that case class comprehensive works on philosophy of Far East and South Asia in 181.9)

Class comprehensive works in 181

.1   **Far East and South Asia**

(Option: To give local emphasis and a shorter number to philosophy of a specific country, class it in this number; in that case class comprehensive works on philosophy of the Far East and South Asia in 181.9)

For philosophy of India, see 181.4

.11   China and Korea

> 181.112–181.115 Schools of Chinese philosophy

Class comprehensive works in 181.11, Buddhist philosophy in 181.043

.112   Confucian [*formerly* 181.09512] and Neo-Confucian philosophy

Class here the Four Books of Confucius

Class the Five Confucian Classics in 299.51282

.114   Taoist philosophy [*formerly* 181.09514]

.115   Mohist, Dialecticianist, Legalist philosophies

.119   Korea

.12   Japan

Class Shinto philosophy in 181.09561

.15   Pakistan and Bangladesh

.16   Indonesia [*formerly also* 181.198]

.17   Philippines [*formerly also* 181.199]

.19	Southeast Asia

Add to base number 181.19 the numbers following —59 in notation 591–597 from Table 2, e.g., philosophy of Thailand 181.193

Indonesia relocated from 181.198 to 181.16; Philippines from 181.199 to 181.17

.2	**Egypt**
.3	**Palestine, Judea, Israel**

Class Jewish philosophy in 181.06

.4	**India**

See also 181.15 for philosophy of Pakistan and Bangladesh

> 181.41–181.48 Schools of Hindu-Brahmanical philosophy

Class comprehensive works in 181.4, Buddhist philosophy in 181.043, Jainist philosophy in 181.044

.41	Sankhya
.42	Mimamsa
.43	Nyaya
.44	Vaisheshika
.45	Yoga

Class here interdisciplinary works on the practice of yoga and yoga as a philosophical school

For physical yoga, see 613.7046; Hindu yogic meditation, 294.543; karma yoga, 294.544

.452	Patanjali's philosophy
.48	Vedanta
.482	Sankaracharya (Advaita)
.483	Ramanujacharya (Visistadvaita)
.484	Dualistic school
.484 1	Madhvacharya (Dvaita)
.484 2	Bhedabheda
.484 3	Nimbarka (Dvaitadvaita)
.484 4	Vallabhacharya (Suddhadvaita)
.5	**Iran (Persia)**
.6	**Iraq**

Class here Assyria, Babylonia, Chaldea, ancient Mesopotamia

.8 **Syria and Lebanon**

Including ancient Phoenicia

.9 **Other**

Example: Arabia

> **182–188 Ancient Western philosophy**

Class comprehensive works in 180

182 **Pre-Socratic Greek philosophies**

.1 **Ionic philosophy**

.2 **Pythagorean philosophy**

.3 **Eleatic philosophy**

.4 **Heraclitean philosophy**

.5 **Empedoclean philosophy**

.7 **Democritean philosophy**

.8 **Anaxagorean philosophy**

183 **Sophistic, Socratic and related Greek philosophies**

.1 **Sophistic philosophy**

.2 **Socratic philosophy**

.4 **Cynic philosophy**

.5 **Cyrenaic philosophy**

.6 **Megaric philosophy**

.7 **Elian and Eretrian philosophies**

184 **Platonic philosophy**

Class here comprehensive works on ancient and modern Platonism

For modern Platonism, see 141.2

185 **Aristotelian philosophy**

For modern Aristotelianism, see 149.91

186 **Skeptic and Neoplatonic philosophies**

.1 **Pyrrhonic philosophy**

.2 **New Academy**

.3 **Eclectic philosophy**

.4   **Neoplatonic philosophy**

Class here Alexandrian philosophy, comprehensive works on ancient and modern Neoplatonism

For modern Neoplatonism, see 141.2

187   **Epicurean philosophy**

188   **Stoic philosophy**

189   **Medieval Western philosophy**

Class here early Christian philosophy

.2   **Patristic philosophy**

.4   **Scholastic philosophy**

For neo-scholasticism, neo-Thomism, see 149.91

.5   **Mystic philosophy**

190   **Modern Western philosophy**

Class here comprehensive works on Christian philosophy, on modern philosophy, on Western philosophy, on European philosophy

Modern philosophy of areas not provided for in 180 is classed here, even if not in the Western tradition, e.g., North American native philosophy 191.08997, traditional African philosophy 199.6

(Option: To give local emphasis and a shorter number to philosophy of a specific country, use one of the following:

(Option A: Place it first by use of a letter or other symbol, e.g., philosophy of Mexico 19M [preceding 191]

(Option B: Class it in 191; in that case class philosophy of United States and Canada in 199.7)

Class ancient, medieval, Oriental philosophy in 180

See Manual at 100, 109 vs. 190; 190

.9   **Historical and geographical treatment**

Class treatment by continent, country, locality in 191–199 (*not* 190.94–190.99)

191   **United States and Canada**

Class here North American philosophy

(Option: To give local emphasis and a shorter number to philosophy of a specific country, class it in this number; in that case class philosophy of United States and Canada in 199.7)

Class Middle American and Mexican philosophy in 199.72

192   **British Isles**

193   **Germany and Austria**

194   **France**

195   **Italy**

196   **Spain and Portugal**

    .1   **Spain**

    .9   **Portugal**

197   **Soviet Union**

       Class philosophy of Soviet Asia in 181.9

    [.1]   **Finland**

       Relocated to 198.8

    [.2]   **Russia, Ukraine, Belorussia**

       Number discontinued; class in 197

198   **Scandinavia**

    .1   **Norway**

    .5   **Sweden**

    .8   **Finland [*formerly* 197.1]**

    .9   **Denmark**

199   **Other geographical areas**

       Add to base number 199 notation 4–9 from Table 2, e.g., Mexican philosophy 199.72; however, class Asiatic philosophy in 181, European philosophy in 190, comprehensive works on North American philosophy in 191

200

---

200 Religion

Beliefs, attitudes, practices of individuals and groups with respect to the ultimate nature of existences and relationships within the context of revelation, deity, worship

Class here comprehensive works on Christianity

(Option: To give preferred treatment or shorter numbers to a specific religion other than Christianity, use one of the four options described at 292–299)

Class comparative religion, works dealing with various religions in 291

See Manual at 100 vs. 200; 133 vs. 200; 200

.1 Philosophy and theory

See Manual at 200.1 vs. 210, 291

.2–.6 Standard subdivisions

.7 Education, research, related topics

.71 Schools and courses

See also 377.1 for religious observances and exercises in nonsectarian schools

.8 Religion with respect to kinds of persons

.9 Historical, geographical, persons treatment of religion

Class here religious situation and conditions

> ## 201–209 Standard subdivisions of Christianity

Class comprehensive works in 200

201 Philosophy and theory of Christianity

Nature, origin, validity of Christian beliefs

Class Christian theology in 230

202 Miscellany of Christianity

203 Dictionaries, encyclopedias, concordances of Christianity

204 Special topics

.5 Christian mythology

Class mythology in the Bible in 220.68, Apocrypha and pseudepigrapha in 229

205 **Serial publications of Christianity**

206 **Organizations of Christianity**

Class the Christian church in 260

207 **Education, research, related topics of Christianity**

Class here Christianity as an academic subject

Comprehensive works on Christian religious education relocated to 268

Class Christian religious education under church auspices at other than the university level in 268

See Manual at 207 vs. 268

.1 **Schools and courses**

.101–.103 In areas, regions, places in general; in the ancient world

[.104–.109] In specific continents, countries, localities in the modern world

Do not use; class in 207.4–207.9

.11 Colleges and universities

Do not use for geographical treatment of colleges and universities; class colleges and universities regardless of denomination in areas, regions, places in general in 207.101; in the ancient world in 207.103; in specific continents, countries, localities in the modern world in 207.4–207.9

Add to base number 207.11 the numbers following 28 in 280.2–289.9, e.g., Roman Catholic seminaries and courses 207.112

.12 Secular secondary schools

Do not use for geographical treatment of secular secondary schools; class secular secondary schools in areas, regions, places in general in 207.101; in the ancient world in 207.103; in specific continents, countries, localities in the modern world in 207.4–207.9

Comprehensive works on Christian education in secondary schools, secondary schools under church auspices relocated to 268.433

.15 Agencies for adult education

Class agencies for adult education under church auspices in 268.434

.3 **Research and topics related to research and education**

Add to base number 207.3 the numbers following —07 in notation 072–079 from Table 1, e.g., museums, collections, exhibits on Christianity 207.34

.4–.9 **Colleges, universities, secular secondary schools in specific continents, countries, localities in the modern world**

Class here specific schools and courses

Do not use for research and miscellaneous educational aspects; class in 207.3

Add to base number 207 notation 4–9 from Table 2, e.g., a seminary in Dublin 207.41835

Secondary schools under church auspices and their courses relocated to 268.433094–268.433099

208 **Christianity with respect to kinds of persons**

209 **Historical, geographical, persons treatment of Christianity and Christian thought**

Observe the table of precedence under 230–280

Class historical, geographical, persons treatment of the organized Christian church in 270

See Manual at 209.2

210 Natural theology

Religious beliefs and attitudes attained through observation and interpretation of evidence in nature, through speculation, through reasoning, but not through revelation

(Option: To give local emphasis and a shorter number to a specific religion other than Christianity, class it in this number, and add to base number 21 the numbers following the base number for that religion in 292–299, e.g., Hinduism 210, Mahabharata 219.23; in that case class natural theology in 200, its subdivisions from 211–218 in 201–208, standard subdivisions of Christianity in 200.1–200.9, standard subdivisions of religion in 200.01–200.09. Other options are described at 292–299)

Class a specific topic treated with respect to religions based on revelation or authority in 291, e.g., concepts of God in world religions 291.211; with respect to a specific religion with the religion, e.g., Christian concepts of God 231

See Manual at 200.1 vs. 210, 291

211 **Concepts of God**

Including anthropomorphism

Class here comprehensive works on God, on The Holy

For existence, knowability, attributes of God, see 212

.2 **Pantheism**

.3 **Theism**

.32 Polytheism

.33 Dualism

.34 Monotheism

.4   **Rationalism (Free thought)**

.5   **Deism**

.6   **Humanism and secularism**

.7   **Agnosticism and skepticism**

.8   **Atheism**

212   Existence, knowability, attributes of God

.1   **Existence**

Including proofs

See Manual at 212.1 vs. 231.042

.6   **Knowability**

Class proofs in 212.1

.7   **Attributes**

Examples: love, omniscience

213   Creation

Including creation of life and human life, evolution versus creation, evolution as method of creation

See Manual at 231.765 vs. 213, 575

214   Theodicy

Vindication of God's justice and goodness in permitting existence of evil and suffering

.8   **Providence**

215   Science and religion

Including cybernetics

Class religion and scientific theories of creation in 213

See also 261.55 for Christianity and science; 291.175 for various religions and science

.1   **Mathematics**

.2   **Astronomy and related topics**

.24   Life on other worlds

.25   Space flight

.3   **Physics**

.4   **Chemistry**

.5   **Geology**

.6   **Paleontology**

.7	**Life sciences**

Class evolution versus creation, evolution as method of creation in 213

For paleontology, see 215.6

.72	Anthropology and ethnology
.74	Biology and natural history

For life on other worlds, see 215.24

.8	**Archaeology**
.9	**Technology**

For space flight, see 215.25

216   Good and evil

For theodicy, see 214

[217]   [Unassigned]

Most recently used in Edition 18

218   Humankind

Including immortality

Class creation, human evolution in 213

[219]   Analogy

Number discontinued; class in 210

220   Bible

Holy Scriptures of Judaism and Christianity

(If option A under 292–299 is chosen, class here sources of the specified religion; class the Bible in 298)

Class Christian Biblical theology in 230, Judaic in 296.31–296.34; Biblical precepts in Christian codes of conduct in 241.52–241.54, in Judaic codes in 296.385

See Manual at 220

SUMMARY

220.01–.09	**Standard subdivisions**
.1–.9	**Generalities**
221	**Old Testament**
222	**Historical books of Old Testament**
223	**Poetic books of Old Testament**
224	**Prophetic books of Old Testament**
225	**New Testament**
226	**Gospels and Acts**
227	**Epistles**
228	**Revelation (Apocalypse)**
229	**Apocrypha, pseudepigrapha, intertestamental works**

.01–.02	Standard subdivisions
[.03]	Dictionaries, encyclopedias, concordances

> Do not use; class dictionaries and encyclopedias in 220.3, concordances in 220.4–220.5

.04	Special topics
.046	Apocalyptic passages

> Class apocalypses in the pseudepigrapha in 229.9; apocalyptic passages in a book or group of books with the book or group of books, e.g., apocalyptic passages in the prophets 224.0046, in the Book of Daniel 224.50046

> *For Revelation (Apocalypse), see 228*

.05–.08	Standard subdivisions
.09	General historical, geographical, persons treatment of the Bible

> Class the canon in 220.12; geography, history, chronology, persons of Bible lands in Bible times in 220.9

SUMMARY

220.1	Origins and authenticity
.3	Encyclopedias and topical dictionaries
.4	Original texts, early versions, early translations
.5	Modern versions and translations
.6	Interpretation and criticism (Exegesis)
.7	Commentaries
.8	Nonreligious subjects treated in the Bible
.9	Geography, history, chronology, persons of Bible lands in Bible times

> **220.1–220.9 Generalities**

> Class comprehensive works in 220, generalities applied to a specific part of the Bible with the part, e.g., a commentary on Job 223.107

.1	**Origins and authenticity**
.12	Canon

> Class here selection of the books accepted as Holy Scripture

.13	Inspiration

> The Bible as revelation (word of God)

> Including the authority of the Bible

.15	Biblical prophecy and prophecies

> Class Christian messianic prophecies in 232.12, Christian eschatological prophecies in 236, Judaic messianic and eschatological prophecies in 296.33

> *See also 224 for prophetic books of the Old Testament*

.3 **Encyclopedias and topical dictionaries**

Class dictionaries of specific texts in 220.4–220.5

> **220.4–220.5 Texts, versions, translations**

Class here critical appraisal of language and style; concordances, indexes, dictionaries of specific texts; complete texts; selections from more than one part; paraphrases

Class comprehensive works in 220.4; texts accompanied by commentaries in 220.77; selections compiled for a specific purpose with the purpose, e.g., selections for daily meditations 242.2

.4 **Original texts, early versions, early translations**

Class here textual (lower) criticism (use of scientific means to ascertain the actual original texts), original texts accompanied by modern translations, comprehensive works on texts and versions

For modern versions and translations, see 220.5

.42 Aramaic

.43 Syriac

.44 Hebrew

.45 Samaritan

.46 Other Semitic

Examples: Arabic, Ethiopic

.47 Latin

Examples: Itala, Vulgate

.48 Greek

.49 Other early versions

Examples: Armenian, Coptic

Gothic relocated to 220.5399

.5 **Modern versions and translations**

Class works containing translations in English and one other modern language with the other language in 220.53–220.59; in two modern languages other than English with the language coming later in Table 6; in more than two modern languages in 220.51.

.51 Polyglot

.52   In English and Anglo-Saxon

Use 220.52001–220.52009 for standard subdivisions

\>   220.520 1–220.520 9 English

Add to the notation for each term identified by * as follows:

01–02   Standard subdivisions
[03]   Dictionaries, encyclopedias, concordances
            Do not use; class in 3
05–08   Standard subdivisions
09   Geographical and persons treatment
            Class historical treatment of the translation in 8
2   Standard editions
3   Concordances, indexes, dictionaries
4   Special editions
            Examples: annotated editions, study editions, editions notable for illustrations
6   Selections
7   Paraphrases
8   History, criticism, explanation of the translation

Class comprehensive works in 220.52

.520 1   English versions before 1582

Examples: Coverdale, Tyndale, Wycliffe

.520 2   *Douay

Class here Rheims-Douay, Rheims-Douay-Challoner versions

See also 220.5205 for Confraternity-Douay-Challoner version

.520 3   *Authorized (King James)

.520 4   Revised

Including English revised (1881–1885), American revised (American standard) (1901)

.520 42   *Revised standard (1946–1957)

.520 5   *Confraternity and *New American

Class here Confraternity-Douay-Challoner version

See also 220.5202 for Rheims-Douay, Rheims-Douay-Challoner versions

.520 6   *New English Bible

.520 7   *Jerusalem Bible

.520 8   Other English translations since 1582

Examples: Good News Bible, New International Version

For translations by individuals, see 220.5209

*Add as instructed under 220.5201–220.5209

.520 9	Translations by individuals

Former heading: Private translations

Examples: Goodspeed, Knox, Moffatt, Phillips

.529	Anglo-Saxon
.53–.59	In other languages

Add to base number 220.5 notation 3–9 from Table 6, e.g., the Bible in Gothic 220.5399 [*formerly* 220.49], in German 220.531

.6 Interpretation and criticism (Exegesis)

Class Christian meditations based on Biblical passages and intended for devotional use in 242.5, Judaic meditations in 296.72; material about the Bible intended for use in preparing Christian sermons in 251, Christian sermons based on Biblical passages in 252; material for preparation of Judaic sermons and texts of Judaic sermons in 296.42

For textual (lower) criticism, see 220.4; commentaries, 220.7

.601	Philosophy and theory (Hermeneutics)
.61	General introductions to the Bible

Including isagogics (introductory studies prior to actual exegesis)

.64	Symbolism and typology

Class here interpretation of specific symbols

.65	Harmonies
.66	Literary criticism

Literary examination of the text in order to reach conclusions about its meaning, structure, authorship, date

Class here higher criticism, internal criticism, redaction criticism

Class the language and style of specific texts in 220.4–220.5

See also 809.93522 for the Bible as literature

.663	Form criticism

Analysis of preliterary or oral forms and traditions in Biblical text

.67	Historical criticism

Interpretation of texts in light of the cultural, historical, religious, sociological milieu in which written

Class form criticism in 220.663

.68	Mythological, allegorical, numerical, astronomical interpretations

Including mythology in the Bible, demythologizing

.7 Commentaries

Criticism and interpretation arranged in textual order

.77	With text

.8	**Nonreligious subjects treated in the Bible**

Use 220.80001–220.80009 for standard subdivisions

Add to base number 220.8 notation 001–999, e.g., natural sciences in the Bible 220.85

Class a religious subject treated in the Bible with the specific religion and topic, e.g., Christian theology 230, Judaic moral virtues based on biblical teaching 296.385; geography, history, chronology, persons of Bible lands in Bible times in 220.9

.9	**Geography, history, chronology, persons of Bible lands in Bible times**

Class general history of areas in the ancient world in 930

.91	Geography

Class here description and civilization

Class civilization treated separately in 220.95

.92	Collected persons

Class an individual person with the part of the Bible in which he is chiefly considered, e.g., Abraham 222.11092

See Manual at 209.2; 220.92

.93	Archaeology (Material remains)
.95	History

Including civilization treated separately

Use 220.95001–220.95009 for standard subdivisions

Class geographical description and civilization treated together in 220.91

.950 5	Bible stories retold

Including picture books

> ## 221–228 Specific parts of the Bible

Add to each subdivision identified by * as follows (regardless of whether the subdivision is treated as a whole or in part):

001–08	Standard subdivisions and generalities
	Add to 0 the numbers following 220 in 220.01–220.8, e.g., interpretation of the work or of a part of the work 06
09	Geography, history, chronology, persons
	Add to 09 the numbers following 221.9 in 221.91–221.95, e.g., biography 092

Class comprehensive works in 220

For Apocrypha, see 229

221   Old Testament

Holy Scriptures of Judaism, Old Testament of Christianity

For historical books, see 222; poetic books, 223; prophetic books, 224

[.03]   Dictionaries, encyclopedias, concordances

> Do not use; class dictionaries and encyclopedias in 221.3, concordances in 221.4–221.5

.04   Special topics

.042   Hagiographa (Writings)

.044   Megillot (Five Rolls)

.046   Apocalyptic passages

> Class apocalyptic passages in a book or group of books with the book or group of books, e.g., apocalyptic passages in the prophets 224.0046, in the Book of Daniel 224.50046

.09   General historical, geographical, persons treatment of the Old Testament

> Class the canon in 221.12; geography, history, chronology, persons of Old Testament lands in Old Testament times in 221.9

.1–.8   Generalities

> Add to base number 221 the numbers following 220 in 220.1–220.8, e.g., Targums 221.42, commentaries 221.7

.9   Geography, history, chronology, persons of Old Testament lands in Old Testament times

> Class general history of ancient areas in 930

.91   Geography

> Class here description and civilization
>
> Class civilization treated separately in 221.95

.92   Persons

> *See Manual at 209.2; 220.92*

.922   Collected treatment

.93   Archaeology (Material remains)

.95   History

> Including civilization treated separately
>
> Use 221.95001–221.95009 for standard subdivisions
>
> Class geographical description and civilization treated together in 221.91

.950 5   Old Testament stories retold

> Including picture books

222   *Historical books of Old Testament

.1   ***Pentateuch (Torah)**

Class here *Hexateuch

For Joshua, see 222.2

.11   *Genesis

.12   *Exodus

For Ten Commandments, see 222.16

.13   *Leviticus

.14   *Numbers

.15   *Deuteronomy

For Ten Commandments, see 222.16

.16   *Ten Commandments (Decalogue)

Class Ten Commandments as code of conduct in Christianity in 241.52, in Judaism in 296.385

.2   ***Joshua (Josue)**

.3   ***Judges and Ruth**

.32   *Judges

.35   *Ruth

.4   ***Samuel**

.43   *Samuel 1

Variant name: Kings 1

.44   *Samuel 2

Variant name: Kings 2

.5   ***Kings**

.53   *Kings 1

Variant name: Kings 3

.54   *Kings 2

Variant name: Kings 4

.6   ***Chronicles (Paralipomena)**

.63   *Chronicles 1 (Paralipomenon 1)

.64   *Chronicles 2 (Paralipomenon 2)

.7   ***Ezra (Esdras 1)**

See also 229.1 for Esdras 1 (also called Esdras 3) of the Apocrypha

*Add as instructed under 221–228

.8   ***Nehemiah (Esdras 2, Nehemias)**

See also 229.1 for Esdras 2 (also called Esdras 4) of the Apocrypha

(.86)   *Tobit (Tobias)

(Optional number; prefer 229.22)

(.88)   *Judith

(Optional number; prefer 229.24)

.9   ***Esther**

(Option: Class here deuterocanonical part of Esther; prefer 229.27)

223   ***Poetic books of Old Testament**

Class here *wisdom literature

For Apocryphal wisdom literature, see 229.3

.1   ***Job**

.2   ***Psalms**

.7   ***Proverbs**

.8   ***Ecclesiastes (Qohelet)**

.9   ***Song of Solomon (Canticle of Canticles, Song of Songs)**

(.96)   *Wisdom of Solomon (Wisdom)

(Optional number; prefer 229.3)

(.98)   *Ecclesiasticus (Sirach)

(Optional number; prefer 229.4)

224   ***Prophetic books of the Old Testament**

Class here Major Prophets

.1   ***Isaiah (Isaias)**

.2   ***Jeremiah (Jeremias)**

.3   ***Lamentations**

(.37)   *Baruch

(Optional number; prefer 229.5)

.4   ***Ezekiel (Ezechiel)**

.5   ***Daniel**

(Option: Class here Song of the Three Children, Susanna, Bel and the Dragon; prefer 229.5 for Song of the Three Children, 229.6 for Susanna, Bel and the Dragon)

.6   ***Hosea (Osee)**

*Add as instructed under 221–228

.7	***Joel**
.8	***Amos**
.9	***Minor prophets**

> *For Hosea, see 224.6; Joel, 224.7; Amos, 224.8*

.91	*Obadiah (Abdias)
.92	*Jonah (Jonas)
.93	*Micah (Micheas)
.94	*Nahum
.95	*Habakkuk (Habacuc)
.96	*Zephaniah (Sophonias)
.97	*Haggai (Aggeus)
.98	*Zechariah (Zacharias)
.99	*Malachi (Malachias)
(.997)	*Maccabees 1 and 2 (Machabees 1 and 2)

> (Optional number; prefer 229.73)

225   New Testament

> *For Gospels and Acts, see 226; Epistles, 227; Revelation, 228*

[.03]   Dictionaries, encyclopedias, concordances

> Do not use; class dictionaries and encyclopedias in 225.3, concordances in 225.4–225.5

.04   Special topics

.046   Apocalyptic passages

> Class apocalyptic passages in a book or group of books with the book or group of books, e.g., in the Gospels 226.0046, in the Gospel of Mark 226.30046

> *For Revelation (Apocalypse), see 228*

.09   General historical, geographical, persons treatment of the New Testament

> Class the canon in 225.12; geography, history, chronology, persons of New Testament lands in New Testament times in 225.9

.1–.8   Generalities

> Add to base number 225 the numbers following 220 in 220.1–220.8, e.g., Authorized Version 225.5203

*Add as instructed under 221–228

.9   **Geography, history, chronology, persons of New Testament lands in New Testament times**

Add to base number 225.9 the numbers following 221.9 in 221.91–221.95, e.g., individual persons 225.92; however, class Jesus Christ, Mary, Joseph, Joachim, Anne, John the Baptist in 232

See Manual at 209.2; 220.92

226   *Gospels and Acts

Class here synoptic Gospels

See Manual at 209.2

.095 05   Gospel stories retold

Class Jesus as a historical figure, biography and specific events in the life of Jesus in 232.9

.1   **Harmonies of the Gospels**

> **226.2–226.5 Specific Gospels**

Class comprehensive works in 226

For miracles, see 226.7; parables, 226.8

.2   ***Matthew**

Class Golden Rule as code of conduct in 241.54

For Sermon on the Mount, see 226.9

.3   ***Mark**

.4   ***Luke**

Class Golden Rule as code of conduct in 241.54

For Sermon on the Mount, see 226.9

.5   ***John**

Class here comprehensive works on Johannine literature

For Epistles of John, see 227.94; Revelation (Apocalypse), 228

.6   ***Acts of the Apostles**

.7   ***Miracles**

Class miracles in the context of Jesus' life in 232.955

.8   ***Parables**

Class parables in the context of Jesus' life in 232.954

.9   ***Sermon on the Mount**

.93   *Beatitudes

.96   *Lord's Prayer

*Add as instructed under 221–228

227   *Epistles

Class here comprehensive works on Pauline epistles

.1   **Romans**

.2   **Corinthians 1**

Class here comprehensive works on the Epistles to the Corinthians

For Corinthians 2, see 227.3

.3   **Corinthians 2**

.4   **Galatians**

.5   **Ephesians**

.6   **Philippians**

.7   **Colossians**

.8   **Other Pauline epistles**

.81   *Thessalonians 1

Class here comprehensive works on the Epistles to the Thessalonians

For Thessalonians 2, see 227.82

.82   *Thessalonians 2

.83   *Timothy 1

Class here comprehensive works on the Epistles to Timothy, on the Pastoral Epistles

For Timothy 2, see 227.84; Titus, 227.85

.84   *Timothy 2

.85   *Titus

.86   *Philemon

.87   *Hebrews

.9   **Catholic epistles**

.91   *James

.92   *Peter 1

Class here comprehensive works on the Epistles of Peter

For Peter 2, see 227.93

.93   *Peter 2

*Add as instructed under 221–228

.94   *John 1

> Class here comprehensive works on the Epistles of John
>
> *For John 2, see 227.95; John 3, 227.96*

.95   *John 2

.96   *John 3

.97   *Jude

228   *Revelation (Apocalypse)

229   Apocrypha, pseudepigrapha, intertestamental works

Apocrypha: works accepted as deuterocanonical in some Bibles

Pseudepigrapha, intertestamental works: works from intertestamental times connected with the Bible but not accepted as canonical

Add to base number 229 as instructed under 221–228, e.g., Authorized Version of the Apocrypha 229.05203

Standard subdivisions and generalities are added for the Apocrypha alone

---

> ### 229.1–229.7 Specific books and works of the Apocrypha
>
> Add to each subdivision identified by † as instructed under 221–228
>
> Subdivisions may be added for a part of any work that has its own number
>
> Class comprehensive works in 229

.1   †Esdras 1 and 2

> Variant names: Esdras 3 and 4
>
> *See also 222.7 for Ezra, 222.8 for Nehemiah*

.2   †Tobit, Judith, Esther

.22   †Tobit (Tobias)

> (Option: Class in 222.86)

.24   †Judith

> (Option: Class in 222.88)

.27   †Deuterocanonical part of Esther

> (Option: Class in 222.9)

.3   †Wisdom of Solomon (Wisdom)

> Class here Apocryphal wisdom literature
>
> (Option: Class in 223.96)
>
> *For Ecclesiasticus, see 229.4*

*Add as instructed under 221–228
†Add as instructed under 229.1–229.7

.4	†**Ecclesiasticus (Sirach)**
	(Option: Class in 223.98)
.5	†**Baruch, Epistle of Jeremiah, Song of the Three Children**
	(Option: Class Baruch in 224.37, Song of the Three Children in 224.5)
.6	†**Susanna, Bel and the Dragon, Prayer of Manasses**
	(Option: Class Susanna, Bel and the Dragon in 224.5)
.7	†**Maccabees (Machabees)**
.73	†Maccabees 1 and 2 (Machabees 1 and 2)
	(Option: Class in 224.997)
.75	†Maccabees 3 and 4 (Machabees 3 and 4)

>   **229.8–229.9 Pseudepigrapha, intertestamental works**

Class comprehensive works in 229.9

For Maccabees 3 and 4, see 229.75

.8	†**Pseudo gospels**

Example: Gospel of Thomas

Including agrapha (Jesus' words not appearing in canonical Gospels) [*formerly* 232.98]

Class comprehensive works on New Testament pseudepigrapha in 229.92

.9	†**Pseudepigrapha**

For pseudo gospels, see 229.8

.91	†Old Testament

For Maccabees 3 and 4, see 229.75

.911	†Historical books
.912	†Poetic books

Example: Odes of Solomon

.913	†Prophetic books

Examples: Apocalypse of Elijah, Ascension of Isaiah, Assumption of Moses, Books of Enoch, Jewish apocalypses

.914	†Testaments

Example: Testament of the Twelve Patriarchs

[.915]	Other books by or about the prophets

Number discontinued; class in 229.91

†Add as instructed under 229.1–229.7

[.918]	Pseudepigrapha in Dead Sea Scrolls	
	Number discontinued; class in 229.91	
.92	†New Testament	Acts of the Apostles

For pseudo gospels, see 229.8

.93   †Epistles

.94   †Apocalypses

> ## 230–280 Christianity

(Option: To give local emphasis and more and shorter numbers to a specific religion other than Christianity, e.g., Buddhism, class it in these numbers, its sources in 220, comprehensive works in 200; in that case class the Bible and Christianity in 298. Other options are described at 292–299)

Unless other instructions are given, observe the following table of precedence for the history of Christianity and the Christian church (except for biography, explained in Manual at 209.2), e.g., Jesuit missions in India 266.254 (*not* 271.53054); persecution of Jesuits by Elizabeth I 272.7 (*not* 271.53042 or 274.206):

Specific topics	220–260
Persecutions in general church history	272
Doctrinal controversies and heresies in general church history	273
Religious congregations and orders in church history	271
Denominations and sects of the Christian church	280
Treatment of the Christian church by continent, country, locality	274–279
General historical, geographical, persons treatment of the Christian church	270
Historical, geographical, persons treatment of Christianity and Christian thought	209

Class comprehensive works in 200

For the Bible, see 220

See Manual at 209.2

> ## 230–270 Specific elements of Christianity

Class here specific elements of specific denominations and sects
    (Option: Class specific elements of specific denominations and sects in 280)

Class comprehensive works in 200

†Add as instructed under 229.1–229.7

230   Christian theology   Christian doctrinal theology

Class here Biblical theology

Class doctrinal controversies in general church history in 273

For Christian moral and devotional theology, see 240; Christian social and ecclesiastical theology, 260

SUMMARY

230.01–.09	**Standard subdivisions**
.1–.9	**Doctrines of specific denominations and sects**
231	**God**
232	**Jesus Christ and his family** **Christology**
233	**Humankind**
234	**Salvation (Soteriology) and grace**
235	**Spiritual beings**
236	**Eschatology**
238	**Creeds, confessions of faith, covenants, catechisms**
239	**Apologetics and polemics**

.01–.03   Standard subdivisions

.04   Specific types of Christian theology

       Class theology of specific denominations and sects in 230.1–230.9

       See Manual at 230.04 vs. 230.092, 230.1–230.9

.042   Theology of Eastern and Roman Catholic churches

       Class specific schools and systems of theology in 230.046

.044   Protestant theology

       Specific schools of Protestant theology relocated to 230.046

.046   Specific schools and systems of theology

       Examples: dispensationalist, evangelical, existentialist, fundamentalist, liberal, liberation, neo-orthodox, process theologies

       Class here specific schools of Protestant theology [*formerly* 230.044]

.05–.09   Standard subdivisions

       See Manual at 230.04 vs. 230.092, 230.1–230.9

.1–.9   Doctrines of specific denominations and sects

Add to base number 230 the numbers following 28 in 281–289, e.g., Methodist doctrines 230.7

(Option: Class here specific doctrines of specific denominations and sects; prefer 231–236. If option is chosen, add as above, then add 0 and to the result add the numbers following 23 in 231–236, e.g., Methodist doctrines on salvation 230.704)

See Manual at 230.04 vs. 230.092, 230.1–230.9; 230.16–230.2

> ## 231–239 Christian doctrinal theology

Class comprehensive works in 230, specific types of Christian doctrinal
theology in 230.042–230.046, comprehensive works on doctrines of specific
denominations and sects in 230.1–230.9

> ## 231–236 Specific topics in Christian doctrinal theology

Class here specific doctrines of specific denominations and sects
  (Option: Class specific doctrines of specific denominations and sects in
  230.1–230.9)

Class comprehensive works in 230

231   God

.04   Special topics

.042   Ways of knowing God

Examples: faith, reason, tradition, proofs

Class revelation in 231.74

See Manual at 212.1 vs. 231.042

.044   General concepts of God

Example: non-Trinitarian concepts

Class here comprehensive works on Holy Trinity

> ## 231.1–231.3 Holy Trinity

Class comprehensive works in 231.044

.1   **God the Father**

.2   **God the Son**

For Jesus Christ, see 232

.3   **God the Holy Spirit**

.4   **Attributes**

Examples: omnipotence, omnipresence, omniscience, transcendence

*For love and wisdom, see 231.6; sovereignty, 231.7; justice and goodness,
231.8*

.5   **Providence**

.6   **Love and wisdom**

.7   **Relation to the world**

    Examples: relation to nature, sovereignty

    Class here God's relation to individual believers

    Class redemption in 234.3, divine law in 241.2, believers' experience of God in 248.2, God's relation to the church in 262.7

    For Providence, see 231.5

.72   Kingdom of God

    Class the Kingdom of God to come in 236

.73   Miracles

    Class here miracles associated with saints

    Stigmata relocated to 248.29

    Class miracles of Jesus in 232.955, miracles associated with Mary in 232.917

.74   Revelation

    Vision and appearing of God, disclosure to men of divine purpose and superhuman knowledge

.745   Prophecy

    Class Biblical prophecy and prophecies in 220.15, messianic prophecies in 232.12, eschatological prophecies in 236

.76   Relation to and action in history

    Examples: covenant relationship, relationship to the Jewish people

.765   Creation

    Including relation of scientific and Christian viewpoints, evolution versus creation, evolution as method of creation

    For creation of humankind, see 233.11

    See Manual at 231.765 vs.213, 575

.8   **Justice and goodness**

    Class here theodicy (vindication of God's justice and goodness in permitting existence of evil and suffering)

    For Providence, see 231.5

232   **Jesus Christ and his family   Christology**

    See Manual at 232

SUMMARY

232.1	**Incarnation and messiahship of Christ**
.2	**Christ as Logos (Word of God)**
.3	**Christ as Redeemer**
.4	**Sacrifice of Christ**
.5	**Resurrection of Christ**
.8	**Divinity and humanity of Christ**
.9	**Family and life of Jesus**

> **232.1–232.8 Christology**

Class comprehensive works in 232, the life of Jesus in 232.9

.1   **Incarnation and messiahship of Christ**

Including typology

.12   Messianic prophecies

.2   **Christ as Logos (Word of God)**

.3   **Christ as Redeemer**

Including atonement

Class comprehensive works on the doctrine of redemption in 234.3

For sacrifice of Christ, see 232.4

.4   **Sacrifice of Christ**

.5   **Resurrection of Christ**

[.6]   **Second Coming of Christ**

Relocated to 236.9

[.7]   **Judgment of Christ**

Relocated to 236.9

.8   **Divinity and humanity of Christ**

Including Person; offices as Prophet, Priest, King; intercession

Class here the hypostatic union

Class non-Trinitarian concepts of Jesus in 232.9

For incarnation, see 232.1; Christ as Logos, 232.2; Christ as Redeemer, 232.3

.9   **Family and life of Jesus**

Class here non-Trinitarian concepts of Jesus

Use 232.9001–232.9009 for standard subdivisions

See Manual at 209.2

.901   Life of Jesus

Class specific events in 232.92, 232.95–232.97

.903	Character and personality of Jesus
.904	Jesus as teacher and exemplar
	Including influence
	Class teachings in 232.954
.908	Historicity of Jesus
.91	Mary, mother of Jesus
	Class here Mariology
	Class Mary's husband and parents in 232.93
.911	Immaculate Conception
.912	Annunciation
.913	Virginity
.914	Assumption (Ascent to heaven)
.915	Sanctity and virtues
.916	Spiritual powers
.917	Miracles and apparitions
.92	Infancy of Jesus
	Including Holy Family
	For Mary, see 232.91; Joseph, 232.932
.921	Nativity
	Including virgin birth
.922	Adoration of the shepherds
.923	Wise men (Magi)
.924	Circumcision
.925	Massacre of innocents
.926	Flight into Egypt
.927	Childhood in Nazareth
.928	Presentation in temple
.929	Jesus among the doctors in the temple
.93	Mary's husband and parents
.932	Joseph
.933	Joachim and Anne

.94   John the Baptist

.95   Public life of Jesus

> Including baptism, temptation, calling of apostles

.954   Teachings

> Class texts and interpretations of New Testament passages narrating parables in 226.8

.955   Miracles

> Class texts and interpretations of New Testament passages narrating miracles in 226.7

.956   Transfiguration

.957   Last Supper

.958   Last words to disciples

.96   Passion and death of Jesus

.961   Betrayal by Judas

.962   Trial and condemnation

.963   Crucifixion and death

.963 5   Seven last words on cross

.964   Burial

.966   Relics of Passion

.967   Descent into hell

.97   Resurrection, appearances, ascension of Jesus

[.98]   Agrapha

> Relocated to 229.8

233   Humankind

> Class relation to God in 231.7, salvation in 234

.1   **Creation and fall**

.11   Creation

> Including relation of human creation and human evolution
>
> Class comprehensive works on creation in 231.765

.14   Original sin and fall

> Class sins in 241.3

.4   **Accountability**

> Including guilt

.5   **Nature**

Including body, soul, spirit; as image and likeness of God, as child of God

Class free will in 233.7

For original sin, see 233.14; death, 236.1; immortality, 236.22

.7   **Freedom of choice between good and evil**

Class predestination and free will in relation to salvation in 234.9

For accountability, see 233.4

234   Salvation (Soteriology) and grace

Including election, innate virtues, merit, universal priesthood

.1   **Kinds and means of grace**

Examples: actual and sanctifying grace

.12   Gifts of the Holy Spirit

Contains wisdom, understanding, counsel, knowledge, fortitude, piety, fear of the Lord

Class here Baptism in the Holy Spirit

For spiritual gifts, see 234.13

.13   Spiritual gifts

Examples: healing, speaking in tongues, interpretation of tongues, prophecy, working of miracles, helps, governments, apostleship, teaching, exhortation, speaking words of wisdom and knowledge

For faith, see 234.2

.16   Sacraments

Class liturgy and ritual of sacraments in 265

.161   Baptism

.161 2   Infant

.161 3   Adult

.162   Confirmation

.163   Eucharist, Holy Communion, Lord's Supper

.164   Holy Orders

.165   Matrimony

.166   Penance

Including confession

.167   Anointing of the sick

.2   **Faith and hope**

> *See also 236 for eschatology, 241.4 for virtues*

.3   **Redemption**

.4   **Regeneration**

.5   **Repentance and forgiveness**

> Including atonement, reconciliation

.6   **Obedience**

.7   **Justification**

.8   **Sanctification and holiness**

.9   **Predestination and free will**

235   Spiritual beings

> *For Mariology, see 232.91*

.2   **Saints**

> Class miracles associated with saints in 231.73

> *For Joseph, see 232.932; Joachim and Anne, 232.933; John the Baptist, 232.94*

> *See Manual at 209.2*

.24   Beatification and canonization

\>   **235.3–235.4 Pure spirits**

> Class comprehensive works in 235

> *For God, see 231*

.3   **Celestial hierarchy**

> Examples: angels, archangels, cherubim, seraphim

.4   **Devils (Demons)**

.47   Satan (Lucifer)

236   Eschatology

> Including Antichrist
>
> Class here Kingdom of God to come

.1   **Death**

.2   **Future state (Life after death)**

> Class resurrection of the dead in 236.8

> *For intermediate state, see 236.4*

.21   Eternity

.22	Immortality

For conditional immortality, see 236.23

.23	Conditional immortality (Annihilationism)
.24	Heaven
.25	Hell
[.3]	**Millennium**

Relocated to 236.9

.4	**Intermediate state**

Probation after death

For purgatory, see 236.5

.5	**Purgatory**
.6	**Limbo of fathers (Limbus patrum)**

Abode of souls of the just who died before the coming of Jesus Christ

.7	**Limbo of infants (Limbus infantium)**

Abode of souls of the unbaptized but just

.8	**Resurrection of the dead**
.9	**Last Judgment and related events**

Examples: Second Coming of Christ [*formerly also* 232.6], Judgment of Christ [*formerly also* 232.7], millennium [*formerly* 236.3], Armageddon, Day of the Lord, end of the world, rapture, tribulation

Class interdisciplinary works on the end of the world in 001.9

[237]	**[Unassigned]**

Most recently used in Edition 16

238	**Creeds, confessions of faith, covenants, catechisms**

Class catechetics in 268, creeds and catechisms on a specific doctrine with the doctrine, e.g., attributes of God 231.4

.1	**Early and Eastern**
.11	Apostles' Creed
.14	Nicene and post-Nicene creeds of the Western Church

Including Constantinopolitan Creed

.142	Nicene Creed
.144	Athanasian Creed

.19   Creeds and confessions of the Eastern Church

> Examples: Confession of Gennadius II, Answers of Jeremiah II, Confession of Metrophanes, Orthodox Confession of Peter Mogila, Confession of Dositheus

.2   Roman Catholic

> Example: Creed of Pius IV

.3–.9   Other

> Add to base number 238 the numbers following 28 in 283–289, e.g., Augsburg Confession 238.41

239   Apologetics and polemics

> Apologetics: systematic argumentation in defense of the divine origin and authority of Christianity
>
> Polemics: refutation of alleged errors in other systems
>
> Class apologetics and polemics on a specific doctrine with the doctrine, e.g., the nature of the church 262.7; apologetics of specific denominations in 230.1–230.9
>
> *See also 273 for doctrinal controversies and heresies in general church history*

.001–.009   Standard subdivisions

.1   Apologetics and polemics in apostolic times

> *For polemics against doctrines of specific groups in apostolic times, see 239.2–239.4*

> **239.2–239.4 Polemics against doctrines of specific groups in apostolic times**

> Class comprehensive works in 239.1

.2   Polemics against Jews in apostolic times

.3   Polemics against pagans and heathens in apostolic times

.4   Polemics against Neoplatonists in apostolic times

> **239.5–239.9 Polemics against doctrines of specific groups in postapostolic times**

> Class comprehensive works in 239; comprehensive postapostolic defenses of and attacks on doctrines of specific denominations or sects in 230.1–230.9; attacks on doctrines of a specific religion with the religion, e.g., doctrines of Judaism 296.31–296.34

.5   Polemics against deists

.6   Polemics against Encyclopedists

.7   Polemics against rationalists, agnostics, apostates, atheists

.8 **Polemics against scientists and materialists**

For polemics against communists, see 239.9

.9 **Polemics against other specific groups in postapostolic times**

Groups not provided for in 239.5–239.8

Examples: communists, secular humanists

240 Christian moral and devotional theology

SUMMARY

241 Moral theology
242 Devotional literature
243 Evangelistic writings for individuals and families
245 Texts of hymns
246 Use of art in Christianity
247 Church furnishings and related articles
248 Christian experience, practice, life
249 Christian observances in family life

241 Moral theology

See Manual at 261.8 vs.241

.04 Specific denominations and sects

Add to base number 241.04 the numbers following 28 in 280.2–289.9, e.g., Protestant moral theology 241.0404

.1 **Conscience**

.2 **Laws and bases of morality**

Examples: divine law, natural law

For codes of conduct, see 241.5

.3 **Sin and vices**

Including specific vices [*formerly also* 241.6]

Class original sin in 233.14

For specific moral issues, see 241.6

See Manual at 241.6 vs.241.3, 241.4

.31 Mortal and venial sin

.32 Sins against the Holy Spirit

.4 **Virtues**

Including specific virtues [*formerly also* 241.6]

Class faith and hope as means of salvation in 234.2

For specific moral issues, see 241.6

See Manual at 241.6 vs.241.3, 241.4

.5   Codes of conduct

> *For specific moral issues, see 241.6*

> **241.52–241.54 Biblical precepts**

> Class comprehensive works in 241.5

.52   Ten Commandments

.53   Sermon on the Mount

.54   Golden Rule

.57   Precepts of the church

> Class church law in 262.9

.6   Specific moral issues

> Add to base number 241.6 the numbers following 17 in 172–179, e.g., the morality of warfare 241.6242, of abortion 241.6976; however, specific vices relocated to 241.3, specific virtues to 241.4

> *See Manual at 241.6 vs. 241.3, 241.4*

242   Devotional literature

> Class here texts of meditations, contemplations, prayers for individuals and families, religious poetry intended for devotional use

> Unless other instructions are given, observe the following table of precedence, e.g., prayers and meditations for daily use based on passages from the Bible 242.2 (*not* 242.5)

Prayers and meditations for use in times of illness, trouble, bereavement	242.4
Prayers and meditations for daily use	242.2
Prayers and meditations for the church year	242.3
Prayers and meditations for specific classes of persons	242.6
Prayers and meditations based on passages from the Bible	242.5
Specific prayers and groups of prayers	242.7
Collections of prayers	242.8

> Class devotional literature on a specific subject with the subject, e.g., meditations on God's providence 231.5

> *For evangelistic writings, see 243; hymns, 245*

> Prayers addressed to spiritual beings other than God are classed in 242.74–242.76

.2   Prayers and meditations for daily use

> Not limited to saints' days or specific parts of the church year

> Including meditations and prayers for Sunday, Sabbath

.3   Prayers and meditations for the church year

.33   Advent and Christmas

.34	Lent

For Holy Week, see 242.35

.35 Holy Week

.36 Easter

.37 Other feast and fast days

Examples: Ascension Day, Ember Days, Rogation Days, saints' days

.4 Prayers and meditations for use in times of illness, trouble, bereavement

.5 Prayers and meditations based on passages from the Bible

Class interpretation and criticism of Bible passages for other than devotional use in 220.6, Bible prayers in 242.722

.6 Prayers and meditations for specific classes of persons

Add to base number 242.6 the numbers following 248.8 in 248.82–248.89, e.g., for young women 242.633; however, class prayers and meditations for use in times of illness, trouble, bereavement in 242.4

Class collections of prayers for specific classes of persons in 242.82–242.89

.7 Specific prayers and groups of prayers

.72 Specific types of prayers

Class here prayers to Father, Son, Holy Spirit

.721 Doxologies (Prayers of praise)

.722 Bible prayers

.723 Prayers of faith

.724 Prayers of thanksgiving

.725 Prayers of penitence

.726 Prayers of petition

> 242.74–242.76 Prayers addressed to spiritual beings other than God

Class comprehensive works in 242.7

.74 To Mary

Including Ave Maria (Hail Mary), Rosary

.75 To Joseph, Joachim, Anne

.76 To saints and angels

For Joseph, Joachim, Anne, see 242.75

.8   Collections of prayers

Use 242.8001–242.8009 for standard subdivisions

For specific prayers and groups of prayers, see 242.7

.801–.809   By adherents of specific denominations and sects

Add to base number 242.80 the numbers following 28 in 281–289, e.g., collections of private prayers by Methodists 242.807

.82–.89   For specific classes of persons

Add to base number 242.8 the numbers following 248.8 in 248.82–248.89, e.g., collections of private prayers for young women 242.833

243   Evangelistic writings for individuals and families

Works designed to convert readers, promote repentance

Class evangelistic sermons in 252.3

[244]   [Unassigned]

Most recently used in Edition 15

245   Texts of hymns

For devotional use of individuals and families

Add to base number 245 notation 1–9 from Table 6, e.g., hymns in German 245.31

Class comprehensive works on texts of hymns in 264.2, musical scores and parts in 782.27, modern metrical versions of Psalms in 223.205

246   Use of art in Christianity

Religious meaning, significance, purpose

Class creation, description, critical appraisal as art in 700

For church furnishings and related articles, see 247

>   246.1–246.4 Schools and styles

Class comprehensive works in 246, specific elements by school and style in 246.5–246.9

.1   Byzantine and Gothic

.2   Early Christian and Romanesque

.4   Renaissance and modern

Including Protestant

>   246.5–246.9 Specific elements

Class comprehensive works in 246

.5   **Icons, symbols, insignia**

.53   Icons

.55   Emblems and symbols

             Examples: banners, incense, votive offerings

             For colors and lights, see 246.6

.558   Crosses and crucifixes

.56   Insignia

             Including insignia of rank

.6   **Colors and lights**

.7   **Musical, rhythmic, dramatic arts**

             Examples: the dance, passion plays, puppet shows

.9   **Architecture**

             Add to base number 246.9 the numbers following 726 in 726.4–726.9, e.g., cathedral church buildings 246.96

247   **Church furnishings and related articles**

             Examples: sculpture, structural decoration, paintings, textiles, plastic arts

.1   **Furniture**

[.11–.18]   [Kinds of furniture]

             Numbers discontinued; class in 247.1

[.3–.8]   **Sculpture, structural decoration, paintings, textiles, plastic arts**

             Numbers discontinued; class in 247

248   **Christian experience, practice, life**

             See Manual at 209.2

SUMMARY

248.06		**Organizations**
	.2	**Religious experience**
	.3	**Worship**
	.4	**Christian life and practice**
	.5	**Witness bearing**
	.6	**Stewardship**
	.8	**Guides to Christian life for specific classes of persons**

.06   Organizations

             Class here pious societies, e.g., sodalities, confraternities

.2   **Religious experience**

.22   Mysticism

.24	Conversion

For moral renewal and commitment, see 248.25

> 248.242–248.246 Conversion from one system of belief to another

Class comprehensive works in 248.24

.242	From Protestantism to Roman Catholicism
.244	From Roman Catholicism to Protestantism
.246	From non-Christianity to Christianity

Class conversion of Christians to another religion with the religion, e.g., conversion of Christians to Judaism 296.71

.25	Moral renewal and commitment
.29	Other

Including stigmata [*formerly also* 231.73], speaking in tongues (glossolalia)

See also 234.13 for spiritual gifts

.3	**Worship**

Class here comprehensive works on worship

Class texts of prayers and devotions in 242

For observances in family life, see 249; public worship, 264

.32	Prayer
.34	Meditation and contemplation
.4	**Christian life and practice**

Class here Christian marriage and family

Class guides to Christian life for specific classes of persons in 248.8

For moral theology, see 241; worship, 248.3; witness bearing, 248.5; stewardship, 248.6

.46	Individual observances

Examples: ceremonial and ritual observances, observance of restrictions and limitations

For asceticism, see 248.47

.463	Pilgrimages
.47	Asceticism

Attitudes and practices aside from and beyond normal moral duties adopted as aids to moral and spiritual development

Examples: practice of celibacy, fasting and abstinence, poverty, solitude, other physical austerities, e.g., flagellation

| .48 | Guides to Christian life by or for adherents of specific denominations and sects |

> Add to base number 248.48 the numbers following 28 in 280.2–289.9, e.g., guides for Roman Catholics 248.482

> Guides to Christian life for specific classes of persons who are adherents of specific denominations and sects relocated to 248.8

.5   Witness bearing

.6   Stewardship

.8   Guides to Christian life for specific classes of persons

> Class here guides to Christian life for specific classes of persons who are adherents of specific denominations and sects [*formerly* 248.48]

> Class a specific aspect with the aspect, e.g., prayer 248.32

> 248.82–248.85 For specific age groups

> Class comprehensive works in 248.8, persons of specific ages in specific occupational groups or experiencing illness, trouble, bereavement in 248.86–248.89

| .82 | Children |

> Through age eleven

| .83 | Young adults |

> Junior-high-school, high-school, college students

| .832 | Young men |

> Class male college students in 248.834

| .833 | Young women |

> Class female college students in 248.834

| .834 | College students |

> Male and female

| .84 | Adults |

> *For persons in late adulthood, see 248.85*

| .842 | Men |

| .842 1 | Fathers |

> Regardless of marital status

| .842 2–.842 9 | By marital status |

> Add to base number 248.842 the numbers following —0865 in notation 08652–08659 from Table 1, e.g., guides for husbands 248.8425

> Class fathers in 248.8421

.843	Women
.843 1	Mothers

Regardless of marital status

.843 2–.843 9	By marital status

Add to base number 248.843 the numbers following —0865 in notation 08652–08659 from Table 1, e.g., guides for wives 248.8435

Class mothers in 248.8431

.844	Married couples

Class husbands in 248.8425, wives in 248.8435

.845	Parents

Class here Christian religious training of children in the home [*formerly also* 649.7], Christian child rearing

For fathers, see 248.8421; mothers, 248.8431

.846	Separated and divorced persons

Class separated and divorced men in 248.8423, separated and divorced women in 248.8433

.85	Persons in late adulthood

>	**248.86–248.89 For occupational classes; persons experiencing illness, trouble, bereavement**

Class comprehensive works in 248.8

.86	Persons experiencing illness, trouble, bereavement
.88	Occupational classes

For religious groups, see 248.89

.89	Religious groups
.892	Secular clergy

Examples: priests, ministers, pastors, rectors, vicars, chaplains, curates, elders, deacons, assistants

.894	Persons in religious orders

Religious and monastic life

.894 2	Men
.894 22	Vocation
.894 25	Selection and novitiate
[.894 28]	Rules

Relocated to 255

.894 3	Women
.894 32	Vocation
.894 35	Selection and novitiate
[.894 38]	Rules

Relocated to 255.9

249   Christian observances in family life

Class here family prayer; family observance of religious restrictions, rites, ceremonies

---

> 250–280 Christian church

Class comprehensive works in 260

250   Local Christian church and Christian religious orders

Class here basic Christian communities

Class the local church in overall church organization in 262.2, public worship in 264, missions in 266, religious training and instruction in 268

SUMMARY

250.1–.9	**Standard subdivisions**
251	**Preaching (Homiletics)**
252	**Texts of sermons**
253	**Pastoral office and work (Pastoral theology)**
254	**Parish government and administration**
255	**Religious congregations and orders**
259	**Activities of the local church**

[.68]   Management

Do not use; class management of the local church in 254, of religious congregations and orders in 255

> 251–254 Local church

Class comprehensive works in 250, special activities of the local church in 259

See Manual at 251–254, 259 vs.260

251   Preaching (Homiletics)

Use 251.001–251.009 for standard subdivisions

Class texts of sermons in 252, pastoral methods in 253.7

.01	Preparation
.02	Sermon outlines

.03   Delivery

   Class here voice, expression, gesture

.07   Radio and television preaching

   Class specific aspects of radio and television preaching in 251.01–251.03

.08   Homiletic illustrations

252   Texts of sermons

   Use 252.001–252.009 for standard subdivisions

   Class sermons on a specific subject with the subject, e.g., God's Providence 231.5

.01–.09   By specific denominations and sects

   Add to base number 252.0 the numbers following 28 in 281–289, e.g., Anglican sermons 252.03

.1   For baptisms, confirmations, weddings, funerals

   Class sermons for memorial occasions in 252.9

.3   For evangelistic meetings

.5   For specific classes of persons

.53   Children

   Through age eleven

.55   Young adults

   Junior-high-school, high-school, college students

   Including academic, chapel, convocation, commencement sermons

.56   Persons in late adulthood, and persons experiencing illness, trouble, bereavement

.58   Occupational classes

   For religious groups, see 252.59

.59   Religious groups

.592   Secular clergy

   Examples: priests, ministers, pastors, rectors, vicars, chaplains, curates, elders, deacons, assistants

.594   Persons in religious orders

.6   For church and public occasions

>   252.61–252.67 Church year

   Class comprehensive works in 252.6

.61   Advent and Christmas

.62	Lent and Holy Week
.63	Easter
.67	Other feast and fast days

        Examples: Ascension Day, Ember Days, Rogation Days, saints' days

.68	Secular occasions

        Examples: elections, holidays, thanksgivings

.7   For consecrations, ordinations, installations

.9   For memorial occasions

253   Pastoral office and work (Pastoral theology)

Class here the work of priests, ministers, pastors, rectors, vicars, curates, chaplains, elders, deacons, assistants, laity in relation to the work of the church at the local level

Class local clergy and laity in relation to the government, organization and nature of the church as a whole in 262.1; the role of clergy in religious education in 268; the ordination of women in 262.14 (unless the work treats the ordination of women only in relation to its effect on the local parish)

.092	Persons treatment

        Class biography of clergy in the period prior to 1054 in 270.1–270.3, in the period subsequent to 1054 in 280

        See Manual at 209.2

.2   Life and person

Including professional and personal qualifications, families of clergy

Class education of the clergy in 207.1, guides to Christian life for secular clergy in 248.892

>   **253.5–253.7 Pastoral duties and responsibilities**

Methods and techniques for clergy and laity

Class comprehensive works in 253, methods for services to specific groups in 259

        For preaching, see 251; parish government and administration, 254

.5   Counseling and spiritual direction

.52	Pastoral psychology
.53	Spiritual direction

.7	**Pastoral methods [*formerly also* 259.7]**

Former heading: Evangelistic methods

Examples: group work, telephone work

.73	Outdoor
[.75]	In prisons

Relocated to 259.5

.76	In homes
.78	Use of radio and television

254   Parish government and administration

Use 254.001–254.009 for standard subdivisions

.01–.09	By specific denominations and sects

Add to base number 254.0 the numbers following 28 in 281–289, e.g., government and administration of Roman Catholic parishes 254.02

.1	**Initiation of new churches**
.2	**In specific kinds of communities**

Class a specific activity in a specific kind of community with the activity, e.g., membership promotion 254.5

.22	Urban
.23	Suburban
.24	Rural
.3	**Use of communications media**

Including use of audiovisual materials

.4	**Public relations and publicity**

For use of communications media, see 254.3

.5	**Membership**

Promotion and growth

.6	**Programs**

Planning and execution

For activities of the local church, see 259

.7	**Buildings, equipment, grounds**
.8	**Finance**

Examples: budget, expenditures, income, methods of raising money

255 Religious congregations and orders

Class here rules [*formerly also* 248.89428], monasticism, comprehensive works on Christian religious congregations and orders

Use 255.001–255.009 for standard subdivisions

When adding from 271 to indicate kinds of orders or specific orders, add only the notation for the kind or order. Do not use the footnote instruction to add as instructed under 271, but add notation from the table under 255.1–255.7 if it applies, or add notation 01–09 from Table 1. For example, the correct number for contemplative orders in the United Kingdom is 255.010941 (*not* 255.01041); for Benedictines in the United Kingdom 255.100941 (*not* 255.1041)

Class guides to Christian life for persons in religious orders in 248.894, specific types of activity of religious congregations and orders with the activity, e.g., sponsoring religious camps 259.8, missionary work 266

> *For religious congregations and orders in church organization, see 262.24; in church history, 271*

.01–.09   Specific kinds

Add to base number 255.0 the numbers following 271.0 in 271.01–271.09 for the kind only, e.g., contemplative orders 255.01; then add notation 01–09 from Table 1, e.g., contemplative orders in the United Kingdom 255.010941

Fuller instructions for use of the add note are given at 255

.1–.7   **Roman Catholic orders of men**

Add to base number 255 the numbers following 271 in 271.1–271.7 for the order only, e.g., Benedictines 255.1; then, for each order having its own number, add further as follows (not as instructed at 271), e.g., Benedictines in the United Kingdom 255.100941, the rule of St. Benedict 255.106:

001–009	Standard subdivisions
02	Constitutions
04	Statutes, ordinances, customs
06	Rule

Fuller instructions for use of the add note are given at 255

.8   **Non-Roman Catholic orders of men**

.9   **Congregations and orders of women**

Class here rules [*formerly also* 248.89438]

Use 255.9001–255.9009 for standard subdivisions

.901–.909   Specific kinds

Add to base number 255.90 the numbers following 271.0 in 271.01–271.09 for the kind only, e.g., contemplative orders 255.901; then add notation 01–09 from Table 1, e.g., contemplative orders in the United Kingdom 255.9010941

Fuller instructions for use of the add note are given at 255

.91–.97   Roman Catholic orders of women

> Add to base number 255.9 the numbers following 271.9 in 271.91–271.97 for the order only, e.g., Dominican sisters 255.972; then, for each order having its own number, add further as instructed under 255.1–255.7 (not as instructed at 271), e.g., Dominicans in the United Kingdom 255.97200941, the rule of the Dominicans 255.97206

> Fuller instructions for use of the add note are given at 255

.98   Non-Roman Catholic orders of women

[256]   [Unassigned]

> Most recently used in Edition 14

[257]   [Unassigned]

> Most recently used in Edition 14

[258]   [Unassigned]

> Most recently used in Edition 17

259   Activities of the local church

> Former heading: Parochial activities by parishes and religious orders

> Not provided for elsewhere

> Class here activities designed to promote religious and social welfare of social groups in community

> Class works limited to social welfare work by religious organizations in 361.75

> *See Manual at 251–254, 259 vs. 260*

.08   History and description with respect to kinds of persons

[.083]   Young people

> Do not use; class in 259.2

.084   Persons in specific stages of adulthood

[.084 6]   Late adulthood

> Do not use; class in 259.3

.086   Persons by social and economic characteristics

[.086 92]   Asocial and antisocial persons

> Do not use; class in 259.5

.087   Gifted persons

> Class handicapped and ill persons in 259.4

[.088 375]   Students

> Do not use; class in 259.2

.1   Activities with families

.2   **Activities with young people**

Class activities with sick and handicapped young people in 259.4, with young delinquents in 259.5

.22   With children

Through age eleven

.23   With young adults

Ages twelve through seventeen; junior-high-school and high-school students

Class activities with college students in 259.24

.24   With college students

.3   **Activities with persons in late adulthood**

Class activities with sick and handicapped persons in late adulthood in 259.4

.4   **Activities with handicapped and ill**

Class here hospital chaplaincy, programs for visiting the sick

.5   **Activities with delinquents and criminals**

Class here pastoral methods in prisons [*formerly* 253.75], prison chaplaincy, activities with asocial and antisocial persons

.6   **Activities with the bereaved**

[.7]   **Pastoral methods**

Relocated to 253.7

.8   **Specific types of activity**

Including recreational and camp programs

Class activities with specific classes of people in 259.2–259.6, revival and camp meetings in 269.24, retreats in 269.6

260   Christian social and ecclesiastical theology

Institutions, services, observances, disciplines, work of Christianity and the Christian church

Class here comprehensive works on the Christian church

For local church and religious orders, see 250; denominations and sects, 280

See Manual at 251–254, 259 vs. 260

.09   Historical, geographical, persons treatment

Class historical, geographical, persons treatment of the Christian church in 270

SUMMARY

261	Social theology and interreligious relations and attitudes
262	Ecclesiology
263	Days, times, places of religious observance
264	Public worship
265	Sacraments, other rites and acts
266	Missions
267	Associations for religious work
268	Religious education
269	Spiritual renewal

261 Social theology and interreligious relations and attitudes

Attitude of Christianity and the Christian church toward and influence on secular matters, attitude toward other religions, interreligious relations

Class here Christianity and culture

Class sociology of religion in 306.6

.1 Role of the Christian church in society

Class specific socioeconomic problems in 261.8

.2 Christianity and other systems of belief

.21 Christianity and irreligion

Including Christianity and communism, Christianity and the apostate and indifferent

.22–.29 Christianity and other religions

Add to base number 261.2 the numbers following 29 in 292–299, e.g., Christianity and Islam 261.27

.5 Christianity and secular disciplines

See Manual at 261.5

.51 Philosophy, logic, related disciplines

Including paranormal phenomena and arts

.515 Psychology

.52 Communications media

Attitude toward and use

Class a specific use of communications media by the church with the use, e.g., in parish administration 254.3

.55 Science

Class the relation of scientific and Christian views on creation in 231.765

.56 Technology

.561 Medicine

.57 Art

.58	Literature

.7   Christianity and political affairs

Including civil war and revolution

Class here Christianity and civil rights

Class Christianity and international affairs in 261.87

See Manual at 322.1 vs.261.7, 291.177

.72	Religious freedom
.73	Theocracy

Supremacy of church over civil government

.8   Christianity and socioeconomic problems

Class here comprehensive works on the Christian view of socioeconomic and political affairs

For Christianity and political affairs, see 261.7

See also 361.75 for welfare services of religious organizations

See Manual at 261.8 vs.241

.83	Social problems
.832	Social welfare problems and services

Add to base number 261.832 the numbers following 362 in 362.1–362.5, e.g., the Christian attitude toward alcoholism 261.832292

Use of this number for comprehensive works on social welfare problems and crime discontinued; class in 261.8

.833	Crime

Add to base number 261.833 the numbers following 364 in 364.1–364.8, e.g., the Christian attitude toward treason 261.833131, toward capital punishment 261.83366

.834	Social structure

Add to base number 261.834 the numbers following 305 in 305.2–305.8, e.g., the Christian attitude toward women 261.8344; however, class Christianity in relation to other religions in 261.22–261.29

.835	Relation of the sexes, marriage, family

Add to base number 261.835 the numbers following 306 in 306.7–306.8, e.g., the Christian attitude toward homosexuality 261.835766

.836	Ecology and population

Add to base number 261.836 the numbers following 304 in 304.2–304.8, e.g., the Christian attitude toward abuse of the environment 261.83628

.85	The economic order

Including management of business enterprises

.87	International affairs
.873	War and peace
.873 2	Nuclear weapons and nuclear war

262   Ecclesiology

Church government, organization, nature

See Manual at 251–254, 259 vs. 260

SUMMARY

262.001–.009	Standard subdivisions
.01–.09	Government and organization of specific denominations and sects
.1	Governing leaders of churches
.2	Local church in church organization
.3	Government and organization of systems governed by papacy and episcopacy
.4	Government and organization of systems governed by election
.5	General councils
.7	Nature of the church
.8	Church and ministerial authority and its denial
.9	Church law and discipline

| .001 | Philosophy and theory |
| .001 1 | Ecumenicalism |

> Do not use for systems; class in 262.001
>
> Class the history of the ecumenical movement in 270.82
>
> *See Manual at 280.042 vs. 270.82, 262.0011*

.001 7	Church renewal
.002–.005	Standard subdivisions
.006	Organizations and management
.006 8	Management

> Do not use notation 068 from Table 1 by itself in 262; however, add notation 0681–0688 as appropriate for particular aspects of administration, e.g., financial administration of the Anglican church 262.030681

| .007–.009 | Standard subdivisions |
| .01–.09 | Government and organization of specific denominations and sects |

> Add to base number 262.0 the numbers following 28 in 281–289, e.g., government and organization of the United Methodist Church 262.076

.1   **Governing leaders of churches**

Authority, function, role

Class biography of church leaders in 270, of leaders of specific denominations in 280

See Manual at 209.2

.11   Apostolic succession

> 262.12–262.15 Governing leaders by rank

Class comprehensive works in 262.1

.12   Bishops and archbishops

.13   Popes and patriarchs

> 262.131–262.136 Popes and their administration

Class comprehensive works in 262.13

.131   Papal infallibility

.132   Temporal power of the pope

.135   College of Cardinals

.136   Administration

Including congregations, tribunals, offices of Curia Romana, Synod of Bishops

For the College of Cardinals, see 262.135

.14   Local clergy

Class here the ordination of women

Add to base number 262.14 the numbers following 28 in 281–289, e.g., local Methodist clergy 262.147

.15   Laity

Body of church members

> 262.17–262.19 Governing leaders by system of government

Class comprehensive works in 262.1, leaders by rank in a specific system of government in 262.12–262.15

.17   Governing leaders in papal and episcopal systems

.18   Governing leaders in presbyterian systems

.19   Governing leaders in congregational systems

.2   **Local church in church organization**

Class government and administration of parishes in 254, of religious congregations and orders in 255

See Manual at 251–254, 259 vs. 260

.22   Parishes

.24   Religious congregations and orders

.26   Small groups

Example: basic Christian communities

> **262.3–262.4 Specific forms of church organization**

Class comprehensive works in 262, comprehensive works on government and organization of specific denominations and sects regardless of form of organization in 262.01–262.09, a specific aspect of government and organization with the aspect, e.g., parishes 262.22

.3   **Government and organization of systems governed by papacy and episcopacy**

Examples: sees, dioceses, cathedral systems

.4   **Government and organization of systems governed by election**

Examples: congregational systems, presbyteries, synods

.5   **General councils**

Add to base number 262.5 the numbers following 28 in 281–289, e.g., ecumenical councils of the Roman Catholic Church 262.52

Class legal acts of general councils in 262.9, nonlegal decrees on a specific subject with the subject, e.g., statements on original sin 233.14

.7   **Nature of the church**

Including God's relation to the church

.72   Attributes, marks, notes

Examples: apostolicity, catholicity, credibility, holiness, infallibility, necessity, visibility and invisibility, unity

.73   Communion of saints

.77   Mystical body of Christ

.8   **Church and ministerial authority and its denial**

Including heresy, schism

.9   **Church law and discipline**

Class here canon (ecclesiastical) law

Class civil law relating to church or religious matters in 340

See also 364.188 for offenses against religion as defined and penalized by the state

---

\>   262.91–262.94 Roman Catholic

Class comprehensive works in 262.9

.91   Acts of the Holy See

Examples: apostolic letters, briefs, encyclicals, papal bulls and decrees

Class acts on specific subjects with the subject, e.g., on the nature of the church 262.7

.92   Early Roman Catholic codes

.922   To Gratian, ca. 1140

.923   Corpus iuris canonici

.924   Quinque compilationes antiquae

.93   Codex iuris canonici (1917)

.931   General principles (Canons 1–86)

.932   Persons (Canons 87–725)

Clergy, religious, laity

.933   Things (Canons 726–1551)

Including sacraments, sacred times and places, worship, teaching office, benefices, temporal goods

.934   Procedure (Canons 1552–2194)

Including trials, cases of beatification and canonization

.935   Crimes and penalties (Canons 2195–2414)

.94   Codex iuris canonici (1983)

.98   Branches and other denominations

Add to base number 262.98 the numbers following 28 in 280.2–289.9, e.g., Anglican ecclesiastical law 262.983

263   Days, times, places of religious observance

.04   Special topics

.042   Holy places

Add to base number 263.042 notation 3–9 from Table 2, e.g., Santiago de Compostela 263.0424611

Class works treating miracles and the shrines associated with them in 231.73; miracles associated with Mary and the shrines associated with them in 232.917; miracles of Jesus and shrines associated with them in 232.955; pilgrimages in 248.463

>   **263.1–263.4 Sabbath and Sunday**

Class comprehensive works in 263

.1   **Biblical Sabbath**

.2   **Observance of the seventh day**

.3   **Sunday**

For Sunday observance, see 263.4

.4   **Sunday observance**

.9   **Church year and other days and times**

Standard subdivisions are added for the church year

See Manual at 394.2682 vs.263.9, 290

.91   Advent and Christmas

.92   Lent and Holy Week

.93   Easter

.97   Other feast and fast days

Examples: Ascension Day, Ember Days, Rogation Days

For specific saints' days, see 263.98

.98   Specific saints' days

264   Public worship

Ceremonies, rites, services (liturgy and ritual)

Class comprehensive works on worship in 248.3; works not limited by denomination or sect about sacraments, other rites and acts in 265; Sunday school services in 268.7

SUMMARY

264.001–.009	**Standard subdivisions**
.01–.09	**By denominations and sects**
.1	**Prayer**
.2	**Music**
.3	**Scripture readings and communion sacrament**
.4	**Responsive readings**
.5	**Creeds and confessions of faith**
.6	**Sermons, exhortations, instructions**
.7	**Prayer meetings, Holy Hours, novenas**
.9	**Sacramentals**

.001   Philosophy and theory

>   Class here liturgical renewal

.002–.009   Standard subdivisions

> 264.01–264.09 By denominations and sects

Class here works limited by denomination or sect about sacraments, other rites and acts [*formerly* 265]

Class comprehensive works in 264; comprehensive works on sacraments, other rites and acts in 265

.01   Early and Eastern churches

Add to base number 264.01 the numbers following 281 in 281.1–281.9, e.g., liturgy and ritual of Eastern Orthodox churches 264.019; then add further from the table under 264.04–264.09, e.g., Eastern Orthodox Mass 264.019036

.02   Roman Catholic Church

Use 264.02001–264.02009 for standard subdivisions

.020 1–.020 9   History, meaning, place of liturgy, ritual, prayers in public worship

Add to base number 264.02 notation 01–09 from the table under 264.04–264.09, e.g., the Mass 264.02036; however, class texts in 264.021–264.029

> 264.021–264.029 Texts of liturgy, ritual, prayers

Class comprehensive works in 264.02

.021   Texts of calendars and ordos

.022   Texts of ceremonials

Ceremonials: canonization of saints, election and coronation of popes, creation of cardinals, other papal functions and services; instructions for bishops

.023   Texts of missals

Class here sacramentaries

For lectionary, see 264.029

.024   Texts of breviaries

For psalters, see 264.028; lectionary, 264.029

.025   Texts of ritual

Class here Pontificale Romanum, Rituale Romanum

Add to base number 264.025 the numbers following 265 in 265.1–265.7, e.g., text of baptism 264.0251

.027   Texts of special books

.027 2   For special times of year

Example: Holy Week

.027 4   For special liturgical services

Examples: funeral services outside the Mass, litanies, novenas, stations of the cross

.028   Texts of psalters

.029   Texts of the lectionary

.03   Anglican churches

Class here the Book of Common Prayer

Use 264.03001–264.03009 for standard subdivisions

.030 1–.030 9   History, meaning, place of liturgy, ritual, prayers in public worship

Add to base number 264.03 notation 01–09 from the table under 264.04–264.09, e.g., prayer 264.0301; however, class texts in 264.031–264.038

>   264.031–264.038 Texts of liturgy, ritual, prayers

Class comprehensive works in 264.03

.031   Texts of calendars, festivals, fasts

.032   Texts of the lectionary and rubrics

.033   Texts of morning prayer and litany

.034   Texts of evening prayer and vespers

.035   Texts of sacraments, ordinances, services

Add to base number 264.035 the numbers following 265 in 265.1–265.7, e.g., text of baptism 264.0351

Class texts of morning prayer and litany in 264.033, texts of evening prayer and vespers in 264.034

.036	Texts of collects, epistles, Gospels
.037	Texts of ordinal, articles, creeds
.038	Texts of psalters
.04–.09	Other specific denominations and sects

Add to base number 264.0 the numbers following 28 in 284–289, e.g., United Methodist services 264.076; then add further as follows:

001–009	Standard subdivisions
01–07	Specific elements

History, meaning, place in public worship, texts

Add to 0 the numbers following 264 in 264.1–264.7, e.g., the Lord's Supper 036, the Lord's Supper in the United Methodist Church 264.076036

081–087	Sacraments

History, meaning, place in public worship, texts

Add to 08 the numbers following 265 in 265.1–265.7, e.g., the ceremony of baptism 081, the ceremony of baptism in the United Methodist Church 264.076081; however, class the Eucharist, Holy Communion, Lord's Supper, Mass in 036

09	Sacramentals, other rites and acts

History, meaning, place in public worship, texts

091	Sacramentals
098–099	Other rites and acts

Add to 09 the numbers following 265 in 265.8–265.9, e.g., funeral services 0985, United Methodist funerals 264.0760985

> **264.1–264.9 Specific elements**

History, meaning, place in public worship, texts

Class comprehensive works in 264, specific elements in the public worship of specific denominations and sects in 264.01–264.09

Specific elements as part of the Mass are classed in 264.36, e.g., Eucharistic prayers (*not* 264.1)

.1	**Prayer**
.13	Texts of prayers

Including litanies

Class comprehensive collections of public and private prayers in 242.8

.2	**Music**

Class here comprehensive works on texts of hymns

Class interdisciplinary works on Christian sacred music in 781.71, on sacred vocal music in 782.22, on hymns in 782.27; texts of hymns for devotional use of individuals and families in 245

.3   **Scripture readings and communion sacrament**

.34   Scripture readings

Class here the common lectionary

.36   Eucharist, Holy Communion, Lord's Supper, Mass

Including specific elements when part of the Mass

For viaticum, see 265.7

.4   **Responsive readings**

.5   **Creeds and confessions of faith**

Class texts in 238

.6   **Sermons, exhortations, instructions**

Class texts of sermons in 252

.7   **Prayer meetings, Holy Hours, novenas**

.9   **Sacramentals**

For consecrations and dedications, see 265.92

265   Sacraments, other rites and acts

Not limited by denomination or sect

Works limited by denomination or sect about sacraments, other rites and acts relocated to 264.01–264.09

>   **265.1–265.7 Sacraments**

Class comprehensive works in 265

For Eucharist, Holy Communion, Lord's Supper, Mass, see 264.36

.1   **Baptism**

.12   Infant

.13   Adult

Class here Christian initiation (baptism and confirmation) of adults, catechumenate

For confirmation, see 265.2

.2   **Confirmation**

.4   **Holy Orders**

.5   **Matrimony**

.6   **Penance**

.61   Contrition

Examination of conscience, prayers preparatory to confession

.62   Confession

.63	Satisfaction

Penitential prayers and acts for the remission of sin

.64	Absolution
.66	Indulgences

.7 Viaticum and anointing of the sick

.8 Rites in illness and death

.82	Religious ceremonies for the afflicted

For viaticum and anointing of the sick, see 265.7

.85	Religious ceremonies for the dead

Class here funeral services

Class the requiem Mass in 264.36

.9 Other acts

Examples: love feasts (agapes), foot washing, laying on of hands, ceremonies of joining a church

.92	Consecrations and dedications
.94	Exorcism

266 Missions

Class here missionary societies, religious aspects of medical missions

Class medical services of medical missions in 362.1

For mission schools, see 377.6

.001–.008	Standard subdivisions
.009	Historical, geographical, persons treatment

Class here joint and interdenominational missions; foreign missions by continent, country, locality served

Class foreign missions originating in specific continents, countries, localities in 266.023; historical, geographical, persons treatment of missions of specific denominations and sects in 266.1–266.9

.02	Kinds of missions
.022	Home missions
.023	Foreign missions

Add to base number 266.023 notation 1–9 from Table 2, e.g., missions originating in France 266.02344; then add 0* and again add notation 1–9 from Table 2 for place served, e.g., French missions to Africa 266.0234406

Class foreign missions characterized only by place served in 266.009

*Add 00 for standard subdivisions; see instructions at beginning of Table 1

.1–.9 **Of specific denominations and sects**

Add to base number 266 the numbers following 28 in 281–289, e.g.,
Seventh-Day Adventist missions 266.6732; Anglican missions serving Africa
266.36

267 Associations for religious work

*For pious societies, see 248.06; religious congregations and orders, 255;
missionary societies, 266*

See Manual at 209.2

.1 **Of both men and women**

.13 Interdenominational and nondenominational

For Moral Rearmament, see 267.16

[.15] Salvation Army

Relocated to 287.96

.16 Moral Rearmament

.18 Of specific branches, denominations, and sects

Add to base number 267.18 the numbers following 28 in 280.2–289.9, e.g.,
Baptist Adult Union 267.186132

.2 **Of men**

.23 Interdenominational and nondenominational

For Young Men's Christian Associations, see 267.3

.24 Of specific branches, denominations, and sects

Add to base number 267.24 the numbers following 28 in 280.2–289.9, e.g.,
Baptist societies 267.246

.3 **Young Men's Christian Associations**

.308 History and description with respect to kinds of persons

Class here work among special classes [*formerly also* 267.36]

[.309] Historical, geographical, persons treatment

Do not use; class in 267.39

.31 Program and objectives

.32 Buildings and equipment

.33 Organization and administration

.34 Staff

.35 Departments

Examples: religious, educational, physical, boys' departments

[.36]	Work among special classes
	Relocated to 267.308
.39	Historical, geographical, persons treatment
	Add to base number 267.39 notation 01–9 from Table 2, e.g., Young Men's Christian Association in New York City 267.397471

.4 Of women

.43 Interdenominational and nondenominational

For Young Women's Christian Associations, see 267.5

.44 Of specific branches, denominations, and sects

Add to base number 267.44 the numbers following 28 in 280.2–289.9, e.g., Baptist societies 267.446

.5 Young Women's Christian Associations

Add to base number 267.5 the numbers following 267.3 in 267.308–267.39, e.g., staff 267.54

.6 Of young adults

.61 Interdenominational and nondenominational

For Young Men's Christian Associations, see 267.3; Young Women's Christian Associations, 267.5

.613 Young People's Society of Christian Endeavor

.62 Of specific branches, denominations, and sects

Add to base number 267.62 the numbers following 28 in 280.2–289.9, e.g., Baptist Young People's Union 267.626132

.7 Of boys

For Young Men's Christian Associations, see 267.3

.8 Of girls

For Young Women's Christian Associations, see 267.5

268 Religious education

Class here comprehensive works on Christian religious education [*formerly* 207], catechetics (the science or art devoted to organizing the principles of religious teaching), curriculums

Class religious education at the university level in 207.11, in secular secondary schools in 207.12; religion and secular education in 377.1; textbooks on a specific subject with the subject, e.g., on missions 266

See Manual at 207 vs. 268

[.068] Management

Do not use; class in 268.1

.08   History and description with respect to kinds of persons

Class education of specific groups in 268.4

.1   **Administration**

Class plant management in 268.2, personnel management in 268.3

.2   **Buildings and equipment**

.3   **Personnel**

Class here preparation, role, training, personnel management

See Manual at 209.2

.4   **Religious education of specific groups**

Former heading: Teaching departments and divisions

Class here curriculums, records and rules, teaching methods, services for specific groups

.43   Specific age groups

.432   Children

Through age twelve

(Option: Class here elementary textbooks on specific subjects; prefer the specific subject, e.g., on missions 266)

See also 372.84 for religion courses in secular elementary schools

.433   Young people

Class here Christian education in secondary schools, secondary school courses in schools run under church auspices [*formerly* 207.12]

Secondary schools under church auspices and their courses in specific continents, countries, localities in the modern world [*formerly* 207.4–207.9] are classed in 268.433094–268.433099

.434   Adults

[.435]   Home departments

Number discontinued; class in 268.4

.5   **Records and rules**

Including attendance, decorations, honor rolls, prizes, promotion

Class records and rules for specific groups in 268.4

.6   **Methods of instruction and study**

Use of this number for curriculums, catechetics discontinued; class in 268

Class methods for specific groups in 268.4

.61   Value and use of textbooks

.62	Textbook method

For value and use of textbooks, see 268.61

.63	Lecture and audiovisual methods
.632	Lecture method
.635	Audiovisual methods
.67	Dramatic method
.68	Laboratory methods
.7	**Services**

Including anniversaries, festivals, music, order of service, rallies, special days

Class services for specific groups in 268.4

.8	**Specific branches, denominations, and sects**

Add to base number 268.8 the numbers following 28 in 280.2–289.9, e.g., Presbyterian religious education 268.85

Class specific elements in religious education by specific denominations and sects in 268.1–268.7

269 Spiritual renewal

.2	**Evangelism**

Class here comprehensive works on evangelism

Class evangelistic writings for individuals and families in 243, witness bearing by individual lay Christians in 248.5, texts of evangelistic sermons in 252.3, missionary evangelization in 266

.24	Revival and camp meetings
.26	Evangelism by radio and television
.4	**Pentecostalism**

Class history of the pentecostal movement in 270.82

.6	**Retreats**

Add to base number 269.6 the numbers following 248.8 in 248.82–248.89, e.g., retreats for men 269.642

270 Historical, geographical, persons treatment of organized Christian church (Church history)

Class here the collected writings of the apostolic and church fathers (patristics) [*formerly* 281.1–281.4]

Observe table of precedence under 230–280

Class historical, geographical, persons treatment of specific denominations and sects in 280

See Manual at 209.2

SUMMARY

270.01–.09	**Standard subdivisions**
.1–.8	**Historical periods**
271	**Religious congregations and orders in church history**
272	**Persecutions in general church history**
273	**Doctrinal controversies and heresies in general church history**
274	**Christian church in Europe**
275	**Christian church in Asia**
276	**Christian church in Africa**
277	**Christian church in North America**
278	**Christian church in South America**
279	**Christian church in other parts of the world**

.01–.06 Standard subdivisions

.07 Education, research, related topics

.072 Research

Class here historiography [*formerly also* 270.09]

.08 History and description with respect to kinds of persons

.09 Areas, regions, places in general, persons

Historiography relocated to 270.072

[.093–.099] Geographical treatment

Do not use; class in 274–279

> **270.1–270.8 Historical periods**

Class comprehensive works in 270

See Manual at 281.1–281.4

.1 **Apostolic period to 325**

.2 **Period of ecumenical councils, 325–787**

.3 **Period of struggle between papacy and empire, 787–1054**

.38 Great schism, 1054

.4 **Period of papal supremacy, 1054–1200**

.5   **Late Middle Ages through the Renaissance, 1200–1517**

.6   **Period of Reformation and Counter-Reformation, 1517–1648**

        Including 17th century

        Class 1648–1699 in 270.7

.7   **Period from Peace of Westphalia through the French Revolution, 1648–1789**

.8   **Modern period, 1789–**

.81   1789–1900

.82   1900–

        Class here ecumenical, pentecostal, charismatic movements

        Add to base number 270.82 the numbers following —0904 in notation 09041–09049 from Table 1, e.g., 1960–1969 in church history 270.826

        See Manual at 280.042 vs.270.82, 262.0011

> ## 271–273 Special topics of church history

        Class comprehensive works in 270

271   **Religious congregations and orders in church history**

        Use 271.001–271.009 for standard subdivisions

        Add 0† to notation for each term identified by *, and to the result add notation 1–9 from Table 2, e.g., collected biography of Benedictines 271.1022, Benedictines in the United Kingdom 271.1041

        Class persecutions involving religious congregations and orders in 272, doctrinal controversies and heresies involving congregations and orders in 273

SUMMARY

271.01–.09	**Specific kinds**
.1	**Benedictines**
.2	**Dominicans (Friars Preachers, Black Friars)**
.3	**Franciscans (Gray Friars)**
.4	**Augustinians**
.5	**Regular clerics**
.6	**Passionists and Redemptorists**
.7	**Roman Catholic orders of men not otherwise provided for**
.8	**Non-Roman Catholic orders of men**
.9	**Congregations and orders of women**

>   271.01–271.09 Specific kinds

        Class comprehensive works in 271

.01   *Contemplative

*Add as instructed under 271

†Add 00 for standard subdivisions; see instructions at beginning of Table 1

.02	*Eremitical
.03	*Teaching
.04	*Preaching
.05	*Military

Class specific orders of knighthood in 271.791

.06	*Mendicant
.07	*Nursing
.08	*Canons regular
.09	Other
.092	*Brothers

See also 271.093 for lay brothers

.093	*Lay brothers
.094	*Third orders

Secular and regular

.095	*Secular institutes

> **271.1–271.8 Specific orders of men**

Class comprehensive works in 271

> **271.1–271.7 Roman Catholic orders of men**

Class comprehensive works in 271

.1	***Benedictines**
.11	*Confederated Benedictines

For Olivetans, see 271.13

.12	*Cistercians (Bernardines)
.125	*Trappists
.13	*Olivetans
.14	*Cluniacs

Including Camaldolese, Silvestrians, Monks of Saint Paul the Hermit

For Carthusians, see 271.71

.16	*Celestines
.17	Mechitarists and Basilians

*Add as instructed under 271

.18	Antonines (Antonians), Maronites, Chaldeans, Syrians
.19	*Canons

Examples: Crosier Fathers, Crosiers of the Red Star, Premonstratensians

Class Augustinians in 271.4

.2   *Dominicans (Friars Preachers, Black Friars)

.3   *Franciscans (Gray Friars)

Including Alcantarines, Observants, Recollects

See also 271.4 for Augustinian Recollects

.36	*Capuchins
.37	*Conventuals
.38	*Third Order Regular

.4   *Augustinians

Including Augustinian Recollects

.42	*Trinitarians
.45	*Mercedarians
.47	*Servites
.49	Other Augustinians

Examples: Brothers Hospitallers of St. John of God, Minims

Teutonic Knights relocated to 271.7914

.5   *Regular clerics

.51	*Theatines
.52	*Barnabites
.53	*Jesuits (Society of Jesus)
.54	*Somaschi
.55	*Camillians
.56	*Minor Clerks Regular (Caracciolini)
.57	*Clerks Regular of the Mother of God
.58	*Piarists

.6   *Passionists and Redemptorists

.62	*Passionists
.64	*Redemptorists

*Add as instructed under 271

.7		**Roman Catholic orders of men not otherwise provided for**
.71		*Carthusians
.73		*Carmelites (White Friars)
.75		*Sulpicians
.76		*Oblates
.77		*Lazarists (Vincentians)
.78		*Christian Brothers (Brothers of the Christian Schools)
.79		Other Roman Catholic orders of men
.791		*Specific orders of knighthood

Class comprehensive works on orders of knighthood in 271.05

.791 2	*Knights of Malta (Knights Hospitalers of St. John of Jerusalem)
.791 3	*Knights Templars
.791 4	*Teutonic Knights [*formerly* 271.49]

.8   **Non-Roman Catholic orders of men**

.9   **Congregations and orders of women**

.900 01–.900 08   Standard subdivisions

.900 09   Historical treatment

[.900 091–.900 099]   Geographical and persons treatment

Do not use; class in 271.9001–271.9009

.900 1–.900 9   Geographical and persons treatment

Add to base number 271.900 notation 1–9 from Table 2, e.g., collected biography of women religious 271.90022, congregations and orders of women in France 271.90044

.901–.909   Specific kinds

Add to base number 271.90 the numbers following 271.0 in 271.01–271.09, e.g., contemplative orders 271.901

\>   271.91–271.98 Specific orders of women

Class comprehensive works in 271.9

\>   271.91–271.97 Roman Catholic orders of women

Class comprehensive works in 271.9

.91   *Sisters of Charity orders

.92   *Sisters of Mercy orders

*Add as instructed under 271

.93	*Sacred Heart orders
.94	*Sisters of Bon Secours
.95	*Little Sisters of the Poor
.97	Other Roman Catholic orders of women
.971	*Carmelites
.972	*Dominicans
.973	*Franciscan orders

Example: Poor Clares

.974	*Ursulines
.975	*Visitation orders
.976	*Saint Joseph orders
.977	*Presentation orders
.98	Non-Roman Catholic orders of women

272 Persecutions in general church history

Regardless of denomination

Class here martyrs

Class relation of state to church in 322.1

> *See also 364.188 for offenses against religion as defined and penalized by the state*

.1	**Of Apostolic Church by imperial Rome**
.2	**By Inquisition**
.3	**Of Waldenses and Albigenses**
.4	**Of Huguenots**
.5	**Of Molinists and Quietists**
.6	**Of Anglican reformers by Mary I**
.7	**Of Roman Church by Elizabeth I and Anglicans**
.8	**Of Quakers, Baptists, witches by Puritans and others of Puritan times**
.9	**Modern persecutions and martyrs**

273 Doctrinal controversies and heresies in general church history

Class persecutions resulting from controversies and heresies in 272, churches founded on specific doctrines in 280

> *See also 239 for apologetics and polemics*

*Add as instructed under 271

.1   **1st-2nd centuries**

> Class here Christian Gnosticism
>
> Class Gnosticism of 3rd century in 273.2, comprehensive works and non-Christian Gnosticism in 299.932

.2   **3rd century**

> Example: Christian Manicheism
>
> Class comprehensive works and non-Christian Manicheism in 299.932
>
> *For Sabellianism, see 273.3*

.3   **Sabellianism**

.4   **4th century**

> Examples: Arianism, Donatism

.5   **5th century**

> Example: Pelagianism

.6   **6th-16th centuries**

> Examples: Albigensianism, Catharism, Waldensianism
>
> Class here antinomianism
>
> Class later antinomianism in 273.7–273.9

.7   **17th century**

> Examples: Jansenism, Molinism, Pietism

.8   **18th century**

> Example: agnosticism

.9   **19th century and later centuries**

> Examples: materialism, modernism

> ## 274–279 Treatment by continent, country, locality
>
> Add to base number 27 notation 4–9 from Table 2, e.g., Christian church in Europe 274, in France 274.4; then to the result add the numbers following 27 in 270.01–270.8, e.g., Christian church in France during the Reformation 274.406
>
> Class comprehensive works in 270, geographical treatment of a specific subject with the subject, using notation 09 from Table 1, e.g., persecutions in France 272.0944

274   ***Christian church in Europe**

275   ***Christian church in Asia**

276   ***Christian church in Africa**

*Add as instructed under 274–279

277   ***Christian church in North America**

278   ***Christian church in South America**

279   ***Christian church in other parts of the world**

280   Denominations and sects of the Christian church

Class here general historical and geographical treatment of, comprehensive works on specific denominations and sects and their individual local churches

(Option: Class here specific elements of specific denominations and sects; prefer 230–270. If option is chosen, add to the number for each specific denomination, sect, group as follows:

001–008	Standard subdivisions
[009]	Historical and geographical treatment
	Do not use; class in 07
02	Basic textual sources
	Class Bible in 220
03–06	Doctrinal, moral, devotional, social, ecclesiastical theology
	Add to 0 the numbers following 2 in 230–260, e.g., the denomination and international affairs 06187
07	Historical and geographical treatment
	Add to 07 the numbers following 27 in 270.1–279, e.g., 20th century 07082)

Class persecution of or by specific churches in 272

See also 273 for doctrines of specific churches considered as heresies

See Manual at 280

SUMMARY

280.01–.09	[Standard subdivisions]
.2–.4	Branches
281	Early church and Eastern churches
282	Roman Catholic Church
283	Anglican churches
284	Protestant denominations of Continental origin and related bodies
285	Presbyterian churches, Reformed churches centered in America, Congregational churches
286	Baptist, Disciples of Christ, Adventist churches
287	Methodist churches; churches uniting Methodist and other denominations; Salvation Army
289	Other denominations and sects

.01–.03   Standard subdivisions

.04   Special topics of general applicability

.042   Relations between denominations

Class the history of the ecumenical movement in 270.82

See Manual at 280.042 vs. 270.82, 262.0011

.05–.09   Standard subdivisions

*Add as instructed under 274–279

> **280.2–280.4 Branches**

Class comprehensive works in 280, specific denominations and sects in 281–289

.2 **Eastern and Roman Catholic churches**

Class specific denominations and sects in 281–282, comprehensive works on Roman Catholic Church and Eastern churches in communion with Rome in 282

.4 **Protestant churches and Protestantism**

Class here dissenters, free churches, nonconformists (British context)

Class specific Protestant denominations in 283–289

281   Early church and Eastern churches

Former heading: Primitive and Oriental churches

> **281.1–281.4 Early church**

Use these subdivisions only for building other numbers in 230–260, e.g., theology in the Ante-Nicene church 230.13; never use them by themselves. Use 281.1 for building numbers for comprehensive works, e.g., theology in the early church 230.11

Collected writings of apostolic and church fathers (patristics) relocated to 270

Class general history in 270.1–270.3, a specific work of an apostolic or church father with the subject, e.g., philosophy 189.2

See Manual at 281.1–281.4

.1 **Apostolic Church to the time of the great schism, 1054**

For Apostolic Church to 100, see 281.2; Ante-Nicene church, 281.3; Post-Nicene church, 281.4

.2 **Apostolic Church to 100**

.3 **Ante-Nicene church, 100–325**

.4 **Post-Nicene church, 325–1054**

.5 **Eastern churches**

Including Catholics of Eastern rites, St. Thomas (Mar Thoma, Syro-Malabar) Christians

For Monophysite churches, see 281.6; Coptic and Ethiopian churches, 281.7; Nestorian churches, 281.8; Eastern Orthodox churches, 281.9

.6 **Monophysite churches**

Example: Eutychian Church

For Coptic and Ethiopian churches, see 281.7

.62   Armenian

| .63 | Jacobite |

Class here Syrian Orthodox Church, Jacobite Patriarchate of Antioch

See also 281.95691 for Eastern Orthodox Church in Syria

.7 **Coptic (Coptic Orthodox) and Ethiopian (Ethiopian Orthodox) churches**

.8 **Nestorian churches**

.9 **Eastern Orthodox churches**

.909 Historical, geographical, persons treatment

Class treatment by continent, country, locality in 281.94–281.99 (*not* 281.9094–281.9099)

[.93] Specific national churches

Relocated to 281.94–281.99

.94–.99 Treatment by continent, country, locality

Class here specific national churches [*formerly also* 281.93]

Add to base number 281.9 notation 4–9 from Table 2, e.g., Russian Orthodox Church 281.947, Orthodox Church in America 281.97

282 **Roman Catholic Church**

Class here the Catholic traditionalist movement, comprehensive works on Roman Catholic Church and Eastern rite churches in communion with Rome

Class Eastern rite churches in communion with Rome in 281.5–281.8; modern schisms in Roman Catholic Church in 284.8

.09 Historical, geographical, persons treatment

Class treatment by continent, country, locality in 282.4–282.9 (*not* 282.094–282.099)

.4–.9 **Treatment by continent, country, locality**

Add to base number 282 notation 4–9 from Table 2, e.g, Roman Catholic Church in Latin America 282.8

> **283–289 Protestant and other denominations**

Class comprehensive works in 280.4

See Manual at 283–289

283 **Anglican churches**

.09 Historical, geographical, persons treatment

Class treatment by continent, country, locality in 283.4–283.9 (*not* 283.094–283.099)

.3   **Specific branches not in communion with the See of Canterbury**

Example: Reformed Episcopal Church and its affiliates

National churches in communion with the See of Canterbury relocated to 283.4–283.9; Church of South India to 287.94

Class treatment of a specific branch by continent, country, locality in 283.4–283.9

See Manual at 283–289

.4–.9   **Treatment by continent, country, locality**

Class here national churches in communion with the See of Canterbury [*formerly also* 283.3]

Add to base number 283 notation 4–9 from Table 2, e.g., Church of England 283.42, Episcopal Diocese of Long Island 283.74721

284   Protestant denominations of Continental origin and related bodies

For Baptist churches, see 286.1–286.5; Church of the New Jerusalem, 289.4; Mennonite churches, 289.7

SUMMARY

284.1	Lutheran churches
.2	Calvinistic and Reformed churches of European origin
.3	Hussite and Anabaptist churches
.4	Albigensian, Catharist, Waldensian churches
.5	Huguenot churches
.6	Moravian churches
.8	Modern schisms in Roman Catholic Church
.9	Arminian and Remonstrant churches

.1   **Lutheran churches**

.109   Historical, geographical, persons treatment

Class treatment by continent, country, locality in 284.14–284.19 (*not* 284.1094–284.1099)

(.12)   (Permanently unassigned)

(Optional number used to provide local emphasis or a shorter number for Lutheran church in a specific country other than the United States; prefer 284.14–284.19)

.13   Specific denominations, branches, synods centered in the United States

Specific denominations, branches, synods centered outside the United States relocated to 284.14–284.19

Class treatment of specific denominations, branches, synods by continent, country, locality in 284.14–284.19

See Manual at 283–289

.131   The American Lutheran Church

.131 2   The Evangelical Lutheran Church

.131 3	United Evangelical Lutheran Church
.131 4	The Lutheran Free Church
.132	The Evangelical Lutheran Synodical Conference of North America

> *For Wisconsin Evangelical Lutheran Synod, see 284.134*

.132 2	The Lutheran Church—Missouri Synod

> *For Synod of Evangelical Lutheran Churches, see 284.1323*

.132 3	Synod of Evangelical Lutheran Churches (Slovak)
.133	The Lutheran Church in America
.133 2	American Evangelical Lutheran Church
.133 3	Augustana Evangelical Lutheran Church
.133 4	Finnish Evangelical Lutheran Church
.133 5	The United Lutheran Church in America
.134	Wisconsin Evangelical Lutheran Synod
.135	The Evangelical Lutheran Church in America
.14–.19	Treatment by continent, country, locality

Class here specific denominations, branches, synods centered outside the United States [*formerly also* 284.13]

(Option: Class Lutheran churches in a specific country other than the United States in 284.12)

Add to base number 284.1 notation 4–9 from Table 2, e.g., Lutheran Church of Sweden 284.1485, Memorial Evangelical Lutheran Church of Washington, D.C. 284.1753

> *See Manual at 284.143*

.2 Calvinistic and Reformed churches of European origin

Class here comprehensive works on Calvinistic churches, on Reformed churches

> *For Huguenot churches, see 284.5; Presbyterian churches, 285; Reformed churches centered in America, 285.7*

> *See also 285.9 for Puritanism*

.209	Historical, geographical, persons treatment

Class treatment by continent, country, locality in 284.24–284.29 (*not* 284.2094–284.2099)

[.23]	Specific churches and branches

Relocated to 284.24–284.29

.24–.29   Treatment by continent, country, locality

> Class here specific churches and branches [*formerly also* 284.23]

> Add to base number 284.2 notation 4–9 from Table 2, e.g., Reformed churches in Holland 284.2492

.3   **Hussite and Anabaptist churches**

> Class here Lollards, Wycliffites

.4   **Albigensian, Catharist, Waldensian churches**

.5   **Huguenot churches**

.6   **Moravian churches**

> *For Hussite churches, see 284.3*

.609   Historical, geographical, persons treatment

> Class treatment by continent, country, locality in 284.64–284.69 (*not* 284.6094–284.6099)

.64–.69   Treatment by continent, country, locality

> Add to base number 284.6 notation 4–9 from Table 2, e.g., Moravian churches in Germany 284.643

.8   **Modern schisms in Roman Catholic Church**

> Examples: Constitutional Church, Gallican schismatic churches, Little Church of France, Old Catholic churches, Philippine Independent Church

.84   Jansenism

.9   **Arminian and Remonstrant churches**

285   **Presbyterian churches, Reformed churches centered in America, Congregational churches**

SUMMARY

285.1	Presbyterian churches of United States origin
.2	Presbyterian churches of British Commonwealth origin
.7	Reformed churches centered in America
.8	Congregationalism
.9	Puritanism

>   **285.1–285.2 Presbyterian churches of United States, of British Commonwealth origin**

> Class comprehensive works on Presbyterian churches, Presbyterian churches of other origin in 285

> (If option under 280 is followed, use 285.001–285.008 for standard subdivisions, 285.02–285.07 for specific elements of Presbyterian churches)

.1   **Presbyterian churches of United States origin**

.109   Historical, geographical, persons treatment

> Class treatment by continent, country, locality in 285.14–285.19 (*not* 285.1094–285.1099)

.13   Specific denominations

> Class treatment of specific denominations by continent, country, locality in 285.14–285.19
>
> *See Manual at 283–289*

.131   United Presbyterian Church in the U.S.A.

.132   Presbyterian Church in the United States of America

.133   Presbyterian Church in the United States

.134   United Presbyterian Church of North America

.135   Cumberland Presbyterian Church

.136   Reformed Presbyterian churches

.137   Presbyterian Church (U.S.A.)

.14–.19   Treatment by continent, country, locality

> Add to base number 285.1 notation 4–9 from Table 2, e.g., the Hudson River Presbytery 285.17473

.2   **Presbyterian churches of British Commonwealth origin**

.209   Historical, geographical, persons treatment

> Class treatment by continent, country, locality in 285.24–285.29 (*not* 285.2094–285.2099)

.23   Specific denominations

> Class treatment by continent, country, locality in 285.24–285.29
>
> *See Manual at 283–289*

.232   United Reformed Church in the United Kingdom

> Class Congregational Church of England and Wales in 285.842

.233   Church of Scotland

.234   Free Church of Scotland

.235   Presbyterian Church of Wales (Welsh Calvinistic Methodist Church)

.24–.29   Treatment by continent, country, locality

> Add to base number 285.2 notation 4–9 from Table 2, e.g., Presbyterianism in Ireland 285.2415, a Church of Scotland parish in Edinburgh 285.24134
>
> Class United Church of Canada in 287.92, Uniting Church in Australia in 287.93

.7   **Reformed churches centered in America**

.709   Historical, geographical, persons treatment

> Class treatment by continent, country, locality in 285.74–285.79 (*not* 285.7094–285.7099)

.73   Specific denominations

> Class treatment of specific denominations by continent, country, locality in 285.74–285.79

> *See Manual at 283–289*

.731   Christian Reformed Church

.732   Reformed Church in America (Dutch)

.733   Reformed Church in the United States (German)

.734   Evangelical and Reformed Church

.74–.79   Treatment by continent, country, locality

> Add to base number 285.7 notation 4–9 from Table 2, e.g., First Reformed Church of Schenectady, N.Y. 285.774744

.8   **Congregationalism**

.809   Historical, geographical, persons treatment

> Class treatment by continent, country, locality in 285.84–285.89 (*not* 285.8094–285.8099)

(.82)   (Permanently unassigned)

> (Optional number used to provide local emphasis or a shorter number for Congregational churches in a specific country other than the United States; prefer 285.84–285.89)

.83   Specific denominations centered in the United States

> Specific denominations centered outside the United States relocated to 285.84–285.89

> Class treatment of specific denominations centered in the United States by continent, country, locality in 285.84–285.89

> *See Manual at 283–289*

.832   Congregational Churches of the United States

.833   Congregational Christian Churches

.834   United Church of Christ

> *For Evangelical and Reformed Church, see 285.734*

.84–.89	Treatment by continent, country, locality

Class here specific denominations centered outside the United States [*formerly also* 285.83]

(Option: Class Congregational churches in a specific country other than the United States in 285.82)

Add to base number 285.8 notations —4–9 from Table 2, e.g., Congregational Church of England and Wales 285.842, Congregational churches in New England 285.874

Class United Church of Canada in 287.92, Uniting Church in Australia in 287.93

.9   Puritanism

286   Baptist, Disciples of Christ, Adventist churches

> **286.1–286.5 Baptist churches**

Class comprehensive works in 286

(If option under 280 is followed, use 286.001–286.008 for standard subdivisions, 286.02–286.07 for specific elements of Baptist churches)

.1   Regular (Calvinistic) Baptists

.109   Historical, geographical, persons treatment

Class treatment by continent, country, locality in 286.14–286.19 (*not* 286.1094–286.1099)

(.12)   (Permanently unassigned)

(Optional number used to provide local emphasis or a shorter number for Regular Baptist churches in a specific country other than the United States; prefer 286.14–286.19)

.13   Specific denominations centered in the United States

Specific denominations centered outside the United States relocated to 286.14–286.19

Class treatment of specific denominations centered in the United States by continent, country, locality in 286.14–286.19

See Manual at 283–289

.131   American Baptist Churches in the U.S.A.

Former name: American (Northern) Baptist Convention

.132   Southern Baptist Convention

.133   National Baptist Convention of the United States of America

.134   National Baptist Convention of America

.135   Progressive National Baptist Convention

.136   American Baptist Association

.14–.19   Treatment by continent, country, locality

> Class here specific denominations centered outside the United States [*formerly also* 286.13]
>
> (Option: Class Regular Baptist churches in a specific country other than the United States in 286.12)
>
> Add to base number 286.1 notation 4–9 from Table 2, e.g., Association of Regular Baptist Churches of Canada 286.171, a Southern Baptist association in Tennessee 286.1768

.2   Freewill Baptists

.3   Seventh-Day Baptists

.4   Old School Baptists

> Examples: Antimission, Hard-Shell, Primitive Baptists

.5   Other Baptist churches and denominations

> Examples: Baptist General Conference, Church of the Brethren, Dunkers

.6   Disciples of Christ (Campbellites)

.609   Historical, geographical, persons treatment

> Class treatment by continent, country, locality in 286.64–286.69 (*not* 286.6094–286.6099)

.63   Specific denominations

> Examples: Christian Church (Disciples of Christ), Churches of Christ
>
> Class treatment of specific denominations by continent, country, locality in 286.64–286.69
>
> *See Manual at 283–289*

.64–.69   Treatment by continent, country, locality

> Add to base number 286.6 notation 4–9 from Table 2, e.g., the Christian Church (Disciples of Christ) in Florida 286.6759

.7   Adventist churches

.709   Historical, geographical, persons treatment

> Class treatment by continent, country, locality in 286.74–286.79 (*not* 286.7094–286.7099)

.73   Specific denominations

> Examples: Advent Christian Church, Church of God General Conference
>
> Class treatment of specific denominations by continent, country, locality in 286.74–286.79
>
> *See Manual at 283–289*

.732   Seventh-Day Adventist Church

.74–.79   Treatment by continent, country, locality

> Add to base number 286.7 notation 4–9 from Table 2, e.g., Seventh-Day
> Adventists in South America 286.78

287   Methodist churches; churches uniting Methodist and other denominations; Salvation Army

SUMMARY

287.1	Wesleyan Methodist Church
.2	Miscellaneous Methodist churches
.4	Primitive Methodist Church
.5	Methodist churches in the British Isles
.6	United Methodist Church
.7	Methodist Protestant Church
.8	Black Methodist churches of United States origin
.9	Churches uniting Methodist and other denominations; Salvation Army

.1   Wesleyan Methodist Church

.109   Historical, geographical, persons treatment

> Class treatment by continent, country, locality in 287.14–287.19 (*not*
> 287.1094–287.1099)

.14–.19   Treatment by continent, country, locality

> Add to base number 287.1 notation 4–9 from Table 2, e.g., Wesleyan
> Methodist Church in New South Wales 287.1944

.2   Miscellaneous Methodist churches

> Examples: Free Methodist Church of North America, Congregational Methodist
> Church [*both formerly* 287.97]

.4   Primitive Methodist Church

.409   Historical, geographical, persons treatment

> Class treatment by continent, country, locality in 287.44–287.49 (*not*
> 287.4094–287.4099)

.44–.49   Treatment by continent, country, locality

> Add to base number 287.4 notation 4–9 from Table 2, e.g., Primitive
> Methodist Church in Kent 287.44223

.5   Methodist churches in the British Isles

.509   Historical, geographical, persons treatment

> Class treatment by country and locality in 287.54 (*not*
> 287.50941–287.50942)

.53   Specific denominations

> Examples: Bible Christians, Methodist New Connexion, Protestant Methodists, United Methodist Church, United Methodist Free Churches, Wesleyan Conference, Wesleyan Reformers, Yearly Conference of People Called Methodists
>
> Class Wesleyan Methodist Church in British Isles in 287.141, Primitive Methodist Church in British Isles in 287.441, treatment of specific denominations by country and locality in 287.54
>
> *See Manual at 283–289*

.532   United Conference of Methodist Churches

.533   Independent Methodists

.534   Wesleyan Reform Union

.54   Treatment by country and locality

> Add to base number 287.54 the numbers following —4 in notation 41–42 from Table 2, e.g., Independent Methodists in Wales 287.5429

.6   **United Methodist Church**

> *See also 287.53 for United Methodist Church in Great Britain*

.609   Historical, geographical, persons treatment

> Class treatment by continent, country, locality in 287.64–287.69 (*not* 287.6094–287.6099)

.63   Specific antecedent denominations

> Class treatment of specific antecedent denominations by continent, country, locality in 287.64–287.69
>
> > *For Methodist Protestant Church, see 287.7; Evangelical United Brethren Church, 289.9*
> >
> > *See Manual at 283–289*

.631   The Methodist Church (1939–1968)

.632   Methodist Episcopal Church

.633   Methodist Episcopal Church, South

.64–.69   Treatment by continent, country, locality

> Add to base number 287.6 notation 4–9 from Table 2, e.g., United Methodist churches in Ohio 287.6771

.7   **Methodist Protestant Church**

.8   **Black Methodist churches of United States origin**

.809   Historical, geographical, persons treatment

> Class treatment by continent, country, locality in 287.84–287.89 (*not* 287.8094–287.8099)

.83   Specific denominations

Examples: African Methodist Episcopal Church, African Methodist Episcopal Zion Church, Christian Methodist Episcopal Church

Class treatment of specific denominations by continent, country, locality in 287.84–287.89

See Manual at 283–289

.84–.89   Treatment by continent, country, locality

Add to base number 287.8 notation 4–9 from Table 2, e.g., Black Methodist churches in Georgia 287.8758, in Liberia 287.86662

See Manual at 283–289

.9   Churches uniting Methodist and other denominations; Salvation Army

.92   United Church of Canada

.93   Uniting Church in Australia

.94   Church of South India [*formerly* 283.3]

.95   Church of North India

.96   Salvation Army [*formerly* 267.15]

[.97]   Free Methodist Church of North America, Congregational Methodist Church

Relocated to 287.2

[288]   Unitarianism, Socinianism, Anti-Trinitarianism

Relocated to 289.1

289   Other denominations and sects

SUMMARY

289.1	**Unitarian and Universalist churches**
.3	**Latter-Day Saints (Mormons)**
.4	**Church of the New Jerusalem (Swedenborgianism)**
.5	**Church of Christ, Scientist (Christian Science)**
.6	**Society of Friends (Quakers)**
.7	**Mennonite churches**
.8	**Shakers (United Society of True Believers in Christ's Second Appearing)**
.9	**Others**

.1   Unitarian and Universalist churches

Class here Unitarianism, Socinianism, Anti-Trinitarianism [*all formerly* 288]

.109   Historical, geographical, persons treatment

Class treatment by continent, country, locality in 289.14–289.19 (*not* 289.1094–289.1099)

.13	Specific denominations

Class treatment of specific denominations by continent, country, locality in 289.14–289.19

See Manual at 283–289

.132	Unitarian Universalist Association
.133	Unitarian churches
.134	Universalist churches
.14–.19	Treatment by continent, country, locality

Add to base number 289.1 notation 4–9 from Table 2, e.g., Unitarianism in Boston 289.174461

(.2) **(Permanently unassigned)**

(Optional number used to provide local emphasis or a shorter number for a specific denomination or sect; prefer the number for the specific denomination or sect in 281–289)

.3 **Latter-Day Saints (Mormons)**

.309   Historical, geographical, persons treatment

Class treatment by continent, country, locality in 289.34–289.39 (*not* 289.3094–289.3099)

.32	Sources (Sacred books)
.322	Book of Mormon
.33	Specific branches

Class treatment of specific branches by continent, country, locality in 289.34–289.39

See Manual at 283–289

.332	Church of Jesus Christ of Latter-Day Saints
.333	Reorganized Church of Jesus Christ of Latter-Day Saints
.34–.39	Treatment by continent, country, locality

Add to base number 289.3 notation 4–9 from Table 2, e.g., Mormons in Utah 289.3792

.4 **Church of the New Jerusalem (Swedenborgianism)**

.409   Historical, geographical, persons treatment

Class treatment by continent, country, locality in 289.44–289.49 (*not* 289.4094–289.4099)

.44–.49	Treatment by continent, country, locality

Add to base number 289.4 notation 4–9 from Table 2, e.g., Swedenborgianism in Europe 289.44

.5   **Church of Christ, Scientist (Christian Science)**

.509   Historical, geographical, persons treatment

>   Class treatment by continent, country, locality in 289.54–289.59 (*not* 289.5094–289.5099)

.52   Sources

>   Writings by Mary Baker Eddy

.54–.59   Treatment by continent, country, locality

>   Add to base number 289.5 notation 4–9 from Table 2, e.g., First Church of Christ, Scientist, Boston 289.574461

.6   **Society of Friends (Quakers)**

.609   Historical, geographical, persons treatment

>   Class treatment by continent, country, locality in 289.64–289.69 (*not* 289.6094–289.6099)

.63   Specific denominations

>   Class treatment of specific denominations by continent, country, locality in 289.64–289.69

>   *See Manual at 283–289*

.64–.69   Treatment by continent, country, locality

>   Add to base number 289.6 notation 4–9 from Table 2, e.g., Quakers in England 289.642

.7   **Mennonite churches**

.709   Historical, geographical, persons treatment

>   Class treatment by continent, country, locality in 289.74–289.79 (*not* 289.7094–289.7099)

.73   Specific branches

>   Examples: Amish, Church of God in Christ, Defenseless Mennonites, General Conference Mennonites, Hutterian Brethren

>   Class treatment of specific branches by continent, country, locality in 289.74–289.79

>   *See Manual at 283–289*

.74–.79   Treatment by continent, country, locality

>   Add to base number 289.7 notation 4–9 from Table 2, e.g., Amish churches in Lancaster County, Pennsylvania 289.774815

.8   **Shakers (United Society of True Believers in Christ's Second Appearing)**

.9   Others

Examples: Church of the Nazarene, Churches of God, Dukhobors, Evangelical Congregational Church, Evangelical United Brethren Church, Messianic Judaism, Plymouth Brethren, United Brethren in Christ

(Option: Class a specific denomination or sect requiring local emphasis in 289.2)

See Manual at 289.9

.92   Jehovah's Witnesses

.94   Pentecostal churches

Examples: Assemblies of God, United Pentecostal Church

Class the pentecostal movement in general church history in 270.82

.95   Independent Fundamentalist and Evangelical churches

Examples: Evangelical Free Church of America, Independent Fundamental Churches of America

Class fundamentalist, evangelical movements in general church history in 270.82

.96   Unification Church

.97   Unity School of Christianity

.98   New Thought

Class eclectic New Thought, comprehensive works in 299.93

290   Comparative religion and religions other than Christianity

See Manual at 290; 394.2682 vs.263.9, 290

SUMMARY

291   Comparative religion
292   Classical (Greek and Roman) religion
293   Germanic religion
294   Religions of Indic origin
295   Zoroastrianism (Mazdaism, Parseeism)
296   Judaism
297   Islam and religions originating in it
299   Other religions

291 Comparative religion

Class here works dealing with various religions, with religious topics not applied to specific religions

Class treatment of religious topics with respect to natural theology in 210, with respect to Christianity in 220–280, with respect to a specific religion other than Christianity in 292–299

(Option: To give preferred treatment or shorter numbers to a specific religion other than Christianity, class it in this number, and add to base number 291 the numbers following the base number for that religion in 292–299, e.g., Hinduism 291, Mahabharata 291.923; if the option is followed, class comparative religion in 290 and its subdivisions in 290.1–290.9, standard subdivisions in 290.01–290.09. Other options are described at 292–299)

See Manual at 200.1 vs.210, 291; 291

SUMMARY

291.01–.09	**Standard subdivisions**
.1	**Religious mythology, social theology, interreligious relations and attitudes**
.2	**Doctrines**
.3	**Public worship and other practices**
.4	**Religious experience, life, practice**
.5	**Moral theology**
.6	**Leaders and organization**
.7	**Missions, religious training and education**
.8	**Sources**
.9	**Sects and reform movements**

[.012]   Classification

Do not use; class in 291.14

.04   Special topics

.042   Prehistoric religions and religions of nonliterate peoples

[.044]   Ancient religions

Number discontinued; class in 291

.046   Religions of 19th and 20th century origin

.06   Organizations

Class management in 291.6, religious organizations in 291.65

.07   Education, research, related topics of religions

Class here education in and teaching of comparative religion, religions as an academic subject

Class comprehensive works on religious education, religious education for the purpose of encouraging believers in religious life and practice in 291.7

.09   Historical, geographical, persons treatment

See Manual at 291.09 vs.294, 299.5

.1   **Religious mythology, social theology, interreligious relations and attitudes**

.13   Mythology and mythological foundations

Stories of primeval history, beings, origins, and customs archetypically significant in the sacred life, doctrine, and ritual of religions

Class sources in 291.8, myths on a specific subject with the subject, e.g., creation myths 291.24

See Manual at 398.2 vs.291.13

.14   Classification of religions

Class here general classes of religions, e.g., monotheistic, nontheistic, pantheistic, polytheistic

.17   Social theologies and interreligious relations and attitudes

Attitudes of religions toward and influences on secular matters, attitudes toward other religions, interreligious relations

.171   Role of organized religions in society

Class specific socioeconomic problems in 291.178

.172   Interreligious relations

Including relations of religions with irreligion

.175   Religions and secular disciplines

Examples: communications media, literature, psychology, science, technology

.177   Religions and political affairs

Attitudes toward and influences on political activities and ideologies

Including civil war and revolution

Class here religions and civil rights

Class religions and international affairs in 291.1787

See Manual at 322.1 vs.261.7, 291.177

.177 2   Religious freedom

.177 3   Theocracy

Supremacy of organized religion over civil government

.178   Religions and socioeconomic problems

For religions and political affairs, see 291.177

See also 361.75 for welfare work of religious organizations

.178 3	Social problems
.178 32	Social welfare problems and services

Add to base number 291.17832 the numbers following 362 in 362.1–362.5, e.g., attitude of religions toward alcoholism 291.17832292

Use of this number for comprehensive works on social welfare problems and crime discontinued; class in 291.1783

.178 33	Crime

Add to base number 291.17833 the numbers following 364 in 364.1–364.8, e.g., attitude of religions toward treason 291.17833131, toward capital punishment 291.1783366

.178 34	Social structure

Add to base number 291.17834 the numbers following 305 in 305.2–305.8, e.g., attitude of religions toward women 291.178344; however, class attitudes toward various religions in 291.172

.178 35	Relation of the sexes, marriage, family

Add to base number 291.17835 the numbers following 306 in 306.7–306.8, e.g., attitude of religions toward homosexuality 291.17835766

.178 36	Ecology and population

Add to base number 291.17836 the numbers following 304 in 304.2–304.8, e.g., attitude of religions toward family planning 291.17836666

.178 5	The economic order

Including management of business enterprises

.178 7	International affairs
.178 73	War and peace

Examples: attitude of religions toward pacifism, conscientious objectors

.178 732	Nuclear weapons and nuclear war
.2	**Doctrines**

Class here comprehensive works on theologians [*formerly* 291.64]; apologetics, polemics

For social theologies, see 291.17; moral theology, 291.5

.21	Objects of worship and veneration

Class here animism, spiritism

.211	God, gods, goddesses, other divinities and deities
.211 3	Male
.211 4	Female

.212	Nature

        Examples: sun, water, fire, trees, sex

.213	Persons

        Examples: ancestors, the dead, heroes, monarchs, saints

.214	Personified abstractions
.215	Good spirits

        Example: angels

.216	Evil spirits

        Examples: demons, devils

.218	Images
.22	Humankind

        Including atonement, creation, repentance, salvation, sin, soul

        Class here comprehensive works on karma

        Class creation of the world in 291.24; a specific aspect of karma with the aspect, e.g., as a concept in Buddhist moral theology 294.35

        For eschatology, see 291.23

.23	Eschatology

        Including death, end of the world, heaven, hell, immortality, other worlds, punishments, purgatory, resurrection, rewards

.237	Reincarnation
.24	Creation and cosmology

        For creation of humankind, see 291.22

.3	**Public worship and other practices**

        Class comprehensive works on worship in 291.43

.32	Divination

        Examples: omens, oracles, prophecies

.33	Witchcraft
.34	Offerings, sacrifices, penances
.35	Sacred places

        Examples: grottoes, holy buildings, pagodas, shrines, temples

.36	Sacred times

        Examples: holy days, liturgic year, religious calendar, religious festivals

.37	Symbolism, symbolic objects, emblems

        Class here the religious use, significance, purpose of the arts in religions

.38 Rites and ceremonies

   Conduct and texts

   Examples: liturgy, music, processions, public feasts and fasts, public prayer

   Class offerings, sacrifices, penances in 291.34; interdisciplinary works on sacred music in 781.7, on sacred vocal music in 782.22

.4 Religious experience, life, practice

.42 Religious experience

   Examples: conversion, enlightenment, moral renewal and commitment

.422 Mysticism

.43 Worship

   Description, interpretation, criticism, history, practical works on prayer, meditation, contemplation

   Including devotional texts

   Class here comprehensive works on worship

   For public worship, see 291.3

.44 Religious life and practice

   Including religious training of children in the home [*formerly also* 649.7]

   For worship, see 291.43; moral theology, 291.5

.446 Individual observances

   Examples: almsgiving, ceremonial and ritual observances, observance of restrictions and limitations, pilgrimages

.447 Asceticism

   Including practice of celibacy, fasting and abstinence, poverty, solitude

.448 Guides to religious life

.5 Moral theology

   Including conscience, duties, sins, vices, virtues

.56 Specific moral issues

   Add to base number 291.56 the numbers following 17 in 172–179, e.g., morality of discriminatory practices 291.5675; however, virtues and vices are classed in 291.5

.6   **Leaders and organization**

>   291.61–291.64 Leaders and their work

Class here role, function, duties

Do not use notation 092 from Table 1 with 291.6 or its subdivisions

Unless other instructions are given, observe the following table of precedence, e.g., clergy who are religious writers 291.61 (*not* 291.64)

Divinely inspired persons	291.63
Persons endowed with supernatural power	291.62
Clergy and counselors	291.61
Interpreters of religion	291.64

Class comprehensive works in 291.6

See Manual at 291: Biography

.61   Clergy and counselors

Examples: heads of religions, gurus, ministers, pastors, priests

.62   Persons endowed with supernatural power

Examples: exorcists, magicians, shamans, sorcerers, thaumaturgists

.63   Divinely inspired persons

Examples: founders of religions, messiahs, prophets

.64   Interpreters of religion

Examples: reformers, writers

Comprehensive works on theologians relocated to 291.2

For clergy and counselors, see 291.61

.65   Organization and organizations

Examples: associations, congregations, institutions, orders, parties

Class laws and decisions in 291.84

.657   Monasticism and monasteries

.7   **Missions, religious training and education**

Class here comprehensive works on religious education

Use of this number for the concept of religious war discontinued; class in 291

Class education in and teaching of comparative religion, of religions as an academic subject in 291.07

.8   **Sources**

Class theology based on sacred sources with theology, e.g., doctrinal theology 291.2

.82   Sacred books and scriptures

.83   Oral traditions

.84   Laws and decisions

> Class civil law relating to religious matters in 340

> > *See also 364.188 for offenses against religion as defined and penalized by the state*

.85   Sources of sects and reform movements

.9   Sects and reform movements

> Class specific aspects of sects and reform movements in 291.1–291.8

> ## 292–299 Religions other than Christianity

> (Options: To give preferred treatment or shorter numbers to a specific religion, use one of the following:

> (Option A: Class the religion in 230–280, its sources in 220, comprehensive works in 200; in that case class the Bible and Christianity in 298

> (Option B: Class in 210, and add to base number 21 the numbers following the base number for the religion in 292–299, e.g., Hinduism 210, Mahabharata 219.23; in that case class natural religion in 200, its subdivisions in 201–209, standard subdivisions of Christianity in 200.1–200.9, standard subdivisions of religion in 200.01–200.09

> (Option C: Class in 291, and add to base number 291 the numbers following the base number for that religion in 292–299, e.g., Hinduism 291, Mahabharata 291.923; in that case class comparative religion in 290 and its subdivisions in 290.1–290.9, standard subdivisions in 290.01–290.09

> (Option D: Class in 298, which is permanently unassigned

> (Option E: Place first by use of a letter or other symbol, e.g., Hinduism 2H0 (preceding 220), or 29H (preceding 291 or 292); add to the base number thus derived, e.g., to 2H or to 29H, the numbers following the base number for the religion in 292–299, e.g., Shivaism 2H5.13 or 29H.513)

> Aside from additions, changes, deletions, exceptions shown under specific entries, add to notation for each term identified by † as follows:

> | | |
> |---|---|
> | 01–05 | Standard subdivisions |
> | 06 | Organizations |
> | | Class management in 6, religious organizations in 65 |
> | 07 | Education, research, related topics |
> | | Class here the religion as an academic subject |
> | | Class comprehensive works on religious education, religious education for the purpose of encouraging believers in religious life and practice in 7 |
> | 08–09 | Standard subdivisions |
> | 1–9 | Specific elements |
> | | Add to base number the numbers following 291 in 291.1–291.9, e.g., organizations 65 |

> Class comprehensive works in 291

> *See Manual at 291*

292   Classical (Greek and Roman) religion

See also 299 for modern revivals of classical religions

.001–.005   Standard subdivisions

.006   Organizations

> Class management in 292.6, religious organizations in 292.65

.007   Education, research, related topics

> Class here classical religion as an academic subject

> Class comprehensive works on religious education, religious education for the purpose of encouraging believers in religious life and practice in 292.7

.008–.009   Standard subdivisions

> 292.07–292.08 By specific culture

> Class comprehensive works in 292, specific elements regardless of culture in 292.1–292.9

.07   Roman

.08   Greek

.1–.9   Specific elements

> Add to base number 292 the numbers following 291 in 291.1–291.9, e.g., mythology 292.13

> Class classical religion as an academic subject in 292.007

293   †Germanic religion

See also 299 for modern revivals of Germanic religion

294   Religions of Indic origin

Including Divine Light Mission, Radha Soami Satsang

See Manual at 291.09 vs. 294, 299.5

SUMMARY

294.3	**Buddhism**
.4	**Jainism**
.5	**Hinduism**
.6	**Sikhism**

.3   Buddhism

See Manual at 291

.306   Organizations

> Class management in 294.36, religious organizations in 294.365

†Add as instructed under 292–299

.307   Education, research, related topics

Class here Buddhism as an academic subject

Class comprehensive works on religious education, religious education for the purpose of encouraging believers in religious life and practice in 294.37

.33   Mythology, social theology, interreligious relations and attitudes

Add to base number 294.33 the numbers following 291.1 in 291.13–291.17, e.g., social theology 294.337

.34   Doctrines and practices

Add to base number 294.34 the numbers following 291 in 291.2–291.4, e.g., religious experience 294.3442

For social theology, see 294.337; moral theology, 294.35

.35–.37   Moral theology, leaders and organization, missions, religious education

Add to base number 294.3 the numbers following 291 in 291.5–291.7, e.g., the Buddha 294.363, Buddhist religious education 294.37

.38   Sources

.382   Sacred books and scriptures (Tripitaka)

Works sacred to both Theravadins and Mahayanists

Class here comprehensive treatment of Theravadin and Mahayanist sacred texts

Class works sacred only to Mahayanists in 294.385

.382 2   Vinayapitaka

.382 3   Suttapitaka

.382 4   Abhidhammapitaka

.383   Oral traditions

.384   Laws and decisions

.385   Sources of branches, sects, reform movements

Examples: Buddhist Tantras, Mahayanist sacred works

.39   Branches, sects, reform movements

Class specific aspects of branches, sects, reform movements in 294.33–294.38

.391   Theravada (Southern, Hinayana) Buddhism

Including Mahasanghika, Saravastivada, Sautrantika schools

.392   Mahayana (Northern) Buddhism

Including Madhyamika, Yogacara (Vijnana) schools

.392 3   Tibetan Buddhism (Lamaism)

See also 299.54 for Bon

.392 5	Tantric Buddhism
.392 6	Pure Land sects
.392 7	Zen

Including Rinzai and Soto

| .392 8 | Nichiren Shoshu and Soka Gakkai |

.4   †Jainism

See Manual at 291

.49   Sects and reform movements

Class specific aspects of sects and reform movements in 294.41–294.48

.492   Svetambara

.493   Digambara

.5   Hinduism

Class here Brahmanism

See Manual at 291

SUMMARY

294.501–.509	**Standard subdivisions**
.51–.53	**Mythology, relations, doctrines, public worship**
.54	**Religious experience, life, practice, moral theology**
.55	**Sects and reform movements**
.56–.57	**Leaders, organization, missions, religious education**
.59	**Sources**

.506   Organizations

Class management in 294.56, religious organizations in 294.565

.507   Education, research, related topics

Class here Hinduism as an academic subject

Class comprehensive works on religious education, religious education for the purpose of encouraging believers in religious life and practice in 294.57

.509   Historical, geographical, persons treatment

.509 013   3999–1000 B.C.

Class here religion of Vedic period

.51–.53   Mythology, relations, doctrines, public worship

Add to base number 294.5 the numbers following 291 in 291.1–291.3, e.g., attitude toward science 294.5175

†Add as instructed under 292–299

.54	Religious experience, life, practice, moral theology
.542–.544	Religious experience, life, practice

Add to base number 294.54 the numbers following 291.4 in 291.42–291.44, e.g., Hindu yogic meditation 294.543

Class public worship in 294.53

For moral theology, see 294.548

.548	Moral theology

Including conscience, dharma, duties, sins, vices, virtues

.548 6	Specific moral issues

Add to base number 294.5486 the numbers following 17 in 172–179, e.g., morality of family relationships 294.54863; however, virtues and vices are classed in 294.548

.55	Sects and reform movements

Class Buddhism in 294.3, Jainism in 294.4, Sikhism in 294.6; a specific aspect of a sect or reform movement with the subject, e.g., doctrines of Vishnuism 294.52

.551	Early
.551 2	Vishnuism

Example: International Society for Krishna Consciousness

.551 3	Shivaism

Including Lingayats

.551 4	Shaktaism

Class here Tantric Hinduism

.551 5	Ganapataism
.551 6	Shanmukaism
.551 7	Sauraism
.555	Ramakrishna movement
.556	Reformed Hinduism
.556 2	Brahma Samaj
.556 3	Arya-Samaj
.56–.57	Leaders, organization, missions, religious education

Add to base number 294.5 the numbers following 291 in 291.6–291.7, e.g., the role of the guru 294.561

Class Hinduism as an academic subject in 294.507

.59	Sources
.592	Sacred books and scriptures

.592 1	Vedic literature

> 294.592 12–294.592 15 The Vedas

Class here Samhitas, Brahmanas, Aranyakas

Class comprehensive works on the Vedas in 294.5921, Upanishads in 294.59218, Vedic religion in 294.509013

.592 12	Rigveda
.592 13	Samaveda
.592 14	Yajurveda
.592 15	Atharvaveda
.592 18	Upanishads
.592 2	Ramayana
.592 3	Mahabharata

For Bhagavad Gita, see 294.5924

.592 4	Bhagavad Gita
.592 5	Puranas
.592 6	Dharmasastras

Including Code of Manu

.593	Oral traditions
.594	Laws and decisions
.595	Sources of sects and reform movements

Example: Hindu tantras

.6   †Sikhism

See Manual at 291

295   †Zoroastrianism (Mazdaism, Parseeism)

Class Mithraism in 299.15

296   Judaism

See Manual at 291

SUMMARY

296.01–.09	**Standard subdivisions**
.1	**Sources**
.3	**Doctrinal, moral, social theology**
.4	**Traditions, rites, public services**
.6	**Leaders, organization, religious education**
.7	**Religious experience, life, practice**
.8	**Sects and movements**

†Add as instructed under 292–299

.06 Organizations

Class management in 296.6, religious organizations in 296.67

.07 Education, research, related topics

Class here Judaism as an academic subject

Class comprehensive works on Judaic religious education, religious education for the purpose of encouraging believers in religious life and practice in 296.68

.1 **Sources**

Class Judaic theology based on these sources in 296.3

For Torah and sacred scripture (Old Testament), see 221

SUMMARY

296.12	**Talmudic literature**
.14	**Midrash**
.15	**Sources of specific sects and movements**
.16	**Cabalistic literature**
.17	**Early rabbinical writings to 1400**
.18	**Halakah (Legal literature)**
.19	**Aggadah (Nonlegal literature)**

> 296.12–296.14 Talmudic literature and Midrash

Class here individual tractates and treatises

Add to each subdivision identified by * as follows (but do not add for individual tractates and treatises, e.g., translations of Pirke Avot 296.123 [not 296.12305]):
001–009   Standard subdivisions
04   Hebrew and Aramaic texts
            Including textual criticism
            Class texts accompanied by commentaries in 07
05   Translations
            Add to 05 notation 1–9 from Table 6, e.g., literature in English 0521
            Class texts accompanied by commentaries in 07
06   Interpretation and criticism (Exegesis)
            Add to 06 the numbers following 220.6 in 220.601–220.68, e.g., historical criticism 067
            For textual criticism, see 04; commentaries, 07
07   Commentaries
            Criticism and interpretation arranged in textual order
            Including texts accompanied by commentaries

Class comprehensive works in 296.1

.12 *Talmudic literature

.123   *Mishnah

*Add as instructed under 296.12–296.14

.124	*Palestinian Talmud (Jerusalem Talmud, Talmud Yerushalmi)
.125	*Babylonian Talmud
	Often called simply the Talmud
.126	Tosefta and Baraita
.126 2	*Tosefta
.126 3	*Baraita
.127	Specific types of Talmudic literature
.127 4	*Halakah
.127 6	*Aggadah
.14	*Midrash
.141	*Halakah
.142	*Aggadah
.15	Sources of specific sects and movements
.155	Qumran community

           Class here comprehensive works on the Dead Sea Scrolls

           Class Old Testament texts in the Dead Sea Scrolls in 221.44, pseudepigrapha in the Dead Sea Scrolls in 229.91

.16	Cabalistic literature

           Example: Zohar

           Class here comprehensive works on cabala

           The text of the Zohar and other religious cabalistic literature is classed here even if the editor introduces and annotates it from an occult or Christian point of view

           Class Judaic mystical experience in 296.712, Judaic mystical movements in 296.8; cabalism associated with a specific religion with the religion, e.g., Christian cabalism 230–280

           See also 135.4 for cabala as a source of occult knowledge

.17	Early rabbinical writings to 1400
.172	Of Maimonides
.179	Responsa
.18	Halakah (Legal literature)

           Class here comprehensive works on Judaic law

           Class Torah in 222.1, Talmudic Halakah in 296.1274, Midrashic Halakah in 296.141, Jewish law relating to secular matters in 340.58

.182	Work of Joseph Caro

*Add as instructed under 296.12–296.14

.19	Aggadah (Nonlegal literature)

Class here comprehensive works on Aggadah

Class Talmudic Aggadah in 296.1276, Midrashic Aggadah in 296.142

See also 296.437 for Passover Haggadah

.3   Doctrinal, moral, social theology

Class here the Thirteen Articles of Faith

> 296.31–296.34 Doctrinal theology (Dogma)

Class here Biblical theology, apologetics, polemics

Class comprehensive works in 296.3

See Manual at 220

.31   God and spiritual beings

.311   God

Including God's special relation to the Jewish people

.315   Angels

.316   Devils (Demons)

.32   Humankind

Including creation, sin, salvation, repentance, atonement, soul

For eschatology, see 296.33

.33   Eschatology

Including death, resurrection, immortality, messianism

.34   Creation

For creation of humankind, see 296.32

.38   Moral and social theology

.385   Moral theology

Including Biblical precepts, conscience, duties, sins, vices, virtues

Class guides to conduct of life in 296.74

.385 6   Specific moral issues

Add to base number 296.3856 the numbers following 17 in 172–179, e.g., morality of family relationships 296.38563; however, virtues and vices are classed in 296.385

.387   Social theology and interreligious relations and attitudes

> Attitude toward other religions, attitude toward and influence on secular matters

> Add to base number 296.387 the numbers following 291.17 in 291.171–291.178, e.g., attitude toward science 296.3875

.4   **Traditions, rites, public services**

> Description, interpretation, conduct, texts of rites and public services

> Class here family celebrations and services, hymns, liturgy, music, prayers, responsive reading, symbolism

> Class comprehensive works on worship in 296.72

.41   Sabbath

.42   Sermons and homiletics

> Class sermons on a specific subject with the subject, e.g., social theology 296.387

.43   Festivals, holy days, fasts

> *For Sabbath, see 296.41*

.431   Rosh Hashanah (New Year)

.432   Yom Kippur (Day of Atonement)

.433   Sukkoth (Feast of Tabernacles)

.435   Hanukkah (Feast of the Dedication)

.436   Purim (Feast of Lots)

.437   Pesach (Passover)

> Class here Passover Haggadah, Seder service

.438   Shabuoth (Feast of Weeks, Pentecost)

.439   Other

> Examples: Lag b'Omer, Tishah b'Ab

.44   Rites and customs for specific occasions

> Example: synagogue dedication

.442   Special rites for male Jews

.442 2   Berith milah (Circumcision)

.442 3   Pidyon haben (Redemption of first-born male)

.442 4   Bar mitzvah

.443   Special rites for female Jews

> Example: bath mitzvah

.444   Marriage and divorce rites and traditions

.445   Burial and mourning rites and traditions

.6   Leaders, organization, religious education

.61   Leaders

Role, function, duties

Example: rabbis

See Manual at 291: Biography

.65   Synagogues and congregations

Role and function

Class history of a specific synagogue in 296.8

.67   Organization and organizations

Examples: associations, institutions, polity

Class here theory and history of organizations other than synagogues and congregations

Class laws and decisions in 296.18

For synagogues and congregations, see 296.65

.673   Young Men's Hebrew Associations

.675   Young Women's Hebrew Associations

.68   Religious education

Including afternoon weekday schools, parochial schools, Sunday and Sabbath schools

Class Judaism as an academic subject in 296.07

.7   Religious experience, life, practice

.71   Religious experience

Examples: conversion, moral renewal and commitment

.712   Mysticism

Class cabalistic literature in 296.16, Judaic mystical movements in 296.8

.72   Worship

Including devotional texts

Class here comprehensive works on worship; description, interpretation, criticism, history, practical works on prayer, meditation, contemplation

Class public worship, family celebrations and services in 296.4

.73   Observance of dietary laws

.74   Religious life and practice

Including asceticism

For moral theology, see 296.385; worship, 296.72; observance of dietary laws, 296.73

.8   Sects and movements

Class specific aspects of sects and movements in 296.1–296.7

.81   Ancient

Examples: Essenes, Hellenistic movement, Karaites, Sadducees, Samaritans, Zealots

.812   Pharisees

.815   Qumran community

.82   Medieval

Example: Sabbatianism

.83   Modern

.832   Orthodox Judaism

.833   Mystical Judaism

.833 2   Hasidism

.833 22   Habad Lubavitch Hasidism

.834   Reform movements

.834 2   Conservative Judaism

.834 4   Reconstructionist Judaism

.834 6   Reform Judaism

297   Islam and religions originating in it

See Manual at 291

SUMMARY

297.01–.09	**Standard subdivisions**
.1	**Sources, social theology, relations, attitudes of Islam**
.2	**Islamic doctrinal theology (Aqaid and Kalam)**
.3	**Islamic public worship and other practices**
.4	**Islamic religious experience, life, practice**
.5	**Islamic moral theology**
.6	**Islamic leaders and organization**
.7	**Islamic missions, religious education, religious wars**
.8	**Islamic sects and reform movements**
.9	**Religions originating in Islam**

.06   Organizations

Class management in 297.6, religious organizations in 297.65

.07 Education, research, related topics

Class here Islamic religion as an academic subject

Class comprehensive works on Islamic religious education, religious education for the purpose of encouraging believers in religious life and practice in 297.7

.1 Sources, social theology, relations, attitudes of Islam

> 297.12–297.14 Sources

Class comprehensive works in 297.1

.12 Sacred books and scriptures

.122 Koran

.122 1 Origin and authenticity

> 297.122 4–297.122 5 Texts

Class comprehensive works in 297.122, texts accompanied by commentaries in 297.1227

.122 4 Arabic texts

Class here textual criticism

.122 5 Translations

Add to base number 297.1225 notation 1–9 from Table 6, e.g., the Koran in English 297.122521

.122 6 Interpretation and criticism (Exegesis)

Add to base number 297.1226 the numbers following 220.6 in 220.601–220.68, e.g., historical criticism 297.12267

For textual criticism, see 297.1224; commentaries, 297.1227

.122 7 Commentaries

Criticism and interpretation arranged in textual order

Including texts accompanied by commentaries

.122 8 Special nonreligious subjects treated in the Koran

.122 9 Individual suras and groups of suras

Origins, authenticity, texts, criticism, interpretation, commentaries, special subjects

.124 Hadith (Traditions)

Use 297.124001–297.124009 for standard subdivisions

.124 01–.124 08 Generalities

Add to base number 297.1240 the numbers following 297.122 in 297.1221–297.1228, e.g., origins 297.12401

>   297.124 1–297.124 8 Specific Hadith

Add to each subdivision identified by * as follows:
001–009   Standard subdivisions
01–09   Generalities
      Add to 0 the numbers following 297.122 in
      297.1221–297.1228, e.g., historical criticism 067

Class comprehensive works in 297.124

.124 1   *Al-Bukhari

.124 2   *Abu Daud

.124 3   *Muslim

.124 4   *Al-Tirmidhi

.124 5   *Al-Nasai

.124 6   *Ibn Majah

.124 7   Other Sunni Hadith

.124 8   Hadith of other sects

.13   Oral traditions

Class Hadith in 297.124

.14   Laws and decisions (Sharia)

Religious and ceremonial

Tawhid relocated to 297.211

Class Islamic law relating to secular matters (Fiqh) in 340.59

.19   Mythology, social theology, relations, attitudes

.197   Social theology and interreligious relations and attitudes

Attitude toward other religions, attitudes toward and influence on secular matters

Add to base number 297.197 the numbers following 291.17 in 291.171–291.178, e.g., attitude toward Judaism 297.1972

.2   Islamic doctrinal theology (Aqaid and Kalam)

Class doctrines concerning Muhammad the Prophet in 297.63

.204   Doctrines of specific sects

Add to base number 297.204 the numbers following 297.8 in 297.81–297.87, e.g., doctrines of Kadarites 297.20435

.21   God and spiritual beings

.211   God

Including Tawhid [*formerly also* 297.14], miracles, revelation

*Add as instructed under 297.1241–297.1248

.215	Angels
.216	Devils (Demons)
.22	Humankind

Including creation, faith, fall, grace, intercession, predestination and free will, repentance, salvation, sin, soul

Class creation of the universe in 297.24

For eschatology, see 297.23

.23	Eschatology

Including day of judgment, death, eternity, future life, heaven, hell, intermediate state, punishment, resurrection, rewards

.24	Other doctrines

Examples: caliphate, creation of the universe, imamat, prophets prior to Muhammad

Class caliphs, imams as leaders in 297.61, caliphate, imamat in Islamic organization in 297.65

.29	Apologetics and polemics

Apologetics: systematic argumentation in defense of the divine origin and authority of Islam

Polemics: refutation of alleged errors in other systems

.291	Polemics against pagans and heathens
.292	Polemics against Judaism
.293	Polemics against Christianity
.294	Polemics against Hinduism
.295	Polemics against other religions
.297	Polemics against rationalists, agnostics, atheists
.298	Polemics against scientists and materialists
.3	**Islamic public worship and other practices**

Use 297.3001–297.3009 for standard subdivisions

.301–.307	Specific sects

Add to base number 297.30 the numbers following 297.8 in 297.81–297.87, e.g., Shiite rites 297.302

.32	Divination

Examples: omens, oracles, prophecies

.33	Occultism

Including amulets, talismans, charms, witchcraft

.35   Sacred places

> Examples: Mecca, Medina, Jerusalem

.36   Sacred times

> Examples: Fridays, Ramadan

> Including comprehensive works on Ramadan

> Class the annual fast of Ramadan as a religious obligation in 297.53

.38   Rites and ceremonies

> Conduct and texts

> Class comprehensive works on worship in 297.43, five religious obligations in 297.51–297.55

.4   Islamic religious experience, life, practice

> Class here Sufism

> Add to base number 297.4 the numbers following 291.4 in 291.42–291.44, e.g., comprehensive works on worship 297.43; however, class the five religious obligations in 297.51–297.55

> Class public worship in 297.38; specific aspects of Sufism with the aspect, e.g., Sufi orders 297.65

> *For moral theology, see 297.5*

.5   Islamic moral theology

> Including conscience, duties, sins, vices, virtues

> *For jihad (holy war), see 297.72*

>   297.51–297.55 Five religious obligations (Pillars of the Faith)

> Class comprehensive works in 297.5

.51   Profession of faith (Shahada)

.52   Prayer five times daily (Salat)

.53   Annual fast of Ramadan

> Class comprehensive works on Ramadan in 297.36

.54   Almsgiving (Zakat)

.55   Pilgrimage to Mecca (Hajj)

.6   **Islamic leaders and organization**

.61   Leaders and their work

        Examples: ayatollahs, caliphs, imams, ulama

        For Muhammad, see 297.63; Muhammad's family and companions, 297.64

        See Manual at 291: Biography

.63   Muhammad the Prophet

.64   Muhammad's family and companions

.65   Organization and organizations

        Examples: caliphate, imamat; associations, congregations, mosques, parties, Sufi orders

        Class doctrines about the caliphate and imamat in 297.24, history of specific congregations and mosques in 297.8

.7   **Islamic missions, religious education, religious wars**

        Class Islam as an academic subject in 297.07

.72   Jihad (Holy war)

.8   **Islamic sects and reform movements**

        Religions originating in Islam relocated to 297.9

        Class specific aspects of sects and reform movements in 297.1–297.7

        For Sufism, see 297.4

.81   Sunnites

.811   Hanafites

.812   Shafiites

.813   Malikites

.814   Hanbalites and Wahhabis

.82   Shiites

.821   Twelvers (Ithna Asharites)

.822   Seveners (Ismailites)

        Examples: Mustalians, Nizaris

.824   Zaydites

.83   Other

.835   Kadarites

.837   Murjiites

.85   Druzes

.86   Ahmadiyya movement

.87	Black Muslim movement

Examples: American Muslim Mission, Nation of Islam, World Community of Islam in the West

.9   Religions originating in Islam [*formerly* 297.8]

Class Sikhism in 294.6

.92	Babism
.93	†Bahai faith

See Manual at 291

(298)   (Permanently unassigned)

(Optional number used to provide local emphasis and a shorter number for a specific religion other than Christianity; prefer the number for the specific religion elsewhere in 292–299; or optional number used for Christianity if option A under 292–299 is chosen. Other options are described at 292–299)

299   Other religions

Examples: Urantia, modern revivals of long dormant religions

(Options for giving local emphasis and shorter numbers for a specific religion are described at 292–299)

If a religion not named in the schedule claims to be Christian, class it in 289.9 even if it is unorthodox or syncretistic

Class syncretistic religious writings of individuals expressing personal views and not claiming to establish a new religion or to represent an old one in 291

SUMMARY

299.1–.4	Of Indo-European, Semitic, North African, North and West Asian, Dravidian origin
.5	Of East and Southeast Asian origin
.6	Originating among Black Africans and people of Black African descent
.7	Of North American native origin
.8	Of South American native origin
.9	Of other origin

.1–.4   Of Indo-European, Semitic, North African, North and West Asian, Dravidian origin

Not otherwise provided for

Add to base number 299 the numbers following —9 in notation 91–94 from Table 5, e.g., Druidism 299.16

.5   Of East and Southeast Asian origin

See Manual at 291.09 vs. 294, 299.5

.51	Of Chinese origin

†Add as instructed under 292–299

.512	†Confucianism

Class Four books of Confucius in 181.09512

See Manual at 291

.514	†Taoism

See Manual at 291

.54	Of Tibetan origin

Class here Bon

.56	Of Japanese and Ryukyuan origin
.561	†Shintoism

See Manual at 291

.57–.59	Other

Add to base number 299 the numbers following —9 in notation 957–959 from Table 5, e.g., Caodaism 299.592

.6 Originating among Black Africans and people of Black African descent

Unless other instructions are given, class complex subjects with aspects in two or more subdivisions of 299.6 in the one coming first in the schedule, e.g., rituals of Yorubas 299.64 (*not* 299.68333)

For Black Muslims, see 297.87

.609	Historical, geographical, persons treatment

Class religions in specific areas in Africa in 299.69

.62	Mythology and mythological foundations

Class myths on a specific subject with the subject, e.g., on a god 299.63

See Manual at 398.2 vs. 291.13

.63	Doctrines

Including gods, goddesses, other supernatural beings

.64	Rituals and ceremonials
.65	Practices

Example: witchcraft

For rituals and ceremonials, see 299.64

.67	Specific cults

Examples: Ras Tafari movement, Umbanda, voodooism

Class voodooism as an occult practice without regard to its religious significance in 133.4

†Add as instructed under 292–299

.68   Of specific groups and peoples

> Add to base number 299.68 the numbers following —96 in notation 961–969 from Table 5, e.g., religion of Yorubas 299.68333

> Class national groups which predominate in specific areas in Africa in 299.69, in other specific areas in 299.609

.69   Of specific areas in Africa

> Add to base number 299.69 the numbers following —6 in notation 61–69 from Table 2, e.g., religions of West Africa 299.696

.7   Of North American native origin

.709   Historical, geographical, persons treatment

> Class religions in specific areas in North America in 299.79

.72–.77   Specific aspects

> Add to base number 299.7 the numbers following 299.6 in 299.62–299.67, e.g., snake dances 299.74

.78   Of specific groups and peoples

> Add to base number 299.78 the numbers following —97 in notation 971–979 from Table 5, e.g., Hopi religion 299.784

.79   Of specific areas in North America

> Add to base number 299.79 the numbers following —7 in notation 71–79 from Table 2, e.g., religions of Indians of Mexico 299.792

.8   Of South American native origin

.809   Historical, geographical, persons treatment

> Religions of specific areas in South America relocated to 299.89

.82–.87   Specific aspects

> Add to base number 299.8 the numbers following 299.6 in 299.62–299.67, e.g., gods and goddesses 299.83

.88   Of specific groups and peoples

> Add to base number 299.88 the numbers following —98 in notation 982–984 from Table 5, e.g., religion of Guaranís 299.883

.89   Of specific areas in South America [*formerly* 299.809]

> Add to base number 299.89 the numbers following —8 in notation 81–89 from Table 2, e.g., religions of Indians of the Amazon 299.8911

.9   Of other origin

.92   Of other ethnic origin

> Aeta, Andamanese, Semang, Papuan, Australian, Malay, Basque, Elamite, Etruscan, Sumerian, Georgian, Ingush, Chechen, Circassian

.93   Of eclectic and syncretistic origin

Religions and applied religious philosophies of eclectic, syncretistic, universal nature

Examples: Eckankar, Great White Brotherhood, New Age religions, New Thought, systems of Bhagwan Shree Rajneesh and Meher Baba, United Church of Religious Science

See also 289.98 for Christian New Thought

.932   Gnosticism

Including Manicheism

Class Christian Gnosticism in 273.1, Christian Manicheism in 273.2

.933   Subud

.934   Theosophy

.935   Anthroposophy

.936   Scientology

Class dianetics in 158.9

300

300 Social sciences

Class here behavioral studies, social studies

Use 300.1–300.9 for standard subdivisions

Class a specific behavioral science with the subject, e.g., psychology 150; military, diplomatic, political, economic, social, welfare aspects of a war with the history of the war, e.g., the Vietnamese War 959.7043

For language, see 400; history, 900

See Manual at 150; 300; 300 vs. 600

SUMMARY

300.1–.9   **Standard subdivisions**
301   **Sociology and anthropology**
302   **Social interaction**
303   **Social processes**
304   **Factors affecting social behavior**
305   **Social groups**
306   **Culture and institutions**
307   **Communities**

.21   Tabulated and related materials

Class statistics in 310

301 Sociology and anthropology

Class here interdisciplinary works on society

Class a specific topic in sociology and anthropology in 302–307; social problems and social welfare in 361–365, a specific aspect of society not provided for in 302–307 with the subject, e.g., general history 900

For criminal anthropology, see 364.2; educational sociology, 370.19; physical anthropology, 573

See Manual at 301; 301 vs. 361–365; 361.1 vs. 362.042, 301

[.019]   Psychological principles

Relocated to 302

.7   **Nonliterate societies**

Use of this number for kinds of societies discontinued; class in 301

[.72]   Nonliterate

Number discontinued; class in 301.7

[.74]   Advanced

Number discontinued; class in 301

> ## 302–307 Specific topics in sociology and anthropology

Unless other instructions are given, class complex subjects with aspects in two or more subdivisions of this schedule in the one coming last in the schedule, e.g., social deterioration during civil wars 303.64 (*not* 303.45); however, class the effect of one factor on another with the factor affected, e.g., the effect of climate on social change 303.4 (*not* 304.25)

Class comprehensive works in 301

See Manual at 150 vs. 302–307; 155.92 vs. 158.2, 302–307; 156 vs.
302–307; 302–307; 320 vs. 302–307

302   Social interaction

Class here the psychological principles of sociology [*formerly also* 301.019], interpersonal relations, social psychology

Class the social psychology of a specific situation with the situation, e.g., of ethnic groups 305.8

See also 155.92 for the effect of social environment upon individuals, 158.2 for
individual aspects of interpersonal relations

See Manual at 150 vs. 302–307; 155.92 vs. 158.2, 302–307; 156 vs. 302–307

SUMMARY

302.01–.09	**Standard subdivisions**
.1	**General topics**
.2	**Communication**
.3	**Social interaction within groups**
.4	**Social interaction between groups**
.5	**Relation of the individual to society**

.015 195   Statistical mathematics

Class here sociometry [*formerly* 302.072]

See Manual at 519.5, T1—015195 vs. 001.422, T1—072

[.019]   Psychological principles

Do not use; class in 302

.072   Research

Sociometry relocated to 302.015195

.1   General topics

.12   Social understanding

Including attribution, risk perception

For social learning, see 303.32; perception of norms, 303.37

.13 Social choice

> Including attraction, influence

.14 Social participation

> Examples: cooperation, voluntarism
>
> Including communalism, competition, encounter groups, sensitivity training
>
> Class here social acceptance, social adjustment, social skills, success
>
> *See also 302.4 for intergroup aspects of participation*

.15 Social role (Role theory)

> Including role conflict

.17 Social dysfunctions

> Dysfunctions affecting a substantial portion of society, e.g., mass hysteria, crazes
>
> Examples: apathy, fear, panic
>
> Class here social psychoanalysis
>
> Class dysfunctional responses of individuals to society in 302.542

.2 **Communication**

> Including semiotics
>
> Class here interdisciplinary works on communication [*formerly* 001.5], mass communication
>
> *For information theory, see 003.54*

.22 Kinds

.222 Nonverbal communication

> Examples: symbols; drumbeats, smoke signals; gestures and body language; flower language
>
> Class here means of nonverbal communication [*formerly* 302.23], interdisciplinary works on nonlinguistic (nonstructured) communication
>
> Class comprehensive works on means of verbal and nonverbal communication in 302.23; manual language for the deaf in 419; symbols in a specific subject with the subject, using notation 0148 from Table 1, e.g., symbols in electrical engineering 621.30148
>
> *For iconography, see 704.9; insignia, 929*

.224 Verbal communication

> Class media in 302.23
>
> *For language, see 400*

.224 2 Oral

> *For conversation, see 302.346*

.224 4	Written

Class here literacy, illiteracy

See also 301.7 for nonliterate societies

.23 Media (Means of communication)

Examples: signs, signboards

Class here mass media, sociology of journalism

Means of nonverbal communication relocated to 302.222

Class the effect of mass media on a specific subject other than social groups with the subject, e.g., on social change 303.4833, on a company's advertising policy 659.111

.230 8 History and description with respect to kinds of persons

Class here the effect of mass media on specific groups, on social stratification [*both formerly* 305]

See Manual at 302.2308

.232 Print media

Class interdisciplinary works on the book in 002

.232 2 Newspapers

.232 4 Periodicals and journals

.234 Motion pictures, radio, television

Class here the electronic media

.234 3 Motion pictures

.234 4 Radio

.234 5 Television

.235 Telephony and telegraphy

.24 Content

Including gossip, rumor

See also 070.1 for the journalistic aspect of content

.25 Failures and disruptions of communication

For censorship, see 303.376

.3 Social interaction within groups

Class here group decision-making processes, group dynamics, negotiation

.33 In abstract and temporary groups

Examples: audiences, bus passengers, communities of interest, crowds, mobs

Class media audiences in 302.23

.34   In small (primary) groups

Groups small enough for all members to engage in face-to-face relationships at one time

Examples: committees, gangs, play groups

Class here friendship

Class the family in 306.85

See also 362.74 for predelinquent gangs, 364.106 for gangs engaging in crime

.346   Conversation

Including conversational rhythm

.35   In hierarchically organized (complex) groups

Class here bureaucracies, organizational behavior

See Manual at 658, T1—068 vs. 302.35

.4   Social interaction between groups

Including in- and out-groups

Class social interaction between a specific group and other groups in 305

.5   Relation of the individual to society

See also 155.92 for psychological effects of the social environment upon the individual

.52   Relation through reference groups

.54   Response of individuals

Including ambition

Class here aggression, dysfunctional responses, individualism

See also 302.17 for mass manifestations of social dysfunction

For conformity, see 303.32

.542   Deviation

Class here madness considered as a form of interaction of individuals with society

.544   Alienation

.545   Isolation

303   Social processes

For social interaction, see 302; factors affecting social behavior, 304

SUMMARY

303.3   **Coordination and control**
.4   **Social change**
.6   **Conflict**

.3 **Coordination and control**

Class here power, policy formulation

Class coordination and control in and through specific institutions in 306

.32 Socialization

Including social learning

Class here conformity

Class interdisciplinary works on child development in 305.231

For education, see 370

.323 By the family

.323 1 By the father

.323 2 By the mother

.324 By the school

.325 By religious organizations

.327 By other instrumentalities

Examples: peer groups, play groups, recreational agencies

.33 Social control

For socialization, see 303.32; social control through specific means, 303.34–303.38

> 303.34–303.38 Social control through specific means

Class comprehensive works in 303.33, socialization through specific means of control in 303.32

.34 Leadership

Including influence, cooperation

.342 Persuasion

By individuals

Class here interdisciplinary works on persuasion

Class specific aspects of persuasion with the subject, e.g., persuasion by media, 302.23, by propaganda 303.375; individual psychology of persuasion 153.852

.35 Utilitarian control

Use of rewards and incentives

.36 Coercion

Examples: authority, punishment, restraint, threat

See also 364.6 for the treatment and punishment of offenders

.37   Normative methods

Including perception of norms

For public opinion, see 303.38

.372   Customs and belief systems

Class here values, social ethics, social justice

See also 361.61 for values in social policy towards welfare problems

See Manual at 303.372 vs. 170

.375   Propaganda

.376   Censorship

See Manual at 303.376 vs. 363.31, 791.4

.38   Public opinion

Class here attitudes, attitude formation and change

Class propaganda in 303.375; public opinion on a specific subject with the subject, e.g., public opinion on racial stereotypes 305.8, on the political process 324

See also 302.12 for social understanding

.385   Prejudice

Class here social stereotypes and stereotyping

Class prejudices held by racial, ethnic, national groups in 303.387; by occupational and miscellaneous social groups in 303.388; prejudices regarding a specific group in 305

.387   Opinions held by racial, ethnic, national groups

Add to base number 303.387 notation 1–9 from Table 5, e.g., opinions of Canadians 303.38711

.388   Opinions held by occupational and miscellaneous groups

Add to base number 303.388 notation 04–99 from Table 7 e.g., opinions of dentists 303.3886176; then add 0* and to the result add notation 1–9 from Table 2, e.g., the opinions of dentists in France 303.3886176044

.4   Social change

Use 303.4 for social evolution in the broadest sense, as the sum total of good and bad (progressive and regressive), fast and slow changes taking place over time. Use 303.42 for detailed analysis of gradual (evolutionary) change as such. Use 303.44 for the study of social evolution considered as constant upward progress or improvement.

Class social change in a specific aspect of society with the subject in sociology, e.g., changes in religious institutions 306.6

[.401 12]   Forecasting and forecasts

Do not use; class in 303.49

*Use 00 for standard subdivisions; see instructions at beginning of Table 1

.42   Gradual (Evolutionary) change

.43   Abrupt (Revolutionary) and disruptive change

.44   Growth and development

   Class here progress, specialization

.45   Deterioration and decay

.48   Causes of change

.482   Contact between cultures

   Class here acculturation, assimilation; social effects of international assistance, of commerce

   Class intercultural education in 370.196

.482 09   Historical and persons treatment

   Class geographical treatment in 303.4821–303.4829 (*not* 303.482091–303.482099)

.482 1–.482 9   Contact between specific areas

   Add to base number 303.482 notation 1–9 from Table 2, e.g., cultural exchanges with China 303.48251; then add 0* and again add notation 1–9 from Table 2, e.g., cultural exchange between China and Japan 303.48251052

   Give priority in notation to the nation most affected. If this cannot be determined, give priority to the one coming first in the sequence of area notations

   (Option: Give priority to the area requiring local emphasis, e.g., libraries in the United States class cultural exchange between the United States and France in 303.48273044)

.483   Development of science and technology

   See Manual at 303.483 vs. 306.45, 306.46

.483 2   Transportation

.483 3   Communication

   Class here information technology

.483 4   Computers

   Class here automation, microelectronics, robots

*Use 00 for standard subdivisions; see instructions at beginning of Table 1

.484	Purposefully induced change

Including dissent, radicalism

Class here social innovation, social reform, social reform movements

Most innovation and reform is directed to a specific end and is classed with the subject, e.g., reform of banking 332.1

Class the political aspects of reform movements in 322.44, the role of reform movements in addressing social problems in 361–365

.485	Natural and manmade disasters

Examples: earthquakes, pandemics, wars

.49	Social forecasts

Class here futurology, social forecasting

Class forecasting in and forecasts of a specific subject with the subject, using notation 0112 from Table 1, e.g., the future of the U.S. Democratic Party 324.27360112

.490 9	Historical and persons treatment

Class geographical treatment in 303.491–303.499 (*not* 303.49091–303.49099)

.491–.499	Forecasts for specific areas

Add to base number 303.49 notation 1–9 from Table 2, e.g., the Communist bloc in the year 2000 303.491717

.6	**Conflict**

Class conflict in a specific area of social relations with the subject in sociology, e.g., racial conflict 305.8; conflicts as historical events in 900, e.g., the disturbances of May-June 1968 centered in Paris 944.0836

.61	Civil disobedience

Examples: hunger strikes, nonviolent action, passive resistance, sit-ins

.62	Civil disorder

For civil war and revolution, see 303.64

.623	Riots
.625	Terrorism

See also 363.32 for the prevention of terrorism

.64	Civil war and revolution

Class terrorism in 303.625

.66   War

Including pacifism, sociology of war

Class war as a cause of social change in 303.485, prevention of war in 327.172, causes of war in 355.027, the art and science of warfare in 355–359; military, diplomatic, political, economic, social, welfare aspects of a specific war with the history of the war, e.g., of the Vietnamese War 959.7043

For civil war, see 303.64

.69   Conflict resolution

Including mediation

Class here conflict management

Class the resolution of specific kinds of conflict with the kind of conflict, e.g., of war 303.66

304   Factors affecting social behavior

.2   Human ecology

Class here anthropogeography, ecological anthropology, human geography

See Manual at 508 vs.574, 910, 304.2

.23   Geographical, space, time factors

Including territoriality, time management

Class aspects of time in specific settings with the subject in 302–307, e.g., in conversation 302.346, in leisure activities 306.4812

.25   Weather and climatic factors

.27   Biological factors

Other than human

.28   Environmental abuse

Class here social consequences of the misuse of resources, of pollution

Use of this number for human activity discontinued; class in 304.2

Class interdisciplinary works on resources in 333.7, on pollution in 363.73

See Manual at 363.7 vs.333.72, 304.28

[.282]   Pollution

Number discontinued; class in 304.28

.5   Genetic factors

Class here sociobiology (biosociology), the study of the genetic bases of human social behavior

Class a specific aspect of sociobiology with the subject in sociology, e.g., the sociobiology of conflict 303.6

See also 574.5 for the sociobiology of plants and animals

.6 **Population**

Class here demography, demographic anthropology, population geography

Class the population of communities in 307.2

For movement of people, see 304.8

.602 1 Statistics

Class here comprehensive works on statistics of population [*formerly also* 312]

.61 Characteristics of populations

Example: density

.62 Growth and decline

See also 304.63 for births, 304.64 for deaths, 304.8 for movement of people

.63 Births

Including birth intervals

Class here comprehensive works on births and deaths

For deaths, see 304.64

See also 304.62 for the growth and decline of populations

.632 Fertility

.634 Family size

.64 Deaths (Mortality)

.645 Life expectancy

Add to base number 304.645 notation 1–9 from Table 2, e.g., life expectancy in Canada 304.64571

[.65] Overpopulation

Relocated to 363.91

.66 Demographic effects of population control efforts

Class population policy, comprehensive works on population control in 363.9

See Manual at 304.66 vs.363.9

[.662] Population quality

Relocated to 363.92

.663 Genocide

[.664] Population quantity

Relocated to 363.91

.666	Family planning

Class here birth control

> *See also 363.96 for family planning programs, 613.9 for birth control techniques*

.667	Abortion
.668	Infanticide
.8	**Movement of people**

For movement to, from, within communities, see 307.2

.809	Historical, geographical, persons treatment

Internal movement in [*formerly also* 304.82] and emigration from specific areas

Class emigration to specific areas in 304.83–304.89

.81	Causes
.82	International movement

Internal movement relocated to 304.809

Class international emigration in 304.809, international immigration in 304.83–304.89

> *See also 325 for political aspects of international movement*

.83–.89	Migration

Add to base number 304.8 notation 3–9 from Table 2, e.g., migration to Australia 304.894; then add 0* and to the result add notation 1–9 from Table 2 for the place of origin, e.g., migration from the United States to Australia 304.894073

*Use 00 for standard subdivisions; see instructions at beginning of Table 1

305   Social groups

General aspects: Social status, role, interactions, problems of social groups; discrimination against and conflict involving social groups

Class here culture and institutions of specific groups other than indigenous racial, ethnic, national groups [*formerly also* 306.08]; subcultures of specific groups; consciousness-raising groups; social stratification, equality, inequality

Observe the following table of precedence, e.g., black Roman Catholic middle-class male youths 305.235 (*not* 305.31, 305.55, 305.62, or 305.896)

Persons by physical and mental characteristics	305.908
Age groups	305.2
Groups by sex	305.3–.4
Social classes	305.5
Religious groups	305.6
Language groups	305.7
Racial, ethnic, national groups	305.8
Occupational and miscellaneous groups (*except* 305.908)	305.9

The effect of mass media on specific groups, on social stratification, relocated to 302.2308

Class the role of specific groups in specific institutions in 306, e.g., women in political institutions 306.2082; specific problems of, welfare services to social groups in 362; a specific aspect of discrimination with the subject, e.g., discrimination in housing 363.51; opinions of specific groups in 303.38

See Manual at 305 vs. 306, 909, 930–990

SUMMARY

305.2	Age groups
.3	Men and women
.4	Women
.5	Social classes
.6	Religious groups
.7	Language groups
.8	Racial, ethnic, national groups
.9	Occupational and miscellaneous groups

.2   Age groups

Class here comprehensive works on the generation gap

For the generation gap within families, see 306.874

.23   Young people

Through age twenty

Class here interdisciplinary works on children

Class a specific aspect of children with the aspect, e.g., social welfare of children 362.7

.231   Child development

Class here interdisciplinary works on child development

Class psychological development of children in 155.4, physical development in 612.65, socialization in 303.32

.232   Infants

Children from birth to age two

.233   Preschool children

Aged three to five

.234   School children

Aged six to eleven

.235   Young adults

Aged twelve to twenty

Class here comprehensive works on young adults aged twelve to twenty and over twenty

Class young adults over twenty in 305.242

.235 5   Development

Class here interdisciplinary works on the development of young adults

Class psychological development of young adults in 155.5, physical development in 612.661

.24   Adults

Class adults of specific sexes in 305.3–305.4

For late adulthood, see 305.26

.242   Early adulthood

Over twenty years of age

Class comprehensive works on young adults, young adults aged twelve to twenty in 305.235

.244   Middle adulthood

Class here middle age

.26   Late adulthood

Class the sociology of retirement in 306.38

See also 646.79 for guides to retirement

.3   Men and women

Including transsexuality

Class here interdisciplinary works on sex role, the sexes, gender identity; adult men and women

Class sex psychology and psychology of the sexes in 155.3, men and women in late adulthood in 305.26; specific aspects of sex role and gender identity with the subject, e.g., psychology of gender identity 155.33; the relations between the sexes and within the sexes in 306.7–306.8; the relation of a specific sex to a specific subject with the subject, using notation 081–082 from Table 1, e.g., women in U.S. history 973.082

For women, see 305.4

.31   Men

Class here interdisciplinary works on men, on males

Class specific aspects of the sociology of men in 305.32–305.38, aspects not provided for in 305.3 with the subject, e.g., legal status of men 346.013

\>   305.32–305.38 Specific aspects of the sociology of men

Class comprehensive works in 305.31

.32   Social role and status of men

Class here discrimination against men, men's movements, e.g., men's liberation movement

.33   Men's occupations

Add to base number 305.33 notation 09–99 from Table 7, e.g., male physicians 305.3361

See also 331 for the economic aspects of men's occupations

.38   Specific kinds of men

Class kinds of men defined by occupation in 305.33

.386–.388   Belonging to various specific religious, language, racial, ethnic, national groups

Add to base number 305.38 the numbers following 305 in 305.6–305.8, e.g., English-speaking men of South Africa 305.38721068

.389   Miscellaneous groups

Add to base number 305.389 the numbers following 305.90 in 305.904–305.906, e.g., widowers 305.389654

.4   **Women**

Class here interdisciplinary works on women, on females

Add to base number 305.4 the numbers following 305.3 in 305.32–305.38, e.g., widows 305.489654

Class specific aspects of the sociology of women not provided for here with the subject outside sociology, e.g., women suffrage in 324.623, economic aspects of women's occupations in 331.4, the legal status of women 346.0134, women's education in 376

.5   **Social classes**

Class here class struggle

Use of this number for equality and inequality discontinued; class in 305

Class the theory of class struggle in Marxism in 335.411

See Manual at 305.9 vs.305.5

.51   General principles

.512   Principles of stratification

.512 2   Caste systems

.513   Social mobility

.52   Upper classes

Class here aristocracy, elites

Class intellectual elites in 305.552

.522   By birth

Class here prominent families

.522 2   Royalty

.522 3   Nobility

.523   By economic status

.523 2   Landowners with large estates and landed gentry

.523 4   Wealthy

For landowners with large estates, see 305.5232

.524   By political status

Examples: cabinet ministers, commissars, judges, legislative representatives

.55   Middle classes (Bourgeoisie)

Class laboring classes in 305.562

.552   Intelligentsia

Class here intellectual elites

.553	Professional classes

Examples: lawyers, nurses, soldiers, teachers

.554	Managerial and entrepreneurial classes

Class farmers in 305.555

.555	Farmers

Worker-managers of their own land

Class agricultural labor in 305.563

.556	White-collar classes

Examples: bookkeepers, bureaucrats, clerks, shop assistants

.56	Lower, alienated, excluded classes

Class here minority groups, nomdominant groups

Class specific minority or nondominant groups with the group, e.g. non-dominant ethnic groups 305.8

.562	Laboring classes (Proletariat)

Including blue-collar workers

Class agricultural workers in 305.563, slaves in 305.567

.563	Agricultural lower classes

Examples: agricultural workers, serfs, sharecroppers

.563 3	Peasants
.567	Slaves
.568	Alienated and excluded classes

Examples: hippies, hoboes, tramps, untouchables

.569	The impoverished

Class problems of and service to the poor in 362.5

.6   Religious groups

Add to base number 305.6 the numbers following —2 in notation 21–29 from Table 7, e.g., Christian Scientists 305.685; then add 0* and to the result add notation 1–9 from Table 2, e.g. Christian Scientists in France 305.685044

Persons occupied with religion relocated to 305.92

.7   Language groups

Add to base number 305.7 notation 1–9 from Table 6, e.g., English-speaking people 305.721; then add 0* and to the result add notation 1–9 from Table 2, e.g., English-speaking people of South Africa 305.721068

*Use 00 for standard subdivisions; see instructions at beginning of Table 1

.8 **Racial, ethnic, national groups**

Class here ethnology, cultural ethnology, ethnography [*all formerly also* 306, 572]; race relations

Use 305.8001–305.8009 for standard subdivisions

Add to base number 305.8 notation 03–99 from Table 5, e.g., Chinese 305.8951, Chinese in the United States 305.8951073

Class unassimilated indigenous racial, ethnic, national groups in 306.08; physical ethnology in 572

> *See also 909.04 for the comprehensive history of specific racial, ethnic, national groups*
>
> *See Manual at 306.08 vs.305.8*

.9 **Occupational and miscellaneous groups**

Use 305.9001–305.9009 for standard subdivisions

Unless otherwise instructed, class complex subjects with aspects in two or more subdivisions of 305.9 in the number coming last, e.g., unemployed bibliographers 305.9091 (*not* 305.90694)

Class here occupational mobility

> *See Manual at at 305.9 vs 305.5*

.904 Persons by kinship characteristics

Add to base number 305.904 the numbers following —04 in notation 043–046 from Table 7, e.g., grandchildren 305.90442

.906 Persons by cultural level, marital status, sexual orientation, special social status

Add to base number 305.906 the numbers following —086 in notation 0863–0869 from Table 1, e.g., homosexuals (including gay liberation movement [*formerly also* 306.766]) 305.90664, veterans 305.90697; however, class members nondominant socioeconomic groups in 305.56; nondominant religious groups in 305.6, of nondominant racial, ethnic, national groups in 305.8; offenders in 364.3; inmates of penal institutions in 365.6

.908 Persons by physical and mental characteristics

Add to base number 305.908 the numbers following —08 in notation 081–082, from Table 7, e.g., gifted persons 305.90829

.909–.999 Persons by occupation

Add to base number 305.9 notation 09–99 from Table 7, e.g., persons occupied with religion 305.92 [*formerly* 305.6], postal workers 305.9383

Class men's occupations in 305.33, women's occupations in 305.43

306   Culture and institutions

Culture: the aggregate of a society's beliefs, folkways, mores, science, technology, values, arts

Institutions: patterns of behavior in social relationships

General aspects: the roles, functions, and patterns within which the groups and members of a society conduct their lives

Class here mass culture, cultural and social anthropology

Ethnology, cultural ethnology, ethnography relocated to 305.8

Class cultural exchange in 303.482, physical anthropology in 573, the history of a specific ethnic group in 900

For customs and folklore, see 390

See Manual at 305 vs. 306, 909, 930–990; 306.4 vs. 306

SUMMARY

306.01–.09	**Standard subdivisions**
.1	**Subcultures**
.2	**Political institutions**
.3	**Economic institutions**
.4	**Cultural institutions**
.6	**Religious institutions**
.7	**Institutions pertaining to relations of the sexes**
.8	**Marriage and family**
.9	**Institutions pertaining to death**

.08   Indigenous racial, ethnic, national groups

Class here culture and institutions, ethnology, race relations of indigenous groups living in distinct communities not integrated in the economic and social life of a nation

Culture and institutions of specific groups other than indigenous racial, ethnic, national groups relocated to 305

Class nonindigenous racial, ethnic, national groups in 305.8

See Manual at 306.08 vs. 305.8

.089   Specific indigenous racial, ethnic, national groups

Add to base number 306.089 notation 03–99 from Table 5, e.g., indigenous North American groups 306.08997, these groups in Mexico 306.08997072

.1   **Subcultures**

Examples: counterculture, drug culture

Use of this number for mass culture discontinued; class in 306

Popular culture relocated to 306.4

Class subcultures of specific groups in 305, drug usage considered as a social problem 362.29

.2   **Political institutions**

Institutions maintaining internal and external peace

Class here comprehensive works on patronage, on client relationships; political sociology

Class political science in 320, law in 340, public administration and military science in 350; patronage and client relationships in a specific institution with the institution, e.g., in systems of production 306.34, in art 306.47

See Manual at 320 vs. 306.2

>   306.23–306.25 Governmental institutions

Class comprehensive works in 306.2

.23   Legislative institutions

.24   Executive institutions

Class military institutions in 306.27, police in 306.28

.25   Judicial institutions

.26   Political parties

.27   Military institutions

Class here military sociology

See also 355 for military science

.28   Police institutions

See also 363.2 for police services

.3   **Economic institutions**

Social arrangements for production, distribution

Class here economic anthropology; economic sociology; sociology of economic development, of consumption

Class specific occupational groups in 305.9, economic institutions relating to housing in 307.336

See also 305.5 for social classes, 330 for economics

.32   Property systems

Example: kinds of land tenure

.34   Systems of production and exchange

Class here the sociology of industrial conflict and relations

See also 302.35 for organizational behavior, 303.482 for commerce (trade) as agent of social change

.342   Capitalism (Free enterprise)

See also 330.122 for economic aspects

.344	Cooperation

See also 334 for economic aspects of cooperatives

.345	Socialism

Class interdisciplinary works on socialism in 335

See Manual at 335 vs.320.53, 306.345

.347	Syndicalism

Class interdisciplinary works on syndicalism in 335.82

See Manual at 335 vs.320.53, 306.345

.349	Agricultural systems

Including the plantation as a system of production

Class here agricultural sociology [*formerly also* 307.72], land tenure systems

Class agricultural production systems not involving the ownership of land in 306.364

.36	Systems of labor

Class here the sociology of work, industrial sociology

Class sociology of industrial conflict and relations in 306.34, economic aspects of work in 331

.361	General aspects

Examples: absenteeism, quality of work life, unemployment

.361 3	Work ethic

Effect of work ethic and its absence on systems of labor

.361 5	Sexual division of labor

.362	Slavery

See also 305.567 for slaves as a social group

.363	Indentured and contract labor

.364	Agricultural systems of labor

Class here agricultural occupations in general; systems of agricultural production not involving ownership of land, e.g., fishing, hunting, gathering systems

Class agricultural slavery in 306.362, indentured and contract labor in agriculture in 306.363

For agricultural shared return systems, see 306.365

.365	Agricultural shared return systems

Class here serfdom, sharecropping

.366	Free labor systems

Class free labor in agricultural systems in 306.364

.368   Nonagricultural occupations

Class here division of labor, occupations considered severally

Class social groups defined by occupation in 305.909–305.999

For sexual division of labor, see 306.3615; agricultural occupations in general, 306.364

.38   Retirement

See also 646.79 for guides to retirement

.4   Cultural institutions

Class here popular culture [*formerly* 306.1]

Including the sociology of witch crazes [*formerly* 900], magic, symbols, eating habits, body shape

Class educational institutions, the sociology of education in 370.19; interdisciplinary works on witch crazes in 133.43

For religious institutions, see 306.6

See Manual at 306.4 vs. 306

.42   Sociology of knowledge

Class here the sociology of the intellectual life, of information

Class specific instances of the sociology of knowledge in 306.44–306.48

.44   Language

Class here sociolinguistics [*formerly* 401.9]

See Manual at 401.43 vs. 412, 415, 306.44, 401.9

.440 89   History and description with respect to racial, ethnic, national groups

Class here ethnolinguistics [*formerly* 408.9]

.446   Bilingualism and multilingualism

Class here biculturalism and multiculturalism in the sense of the prevalence among residents in an area of divergent cultural traditions centered upon different languages

Class the treatment of bilingualism and multilingualism in the context of language planning and policy formulation in 306.449

Use 306.4 for biculturalism and multiculturalism in which the difference in language is not a central element

See also 404.2 for linguistic aspects of bilingualism

.449	Language planning and policy

Class here the development of policies on language to solve the communication problems of a community that uses more than one language

.449 09	Historical and persons treatment

Class treatment by specific continents, countries, localities in the modern world in 306.4494–306.4499 (*not* 306.449094–306.449099)

.449 4–.449 9	Treatment by specific continent, country, locality in the modern world

Add to base number 306.449 notation 4–9 from Table 2, e.g., language policy of India 306.44954

.45	Science

Class here works contrasting the scientific and the humanistic cultures

See Manual at 303.483 vs. 306.45, 306.46

.46	Technology

See Manual at 303.483 vs. 306.45, 306.46

.461	Medicine

Class here the sociology of medicine, of health, of illness

Class social aspects of medical welfare problems and services in 362.1042

.47	Art

Class the sociology of arts and crafts in 306.489

.48	Recreation
.481	General topics

Examples: play, pleasure, wit and humor

.481 2	Leisure

Class here free time

.482	Gambling
.483	Sports

Class gambling on athletic events in 306.482

.484	Music, dance, theater
.485	Television, radio, motion pictures
.487	Hobbies and games

Class sports in 306.483, gambling on games in 306.482

.488	Reading
.489	Arts and crafts

.6   **Religious institutions**

To be classed here, the institutions must be considered from a secular, nonreligious viewpoint

Class here sociology of religion

Add to base number 306.6 the numbers following 2 in 230–290, e.g., Sunday school as a social institution 306.668, the synagogue as a social institution 306.69665

Use 306.63 for comprehensive works on Christian institutions

Class general works on religious institutions in countries where a specific religion predominates in 306.609 unless viewed as representative of the specific religion

> *See also 291.17 for social theology, 261 for Christian social theology*

.7   **Institutions pertaining to relations of the sexes**

Class here interdisciplinary works on sex [*formerly* 612.6], sexual love, sexual relations

Unwed parenthood relocated to 306.856

> *For sexual ethics, see 176; problems and controversies concerning various sex relations, 363.4; sex offenses, 364.153; sex customs, 392.6; sex hygiene, 613.95; sex techniques, 613.96; sex practices viewed as treatable disorders, 616.8583*

> *See Manual at 155.34 vs. 306.7*

.73   General institutions

Class here dating behavior

Group sex relocated to 306.77

> *For marriage, see 306.81*

.732   Celibacy

.734   Courtship

> *See also 392.4 for customs of courtship*

.735   Cohabiting

Former heading: Nonmarital relations

Including ménage à trois, free love

.736   Extramarital relations

[.737]   Illegitimacy

Relocated to 306.874

.738   Homosexual marriage

.74 Prostitution

See also 331.76130674 for prostitution as an occupation, 363.44 for prostitution as a social problem, 364.1534 for prostitution as a crime

.742 By females

Class child prostitution in 306.745

.743 By males

Class child prostitution in 306.745

.745 By children

.76 Sexual orientation

Class practices associated with specific orientations in 306.77

.762 Neutral sexual orientation

.764 Heterosexuality

.765 Bisexuality

.766 Homosexuality

Gay liberation movement relocated to 305.90664

.766 2 Male homosexuality

.766 3 Female homosexuality (Lesbianism)

.77 Sexual practices

Examples: group sex [*formerly* 306.73], fetishism, transvestism

See also 363.47 for pornography as a social problem, 364.174 as an offense against public morals, 364.153 as a sex crime

.772 Masturbation

.773 Sodomy

For oral sex, see 306.774

.774 Oral sex

.775 Sadism

Class here sado-masochism

For masochism, see 306.776

.776 Masochism

[.777] Incest

Relocated to 306.877

[.778] Group sex

Number discontinued; class in 306.77

[.779] Bestiality

Number discontinued; class in 306.77

.8   **Marriage and family**

See also 362.8286 for premarital and marriage counseling

SUMMARY

306.81	**Marriage**
.82	**Patterns in mate selection**
.83	**Types of kinship systems**
.84	**Types of marriage**
.85	**The family**
.87	**Intrafamily relationships**
.88	**Alteration of family arrangements**
.89	**Separation and divorce**

.81   Marriage

Class here interdisciplinary works on marriage

Class homosexual marriage in 306.738, patterns of mate selection 306.82, alteration of the marriage arrangements 306.88, other aspects of marriage with the subject, e.g., sexual techniques 613.96

For types of marriage, see 306.84

.82   Patterns in mate selection

Examples: endogamy, exogamy

Class courtship in 306.734

See also 392.4 for the customs of mate selection, 646.77 for practical guidance on choosing a mate and for dating behavior

.83   Types of kinship systems

Examples: matrilineal, patrilineal, totemic

.84   Types of marriage

Examples: common-law marriage, remarriage

.842   By number of spouses

.842 2   Monogamy

.842 3   Polygamy and polyandry

.843   Interreligious marriage

Marriages in which the spouses belong to different religions or different branches of the same religion

.845   Intercultural marriages

Class here marriages between citizens of different countries

.846   Interracial marriages

Class here miscegenation

.85   The family

Including the nonconsanguinal family

Class here interdisciplinary works on the family

Class a specific aspect of the family with the subject, e.g., kinship systems 306.83, achieving harmonious family relations 646.78

For intrafamily relationships, see 306.87; alteration of family arrangements, 306.88

See also 155.924 for the psychological influence of the family on individual members

.852   The rural family

See also 307.72 for rural sociology

.853   The suburban family

See also 307.74 for suburban communities

.854   The urban family

See also 307.76 for urban sociology

.855   The nuclear family

Class the single-parent family in 306.856

.856   The single-parent family

Class here unwed parenthood [*formerly* 306.7], divorced families with single-parent custody

.857   The extended family

Class kinship systems in the extended family in 306.83

.858   The patriarchal family

.859   The matriarchal family

.87   Intrafamily relationships

Example: in-law relationships

Including birth order

For alteration of family arrangements, see 306.88

See also 362.82 for social services to families, 646.78 for practical guides to harmonious family relationships

.872   Husband-wife relationship

See also 613.96 for sexual techniques

.874   Parent-child relationship

> Examples: illegitimacy [*formerly* 306.737], stepparent-stepchild relationship, adopted children, only child, youngest child
>
> Class here the generation gap within families
>
> Class comprehensive works on the generation gap in 305.2
>
> *See also 649 for child rearing (parenting)*

.874 2   Father-child relationship

> Class here the sociology of fatherhood

.874 3   Mother-child relationship

> Class here the sociology of motherhood

.874 5   Grandparent-child relationship

.875   Sibling relationships

.875 2   **Brother-brother relationship**

.875 3   **Brother-sister relationship**

.875 4   **Sister-sister relationship**

.877   Incest [*formerly* 306.777]

.88   Alteration of family arrangements

> Examples: desertion, death
>
> *For separation and divorce, see 306.89*

.89   Separation and divorce

> Including the binuclear family, shared custody
>
> Class the parent-child relationship in divorced families in 306.874, divorced families with single-parent custody in 306.856

.9   **Institutions pertaining to death**

> Class here interdisciplinary works on death
>
> Class specific aspects of death with the subject, e.g., the psychology of death 155.937, funeral rites and ceremonies 393.9

307   Communities

> *See Manual at 307*

> **307.1–307.3 Specific aspects of communities**

Add to the notation for each term identified by * as follows:
01–09   Standard subdivisions
1   Specific kinds of communities
          Add to 1 the numbers following 307.7 in 307.72–307.77, e.g.,
          cities 16

Class comprehensive works in 307

.1   ***Planning and development**

.12   *Planning

> *See also 711 for the physical aspect of city planning*
>
> *See Manual at 711 vs.307.12*

.14   *Development

> Class here human settlement
>
> Class resettlement in 307.2, redevelopment in 307.34

.2   ***Population**

> Size, composition; movement to, from, within communities
>
> Including decentralization, resettlement

.24   *Movement from rural to urban communities

> Class here the rural exodus

.26   *Movement from urban to rural communities

> Class here the urban exodus

.3   ***Structure**

> Class movement within communities in 307.24

.32   *Physical setting

.33   *Patterns of use

.332   *Industrial use

.333   *Commercial use

.334   *Recreational use

.336   *Residential use

> Including housing succession
>
> Class here housing patterns, sociology of housing
>
> *See also 363.58 for housing programs*
>
> *See Manual at 307.336 vs.307.34, 363.5*

*Add as instructed under 307.1–307.3

.336 2		*Neighborhoods
		Class ghettos in 307.3366
.336 4		*Slums
.336 6		*Ghettos
.34		*Redevelopment
		Class community planning in 307.12
		See Manual at 307.336 vs. 307.34, 363.5
.342		*City core
.344		*Slum clearance
.346		*Parks and recreational facilities

.7 **Specific kinds of communities**

Class specific aspects of specific kinds of communities in 307.1–307.3

.72 Rural communities

Class here rural sociology, rural villages

Including plantations considered as communities

Agricultural sociology relocated to 306.349

Class the plantation considered as a system of production in 306.349

.74 Suburban communities

.740 9 Historical and geographical communities

Specific suburban communities relocated to 307.7609

.76 Urban communities

Class here urban sociology, interdisciplinary works on cities

Class suburban communities in 307.74

.760 9 Historical and geographical treatment

Class here specific suburban communities [*formerly also* 307.7409], specific urban communities regardless of size [*formerly also* 307.762–307.764] or kind [*formerly also* 307.766–307.768]

> 307.762–307.764 Urban communities by size

Class comprehensive works in 307.76

Specific urban communities regardless of size relocated to 307.7609

.762 Small urban communities

Class here comprehensive works on villages

For rural villages, see 307.72

*Add as instructed under 307.1–307.3

.763	Medium-sized urban communities
.764	Large urban communities

Class here metropolitan areas as communities

For medium-sized communities, see 307.763

> 307.766–307.768 Urban communities by kind

Class comprehensive works in 307.76

Specific urban communities regardless of kind relocated to 307.7609

.766	Mining and industrial towns .

Class company towns in 307.767

.767	Company towns
.768	New towns
.77	Self-contained communities
.772	Tribal communities

Class tribal communities considered in the context of culture and institutions of indigenous racial, ethnic, national groups in 306.08

.774	Communes

Class kibbutzim in 307.776

.776	Kibbutzim

[308] [Unassigned]

Most recently used in Edition 16

[309] [Unassigned]

Most recently used in Edition 18

310 General statistics

Interdisciplinary collections of quantitative data

Class statistics of a specific subject, other than general statistics of a place, with the subject, using notation 021 from Table 1, e.g., statistics on deaths by crimes of violence 364.15021

See also 001.4225 for analysis of statistical data, 001.4226 for presentation of statistical data

.9 Historical, geographical, persons treatment

Class general statistics of specific continents, countries, localities in modern world in 314–319 (*not* 310.94–310.99)

[311] **[Unassigned]**

Most recently used in Edition 17

[312] **Statistics of populations (Demographic statistics)**

Comprehensive works relocated to 304.6021; statistics of a specific demographic topic to the topic with use of notation 021 from Table 1, e.g., statistics on deaths by crimes of violence 364.15021

[313] **[Unassigned]**

Most recently used in Edition 14

> **314–319 General statistics of specific continents, countries, localities in modern world**

Add to base number 31 notation 4–9 from Table 2, e.g., statistics of France 314.4

Class comprehensive works in 310

314 ***Of Europe**

315 ***Of Asia**

316 ***Of Africa**

317 ***Of North America**

318 ***Of South America**

319 ***Of other parts of the world   *Of Pacific Ocean Islands**

320 **Political science (Politics and government)**

For law, see 340; public administration and military science, 350

See also 306.2 for sociology of political institutions and processes

See Manual at 320; 320 vs.302–307; 320 vs.306.2; 320 vs.909, 930–990

SUMMARY

320.01–.09	**Standard subdivisions**
.1–.9	**[Structure and functions, ideologies, situation and conditions, and related topics]**
321	**Systems of governments and states**
322	**Relation of the state to organized groups and their members**
323	**Civil and political rights**
324	**The political process**
325	**International migration and colonization**
326	**Slavery and emancipation**
327	**International relations**
328	**The legislative process**

*Add as instructed under 314–319

SUMMARY

320.01–.09	Standard subdivisions
.1	The state
.3	Comparative government
.4	Structure and functions of government
.5	Political ideologies
.6	Policy formulation
.8	Local government
.9	Political situation and conditions

.01   Philosophy and theory

.011   General theory; systems

Class here nature, legitimacy, role of government [*all formerly* 320.2]; political justice, political change

Class persons treatment of general theory in 320.092, specific theories in the sense of ideologies in 320.5; theories on specific aspects of government with the aspect, e.g., the social contract as a theory of the origin of the state 320.11

See Manual at 320.011 vs. 320.5

.011 3   Systems analysis

The word "systems" here refers only to concepts derived from 003, e.g., systems theory, models

Add to base number 320.0113 the numbers following 003 in 003.1–003.8, e.g., computer modeling and simulation 320.01133, forecasting and forecasts 320.01132; however, class forecasting and forecasts for a specific period or area in 320.9

.014   Language (Terminology) and communication

Class here political persuasion and propaganda

Class interdisciplinary works on persuasion in 303.342, on propaganda in 303.375

.019   Psychological aspects

Including political decision making

Class political persuasion and propaganda in 320.014

.02–.08   Standard subdivisions

.09   Historical, geographical, persons treatment of political science (politics and government) as a discipline

Class historical and geographical treatment of politics and government, forecasting and forecasts in a specific period or area in 320.9

.092   Political philosophers and scientists

Biography of political thinkers identified with specific ideologies relocated to 320.5

.1	**The state**

Class systems by which states are organized in 321

See Manual at 320

.101	Philosophy and theory

Class theories of origin of the state in 320.11

.11	Theories of origin

Class here the social contract

.12	Territory

Class here geopolitics

Class geopolitics in international relations in 327.101, territory in international law in 341.42, history of territorial changes in 911

.15	Sovereignty

Class here national self-determination

Class states with restricted sovereignty in 321.08

Use of this number for elements discontinued; class in 320.1

[.156]	Population

Number discontinued; class in 320.1

[.157]	Sovereignty

Number discontinued; class in 320.15

[.17]	Emerging states

Number discontinued; class in 320.1

[.2]	**Government**

Use of this number for comprehensive works on government discontinued; class in 320

Nature, legitimacy, role of government relocated to 320.011

.3	**Comparative government**

Class comparison of a specific subject with the subject, e.g., comparison of committee systems in different legislatures 328.365

.309	Historical, geographical, persons treatment

Class a comparison of two governments, if neither predominates, with the one coming first in Table 2

.4   **Structure and functions of government**

Class here civics

Relation of local government to higher levels of government relocated to 320.8

Class analysis of systems by which government is structured in 321

For comparative government, see 320.3

See Manual at 350.354 vs. 320.4, 320.9

.404   Separation of powers

Class here relation of executive branch to other branches [*formerly also* 351.0037], branches of government

Class separation of powers in specific areas in 320.41–320.49, cabinet system of executives in 321.8043, legislative control and oversight of executive branch in 328.3456

For legislative branch, see 328; judicial branch, 347; executive branch, 350

.404 9   Vertical separation of powers

Class here relation of a central government with regional subordinate jurisdictions

Class systems of relating federal to regional governments in 321.023

For relation of local government to higher levels of government, see 320.8

.409   Historical and persons treatment

Class geographical treatment in 320.41–320.49

.41–.49   Geographical treatment

Class here systems of state and government in specific states

Add to base number 320.4 notation 1–9 from Table 2, e.g., structure of government in Cuba 320.47291; then to the result add standard subdivisions as modified under 320.4, e.g., separation of powers in Cuba 320.4729104

.5   **Political ideologies**

Class here biography of political thinkers identified with specific ideologies [*formerly 320.092*]

Except as provided under 320.53209, use notation 09 from Table 1 for variants of basic ideologies formulated and practiced in specific nations, e.g., Titoism 320.532309497, Nazism 320.5330943, apartheid 320.560968

Class ideologies respecting a specific aspect of state or government with the subject, e.g., respecting revolution 321.094

See Manual at 320.011 vs. 320.5; 320.5 vs. 320.9, 324

.51	Liberalism
.512	Traditional liberalism

Ideologies and theories stressing rationalism, individualism, limited government

Including libertarianism

See also 320.52 for conservatism

.513	Modern liberalism

Ideologies and theories stressing responsibility of the state for the welfare of its citizens

.52	Conservatism

Ideologies and theories stressing limits of human reason and virtue, value of tradition, caution in effecting social change

See also 320.512 for traditional liberalism

.53	Collectivism and fascism

Class here the new left, radicalism, totalitarianism, comprehensive works on authoritarianism

Class religiously oriented authoritarianism in 320.55

See Manual at 335 vs. 320.53, 306.345

> 320.531–320.532 Specific collectivist ideologies

Class comprehensive works in 320.53

.531	Socialism

Nonauthoritarian systems

See also 320.532 for authoritarian systems of socialism

.531 2	Non- and quasi-Marxian socialism

Examples: Christian socialism, Fabian socialism

.531 5	Marxian socialism (Social democracy, Democratic socialism)
.532	Communism

Class here comprehensive works on Marxian systems of collectivism, authoritarian systems of socialism

Class nonauthoritarian Marxian socialism in 320.5315

.532 09	Historical, geographical, persons treatment

Class communism as formulated and practiced in the Soviet Union in 320.5322, other systems as formulated and practiced in specific nations in 320.532309, e.g., Maoism 320.53230951

.532 2	Marxism-Leninism

Class here communism as formulated and practiced in the Soviet Union

Class variant forms of communism in 320.5323

For Trotskyism, see 320.5323

.532 3	Variant forms of communism

Systems of communism, of Marxism-Leninism, other than ones accepted in Soviet Union

Including Trotskyism

.533	Fascism
.54	Nationalism

Class here ethnic nationalism, "pan" movements

.540 956 94	Zionism [*formerly* 956.54001]
.549	Regional nationalism

Nationalism not centered around either a single language or a single existing state, e.g., Pan-Slavism (320.5490947)

.55	Religiously oriented theories and ideologies

Example: theocracy

For Christian socialism, see 320.5312

.56	Racism

Ideologies based on the assumption of racial superiority

See also 320.5330943 for Nazism

.57	Anarchism
.6	**Policy formulation**

Class here planning, formulation of programs and proposals, policy studies

Class a specific aspect of policy formulation with the aspect, e.g., formulating political party programs 324.23, legislative lobbying 328.38, policy making in public administration 351.0072; policy formulation and public policy in specific subjects with the subject, e.g., policies for economic development 338.9, social policy 361.61

.8 **Local government**

Class here relation of local government to higher levels of government [*formerly* 320.4], boundaries, forms, kinds, structure and function

Class systems of relating local government to higher levels of government when considered in areas larger than a nation in 321.01

See also 352 for local administration

.83 Intermediate levels

Government levels between national, state, or large provincial government and local municipalities

Examples: counties, districts, arrondissements, provinces with limited areas

.84 Rural government

.85 City government

Including incorporation

Class here urban government

See also 352.003 for administrative aspects of municipal incorporation

.854 Forms of government

Examples: commission, council-manager, mayor-council

.859 Annexation

See also 352.006 for administrative aspects of annexation

.9 **Political situation and conditions**

Class here historical and geographical treatment of politics and government; history, description, critical appraisal of political institutions and forms

Use 320.9001–320.9008 for standard subdivisions

Add to base number 320.9 notation 01–99 from Table 2, e.g., political conditions in Egypt 320.962

Class general political history in 900

See Manual at 320; 320 vs.909, 930–990; 320.5 vs.320.9, 324; 350–354 vs.320.4, 320.9

321 Systems of governments and states

Class here method of selection of chief executive [*formerly also* 351.0034], kinds of states

Unless other instructions are given, use 321 only for considerations of "system" or "kind," and only for areas broader than a specific state. Use 320.4 for structure and functions of governments of any system or kind, and for the system or systems of any specific state

Use 321.001–321.009 for standard subdivisions

Class interdisciplinary works on systems which have corresponding political and economic manifestations in 330.1 and 335

.01   **Systems of relating the parts to the whole**

Example: unitary systems (systems in which full control is vested in central governments)

Class systems of relating the whole to the parts in nation states in 321.05, in ideal states in 321.07

For federal systems, see 321.02; empires, 321.03; proposed regional and world unions, 321.04

.02   **Federal systems**

Class here confederations

Class proposed regional and world federations in 321.04

.023   **Systems of relating federal and regional governments**

Class systems of relating federal and regional governments in specific nations in 320.4

.03   **Empires**

Systems in which a group of nations are governed by a single sovereign power

Class here specific empires

See also 325.32 for imperialism as a policy of extending dominion

.04   **Proposed regional and world unions**

Unitary or federal

Class here specific proposed regional and world unions, interdisciplinary works on supranational states

For empires, see 321.03

.05   **Nation states**

States considered as political embodiments of racial or ethnic groups

The terms ''national state'' or ''nation'' used to cover any sovereign state are classed in 320.1

.06   **Small states**

Including city-states, ministates

See also 320.85 for cities as local governments, 327.101 for international role of small states

.07   **Ideal states (Utopias)**

Including anarchy as an ideal system

Class proposed regional and world unions in 321.04

.08   **States with restricted sovereignty**

Examples: mandates, protectorates

.09	Change in system of government

Including coup d'état

Class here change in system of government in specific nations

Use 321.09 only for the process of change. For the preceding and following system or systems in general, use a number for the system or systems in 321; for the preceding and following system or systems in a specific nation, use notation for the nation in 320.4

.094	Revolution

Class interdisciplinary works on revolution in 303.64

.1 Systems of government among nonliterate peoples, ancient and medieval systems of government

.12	Systems of government among nonliterate peoples

Ancient and modern

Class here systems of government among nonliterate people in specific areas

.14	Ancient and medieval systems of government

Class feudal system in 321.3, pure democracy in 321.4, elitist systems in 321.5

> **321.3–321.9 Systems of government defined by source or exercise of authority**

Class comprehensive works in 321

.3 Feudal system

.4 Pure democracy

.5 Elitist systems

Examples: aristocracy, oligarchy, plutocracy, theocracy

Autocracy relocated to 321.6

.6 Absolute monarchy

Class here autocracy [*formerly* 321.5]

Class ancient absolute monarchy in 321.14

.8 Democratic systems

For pure democracy, see 321.4

.804	Systems of selecting chief executives
.804 2	Presidential system

A system in which the real executive power is exercised by a president chosen independently of the legislature

.804 209 73	In United States

> Class here method of selection of president [*formerly also* 353.034], methods of selection of governors [*formerly also* 353.9134]

.804 209 74–.804 209 79	In specific states of United States

> Class here methods of selection of governors [*formerly also* 353.97 with use of notation 034 from table at 353.97–353.99]

> *For Hawaii, see 321.804209969*

.804 209 969	In Hawaii

> Class here method of selection of governor [*formerly also* 353.9969034]

.804 3	Cabinet system

> A system in which the real executive power is exercised by a cabinet of ministers chosen by the legislature and responsible to it

.86	Republics

> Class selection of executives in 321.804

.87	Limited monarchies

> Class selection of executives in 321.804

.9   Authoritarian systems

> *For elitist systems, see 321.5; absolute monarchy, 321.6*

.92	Communist
.94	Fascist

> Including Nazi system

322   Relation of the state to organized groups and their members

Relation of the state to groups other than regular political parties

Class groups organized for a specific purpose not provided for here with the purpose, e.g., groups organized to promote political rights 323.5

.1   Religious organizations and groups

Class here church and state

> *See Manual at 322.1 vs. 261.7, 291.177*

.2   Labor movements and groups

Including general strikes

Class general strikes directed primarily toward employers, or focused upon limited economic objectives in 331.8925

> *See also 323.3223 for relation of the state to the unorganized working class*

.3   Business and industry

.4 **Political action groups**

Class here protest groups; nonelectoral tactics used by political action groups, e.g., civil disobedience, passive resistance; specific kinds of confrontations between such groups and constituted authorities, e.g., riots

Class interdisciplinary works on conflicts and their resolution in 303.6, political action committees (U.S. fund-raising groups) in 324.4

.42 Revolutionary and subversive groups

Class here revolutionary and subversive activity of political parties, military and direct action branches of such parties

Class comprehensive works on parties and international movements engaged in both nonviolent political activity and revolutionary activity in 324

.420 9 Historical, geographical, persons treatment

Class here specific revolutionary and subversive groups irrespective of political persuasion or stated goals, e.g., Palestine Liberation Organization 322.42095694, Ku Klux Klan 322.420973

See also 909 and 930–990 for the impact of revolutionary and subversive groups on general history

.43 Pressure groups

Groups striving for immediate and relatively limited goals

Class the role of pressure groups in the political process in 324.4; specific pressure groups with their goal, e.g., a group working for better law enforcement 363.23

.44 Reform movements

Groups seeking to change a substantial social function

Use of this number for protest movements discontinued; class in 322.4

Class a specific reform movement with the social function it seeks to reform, e.g., the woman suffrage movement 324.623, welfare reform 361.68

See Manual at 361.23–361.24 vs. 322.44

.5 **Military organizations (Armed forces)**

323 Civil and political rights

Class here the relation of the state to its residents; individual freedom, human rights, rights of mankind

Class relation of the state to political parties and related organizations in 324, e.g., to political parties 324.204; law of civil rights in 342.085; welfare aspects of human rights in 361.614

For relation of the state to organized groups and their members, see 322

SUMMARY

323.01–.09   **[Standard subdivisions, citizen participation, resistance and repression]**
     .1   **Civil rights of nondominant aggregates, political rights of nondominant aggregates**
     .3   **Civil and political rights of other social aggregates**
     .4   **Specific civil rights; limitation and suspension of civil rights**
     .5   **Political rights**
     .6   **Citizenship and related topics**

.01   Philosophy and theory

> Class here natural rights [*formerly* 323.401]

.04   Special topics

.042   Participation of citizens in governmental processes

> Class here participatory democracy

> Class citizen participation in a specific issue with the issue, e.g., participation in public school evaluation 379.154

.044   Resistance and repression

> Class limitation and suspension of civil rights in 323.49

[.08]   History and description with respect to kinds of persons

> Do not use; class civil and political rights of nondominant aggregates in 323.1, of other social aggregates in 323.3

.1   **Civil rights of nondominant aggregates [*formerly also* 323.423], political rights of nondominant aggregates**

> Use of this number for comprehensive works on the relation of the state to social aggregates discontinued; class in 323

> Class specific nondominant aggregates other than members of racial, ethnic, national groups in 323.3; specific civil rights of specific nondominant aggregates in 323.4, specific political rights in 323.5

.109   Historical, geographical, persons treatment

> Class treatment by specific continents, countries, localities in 323.13–323.19 (*not* 323.1093–323.1099)

.11   Members of racial, ethnic, national groups

.110 9   Historical, geographical, persons treatment

> Class comprehensive works on members of racial, ethnic, national groups in specific areas in 323.13–323.19 (*not* 323.11093–323.099); members of specific racial, ethnic, national groups in specific places in 323.111–323.119

.111–.119   Members of specific racial, ethnic, national groups

> Add to base number 323.11 notation 1–9 from Table 5, e.g., relation of the state to Jews 323.11924, to Afro-Americans 323.1196073

> (Option: Class relation of the state to North American native races in 970.5 rather than 323.1197, to South American native races in 980.5 rather than 323.1198; prefer 323.1197 and 323.1198)

> Class members of specific racial, ethnic, national groups who are also members of other social aggregates in 323.3

.13–.19   Comprehensive treatment of nondominant aggregates, of racial, ethnic, national aggregates by specific continents, countries, localities

> Add to base number 323.1 notation 3–9 from Table 2, e.g., relation of the Soviet state to national minorities 323.147

> Class treatment of specific racial, ethnic, national groups in specific continents, countries, localities in 323.111–323.119; of other specific nondominant social aggregates in specific continents, countries, localities in 323.3

.3   **Civil and political rights of other social aggregates**

> Other than members of racial, ethnic, national groups

> Class a specific civil right of a specific social aggregate in 323.4, specific political rights in 323.5

.32   Socioeconomic classes

> Add to base number 323.32 the numbers following —086 in notation 0862–0869 from Table 1, e.g., the working class 323.3223, intellectuals 323.3231

.34   Women

> Class women of specific socioeconomic classes in 323.32

.35   Age groups

> Class age groups of a specific socioeconomic class in 323.32, women of a specific age group in 323.34

.352   Young people

> Class here children

.353   Middle-aged adults

> Use of this number for adults discontinued; class in 323

.354   Adults in later stage of life

.4   **Specific civil rights; limitation and suspension of civil rights**

> Do not use standard subdivisions; class in 323.01–323.09

> Use of this number for comprehensive works on civil rights discontinued; class in 323

[.401]	Natural rights
	Relocated to 323.01
.42	Equal protection of laws
.422	Procedural rights
	Examples: habeas corpus, trial by jury
[.423]	Civil rights of nondominant aggregates
	Relocated to 323.1
.43	Personal security
	Including right to bear arms
	Class right to privacy in 323.448
.44	Freedom of action (Liberty)
	Class here intellectual freedom
	For rights of assembly and association, see 323.47; right of petition, 323.48
.442	Freedom of conscience and religion
.443	Freedom of speech
.445	Freedom of publication
	Including right to information
	Class here freedom of information, freedom of press
.448	Right to privacy
.448 2	Freedom from government surveillance
	Surveillance by interception of mail, electronic monitoring, other means
	Class governmental databases in 323.4483
.448 3	Freedom from misuse of information in databases
	In governmental and private databases
.46	Economic rights (Property)
	Including employment rights, freedom of contract
	Class here property rights
	See Manual at 323.46 vs. 361.614
.47	Rights of assembly and association
.48	Right of petition
	Class here comprehensive works on rights of petition and assembly
	For right of assembly, see 323.47

.49	Limitation and suspension of civil rights

Including harassment through abuse of laws, e.g., detention of dissidents for alleged mental health problems

Class limitation and suspension of specific rights in 323.42–323.48

[.490 8]	History and description with respect to kinds of persons

Do not use; class limitation and suspension of rights of nondominant aggregates in 323.1, of other social aggregates in 323.3

.5	**Political rights**

Examples: rights to be represented, to hold office

Voting rights relocated to 324.62

Class right of assembly in 323.47, of petition in 323.48; exercise of political rights in 324

[.508]	History and description with respect to kinds of persons

Do not use; class political rights of nondominant aggregates in 323.1, of other social aggregates in 323.3

.6	**Citizenship and related topics**
.62	Acquisition of citizenship

For acquisition of citizenship by marriage, see 323.636

.622	By birth
.623	By naturalization
.629	By other ways

Examples: by adoption, land purchase, length of residence

.63	Relation of the state to aliens and persons with citizenship problems
.631	Aliens

Including asylum

Class naturalization of aliens in 323.623

.632	Stateless persons
.634	Persons with dual nationality
.636	Married people of differing nationality

Including acquisition of citizenship by marriage

.64	Expatriation and repatriation
.65	Duties and obligations of citizens

Including loyalty

.67	Passports and visas

324   The political process

Class here elections

See Manual at 320 vs. 909, 930–990; 320.5 vs. 320.9, 324

SUMMARY

324.01–.09	**Standard subdivisions**
.1	**International party organizations, auxiliaries, activities**
.2	**Political parties**
.3	**Auxiliary organizations**
.4	**Interest and pressure groups**
.5	**Nomination of candidates**
.6	**Election systems and procedures; suffrage**
.7	**Conduct of election campaigns**
.9	**Historical and geographical treatment of elections**

.025   Directories of persons and organizations

Class here lists and directories of elected officials [*formerly also* 351.22]

Class lists and directories of elected officials of specific jurisdictions in 324.9

.09   Historical, geographical, persons treatment

Class historical and geographical treatment of elections in 324.9

.1   International party organizations, auxiliaries, activities

Not directly controlled by specific national parties

Class revolutionary and subversive activities, direct action branches of party organizations in 322.42

See Manual at 324.1 vs. 324.2, 324.209, 324.21

>   324.13–324.17 International organizations, auxiliaries, activities of parties identified primarily by position on right-to-left spectrum

Class comprehensive works in 324.1; organizations, auxiliaries, activities of parties not primarily identified by position on right-to-left spectrum in 324.18

.13   Of rightist parties

Including international anticommunist leagues and their activities, monarchist parties

.14   Of conservative parties

.15   Of centrist parties

.16   Of liberal parties

For social democratic parties, see 324.172

.17	Of leftist and labor oriented parties

Including First International

.172	Of social democratic parties
.174	Of nonauthoritarian socialist parties

Including Second and Socialist Internationals

For social democratic parties, see 324.172

.175	Of communist parties

Including Third (Communist) and Fourth (Trotskyist) Internationals, Cominform

.18	Other parties

Regardless of position on rightist to leftist spectrum

Examples: environmentalist, libertarian parties

.182	Religious parties
.183	Nationalist parties
.2	**Political parties**

Class revolutionary and subversive activities, direct action branches of parties in 322.42, international organizations and activities of parties in 324.1, auxiliary organizations in 324.3

See Manual at 324.1 vs.324.2, 324.209, 324.21

[.202 3]	Politics as a profession, occupation, hobby

Do not use; class in 324.22

.204	Relation of political parties to state and government

Including political patronage

.209	Historical, geographical, persons treatment

Class here treatment in continents and regions in modern world larger than countries [*formerly* 324.24–324.29]

Class treatment in specific countries and parts of countries in modern world in 324.24–324.29 (*not* 324.2094–324.2099)

See Manual at 324.1 vs.324.2, 324.209, 324.21; 324.24–324.29 and 324.29

.21   Kinds of parties

Class here organization, membership, finance of parties

Treatment in specific countries and parts of countries in modern world of organization, membership, finance of parties in general relocated to 324.24–324.29

Add to base number 324.21 the numbers following 0 in notation 02–08 from table under 324.24–324.29, e.g., centrist parties 324.215

Class leadership of specific kinds of parties in 324.22; programs and ideologies of specific kinds of parties in 324.23; specific parties and kinds of parties in a specific country or part of a country in modern world in 324.24–324.29

For leadership, see 324.22; campaign finance, 324.78

See Manual at 324.1 vs. 324.2, 324.209, 324.21

.22   Leadership

Including selection of leaders

Class here politicians as a type of person; politics as a profession, occupation, hobby

Treatment in specific countries and parts of countries in modern world of leadership of parties in general relocated to 324.24–324.29

Class leadership of specific parties and kinds of parties in a specific country or part of a country in modern world in 324.24–324.29

For nomination of candidates, see 324.5

.23   Programs and ideologies

Class here platforms, campaign literature and propaganda, and works about them

Add to base number 324.23 the numbers following 0 in notation 02–08 from table under 324.24–324.29, e.g., programs of centrist parties 324.235

Treatment in specific countries and parts of countries in modern world of programs and ideologies of parties in general relocated to 324.24–324.29

Class programs and ideologies of specific parties and kinds of parties in a specific country or part of a country in modern world in 324.24–324.29; campaign literature and propaganda on a specific subject with the subject, e.g., on United States participation in the Vietnamese War 959.7043373

.24–.29   Parties in specific countries in modern world

Class here treatment in specific countries and parts of countries of organization, membership, finance of parties in general [*formerly* 324.21]; of leadership of parties in general [*formerly* 324.22], of programs and ideologies of parties in general [*formerly* 324.23], of auxiliary organizations and nominations of specific parties

Except where specifically instructed to the contrary below, add to base number 324.2 notation 4–9 from Table 2 for specific country, e.g., parties of France 323.244; then add further as follows:

001–009	Standard subdivisions
02	Historical parties
	Parties existing prior to 1945 and no longer in existence
	Class comprehensive works on historical parties in 324.212
>03–08	Recent parties
	Parties founded or remaining in existence since 1945
	Class comprehensive works on parties in specific countries in base number for the country in 324.24–324.29, comprehensive works on specific kinds of parties in 324.21
>03–07	Recent parties identified primarily by position on right-to-left spectrum
	Class comprehensive works in base number for the country in 324.24–324.29, other recent parties not primarily identified by position on right-to-left spectrum in 08
	See Manual at 324.24–324.29
03	Rightist parties
	Including monarchist parties
	Sectionalist parties relocated to 08, nationalist parties to 083
038	Fascist and Nazi parties
04	Conservative parties
05	Centrist parties
06	Liberal parties
	For social democratic parties, see 072
07	Leftist and worker parties
072	Social democratic parties
074	Nonauthoritarian socialist parties
	For social democratic parties, see 072
075	Communist parties
08	Other recent parties
	Not primarily identified by position on right-to-left spectrum
	Examples: sectionalist [*formerly* 03], environmentalist, libertarian, separatist parties
	See Manual at 324.24–324.29
082	Religious parties
083	Nationalist parties [*formerly* 03]

(Option: Arrange specific parties of a specific country alphabetically, e.g., Labour Party of United Kingdom 324.241)

Treatment of parties in continents and regions in modern world larger than countries relocated to 324.209

(continued)

.24–.29　　Parties in specific countries in modern world (continued)

Class comprehensive works on parties in 324.2, on specific kinds of parties in 324.21, on party leadership in 324.22, on party programs and ideologies in 324.23; treatment in specific countries of party auxiliary organizations in general in 324.309, of party nominations in general in 324.509

See Manual at 324.24–324.29 and 324.209; 324.24–324.29

Special developments follow for selected specific countries whose party systems deviate from the above pattern

SUMMARY

324.241	**Parties of United Kingdom**
.268	**Parties of Republic of South Africa**
.271	**Parties of Canada**
.273	**Parties of United States**
.274–.279	**Parties of states of United States and District of Columbia**
.294	**Parties of Australia**
.296 9	**Parties in Hawaii**

.241　　Parties of United Kingdom

Use 324.241001–324.241009 for standard subdivisions

.241 02　　Historical parties

Parties existing prior to 1945 and no longer in existence

Class here parties of Great Britain before union with Ireland, of England and Wales before union with Scotland

.241 04　　Conservative Party

.241 06　　Liberal Party

.241 07　　Labour Party

.241 09　　Other parties

Add to base number 324.24109 the numbers following 0 in 03–08 from table under 324.24–324.29, e.g., Communist Party 324.2410975

.268　　Parties of Republic of South Africa

Use 324.268001–324.268009 for standard subdivisions

.268 02　　Historical parties

Parties existing prior to 1945 and no longer in existence

> 324.268 03–324.268 08 Recent parties [*formerly also* 324.26809]

Parties founded or remaining in existence since 1945

Class comprehensive works in 324.268

> 324.268 03–324.268 07 Recent parties identified primarily by position on right-to-left spectrum

Class comprehensive works in 324.268, other recent parties not primarily identified by position on right-to-left spectrum in 324.26808

.268 03   Rightist parties

National party relocated to 324.268083

.268 038   Fascist and Nazi parties

.268 04   Conservative parties

Union Party relocated to 324.26808

.268 05   Centrist parties

United Party relocated to 324.26808

.268 06   Liberal parties

Including Liberal Party [*formerly* 324.26807]

For social democratic parties, see 324.268072

.268 07   Leftist and worker parties

Liberal Party relocated to 324.26806

.268 072   Social democratic parties

.268 074   Nonauthoritarian socialist parties

For social democratic parties, see 324.268072

.268 075   Communist parties

.268 08   Other recent parties

Not primarily identified by position on right-to-left spectrum

Examples: Union Party [*formerly* 324.26804], United Party [*formerly* 324.26805]; environmentalist, libertarian, sectionalist, separatist parties

.268 082   Religious parties

.268 083   National parties

Example: National Party [*formerly* 324.26803], African National Congress

[.268 09]   Other parties

Relocated to 324.26803–324.26808

[.268 2–.268 7]	Parties of provinces of South Africa
	Numbers discontinued; class in 324.268
.271	**Parties of Canada**
	Use 324.271001–324.271009 for standard subdivisions
.271 02	Historical parties
	Parties existing prior to 1945 and no longer in existence
.271 04	Progressive Conservative Party
.271 05	Social Credit Party
.271 06	Liberal Party
.271 07	New Democratic Party
.271 09	Other parties

Add to base number 324.27109 the numbers following 0 in 03–08 from table under 324.24–324.29, e.g., nationalist parties 324.2710983

.271 1–.271 9	Parties of provinces and territories of Canada

Add to base number 324.271 the numbers following —71 in notation 711–719 from Table 2 for province or territory, e.g., parties in Quebec 324.2714; then to the result add the numbers following 324.271 in 324.271001–324.27109, e.g., Parti québécois 324.2714098

.273	**Parties of United States**

Class parties in specific states and the District of Columbia in 324.274–324.279

.273 2	Historical parties

Parties existing prior to 1945 and no longer in existence

Examples: American (''Know-Nothing'') Party, Free Soil Party

.273 22	Federalist Party
.273 23	Whig Party
	Including National Republican Party
.273 26	Jeffersonian Republican Party
	Including Antifederalist Party
.273 27	Populist and progressive parties
	Example: Progressive (''Bull Moose'') Party
	See also 324.2737 for the Progressive Party (1948)
.273 3	Nationalist parties of the right
	Example: American Independent Party
	Including sectionalist parties, e.g., States' Rights Party (Dixiecrats)
.273 38	American Nazi Party

.273 4	Republican Party
.273 6	Democratic Party
	Including Democratic Republican Party
.273 7	Leftist and worker parties
	Examples: Progressive Party (1948), Socialist Labor Party, Socialist Workers Party
.273 75	Communist Party
.273 8	Other recent parties
	Examples: environmentalist, libertarian, prohibitionist, religious, separatist parties
	See also 324.2733 for sectionalist parties

.274–.279 **Parties of states of United States and District of Columbia**

Add to base number 324.27 the numbers following —7 in notation 74–79 from Table 2 for state or District of Columbia, e.g., parties in California 324.2794; then add 0*, and to the result, except for New York, add the numbers following 324.273 in 324.27301–324.2738, e.g., Republican Party in California 324.279404

Class comprehensive works in 324.273

For parties in Hawaii, see 324.2969

A special development for New York follows

.274 7	Parties in New York
	Use 324.2747001–324.2747009 for standard subdivisions
.274 702	Historical parties
	Add to base number 324.274702 the numbers following 324.2732 in 324.27322–324.27327, e.g., Whig Party 324.2747023
.274 703	Conservative Party
.274 704	Republican Party
.274 706	Democratic Party
.274 707	Liberal Party
.274 709	Other parties
	Add to base number 324.274709 the numbers following 0 in 03–08 from table under 324.24–324.29, e.g., Communist Party 324.27470975

*Add 00 for standard subdivisions; see instructions at beginning of Table 1

.294   Parties of Australia

        Use 324.294001–324.294009 for standard subdivisions

.294 02   Historical parties

        Parties existing prior to 1945 and no longer in existence

.294 04   Country Party

.294 05   Liberal Party

.294 06   Democratic Labour Party

.294 07   Labour Party

.294 09   Other parties

        Add to base number 324.29409 the numbers following 0 in 03–08 from table under 324.24–324.29, e.g., Communist Party 324.2940975

.294 1–.294 8   Parties in states and territories of Australia

        Add to base number 324.294 the numbers following —94 in notation 941–948 from Table 2 for state or territory, e.g., parties in New South Wales 324.2944; then to the result add the numbers following 324.294 in 324.294001–324.29409, e.g., Labour Party in New South Wales 324.294407

.296 9   Parties in Hawaii

        Use 324.2969001–324.2969009 for standard subdivisions

        Add 0 to base number 324.2969, and to the result add the numbers following 324.273 in 324.2732–324.2738, e.g., Democratic Party in Hawaii 324.296906

.3   Auxiliary organizations

Organizations attached to political parties, e.g., political clubs, women's organizations, youth groups, sports clubs, communist front organizations

Class revolutionary and subversive action arms of political parties in 322.42, auxiliary organizations of international party organizations in 324.1, of specific parties in 324.24–324.29

.4   Interest and pressure groups

Class here the influence and activities of groups in extragovernmental processes; political action committees (PACs, U.S. fund-raising groups); comprehensive works on executive- and legislative-branch lobbying

Class comprehensive works on interest groups in 322.4, on pressure groups in 322.43; legislative-branch lobbying in 328.38, lobbying for a specific goal with the goal, e.g., for penal reform 364.6

.5   **Nomination of candidates**

Class here selection of convention delegates, campaigns for nomination

Use 324.5 for works on campaigns for nomination and their results (e.g., delegate counts and primary returns) only if two or more parties are involved. Use 324.24–324.29 if only one party's nomination is involved; 324.9 if both nomination and election campaigns are involved; 930–990 if there is emphasis on the effect of the nomination campaign on general history

Class nomination procedures of specific parties in 324.24–324.29

.52   By caucuses and co-option

.54   By primaries

.56   By nominating conventions

See also 324.21 for convention finance

.6   **Election systems and procedures; suffrage**

Example: procedures for contested elections

Class here comprehensive works on systems and procedures for nominations and elections

Class conduct of election campaigns in 324.7

For nomination of candidates, see 324.5

See Manual at 324.6 vs. 342.07

.609   Historical, geographical, persons treatment [*all formerly* 324.9]

.62   Suffrage

Class here voting rights [*formerly also* 323.5], qualifications for voting

.623   Women's suffrage

.63   Electoral systems

Examples: direct and indirect elections, electoral colleges, proportional representation

.64   Registration of voters

.65   Voting procedures

Former heading: Polling

Example: absentee voting

Including ballots and ballot systems, counting and certification of votes, election officials, voting machines

.66   Election frauds

Class irregularities in campaign finance in 324.78

.68   Recall

Removal of an official from office by popular vote

.7   Conduct of election campaigns

> Former heading: Practical politics
>
> Class conduct of nomination campaigns in 324.5

.72   Strategy

> Including citizen participation
>
> *For use and effect of media, see 324.73*

.73   Use and effect of media

.78   Campaign finance

> *See also 324.21 for party finance*

.9   Historical and geographical treatment of elections

> Class here campaigns, election returns and results, studies of voting behavior
>
> Historical, geographical, persons treatment of election systems and procedures relocated to 324.609
>
> Class platforms, campaign literature and propaganda, and works about them in 324.23

.901–.905   Historical periods

> Add to base number 324.90 the numbers following —090 in notation 0901–0905 from Table 1, e.g., election campaigns in the 19th century 324.9034

.91–.99   Geographical treatment

> Add to base number 324.9 notation 1–9 from Table 2, e.g., political campaigns in the United Kingdom 324.941; then to the result add historical period numbers from appropriate subdivisions of 930–990, e.g., the election campaign of 1966 in the United Kingdom 324.9410856. In all cases use one 0* except 00* for North America and South America, e.g., the election of 1964 in the United States 324.9730923, elections in South America between the World Wars 324.980033

325   International migration and colonization

> Including involuntary population transfer, population exchange
>
> Class interdisciplinary works on international movement of people in 304.82

.09   Historical, geographical, persons treatment

> Class treatment by specific continents, countries, localities in modern world in 325.4–325.9 (*not* 325.094–325.099)

.1   Immigration

.109   Historical, geographical, persons treatment

> Class immigration in specific continents, countries, localities in modern world in 325.4–325.9 (*not* 325.1094–325.1099)

*Use extra 0s for standard subdivisions; see instructions at beginning of Table 1

.2   Emigration

.209   Historical and geographical treatment

> Class treatment by specific continents, countries, localities in
> 325.23–325.29 (*not* 325.2093–325.2099)

.21   Political refugees

> Class here displaced persons

.210 9   Historical, geographical, persons treatment

> When treatment is of refugees from one country in another country,
> class in country of origin, e.g., Polish political refugees in Canada
> 325.21094380971

.23–.29   Emigration from specific continents, countries, localities

> Add to base number 325.2 notation 3–9 from Table 2, e.g., emigration from
> Japan 325.252, emigration from Japan to the United States 325.2520973

.3   Colonization

> Class here the exercise of political dominion over distant territories

.309   Historical, geographical, persons treatment

> Class colonization in specific places in modern world in 325.4–325.9
> (*not* 325.3094–325.3099), colonization by specific countries in
> 325.33–325.39 (*not* 325.3093–325.3099)

.31   Colonial administration and policy

> Class public administration of specific colonies in 354

.310 9   Historical, geographical, persons treatment

> Class administration of and policy with respect to already acquired
> colonies in 325.313–325.319 (*not* 325.31093–325.31099);
> comprehensive works on colonial policy of specific countries in
> 325.33–325.39 (*not* 325.31093–325.31099); internal administration
> of specific colonies in 354

.313–.319   Administration of and policy in respect to already acquired colonies

> Add to base number 325.31 notation 3–9 from Table 2, e.g., policies of
> the United Kingdom in its colonies 325.3141, policies of the United
> Kingdom in its Indian empire 325.31410954

.32   Imperialism

> Class comprehensive works on foreign policy in 327

.33–.39   Colonization by specific countries

> Class here comprehensive works on colonial policy of specific countries

> Add to base number 325.3 notation 3–9 from Table 2, e.g., colonization by the United Kingdom 325.341, colonization by the United Kingdom in West Africa 325.3410966

> Class colonial policy of specific countries with respect to already acquired colonies in 325.31

.4–.9   International migration to and colonization in specific continents, countries, localities in the modern world

> Class here comprehensive works on treatment of international migration and colonization limited by specific places

> Add to base number 325 notation 4–9 from Table 2, e.g., migration to Israel 325.5694

> Class emigration to specific continents, countries, localities from specific continents, countries, localities in 325.23–325.29; colonization in specific continents, countries, localities by specific countries in 325.33–325.39

326   Slavery and emancipation

> Class interdisciplinary works on slavery in 306.362

327   International relations

> Class interdisciplinary works on relations among countries in 303.482, imperialism as national policy in 325.32, military science in 355; international relations with respect to a specific subject with the subject, e.g., trade negotiations between Germany and Japan 382.0943052

> *See Manual at 341 vs. 327*

[.01]   Philosophy and theory

> Do not use; class 327.101

.06   Organizations

> Class organizations established by two or more governments in 341.2

[.068]   Management

> Do not use; class in 351.89

.09   Historical and geographical treatment

> Class here diplomatic history, international relations of or in specific areas or blocs, e.g., international relations in the Middle East 327.0956, foreign relations of the Communist bloc 327.091717

> Class foreign relations and diplomatic history of specific nations in 327.3–327.9 (*not* 327.093–327.099)

.092   Persons

> Diplomats relocated to 327.2092

.1 **Generalities of international relations**

Class here foreign policy, imperialism in international relations, international politics, power politics

Unless otherwise instructed, class generalities of international relations of specific nations in 327.3–327.9

.101 Philosophy and theory of international relations

Including the role and position of small states, the economic bases of international relations

Class here geopolitics in international relations, the nature of power in international relations

Class comprehensive works on geopolitics in 320.12

[.101 1] Geopolitics

Number discontinued; class in 327.101

.11 Specific means of attaining foreign policy goals

Use of this number for international politics discontinued; class in 327.1

For espionage and subversion, see 327.12; propaganda and war of nerves, 327.14; diplomacy, 327.2

.111 Economic activities

Example: foreign aid

Class boycotts and sanctions in 327.117

.112 Balance of power system

.114 Spheres of influence

.116 Alliances

Class here collective security

.117 Use of force and threats of force

Including boycotts and sanctions

Class war of nerves in 327.14, war in 355.02

.12 Espionage and subversion

Class here interdisciplinary works on espionage, subversion, intelligence gathering

Class military espionage and subversion in 355.343

.120 9 Historical, geographical, persons treatment

Class here comprehensive works on espionage and subversion in specific nations

Class espionage and subversion by specific nations in 327.123–327.129

.123–.129   Espionage and subversion by specific nations [*formerly* 327.3–327.9]

> Add to base number 327.12 notation 3–9 from Table 2, e.g., espionage by France 327.1244, then add 0* and to the result add notation 1–9 from Table 2, e.g., espionage by France in the Communist bloc 327.124401717

.14   Propaganda and war of nerves

> Including disinformation activities

> Class interdisciplinary works on propaganda in 303.375, comprehensive works on political propaganda in 320.014

.16   International conflict

> Class war in 355.02, of conflict involving specific means of attaining foreign policy goals in 327.11

> *See also 327.17 for peaceful resolution of conflict*

.17   International cooperation

> Class here internationalism, resolution of conflict

> Activities of nongovernmental organizations, movements, and individuals of specific nations are classed here, not with the foreign relations of specific nations in 327.3–327.9

> Class international organizations in 341.2

.172   Promotion of peace and international order

.174   Disarmament and arms control

.2   **Diplomacy**

> Use 327.2 for the methods and style of diplomacy (including protocol); 327 for the substance and content of diplomatic relations

> Class laws and rules governing diplomatic conduct in 341.33; customs of diplomacy in 399

.202 5   Directories

> Class here diplomatic lists [*formerly also* 351.892]

.209 2   Persons treatment of diplomats [*formerly also* 327.092]

> Persons treatment of nonambassadorial diplomats of specific nations relocated to 327.3–327.9

*Add 00 for standard subdivisions; see instructions at beginning of Table 1

.3–.9   Foreign relations of specific nations

Class here persons treatment of nonambassadorial diplomats of specific nations [*formerly* 327.2092]

Add to base number 327 notation 3–9 from Table 2, e.g., foreign relations of Brazil 327.81; then, for the relations between that nation and another nation or region, add 0* and to the result add notation 1–9 from Table 2, e.g., relations between Brazil and France 327.81044, between Brazil and the Arab world 327.810174927

Give priority in notation to the nation emphasized. If the emphasis is equal, give priority to the one coming first in the sequence of area notations

(Option: Give priority in notation to the nation requiring local emphasis, e.g., libraries in the United States class foreign relations between the United States and France in 327.73044)

Espionage and subversion by specific nations relocated to 327.123–327.129

328   The legislative process

Class here the legislative branch

See Manual at 320 vs. 909, 930–990

.068   Management

Class here public administration of legislative branch

Class public administration of legislative branch of specific jurisdiction in 328.4–328.9, using standard subdivision notation 0068 from table under 328.4–328.9

.09   Historical, geographical, persons treatment

Class the legislative process in specific jurisdictions in modern world in 328.4–328.9 (*not* 328.094–328.099)

.1   Rules and procedures of legislative bodies

Including rules and procedures for reporting legislative sessions, e.g., television coverage

Class comprehensive rules of order in 060.42; rules and procedures of committees of legislative bodies in 328.3653; rules and procedures of specific legislative bodies in the modern world in 328.4–328.9, using notation 05 from the add table under 328.4–328.9, e.g., rules of Canadian Parliament 328.7105

.2   Initiative and referendum

Use of this number for the legislative function discontinued; class in 328

.209   Historical, geographical, persons treatment

Class treatment in specific jurisdictions in the modern world in 328.24–328.29 (*not* 328.2094–328.2099)

.24–.29   Treatment in specific jurisdictions in the modern world

Add to base number 328.2 notation 4–9 from Table 2, e.g., initiative in California 328.2794

*Add 00 for standard subdivisions; see instructions at beginning of Table 1

.3   Legislative bodies

Use of this number for the legislative branch discontinued; class in 328

Class legislative bodies of specific jurisdictions in the modern world in 328.4–328.9, using notation 07 from the add table under 328.4–328.9

SUMMARY

328.301–.309	**Standard subdivisions and legislative reform**
.31	**Upper houses**
.32	**Lower houses**
.33	**Members and membership**
.34	**Powers, privileges, restrictions**
.35	**Sessions**
.36	**Internal organization and discipline**
.37	**Enactment of legislation**
.38	**Lobbying**
.39	**Forms of legislative bodies**

.304   Special topics

.304 2   Legislative reform

Class reform of the basis of representation in 328.334, of internal organization in 328.36

.306   Organizations and management

Class auxiliary legislative organizations in 328.361

.306 01   Interparliamentary unions

.306 8   Management

Class management of members' offices in 328.331068

.309   Historical, geographical, persons treatment

Class legislative bodies of specific jurisdictions in modern world in 328.4–328.9 (*not* 328.3094–328.3099)

.31   Upper houses

Class comprehensive works on upper and lower houses in 328.3, a specific aspect of upper houses with the aspect, e.g., treaty making power 328.346

.32   Lower houses

Class a specific aspect of lower houses with the aspect, e.g., basis of representation 328.334

.33   Members and membership

Including qualifications, terms of office

Class comprehensive persons treatment of members in 328.092, persons treatment of members of specific legislative bodies in the modern world in 328.4–328.9

.331   Work and activity of individual members

Class here constituency services, work of members' offices

.333	Compensation
.334	Basis of representation
.334 5	Election districts
	Other than districts used in proportional representation
	Class here apportionment and reapportionment, redistricting
[.334 52–.334 54]	Apportionment and reapportionment, redistricting
	Numbers discontinued; class in 328.3345
.334 55	Gerrymandering
.334 7	Proportional representation
.34	Powers, privileges, restrictions
.341	General powers
	For treaty and war powers, see 328.346
.341 2	Financial power
	Power over appropriation, borrowing and lending, currency, taxation
.341 3	General economic and public welfare powers
.345	Extralegislative powers
	Including control and oversight of the judicial branch
.345 2	Investigative power
	Including ombudsman role
	Class interdisciplinary works on ombudsmen in 351.91
.345 3	Judicial power
	Example: power to impeach
.345 4	Electoral power
.345 5	Power over appointments
.345 6	Control and oversight of executive branch [*formerly also* 351.0075]
	Class here general relations with executive branch
	Class cabinet system of executives in 321.8043, control of foreign relations in 328.346
	For ombudsman role, see 328.3452
.346	Treaty and war powers
	Class here control of foreign relations
.347	Personal privileges and immunities of legislators
	For personal immunities, see 328.348
.348	Personal immunities of legislators

.349   Restrictions on legislative power

> Examples: constitutional restrictions, checks exercised by other branches and by the electorate

.35   Sessions

> Class a specific aspect of legislative sessions with the aspect, e.g., internal organization of a session 328.36

.36   Internal organization and discipline

> *For rules, see 328.1*

.361   Auxiliary organizations

> Bodies set up to provide information, other assistance to legislative bodies

> Class legislative reference bureaus in 027.65

.362   Officers and leaders

> Class party organization in legislative bodies in 328.369

.365   Committees

> Class committee hearings and reports on a specific subject with the subject, e.g., general reports on military affairs 355; however, if the hearings and reports emphasize proposed legislation, class with the subject in law, e.g., hearings on bills governing armed services 343.013

[.365 2]   Organization, jurisdiction, membership

> Number discontinued; class in 328.365

.365 3   Rules

> Including rules of specific committees, of specific types of committees

.365 7   Specific types of committees

> Examples: standing, special, select, interim, joint, conference committees

> Class rules of specific types of committees in 328.3653, committees of specific subject jurisdiction in 329.3658

.365 8   Committees of specific subject jurisdiction

> Examples: education, foreign relations, rules committees

> Class rules of committees of specific subject jurisdiction in 328.3653

.366   Discipline of members

.369   Party organization in legislative bodies

> Class here opposition, opposition parties, party caucuses

.37	Enactment of legislation

Including repeal of legislation

See also 328.365 for committee procedures

.372	Origin

Submission by members, by executive, by outside interests

.373	Drafting
.375	Passage

Including votes and voting procedures

.377	Enactment of resolutions
.378	Enactment of specific types of legislation

Examples: public and private laws

For enactment of resolutions, see 328.377; enactment of budgets, 351.7223

.38	Lobbying
.39	Forms of legislative bodies

Examples: unicameral, bicameral

Class upper houses in 328.31, lower houses in 328.32

.4–.9   The legislative process in specific jurisdictions in the modern world

Add to base number 328 notation 4–9 from Table 2, e.g., the legislative process in Canada 328.71; then add further as follows:

001–008	Standard subdivisions
[009]	Historical and persons treatment
	Do not use; class in 09
01	Journals and calendars
02	Debates
03	Abstracts
04	Other documents
	Class here series of miscellaneous parliamentary papers and documents
05	Rules and procedures
	Including legislative manuals
	Class committee rules in 07653
07	The legislative body
	Add to 07 the numbers following 328.3 in 328.304–328.39, e.g., specific committees 07658
09	Historical and persons treatment

Class initiative and referendum in specific jurisdictions in the modern world in 328.24–328.29

[329]   [Unassigned]

Most recently used in Edition 18

330   Economics

Unless other instructions are given, observe the following table of precedence, e.g., finance as an economic factor in international economics 332.042 (*not* 337)

Cooperatives	334
Public finance	336
Factors of production	331–333
Production, Commerce (381–382), Transportation (385–388)	338
Macroeconomics and related topics	339
International economics	337
Socialism and related systems	335

Class economics of communication in 384, of transportation in 388

For commerce, see 380.1

See Manual at 650 vs. 330

SUMMARY

330.01–.09   **Standard subdivisions**
  .1   **Systems and theories**
  .9   **Economic situation and conditions**

331   **Labor economics**
  .01–.09   **Standard subdivisions**
  .1   **Labor force and market**
  .2   **Compensation and other conditions of employment**
  .3   **Workers of specific age groups**
  .4   **Women workers**
  .5   **Special categories of workers other than by age or sex**
  .6   **Categories of workers by racial, ethnic, national origin**
  .7   **Labor by industry and occupation**
  .8   **Labor unions (Trade unions), labor-management (collective) bargaining and disputes**

332   **Financial economics**
  .01–.09   **Standard subdivisions**
  .1   **Banks and banking**
  .2   **Specialized banking institutions**
  .3   **Credit and loan institutions**
  .4   **Money**
  .5   **Other mediums of exchange**
  .6   **Investment and investments**
  .7   **Credit**
  .8   **Interest and discount**
  .9   **Counterfeiting, forgery, alteration**

333	**Land economics**	
	.001–.009	Standard subdivisions
	.01–.08	[Theories and land surveys]
	.1	Public ownership and control of land and other natural resources
	.2	Ownership and control of land and natural resources by nongovernmental collectivities
	.3	Individual (Private) ownership and control of land and natural resources
	.4	Absentee ownership
	.5	Renting and leasing land and natural resources
	.7	Natural resources and energy
	.8	Subsurface resources
	.9	Other natural resources
334	**Cooperatives**	
	.01–.09	Standard subdivisions
	.1	Building and housing
	.2	Banking and credit
	.5	Consumer cooperatives
	.6	Production
	.7	Benefit societies
335	**Socialism and related systems**	
	.02	Utopian systems and schools
	.1	Systems of English origin
	.2	Systems of French origin
	.3	Systems of American origin
	.4	Marxian systems (Marxism)
	.5	Democratic socialism
	.6	Fascism
	.7	Christian socialism
	.8	Other systems
	.9	Voluntary socialist and anarchist communities
336	**Public finance**	
	.001–.008	Standard subdivisions
	.01–.09	[Governmental level; revenue; historical, geographical, persons treatment]
	.1	Nontax revenues
	.2	Taxes and taxation
	.3	Public borrowing, debt, expenditure
	.4–.9	Public finance of specific continents, countries, localities in modern world
337	**International economics**	
	.09	Historical, geographical, persons treatment
	.1	Multilateral economic cooperation
	.3–.9	Foreign economic policies and relations of specific jurisdictions and groups of jurisdictions
338	**Production**	
	.001–.009	Standard subdivisions
	.01–.09	[General topics]
	.1	Agriculture
	.2	Extraction of minerals
	.3	Other extractive industries
	.4	Secondary industries and services
	.5	General production economics
	.6	Organization of production
	.7	Business enterprises and their structure
	.8	Combinations
	.9	Economic development and growth

339	Macroeconomics and related topics
.2	Distribution of income and wealth
.3	National product, wealth, income accounts and accounting
.4	Factors affecting national product, wealth, income
.5	Macroeconomic policy

.01   Philosophy and theory

Class theories in 330.1

.015 1   Mathematical principles

See also 330.1543 for mathematical economics as a school of thought

.015 195   Statistical mathematics

Class here econometrics [*formerly* 330.028]

See Manual at 519.5, T1—015195 vs. 001.422, T1—072

.02   Miscellany

.028   Auxiliary techniques and procedures; apparatus, equipment, materials

Econometrics relocated to 330.015195

.03–.08   Standard subdivisions

.09   Historical, geographical, persons treatment of economics as a discipline

Class economic situation and conditions in 330.9

.1   Systems and theories

.12   Systems

.122   Free enterprise economy

Usually synonymous with capitalism

Including open economy (the economy of an area in which trade with other areas is unrestricted)

Class laissez-faire economic theory in 330.153

See also 382.7 for trade barriers and restrictions

.124   Planned economies

Class socialism and related systems in 335

.126   Mixed economies

Example: welfare state systems

Including interventionism

See also 330.1556 for welfare economics as a school of economic thought

.15	Schools of economic thought

Example: Chicago school of economics

Including supply-side economics

.151	Pre-classical schools

For physiocracy, see 330.152

.151 2	Ancient and medieval theories
.151 3	Mercantilism
.152	Physiocracy

Class here the school of Quesnay

.153	Classical economics

Class here the school of Smith, Malthus, Ricardo, Mill, Bastiat, Say; laissez-faire economic theory

See also 330.157 for neoclassical school

.154	Methodological schools

Schools based on employment of specific methods of analysis

.154 2	Historical school

Class here the school of Roscher, Knies, Hildebrand, Schmoller, Bücher, Knapp

.154 3	Mathematical economics

Class here the schools of Cournot, Dupuit, Pareto

Class mathematics applied to economics as a whole in 330.0151

See also 330.157 for the marginal utility school

.155	Miscellaneous schools

Only those named below

Including ethical, institutional, romantic, social justice schools; universalism; single-tax school

Neoclassical school relocated to 330.157

.155 6	Welfare economics school
.156	Keynesianism
.157	Marginal utility school

Variant names: neoclassical [*formerly also* 330.155], Austrian school

Class here the school of W.S. Jevons, Menger, Walras, Wieser, Böhm-Bawerk, Von Mises

See also 330.1543 for the mathematical economics school of Cournot, Dupuit, Pareto

(.159)	Socialist and related schools

          (Optional number; prefer 335)

          Add to base number 330.159 the numbers following 335 in 335.1–335.9, e.g., Marxian systems 330.1594

.16   Theories of wealth

.17   Theories of property

.9   Economic situation and conditions

Class here works describing situation and conditions at both the macroeconomic (aggregate) level and the microeconomic level (level of the individual unit, such as the household or firm)

Class policies to promote economic growth and development in 338.9, macroeconomic policies in 339.5

.901–.905   Historical periods

Add to base number 330.90 the numbers following —090 in notation 0901–0905 from Table 1, e.g., economic situation in 1960–1969 330.9046

.91–.99   Geographical treatment (Economic geography)

(Option: Class in 910.133)

Add to base number 330.9 notation 1–9 from Table 2, e.g., economic situation and conditions in France 330.944; then add 0* (except 00 for North and South America) and to the result add historical period numbers from appropriate subdivisions of 930–990, e.g., economic situation and conditions in France under Louis XIV 330.944033, in the United States during Reconstruction period 330.97308, in South America in 20th century 330.98003

> **331–333 Labor, financial, land economics**

Class comprehensive works on labor, financial, land economics in 330; comprehensive works on labor, capital, land considered as factors of production in 338.01

*Add 00 for standard subdivisions; see instructions at beginning of Table 1

331   Labor economics

Class here industrial relations, interdisciplinary works on labor

Unless other instructions are given, observe the following table of precedence, e.g., compensation of women in banking 331.42813321 (*not* 331.2813321 or 331.7613321)

Choice of vocation	331.702
Labor force by personal characteristics	331.3–.6
Labor force and market	331.1
Compensation and other conditions of employment	331.2
Labor unions (Trade unions), labor-management (collective) bargaining and disputes	331.8
Labor by industry and occupation (*except* 331.702)	331.7

Class economic conditions of laboring classes in 330.9, full employment policies in 339.5

See also 305.562 for sociology of laboring classes, 306.36 for sociology of labor, 350.1 for personnel management in government, 658.3 for comprehensive works on personnel management

See Manual at 331 vs.331.8; 658.3 vs.331

SUMMARY

331.01–.09	**Standard subdivisions**
.1	**Labor force and market**
.2	**Compensation and other conditions of employment**
.3	**Workers of specific age groups**
.4	**Women workers**
.5	**Special categories of workers other than by age or sex**
.6	**Categories of workers by racial, ethnic, national origin**
.7	**Labor by industry and occupation**
.8	**Labor unions (Trade unions), labor-management (collective) bargaining and disputes**

.01   Philosophy and theory

.011   Rights and position of labor

Examples: right of labor to what it produces, right to earn a living

Including relation of labor to capital

Do not use for systems theory, analysis, design; class in 331.01

Class open shop, right-to-work in 331.8892

.011 2   Industrial democracy

Determination of a company's policies affecting the welfare of its workers by joint action of management and worker representatives

Class role of labor unions in industrial democracy in 331.88, producer cooperatives in 334.6, guild socialism in 335.15, syndicalism in 335.82, worker control of industry in 338.6

See also 658.3152 for employee representation in management discussed from the managerial viewpoint

| .012 | Satisfactions and dissatisfactions of labor |

Do not use for classification of occupations; class in 331.70012

| .013 | Freedom, dignity, value of labor |

| .04 | Industrial relations in specific industries and occupations and specific groups of industries and occupations |

| .041 | In industries and occupations other than extractive, manufacturing, construction |

Class here industrial relations in service industries and occupations

Add to base number 331.041 notation 001–999, e.g., industrial relations in clerical occupations 331.04165137

| .042–.049 | In extractive, manufacturing, construction industries and occupations |

Add to base number 331.04 the numbers following 6 in 620–690, e.g., industrial relations in chemical industries 331.046

.1 Labor force and market

Comprehensive works on employment and unemployment are classed in this number; however, works that merely give the number and characteristics of employed and unemployed workers without discussing the labor market are classed in 331.11. If in doubt, prefer 331.1

SUMMARY

331.11	Labor force
.12	Labor market
.13	Maladjustments in labor market

| .11 | Labor force |

All who are employed or available for employment

Class here human resources, man- and womanpower, labor supply, size of labor force

Comprehensive works on labor force and labor market are classed in 331.1. Works that discuss the labor force only in relation to the demand for labor are classed in 331.12. Employment and labor actively employed are classed in 331.125

See also 331.123 for demand (need, requirements) for labor, 331.8732 for union membership

| .111 | Geographical distribution |

Examples: urban, rural

| .114 | Qualifications and personal characteristics |

| .114 2 | Qualifications |

Including innate physical and mental capacity

| .114 22 | By level of skills |

Examples: skilled, semiskilled, unskilled

.114 23	By level of education
.114 24	By level of experience
.114 3	Personal characteristics

Class workers with specific characteristics in 331.3–331.6

.117	Systems of labor

See also 306.36 for social aspects of systems of labor

.117 2	Free labor
.117 3	Compulsory labor
.117 32	State labor (Drafted workers)
.117 34	Slave labor
.118	Labor productivity
.119	Labor force in specific industries and occupations and groups of industries and occupations

Class comprehensive works on labor in specific industries and occupations and groups of industries and occupations in 331.7

.119 04	Special topics
.119 042	Labor force in general categories of occupations

Examples: civilian, governmental (public service), nongovernmental, nonagricultural, service, white-collar occupations

.119 1	In industries and occupations other than extractive, manufacturing, construction

Add to base number 331.1191 notation 001–999, e.g., labor force in stenography 331.11916513741; however, class labor force in general categories of occupations, e.g., governmental (public service) occupations, in 331.119042

.119 2–.119 9	In extractive, manufacturing, construction industries and occupations

Add to base number 331.119 the numbers following 6 in 620–690, e.g., labor force in automobile manufacturing 331.119292

.12   Labor market

The activities of and opportunities for buying and selling labor

Class here supply of labor in relation to demand

Use of this number for comprehensive works on labor force and labor market discontinued; class in 331.1

For maladjustments in labor market, see 331.13

SUMMARY

331.120 4	**Special topics**
.120 42	**Government policy on the labor market**
.123	**Demand (Need, Requirements) for labor**
.124	**Job vacancies (Openings, Opportunities)**
.125	**Labor actively employed**
.126	**Turnover**
.127	**Mobility of labor**
.128	**Placement**
.129	**Labor market by industry and occupation**

.120 4   Special topics

.120 42   Government policy on the labor market

General aspects: developing, utilizing, employing needed labor

Here are classed government labor policies and programs discussed in terms of broader purposes than just combating unemployment, e.g., public service employment as a countercyclical measure to provide both jobs for the unemployed and assistance to distressed areas and state and local governments. Works about government labor policies and programs that discuss them solely in terms of prevention and relief of unemployment are classed in 331.1377

Class policies designed to secure full employment through fiscal and monetary policy in 339.5; policy with respect to a specific aspect of labor force and market with the subject, e.g., assistance in finding jobs 331.128

See also 362.85 for social programs for laboring classes, 370 for education

.123   Demand (Need, Requirements) for labor

Class job vacancies (openings, opportunities) in 331.124, shortages and surpluses in 331.136

.123 1   In industries and occupations other than extractive, manufacturing, construction

Class here demand (need, requirements) for labor in service industries and occupations

Add to base number 331.1231 notation 001–999, e.g., demand for teachers 331.12313711

.123 2–.123 9   In extractive, manufacturing, construction industries and occupations

Add to base number 331.123 the numbers following 6 in 620–690, e.g., demand for carpenters 331.12394

.124	Job vacancies (Openings, Opportunities)
.124 1	In industries and occupations other than extractive, manufacturing, construction

Class here job vacancies (openings, opportunities) in service industries and occupations

Add to base number 331.1241 notation 001–999, e.g., opportunities in librarianship 331.124102

.124 2–.124 9	In extractive, manufacturing, construction industries and occupations

Add to base number 331.124 the numbers following 6 in 620–690, e.g., opportunities in paper manufacture 331.12476

.125	Labor actively employed

That portion of the total available supply of labor employed at any given time

Including types of employment

Class here utilization of human resources, employment, comprehensive works on employment and compensation

Use of this number for comprehensive works on employment and unemployment discontinued; class in 331.1

Class compensation in 331.21

See also 331.126 for turnover, 331.137 for unemployment

.125 1	In industries and occupations other than extractive, manufacturing, construction

Class here labor actively employed in service industries and occupations

Add to base number 331.1251 notation 001–999, e.g., labor actively employed in education 331.125137

.125 2–.125 9	In extractive, manufacturing, construction industries and occupations

Add to base number 331.125 the numbers following 6 in notation 620–690, e.g., labor actively employed in the plumbing industry 331.125961

.126	Turnover
.127	Mobility of labor
.127 09	Historical and persons treatment

Class geographical treatment in 331.1279

.127 2	Interoccupational mobility
.127 9	Geographical mobility
.127 91	International mobility

Example: brain drain

.127 93–.127 99	Within specific countries and lesser areas

Add to base number 331.1279 notation 3–9 from Table 2, e.g., mobility of labor within Canada 331.127971

Class mobility between countries and continents in 331.12791

.128	Placement

Formal and informal arrangements for matching people and jobs

Class here employment agencies, job banks, labor exchanges, sources of job information

Class lists of job openings in 331.124

See also 362 for employment services viewed as a solution to social problems; 650.14 for success in, techniques of job hunting

.129	Labor market by industry and occupation

Class specific aspects of labor market by industry and occupation in 331.123–331.128

.129 04	Special topics
.129 042	Labor market by general categories of occupations

Examples: civilian, governmental (public service), nongovernmental, nonagricultural, service, white-collar occupations

.129 1	Labor market by industries and occupations other than extractive, manufacturing, construction

Add to base number 331.1291 notation 001–999, e.g., labor market in stenography 331.12916513741; however, class labor market in general categories of occupations, e.g., governmental (public service) occupations, in 331.129042

.129 2–.129 9	Labor market by extractive, manufacturing, construction industries and occupations

Add to base number 331.129 the numbers following 6 in notation 620–690, e.g., labor market in automobile manufacturing 331.129292

.13	Maladjustments in labor market

Including underemployment, underemployed

.133	Discrimination in employment

General aspects: history, description, extent

Class here equal employment opportunity programs

Class discrimination in relation to a specific aspect of industrial relations with the subject, e.g., discrimination as a factor affecting compensation 331.2153, discrimination by unions 331.8732

See also 351.104 for personnel policies on discrimination in government, 658.3 for comprehensive works about personnel policies on discrimination

.136	Labor shortages and surpluses
.137	Unemployment

Class here unemployed

.137 04	Kinds of unemployment

See Manual at 331.13704 vs. 331.1372

.137 041	Structural unemployment

Unemployment resulting from changes in the overall environment, principally changes in population, government policies, technology, and consumer tastes, but not from a general economic recession

Class technological unemployment in 331.137042

.137 042	Technological unemployment

Including unemployment due to automation

.137 044	Seasonal unemployment
.137 045	Frictional unemployment

Irreducible minimum of people out of work because of need or desire to change jobs

.137 047	Cyclical unemployment

Unemployment due to economic fluctuations

[.137 09]	Historical, geographical, persons treatment

Do not use; class in 331.1379

> 331.137 2–331.137 7 Specific elements of unemployment

Class comprehensive works in 331.137

.137 2	Causes of unemployment

Class macroeconomic causes in 339

See Manual at 331.13704 vs. 331.1372

.137 3	Effects of unemployment
.137 4	Distribution and incidence of unemployment
.137 7	Prevention and relief of unemployment

Class a specific measure of prevention or relief with the subject, e.g., work sharing 331.2572, economic stabilization 339.5, welfare 362.85

See also 331.12042 for government labor policies with broader purposes than just combating unemployment

| .137 8 | Unemployment among general classes of labor, in specific industries and occupations, in specific groups of industries and occupations |

Class specific elements regardless of class, industry, occupation in 331.1372–331.1377

| .137 804 | General classes of unemployed |

Persons with various degrees of education, skill, experience

Class unemployed persons having specific personal characteristics in 331.3–331.6

| .137 81 | Unemployment in industries and occupations other than extractive, manufacturing, construction |

Class here unemployment in service industries and occupations

Add to base number 331.13781 notation 001–999, e.g., unemployment in clerical occupations 331.1378165137

| .137 82–.137 89 | Unemployment in extractive, manufacturing, construction industries and occupations |

Add to base number 331.1378 the numbers following 6 in 620–690, e.g., unemployment in the automobile industry 331.1378292

| .137 9 | Historical, geographical, persons treatment |

Add to base number 331.1379 notation 01–99 from Table 2, e.g., unemployment in the United States 331.137973

Class historical and geographical treatment of specific elements of unemployment in 331.1372–331.1377, of unemployment among general classes of labor and in specific industries and occupations in 331.1378

.2 Compensation and other conditions of employment

Collective bargaining on compensation and other conditions of employment is classed in 331.89, but the compensation and other conditions that result from such bargaining are classed here

See also 658.312 for compensation and other conditions of employment discussed from the managerial viewpoint

SUMMARY

331.204	**In specific industries and occupations and specific groups of industries and occupations**
.21	**Compensation**
.22	**Compensation differentials**
.23	**Guaranteed-wage plans**
.25	**Other conditions of employment**
.28	**Compensation in specific industries and occupations and specific groups of industries and occupations**
.29	**Historical, geographical, persons treatment of compensation**

| .204 | In specific industries and occupations and specific groups of industries and occupations |

.204 1	In industries and occupations other than extractive, manufacturing, construction

Class here compensation and other conditions of employment in service industries and occupations

Add to base number 331.2041 notation 001–999, e.g., compensation and other conditions of employment in clerical occupations 331.204165137

.204 2–.204 9	In extractive, manufacturing, construction industries and occupations

Add to base number 331.204 the numbers following 6 in 620–690, e.g., compensation and other conditions of employment in chemical industries 331.2046

.21	Compensation

Class here wages, comprehensive works on wage-price policy

Class wage-price controls to combat inflation in 332.415, price policy in 338.52, wage-price policy as a factor in economic stabilization 339.5

For compensation differentials, see 331.22; fringe benefits, 331.255; compensation in specific industries and occupations, 331.28

.210 1	Theories

Examples: bargain theory, marginal productivity theory, national income theory, subsistence theory ("iron law"), wages fund theory

[.210 9]	Historical, geographical, persons treatment

Do not use; class in 331.29

.215	Factors affecting compensation

Including methods of determination, e.g., intra- and interindustry comparison; criteria used in determination, e.g., cost of living as a compensation determinant

Class minimum wage policies in 331.23

See also 332.415 for wage-price controls to combat inflation, 339.5 for wage control as a factor in economic stabilization

.215 3	Discrimination and anti-discrimination policies

Class here comparable worth, equal pay for equal work

.216	Methods of compensation
.216 2	Time payments

Examples: hourly, weekly, monthly, annual periods

Class guaranteed-wage plans in 331.23

.216 4	Incentive compensation

Examples: stock ownership and purchase plans [*formerly* 331.255], transfer of stock and stock options to employees, profit-sharing; bonuses, group incentives; piecework, combined time- and piecework

Class tips in 331.2166

.216 6	Other compensation

.216 6   Other compensation

Examples: professional and subcontracting fees, tips, weighting

.22   Compensation differentials

Differences among industries, occupations, regions

Including comparison among firms in the same industry

Class determination of compensation, factors affecting compensation in 331.215

See also 331.29 for general surveys of compensation in an area, not emphasizing differences

.23   Guaranteed-wage plans

Including minimum wage

Class guaranteed minimum income in 362.582

.25   Other conditions of employment

Examples: economic aspects of physical working conditions, e.g., space, ventilation, working facilities; quality of work life

Including telecommuting

.252   Pensions

Including retirement age

Class here retirement benefits, interdisciplinary works on pensions

Class comprehensive works on administration of pensions in 658.3253, pensions provided by unions in 331.8735, annuities resulting from retirement and estate planning in 332.02401, public administration of pensions for government (public service) employees in 351.5, pensions (annuities) provided through insurance in 368.37, government pension plans for the population at large in 368.43

Pensions for government (public service) employees are classed in 331.2529135

.252 2   Pension reform

Including preservation and transfer of vested rights in pensions

.252 9   Pensions in specific industries and occupations and groups of industries and occupations

.252 91   In industries and occupations other than mining, manufacturing, construction

Class here pensions in service industries and occupations

Add to base number 331.25291 notation 001–999, e.g., veterans' pensions 331.25291355 [*formerly* 355.1151], pensions for government employees in general 331.2529135

.252 92–.252 99   In extractive, manufacturing, construction industries and occupations

Add to base number 331.2529 the numbers following 6 in 620–690, e.g., pensions in construction trades 331.252924

.255	Fringe benefits

.255   **Fringe benefits**

Examples: health and welfare programs, insurance, unemployment compensation

Class here interdisciplinary works on fringe benefits

Class transfer of stock and stock options in 331.2164, fringe benefits provided by unions in 331.8735, fringe benefits for veterans of military service and their survivors in 362.86, benefits provided through insurance in 368.3, benefits provided through government-sponsored social insurance in 368.4, comprehensive works on administration of employee benefits in 658.325

Stock ownership and purchase plans relocated to 331.2164

For pensions, see 331.252

.257   **Hours**

.257 2   **Work day and week**

Including job sharing, work sharing, part-time employment

Class here flexible working hours, shift work

.257 22   **Work week**

Including compressed work schedules, e.g., four-day forty-hour week

.257 23   **Work day**

Example: eight-hour day

For rest periods, see 331.2576

.257 4   **Night, holy day, Sunday, holiday work**

See also 331.2572 for shift work

.257 6   **Leave and rest periods (breaks)**

Examples: paid vacations and holidays

.257 62   **Sick leave**

.257 63   **Special-purpose leave**

Examples: educational and paternity leave, sabbaticals

Class maternity leave in 331.44

.259	Training, worker security, regulation of worker conduct

.259 2   Training

Class here interdisciplinary works on vocational training

Class vocational training conducted by an educational system at the secondary level in 373.2, at the adult level in 374.013; managerial aspects of training by the employer in 658.3124

.259 22   Apprenticeship

Class apprentices as a special class of workers in 331.55, work experience as part of education in 371.38

.259 24   Retraining

.259 6   Worker security

Examples: employment security, job tenure

Including right to organize, rights of transfer and promotion, seniority

.259 8   Regulation of worker conduct

Including absenteeism, discipline

.28   Compensation in specific industries and occupations and specific groups of industries and occupations

Class specific elements of compensation in specific industries and occupations in 331.21–331.23

.281   In industries and occupations other than extractive, manufacturing, construction

Class here compensation in service industries and occupations

Add to base number 331.281 notation 001–999, e.g., compensation of bankers 331.2813321

.282–.289   In extractive, manufacturing, construction industries and occupations

Add to base number 331.28 the numbers following 6 in 620–690, e.g., compensation in the mining industry 331.2822, average factory compensation 331.287

.29   Historical, geographical, persons treatment of compensation

Add to base number 331.29 notation 01–99 from Table 2, e.g., compensation in Australia 331.2994

Class historical, geographical, persons treatment of specific elements of compensation in 331.21–331.23, of compensation in specific industries and occupations in 331.28

General surveys of compensation in an area are classed here, but surveys that emphasize the differences in compensation among industries, occupations, and regions are classed in 331.22. If in doubt, prefer 331.29

Wage-price policies of specific jurisdictions are classed here; but if the policies are discussed in relation to stabilizing the economy, they are classed in 339.5

> ### 331.3–331.6 Labor force by personal characteristics

Class here labor force and market, compensation and other conditions of employment, specific industries and occupations, labor unions, labor-management bargaining with respect to special classes of workers

Unless other instructions are given, class complex subjects with aspects in two or more subdivisions of this schedule in the number coming first in the schedule, e.g., young Chinese women 331.344089951 (*not* 331.4 or 331.6251)

Class comprehensive works in 331.1143; choice of vocation for persons with specific personal characteristics in 331.702; employment services as a form of social service to persons with specific personal characteristics in 362.6–362.8, e.g., sheltered employment for aged people 362.64

.3   Workers of specific age groups

.31   Children

Through age thirteen

.34   Young people

Through age thirty-five

For children, see 331.31; young people in specific industries and occupations, 331.38

.341–.342   Specific aspects of employment of young people

Add to base number 331.34 the numbers following 331 in 331.1–331.2, e.g., training of young workers in 331.342592

Class specific aspects of employment of specific kinds of young people in 331.344–331.346

.344–.346   Employment of specific kinds of young people

Add to base number 331.34 the numbers following 331 in 331.4–331.6, e.g., Afro-American youth 331.346396073; however, class apprentices in 331.55

.347   Persons aged 14 through 20

Class specific aspects of employment of persons aged 14 through 20 in 331.341–331.342, employment of specific kinds of persons aged 14 through 20 in 331.344–331.346

.348   Persons aged 21 through 35

Class specific aspects of employment of persons aged 21 through 35 in 331.341–331.342, employment of specific kinds of persons aged 21 through 35 in 331.344–331.346

.38   Young people in specific industries and occupations and specific groups of industries and occupations

        Children and young adults

        Class specific aspects of employment of young people in specific industries and occupations in 331.341–331.342, employment of specific kinds of young people in specific industries and occupations in 331.344–331.346

.381   In industries and occupations other than extractive, manufacturing, construction

          Class here young people in service industries and occupations

          Add to base number 331.381 notation 001–999, e.g., young people in clerical occupations 331.38165137

.382–.389   In extractive, manufacturing, construction industries and occupations

          Add to base number 331.38 the numbers following 6 in 620–690, e.g., young textile workers 331.3877

.39   Other age groups

.394   Middle-aged workers

.398   Older workers

        Former heading: Aged 65 and over

.398 8   In specific industries and occupations and specific groups of industries and occupations

.398 81   In industries and occupations other than extractive, manufacturing, construction

          Class here older workers in service industries and occupations

          Add to base number 331.39881 notation 001–999, e.g., older workers in clerical occupations 331.3988165137

.398 82–.398 89 In extractive, manufacturing, construction industries and occupations

          Add to base number 331.3988 the numbers following 6 in 620–690, e.g., older agricultural workers in 331.39883

.4   **Women workers**

      See also 305.43 for sociological aspects of women's occupations

.41–.42   Specific aspects of employment of women

        Add to base number 331.4 the numbers following 331 in 331.1–331.2, e.g., discrimination against women 331.4133, compensation of women in banking 331.42813321

        Class specific aspects of employment of married women in 331.43, of working mothers in 331.44; women with respect to labor unions and collective bargaining in 331.47

.43   Married women

        Class working mothers in 331.44

.44	Working mothers

Including expectant mothers, maternity leave

.47	Labor unions (trade unions) and labor-management (collective) bargaining

Add to base number 331.47 the numbers following 331.8 in 331.87–331.89, e.g., women in labor unions 331.478

.48	Women workers in specific industries and occupations and specific groups of industries and occupations

Class specific aspects of employment of women in specific industries and occupations in 331.41–331.42, married women in specific industries and occupations in 331.43, working mothers in specific industries and occupations in 331.44

.481	In industries and occupations other than extractive, manufacturing, construction

Class here women in service industries and occupations

Add to base number 331.481 notation 001–999, e.g., women in advertising 331.4816591

.482–.489	In extractive, manufacturing, construction industries and occupations

Add to base number 331.48 the numbers following 6 in 620–690, e.g., women pulp and paper workers 331.4876

.5	**Special categories of workers other than by age or sex**

For categories of workers by racial, ethnic, national origin, see 331.6

.51	Prisoners and ex-offenders

Examples: political and war prisoners

.52	Veterans

Class here nonmilitary labor of former members of the armed forces

See also 331.25291355 for pensions received because of military service, 331.761355 for military labor

.54	Workers in special economic situations

Class here economically disadvantaged workers not provided for elsewhere

.542	Contract workers

.544	Migrant and casual workers

Migrant workers: workers who regularly shift from one work area to another throughout the year, e.g., agricultural workers following seasonal planting and harvests in various areas

Standard subdivisions are added for migrant workers alone

See also 331.62 for immigrant and alien workers

.55   Apprentices

[*Formerly also* 607.33 or with the specific subject with use of notation 073 from Table 1]

Class training of apprentices in 331.25922

.59   Workers with physical and mental disabilities

Example: developmentally disabled workers

Standard subdivisions are added for workers with physical and mental disabilities and for workers with physical disabilities alone

Add to base number 331.59 the numbers following —087 in notation 0871–0875 in Table 1, e.g., workers with impaired vision 331.591

.6   **Categories of workers by racial, ethnic, national origin**

.62   Immigrants and aliens

See also 331.544 for migrant workers

.620 9   Historical, geographical, persons treatment

Class here immigrant and alien workers in specific areas, e.g., immigrant workers in Canada 331.620971

Class immigrant and alien workers from specific jurisdictions in 331.621–331.629

.621–.629   Immigrants and aliens by place of origin

Add to base number 331.62 notation 1–9 from Table 2, e.g., immigrant workers from China 331.6251; then, for area located, add 0* and again add notation 1–9 from Table 2, e.g., immigrant workers from China in California 331.62510794

See also 331.6209 for immigrant and alien workers in specific areas

.63   Native-born nonindigenous ethnic groups

Use 331.63001–331.63009 for standard subdivisions

Add to base number 331.63 notation 03–99 from Table 5, e.g., Afro-Americans 331.6396073, Afro-American workers in Alabama 331.63960730761

.69   Indigenous ethnic groups

Use 331.69001–331.69009 for standard subdivisions

Add to base number 331.69 notation 03–99 from Table 5, e.g., Black South Africans in South Africa 331.69968, North American native peoples in North America 331.6997

*Add 00 for standard subdivisions; see instructions at beginning of Table 1

.7   **Labor by industry and occupation**

Including professional relationships

Use 331.7001–331.7009 for standard subdivisions

Class professional relationships in a specific industry or occupation with the industry or occupation, using notation 023 from Table 1, e.g., professional relationships in law 340.023

.702   Choice of vocation

Class here choice of vocation for persons with specific personal characteristics, e.g., veterans; interdisciplinary works describing vocations and occupational specialties; interdisciplinary works on career opportunities and vocational counseling

Class studies of vocational interest in 158.6; vocational counseling in schools in 371.425; job hunting in 650.14; descriptions of, career opportunities in, choice of vocation with regard to specific vocations and occupational specialties with the subject, using notation 023 from Table 1, e.g., accounting 657.023

.702 3   For persons at specific educational levels

.71   Professional and managerial occupations

Class specific professional and managerial occupations in 331.761

.712   Professional

.714   Managerial

.76   Specific industries and occupations

Class specific groups of occupations in 331.79

.761   Industries and occupations other than extractive, manufacturing, construction

Add to base number 331.761 notation 001–999, e.g., labor in the banking industry 331.7613321; however, class governmental (public service) occupations in 331.795

.762–.769   Extractive, manufacturing, construction industries and occupations

Add to base number 331.76 the numbers following 6 in 620–690, e.g., food processing 331.7664

.79   Specific groups of occupations

Unless other instructions are given, class complex subjects with aspects in two or more subdivisions of 331.79 in the one coming last, e.g., white-collar governmental (public-service) occupations 331.795 (*not* 331.792)

Class agricultural occupations in 331.763

For professional and managerial occupations, see 331.71

.792   White-collar occupations

.793   Service occupations

.794   Industrial occupations

Including the work of artisans and supervisors; skilled, semiskilled work

For unskilled work, see 331.798

.795   Governmental (public service) occupations

Occupations of elected and appointed civil servants

.798   Unskilled work

.8   Labor unions (Trade unions), labor-management (collective) bargaining and disputes

Class here interdisciplinary works on labor movements

Class comprehensive works on industrial democracy in 331.0112; specific aspects of the labor movement with the aspect, e.g., political activities of labor movements 322.2

See Manual at 331 vs.331.8

SUMMARY

331.87	Labor union organization
.88	Labor unions (Trade unions)
.89	Labor-management (Collective) bargaining and disputes

.87   Labor union organization

See also 331.88 for comprehensive works about labor unions

.871   Constitutions, bylaws, rules

.872   Levels of organization

Examples: locals, nationals, federations

.873   Specific aspects of union organization

Example: discipline of members

.873 2   Membership and membership policies

Including discrimination by unions

Class discrimination by unions against workers with specific personal characteristics in 331.3–331.6, e.g., discrimination against women 331.47732

.873 3   Officers and leaders

.873 5   Benefits, funds, property

.874   Union elections and conventions

.88   Labor unions (Trade unions)

Class here unions organized along religious lines, e.g., Christian trade unions

For labor union organization, see 331.87

See also 322.2 for political activities of labor unions, 658.3153 for the managerial viewpoint on labor unions

.880 1   Theory of unions

Examples: countermonopoly theory; theories of unions as instruments of class struggle, as instruments of industrial democracy, as instruments for worker control of industry

Including anti-union theories

See also 331.0112 for industrial democracy, 338.6 for worker control of industry

.880 4   Special topics

.880 41   White-collar unions

.880 42   Blue-collar unions

.880 9   Historical, geographical, persons treatment of labor unions

.880 91   Treatment by areas, regions, places in general

Class here international unions

Class international unions with members from only two countries in 331.88094–331.88099, using the comprehensive notation from Table 2 for the two countries, e.g., unions with United States and Canadian workers in 331.88097

.881   Labor unions (Trade unions) in specific industries and occupations and specific groups of industries and occupations

.881 1   In industries and occupations other than extractive, manufacturing, construction

Class here labor unions (trade unions) in service industries and occupations

Add to base number 331.8811 notation 001–999, e.g., teachers' unions 331.88113711

.881 2–.881 9   In extractive, manufacturing, construction industries and occupations

Add to base number 331.881 the numbers following 6 in 620–690, e.g., garment workers' unions 331.88187

.883   Kinds of unions

Class specific kinds of unions in specific industries and occupations in 331.881

For revolutionary unions, see 331.886

.883 2	Craft unions

Unions of workers practicing a specific trade or occupation regardless of the industry in which they are employed

Class semi-industrial unions in 331.8833

.883 3	Industrial unions

Unions in a specific industry or group of industries regardless of craft or occupation practiced

Class here semi-industrial unions (those representing many but not all of the workers in an industry, e.g., a union that represents all except the maintenance workers)

.883 4	Company unions

Unaffiliated labor unions of the employees of a single firm

.886	Revolutionary unions

Example: Industrial Workers of the World (IWW)

.889	Union security arrangements

.889 2	Shop arrangements

Examples: closed shop, open shop, union shop

Including preferential hiring, right to work, sole bargaining rights

Class right to work as a government measure to deal with labor-management (collective) bargaining and disputes in 331.898

.889 4	Control of hiring and layoffs

Examples: hiring halls, licenses, control of apprenticeships

.889 6	Dues checkoff, make-work arrangements (featherbedding), control of grievance procedures

Use of this number for other union security measures discontinued; class in 331.889

.89	Labor-management (Collective) bargaining and disputes

Here is classed the process of collective bargaining on compensation and other conditions of employment; however, the compensation and other conditions that result are classed in 331.2

See also 658.3154 for works treating collective bargaining from the managerial viewpoint

See Manual at 331 vs.331.8

SUMMARY

331.890 4	**In specific industries and occupations and specific groups of industries and occupations**
.891	**Procedures**
.892	**Strikes**
.893	**Other labor measures**
.894	**Management measures**
.898	**Government measures**

.890 4	In specific industries and occupations and specific groups of industries and occupations
.890 41	In industries and occupations other than extractive, manufacturing, construction

> Class here labor-management (collective) bargaining and disputes in service industries and occupations

> Add to base number 331.89041 notation 001–999, e.g., labor-management bargaining in hospitals 331.8904136211

.890 42–.890 49	In extractive, manufacturing, construction industries and occupations

> Add to base number 331.8904 the numbers following 6 in 620–690, e.g., labor-management bargaining and disputes in the garment industry 331.890487

.891	Procedures
.891 2	Preliminaries

> Examples: organizing, winning recognition, negotiation of contract

.891 4	Conciliation measures
.891 42	Mediation
.891 43	Arbitration
.891 5	Negotiation during life of contract

> Including cancellation of labor contracts

.892	Strikes

> *See also 331.8914 for conciliation measures*

.892 01	Theory of strikes

> Including right to strike, general theories about effects of strikes

> Effects of strikes on specific things are classed with the thing, e.g., effect of strikes on profitability of mining industries 338.23

[.892 09]	Historical, geographical, persons treatment

> Do not use; class in 331.8929

.892 1	Strike votes

> 331.892 2–331.892 6 Kinds of strikes

Unless other instructions are given, observe the following table of precedence, e.g., union-authorized general strikes 331.8925 (*not* 331.8922)

General strikes	331.8925
Sympathetic strikes	331.8923
Protest stoppages, sit-down strikes	331.8926
Unauthorized (Wildcat) strikes	331.8924
Union-authorized strikes	331.8922

Class comprehensive works in 331.892, specific kinds of strikes in specific industries and occupations in 331.8928

.892 2   Union-authorized strikes

Former heading: Organized

Not otherwise provided for

Examples: economic, jurisdictional strikes

Class here official strikes

.892 3   Sympathetic strikes

.892 4   Unauthorized (Wildcat) strikes

Not provided for elsewhere

Class here unofficial strikes

.892 5   General strikes

Work stoppages throughout an area

Class interdisciplinary works on general strikes in 322.2

.892 6   Protest stoppages, sit-down strikes

Use of this number for other strikes discontinued; class in 331.892

Class protest stoppages throughout an area in 331.8925

.892 7   Picketing

.892 8   Strikes in specific industries and occupations and specific groups of industries and occupations

.892 81   In industries and occupations other than extractive, manufacturing, construction

Class here strikes in service industries and occupations

Add to base number 331.89281 notation 001–999, e.g., teachers' strikes 331.892813711

.892 82–.892 89   In extractive, manufacturing, construction industries and occupations

Add to base number 331.8928 the numbers following 6 in 620–690, e.g., strikes of rubber workers 331.8928782

.892 9   Historical, geographical, persons treatment

Add to base number 331.8929 notation 01–99 from Table 2, e.g., strikes in Great Britain 331.892941

Class specific aspects of strikes in specific periods and places in 331.8921–331.8927, strikes in specific industries and occupations in specific periods and places in 331.8928

.893   Other labor measures

Examples: boycotts, injunctions, political action, sabotage

Class here comprehensive works on labor violence

Class violence in strikes in 331.892

.894   Management measures

Examples: blacklisting, white-listing, injunctions, labor espionage, lockouts, political action, yellow-dog contracts

.898   Government measures

Example: right-to-work policy

Class comprehensive works on right to work in 331.8892

For conciliation measures, see 331.8914

.898 2   Strike requirements

Examples: purpose, notice, cooling-off periods, exhaustion of other means

.898 4   Use of troops

332   Financial economics

For public finance, see 336

See Manual at 332 vs. 338, 658.15; 339 vs. 332, 336

SUMMARY

332.01–.09	**Standard subdivisions**
.1	**Banks and banking**
.2	**Specialized banking institutions**
.3	**Credit and loan institutions**
.4	**Money**
.5	**Other mediums of exchange**
.6	**Investment and investments**
.7	**Credit**
.8	**Interest and discount**
.9	**Counterfeiting, forgery, alteration**

.024   Personal finance

Class management of personal expenditure in 640.42, a specific aspect of personal finance not provided for here with the subject, e.g., investment 332.678, consumer information 381.33

See Manual at 332.024 vs. 640.42

.024 001–.024 007   Standard subdivisions

.024 008	Personal finance with respect to groups of persons
[.024 008 1–.024 008 8]	Personal finance with respect to specific miscellaneous kinds of persons

> Do not use; class in 332.02403–332.02499

.024 009	Historical, geographical, persons treatment
.024 01	Increasing income, net worth, financial security

Including financial independence; estate planning; planning for retirement, e.g., Individual Retirement Accounts (IRAs) and Keogh plans

Class works on increasing income, net worth, financial security for specific classes of persons in 332.02403–332.02499

.024 02	Personal financial problems

Examples: debt management; coping with depression, inflation

Class special problems for specific classes of persons in 332.02403–332.02499

.024 03–.024 99	Personal finance for specific classes of persons

Add to base number 332.024 notation 03–99 from Table 7, e.g., personal finance for single people 332.0240652

.04	Special topics
.041	Capital

Class international aspects of capital in 332.042

.041 2	Working capital

Examples: cash, short-term money claims, inventories

.041 4	Fixed (Investment) capital

Instruments of production with economic life span measured in years, e.g., factories, machinery; and funds invested in them

For land, see 333

.041 5	Capital formation and saving

Class here interdisciplinary and general economic studies of the ways, means, and problems of raising money for investment in capital assets

Class capital formation discussed in relation to production in specific kinds of industries in 338.1–338.4, financing of firms in 338.6041, savings and investment as a factor affecting national income in 339.43

[.041 506 8]	Management

Do not use; class in 658.1522

.041 52	Self-financing

Use by an individual of his own savings, or by an enterprise of its retained profits, for investment in own business

Class here procurement of capital from internal sources

See also 658.15226 for managerial aspects of self-financing

.041 54	External sources of capital
.042	International finance

Including international capital movements

Class international banks and banking in 332.15, exchange of currencies in 332.45, international exchange of securities in 332.65, international investment in 332.673

See also 337 for international economics

.06	Organizations

Class financial institutions and their management in 332.1

.1	**Banks and banking**

Class here government guaranty of deposits; bank failures; comprehensive works on money and banking, on financial institutions and their functions

Class credit unions in 334.22

For specialized banking institutions, see 332.2; credit and loan institutions, 332.3; money, 332.4; credit, 332.7

See Manual at 332.7 vs.332.1

.11	Central banks

Specific central banks are classed here, e.g., the U.S. Federal Reserve System 332.110973

.112	Relation to monetary policy

Including issuance of bank notes

Purchase of government securities relocated to 332.114

Class role of central bank in carrying out macroeconomic policy in 339.53

For reserve requirements, interest rates, see 332.113; open market operations, 332.114

.113	Relation to private banks

Including clearance, interest (discount) rates, loans, reserve requirements

.114	Open-market operations

Example: purchase of government securities [*formerly also* 332.112]

.12	Commercial banks

Class here clearing banks, clearing houses

Savings departments relocated to 332.1752

Class clearing services in 332.178

For multiple banking, see 332.16; banking services of commercial banks, 332.17

See Manual at 658.15 and T1—0681

.122	Incorporated banks

Class here chartered banks

.122 3	National banks

See also 332.11 for central banks

.122 4	State and provincial banks
.123	Unincorporated (Private) banks
.15	International banks and banking

Class here international operations of commercial and other banks, the role of banks in international borrowing and debt

See also 336.3435 for comprehensive works on international borrowing and debt

.152	For monetary stabilization and balance of payments

Example: International Monetary Fund

.153	For development of resources and production

Examples: International Development Association, International Finance Corporation

Class here comprehensive works on development banks

Class development banks serving one country in 332.28

.153 2	International Bank for Reconstruction and Development (World Bank)
.153 4	European Investment Bank
.153 8	Interamerican Development Bank
.154	For promotion and facilitation of trade
.155	For international settlements

Example: Bank for International Settlements

.16	Multiple banking

Examples: branch, chain, group, interstate banking; bank mergers, syndicates, holding companies

.17	Banking services of commercial banks

Class here comprehensive works on services of banks

Class services of specialized banking institutions in 332.2

> *For international operations, see 332.15*

> *See also 332.7 for credit functions not limited to a specific type of financial institution*

.175	General banking services
.175 2	Deposits

Examples: demand deposits (checking accounts); time deposits, e.g., certificates of deposit, savings accounts; NOW (negotiable order of withdrawal) accounts

Including savings departments [*formerly* 332.12]

.175 3	Loans
.175 4	Investments

> *See also 332.66 for investment banks and banking*

.178	Special banking services

Examples: credit cards; debit and smart cards; safe-deposit services; trust services

Including clearing services

> *See also 332.765 for works that discuss credit cards as offered by multiple types of institutions or without regard to type of institution*

.2	**Specialized banking institutions**

Class international banks in 332.15, e.g., international development banks 332.153; cooperative banking in 334.2

> *For agricultural institutions, see 332.31; investment banking, 332.66*

.21	Savings banks

Examples: government and stock savings banks

Class here mutual savings banks

Class comprehensive works on thrift institutions in 332.32

> *For postal savings banks, see 332.22*

.22	Postal savings banks
.26	Trust companies
.28	Development banks serving one country

Class banks for development of agriculture in 332.31

> *See also 332.153 for international development banks*

.3 **Credit and loan institutions**

> Included here are credit and loan functions of enterprises whose primary function is not credit and loan, e.g., retail stores, travel agencies. Credit and loan functions of insurance companies, however, are classed in 332.38

.31 Agricultural institutions

> Example: land banks

.32 Savings and loan associations

> Variant names: building and loan associations, home loan associations, mortgage institutions

> Class here comprehensive works on thrift institutions

> Class savings banks in 332.21, credit unions in 334.22

.34 Loan brokers

> Examples: chattel-loan brokers, pawnbrokers, salary-loan brokers

.35 Consumer and sales finance institutions

.37 Industrial banks

> Financial institutions organized to extend loans to employees

> Class here labor banks

> > *For credit unions, see 334.22*

> > *See also 332.35 for banks specializing in consumer loans*

.38 Insurance companies

> Credit and loan functions

> > *See also 368.0065 for interdisciplinary works on insurance companies*

.4 **Money**

> Class here comprehensive works on mediums of exchange

> Class comprehensive works on money and banking in 332.1, mediums of exchange other than money in 332.5

SUMMARY

332.401–.404	**[Theories; forms and units of money]**
.41	**Value of money**
.42	**Monetary standards**
.45	**Foreign exchange**
.46	**Monetary policy**
.49	**Historical, geographical, persons treatment of money and monetary policy**

.401 Theories

> Examples: circulation and velocity theory, equation of exchange theory, income and cash balance theories, quantity theory, supply and demand theory

.404	Forms and units of money
.404 2	Gold and silver coins
.404 3	Token coins

Coins with an intrinsic value less than their nominal value

Class here coins made of nonprecious metals

.404 4	Paper money
.404 8	Decimalization of currency
[.409]	Historical, geographical, persons treatment

Do not use; class in 332.49

.41	Value of money

Class here inflation, stagflation, deflation

Class the personal financial problem of coping with changing value of money in 332.02402

See also 331.1372 for effects of inflation on unemployment

See Manual at 332.41 vs. 339.41, 339.42

.414	Factors affecting fluctuations in value

Examples: devaluation, variations in quantity

For stabilization measures, see 332.415

.415	Stabilization measures

Including wage-price controls to combat inflation

Class monetary policy in 332.46, fiscal policy in 336.3

See also 339.5 for comprehensive works on economic stabilization policies

.42	Monetary standards
.420 4	Special topics
.420 42	Official status of money

Including credit money

Class here legal tender

See also 343.032 for monetary law

[.420 422–.420 424]	Standard and credit money

Numbers discontinued; class in 332.42042

> 332.422–332.425 Commodity standards

Systems in which value of monetary unit is kept equal to value of a designated quantity of a particular commodity or group of commodities

Class comprehensive works in 332.42

.422   Monometallic standards

.422 2   Gold standards

Examples: gold coin, gold bullion, gold exchange standards

.422 3   Silver standards

.423   Bimetallic standards

Free concurrent coinage of two metals, without limitation as to quantity or ratio of the metals

Class here bimetallic standards based on gold and silver

.424   Symmetallic standards

Coinage from an amalgam of two or more metals in a required proportion

.425   Composite commodity standards

Staple commodities in predetermined proportions

.427   Fiat money

Controlled and free forms of nonredeemable (inconvertible) currencies not kept equal to units of any commodity or group of commodities

.45   Foreign exchange

Exchange of one country's currency for another's

Including the Eurocurrency and Eurodollar market, special drawing rights

Class here currency convertibility, forward exchange, international monetary systems

Class comprehensive works on international finance in 332.042, investment in Eurobonds in 332.6323, government Eurobonds in public finance in 336.31, balance of payments in 382.17

.452   With a gold standard

Monetary units of exchanging countries defined in terms of gold, currencies freely convertible into gold, full freedom to import and export gold

Including devaluation

Class effect of devaluation on internal economy of devaluing country in 332.414

.454   With a paper standard

Monetary units of exchanging countries not defined in terms of gold or any other item of intrinsic value

Class regulation of exchange in 332.4564

.456   Exchange rates and their determination

.456 09   Exchange rates of specific currencies and groups of currencies

Add to base number 332.45609 notation 1−9 from Table 2 e.g., exchange rates of currency of United Kingdom 332.4560941; then add 0* and again add notation 1−9 from Table 2, e.g., exchange rate between currencies of United Kingdom and United States 332.4560941073

Give priority in notation to the currency of a jurisdiction or group of jurisdictions coming first in the sequence of area notations (Option: Give priority in notation to the currency of the jurisdiction requiring local emphasis, e.g., libraries in United States class exchange rate between currencies of United States and United Kingdom in 332.4560973041)

.456 2   Determination by supply and demand

Class here floating exchange rate

.456 4   Determination by government regulation of exchange rates

For determination by international agreement, see 332.4566

.456 6   Determination by international agreement

Class here international monetary policy, international monetary reform

For International Monetary Fund, see 332.152

.46   Monetary policy

Class here managed currency [*formerly* 332.56]

Including minting policies and practices

Class use of monetary policy for economic stabilization in 339.53, relation of central banks to monetary policy in 332.112

[.460 9]   Historical, geographical, persons treatment

Do not use; class in 332.49

.49   Historical, geographical, persons treatment of money and monetary policy

Add to base number 332.49 notation 01−99 from Table 2, e.g., money and monetary policy in India 332.4954

.5   **Other mediums of exchange**

Including barter instruments

*Add 00 for standard subdivisions; see instructions at beginning of Table 1

.55	Commercial paper
	Use of this number for barter instruments discontinued; class in 332.5
	Class comprehensive works on commercial paper, commercial paper as a credit instrument in 332.77

| .56 | Social credit money |
| | Managed currency relocated to 332.46 |

.6   Investment and investments

Class here investment prospectuses [*formerly also* with the subject with use of notation 029 from Table 1], portfolio analysis and management

Class description and analysis of business enterprises issuing securities in 338.7–338.8

| [.601 12] | Forecasting and forecasts |
| | Do not use; class in 332.678 |

SUMMARY

332.604	**Special topics**
.604 2	**Investment for specific purposes**
.62	**Brokerage firms**
.63	**Forms of investment**
.64	**Exchange of securities and commodities**
.65	**International exchange of securities**
.66	**Investment banks and banking**
.67	**Investments by field of investment, kind of enterprise, kind of investor; investment guides**

| .604 | Special topics |

| .604 2 | Investment for specific purposes |
| | Examples: investment for hedges against inflation, for tax advantages |

.62	Brokerage firms
	Example: discount brokers
	Including investment counselors
	Class real estate brokerage in 333.33

.63	Forms of investment
	Examples: art, coins, stamps
	Class here speculation in specific forms of investment [*formerly also* 332.645]
	Class speculation in multiple forms of investment in 332.645, investment in specific kinds of businesses regardless of form in 332.67
	See also 332.0414 for comprehensive works on fixed (investment) capital, 332.62 for brokerage firms

.632	**Securities, real estate, commodities**

Class here evaluation of growth potential, safety features, yield; speculation in securities; comprehensive works on financial futures

Standard subdivisions are added for securities, real estate, commodities; for securities

Class foreign exchange futures in 332.45; buying and selling procedures for securities and commodities in 332.64, for real estate in 333.33

.632 04   Special topics

.632 042   Evaluation techniques for securities, real estate, commodities

Examples: analyzing corporate balance sheets, reading financial pages and ticker tapes

.632 044   General types of securities

Examples: corporate securities; fixed rate, variable rate securities; gilt-edged securities

See Manual at 332.632044 vs.332.6323

.632 2   Stocks (Shares)

Including rights and warrants

See Manual at 332.6322 vs.332.6323

.632 21   Valuation

Including dividends paid, price-earnings ratio

For prices, see 332.63222

.632 22   Prices

.632 220 21   Tabulated and related materials

Do not use for statistics; class in 332.63222

.632 23   Common stock

Class valuation in 332.63221, prices in 332.63222, speculation in 332.63228

Most works about penny stocks emphasize speculation and are classed in 332.63228

.632 25   Preferred stock

Class valuation in 332.63221, prices in 332.63222, speculation in 332.63228

.632 28   Speculation

Examples: stock options, put and call transactions for stock [*both formerly* 332.6452], buying on margin, stock index futures

.632 3	Bonds

Class here interest rate futures and options, mortgage bonds and certificates

See Manual at 332.632044 vs. 332.6323; 332.6322 vs. 332.6323

.632 32 Government bonds, notes, certificates, bills

Example: treasury bills

For municipal bonds, see 332.63233

.632 33 Municipal bonds

.632 34 Corporate bonds

.632 4 Real estate

See also 332.72 for real estate finance, 333.33 for real estate business

---

\> 332.632 42–332.632 44 Types of investment in real estate

Class comprehensive works in 332.6324

.632 42 Land

Class sale of real estate in 333.333

.632 43 Buildings and other fixtures

See also 643.12 for how to select a home, 647.92–647.94 for management of multiple dwellings

.632 44 Mortgages

See also 332.6323 for mortgage bonds and certificates

.632 47 Real estate investment trusts

Including real estate syndication

.632 7 Investment company securities

Including investment trusts, money market funds, mutual funds, unit trusts

For real estate investment trusts, see 332.63247

.632 8 Commodities

Class here commodity futures and options, speculation in commodities

See also 332.644 for exchange of commodities and commodities exchanges

.64   **Exchange of securities and commodities**

Class here buying and selling of securities and commodities; organization, procedures, activities of organized exchanges

See also 332.632 for advice on investing in specific forms of securities and commodities, 332.678 for general investment guides

.642   **Exchange of securities and securities exchanges**

Add to base number 332.642 notation 4–9 from Table 2, e.g., exchange of securities in the Netherlands 332.642492

When adding from Table 2 for a specific exchange, use the number for the primary area served by the exchange, e.g., New York Stock Exchange 332.64273, Pacific Stock Exchange 332.64279

Class brokerage firms in 332.62, speculation in 332.632

For over-the-counter market, see 332.643; international exchange of securities, 332.65

.643   **Over-the-counter market**

.644   **Exchange of commodities and commodities exchanges**

Class here commodity futures and options markets

Class speculation in 332.6328

.644 1   Products of agriculture

Add to base number 332.6441 the numbers following 63 in 633–638, e.g., soybeans 332.6441334

.644 2   Products of mineral industries

Add to base number 332.6442 the numbers following 553 in 553.2–553.9, e.g., copper 332.644243

.645   **Speculation**

Speculation in multiple forms of investment

Examples: arbitrage, buying on margin, futures, hedging, put and call transactions

Speculation in specific forms of investment relocated to 332.63

Class guides to speculation in 332.678

See also 332.45 for speculation in foreign exchange

[.645 2]   Put and call transactions

Use of this number for put and call transactions for multiple forms of investment discontinued; class in 332.645

Stock options, put and call transactions for stock relocated to 332.63228

.65 International exchange of securities

Sale and purchase of securities offered by nationals of one jurisdiction to nationals of another jurisdiction

Class international sale and purchase of specific kinds of securities in 332.632

.66 Investment banks and banking

Investment banking: underwriting and sale of security issues

Class here issuing houses

Class international investment banks and banking in 332.15

.67 Investments by field of investment, kind of enterprise, kind of investor; investment guides

Class investment in specific forms of securities in 332.63, e.g., investment in railroad stocks 332.6322 (*not* 332.6722); specific aspects of investment in 332.64–332.66, e.g., speculation by pension funds 332.645 (*not* 332.67254)

.671 Investment in specific kinds of enterprises and by specific kinds of investors

Add to base number 332.671 the numbers following 332.672 in 332.6722–332.6725, e.g., investments by government agencies 332.67152

Class domestic investment in 332.672, international investment in 332.673

.672 Domestic investment

.672 2 In specific kinds of enterprises

Examples: insurance companies, railroads

Including investment in small business

Class investment in specific kinds of enterprises by specific kinds of investors in 332.6725

See Manual at 332 vs. 338, 658.15

.672 5 By specific kinds of investors

.672 52 By governments and their agencies

.672 53 By private investors

For investment by specific kinds of institutions, see 332.67254; by specific kinds of individuals, 332.67255

.672 54 By specific kinds of institutions

Examples: by life insurance companies, pension funds

Class investments by banks in 332.1754

.672 55 By specific kinds of individuals

Examples: by attorneys, physicians, middle-income investors

.673 International investment

Class international investment banking in 332.15, specific forms of international investment in 332.63, history and description of international business ventures and subsidiaries in 338.88

For international exchange of securities, see 332.65

See also 658.1149 for initiation of international business enterprises (including subsidiaries)

.673 09 Historical, geographical, persons treatment

Class here the advantages and disadvantages of establishing businesses in specific areas, investment in specific areas not originating in other specific areas

Class the advantages and disadvantages of establishing businesses in specific areas resulting from government policy in 332.6732, investment originating in specific continents and countries in 332.6733–332.6739 (*not* 332.673093–332.673099)

See also 338.09 for works describing where in fact industry is located

See Manual at 338.09 vs. 338.6042, 332.67309, 346.07, 658.11, 658.21, T1—068

.673 1 By specific kinds of investors

Class investment by specific kinds of investors originating in specific continents and countries in 332.6733–332.6739

.673 12 By governments

.673 14 By private investors

Institutional and individual

.673 2 Government policy

Including international control

.673 22 Incentives and obstacles in country of investment

Add to base number 332.67322 notation 3–9 from Table 2, e.g., incentives and obstacles in Brazil 332.6732281

.673 24 Incentives and obstacles in country of investor

Add to base number 332.67324 notation 3–9 from Table 2, e.g., incentives and obstacles to overseas investment by British citizens 332.6732441

.673 3–.673 9 Investment originating in specific continents and countries

Add to base number 332.673 notation 3–9 from Table 2, e.g., British foreign investments 332.67341; then, for place of investment, add 0* and to the result add notation 1–9 from Table 2, e.g., British foreign investments in Brazil 332.67341081

Class policies of specific governments in 332.6732

*Add 00 for standard subdivisions; see instructions at beginning of Table 1

.678 Investment guides

Including forecasting, formula plans, speculation

Class guides to specific forms of investment in 332.63, to investment by type of investor, type of enterprise, field of investment in 332.67

.7 Credit

Class here comprehensive works on specific types of credit

Class credit functions of specific types of financial institutions in 332.1–332.3

For interest and discount, see 332.8

See Manual at 332.7 vs. 332.1

.71 Agricultural credit

.72 Real-estate finance and mortgages

Class here discrimination in mortgage loans; mortgage delinquencies and defaults

Class finance on farm real estate in 332.71

See also 332.32 for mortgage institutions, 332.6323 for mortgage bonds and certificates, 332.63244 for mortgages as an investment

.722 Home (Residential) finance

.74 Other forms of credit

.742 Commercial, mercantile, industrial

Examples: export credit, small business loans

.743 Personal loans

Example: chattel mortgages

Including consumer credit

.75 Credit restrictions and collapse

Class here bankruptcy

.76 Credit instruments

Examples: checks, debit cards, money orders

Class certificates of deposit in 332.1752

For commercial paper, see 332.77

.765 Credit cards

Class here comprehensive works on credit cards

Class credit cards issued by specific types of financial institutions in 332.1, e.g., commercial banks 332.178

.77	Commercial paper

Examples: acceptances, drafts, promissory notes

Including letters of credit

Class here comprehensive works on commercial paper

Class commercial paper as an exchange medium in 332.55

.8   Interest and discount

.82   Interest

> *For usury, see 332.83*
>
> *See also 332.6323 for interest rate futures*

.83   Usury

.84   Discount and rediscount

.9   Counterfeiting, forgery, alteration

> *See also 364.133 for counterfeiting as a crime, 364.163 for forgery as a crime, 737.4 for counterfeit coins, 769.55 for counterfeit paper money, 769.562 for counterfeit stamps*

333   Land economics

Land: the sum total of natural and man-made resources over which possession of the earth gives control

SUMMARY

333.001–.009	**Standard subdivisions**
.01–.08	**[Theories and land surveys]**
.1	**Public ownership and control of land and other natural resources**
.2	**Ownership and control of land and other natural resources by nongovernmental collectivities**
.3	**Individual (Private) ownership and control of land and other natural resources**
.4	**Absentee ownership**
.5	**Renting and leasing land and other natural resources**
.7	**Natural resources and energy**
.8	**Subsurface resources**
.9	**Other natural resources**

.001   Philosophy and theory

Class theories in 333.01

.001 2   Classification

Class land classification in 333.73012

.002–.009   Standard subdivisions

.01   Theories

.012 Rent

Return produced by ownership of land after deduction of all outlays for labor and capital

Including Ricardo's theory of earning power of land in terms of its marginal productivity

See also 333.5 for renting and leasing land and natural resources

.08 Land surveys

Class here work of chartered surveyors (United Kingdom)

Class specific kinds of land surveys with the topic, e.g., public land surveys 333.18, land use surveys 333.7313

See also 526.9 for surveying techniques, 631.47 for surveys that focus on agricultural use of soils

> **333.1–333.5 Ownership and control of land and other natural resources**

Ownership: right to possession and use of land and other natural resources; right to transfer of possession and use

Control limited to the kind of control that stems from ownership

Class here ownership and control of specific kinds of natural resources

Class comprehensive works in 333.3

See also 333.7–333.9 for usage of land and other natural resources, for control of such usage not stemming from ownership

See Manual at 333.1–333.5 vs. 333.73–333.78; 333.1–333.5 vs. 346.043

.1 **Public ownership and control of land and other natural resources**

Public control of privately owned lands and other natural resources relocated to 333.717, comprehensive works on land policy to 333.73

See also 333.2 for ownership and control of land by peoples subordinate to another jurisdiction, 343.02 for law of public property

.11 Acquisition and disposal of specific kinds of lands

Examples: forests, highways and streets, recreational lands

.13 Acquisition

Examples: expropriation, purchase

Including eminent domain

Class here evaluation of lands for government acquisition

Class acquisition of specific kinds of land in 333.11

For nationalization, see 333.14

.14 Nationalization

.16	Disposal

> Examples: grants, leases, sale
>
> Class disposal of specific kinds of land in 333.11

.18	Public land surveys

> *See also 333.08 for comprehensive works on land surveys, 333.7313*
> *for surveys of public land use, 526.9 for surveying techniques*

.2   Ownership and control of land and natural resources by nongovernmental collectivities

> Examples: common lands; open-field system; ownership and control of land by peoples subordinate to another jurisdiction, e.g., Amerindian lands in the United States
>
> Including enclosure of common lands
>
> *For corporate ownership, see 333.324*

.3   Individual (Private) ownership and control of land and natural resources

> Including subdivision of private land
>
> Class here comprehensive works on land tenure, on ownership and control of land and other natural resources
>
> Use of this number for comprehensive works on ownership and use of land and other natural resources discontinued; class in 333
>
> *For public ownership and control, see 333.1; ownership and control by*
> *nongovernmental collectivities, 333.2; absentee ownership, 333.4*

.31	Land reform

> Class here land redistribution, settlement and resettlement of people on the land
>
> Add to base number 333.31 notation 4–9 from Table 2, e.g., land reform in Latin America 333.318
>
> *See also 333.2 for enclosure of common lands*

.32	Types of tenure
.322	Feudal tenure
.323	Individual tenure

> *For corporate ownership, see 333.324*

.323 2	Complete ownership (Fee simple)

> Full right to possession, use, transfer of possession and use

.323 4	Qualified ownership

> Ownership with restrictions on use or transfer
>
> Examples: entails, life estates, time-sharing

.324	Corporate ownership
.33	Transfer of possession and right to use

> Including consolidation of holdings
>
> Class here comprehensive works on real estate business
>
> Class government acquisition and disposal in 333.1, land reform in 333.31
>
> *For renting and leasing, see 333.5; real estate development, 333.7315*
>
> *See also 332.6324 for real estate investment, 332.72 for real estate finance*

.332	Value and price of land

> Class here valuation (appraisal)
>
> Class value and price of specific kinds of land in 333.335–333.339; valuation for government acquisition and disposal in 333.11–333.16, for tax purposes in 352.72421

.332 2	Real estate market

> Class here economic and social factors affecting exchange of real estate
>
> Class price in 333.3323

.332 3	Price
.332 302 1	Tabulated and related materials

> Do not use for statistics; class in 333.3323

.333	Sale and gift

> Class sale and gift of specific kinds of land in 333.335–333.339

> 333.335–333.339 Transfer of possession and use of specific kinds of land, other natural resources, real estate

Except for additions, changes, deletions, exceptions shown under specific entries, add to each term identified by * as follows:

2	Value and price
	Class here valuation (appraisal)
22	Real estate market
	Class here economic and social factors affecting exchange of real estate
	Class price in 23
23	Price
3	Sale and gift
5	Renting and leasing
	Add to 5 the numbers following 333.5 in 333.53–333.56, e.g., share renting 563

Class comprehensive works in 333.33

.335	*Rural lands *Agricultural lands

.335 563   Share and percentage renting

Example: sharecropping [*formerly also* 333.563]

.335 7   *Forest lands

.336   *Industrial lands

Including transportation space, e.g., airport space, railroad rights-of-way

See also 333.338 for works that emphasize buildings and other fixtures

.337   *Urban lands

Residential and commercial lands

For industrial lands, see 333.336

See also 333.338 for works that emphasize buildings and other fixtures

.338   Buildings and other fixtures   *Residential buildings

Examples: apartments, condominiums, mobile homes

.338 7   *Commercial and industrial buildings

.339   Other natural resources

Appraisal, gift, leasing, renting, sale, market

Examples: rights to use of minerals, water, air space

[.38]   Subdivision and development

Number discontinued; class subdivision in 333.3

Development relocated to 333.715

.4   Absentee ownership

.5   Renting and leasing land and natural resources

Class renting and leasing specific kinds of land and natural resources in 333.335–333.339

.53   Tenancy

Examples: tenancy for years (for a specified time period), tenancy from year to year, tenancy at will

For landlord-tenant relations, see 333.54

.54   Landlord-tenant relations

.56   Types of renting

.562   Cash renting

.563   Share and percentage renting

Sharecropping relocated to 333.335563

*Add as instructed under 333.335–333.339

.7   **Natural resources and energy**

Aspects other than ownership

Class here raw materials; interdisciplinary works on the environment, on waste resources

Except for additions, changes, deletions, exceptions shown under specific entries, add to notation for each term identified by * as follows:

1	General topics
	Class general topics of a specific kind of resource with the kind, e.g., control of usage of mountains as recreational areas 333.784 (*not* 333.7817)
11	Reserves (Stock, Supply)
	Quantity available for use
	Including shortages
12	Requirements (Need, Demand)
13	Consumption (Use, Utilization)
	Class consumption control in 17, specific uses in 333.7–333.9 without adding notation 13
137	Abuse and wastage
	Class here description of abused resources, consequences of abuse and wastage
	Class reclamation, rehabilitation, restoration of abused resources in 153; pollution in 363.73
14	Impact studies
	Studies of actual impacts are classed with the thing affected, studies of projected impacts with the program or development being planned
	Class studies emphasizing abuse and wastage in 137
>15–17	Management and control
	Class here citizen participation, planning, policy
	Class comprehensive works in 333.7–333.9 without adding from this table
15	Development
152	Improvement
153	Reclamation, rehabilitation, restoration
	Class reclamation that is not restoration to a previous state in 152
158	Subsidies
16	Conservation and protection
	Class control of usage in 17
17	Control of usage
	Examples: allocation, price control, rationing
	Including ways and means of efficient use
	Class control of specific uses in 333.7–333.9 without adding notation 17

Class interdisciplinary works on consumption in 339.47; ownership of land and other natural resources in 333.1–333.5; natural resources other than land in 333.8–333.9; economic geology in 553; other aspects of the environment with the aspect, e.g., environmental protection 363.7

See Manual at 333.7–333.9; 363; 363.6 vs. 333.7

SUMMARY

333.71	**General topics**
.72	**Conservation and protection**
.73	**Land**
.74	**Pasture (Grazing) lands**
.75	**Forest lands**
.76	**Rural lands Agricultural lands**
.77	**Urban lands**
.78	**Recreational and wilderness areas**
.79	**Energy**

.71   General topics

Add to base number 333.71 the numbers following 1 in notation 11–17 from table under 333.7, e.g., development 333.715 [*formerly also* 333.38], reclamation 333.7153 [*formerly also* 333.72], public control of privately owned lands and other natural resources 333.717 [*formerly* 333.1]; however, class conservation and protection in 333.72

.72   Conservation and protection

Reclamation relocated to 333.7153

Class conservation of specific types of natural resources in 333.73–333.95

See Manual at 363.7 vs. 333.72, 304.28

.73   Land

Class here comprehensive works on land policy [*formerly also* 333.1], kinds of land by physical condition, e.g., humid land, mountainous land

Class kinds of land by use in 333.74–333.78; shorelands and related areas in 333.917; submerged lands, wetlands, in 333.918

See Manual at 333.1–333.5 vs. 333.73–333.78

.731   General topics

Add to base number 333.731 the numbers following 1 in notation 11–17 from table under 333.7, e.g., real estate development 333.7315, comprehensive works on soil and water conservation 333.7316

Class comprehensive works on real estate business in 333.33, soil and water conservation in rural lands in 333.7616, real estate development in urban lands in 333.7715, zoning of urban lands in 333.7717, water conservation in 333.9116, pollution control in 363.73966

.736   *Arid and *semiarid lands

Class here desertification

.74   *Pasture (Grazing) lands

See Manual at 333.1–333.5 vs. 333.73–333.78

*Add as instructed under 333.7

.75	Forest lands

Class here timber resources

Add to base number 333.75 notation 11–17 from table under 333.7, e.g., supply of timber in nature 333.7511, demand for timber 333.7512 [*both formerly also* 338.1749]

Wood as a fuel relocated to 333.9539

Class parks, recreational, wilderness areas in 333.78

See Manual at 333.1–333.5 vs. 333.73–333.78; 333.75 vs. 338.1749

.76	*Rural lands *Agricultural lands

Class rural recreational lands in 333.78

Rural lands of a specific physical condition, if not devoted to a specific use, are classed in 333.73. For example, semiarid lands in general are classed in 333.736; however, semiarid lands devoted to grazing are classed in 333.74

For pasture lands, see 333.74; forest lands, 333.75

See Manual at 333.1–333.5 vs. 333.73–333.78

.765	*Mined lands *Surface-mined lands
.77	*Urban lands

Examples: civic, commercial, industrial, residential lands; highways and streets

Class urban mined lands in 333.765, urban recreational lands in 333.78

See Manual at 333.1–333.5 vs. 333.73–333.78

[.772]	Highways and streets

Number discontinued; class in 333.77

.78	*Recreational and wilderness areas

Class wildlife and wildlife refuges in 333.95

See also 363.68 for park and recreation services

See Manual at 333.1–333.5 vs. 333.73–333.78

.782	*Wilderness areas

For specific kinds of wilderness areas, see 333.784

See also 333.95 for wildlife and wildlife refuges

.783	*Parks

*Add as instructed under 333.7

.784   Specific kinds of recreational and wilderness areas

Examples: coastlines, forests, mountains

>   333.784 4–333.784 6 Recreational use of water

Class here recreational use of land adjoining water, e.g., beaches, shores

Class comprehensive works in 333.784

See also 333.91 for comprehensive works on uses of water and land adjoining it

.784 4   Lakes

.784 5   Rivers and streams

.784 6   Reservoirs

See also 333.7844 for lakes

.79   Energy

Class here production of energy [*formerly* 338], interdisciplinary works on energy

Power resources are classed here. A work that discusses only electric power is classed in 333.7932

Class extraction of energy resources and comprehensive works on the economics of mineral fuels in 338.2; interdisciplinary works on mineral fuels in 553; specific forms of energy, specific energy resources not provided for here with the subject, e.g., fossil fuels 333.82, geothermal energy 333.88, hydroelectricity 333.914, wind energy 333.92, biomass as an energy resource 333.9539; noneconomic aspects with the aspect, e.g., energy management 658.2, fuel technology 662.6

.791   General topics

Add to base number 333.791 the numbers following 1 in notation 11–17 from table under 333.7, e.g., energy development and production 333.7915

Class utilization of waste heat in 333.793

.792   Primary forms of energy

Resources used directly to perform work, to produce other forms of energy

.792 3   †Solar energy

Including electricity derived from solar energy, e.g., with photovoltaic cells

Class distribution of electricity derived from solar energy in 333.7932

.792 33   Financial aspects

Including prices

†Add as instructed under 333.7, except use 15 for both development and generation of energy

.792 4   †Nuclear energy

                               Class here electricity derived from nuclear energy

                               Class distribution of electricity derived from nuclear energy in
                               333.7932, nuclear fuels in 333.85

.792 43   Financial aspects

                               Including prices

.793   Secondary forms of energy

                               Energy produced through use of other resources

                               Including cogeneration of electric power and heat, district heating

                               Class secondary forms of energy derived from specific resources with the
                               resource, e.g., electricity derived from nuclear energy 333.7924;
                               economics of synthetic fuel production 338.4766266

.793 2   †Electrical energy

                               Including rural electrification [*formerly* 621.393], distribution of
                               electrical energy regardless of resource from which the electricity was
                               derived

                               Class here electricity derived from fossil fuels [*formerly* 333.82],
                               electrical utilities [*formerly* 363.62], comprehensive works on
                               electrical energy

                               Electricity derived from a specific resource is classed with the
                               resource, e.g., from water 333.914. The two exceptions are for
                               electricity derived from fossil fuels and for distribution of electricity

.793 23   Financial aspects

.793 231   Prices

.793 8   †Energy from waste materials

                               Class energy from biological wastes in 333.9539, the chemical
                               technology of energy from waste materials in 662.87

.794   †Renewable energy resources

                               Class here alternative energy resources

                               Class specific renewable and alternative energy resources with the
                               resource, e.g., solar energy 333.7923

.796   Energy for specific uses

                               Example: energy for military use

                               Unless other instructions are given, class complex subjects with aspects
                               in two or more subdivisions of 333.796 in the one coming last, e.g.,
                               energy use in school buildings 333.7964 (not 333.7962)

                               Class a specific kind of energy for specific uses with the kind of energy,
                               e.g., energy from petroleum for transportation use 333.8232 (*not*
                               333.7968)

†Add as instructed under 333.7, except use 15 for both development and generation of energy

[.796 01–.796 09]	Standard subdivisions
	Do not use; class in 333.7901–333.7909

.796 2   *For use in buildings and offices

        Including use in construction

            See also 624 for technical aspects of energy use in construction

.796 3   *For residential and domestic use

.796 4   *Social service institutions

        Examples: churches, hospitals, prisons, schools

.796 5   *For industrial use

        Class here manufacturing use

        Class energy use in construction of buildings in 333.7962

            For food processing use, see 333.7966

.796 6   *For use in agriculture and food processing

.796 8   *For use in transportation and commerce

        Standard subdivisions are added for transportation

.796 89   *For commercial use

.8   Subsurface resources

Class here supply in storage, shortages, surpluses, demand, and projections of these [*all formerly also* 338.27], strategic materials

Add to base number 333.8, and also to each subdivision identified by ‡, as instructed under 333.7; however, use 11 only for reserves in storage, and do not use 15 development; class reserves in nature in 553, development in 338.2

Class extraction of subsurface resources and comprehensive works on the economics of subsurface resources in 338.2, interdisciplinary works on subsurface resources in 553

    For ground water, see 333.9104

    See Manual at 333.7–333.9; 333.8 vs. 338.2, 553; 553

.82   ‡Fossil fuels

        Electricity derived from fossil fuels relocated to 333.7932

.822   ‡Coal

.823   ‡Oil and natural gas

.823 2   ‡Oil

        Petroleum in its narrow sense

        Gasoline relocated to 338.4766553827

*Add as instructed under 333.7

‡Add as instructed under 333.7, except use 11 only for reserves in storage and do not use 15 development; class reserves in nature in 553, development in 338.2

.823 3	‡Natural gas

        See also 363.63 for gas distribution services of public utilities

.85   ‡Minerals

        Add to base number 333.85 the numbers following 553 in 553.2–553.9, e.g., tin 333.85453, uranium 333.854932; however, class fossil fuels in 333.82, ground water in 333.9104

        Class comprehensive works on the economics of minerals in 338.2, interdisciplinary works on nonmetallic minerals in 553, interdisciplinary works on metals in 669

.88   *Geothermal energy

        Class here subsurface thermal waters [*formerly also* 333.9104], thermal waters [*formerly* 553.7], electricity derived from geothermal energy

        Class distribution of electricity derived from geothermal energy in 333.7932

.9   **Other natural resources**

        Add to each subdivision identified by * as instructed under 333.7

        See Manual at 333.7–333.9

SUMMARY

	333.91	**Water**
	.92	**Air**
	.94	**Space**
	.95	**Biological resources**

.91   Water

        Class here aquatic resources, land adjoining water, comprehensive works on the economics of water resources

        Use 333.91001–333.91009 for standard subdivisions

        Class interdisciplinary works on water in 553.7; a specific aquatic resource with the subject, e.g., minerals 333.85, fish 333.956; a specific aspect of water not provided for here with the subject, e.g., recreational use of water and land adjoining it 333.7844–333.7846, regulation and control of distribution of water to consumers 363.61

        See Manual at 363.61; 553

[.910 2]   Surface water

        Number discontinued; class in 333.91

.910 4   †Ground (Subsurface) water

        Subsurface thermal waters relocated to 333.88

*Add as instructed under 333.7

†Add as instructed under 333.7, except use 11 only for reserves in storage; class reserves in nature in 553.7

‡Add as instructed under 333.7, except use 11 only for reserves in storage and do not use 15 development; class reserves in nature in 553, development in 338.2

.911	General topics of water

Class general topics of a specific kind of water with the kind, e.g., general topics of rivers and streams 333.91621

.911 1	Reserves (Stock, Supply)

Class here only reserves in storage, e.g., in reservoirs and storage tanks

Class reserves in nature in 553.7

.911 2	Requirements (Need, Demand) [*formerly also* 628.17]
.911 3	Use (Utilization) [*formerly also* 628.17]

Class here comprehensive works on proprietary uses of water, on resource economics of consumption of water [*both formerly* 333.912]

Class water for specific uses in 333.912–333.915

.911 37	Abuse and wastage

Class reclamation, rehabilitation, restoration of abused water in 333.91153; water conservation in 333.9116; water pollution in 363.7394

.911 4	Impact studies

Class studies emphasizing abuse and wastage in 333.91137

.911 5–.911 7	Management and control of water

Add to base number 333.91 notation 15–17 from the table under 333.7, e.g., water conservation 333.9116

>	333.912–333.915 Water for specific uses

Class comprehensive works in 333.91

For recreational use, see 333.7844–333.7846

.912	†Water for domestic (residential) and industrial uses

Comprehensive works on proprietary uses of water, on resource economics of consumption of water relocated to 333.9113

.912 2	For domestic (residential) use

Examples: drinking and washing

.912 3	For industrial use

Class water for generation of energy in 333.914, water for transportation in 333.915

.913	†Water for irrigation

†Add as instructed under 333.7, except use 11 only for reserves in storage; class reserves in nature in 553.7

.914   Water for generation of energy

Example: thermal ocean power conversion

Class here hydroelectricity

Add to base number 333.914 notation 11–17 from table under 333.7, except use 11 for energy-producing potential of water and 15 for both development and generation of energy, e.g., potential hydroelectric energy resources of Idaho 333.9141109796, hydropower generation in the Columbia River basin 333.9141509797

Use of this number for other nonproprietary uses of water discontinued; class in 333.91

.915   †Water for transportation

> 　　　　333.916–333.918 Specific kinds of water and land adjoining it

Class comprehensive works in 333.91, specific uses of specific kinds of water in 333.912–333.915

.916   Bodies of water

Class lands adjoining specific kinds of bodies of water in 333.917

.916 2   †Rivers and streams

Class river basins in 333.73

.916 3   †Lakes and ponds

For salt-water lakes, see 333.9164

.916 4   Oceans and seas

Including bays, gulfs, estuaries, salt-water lakes

Add to base number 333.9164 notation 11–17 from table under 333.7, e.g., conservation and protection of seas 333.916416; however, use 11 only for reserves in storage; class reserves in nature with the subject, e.g., oceans 551.46

.917   *Shorelands and related areas

Examples: beaches, coasts, shores

Class here tidelands in the sense of lands that are overflowed by the tide but exposed by low water

Submerged lands and wetlands related to specific types of bodies of water, tidelands in the sense of lands underlying the ocean beyond the low tidemark but within a nation's territorial waters, continental shelves relocated to 333.918

Class river basins in 333.73, recreational use of shorelands and related areas in 333.784

*Add as instructed under 333.7

†Add as instructed under 333.7, except use 11 only for reserves in storage; class reserves in nature in 553.7

.918   *Submerged lands and wetlands

Class here submerged lands and wetlands related to specific types of bodies of water, tidelands in the sense of lands underlying the ocean beyond the low tidemark but within a nation's territorial waters, continental shelves [*all formerly* 333.917]

Class recreational use in 333.784

See also 333.916 for works focusing on bodies of water rather than the land they submerge

.92   *Air

Class here wind energy, use of wind for generation of electricity

.94   Space

See Manual at 333.94 vs. 338.0919

.95   *Biological resources

Class here biosphere, wildlife, wildlife refuges

.952   *Aquatic biological resources

Class specific aquatic organisms and groups of organisms in 333.953–333.959

.953   *Plant resources

Class forests, comprehensive works on timber resources in 333.75

.953 9   Plant resources for generation of energy

Class here wood as a fuel [*formerly also* 333.75], interdisciplinary works on biomass as an energy resource

Add to base number 333.9539 notation 11–17 from table under 333.7, except use 15 for both development and generation of energy, e.g., generation of energy from biomass 333.953915

Class animal biomass as an energy resource in 333.954

.954   *Animal resources

Class here game

For invertebrates, see 333.955; fish, 333.956; amphibians and reptiles, 333.957; birds, 333.958; mammals, 333.959

See Manual at 333.954 vs. 338.37

.955   *Invertebrates

Examples: insects, shellfish

.956   *Fish

Class here comprehensive works on finfish and shellfish

For shellfish, see 333.955

.957   *Amphibians and reptiles

*Add as instructed under 333.7

.958	*Birds
.959	*Mammals

334 Cooperatives

Voluntary organizations or enterprises owned by and operated for the benefit of those using the services

[.060 1] International organizations

Do not use; class in 334.0919

.091 9 International associations of cooperatives

Do not use for cooperatives in space; class in 334.09

.1 Building and housing

.2 Banking and credit

.22 Credit unions

See also 332.32 for comprehensive works on thrift institutions

.5 Consumer cooperatives

Class comprehensive works on cooperative marketing in 334.6813801, consumer housing cooperatives in 334.1

[.506 8] Management of consumer cooperatives

Relocated to 658.8707

.6 Production

.68 In specific industries and groups of industries

.681 Other than extractive, manufacturing, construction

Class here service industries

Add to base number 334.681 notation 001–999, e.g., cooperative marketing by producers and comprehensive works on cooperative marketing 334.6813801, cooperative legal services 334.68134; however, class banking and credit in 334.2, consumers' cooperatives in 334.5

.682–.689 Extractive, manufacturing, construction

Add to base number 334.68 the numbers following 6 in 620–690, e.g., cooperative cattle production 334.68362; however, class building cooperatives in 334.1, kibbutzim and moshavim in Israel in 335.95694, Soviet collective farms in 338.7630947

Cooperative marketing by producers is classed in 334.6813801, e.g., cooperative domestic marketing of cattle by producers 334.6813814162

.7 Benefit societies

Examples: benevolent, friendly, mutual-aid, provident societies

See also 368 for insurance

*Add as instructed under 333.7

335   Socialism and related systems

Class here state socialism, interdisciplinary works on political and economic aspects of socialism and related systems

(Option: Class in 330.159)

Use 335.001–335.009 for standard subdivisions

Class socialism and communism as political ideologies in 320.53; socialist and communist political parties in 324.217; a specific topic of economics treated from a socialist or communist point of view with the subject in economics, e.g., interest 332.82

The term "socialism" is often used in narrow senses to mean communism (335.43) or democratic socialism (335.5)

Comparisons of Communism (Marxism-Leninism) with other systems are classed in 335.437

> *See Manual at 335 vs. 320.53, 306.345*

SUMMARY

335.02	**Utopian systems and schools**
.1	**Systems of English origin**
.2	**Systems of French origin**
.3	**Systems of American origin**
.4	**Marxian systems**
.5	**Democratic socialism**
.6	**Fascism**
.7	**Christian socialism**
.8	**Other systems**
.9	**Voluntary socialist and anarchist communities**

.02   Utopian systems and schools

Class specific utopian systems in 335.1–335.3

> *See also 301 for ideal societies, 321.07 for ideal states*

> ### 335.1–335.3 Non- and quasi-Marxian socialism

Class comprehensive works in 335

> *For national socialism, see 335.6; Christian socialism, 335.7; voluntary socialist communities, 335.9*

.1   **Systems of English origin**

.12   Utopian socialism

Example: Owenism

.14   Fabian socialism

.15   Guild socialism

.2   **Systems of French origin**

Examples: Babouvism, Icarianism

.22	Saint-Simonism
.23	Fourierism (Phalansterianism)
.3	**Systems of American origin**
.4	**Marxian systems**

Class here Marxism

Class democratic Marxian systems in 335.5

See Manual at 335.4 vs. 335.401, 335.411

.401	Philosophy and related topics

Comprehensive works on theory of Marxian systems are classed in 335.4

Class philosophical foundations in 335.411

See Manual at 335.4 vs. 335.401, 335.411

.41	Philosophic foundations, economic concepts, aims

Example: social ownership of means of production

.411	Philosophic foundations

Example: theory of class struggle

Class the philosophic foundations of Marxian economics in 335.412

See Manual at 335.4 vs. 335.401, 335.411

.411 2	Dialectical materialism

See Manual at 146.32 vs. 335.4112

.411 9	Historical materialism
.412	Economic concepts

Example: labor theory of value

[.413]	Aims

Number discontinued; class in 335.41

> 335.42–335.43 Marxian doctrines and systems characteristic of specific historical periods and regions

Class comprehensive works in 335.4

.42	Early period
.422	Communism (1848–1875)

Period of Communist manifesto

.423	Scientific socialism (1875–1917)

For democratic socialism, see 335.5

.43	**Communism (Marxism-Leninism)**

Communism of post-1917 period

Class here Soviet communism, communist theory and practice of democratic centralism

Class communism as a political ideology in 320.532

.433	Trotskyite doctrines
.434	National variants as schools of thought

Use 335.4309 for communism in specific nations viewed as actual economic systems rather than schools of thought, e.g., Cuban communism as an existing system 335.43097291 (*not* 335.4347)

Soviet communism as a school of thought is classed in 335.43, as the actual economic system of the Soviet Union in 335.430947

.434 4	Yugoslav communism

Class here Titoism

.434 5	Chinese communism

Class here Maoism

.434 7	Cuban communism (Castroism)

Including ideas of Che Guevara

[.436]	Critical works

Number discontinued; class in 335.43

.437	Comparative studies

Comparison of communism with capitalism, cooperation, democratic socialism, other forms of collectivism

.5	**Democratic socialism**

Marxian and non-Marxian socialism pursued through persuasion and consent of the electorate in a nonauthoritarian state

Use of this number for state socialism discontinued; class in 335

Class Christian socialism in 335.7, voluntary socialist communities in 335.9

For Fabian socialism, see 335.14

.6	**Fascism**

Examples: falangism, national socialism

See also 320.533 for fascism as a political ideology

.7	**Christian socialism**

Class voluntary Christian socialist communities in 335.9

See also 320.5312 for Christian socialism as a political ideology

.8	**Other systems**

.82   Syndicalism

Class here anarcho-syndicalism

.83   Anarchism

Class anarchism as a political ideology in 320.57, anarcho-syndicalism in 335.82, voluntary anarchist communities in 335.9

.9   Voluntary socialist and anarchist communities

Use 335.9 only for truly voluntary communities. Use 338.7 for communes or collectives imposed by force, if discussed as organizations of production

Add to base number 335.9 notation 3–9 from Table 2, e.g., kibbutzim and moshavim in Israel 335.95694, voluntary socialist communities in the United States 335.973

See also 307.774 for interdisciplinary and sociological studies of communes, 307.776 for interdisciplinary and sociological studies of kibbutzim

336   Public finance

Class here intergovernmental fiscal relations

Class financial administration of governments in 351.72

See also 351.725 for administration of fiscal relations between governmental units

See Manual at 336 vs. 351.72; 339 vs. 332, 336

SUMMARY

336.001–.008	**Standard subdivisions**	
.01–.09	**[Governmental level; revenue; historical, geographical, persons treatment]**	
.1	**Nontax revenues**	
.2	**Taxes and taxation**	
.3	**Public borrowing, debt, expenditure**	
.4–.9	**Public finance of specific continents, countries, localities in modern world**	

.001–.005   Standard subdivisions

.006   Organizations and management

.006 01   International organizations

Class associations of sovereign states in 336.0916

.007–.008   Standard subdivisions

[.009]   Historical, geographical, persons treatment

Do not use; class treatment by governmental level in 336.01; areas, regions, places in general, persons, ancient world in 336.09; continents, countries, localities in modern world in 336.4–336.9

.01	By governmental level

Here are classed works about multiple jurisdictions at the same level, e.g., public finance at the state level in the United States 336.01373. Works about a single jurisdiction are classed in 336.093 or 336.4–336.9, e.g., public finance at the national level in the United States 336.73 (*not* 336.01273)

.012	National

Add to base number 336.012 notation 1–9 from Table 2, e.g., national public finance in Europe 336.0124

.013	State and provincial

Add to base number 336.013 notation 1–9 from Table 2, e.g., provincial public finance in Canada 336.01371

.014	Local

Add to base number 336.014 notation 1–9 from Table 2, e.g., local public finance in Pennsylvania 336.014748

.02	Revenue

Add to base number 336.02 notation 1–9 from Table 2, e.g., revenue in Great Britain 336.0241

Class specific forms of revenue in 336.1–336.2

.09	Historical, geographical, persons treatment, associations of sovereign states

Class continents, countries, localities in the modern world in 336.4–336.9

.090 1–.090 5	Historical periods

Add to base number 336.090 the numbers following —090 in notation 0901–0905 from Table 1, e.g., public finance in the 19th century 336.09034

.091	Areas, regions, places in general; associations of sovereign states
.091 6	Associations of sovereign states
.091 62	League of Nations
.091 63	United Nations
.091 68	Regional associations

Example: League of Arab States

Class regional associations limited to specific continents in 336.4–336.9

.091 7	Socioeconomic regions

Add to base number 336.0917 the numbers following —17 in —171–177 from Table 2, e.g., public finance in developing countries 336.091724

.092	Persons

.093   The ancient world

             Add to base number 336.093 the numbers following —3 in notation 31–39 from Table 2, e.g., public finance in the Roman Empire 336.0937

>   **336.1–336.2 Revenues**

          Class comprehensive works in 336.02

.1   **Nontax revenues**

          For public borrowing, see 336.34

>   336.11–336.15 Commercial revenues

          Class comprehensive works in 336.1

          For revenue from public industries and services, see 336.19

.11   From rents and franchises

.12   From public lands

          Including mineral rights

          Class income from rental of land and leasing of mineral rights in 336.11

.15   From deposits, investments, loans

.16   Administrative revenues

          Examples: fees for services rendered, for licenses; fines; gifts; profits on coinage

          For franchises, see 336.11

.17   Revenues from lotteries

.18   Inter- and intragovernmental revenues

.182   From reparations and interest on war loans

.185   From one government unit to another

          Examples: grants from higher units, payment in lieu of taxes, technical assistance funds

.188   From international grants

.19   Revenue from public industries and services

.2   Taxes and taxation

Class here interdisciplinary works on taxes and taxation

Class tax law in 343.04, tax administration in 351.724

See Manual at 336.2 vs. 351.724, 343.04

SUMMARY

336.200 1–.200 9	**Standard subdivisions**
.201–.207	**General topics**
.22	**Real property taxes**
.23	**Personal property taxes**
.24	**Income taxes**
.25	**Poll taxes**
.26	**Customs taxes (Customs duties)**
.27	**Other taxes**
.29	**Principles of taxation**

.200 1–.200 8   Standard subdivisions

.200 9   Historical, geographical, persons treatment

Class treatment by governmental level in 336.201

>   336.201–336.207 General topics

Observe the following table of precedence, e.g., reform of business taxes 336.207 (*not* 336.205)

Business taxes	336.207
Provisions that allow tax avoidance	336.206
Taxes by governmental level	336.201
Tax reform	336.205

Class comprehensive works in 336.2

.201   Taxes by governmental level

Here are classed works about multiple jurisdictions at the same level, e.g., state taxes in the United States 336.201373. Works about a single jurisdiction are classed in 336.2009, e.g., federal taxes in the United States 336.200973 (*not* 336.201273)

.201 2   National taxes

Add to base number 336.20212 notation 1–9 from Table 2, e.g., national taxes in Europe 336.20124

.201 3   State and provincial taxes

Add to base number 336.2013 notation 1–9 from Table 2, e.g., provincial taxes in Canada 336.201371

.201 4   Local taxes and rates

Add to base number 336.2014 notation 1–9 from Table 2, e.g., local taxes in Pennsylvania 336.2014748

.205   Tax reform

Including proposals and innovations

.206   Provisions that allow tax avoidance

Former heading: Reductions in taxes

Examples: tax credits, deductions, incentives, loopholes, rebates

Class here tax expenditure (tax deductions, exemptions, credits, by which a government ''spends'' revenue by not collecting it)

.207   Business taxes

Examples: taxes on industry, manufacturing, small business, international business

.22   Real property taxes

Taxes on land, buildings, permanent improvements

Class here rates (United Kingdom), comprehensive works on property taxes

For personal property taxes, see 336.23

.222   Rates, assessment, valuation

Class rates (percentages), assessment, valuation of specific kinds of real property in 336.225

.225   Specific kinds of real property

Examples: farm, residential, commercial property

.23   Personal property taxes

On tangible and intangible property

Including mobile homes

.24   Income taxes

Class here comprehensive works on taxes on personal wealth

For property taxes, see 336.22; estate, inheritance, gift taxes, 336.276

.241   General topics

Class general topics applied to personal income tax in 336.242, general topics applied to corporate income tax in 336.243

.241 5   Reform

Class reform of taxes on business income in 336.2417

.241 6   Provisions that allow tax avoidance

Former heading: Reductions and rebates

Class provisions allowing avoidance of taxes on business income in 336.2417

.241 7   Taxes on business income

.242	Personal (Individual) income taxes
	See also 362.582 for negative income tax
.242 1	General topics
	Class general topics applied to taxes on specific kinds of personal income in 336.2422–336.2428
.242 15	Reform
.242 16	Provisions that allow tax avoidance
	Former heading: Reductions and rebates
.242 2	Income from wages
	Including withholding tax
.242 3	Self-employment income
	Examples: income from individual proprietorships, from partnerships
.242 4	Income from property transfers
	Capital gains and losses
	Class here comprehensive works on taxation of individual and corporate capital gains and losses
	Class taxation of corporate capital gains in 336.243
.242 6	Interest income
	Class here comprehensive works on taxation of individual and corporate interest income
	Class taxation of corporate interest income in 336.243
.242 8	Retirement income
.243	Corporate income taxes
	Examples: capital gains taxes, interest income
	Class business taxes in 336.207
.243 1	General topics
	Class general topics applied to profits taxes in 336.2432
.243 15	Reform
.243 16	Provisions that allow tax avoidance
	Former heading: Reductions
	Example: oil depletion allowance
.243 2	Profits taxes
	Examples: excess and undistributed profits taxes
.249	Social security taxes
	See also 368.4 for social security benefits
	See Manual at 336.249 vs. 368.401, 368.4011

.25	Poll taxes
.26	Customs taxes (Customs duties)

See also 382.7 for interdisciplinary works on tariff policy

.263	Export and transit taxes
.264	Import taxes

For import tax schedules, see 336.265; import taxes on specific commodities, 336.266

.265	Import tax schedules

For import tax schedules on specific commodities, see 336.266

.266	Import taxes and tax schedules on specific commodities

Add to base number 336.266 notation 001–999, e.g., taxes on paintings 336.26675

.27	Other taxes
.271	Excise and related taxes

Examples: luxury, use taxes

.271 3	Sales taxes
.271 4	Value added taxes
.271 6	Severance taxes
.272	Stamp taxes and revenue stamps
.276	Estate, inheritance, gift taxes
.278	Taxes on specific commodities, services, industries

Add to base number 336.278 notation 001–999, e.g., coal industry taxes 336.2783382724

Class a specific kind of tax on a specific commodity, service, industry with the kind of tax, e.g., import taxes on coal 336.26655324, severance taxes on coal 336.2716

.29	Principles of taxation

Class principles of specific kinds of taxes in 336.22–336.27

.291	General principles

Examples: adequacy (yield), certainty, diversity, economy and convenience of collection, justice

.293	Kinds of rate

Examples: progressive, proportional, regressive rates

.294   Incidence

        The final burden of tax payment and the people on whom it falls

        Including direct, indirect, double taxation

        Class incidence of a specific tax with the tax, e.g., incidence of income tax 336.24

.3   **Public borrowing, debt, expenditure**

        Class here fiscal policy, comprehensive works on monetary and fiscal policy

        Class use of fiscal and monetary policy in economic stabilization in 339.5

        For monetary policy, see 332.46

.31   Public (Government) securities

        Example: government Eurobonds [*formerly also* 336.3435]

        Class investment in government securities in 332.63232

        For short term securities, see 336.32

.32   Short term securities

        Examples: certificates of indebtedness, treasury bills and notes

.34   Public borrowing and public debt

        For public securities, see 336.31; debt management, 336.36

.340 9   Historical, geographical, persons treatment

        Class treatment by governmental level in 336.343

.343   By governmental level

        Here are classed works about multiple jurisdictions at the same level, e.g., public borrowing and public debt at the state level in the United States 336.343273, international debt in Latin America 336.3435098. Works about a single jurisdiction are classed in 336.3409, e.g., borrowing and debt at the national level in the United States 336.340973 (*not* 336.343373)

        Class flotation of loans regardless of level in 336.344, limitation of indebtedness regardless of level in 336.346

.343 1   Local level

        Add to base number 336.3431 notation 1–9 from Table 2, e.g., local borrowing in Pennsylvania 336.3431748

.343 2   State and provincial level

        Add to base number 336.3432 notation 1–9 from Table 2, e.g., provincial borrowing and public debt in Canada 336.343271

.343 3   National level

        Add to base number 336.3433 notation 1–9 from Table 2, e.g., national borrowing and public debts in Europe 336.34334

        Class borrowing by one nation from another nation in 336.3435

.343 5 International level

>Borrowing by one nation from another, public debts owed by one nation to another

>Class here comprehensive works on international borrowing and debts

>Government Eurobonds relocated to 336.31

>Class role of banks in international borrowing and debts in 332.15

.344 Flotation of loans

>Including allotments, subscriptions, compulsory loans, marketability

>Class government securities in 336.31

.346 Limitation of public indebtedness

.36 Debt management

>Class debt limits (ceilings) in 336.346

>*See also 339.523 for deficit financing*

.363 Repayment and redemption

>Including sinking funds

.368 Repudiation and abrogation

>Class here public insolvency

.39 Expenditure

>General aspects: character, principles, justification

>Class tax expenditure in 336.206, economic effects of expenditure in 339.522

>*See Manual at 336 vs. 351.72*

.4–.9 Public finance of specific continents, countries, localities in modern world

>Add to base number 336 notation 4–9 from Table 2, e.g., public finance of Australia 336.94

337 International economics

>Class here international economic planning; comprehensive works on international economic relations, on international economic cooperation

>Class a specific aspect of international economics not provided for here with the aspect, e.g., international (multinational) business enterprises 338.88, foreign trade 382

>*See also 341.75 for international economic law*

.09 Historical, geographical, persons treatment

>Class foreign economic policies and relations of specific jurisdictions and groups of jurisdictions in 337.3–337.9 (*not* 337.093–337.099)

.1 **Multilateral economic cooperation**

Former heading: Spheres of economic cooperation

Class here economic integration, multilateral agreements and multistate organizations for economic cooperation

Class bilateral economic cooperation in 337.3–337.9, trade agreements in 382.9

See also 341.2 for interdisciplinary works on international organizations

See Manual at 337.1 vs. 337.3–337.9

.109 Historical and persons treatment

Class geographical treatment in 337.11–337.19

.11 In areas, regions, places in general

Add to base number 337.11 the numbers following —1 in notation 17–18 from Table 2, e.g., multilateral economic cooperation in the Western Hemisphere 337.11812

.14 European multilateral cooperation

.142 European Economic Community (European Common Market, EEC)

.143 European Free Trade Association (EFTA)

.147 Council for Mutual Economic Assistance (COMECON)

Former heading: East European Economic Organization

.15–.19 Multilateral cooperation in other continents

Add to base number 337.1 notation 5–9 from Table 2, e.g., Andean Group 337.18

.3–.9 **Foreign economic policies and relations of specific jurisdictions and groups of jurisdictions**

Class here bilateral economic cooperation

Add to base number 337 notation 3–9 from Table 2, e.g., economic policy of United Kingdom 337.41; then, for foreign economic relations between two jurisdictions or groups of jurisdictions, add 0* and to the result add notation 1–9 from Table 2, e.g., economic relations between United Kingdom and France 337.41044

Give priority in notation to the jurisdiction or group of jurisdictions emphasized. If the emphasis is equal, give priority to the one coming first in the sequence of area notations
(Option: Give priority in notation to the jurisdiction or group of jurisdictions requiring local emphasis, e.g., libraries in the United States class foreign economic relations between the United States and France in 337.73044)

Class multilateral economic cooperation in 337.1

See Manual at 337.1 vs. 337.3–337.9

*Add 00 for standard subdivisions; see instructions at beginning of Table 1

338   Production

Class here comprehensive works on the economic and technical aspects of industry and production, e.g., the economy and technology of the automotive industry 338.476292

Production of energy relocated to 333.79, production economics of insurance industry to 368

Class specific factors of production in 331–333; production economics of financial industries in 332, of real estate business in 333.33; economics of cooperative production in 334; commerce, communications, transportation in 380; production technology in 620–690

See Manual at 332 vs. 338, 658.15; 363.5, 363.6, 363.8 vs. 338

SUMMARY

338.001–.009	**Standard subdivisions**
.01–.09	**[General topics]**
.1	**Agriculture**
.2	**Extraction of minerals**
.3	**Other extractive industries**
.4	**Secondary industries and services**
.5	**General production economics**
.6	**Organization of production**
.7	**Business enterprises and their structure**
.8	**Combinations**
.9	**Economic development and growth**

.001   Philosophy and theory

         Class a specific theory with the subject, e.g., law of diminishing marginal utility 338.5212

.001 12   Forecasting and forecasts

         Class forecasting and forecasts of commodities and services in 338.020112, general production forecasting and forecasts in 338.544

.002–.008   Standard subdivisions

.009   Historical, geographical, persons treatment of general principles and theories

         Class historical, geographical, persons treatment of production in 338.09

.01   Factors of production

         Class here comprehensive and theoretical works on factors of production

         Class labor in 331, capital in 332, land in 333, factors of production as part of industrial conditions and situation in 338.09, factors of production as costs of production in 338.512

.02	**Commodities and services**

> Class general production economics in 338.5, consumption in 339.47, shipments and sales in 380–382

.020 12	Classification

> Class here standard industrial classifications

.04	**Entrepreneurship**
.06	**Production efficiency**

> Including cost-output ratio

> Class conservation of energy in 333.7916

.064	**Effect of technological innovations**

> Class here the effect of automation, comprehensive works on the effect of technological innovations on the economy

> Class the effect of technological innovations on a specific aspect of the economy with the aspect, e.g., effect on working conditions 331.25, effect on banking 332.1

> > *See also 303.483 for the effect of technological innovation on society*

.09	**Historical, geographical, persons treatment of production**

> Class here existing and potential resources for production, industrial conditions and situation, industrial surveys, location of industry, productivity

> Add to base number 338.09 notation 01–9 from Table 2, e.g., industrial surveys of Canada 338.0971

> Class a specific resource with the resource, e.g., water for power 333.914

> > *See also 338.6042 for the rationale for and process of locating business enterprises*

> > *See Manual at 333.94 vs. 338.0919; 338.09 vs. 338.6042, 332.67309, 346.07, 658.11, 658.21, T1—068*

> **338.1–338.4 Specific kinds of industries**

> Class here finance of specific kinds of industries [*formerly also* 338.6041], general production economics of specific kinds of industries

> Class comprehensive works in 338; financial industries in 332; real estate business in 333.33; energy production in 333.79; cooperatives in specific kinds of industries in 334; commerce, communications, transportation in 380; organization of production in specific kinds of industries in 338.6; business enterprises other than cooperatives in specific kinds of industries in 338.7–338.8; biographies of entrepreneurs in specific kinds of industries in 338.6–338.8, e.g., biographies of small-business owners 338.642092, biographies of entrepreneurs in textile manufacturing 338.76770092; biographies of people known for their contributions in technology in 600, e.g., biographies of mining engineers 622.092

> **338.1–338.3 Primary (Extractive) industries**

Class comprehensive works in 338

.1   **Agriculture**

See also 334.683 for agricultural cooperatives

See Manual at 631.558 vs. 338.1

.13   Financial aspects

Class here capital formation and other investment in agriculture, costs, prices received by farmers, farm income

Add to base number 338.13 the numbers following 63 in 633–638, e.g., prices of rice 338.13318

Class government policies that affect financial aspects in 338.18, food prices in 338.19

See also 338.16 for production efficiency

See Manual at 332 vs. 338, 658.15

.14   Factors affecting production

Examples: drought, plant and animal diseases, shortages of materials and equipment used in farming

Class financial factors in 338.13, production efficiency in 338.16, surpluses and shortages of farm products in 338.17, government policies in 338.18

[.15]   Surpluses and shortages of farm products

Relocated to 338.17

.16   Production efficiency

Including cost-output ratio, size of farm, use of labor

Class here science, technological innovation in agriculture

Class energy conservation in agriculture in 333.7966

See also 338.14 for factors affecting production

.161   Mechanization

Class here automation

Class mechanization of harvesting methods in 338.163

.162   Agricultural methods

Examples: crop rotation; use of plant nutrients, of insecticides

For harvesting methods, see 338.163

.163   Harvesting methods

.17   Products

Including the seed industry as a whole

Specific kinds of seed are classed with the kind

Class here surpluses and shortages of farm products [*formerly* 338.15], forecasts and projections of supply and demand

Add to base number 338.17 the numbers following 63 in 633–638, e.g., rice or seed rice 338.17318, forestry 338.1749, forest products 338.17498; however, supply of timber in nature relocated to 333.7511, demand for timber relocated from 338.1749 to 333.7512

Class specific elements of production applied to specific products and groups of products in 338.13–338.16, 338.18; supply, surpluses, shortages of food in 338.19; specific producers in 338.763

See Manual at 333.75 vs. 338.1749

.18   Government farm policies

Examples: acreage allotments, agricultural credit, drought relief, price supports, subsidies

Class government policies with respect to food supply in 338.19

.180 9   Historical, geographical, persons treatment

Class treatment by specific continents, countries, localities in 338.183–338.189 (*not* 338.18093–338.18099)

.181   International policies

Policies and programs of international bodies

.183–.189   Treatment by specific continents, countries, localities

Add to base number 338.18 notation 3–9 from Table 2, e.g., government farm policies of India 338.1854

.19   Food supply

Class here economic causes and effects of, economic remedies for maladjustments in food supply; measures for attaining and maintaining adequate amounts of food; food requirements (demand); reserves (stocks, supply) of food; prices of food to the consumer; comprehensive works on the economics of production, storage, distribution of food

Add to base number 338.19 notation 1–9 from Table 2, e.g., food supply in Africa 338.196

Class interdisciplinary works on food supply in 363.8, production of food in 338.13–338.18, supply of specific food commodities in 338.17, food processing in 338.47664

See Manual at 363.5, 363.6, 363.8 vs. 338; 363.8 vs. 338.19

.2 **Extraction of minerals**

Class here extraction of energy resources, comprehensive works on the economics of extraction and processing of minerals and energy resources

Class conservation of mineral and energy resources in 333.7–333.9, processing of minerals and raw materials of energy in 338.47

See Manual at 333.8 vs. 338.2, 553

.23 Financial aspects

Class here capital formation and other investment in industries engaged in extraction of minerals; costs, income, prices

Add to base number 338.23 the numbers following 553 in 553.2–553.9, e.g., tin 338.23453

Class production efficiency in 338.26

See Manual at 332 vs. 338, 658.15

.26 Production efficiency

Including automation, cost-output ratio, effect of technological innovation, factors of production

Class energy conservation in mineral extraction industries in 333.7965

.27 Products

Add to base number 338.27 the numbers following 553 in 553.2–553.9, e.g., water 338.277

Supply in storage, shortages, surpluses, demand, and projections of these relocated to 333.8

Class specific elements of production applied to specific products in 338.23–338.26, specific producers in 338.76

See also 553.2–553.9 for supply in nature

.3 **Other extractive industries**

Including financial aspects, production efficiency

See Manual at 332 vs. 338, 658.15

.37 Products

Class specific producers in 338.76

See Manual at 333.954 vs. 338.37

.371 Products of culture of invertebrates and cold-blooded vertebrates

Add to base number 338.371 the numbers following 639 in 639.3–639.7, e.g., culture of oysters 338.37141; however, class insect culture in 338.178

Class comprehensive works on fishing and the culture of fish and other water animals in 338.3727

.372   Products of fishing, whaling, hunting, trapping

                     Add to base number 338.372 the numbers following 59 in 592–599, e.g.,
                     sponges 338.37234

                     Class the culture of invertebrates and cold-blooded vertebrates in
                     338.371

                     See Manual at 338.372

.4   Secondary industries and services

.43   Financial aspects

                     Class here capital formation and other investment in secondary industry and
                     services; costs, income, prices

                     Use 338.430001–338.430009 for standard subdivisions

                     Add to base number 338.43 notation 001–999, e.g., automobile prices
                     338.436292; however, class financial aspects of financial industries in 332;
                     of real estate business in 333.33; of energy production in 333.79; of
                     cooperative production in 334; of the insurance industry in 368.01; of
                     commerce, communications, transportation in 380

                     Class production efficiency in 338.45

                     See Manual at 332 vs. 338, 658.15

.45   Production efficiency

                     Including cost-output ratio, factors of production (land, labor, capital),
                     production capacity

                     Class energy conservation in secondary industries in 333.7916

.454   Automation

                     For automation in specific industries, see 338.456

.456   Production efficiency in specific industries and groups of industries

                     Class here automation in specific industries

.456 1   Other than extractive, manufacturing, construction

                     Class here service industries

                     Add to base number 338.4561 notation 001–999, e.g., production
                     efficiency in hospital services 338.456136211; however, class
                     production efficiency in financial industries in 332; in real estate
                     business in 333.33; in cooperative enterprises in 334; in the insurance
                     industry in 368; in commerce, communications, transportation in 380

.456 2–.456 9   Manufacturing and construction

                     Add to base number 338.456 the numbers following 6 in 620–690,
                     e.g., power equipment in textile manufacture 338.456770285;
                     however, class production efficiency in energy production in 333.79,
                     in cooperative enterprises in 334

.46   Professional services

> Class specific elements of production applied to professional services in 338.43–338.45, specific professional services in 338.47

.47   Goods and services

> Class here quantities produced, shortages, surpluses, stockpiles, forecasts and projections of supply and demand

> Use 338.470001–338.470009 for standard subdivisions

> Add to base number 338.47 notation 001–999, e.g., the product gasoline 338.4766553827 [*formerly also* 333.8232], tourist industry 338.4791; however, class production economics of financial industries in 332; of real estate business in 333.33; of energy production in 333.79; of cooperative enterprises in 334; of the insurance industry in 368; of commerce, communications, transportation in 380

> Class comprehensive works on professional services in 338.46, specific elements of production applied to specific goods and services in 338.43–338.45, specific producers in 338.76

.48   Government policies

> Class government policies with respect to a specific aspect of secondary industries and services in 338.43–338.47

.5   General production economics

> Including risk

> Class here microeconomics (economics of the firm)

> Class production economics of specific kinds of industries in 338.1–338.4

> *For organization of production, see 338.6*

[.501 12]   Forecasting and forecasts

> > Do not use; class in 338.544

.51   Costs

.512   Factors of production as costs of production

> > Including law of diminishing marginal returns, of factoral proportions

.514   Elements in cost calculation

.514 2   Kinds of cost

> > Examples: average, fixed, marginal, total, variable

.514 4   Size of enterprise

> > Including economies and diseconomies of scale, use of technology

.516   Profit

> > Including relation of marginal cost to marginal revenue

.52	Prices

Class here determination, effects of changes, comprehensive works on prices

Class effect of money on prices in 332.41, effect of costs on prices in 338.516, effects of prices on the whole economy in 339.42

.520 1   Philosophy and theory

Class specific theories in 338.521

.520 2   Miscellany

.520 21   Tabulated and related materials

Do not use for statistics; class in 338.528

.521   Price theories

Class here law of supply and demand, theories of value

Class Marxian labor theory of value in 335.412

See also 333.7 for supply and demand for natural resources and energy, 338.1–338.4 for supply and demand for specific products

.521 2   Theory of demand

Example: law of diminishing marginal utility

Including price-demand relationship

.521 3   Theory of supply

Including price-supply relationship

> 338.522–338.526 Price determination

Class comprehensive works in 338.52

.522   Price determination in free markets

Example: determination in market for brand-name products

Including interproduct competition, e.g., butter versus margarine

.523   Price determination in controlled markets

Determination by oligopolies, monopolies

Including price leadership

.526   Prices determination by government regulation

.528   Levels

Class here statistics, indexes

.528 021   Tabulated and related materials

Do not use for statistics; class in 338.528

.54	Economic fluctuations
	Example: seasonal variations
	Including secular trends
[.540 112]	Forecasting and forecasts
	Do not use; class in 338.544
.542	Business cycles
	Including prosperity, recession, depression, recovery; panics
	Class remedial measures in 338.543
.543	Remedial and preventive action
	Class economic stabilization in 339.5
.544	General production forecasting and forecasts
	See also 658.40355 for forecasting as a technique of managerial decision-making
.544 2	Methods of forecasting
	Class economic forecasting in 330.0112
.544 3	Forecasts
	Class forecasts of economic situation in 330.900112
.6	**Organization of production**
	Class here organization of production in specific kinds of industries
	Including worker control of industry
	Class guild socialism in 335.15, syndicalism in 335.82, the role of unions in achieving worker control of industry in 331.8801
	For business enterprises and their structure, see 338.7
	See Manual at 338.76
.604	Special topics
.604 1	Finance
	Finance of specific kinds of industries relocated to 338.1–338.4
.604 2	Location
	Class here proximity to sources of power, raw materials, labor supply, transportation, markets
	See Manual at 338.09 vs. 338.6042, 332.67309, 346.07, 658.11, 658.21, T1—068
.604 6	Specialization
	Including law of comparative advantage
.604 8	Competition and restraint
	Class monopoly and monopolies in 338.82

.61		Private enterprise

Class specific systems of private enterprise in 338.63, specific sizes of private enterprise in 338.64

.62   Public enterprise

.63   Systems of production

> *For factory system, see 338.65*

.632   Guild system

.634   Domestic system

> Class here cottage industry

.64   Size of enterprises

Class relation of size of enterprise to cost of production in 338.5144, specific types of enterprises of specific sizes in 338.7–338.8

.642   Small business

> Including custom production

> Class here small industries

.642 089   Racial, ethnic, national groups

> Class minority enterprises in 338.6422

.642 2   Minority enterprises

> Class handicraft industries operated by minorities in 338.6425

.642 5   Handicraft industries

.644   Big business

> Class here large industry

> Class monopoly and monopolies in 338.82

.65   Factory system

.7   **Business enterprises and their structure**

Not limited to private or capitalist enterprises

Class here interdisciplinary works on business enterprises, on organizations for production

> *For cooperatives, see 334; combinations, 338.8*

> *See Manual at 338.76*

.71   Formation and dissolution of business enterprises

\>   338.72–338.74 Specific kinds of business enterprises

Class comprehensive works in 338.7, specific kinds of business enterprises in specific industries and groups of industries in 338.76

.72	Individual proprietorships
.73	Partnerships
.74	Corporations

Open and closed

Class government corporations as part of the public administrative process in 351.0092

.76	Business enterprises in specific industries and groups of industries

Class here specific individual business enterprises, biographies of entrepreneurs in specific fields

Class business enterprises engaged in trade in 380.1; biographies of people known for their contribution to technology in 600, using notation 092 from Table 1, e.g., biographies of mining engineers 622.092

See Manual at 338.76

.761	Other than extractive, manufacturing, construction

Class here service industries

Add to base number 338.761 notation 001–999, e.g., law firms 338.76134; however, class financial institutions in 332.1–332.6; real estate business enterprises in 333.33; cooperative enterprises in 334; insurance companies in 368.0065; enterprises engaged in commerce, communications, transportation in 380

.762–.769	Extractive, manufacturing, construction

Add to base number 338.76 the numbers following 6 in 620–690, e.g., agriculture 338.763; however, class enterprises engaged in production of energy in 333.79, cooperative enterprises in 334.682–334.689

.8	**Combinations**

Organization and structure for massive production and control of production

Class here antitrust policies, economic concentration, comprehensive works on combinations and their practices

To be classed here, works about specific individual enterprises must stress that they are combinations; otherwise, the works are classed in 338.76

.804	Special topics
.804 2	Kinds of combinations

Examples: horizontal, vertical, conglomerate

.82	Restrictive practices

Class here monopoly and monopolies, oligopoly and oligopolies

Use of this number for comprehensive works on combinations and their practices discontinued; class in 338.8

Class price determination in 338.523, restrictive practices of international (multinational) business enterprises in 338.884

.826 In specific industries, groups of industries, fields of enterprise

.826 1 Other than extractive, manufacturing, construction

Class here service industries

Add to base number 338.8261 notation 001–999, e.g., restrictive practices in publishing 338.82610705; however, class restrictive practices by combinations in the financial industries in 332.1–332.6; in real estate business in 333.33; in cooperative enterprise in 334; in the insurance industry in 368; in commerce, communications, transportation in 380

.826 2–.826 9 Extractive, manufacturing, construction

Add to base number 338.826 the numbers following 6 in 620–690, e.g., restrictive practices by combinations engaged in computer engineering 338.8262139; however, class restrictive practices by combinations engaged in energy production in 333.79, by cooperatives in 334

> 338.83–338.87 Specific forms of combinations and their practices

Class comprehensive works in 338.8, international combinations regardless of form in 338.88

.83 Mergers and amalgamations

.836 In specific industries, groups of industries, fields of enterprise

.836 1 Other than extractive, manufacturing, construction

Class here service industries

Add to base number 338.8361 notation 001–999, e.g., mergers of publishers 338.83610705; however, class mergers and amalgamations of financial institutions in 332.1–332.6, of real estate business enterprises in 333.33, of cooperatives in 334, of enterprises in the insurance industry in 368, of enterprises engaged in commerce, communications, transportation in 380

.836 2–.836 9 Extractive, manufacturing, construction

Add to base number 338.836 the numbers following 6 in 620–690, e.g., mergers of automobile companies 338.836292; however, class mergers and amalgamations of enterprises engaged in energy production in 333.79, of cooperatives in 334

.85 Trusts

.86 Holding companies

.87 Informal arrangements

Examples: cartels, interlocking directorates, pools

.88 International (Multinational) business enterprises and their activities

.880 9 Historical and persons treatment

Class geographical treatment in 338.888–338.889

.

> 338.881–338.884 Specific aspects of international (multinational) business enterprises and their activities

Class comprehensive works in 338.88, specific aspects of international enterprises engaged in specific fields and their activities in 338.887, of foreign-owned enterprises in specific areas and their activities in 338.888–338.889

.881   Growth, expansion, power

See also 322.3 for political influence

.883   Role in international economic development

.884   Restrictive practices and their control

International monopoly, oligopoly

.887   Multinational business enterprises in specific industries, groups of industries, fields

.887 1   Other than extractive, manufacturing, construction

Class here service industries

Add to base number 338.8871 notation 001–999, e.g., multinational enterprises engaged in advertising 338.88716591; however, class multinational enterprises in financial industries in 332.1–332.6; in real estate business in 333.33; multinational cooperatives in 334; multinational enterprises in the insurance industry in 368; in commerce, communications, transportation in 380

.887 2–.887 9   Extractive, manufacturing, construction

Add to base number 338.887 the numbers following 6 in 620–690, e.g., multinational enterprises engaged in mining petroleum and natural gas 338.88722338; however, class multinational enterprises engaged in energy production in 333.79, multinational cooperatives in 334

.888   Foreign-owned enterprises by location of operations

Add to base number 338.888 notation 1–9 from Table 2, e.g., foreign-owned enterprises in Europe 338.8884

Class foreign-owned enterprises in specific industries and groups of industries in 338.887, enterprises owned by inhabitants of one nation in another nation in 338.889

See Manual at 338.888–338.889

.889   Foreign-owned enterprises by owner

Add to base number 338.889 notation 1–9 from Table 2, e.g., foreign enterprises owned by United States nationals 338.88973; then, for area in which enterprise is located, add 0* and again add notation 1–9 from Table 2, e.g., enterprises owned by United States nationals in Canada 338.88973071

Class foreign-owned enterprises in specific industries or groups of industries in 338.887, foreign-owned enterprises in a specific area without regard to area of ownership in 338.888

See Manual at 338.888–338.889

.9   **Economic development and growth**

Including autarky and interdependence

Class here economic planning, government policies and programs

Class economic development and growth with respect to a specific subject with the subject, e.g., international economic development and growth 337, economic development and growth with respect to specific kinds of industries 338.1–338.4

.900 1–.900 8   Standard subdivisions

.900 9   Historical, geographical, persons treatment

Class treatment by country and locality in 338.93–338.99 (*not* 338.90093–338.90099)

.91   International development and growth

Foreign economic assistance (foreign aid)

Including technical assistance

Class here assistance (aid) by international organizations

Class foreign economic policies and relations of specific jurisdictions and groups of jurisdictions in 337.3–337.9

.910 9   Assistance to specific jurisdictions and groups of jurisdictions

Class assistance given by specific jurisdictions and groups of jurisdictions to other jurisdictions in 338.911–338.919

.911–.919   International assistance (Aid) by specific jurisdictions and groups of jurisdictions

Add to base number 338.91 notation 1–9 from Table 2, e.g., assistance by United Kingdom 338.9141; then, for assistance by a specific jurisdiction or group of jurisdictions to another jurisdiction or group of jurisdictions, add 0* and again add notation 1–9 from Table 2, e.g., assistance by United Kingdom to Nigeria 338.91410669

.92   Specific policies

Class specific policies in specific continents, countries, localities in 338.93–338.99

*Add 00 for standard subdivisions; see instructions at beginning of Table 1

.922   Subsidies and grants

.924   Nationalization

.926   Information policy

> Class here science policy, technology transfer
>
> *See Manual at 500 vs. 338.926, 351.855*

.927   Appropriate technology

> Class here alternative technology

.93–.99   Economic development and growth in specific continents, countries, localities

> Add to base number 338.9 notation 3–9 from Table 2, e.g., economic policies of United Kingdom in 338.941; then add 0* and to the result add the numbers following 338.92 in 338.922–338.927, e.g., subsidies in United Kingdom 338.94102

339   Macroeconomics and related topics

> *For economic fluctuations, see 338.54*
>
> *See Manual at 339 vs. 332, 336*

SUMMARY

339.2	**Distribution of income and wealth**
.3	**National product, wealth, income accounts and accounting**
.4	**Factors affecting national product, wealth, income**
.5	**Macroeconomic policy**

[.01]   Philosophy and theory

> Do not use; class in 339.3

.2   **Distribution of income and wealth**

> Standard subdivisions are added for either or both of the topics named in the heading
>
> Class national wealth and income accounts and accounting in 339.3; specific aspects of income distribution in 339.4; transfer payments, redistribution of income in 339.52

.21   Functional distribution of income and wealth

> Functional distribution of income: division of nation's income among factors of production: land (rent, rental income), labor (wages, salaries), capital (interest), entrepreneurship (proprietor's income), corporate profits
>
> Standard subdivisions are added for either or both of the topics named in the heading

*Add 00 for standard subdivisions; see instructions at beginning of Table 1

.22	**Personal distribution of income and wealth**

Division of nation's income and wealth among families and individuals

Including consumer income, household income

Standard subdivisions are added for either or both of the topics named in the heading

Class income-consumption relations (household budget) in 339.41, poverty in 339.46

See Manual at 339.32 vs. 339.22

.23	**Input-output accounts (Interindustry accounts)**

Accounts and analysis of goods and services provided by each industry for all other industries and consuming units

Including data on specific industries

.26	**Flow-of-funds accounts**

Sources of funds paid to and use of funds by various sectors of the economy

.3	**National product, wealth, income accounts and accounting**

Class here macroeconomic theory; product, wealth, income accounts and accounting of other types of areas, e.g., states, provinces; interdisciplinary works on national product, wealth, income

Class macroeconomic policy in 339.5

For distribution of income and wealth, see 339.2; factors affecting national product, wealth, income, 339.4

.309	**Historical, geographical, persons treatment**

Class product, wealth, income accounts and accounting of specific countries and localities in 339.33–339.39 (*not* 339.3093–339.3099)

.31	**Gross product accounts and accounting**

Class here gross domestic product (GDP), gross national product (GNP)

See also 339.32 for net national product (NNP)

.310 9	**Historical, geographical, persons treatment**

Class gross product accounts and accounting of specific countries and localities in 339.33–339.39 (*not* 339.31093–339.31099)

.32	**Other kinds of national accounts and accounting**

Examples: net national product (NNP), national income (NI), personal income (PI), disposable personal income (DPI)

See Manual at 339.32 vs. 339.22

.320 9	**Historical, geographical, persons treatment**

Class kinds of national accounts and accounting of specific countries and localities in 339.33–339.39 (*not* 339.32093–339.32099)

.33–.39   Product, wealth, income accounts of specific countries and localities

Add to base number 339.3 notation 3–9 from Table 2, e.g., gross national product of the United States 339.373

.4   **Factors affecting national product, wealth, income**

For economic stabilization, see 339.5

.41   Income and its relation to consumption

Including consumer responses to decreases and increases in income, the effect of consumption on income (the accelerator), household budgets as a measure of relation of income to consumption

Class effects of prices on consumption in 339.42; the multiplier, the relation of consumption and savings in 339.43

See Manual at 332.41 vs. 339.41, 339.42

.42   Cost of living (Prices)

Including effect of prices on consumption; the total effects of rising costs of a commodity on the consumer, e.g., the total effects of rising energy costs on the consumer

Class price statistics and indexes in 338.528

See Manual at 332.41 vs. 339.41, 339.42

.43   Savings and investment

Example: capital formation

Including effect of investment on income (the multiplier), relation of consumption and savings

.46   Economic causes and effects of poverty

See also 362.51 for social causes of poverty, 362.53 for social effects of poverty

.47   Consumption (Spending)

Class here standard of living, interdisciplinary works on consumption

Class the social aspects of consumption in 306.3; consumption viewed in light of its effect on the future supply of natural resources and energy in 333.7–333.9 with notation 13 from the add table under 333.7; consumption as a factor in shortages and surpluses of products in 338; consumption in relation to income in 339.41, in relation to cost of living in 339.42, in relation to savings and investment in 339.43, in relation to poverty in 339.46; government spending in 339.522; works discussing consumption as sales or marketing opportunities (e.g., results of market studies) or as a measure of the volume, value, or kind of trade in 380–382

For consumption of specific commodities and services, of specific groups of commodities and services, see 339.48

.48   Consumption of specific commodities and services, of specific groups of commodities and services

Add to base number 339.48 notation 001–999, e.g., consumption of agricultural products 339.4863

.49   Conservation of national resources

National resources consist of natural resources; human resources; resources that result from human activities, e.g., housing

Add to base number 339.49 notation 1–9 from Table 2, e.g., conservation of the national resources of India 339.4954

Class conservation of natural resources in 333.72

.5   **Macroeconomic policy**

Class here economic stabilization and growth, equilibrium, full employment policies, incomes policies

Class measures to combat inflation in 332.415, to control economic fluctuations in 338.543, to promote growth and development in 338.9

.52   Use of fiscal policy

Class here income redistribution

.522   Government spending

Including transfer payments

.523   Budget surpluses and deficits

.525   Taxation

.53   Use of monetary policy

Examples: discount rates offered by central banks, reserve requirements imposed on banks, open-market operations, regulation of bank credit

340   Law

Class here jurisprudence

Classification numbers for works on law (other than international law, law in general, kinds of law in general, and the law of a jurisdiction or area in general) are built from four elements:
(1)   34, the base number, indicating law
(2)   A digit indicating the specific branch of law, as follows:
        2 Constitutional and administrative law
        3 Military, defense, tax, economic law
        4 Social, labor, welfare, health, safety, education, cultural law
        5 Criminal law
        6 Private law
        7 Civil procedure and courts
        8 Laws (Statutes), regulations, cases
(3)   A group of digits beginning with 0 indicating a topic subordinate to the specific branch of law
        Example: 05 Procedure (under 5 Criminal law)
(4)   Notation from Table 2 indicating the jurisdiction or place
        Example: 94 Australia

(continued)

340   Law (continued)

Arrange these elements as follows:
- (1)   Base number 34
- (2)   Notation for the branch of law
- (4)   Notation from Table 2 for jurisdiction or place
- (3)   Notation for the subordinate topic in the branch of law, e.g., criminal procedure of Australia 345.9405

Class comprehensive works on the law of specific jurisdictions and areas in the modern world in 349

(Option: To give preferred treatment to the law of a specific jurisdiction, to jurisdictions in general, to branch of law and its subordinate topics, or to subject, use one of the following:

(Option A: To give local emphasis and a shorter notation to the law of a specific jurisdiction or area, arrange the elements as follows:
- (1)   Base number 34
- (2)   Notation for the branch of law
- (3)   Notation for subordinate topic, e.g., (assuming Australia to be the jurisdiction given preferred treatment), criminal procedure of Australia 345.05

(To class the law of a jurisdiction subordinate to the emphasized jurisdiction or area, insert between 2) and 3) a shortened notation from Table 2 derived by dropping from the given area number for a jurisdiction all digits that apply to larger areas. For instance, the number for criminal procedure of New South Wales, a state of Australia, e.g., 345.405. For subordinate jurisdictions of a country with irregular notation, i.e., each country the number for whose subdivisions are coordinate with the number for the entire country (e.g., the Sudan having notation 624, the provinces of the Sudan having notation 625–629), add to the three digits that part of the notation from Table 2 that changes, e.g., criminal procedure of the Darfur region 345.705. Add 00 before adding notation for Table 1 to general works on the law of a jurisdiction or area, e.g., a directory of lawyers in Australia 349.40025

(Class comprehensive works on the law of the preferred jurisdiction or area in 342, comparative law and the law of other jurisdictions and areas in 349

(Option B: To arrange by jurisdiction or area arrange the elements as follows:
- (1)   Base number 34
- (4)   Notation from Table 2, followed by a 0
- (2)   Notation for the branch of law
- (3)   Notation for the subordinate topic without the initial 0, e.g., criminal procedure of Australia 349.4055, of New South Wales 349.44055, texts of the welfare laws of Sydney 349.44104302632. Add 00 before adding notation from Table 1 to general works on the law of a jurisdiction or area, e.g., a directory of lawyers in Australia 349.40025

(Class comparative law in 342 where full instructions are given

(Option C: Class law of a specific discipline or subject with the discipline or subject, using notation 026 from Table 1, e.g., law of education 370.26)

See Manual at 340; 363 vs. 340, 350–354

SUMMARY

340.01–.09	Standard subdivisions
.1	Philosophy and theory of law
.2	Comparative law
.3	Law reform
.5	Legal systems
.9	Conflict of laws
341	International law
.01–.09	Standard subdivisions
.1	Sources of international law
.2	The world community
.3	Relations between states
.4	Jurisdiction and jurisdictional relations of states
.5	Disputes and conflicts between states
.6	Law of war
.7	International cooperation
342	Constitutional and administrative law
.001–.009	Standard subdivisions
.02	Basic instruments of government
.03	Revision and amendment of the basic instruments of government
.04	Structure, powers, functions of governments
.05	Legislative branch of government
.06	Executive branch of government
.07	Election law
.08	Jurisdiction of governmental units over persons
.09	Local government
.3–.9	Specific jurisdictions and areas
343	Military, tax, trade, industrial law
.001–.009	Standard subdivisions
.01	Military, defense (national security), veterans' law
.02	Law of public property
.03	Law of public finance
.04	Tax law
.05	Kinds of taxes by base
.06	Kinds of taxes by incidence
.07	Regulation of economic activity
.08	Regulation of trade
.09	Control of public utilities
.3–.9	Specific jurisdictions and areas
344	Social, labor, welfare, health, safety, education, cultural law
.001–.009	Standard subdivisions
.01	Labor
.02	Social insurance
.03	Welfare
.04	Public health
.05	Public safety
.06	Public works
.07	Education and schools
.08	Educational and cultural exchanges
.09	Culture and religion
.3–.9	Specific jurisdictions and areas

345	**Criminal law**	
.001–.009	Standard subdivisions	
.01	Criminal courts	
.02	Crimes (Offenses)	
.03	Criminals (Offenders)	
.04	Liability, responsibility, guilt	
.05	General criminal procedure	
.06	Evidence	
.07	Trials	
.08	Juvenile procedure	
.3–.9	Specific jurisdictions and areas	

346 Private law
.001–.009 Standard subdivisions, equity
.01 Persons and domestic relations
.02 Contracts and agency
.03 Torts (Delicts)
.04 Property
.05 Inheritance, succession, fiduciary trusts, trustees
.06 Organizations (Associations)
.07 Commercial law
.08 Banking and insurance
.09 Securities and negotiable instruments
.3–.9 Specific jurisdictions and areas

347 Civil procedure and courts
.001–.009 Standard subdivisions
.01 Courts
.02 Courts with general original jurisdiction
.03 Courts with appellate jurisdiction
.04 Courts with specialized jurisdiction
.05 General considerations of procedure
.06 Evidence
.07 Trials
.08 Appellate procedure
.09 Arbitration, mediation, conciliation
.3–.9 Specific jurisdictions and areas

348 Laws (Statutes), regulations, cases
.001–.009 Standard subdivisions, codification
.01 Preliminary materials
.02 Laws (Statutes) and regulations
.04 Cases
.05 Advisory opinions of attorneys-general (ministers of justice)
.3–.9 Specific jurisdictions and areas

349 Law of specific jurisdictions and areas

[.01] Philosophy and theory of law

Do not use; class in 340.1

.02 Miscellany of law

.023 Law as a profession, occupation, hobby

See Manual at 340.023

.03 Encyclopedias [*formerly* 348.06], dictionaries, concordances of law

.05–.08 Standard subdivisions of law

.09   Historical, geographical, persons treatment of law

> Class comprehensive works on the law of specific jurisdictions and areas in the modern world in 349, the historical and geographical treatment of the law of traditional societies in 340.52

[.093]   Treatment by specific jurisdictions and areas in the ancient world

> Do not use; class in 340.53

.1   **Philosophy and theory of law**

> *For the theory of specific legal systems, see 340.5*

.109   Legal theories and schools

> Biography, description, critical appraisal of the work of individual theorists

> Do not add notation from Table 2 for the locale of the theorist

.11   Special topics

> Including the origin, sources, nature, limits of law; rule of law; legal reasoning; justice, injustice

.112   Law and ethics

> Including human rights, the law and morality, legal positivism, natural law

.115   Law and society

> Including distributive justice

> Class here sociological jurisprudence

.2   **Comparative law**

> Class the comparison of specific branches of law in 342–347

> (If option A under 340 is chosen, class comparative law in 349

> (If option B under 340 is chosen, class comparative law in 342)

.3   **Law reform**

.5   **Legal systems**

> History and theory

> Class here customary law

> Class religious laws of a specific religious body with the body, e.g., Christian canon law 262.9, Islamic law relating to religious matters 297.14; a specific subject in a specific system of law with the subject in law, e.g., juristic persons in ancient Roman law 346.37013, in Byzantine law 346.495013, in civil law 346.013

.52   Law of traditional societies

Former heading: Law of nonliterate peoples

Class here ethnological jurisprudence

Add to base number 340.52 notation 4–9 from Table 2, e.g., traditional law of the Sahara 340.5266

Law of traditional societies in the ancient world relocated to 340.53

.53   Ancient law

Class here law of traditional societies in the ancient world [*formerly* 340.52]

Add to base number 340.53 the numbers following —3 in notation 31–39, e.g., the law of ancient Greece 340.538

Class ancient Oriental law in 340.58

For Roman law, see 340.54

.54   Roman law

Including Byzantine law

Class comprehensive works on Roman-derived law in specific jurisdictions and areas in the modern world in 349

For medieval Roman law, see 340.55

>   340.55–340.59 Medieval, modern, Oriental systems of law

Class comprehensive works in 340.5, comprehensive works on the law of specific jurisdictions and areas in the modern world in 349

.55   Medieval European law

Including feudal law, medieval Roman law

Class medieval civil law in 340.56, medieval common law in 340.57

.56   Civil law systems

Systems of law derived from Roman law

Including Roman-Dutch law

See Manual at 340: Terminology and notation used

.57   Common law systems

See Manual at 340.57

.58   Oriental law

Indigenous systems

Class systems of law in Oriental countries derived from a European system with the system from which derived, e.g., civil law 340.56

For Islamic law, see 340.59

.59   Islamic law (Fiqh)

>Law relating to secular matters

.9   **Conflict of laws**

>The body of rules governing the choice of jurisdiction in cases in private law which fall under the laws of two or more such jurisdictions

>Class here private international law

>Add to base number 340.9 the numbers following 346.0 in 346.01–346.09, e.g., conflict of divorce laws 340.9166

>Class domestic conflict of laws in 342.042

>*See Manual at 340.9*

341   **International law**

>*See Manual at 341*

SUMMARY

341.01–.09	**Standard subdivisions**
.1	**Sources of international law**
.2	**The world community**
.3	**Relations between states**
.4	**Jurisdiction and jurisdictional relations of states**
.5	**Disputes and conflicts between states**
.6	**Law of war**
.7	**International cooperation**

.01   Philosophy and theory

>Class critical works on individual publicists (theorists) in 341.1

.02   Miscellany

.026   Treaties and cases

>Texts of treaties and judicial decisions; guides

>Class here conventions, protocols

>Class comprehensive works on treaties in 341.37; treaties as a source of international law in 341.1; treaties and cases on a specific subject with the subject in international law, using this extended notation 026, e.g., collections of treaties on air transportation 341.7567026

>*See Manual at 341.026*

>   341.026 1–341.026 6 Texts of treaties

>Class comprehensive works in 341.026

>   341.026 1–341.026 3 Series of treaties compiled by international organizations

>Class comprehensive works in 341.026, specific kinds of treaties regardless of compiling organization in 341.0265–341.0266

.026 1	League of Nations series of treaties

Class a League of Nations series relating to a specific area in 341.0264

.026 2	United Nations series of treaties

Class a United Nations series relating to a specific area in 341.0264

.026 3	Series of treaties compiled by regional organizations

Add to base number 341.0263 the numbers following 341.24 in 341.242–341.249, e.g., a series compiled by the Organization of American States 341.02635

.026 4	Collections of treaties by area

Add to base number 341.0264 notation 1–9 from Table 2, e.g., treaties on the Philippines 341.0264599

Class collections of treaties relating to a specific area compiled by regional organizations in 341.0263, collections of specific kinds of treaties by area in 341.0265–341.0266

> 341.026 5–341.026 6 Kinds of treaties

Collections and individual treaties

Class comprehensive works in 341.026

.026 5	Multilateral treaties

Class an agreement between an international organization and a specific country in 341.026, treaties on a specific subject with the subject in international law, e.g., a pollution control treaty between the World Health Organization and Spain 341.7623026

.026 6	Bilateral treaties

Add to base number 341.0266 notation 3–9 from Table 2, e.g., treaties of the United Kingdom 341.026641; then add 0* and again add notation 3–9 from Table 2, e.g., treaties between the United Kingdom and France 341.026641044

Give priority in notation to the country coming first in the sequence of area notations
(Option: Give priority in notation to the country requiring local emphasis, e.g., libraries in the United States class treaties between the United Kingdom and the United States in 341.026673041)

.026 7	Codification

*Add 00 for standard subdivisions; see instructions at beginning of Table 1

.026 8	Cases

Decisions and reports

Class here general collections of cases on international matters tried in any court system

Add to base number 341.0268 notation 4–9 from Table 2, e.g., cases brought by the United Kingdom 341.026841; then, for cases brought by that nation against another nation, add 0* and again add notation 4–9 from Table 2, e.g., cases brought by the United Kingdom against the United States 341.026841073
>(Option: Give priority in notation to the nation requiring local emphasis, e.g., libraries in the United States class all cases involving the United States and the United Kingdom in 341.026873041)

.04	Relation of international and domestic law

Class here works on whether domestic or international law prevails in a certain situation

Class the law of a nation or lesser jurisdiction that carries out the provisions of an international agreement in 342–347

.1	**Sources of international law**

Treaties, judicial decisions, custom, general principles of law, works of publicists (theorists)

Class here critical works on individual publicists (theorists)

Class texts of treaties and reports of judicial decisions in 341.026; writings of publicists with the subject in international law, e.g., international rivers 341.442

.2	**The world community**

Class here international persons and personality, privileges and immunities for international organizations

Class administration of international organizations in 354.1

SUMMARY

341.21	**World government**
.22	**League of Nations**
.23	**United Nations**
.24	**Regional associations and organizations**
.26	**States**
.27	**Semisovereign and dependent states**
.28	**Nonself-governing territories**
.29	**Areas having special status in international law**

.21	World government

Proposals and schemes

*Add 00 for standard subdivisions; see instructions at beginning of Table 1

> 341.22–341.24 Corporate bodies

Class here officials and employees of international organizations

Class comprehensive works in 341.2, legal aspects of a specialized world agency with the subject with which it deals in international law, e.g., the World Health Organization 341.765

.22 League of Nations

Add to base number 341.22 the numbers following 341.23 in 341.231–341.239, e.g., Covenant of the League 341.222

.23 United Nations

.230 13 Value

Evaluation of and opinions about the effectiveness and worth of the United Nations

[.230 68] Management

Do not use; class in 341.233

.231 †Functions and activities

Class the functions and activities of specific branches in 341.232; a specific activity or function with the activity or function in international law, e.g., role in the peaceful settlement of disputes 341.523

.232 †Organization

Including charter

Class here rules of procedure

Class officials and employees in 341.233

.232 2 †General Assembly

.232 3 †Security Council

.232 4 †Secretariat

Including Secretary General

.233 †Management

Including admission, membership

For organization, see 341.232

.234–.239 General relations with specific nations

Add to base number 341.23 notation 4–9 from Table 2, e.g., relations with the United States 341.2373

Class relations dealing with a specific subject with the subject in international law, e.g., United Nations peacekeeping operations 341.584

.24 Regional associations and organizations

†Add extended notation 026 as instructed under 341.026

.242	European regional associations and organizations
.242 2	†European Economic Community (European Common Market)

European Parliament relocated to 341.2424

Class laws promulgated by the European Economic Community with the subject in international law, e.g., economic enactments 341.750614; nonlegal aspects with the subject outside of law, e.g., general economic activities 337.142

.242 4	European Parliament [*formerly* 341.2422]
.242 7	Council for Mutual Economic Assistance
.243	Atlantic regional associations and organizations
.245	Western Hemisphere regional associations and organizations
.246	Pacific regional associations and organizations
.247	Asian regional associations and organizations
.247 3	Far East regional associations and organizations

Example: ASEAN (Association of South East Asian Nations)

.247 7	Western Asia regional associations and organizations

Example: Arab League

Class here Middle East organizations

.249	African regional associations and organizations

For the Arab League, see 341.2477

> 341.26–341.29 Territorially organized bodies

Class comprehensive works in 341.2

.26	States

General aspects: sovereignty, origin, succession, termination

Including the recognition of states and governments, mergers of states

Class here liability of states

Class the liability of states with respect to a specific subject with the subject in international law, e.g., liability for the safety of diplomatic personnel 341.33, liability for damages caused by testing nuclear weapons 341.734

For semisovereign and dependent states, see 341.27; relations between states, 341.3; jurisdiction of states, 341.4

.27	†Semisovereign and dependent states

Examples: mandates, protectorates, trusteeships

Standard subdivisions may be added to semisovereign and dependent states, to semisovereign states alone, to dependent states alone

†Add extended notation 026 as instructed under 341.026

.28 †Nonself-governing territories

Including colonies

.29 †Areas having special status in international law

Example: partitioned areas, e.g., Antarctica, Berlin, Cyprus

.3 †Relations between states

For jurisdictional relations, see 341.4; disputes and conflicts, 341.5; international cooperation, 341.7

.33 †Diplomatic law

Including legal aspects of the status, privileges, immunities, functions of diplomatic personnel and agencies; delegations to international organizations and their staffs

Class officials and employees of international organizations in 341.22–341.24, consular law in 341.35, diplomacy in 327.2

.35 †Consular law

Including status, role, function, privileges, immunities of consular officials and employees

.37 Treaties

General aspects: negotiation and ratification, validity and binding force, termination, interpretation

Including the making of treaties

Class texts of treaties in 341.026, treaties on a specific subject with the subject in international law, adding extended subdivision 026, e.g, a disarmament treaty between the Soviet Union and the United States 341.733026647073

.4 †Jurisdiction and jurisdictional relations of states

Class here servitudes and easements, right of innocent passage; extraterritoriality

SUMMARY

341.42	**Territory**
.44	**Bodies of water**
.45	**High seas**
.46	**Airspace**
.47	**Extraterrestrial space**
.48	**Jurisdiction over persons**

> 341.42–341.47 Jurisdiction over physical space

Class comprehensive works in 341.4

†Add extended notation 026 as instructed under 341.026

.42	†Territory

General aspects: acquisition, boundaries, border disputes

Class mergers of states in 341.26, boundary rivers in 341.442

.44	†Bodies of water

For the high seas, see 341.45

.442	†Rivers

National, semi-national, boundary, internationalized rivers

Including combined river, lake, canal systems, e.g., Saint Lawrence Seaway

.444	†Lakes and landlocked seas

Class combined river, lake, canal systems in 341.442

.446	†Canals and straits

Class combined river, lake, canal systems in 341.442

.448	†Territorial waters

Including bays, continental shelves

Class access to the sea, comprehensive works on ocean and sea waters in 341.45

.45	†High seas

Class here comprehensive works on ocean and sea waters

Class the development and conservation of sea resources in 341.762, pollution of ocean resources in 341.7623, fisheries in 341.7622, oceanographic research in 341.76755

For territorial waters, see 341.448

.46	†Airspace

Class meteorological research in 341.76755

.47	†Extraterrestrial space

Including the moon, planets

Class space research in 341.76752

.48	†Jurisdiction over persons

Including jurisdiction of the state over its nationals in other areas

Class here jurisdiction over personal property

Class private international law in 340.9

.481	†Human rights

Including natural rights

See also 340.112 for natural law

†Add extended notation 026 as instructed under 341.026

| .482 | †Nationality and citizenship |
| .484 | †Jurisdiction over aliens and alien property |

Rights and obligations of aliens

Class liability of states for aliens in 341.26, criminal jurisdiction over aliens in 341.488

For stateless persons and refugees, see 341.486

.484 2	†Immigration, passports, visas
.484 4	†Double taxation
.484 6	†Nationalization (Expropriation) of alien property
.486	†Jurisdiction over stateless persons and refugees
.488	†Criminal jurisdiction

Over citizens, aliens

Including extradition, right of asylum

Use of this number for extraterritoriality discontinued; class in 341.4

Class international crimes in 341.77

| .5 | **†Disputes and conflicts between states** |

Class disputes on a specific subject with the subject in international law, e.g., jurisdictional disputes 341.4

For law of war, see 341.6

| .52 | †Peaceful settlement |

Including mediation

For adjudication, see 341.55

| .522 | †Arbitration |
| .523 | †Role of international organizations |

Class peace conferences in 341.73

| .55 | †Adjudication |

Courts and court procedure

Including the role of domestic courts in adjudicating matters of public international law, interpretation of general international law in courts, adjustment of nonwar claims

Class the interpretation of a specific subject with the subject in international law, e.g., interpretation of human rights 341.481

| .552 | †International Court of Justice (World Court) |

†Add extended notation 026 as instructed under 341.026

.58	†Coercive methods of settlement short of war

.58   †Coercive methods of settlement short of war

Example: ultimatums

Including the role of international organizations

.582   †Sanctions

Examples: boycotts, embargoes, reprisals, severing diplomatic relations

.584   †Intervention

Examples: blockades, deploying peacekeeping observers and forces

.6   †Law of war

.62   General considerations

Examples: legality, justification, opening of hostilities

Including aggression

.63   †Conduct of war

Including intercourse between belligerents, prize law

.64   †Neutrality and neutral states

Class the status of nationals of neutral nations in 341.67

.65   †Treatment of prisoners

Including the granting of quarter

.66   Termination of war

General aspects: treaties, laws of occupation

Including indemnification, reparations, restitution

Class here military government of occupied countries

Class texts of treaties in 341.026; war claims by private individuals of one country against another country in 340.9

.67   †Individuals

Status of enemy aliens and their property, nationals of neutral nations, combatants, noncombatants, war victims

For treatment of prisoners, see 341.65

.68   †International law and civil war

Including the responsibility of the state for acts of unsuccessful insurgent governments

.69   †War crimes

Class here trials of war criminals, e.g., the Tokyo war crime trials 341.690268

†Add extended notation 026 as instructed under 341.026

.7 †**International cooperation**

SUMMARY

341.72	**Defense and mutual security**
.73	**Peace and disarmament**
.75	**International economic law**
.76	**Social law and cultural relations**
.77	**International criminal law**
.78	**International judicial cooperation**

.72 †Defense and mutual security

Including civil defense, international security forces

Class here the legal aspects of international mutual security pacts, e.g., NATO (North Atlantic Treaty Organization)

Class specific aspects and activities of international mutual security pacts with the subject in 001–999, e.g., military aspects 355.031

.722 †Peaceful (Friendly) occupation

.725 †Military installations

Class here military bases

.728 †Military assistance

Including military missions, loan and sale of equipment

.73 †Peace and disarmament

Class here peace conferences, general efforts to gain acceptance of the renunciation of war as an instrument of national policy

Class peaceful settlement of disputes in 341.52

.733 †Disarmament

Including suspension of weapons testing

Class the abolition and control of specific kinds of weapons in 341.734–341.738

.734 †Control of nuclear weapons

During time of peace

.735 †Control of chemical and biological weapons

During time of peace

.738 †Control of strategic weapons

During time of peace

Class control of nuclear strategic weapons in 341.734, control of chemical and biological strategic weapons in 341.735

.75 †International economic law

Class double taxation for individuals and corporate bodies in 341.4844, fisheries in 341.7622, labor in 341.763

†Add extended notation 026 as instructed under 341.026

.750 6	International economic organizations
.750 61	Permanent government organizations
.750 614	European Economic Community (European Common Market)

Economic functions

.751   †Money and banking

Class here foreign loans, international financial law, international fiscal law

Add to base number 341.751 the numbers following 332 in 332.1–332.9, e.g., foreign exchange law 341.75145; however, class investment and investments in 341.752

Class banking for international economic and social development in 341.759

.752   †Investment and investments

Add to base number 341.752 the numbers following 332.6 in 332.62 to 332.67, e.g., exchange of securities 341.75242

Class the law of a specific jurisdiction with respect to foreign investments in 346.092, law with respect to investment by foreign nationals in 346.07

.753   †Organization and conduct of business

Including combinations, monopoly, unfair competition, restraint of trade; contracts

.754   †Trade and commerce

Including standardization, tourism

.754 3   †Tariffs

Including free trade

Class tariffs on specific commodities in 341.7547

.754 7   Trade in specific commodities

Add to base number 341.7547 the numbers following 380.14 in 380.141–380.145, e.g., rice 341.75471318

.755   †Power and power resources

.756   †Transportation

.756 5   †Railroad transportation

.756 6   †Water transportation (Maritime law)

Add to base number 341.7566 the numbers following 343.096 in 343.0962–343.0968, e.g., registry of ships 341.75665

Class the right to use territorial waters, ports, roadsteads, harbors, other bodies of water in 341.44

See also 341.63 for prize law

†Add extended notation 026 as instructed under 341.026

.756 7	†Air and space transportation

Add to base number 341.7567 the numbers following 343.097 in 343.0975–343.0979, e.g., space transportation 341.75679

Class the right to overfly, to use airports and landing fields in 341.46

.756 8	†Road and highway transportation

Add to base number 341.7568 the numbers following 343.094 in 343.0942–343.0948, e.g., international recognition of drivers' licenses 341.75686

.756 9	†Transportation of specific goods

Examples: animals, hazardous materials

.757	†Communications
.757 3	†Postal communications
.757 7	†Telecommunications

Examples: amateur radio transmission, computer communications

Including communication satellites

.758	Intangible property

Class here intellectual property, industrial property (intangible property of an industrial nature, e.g., business names, licensing, franchising, goodwill)

.758 2	†Copyright
.758 4	†Design protection
.758 6	†Patents
.758 8	†Trademarks
.759	†Economic and social development

Including economic and technical assistance, technology transfer, voluntary service groups

Class the conservation and development of natural resources in 341.762, technology transfer in a specific industry with the industry, e.g., in telecommunications 341.7577

.759 2	†Food and agricultural assistance

Class food relief in 341.766

.76	†Social law and cultural relations

Including social security, UNICEF

For economic and social development, see 341.759

.762	†Conservation and development of natural resources

Example: weather control

Class here environmental protection

†Add extended notation 026 as instructed under 341.026

.762 1	†Seabed (Ocean bottom)
.762 2	†Fisheries

.762 2 Including whaling, sealing, fishery of invertebrates

.762 3 †Pollution control

Class the control of the pollution of specific resources in 341.7625

.762 5 Protection of specific resources

Class the protection of marine life in 341.7622

.762 53 †Water pollution

.763 †Labor

.763 2 †Conditions in specific industries

Class wages in specific industries in 341.7636

.763 6 †Wages

.765 †Public health

.766 †Welfare services

Class public health in 341.765

.767 †Educational, scientific, technological, cultural relations

.767 2 †Exchanges of information

Class exchanges of information in specific fields in 341.7675–341.7677

.767 3 †Exchanges of persons

Including exchanges of students and teachers

Class exchanges of persons in specific fields in 341.7675–341.7677

.767 5 †Cooperation in scientific and technological research

.767 52 †Astronomical and space research

Including the tracking of satellites

.767 53 †Physical sciences and technology

Including nuclear research

.767 54 †Chemical sciences and technology

.767 55 †Geological, meteorological, oceanographic sciences

.767 57 †Biological and agricultural research

.767 7 †Cooperation in arts and archaeology

Including the preservation of antiquities

†Add extended notation 026 as instructed under 341.026

.77   †International criminal law

             Including pornography, slave trade, tax evasion

             Class criminal jurisdiction in 341.488

             For war crimes, see 341.69

.772   †Hijacking

             Class here piracy

.773   †Terrorism

.775   †Drug traffic

.778   †Genocide

.78   †International judicial cooperation

             Examples: judicial assistance, letters rogatory

             Including the status of the judgments of foreign courts

             For extradition, see 341.488

> ## 342–348 Branches of the law of specific jurisdictions and laws, regulations, cases

    Class comprehensive works in 349

> ## 342–347 Law of specific jurisdictions

    Class here the law of specific areas

    Add to each subdivision identified by * the following extended notation:

026	Laws, regulations, cases, procedure, courts
	Standard subdivisions may be added to 026 and its subdivisions
0262	Preliminary materials
	Examples: bills, hearings, reports, executive messages, statements of witnesses, legislative histories, slip laws
	Commentaries and critical works are classed in the number for the specific topic in 342–347 without further subdivision
	See Manual at 342–347
0263	Laws and regulations
	Commentaries and criticism are classed in the number for the specific topic in 342–347 without further subdivision
02632	Individual laws [*formerly* 02633] and collected laws
	Including proposed, uniform, model codes
[02633]	Individual laws
	Relocated to 02632
02636	Administrative regulations
	Collections and individual regulations

                                                         (continued)

†Add extended notation 026 as instructed under 341.026

> ## 342–347 Law of specific jurisdictions (continued)

02638	Guides to laws and regulations
	Digests, citators, checklists, tables, indexes
0264	Cases
	Do not use for casebooks, for popular works
02642	Reports
02643	Court decisions
	Class here official court decisions
	Class treatises on court decisions and popular treatment of the cases with the subject in law without further subdivision
02646	Decisions (Rulings) of regulatory agencies
02648	Guides to cases
	Examples: digests, citators, checklists, tables, indexes
	Including loose-leaf services
	Class here guides to laws, regulations, cases
	For guides to laws and regulations, see 02638
0265	Advisory opinions of attorneys-general (ministers of justice)
0269	Courts and procedure
	Including administrative courts, regulatory agencies; practice, rules, form books

(Option: Class laws, regulations, cases on specific subjects in law in 348, courts and procedure in specific fields in 347)

Class comprehensive works in 340, comprehensive works on the law of specific jurisdictions and areas in the modern world in 349; general laws, regulations, cases in 348

342   *Constitutional and administrative law

Class here comprehensive works on public law, on constitutional law

(If Option A under 340 is chosen, class here comprehensive works on the law of the preferred jurisdiction. Class specific branches of the law of the preferred jurisdiction in 342–348

(If Option B under 340 is chosen, class here comparative law and law without jurisdiction by adding to base number 342 the numbers following 34 in 342–348, but omitting the first 0 after the decimal point, e.g., comparative criminal procedure 342.55 [not 342.505])

Use 342.001–342.009 for standard subdivisions

For international law, see 341; military, tax, trade, industrial law, 343; social, labor, welfare, health, safety, education, cultural law, 344; criminal law, 345

*Add extended notation 026 as instructed under 342–347

SUMMARY

342.02	**Basic instruments of government**
.03	**Revision and amendment of the basic instruments of government**
.04	**Structure, powers, functions of government**
.05	**Legislative branch of government**
.06	**Executive branch of government**
.07	**Election law**
.08	**Jurisdiction of governmental units over persons**
.09	**Local government**
.3–.9	**Specific jurisdictions and areas**

.02   *Basic instruments of government

Class here constitutions, municipal charters

Class constitutional provisions dealing with a specific subject with the subject in law, e.g., individual rights 342.085

For revision and amendment, see 342.03

[.020 9]   Historical, geographical, persons treatment

Do not use; class in 342.029

.023   Texts of constitutions

Including annotated texts, texts of proposed constitutions

.024   Sources

Class commentary on source documents without text in 342.0292

.024 2   Convention proceedings

Including debates, journals, minutes

.024 3   Other convention documents

Examples: enabling acts, memoranda, proposals, rules

.029   Constitutional history

Including ratification

For sources, see 342.024

.029 2   History of conventions

Class constitutional conventions dealing with revision and amendment of constitutions in 342.03, proceedings and documents of conventions in 342.024

.03   Revision and amendment of the basic instruments of government

Class here constitutional reform

Class proposals for and formation of new constitutions in 342.02; amendments dealing with a specific subject with the subject in law, e.g., an amendment prohibiting sale and consumption of alcoholic beverages 344.0541

*Add extended notation 026 as instructed under 342–347

[.030 9]	Historical, geographical, persons treatment
	Do not use; class in 342.039
.032	*Amendment procedure
.035	Proposed and pending amendments
	Class here texts of constitutional amendments
	Class texts of proposed constitutions in 342.023
.039	History of amendments
	Including defeated amendments
.04	*Structure, powers, functions of government
	Class government corporations in 346.067
.041	*Powers and functions of government
	For jurisdiction over persons, see 342.08
.041 2	*Conduct of relations with foreign governments
	Including the power to wage war, to acquire territory from and cede it to other jurisdictions, to regulate reception of and relations with diplomatic and consular personnel
	Class military and defense law in 343.012–343.019
	See also 342.0418 for police powers, 342.062 for war and emergency powers of the executive
.041 3	*Jurisdiction over territory, dependencies, colonies
	Including annexation
	Class the power to acquire territory from foreign jurisdictions in 342.0412
.041 8	*Police powers
	Powers to exercise control in the interests of general security, health, safety, morals, welfare
	Class individual rights in 342.085; exercise of a specific police power with the power in law, e.g., exclusion of undesirable aliens 342.082, regulation of public health 344.04
	See also 342.062 for war and emergency powers of the executive
.042	*Levels of government
	Including federalism, federal structure; relations between levels, relations between subordinate units of the same level; domestic conflict of laws; home rule; interstate compacts
	Class interstate compacts on a specific subject with the subject in law, e.g., compacts on seaports and their facilities 343.0967

*Add extended notation 026 as instructed under 342–347

.044   *Branches of government

Including the distribution and separation of powers, relations between branches

Class relations of a specific branch of government with government institutions at a different level in 342.042

For the legislative branch, see 342.05; the executive branch, 342.06; the judicial branch, 347

.05   *Legislative branch of government

Class here lobbying

Class relations of the legislative branch with government institutions at a different level in 342.042

.052   *Powers, functions, duties

.053   *Basis of representation

Example: proportional representation

Including apportionment, districting

.055   *Membership

Including modes of selection, terms of office; immunities, privileges, qualifications; conduct, discipline of members; salaries, expenses, retirement

.057   *Organization and procedure

Including the organization and procedure of committees

.06   *Executive branch of government

Including terms of office, modes of selection; powers, functions, duties; immunities, privileges, qualifications; conduct, discipline; salaries, expenses, retirement

Class here the relation of the executive branch to the fundamental instrument of government [*formerly also* 351.003], administrative law

Class relations of the executive branch with governmental institutions at a different level in 342.042

See Manual at 342.06

.062   *Chief and deputy chief executives

Including martial law, provisional courts, war and emergency powers

.064   *Executive departments and ministries

Class departments and ministries dealing with a specific subject with the subject in law, e.g., revenue agencies 343.036

*Add extended notation 026 as instructed under 342–347

.066   *Administrative procedure

Legislative and judicial functions of the executive branch

Class privacy in 342.0858

See also 344.0531 for information control laws

.066 2   *Public records

Class here the right to information, sunshine laws [*both formerly* 342.0853], privacy of government records

.066 4   *Regulatory agencies and administrative courts

Including hearing examiners

Class the executive function of administering and enforcing the law in 350–354; regulatory agencies, administrative courts dealing with a specific subject with the subject in law, using notation 0269 from the table under 342–347, e.g., agencies regulating civil aeronautics 343.0970269

.066 7   *Ombudsmen

.068   *Officials and employees

Including the personal liability of government officials

Class here civil service

Class labor-management bargaining in government service in 344.018

.068 4   *Employee rights and discipline

Including security measures, political activity of employees, loyalty oaths, conflict of interest

.068 6   *Conditions of employment

Examples: pay, fringe benefits, retirement, tenure, leave, job classification, training

.07   *Election law

Class apportionment, districting in 342.053, modes of selecting legislators in 342.055, modes of selecting executives in 342.06

See Manual at 324.6 vs. 342.07

.072   *Voting rights and qualifications for voting

Examples: requirements with respect to age, sex, race, residence, education

.075   *Election procedures

Examples: absentee voting, conduct of polling, registration and enumeration of voters, type of ballot

.078   *Campaign practices

Including finance

*Add extended notation 026 as instructed under 342–347

.08   *Jurisdiction of governmental units over persons

Examples: residence status of persons in local jurisdictions, census law

.082   *Entrance to and exit from national domain

Immigration, emigration, passports, visas, quotas

Class entry and exit of diplomatic and consular personnel in 342.0412

.083   *Citizenship and nationality

Including status of aliens, asylum

Class status of diplomatic and consular personnel in 342.0412

.085   *Individual activities

Including the individual rights of servicemen

Class here comprehensive works on individual rights, on the capacity and status of persons

Class claims of the denial of constitutional rights to specific social groups in 342.087, to aliens in 342.083; specific claims with the subject in law, e.g., land claims in the United States 346.730432; a specific right not provided for here with the right, e.g., right to vote 342.072, right to education 344.079

.085 2   *Religious activities

.085 3   *Promulgation of information and opinion

Including academic freedom, freedom of speech, freedom of the press

Right to information, sunshine laws relocated to 342.0662

Class promulgation of political opinion in 342.0854, the relation of press freedom to the judicial process in 347.05

See also 342.0662 for access to public records, 344.0531 for censorship and information control laws, 344.0547 for obscenity and pornography laws

.085 4   *Political activity

Including civil disobedience and dissent, rights of petition and assembly

Class election law in 342.07

.085 8   *Maintenance of privacy

Class privacy of government records in 342.0662

.087   *Social groups

General aspects: legal status, disabilities, restrictions

Including slavery

See also 342.085 for individual rights

.087 2   *Indigenes and aborigines

*Add extended notation 026 as instructed under 342–347

.087 3   *Racial, ethnic, national groups

Class here affirmative action

Class indigenes and aborigines of specific racial, ethnic, national groups in 342.0872

.087 8   *Women

.088   *Government liability

Examples: for abuse of power, corruption, denial of civil rights

Class liability in a specific field with the field in law, e.g., liability of government for activity of military units 343.013, liability of schools, school officials, school districts 344.075

.09   *Local government

Examples: municipal corporations, municipal governments

Class specific local governments in 342.3–342.9; a specific aspect of local government with the aspect in law, e.g., local real estate taxation 343.054

See also 342.042 for home rule

.3–.9   Specific jurisdictions and areas

Add to base number 342 notation 3–9 from Table 2, e.g., constitutional and administrative law of Australia 342.94, of New South Wales 342.944, of African states 342.6; then to the result add the numbers following 342 in 342.001–342.09, e.g., election law of Australia 342.9407, of New South Wales 342.94407, of African states 342.607, administrative regulations for elections in Australia 342.940702636

343   Military, tax, trade, industrial law

Use 343.001–343.009 for standard subdivisions

SUMMARY

343.01	Military, defense (national security), veterans' law
.02	Law of public property
.03	Law of public finance
.04	Tax law
.05	Kinds of taxes by base
.06	Kinds of taxes by incidence
.07	Regulation of economic activity
.08	Regulation of trade
.09	Control of public utilities
.3–.9	Specific jurisdictions and areas

.01   Military, defense (national security), veterans' law

Class here war and emergency legislation

Class military appropriations in 355.622

For war claims, see 341.66; martial law, 342.062

*Add extended notation 026 as instructed under 342–347

.011   *Veterans' law

                 Class here veterans' welfare law [*formerly also* 344.03286]

                 Class veterans' insurance claims in 346.086364

.011 2   *Veterans' pensions

                 Including benefits to survivors of veterans

.011 3   *Education and training for veterans

.011 4   *Employment for veterans

.011 5   *Health care and rehabilitation for veterans

                 Class compensation for disability in 343.0116

.011 6   *Disability compensation for veterans

>   343.012–343.019 National security and military law

                 Class comprehensive works in 343.01, military assistance to foreign nations in 342.0412, civilian employees of military services in 342.068; a specific aspect of military, war, defense, emergency legislation not provided for here with the aspect in law, e.g., regulation of industry 343.07

.012   *Manpower procurement

                 Examples: recruitment

                 Class individual rights of servicemen in 342.085, reserve officers' training corps and military academies in 344.0769

.012 2   *Draft and selective service

                 Including draft resistance

                 Class treatment of conscientious objectors in 343.0126

.012 6   *Conscientious objectors

                 Including amnesty

.013   *Military services

                 Including organization, training, rank, pay, promotion, demotion, leave, allowances, living conditions

                 For discipline and conduct, see 343.014; law governing armies, 343.015; specific military services, 343.016–343.019

.014   *Discipline and conduct

                 Including awards and incentives, enforcement, medals, offenses

.014 3   *Military legal procedure and courts

                 Including procedural rights of servicemen in military courts

                 Class general rights of servicemen in 342.085, procedural rights in nonmilitary courts in 347; international war crime trials in 341.69

*Add extended notation 026 as instructed under 342–347

.014 6   *Military penology

                 Including probation and parole

                 Class military prisons in 344.03548

.015   *Laws governing armies

                 Class specific services in 343.016–343.019

.016–.019   Specific military services

                 Add to base number 343.01 the numbers following 35 in 356–359, e.g., naval law 343.019

                 Class comprehensive works in 343.013, discipline and conduct of specific services in 343.014, manpower of specific services in 343.012, the law governing armies in 343.015

.02   *Law of public property

                 General aspects: acquisition, disposal, regulation and control

.023   *Personal property

.025   *Real property

.025 2   *Acquisition

                 Including appraisal, eminent domain (expropriation), condemnation, nationalization

                 Class the acquisition of territory from other jurisdictions in 342.0412

.025 3   *Disposal

                 Sale and grant

                 Class cession of territory to other jurisdictions in 342.0412

.025 6   *Control and use of public real property

                 Including construction and maintenance of government buildings

                 Class comprehensive works on the control and use of public and private real property, control of natural resources in 346.044, regulation of construction operations in 343.07869

.03   *Law of public finance

                 For government securities, see 346.0922

.032   *Monetary law

                 Currency, coinage, foreign exchange

                 Including commemorative medals and coins that are legal tender, limitations on the amount of metal used in coinage

                 Class here monetary policy, indexation

                 Class comprehensive works on commemorative medals in 344.091, international law of monetary exchange in 341.751, central banks and banking in 346.082

*Add extended notation 026 as instructed under 342–347

.034	*Budgeting and expenditure

Including accounting and auditing procedures, revenue sharing

Class here fiscal policy, economic stabilization, grants-in-aid, intergovernmental financial relations

Class the budget and its preparation in 351.722; revenue law, revenue sharing as revenue in 343.036; regulation of prices in 343.083; bills for authorization and reauthorization of expenditure for a specific purpose with the purpose in law, e.g., for price supports 343.0742

.036	*Revenue law

For public borrowing and debt, see 343.037; tax law, 343.04

.037	*Public borrowing and debt
.04	*Tax law

Class here tax planning, tax avoidance in general [*formerly also* 343.0523], internal revenue law, tax auditing

Class interdisciplinary works on taxes in 336.2, double taxation in 341.4844, fiscal policy in 343.034, tax planning applied to a specific kind of tax in 343.05–343.06, tax shelters and investment credit in 343.0523; tax evasion in 345.0233

For specific kinds of taxes, see 343.05–343.06

See Manual at 336.2 vs. 351.724, 343.04

.042	*Assessment and collection

Including corvee, payment-in-kind, tax accounting, tax appeal

Class assessment and collection of taxes at specific levels in 343.043, of specific kinds of taxes in 343.05–343.06; tax evasion in 345.0233

.043	Taxes by level

National, state, local

Class here only comprehensive works and comparisons, e.g., national taxes in North America 343.7043, state taxes in the United States 343.73043, local taxes of the jurisdictions of Pennsylvania 343.748043

Class taxes of a specific jurisdiction in 343.04, specific kinds of taxes regardless of level in 343.05–343.06, e.g., income tax law of Michigan 343.774052

>	343.05–343.06 Specific kinds of taxes

Class comprehensive works in 343.04; social security taxes in 344.02

*Add extended notation 026 as instructed under 342–347

.05   Kinds of taxes by base

SUMMARY

343.052	**Income tax**
.053	**Estate, inheritance, gift taxes**
.054	**Property taxes**
.055	**Excise and transaction taxes**
.056	**Customs taxes (Tariff)**
.057	**Stamp taxes and duties**

.052   *Income tax

         Class the internal revenue code in 343.04

.052 04   Special topics

.052 042   *Assessment of income taxes

.052 044   *Preparation of returns

.052 3   *Reductions in tax

         Tax planning, tax avoidance in general relocated to 343.04

.052 32   *Charitable deductions

.052 33   *Individual retirement accounts

         Including Keogh plans

.052 34   *Depreciation and depletion allowances

.052 36   *Business losses

         Including bad debts

.052 4   Taxes on specific types of income

         Examples: proceeds from insurance, retirement income; income from rents, royalties, securities transactions

         Class reductions in taxes on specific types of income in 343.0523

.052 42   *On wages and salaries

         Including payroll, withholding taxes

.052 44   *On profits

.052 45   *On capital gains

.052 46   *On investment income

         Examples: income from bonds, deposits, stocks

         For taxes on capital gains, see 343.05245; taxes on real-estate transactions, 343.0546

.052 48   *On income from foreign sources

         Class taxes on specific types of income from specific foreign sources in 343.05242–343.05246

*Add extended notation 026 as instructed under 342–347

.052 6	Income taxes by incidence

Including taxes on self-employed persons, on the aged, on citizens resident in foreign countries

Class here domestic double taxation

Add to base number 343.0526 the numbers following 343.06 in 343.062–343.068, e.g., corporation income taxes 343.05267; however, class reduction in taxation regardless of incidence in 343.0523, taxes on specific types of income regardless of incidence in 343.0524

.053	*Estate, inheritance, gift taxes

Class here estate planning

Class taxes on fiduciary trusts in 343.05264

.053 2	*Inheritance taxes
.053 5	*Gift taxes
.054	*Property taxes

On real and personal property

.054 2	*Assessment
.054 3	*Exemptions
.054 6	*Taxes on real-estate transactions

Class here taxes incident upon the sale of real estate, e.g., sales tax

Class other real estate tax aspects with the aspect in law, e.g., tax assessment 343.0542

.055	Excise and transaction taxes

Examples: luxury, severance, transfer, turnover, use, value-added taxes; user fees

Class taxes on real-estate transactions in 343.0546

.055 2	*Sales taxes

Class sales taxes on specific commodities and services in 343.0558

.055 3	*Excise taxes

Class excise taxes on specific commodities and services in 343.0558

.055 8	*Taxes on specific commodities and services

Add to base number 343.0558 the numbers following 380.14 in 380.141–380.145, e.g., taxes on cigarettes 343.0558567973

.056	*Customs taxes (Tariff)
.057	*Stamp taxes and duties

*Add extended notation 026 as instructed under 342–347

.06 Kinds of taxes by incidence

Class taxes on specific bases regardless of incidence in 343.05

.062 *On individuals

Class here poll tax

.064 *On fiduciary trusts

Including pension trusts

.066 *On organizations

Class here the status of tax-exempt organizations

For taxes on corporations, see 343.067

.066 2 *Partnerships

.066 8 *Charitable foundations and trusts

.067 *On corporations

.068 *On business enterprises

Including small business taxes

Class taxes on specific types of business organizations in 343.066, on individuals engaged in business in 343.062

.07 *Regulation of economic activity

Examples: daylight saving, nationalization of industry, rationing

Class here comprehensive works on the regulation of small business, licensing, industry and trade

Class regulation of the practice of specific occupations in 344.01, public health and safety measures in 344.04, regulation of organizations in 346.06

For regulation of trade, see 343.08

See also 346 for the impact of economic activity upon private persons and corporate bodies

.071 *Consumer protection

Class a specific aspect of consumer protection with the aspect, e.g., protection against misleading advertising 343.082

> 343.072–343.075 Specific aspects of regulation

Class comprehensive works in 343.07; regulation of specific industries and services regardless of aspect in 343.076–343.078, of public utilities regardless of aspect in 343.09; a specific aspect of industrial regulation not provided for here with the aspect in law, e.g., wages 344.0121

*Add extended notation 026 as instructed under 342–347

.072	*Unfair practices
	Including industrial espionage, rebates
.072 1	*Antitrust law
	Class here competition law
.072 3	*Restraint of trade
.072 5	*Price fixing and discrimination
.074	*Economic assistance
	Class here technology transfer
	Class assistance to specific industries and services in 343.076–343.078

> 343.074 2–343.074 6 Domestic assistance

Class comprehensive works in 343.074

.074 2	Specific kinds of assistance
	Examples: loans, price supports, subsidies, mortgage insurance
.074 5	*Rural development
	Class assistance to agriculture in 343.076, specific kinds of assistance to rural areas in 343.0742
.074 6	*Regional development
	Class development of rural regions in 343.0745, specific kinds of assistance in 343.0742
.074 8	*Foreign assistance
.075	*Production controls
	Quantity and quality controls
	Including weights and measures, packaging (containers)
	Class subsidies in 343.0742
	See also 344.042 for product control

> 343.076–343.078 Regulation of specific industries and services

Class here works on the regulation of the production of and trade in specific goods and services

Class comprehensive works in 343.07

For public utilities, see 343.09

*Add extended notation 026 as instructed under 342–347

.076　　　　　　　　*Agriculture and agricultural industries

Class here acreage allotments, price supports, production quotas, production controls

Add to base number 343.076 the numbers following 63 in 633–639, e.g., forest products 343.076498

Class trade in specific commodities in 343.0851

See also 344.049 for veterinary public health

.077　　　　　　　　*Mineral industries

Exploration for and extraction of minerals

Class conservation of minerals in 346.04685, mineral rights in 346.043

.077 2　　　　　　　*Extraction of petroleum and gases

.077 5　　　　　　　*Mining

.077 52　　　　　　　　*Coal

.077 55　　　　　　　　*Nonfuel minerals

.078　　　　　　　　*Secondary industries and services

Add to base number 343.078 notation 001–999, e.g., regulation of the shipbuilding industry 343.07862382; however, class regulation of health services in 344.04; regulation of closely regulated industries, such as transportation and communication, in 343.09; regulation of marketing relocated from 343.0786588 to 343.084, of the advertising industry from 343.0786591 to 343.082

See Manual at 343.078 vs. 343.08

.08　　　　　　　　*Regulation of trade

Including warranties and guarantees

Class here commodity exchanges and exchange transactions

Class comprehensive works on the regulation of trade and industry in 343.07, regulation of real-estate business in 346.0437, of banks in 346.082, of insurance companies and agencies in 346.086, of organizations engaged in marketing securities in 346.0926

See Manual at 343.078 vs. 343.08

\>　　　　　343.082–343.084 Labeling, advertising, prices, marketing

Class comprehensive works in 343.08; labeling, advertising, prices, and marketing of specific commodities in 343.085; in specific kinds of trade 343.087–343.088

*Add extended notation 026 as instructed under 342–347

.082 *Advertising and labeling

Class here regulation of the advertising industry [*formerly also* 343.0786591]

Class restrictions on the posting of advertisements in 346.045

.083 *Prices

Class price supports of specific materials and products in 343.076–343.078

.084 *Marketing

Including quotas, agreements, restrictions

Class here the regulation of marketing [*formerly also* 343.0786588]

Class the law of sale in 346.072

.085 Specific commodities

Add to base number 343.085 the numbers following 380.14 in 380.141–380.145, e.g., rice 343.0851318

Class a specific kind of trade in a specific commodity in 343.087–343.088

> 343.087–343.088 Specific kinds of trade

Class comprehensive works in 343.08

.087 *Foreign (International) trade

Class here general customs law, the combined treatment of trade, tariffs, and general shipping

Class tariffs in 343.056

.087 1–.087 5 Specific commodities

Add to base number 343.087 the numbers following 380.14 in 380.141–380.145, e.g., rice 343.0871318

.087 7 *Imports

Class importation of specific commodities in 343.0871–343.0875

.087 8 *Exports

Class exportation of specific commodities in 343.0871–343.0875

.088 *Domestic trade

Including trade on days of religious observance, e.g., on Sunday

.088 1–.088 5 Specific commodities

Add to base number 343.088 the numbers following 380.14 in 380.141–380.145, e.g., rice 343.0881318

*Add extended notation 026 as instructed under 342–347

.088 7		*Retail trade

Class retail trade in specific commodities in 343.0881–343.0885

.088 8		*Wholesale trade

Class wholesale trade in specific commodities in 343.0881–343.0885

.09		*Control of public utilities

Class here closely regulated industries

SUMMARY

343.091	General considerations
.092	Water and power supply
.093	Transportation
.094	Road and highway transportation
.095	Rail transportation
.096	Water transportation
.097	Air and space transportation
.098	Local transportation
.099	Communications

.091		*General considerations

Examples: rates, rate-making, operations, facilities, services

Class general considerations applied to specific utilities in 343.092–343.099

> 343.092–343.099 Specific utilities

Class comprehensive works in 343.09

.092		*Water and power supply
.092 4		*Water supply and power
.092 5		*Nuclear energy
.092 6		*Oil and gas

Class extraction of oil and gas in 343.0772, processing in 343.0786655–343.0786657

.092 7		*Coal

Class extraction of coal in 343.07752, processing in 343.07866262

.092 8		*Solar energy
.092 9		*Electric power

Including cogeneration of heat and electricity

Class a specific source of electric power with the source in law, e.g., nuclear power 343.0925

*Add extended notation 026 as instructed under 342–347

.093	*Transportation

Example: pipelines

Class here safety in transportation, comprehensive works on the law of carriers

Class the private law of transportation accidents in 346.0322, transportation insurance in 346.0862

For specific modes of transportation, see 343.094–343.098

.093 2	*Freight
.093 3	*Passenger

Class here mass transportation

> **343.094–343.098 Specific modes of transportation**

Class comprehensive works in 343.093

> **343.094–343.097 Nonlocal transportation**

Class comprehensive works in 343.093

See also 343.098 for local transportation

.094	*Road and highway transportation

Class police traffic services in 344.052332, traffic offenses in 345.0247

.094 2	*Roads and highways

General aspects: construction, finance, condition

.094 4	*Vehicles

Including licensing, registration, equipment, safety devices, warranty, accessories, size, weight, load, inspection, product recall

Class property laws relating to vehicles in 346.047, vehicle operation in 343.0946, vehicle product liability in 346.038, vehicle insurance in 346.086092, commercial services using vehicles in 343.0948

.094 6	*Vehicle operation and traffic control

Including drivers' licenses, traffic signals, speed limits

.094 8	*Commercial services

Class commercial vehicles in 343.0944, operation in 343.0946; local services in 343.0982

.094 82	*Bus
.094 83	*Truck

*Add extended notation 026 as instructed under 342–347

.095   *Rail transportation

.095 2   *Stationary facilities

Examples: tracks, yards, stations, signals

.095 5   *Rolling stock

Examples: locomotives, cars

.095 8   *Services

Examples: passenger, freight

.096   *Water transportation

Including domestic prize law

Class here maritime, admiralty law

Class international maritime law in 341.7566; a specific subject of maritime or admiralty law not provided for here with the subject in law, e.g., maritime contracts 346.02

>   343.096 2–343.096 4 Specific kinds of water transportation

Class comprehensive works in 343.096; facilities, operations, services of specific kinds of transportation in 343.0965–343.0968

.096 2   *Ocean transportation

Class interoceanic waterways in 343.0964

.096 4   *Inland waterway

Including interoceanic canals

>   343.096 5–343.096 8 Facilities, operations, services

Class comprehensive works in 343.096

.096 5   *Ships

Including papers, registry, qualifications of officers and crew

.096 6   *Navigation and rule of the road

.096 7   *Ports and harbors

Including services, e.g., piloting, warehousing, towing and tug services

.096 8   *Services

Passenger, freight

Class here salvage operations

For services of ports and harbors, see 343.0967

*Add extended notation 026 as instructed under 342–347

.097	*Air and space transportation

> 343.097 5–343.097 8 Air transportation

Class comprehensive works in 343.097

.097 5	*Aircraft
	Including papers, registry, qualifications of officers and crew
.097 6	*Air navigation and traffic control
.097 7	*Airports and landing fields
	Including services, e.g., hangars
	For traffic control, see 343.0976
.097 8	*Air transportation services
	Passenger, freight
	For services of airports and landing fields, see 343.0977
.097 9	*Space transportation
.098	*Local transportation
	Class police traffic services in 344.052332, traffic offenses in 345.0247
	For local water transportation, see 387; local air transportation, 387.7
.098 1	*Pedestrian traffic
	Including footpaths and trails
.098 2	*Street traffic
.098 3	*Rail traffic
	Surface, subsurface, elevated
.099	*Communications
	Class here mass media law
.099 2	*Postal service
	Class postal offenses in 345.0236
.099 23	*Revenue and rates
.099 25	*Postal organization
	Including routes
.099 4	*Telecommunication
	Including the fairness doctrine
.099 42	*Telegraph
.099 43	*Telephone
.099 44	*Computer communications

*Add extended notation 026 as instructed under 342–347

.099 45	*Radio

Use of this number for electronic communication discontinued; class in 343.0994

.099 46	*Television

Including cable television (CATV)

.099 8	*Press law

Class here publishing law

Class libel in 346.034, freedom of the press in 342.0853, censorship in 344.0531

.099 9	*Information storage and retrieval

Class here comprehensive works on computer law

Class a specific aspect with the aspect in law, e.g., invasion of privacy 342.0858

.3–.9 Specific jurisdictions and areas

Add to base number 343 notation 3–9 from Table 2, e.g., miscellaneous public law of Australia 343.94, of New South Wales 343.944, of African states 343.6; then to the result add the numbers following 343 in 343.001–343.099, e.g., tax law of Australia 343.9404, of New South Wales 343.94404, of African states 343.604, administrative regulations on taxes of Australia 343.940402636

344 Social, labor, welfare, health, safety, education, cultural law

Use 344.001–344.009 for standard subdivisions

SUMMARY

344.01	Labor
.02	Social insurance
.03	Welfare
.04	Public health
.05	Public safety
.06	Public works
.07	Education and schools
.08	Educational and cultural exchanges
.09	Culture and religion

.01	*Labor

Class here fees, wages, licensing for specific occupations and professions

Add to base number 344.01 the numbers following 331 in 331.1–331.8, e.g., child labor law 344.0131; however, class government officials and employees in 342.068, military personnel in 343.013–343.019, medical personnel in 344.041, certification and licensing of teachers in 344.078

*Add extended notation 026 as instructed under 342–347

.02	*Social insurance
	See also 344.03 for social welfare law
.021	*Workers' (Workmen's) compensation insurance
	Class disability compensation for veterans in 343.0116
.021 7	In specific occupations and industries
	Class workmen's compensation insurance for specific disablements and injuries in specific occupations and industries in 344.0218
.021 8	For specific disablements and injuries
.022	*Accident and health insurance
	Including insurance for special groups, e.g., Medicaid
	Class health benefits for veterans in 343.0115
.022 4	*Maternity insurance
.022 6	*Accident and health insurance for the aged
	Example: Medicare
.023	*Old age and survivors' insurance
	Example: social security (United States)
	Class accident and health insurance for the aged in 344.0226
.024	*Unemployment insurance
.028	*Insurance against crimes of violence
.03	*Welfare
.031	Specific topics of welfare in general
	Add to base number 344.031 the numbers following 361 in 361.02–361.8, e.g., laws governing charitable trusts 344.0317632
.032	*Social welfare problems and services
	Add to base number 344.032 the numbers following 362 in 362.04–362.8, e.g., health services law 344.0321, child welfare law 344.0327; however, class mental and emotional illnesses and disturbances in 344.044, adoption of children in 346.0178; veterans welfare relocated from 344.03286 to 343.011
	Class medical personnel and their activities in 344.041
.033	*Food supply
.035	*Penal institutions
	Add to base number 344.035 the numbers following 365 in 365.3–365.7, e.g., law governing convict labor 344.03565

*Add extended notation 026 as instructed under 342–347

.04   *Public health

For public safety, see 344.05

SUMMARY

344.041	**Medical personnel and their activities**
.042	**Product control**
.043	**Control of disease**
.044	**Mental health services and services to substance abusers**
.045	**Disposal of the dead**
.046	**Control of the environment**
.047	**Safety**
.048	**Birth control**
.049	**Veterinary public health**

.041   *Medical personnel and their activities

Class military medicine in 343.013, medical malpractice in 346.0332, hospitals and their services in 344.03211

For control of disease, see 344.043

.041 2   *Physicians and surgeons and their activities

Including informed consent

.041 3   *Dentists and dentistry

Including dental technicians, dental assistants

.041 4   *Nurses and nursing

.041 5   *Midwives and midwifery

.041 6   *Pharmacists and pharmacy

.041 9   Specific problems in medical practice

.041 92   *Abortion

Class abortion control in 344.0546, abortion for birth control in 344.048, criminal abortion in 345.0285

.041 94   *Oversight of the human body and its parts

Including preservation of life through freezing, blood transfusion, organ donation, transplants

.041 96   *Human experimentation

Example: medical genetics

.041 97   *Terminal care

Class here euthanasia, the right to die

.042   *Product control

Control for purity, safety

Including recall of unsafe products

See also 343.0944 for motor vehicle recall

*Add extended notation 026 as instructed under 342–347

.042 3	*Food, drugs, cosmetics, clothing, toys
.042 32	*Food
	Including food additives
.042 33	*Drugs
.042 35	*Clothing and toys
.042 4	*Chemicals

Class cosmetics in 344.0423, food additives in 344.04232, drugs in 344.04233

| .043 | *Control of disease |

Control of carriers, quarantine, immunization measures

Including the control of disease in a specific site, e.g., in a factory

| .043 6–.043 8 | Control of specific diseases |

Add to base number 344.043 the numbers following 61 in 616–618, e.g., control of AIDS 344.04369792; however, class control of mental diseases in 344.044

| .044 | *Mental health services and services to substance abusers |

Class the capacity and status of persons of unsound mind in 346.0138

| .044 6 | *To substance abusers |

Class here addiction

Class the control of trade in alcoholic beverages and narcotics in 344.054

.044 61	*Alcoholics
.044 63	*Narcotics addicts
.045	*Disposal of the dead
.046	*Control of the environment

Class conservation of natural resources in 346.044

| .046 2 | *Waste disposal |

Including recycling

| .046 22 | Kinds of waste |

Examples: sewage; solid, chemical, animal wastes

Class disposal of specific kinds of wastes into specific environments in 344.04626

| .046 26 | Disposal into specific environments |

Examples: dumping into rivers, oceans

*Add extended notation 026 as instructed under 342–347

.046 3	Pollution and noise control
.046 32	*Pollution control

Class waste disposal in 344.0462

For control of specific pollutants, see 344.04633; control of pollution of specific environments, 344.04634

.046 33	Control of specific pollutants

Examples: oil, pesticides

Class pollution of specific environments by specific pollutants in 344.04634

.046 34	Control of the pollution of specific environments

Example: soil pollution

Including acid rain

.046 342	*Air
.046 343	*Water
.046 38	*Noise control
.046 4	*Sanitation in places of public assembly

Examples: hotels, restaurants

For industrial sanitation, see 344.0465

.046 5	*Industrial sanitation and safety
.047	*Safety

Class transportation safety in 343.093, product safety in 344.042

For industrial safety, see 344.0465; public safety, 344.05

.047 2	*Safety in the use of hazardous materials and devices

Class safety in the use of hazardous materials in industry in 344.0465

.047 6	*Safety in recreation
.048	*Birth control
.049	*Veterinary public health
.05	Police services, other aspects of public safety, controversies related to public morals and customs

Add to base number 344.05 the numbers following 363 in 363.2–363.4, e.g., fire protection 344.0537

For criminal investigation and law enforcement, see 345.052

.06	*Public works

Use 344.060001–344.060009 for standard subdivisions

Add to base number 344.06 notation 001–999, e.g., public housing 344.063635

*Add extended notation 026 as instructed under 342–347

.07   *Education and schools

Unless other instructions are given, class complex subjects with aspects in two or more subdivisions of this topic in the number coming last in the schedule, e.g., finance of elementary public schools by local governments 344.07682 (*not* 344.074, 344.073, or 344.071)

For educational exchanges, see 344.08

>   **344.071–344.074 Kinds of education and schools**

Class comprehensive works in 344.07

.071   *Public education and schools

.072   *Private education and schools

.073   By level of government

National, state, local

.074   By level of education

Elementary, secondary, higher

.075   *Liability of schools, school officials, school districts

.076   *Finance of education

Public and private

Class financial aid to students in 344.0795

.076 2   *Financial resources

Examples: tax receipts, investments, natural resources, land

For aid to education, see 344.0763

.076 3   *Aid to education

By higher levels of government

.076 5   *Expenditure

.076 7   Specific kinds of schools

Examples: trade, vocational schools

.076 8   Specific levels of education and schools

.076 82   *Preschool and elementary education

Secondary education relocated to 344.07683

.076 83   *Secondary education [*formerly* 344.07682]

.076 84   *Higher education

Adult education relocated to 344.07685

.076 85   *Adult education [*formerly* 344.07684]

*Add extended notation 026 as instructed under 342–347

.076 9   Specific educational programs

> Examples: medical and public health education, programs for exceptional students
>
> Including schools devoted to specific educational programs, e.g., military, merchant marine academies

.077   *Content of education

> General aspects: curriculums, courses of study, textbooks

.078   *Teachers and teaching

> Including examination, certification, registration, appointment of teachers
>
> Class employment rights in 344.012

.079   *Students

> Including compulsory education, right to education, authority of the law over students, testing

.079 1   *Education of exceptional students

> Add to base number 344.0791 the numbers following 371.9 in 371.91–371.97, e.g., education of blind students 344.079111
>
> Class finance in 344.0769

.079 2   *Attendance

> Including truancy, school year and day

.079 3   *Discipline and student rights

> Class general rights of students in 342.085

.079 4   *Student services

> Examples: counseling, personnel services
>
> *See also 344.0327 for child welfare*

.079 42   *School lunches

.079 5   *Financial aid to students

> Examples: scholarships, loans

.079 6   *Religion in schools

.079 8   *Segregation and discrimination

.08   *Educational and cultural exchanges

.09   *Culture and religion

> Examples: language code (the official language or languages of a specific jurisdiction), flag code

.091   *Historic commemoration and patriotic events

> Class commemorative medals and coins that are legal tender in 343.032

*Add extended notation 026 as instructed under 342–347

.092	*Libraries and archives
.093	*Museums and galleries
.094	*Historic preservation and monuments

.094 *Historic preservation and monuments

> Including antiquities, historical buildings, historical parks

> Class historic commemoration and patriotic events in 344.091

.095 *Science and technology

> Add to base number 344.095 the numbers following 341.7675 in 341.76752–341.76757, e.g., oceanographic law 344.0955

.096 *Religion

.097 *Arts and humanities

> *For museums and galleries, see 344.093*

.099 *Amusements

> Professional and amateur

> Examples: boxing, horse racing

> Class gambling in 344.0542, arts and humanities in 344.097

.3–.9 Specific jurisdictions and areas

> Add to base number 344 notation 3–9 from Table 2, e.g., social law of Australia 344.94, of New South Wales 344.944, of African states 344.6; then to the result add the numbers following 344 in 344.001–344.099, e.g., labor law of Australia 344.9401, of New South Wales, 344.94401, of African states 344.601, administrative regulations on labor in Australia 344.940102636

345 *Criminal law

> Class comprehensive works on civil and criminal courts and procedures in 347

> Use 345.001–345.009 for standard subdivisions

> *See Manual at 345*

SUMMARY

345.01	**Criminal courts**
.02	**Crimes (Offenses)**
.03	**Criminals (Offenders)**
.04	**Liability, responsibility, guilt**
.05	**General criminal procedure**
.06	**Evidence**
.07	**Trials**
.08	**Juvenile procedure**
.3–.9	**Specific jurisdictions and areas**

*Add extended notation 026 as instructed under 342–347

.01   *Criminal courts

Courts specializing in criminal cases, general and other specialized courts considered with respect to their functions in criminal cases

General aspects: jurisdiction, officials, court management

Including public prosecutors, public defenders, legal aid

Class here appellate courts devoted exclusively to criminal cases

Class appellate courts hearing both civil and criminal cases in 347.03, military courts in 343.0143

For juvenile courts, see 345.081

>   345.02–345.04 General considerations

Class comprehensive works in 345

.02   *Crimes (Offenses)

Class here specific trials of specific crimes and classes of crime, e.g., trials of offenses against the person 345.025, a specific trial for murder 345.02523

Add to base number 345.02 the numbers following 364.1 in 364.13–364.18, e.g., white-collar crime 345.0268

See Manual at 345.02 vs. 346.03

.03   *Criminals (Offenders)

Examples: accomplices, juvenile delinquents, recidivists

.04   *Liability, responsibility, guilt

Including the capacity to commit a crime; criminal intent; double jeopardy; defenses, e.g., duress; defenses for a specific crime, e.g., self-defense

.05   *General criminal procedure

Including judicial error

Class here administration of criminal justice, criminal practice, court rules

Class interdisciplinary works on criminal justice in 364, procedure in specific courts devoted exclusively to criminal cases in 345.01, in specific courts hearing both civil and criminal cases in 347.02–347.04

For evidence, see 345.06; trials, 345.07; juvenile procedure, 345.08

.050 4   Special topics

.050 42   *Prosecution

Class public prosecutors in 345.01

.050 44   *Defense

Class public defenders in 345.01, right to counsel in 345.056, defenses in 345.04

*Add extended notation 026 as instructed under 342–347

.052	*Criminal investigation and law enforcement

Examples: surveillance, interception of communication (wiretapping, opening mail), warrants, extradition, interrogation, judicial assistance

Class here police manuals on what the police may legally do in the course of carrying out their duties

Class rights of suspects in 345.056, admissibility of the results of investigative procedures as evidence in 345.06

.052 2	*Search and seizure
.052 7	*Arrests

Including preventive detention

.056	*Rights of suspects

Examples: speedy trial, jury trial, services of counsel, habeas corpus, protection from self-incrimination

Including the effect of press coverage on fair trial

Class legal aid in 345.01

.06	*Evidence

Class here confessions

Add to base number 345.06 the numbers following 347.06 in 347.062–347.067, e.g., expert testimony 345.067

.07	*Trials

Class comprehensive works on appellate procedure in criminal cases in 347.08, trials of specific offenses in 345.02, hearings and trials in juvenile cases in 345.087

.072	*Pretrial procedure

Examples: preliminary hearings, discovery, pretrial release, plea bargaining, arraignment, pleadings, grand jury proceedings, indictment, summons

.075	*Trial (Courtroom) procedure

Examples: juries and jury selection; opening statements, examination of witnesses, summations by prosecution and defense; instructions to jury, verdicts

For final disposition of cases, see 345.077

.077	*Final disposition of cases

Examples: probation, parole, pardon, rehabilitation (reinstatement, after service of sentence, of a criminal's personal rights lost by judicial sentence)

.077 2	*Sentencing

For specific penalties, see 345.0773

*Add extended notation 026 as instructed under 342–347

.077 3	*Specific penalties
	Example: death penalty
.08	*Juvenile procedure
	Class juvenile offenders in 345.03, liability of juveniles in 345.04
.081	*Juvenile courts
	General aspects: jurisdiction, officials, court management
.087	*Hearings and trials
	Contains trial and pretrial procedure, disposition of cases
	Including probation and parole

.3–.9   Specific jurisdictions and areas

Add to base number 345 notation 3–9 from Table 2, e.g., criminal law of Australia 345.94, of New South Wales 345.944, of African states 345.6; then to the result add the numbers following 345 in 345.001–345.087, e.g., the law of evidence in Australia 345.9406, in New South Wales 345.94406, in African states 345.606, decisions on evidence in Australia 345.940602643

Special developments for Scotland and England follow

.411	Criminal law of Scotland
.411 01	*Criminal courts
	General aspects: jurisdiction, officials, court management
	Including Lord Advocate, Solicitor-General, Crown Counsel, procurators fiscal, legal aid
	Class here appellate courts devoted exclusively to criminal cases
	Class appellate courts hearing both civil and criminal cases in 347.41103
	For Children's Hearings (juvenile courts), see 345.41108
.411 012	*District Court
.411 014	*Sheriff Court
.411 016	*High Court of Justiciary
.411 016 2	*Court of First Instance
.411 016 3	*Court of Appeal
.411 02–.411 07	General considerations and procedure
	Add to base number 345.4110 the numbers following 345.0 in 345.02–345.07, e.g., general criminal procedure 345.41105
.411 08	Juvenile procedure
	Including Children's Hearings (juvenile courts)
	Class juvenile offenders in 345.41103, liability of juveniles in 345.41104

*Add extended notation 026 as instructed under 342–347

.42	Criminal law of England
.420 1	*Criminal courts

General aspects: jurisdiction, officials, court management

Including Attorney-General, Director of Public Prosecutions, legal aid

Class here appellate courts devoted exclusively to criminal cases

Class appellate courts hearing both civil and criminal cases in 347.4203, juvenile courts in 345.4208

.420 12	*Magistrates Court

Comprehensive works

Class civil jurisdiction of Magistrates Court in 347.42023

.420 14	*Crown Court
.420 16	*Divisional Court of Queen's Bench Division of High Court of Justice
.420 18	*Criminal Division of Court of Appeal
.420 2–.420 8	General considerations, procedure, juvenile courts and procedure

Add to base number 345.420 the numbers following 345.0 in 345.02–345.08, e.g., juvenile procedure 345.4208

346 *Private law

Class private international law in 340.9

SUMMARY

346.001–.009	**Standard subdivisions**
.01	**Persons and domestic relations**
.02	**Contracts and agency**
.03	**Torts (Delicts)**
.04	**Property**
.05	**Inheritance, succession, fiduciary trusts, trustees**
.06	**Organizations (Associations)**
.07	**Commercial law**
.08	**Banking and insurance**
.09	**Securities and negotiable instruments**
.3–.9	**Specific jurisdictions and areas**

.001–.003	Standard subdivisions
.004	*Equity
.005–.009	Standard subdivisions
.01	Persons and domestic relations
.012	*Persons

Examples: names, domiciles, births, deaths

For capacity and status of persons, see 346.013

*Add extended notation 026 as instructed under 342–347

.013   *Capacity and status of persons

         Capacity: the attribute of persons (personal or corporate) which enables them to perform civil or juristic acts

         Including capacity and status of aged persons; of slaves; of racial, ethnic, national, economic groups; of handicapped persons

         Class individual rights in 342.085, rehabilitation of criminals (reinstatement, after service of sentence, of a criminal's personal rights lost by judicial sentence) in 345.077

.013 4   *Women

.013 5   *Minors

         Including age of majority

.013 8   *Mentally handicapped and disturbed persons

.015   *Domestic relations (Family law)

         For marriage, see 346.016; parent and child, 346.017

.016   *Marriage

         Examples: certificates, solemnization, common-law marriage, invalid and voidable marriages, antenuptial contracts

         Class law relating to the property of married persons in 346.04

.016 3   *Husband and wife

         Rights and duties

         Including the legal status of homemakers

         Class the civil status of married women in 346.0134

.016 6   *Divorce, separation, annulment

         Including alimony

         Class child support in 346.0172

.017   *Parent and child

         Including custody, illegitimacy, legitimation, visitation rights

         Class here parental rights and duties, surrogate parenthood

.017 2   *Child support

.017 5   *Paternity

.017 8   *Adoption

.018   *Guardian and ward

*Add extended notation 026 as instructed under 342–347

.02   *Contracts and agency

> Class the law of contracts on a specific subject not provided for here with
> the subject in law, e.g., a partnership contract 346.0682; the contract itself
> with the subject outside law: if governmental in 351–354, e.g., civil defense
> contracts 351.755; if nongovernmental with the specific subject using
> notation 0687 from Table 1, e.g., roofing contracts 695.0687

> *See Manual at 346.02*

> ## 346.022–346.025 Contracts

> Class here liability

> Class comprehensive works in 346.02, sale in 346.072, loan in 346.073, other
> contracts dealing with a specific subject not provided for here with the subject
> in law, e.g., contracts of partnership 346.0682

> *For extracontractual liability, see 346.03; criminal liability, 345.04;
> government liability, 342.088; liability of schools, school officials, school
> districts, 344.075*

.022   *General considerations of contracts

> Examples: parties to contract, consideration, void and voidable contracts,
> assignments, rescission, breach of contract, remedies

> Class general considerations of contracts applied to specific kinds of
> contracts in 346.023–346.025

.023   *Public (Government) contracts

> Including war, defense, research and development contracts

.024   *Contracts of service

> Including master-servant relationships, mechanics' liens

> Class contracts of service involving bailments in 346.025, agency in
> 346.029, labor contracts in 344.01891

> *See also 346.074 for liens in secured transactions*

.025   *Contracts involving bailments

> Examples: deposit of goods in warehouses, consignment of goods for
> transportation, property of guests in inns and hotels, pledges (pawns)

.029   *Agency and quasi contract

> Including power of attorney, unjust enrichment

.03   *Torts (Delicts)

> Class here defenses, extracontractual liability; liability for the torts of others,
> e.g., employees

> Class remedies in 347.077

> *See Manual at 345.02 vs. 346.03*

*Add extended notation 026 as instructed under 342–347

.031   Liability of specific classes of persons

                  Examples: employers, directors of corporations, hospitals

                  Class liability of specific classes of persons in specific situations in
                  346.032–346.038

.032   *Negligence

                  Including contributory negligence

                  Class malpractice in 346.033

.032 2   *Accidents

                  Examples: transportation accidents, industrial accidents

                  Class accidents resulting in personal injury and death in 346.0323

.032 3   *Personal injury and wrongful death

.033   *Torts against the person

                  Examples: assault and battery, false arrest and illegal confinement, abuse
                  of legal process, invasion of privacy, malpractice

                  For accidents, see 346.0322; defamation, 346.034

.033 2   *Medical malpractice

.034   *Libel and slander (Defamation)

.036   *Torts involving property

                  Examples: trover and conversion, trespass, deceit and fraud, nuisance,
                  wrongful entry

                  Class wrongful entry as an invasion of privacy in 346.033

.038   *Product liability

                  Class here strict liability

[.038 2]   Product liability

                  Number discontinued; class in 346.038

.04   *Property

                  Class here marital property

                  For public property, see 343.02

SUMMARY

346.042	**Kinds of interest in property**
.043	**Real property**
.044	**Government control and regulation of real property**
.045	**Regional and city planning**
.046	**Government control and regulation of specific kinds of land and natural resources**
.047	**Personal property**
.048	**Intangible property**

*Add extended notation 026 as instructed under 342–347

.042	Kinds of interest in property
	Joint, community, separate property
	Examples: future interests (executory interests, expectancies)
.043	*Real property
	Land, permanent fixtures, natural resources
	Including mobile homes, swimming pools
	For government control and regulation, see 346.044
	See Manual at 333.1–333.5 vs. 346.043
.043 2	*Ownership (Land tenure)
	Types of estate, e.g., fee simple, joint tenancy; incidents of ownership, e.g., boundaries, water rights (riparian rights)
	Including ejectment, recovery, squatter's right, surveying
.043 3	*Horizontal property (Condominiums) and cooperative ownership
	Including time-sharing
.043 4	*Tenancy
	Class here landlord and tenant
	Class ejectment in 346.0432
.043 44	*Rent
	Including rent control
.043 46	*Leases
.043 462	*Commercial leases
.043 48	*Farm tenancy
	Class specific aspects of farm tenancy in 346.04344–346.04346
.043 5	*Easements and servitudes
	Including right of way
.043 6	*Transfer
	Including restrictions on alienation, consolidation of land holdings
	Class inheritance and succession in 346.052–346.057
	For conveyancing, see 346.0438
.043 62	*Acquisition and purchase
	Example: preemption
	See also 341.754 for preemption in international law
.043 63	*Sale
	Class the real-estate business in 346.0437

*Add extended notation 026 as instructed under 342–347

| .043 64 | *Mortgages |
| | Class here foreclosure |

| .043 7 | *Real-estate business |

Including valuation of real property

Class regulation of a specific general administrative function of the real estate business with the function in law, e.g., organization 346.065, wages 344.0121

| .043 73 | *Closing and settlements |

Including escrows

| .043 77 | *Subdivision |

| .043 8 | *Conveyancing |

Including deeds, registration and description of land, titles, abstracts of title, title investigations

| .044 | *Government control and regulation of real property |

Class here land reform; conservation, regulation, control of natural resources; comprehensive works on government control and regulation of public and private real property

Class government as landlord or tenant in 346.0434

For rent control, see 346.04344; regional and city planning, 346.045; control of specific kinds of land and natural resources, 346.046

See also 343.0256 for the control and use of public real property

| .045 | *Regional and city planning |

Including zoning, land use, building codes that relate to regional or city planning or land use, restrictions on the posting of advertisements

Class regulations governing the construction of buildings in 343.07869

| .046 | Government control and regulation of specific kinds of land and natural resources |

Add to base number 346.046 the numbers following 333 in 333.7–333.9, e.g., control of recreational lands 346.04678

| .047 | *Personal property |

Movable property

Including leasing, e.g., of computers

Class mobile homes in 346.043

For intangible property, see 346.048; sale, 346.072

*Add extended notation 026 as instructed under 342–347

.048   *Intangible property

         Including public lending rights

         Class here intellectual property, industrial property (intangible property of an industrial nature, e.g., business names, licensing, franchising, goodwill)

         For negotiable instruments, see 346.096

.048 2   *Copyright

.048 4   *Design protection

.048 6   *Patents

.048 8   *Trademarks

.05   *Inheritance, succession, fiduciary trusts, trustees

.052   *Inheritance and succession

         Including intestate succession

         Class here probate practice, estate planning

         Class estate planning to avoid taxes in 343.053

         For testate succession, see 346.054; administration of estates, 346.056

.054   *Wills (Testate succession)

.056   *Administration of estates

         Including execution of wills

         For unclaimed estates, see 346.057

.057   *Unclaimed estates

.059   *Fiduciary trusts and trustees

.06   *Organizations (Associations)

         Organization, ownership, management

         Class here the organization of associations engaged in specific types of enterprises, e.g., organization of railroad companies

         Class the organization of labor unions in 344.0188

SUMMARY

346.062	**General considerations**
.063	**Accounting**
.064	**Nonprofit organizations**
.065	**Business enterprises**
.066	**Corporations (Companies)**
.067	**Government corporations**
.068	**Unincorporated business enterprises**

*Add extended notation 026 as instructed under 342–347

.062   *General considerations

Examples: registration, meetings

Class general considerations of specific kinds of organizations in 346.064–346.068

.063   *Accounting

Class accounting for specific kinds of organizations in 346.064–346.068

\>   346.064–346.068 Specific kinds of organizations

Class here accounting, meetings, registration

Class comprehensive works in 346.06

.064   *Nonprofit organizations

Examples: unincorporated societies, trade and professional associations, nonprofit corporations

Including charitable trusts and foundations

.065   *Business enterprises

Including valuation, the sale of businesses, record requirements for businesses

Class record requirements for a specific kind of organization with the kind, e.g., record requirements for a government corporation 346.067; record requirements for a specific subject with the subject in law, e.g., workmen's compensation insurance records 344.021

For corporations, see 346.066; unincorporated business organizations, 346.068

.065 2   *Small business

Class small corporations in 346.066

.066   *Corporations (Companies)

Class comprehensive works on corporate and commercial law in 346.07, government corporations in 346.067, municipal corporations in 342.09

\>   346.066 2–346.066 6 Specific aspects of corporate law

Class comprehensive works in 346.066

.066 2   *Organization

Including charters, bylaws, promotion, investment banking, liquidation

.066 22   *Incorporation

.066 26   *Reorganization

Including acquisitions and mergers

*Add extended notation 026 as instructed under 342–347

| .066 4 | *Management |
| | Including records |

.066 42   *Officers

.066 45   *Meetings

                    Class shareholders' meetings in 346.0666

.066 48   *Accounting

.066 6   *Securities and security holders

                    Including shareholders' voting and meetings

                    Class securities marketing in 346.092; tender offers with the subject in law to which they apply, e.g., tender offers for settlement of debts 346.077, for treasury bills 346.0922

.066 8   Kinds of corporations (companies)

                    Examples: close corporations, family corporations, limited companies, private companies, public limited companies; cooperatives, holding companies, credit unions

                    Class specific aspects of corporate law applied to specific kinds of corporations in 346.0662–346.0666

                        For nonprofit corporations, see 346.064; government corporations, 346.067

.067   *Government corporations

                    Example: quangos

                    Class municipal corporations in 342.09

.068   *Unincorporated business enterprises

                    Examples: horse syndicates, land trusts, sole traders

.068 2   *Partnerships

.07   *Commercial law

                    Class here comprehensive works on business law; laws of a specific jurisdiction governing business investment by foreign nationals, e.g., laws of China governing the conduct of business in China by foreign nationals 346.5107

                    Class a specific topic of commercial law, of business law not provided for here with the subject, e.g., tax law 343.04, insurance law 346.086

                      See Manual at 338.09 vs. 338.6042, 332.67309, 346.07, 658.11, 658.21, T1—068

.072   *Sale

                    Class conditional and secured sales transactions in 346.074; the sale of real property in 346.04363, of business enterprises in 346.065

*Add extended notation 026 as instructed under 342–347

.073   *Loan

Including agricultural and consumer credit, interest, usury, truth in lending

Class secured loan transactions in 346.074

.074   *Secured transactions

Examples: chattel mortgages; liens, suretyship and guaranty; conditional sales (installment sales, hire-purchase); securities for bankers' advances

Class real-estate mortgages in 346.04364, mortgage insurance as a form of economic assistance in 343.0742

See also 346.024 for mechanics' liens

.077   *Debtor and creditor

Including the collection of debts, creditors' remedies, debtors' relief

For bankruptcy, see 346.078

.078   *Bankruptcy

Including receivership

Class here insolvency

.08   Banking and insurance

.082   *Banks and banking

Add to base number 346.082 the numbers following 332 in 332.1–332.3, e.g., branch banking 346.08216

Class investment banking in 346.0662; regulation of a specific general administrative function of banks with the function in law, e.g., corporate organization 346.0662, wages 344.0121

For loan, see 346.073

.086   *Insurance

Add to base number 346.086 the numbers following 368 in 368.01–368.88, e.g., fire insurance 346.08611; however, class social insurance in 344.02

Class regulation of a specific general administrative function of insurance companies and agencies with the function in law, e.g., corporate organization 346.0662, wages 344.0121

.09   *Securities and negotiable instruments

.092   *Securities

Exchange, transfer, sale, marketing

Class the initial promotion of securities in 346.0662; what a corporation must do to make certain a security is valid in 346.0666

See also 346.074 for the security a borrower must provide to assure that he will repay a debt

*Add extended notation 026 as instructed under 342–347

.092 2	Specific types of securities
	Examples: bonds, stocks, mutual funds
	Including government securities
	Class organizations marketing specific types of securities in 346.0926
.092 6	*Marketing agents and arrangements
	Examples: dealers, brokers, stock exchanges
	Including private placement of securities, par value modification
	Class investment banking in 346.0662; regulation of a specific general administrative function of organizations engaged in marketing securities with the function in law, e.g., organization 346.065, wages 344.0121
.096	*Negotiable instruments
	Examples: checks (cheques), bills of exchange, drafts, trade acceptances, promissory notes, warehouse receipts
	For securities, see 346.092

.3–.9   Specific jurisdictions and areas

Add to base number 346 notation 3–9 from Table 2, e.g., private law of Australia 346.94, of New South Wales 346.944, of African states 346.6; then to the result add the numbers following 346 in 346.001–346.096, e.g., property law of Australia 346.9404, of New South Wales 346.94404, of African states 346.604, property laws of Australia 346.94040263

347   *Civil procedure and courts

Class here comprehensive works on civil and criminal procedure, the judicial branch of government, administration of justice

(Option: Class here courts and procedure in specific fields of law; prefer specific subject, using notation 0269 from the table under 342–347)

Use 347.001–347.009 for standard subdivisions

Class criminal procedure and courts in 345

For administrative procedure, see 342.066

See Manual at 347

SUMMARY

347.01	Courts
.02	Courts with general original jurisdiction
.03	Courts with appellate jurisdiction
.04	Courts with specialized jurisdiction
.05	General considerations of procedure
.06	Evidence
.07	Trials
.08	Appellate procedure
.09	Arbitration, mediation, conciliation
.3–.9	Specific jurisdictions and areas

*Add extended notation 026 as instructed under 342–347

| .01 | *Courts |

Class juvenile procedure and courts in 345.08; provisional courts in 342.062; courts dealing with a specific subject with the subject in law, using notation 0269 from the table under 342–347, e.g., tax courts 343.040269

For courts with specific kinds of jurisdiction, see 347.02–347.04

| .012 | *General considerations |

Powers, functions, jurisdiction, organization

Including judicial review, the power to use contempt of court prerogative, judicial discretion, judicial error

Class contempt of court as an offense in 345.0234

| .013 | *Judicial administration (Court management) |

Effect of court work loads, calendars, records, staffing on the administration of justice

Including judicial statistics, the cost of running a court in the cost-benefit sense

Class judges in 347.014, other court officials in 347.016

| .014 | *Judges |

General aspects: appointment, tenure, retirement, removal, discipline

Class a judge associated with a specific court with the court, e.g., judges of the High Court of Justice in England 347.4202534, judges of a juvenile court 345.081

| .016 | Other officials |

Examples: marshals, sheriffs, constables, clerks, court reporters, coroners, justices of the peace, notaries

| .017 | *Legal aid |

Class here interdisciplinary works on legal aid

Class legal aid in criminal cases in 345.01, as a welfare service in 362.58

> 347.02–347.04 Courts with specific kinds of jurisdiction

Class here procedure in specific courts

Add to each subdivision identified by ‡ as follows:
2   General considerations
           Examples: powers, functions, jurisdiction, organization
3   Judicial administration
34   Judges
36   Other officials
5   Rules

Class comprehensive works in 347.01

*Add extended notation 026 as instructed under 342–347

> 347.02–347.03 Courts with general jurisdiction

Class comprehensive works in 347.01, procedure in specific levels of courts in 347.05–347.08

.02 *‡Courts with general original jurisdiction

Class here courts of countries and states of the United States that have names such as Circuit, District, County, Municipal, Superior Court

.03 Courts with appellate jurisdiction

Class here comprehensive works on appellate courts

Class appellate courts with specialized jurisdiction in 347.04, those devoted exclusively to criminal cases in 345.01

.033 *‡Intermediate

.035 *‡Courts of last resort (Supreme courts)

.04 Courts with specialized jurisdiction

General aspects: powers, functions, jurisdiction, organization, judges, other officials, rules, procedure

Example: admiralty courts, claims courts

Class courts dealing with a specific subject with the subject in law, using notation 0269 from the table under 342–347, e.g., tax courts 343.040269

> 347.05–347.08 Procedure

Class here procedure in specific levels of courts

Class comprehensive works in 347.05

.05 *General considerations of procedure

Class here comprehensive works on procedure, the relation of a fair trial to freedom of the press

Class procedure in specific courts in 347.02–347.04; procedure with respect to a specific subject with the subject in law, using notation 0269 from the table under 342–347, e.g., court procedure in tax matters 343.040269

For evidence, see 347.06; trials, 347.07; appellate procedure, 347.08

.050 4 *Practice

The form, manner, order of instituting and conducting a suit, court case, or other judicial proceeding through its successive stages to its end in accordance with rules and principles laid down by law or by regulations and precedents of the courts

Class trial practice in 347.07

*Add extended notation 026 as instructed under 342–347
‡Add as instructed under 347.02–347.04

.051   *Court rules

> Class rules of specific courts, of courts having specific kinds of jurisdiction in 347.02–347.04

.052   Motions, limitation of actions, parties to trial, jury trial

> Class here advocacy

.053   Kinds of actions

> Examples: civil, class, personal, statutory

.055   Forms and form books

> Class forms and form books on a specific subject with the subject in law, using notation 0269 from the table under 342–347

.06   *Evidence

.062   *Admissibility

.064   Kinds

> Examples: circumstantial, demonstrative, documentary, hearsay, physical, presumptive, prima facie

> Including methods of interpreting records for trial practice, e.g., accounting records, hospital records

> *For witnesses, see 347.066*

.066   *Witnesses

> General aspects: capacity, privileges and immunities, privileged communications, compulsion of attendance

> Class examination of witnesses in 347.075

> *For expert testimony, see 347.067*

.067   *Expert testimony

> Class medical jurisprudence, forensic medicine, forensic psychiatry in 614.1; the use of science in detecting crime in 363.25

.07   *Trials

> Class a trial dealing with a specific subject with the subject in law, using notation 0269 from the table under 342–347, e.g., a product liability trial 346.0380269

.072   *Pretrial procedure

> Examples: pleading, publication of notice, service of process, pretrial discovery procedures, pretrial conferences, motions

.075   *Trial (Courtroom) procedure

> Examples: opening statements, examination of witnesses, summations, verdicts

*Add extended notation 026 as instructed under 342–347

.075 2		*Juries and their selection

Class instructions to juries in 347.0758

.075 8		*Instructions to juries
.077		*Judgments

Including remedies, executions of judgment, costs, attachment and garnishment

.08	*Appellate procedure

Class here comprehensive works on appeals in criminal cases

Class procedure in specific appellate courts hearing both civil and criminal cases, specific appellate courts devoted exclusively to civil cases in 347.03–347.04; procedure in appellate courts devoted exclusively to criminal cases in 345.01

.09	*Arbitration, mediation, conciliation

Class here dispute resolution

.3–.9	**Specific jurisdictions and areas**

Add to base number 347 notation 3–9 from Table 2, e.g., civil procedure and courts of Australia 347.94, of New South Wales 347.944, of African states 347.6; then to the result add the numbers following 347 in 347.001–347.09, e.g., the law of evidence in Australia 347.9406, in New South Wales 347.94406, in African states 347.606; Australian court decisions on evidence in 347.940602643

Special developments for Scotland, England, the United States follow

.411	Civil procedure and courts of Scotland
.411 01	*Courts

Add to base number 347.41101 the numbers following 347.01 in 347.012–347.017, e.g., general considerations 347.411012

For courts with specific kinds of jurisdiction, see 347.41102–347.41104

> 347.411 02–347.411 04 Courts with specific kinds of jurisdiction

Add to each subdivision identified by ‡ as instructed under 347.02–347.04, e.g., jurisdiction of the Sheriff Court 347.4110212

Class comprehensive works in 347.41101

> 347.411 02–347.411 03 Courts with general jurisdiction

Class comprehensive works in 347.41101, procedure in specific levels of courts in 347.41105–347.41108

.411 02	*Courts with original jurisdiction

*Add extended notation 026 as instructed under 342–347

.411 021	*‡Sheriff Court

Comprehensive works

Class criminal jurisdiction of Sheriff Court in 345.411014, appellate jurisdiction of Sheriff-Principal in 347.411032

.411 023	*‡Court of Session

For Outer House, see 347.411024; Inner House, 347.411035

.411 024	*‡Outer House of Court of Session
.411 03	Courts with appellate jurisdiction

Class here comprehensive works on appellate courts

Class appellate courts devoted exclusively to criminal cases in 345.41101, appellate courts with specialized jurisdiction in 347.41104

.411 032	*‡Sheriff-Principal
.411 035	*‡Inner House of Court of Session
.411 039	*‡House of Lords (Court of last resort)
.411 04	Courts with specialized jursidiction

General aspects: powers, functions, jurisdiction, organization, judges, other officials, rules, procedure

Examples: Licensing Courts, Licensing Appeals Courts, Court of the Lord Lyon

Class courts dealing with a single specific subject with the subject in law, using notation 0269 from the table under 342–347, e.g., Court of Exchequer 343.411040269

.411 05–.411 09	Procedure and arbitration

Add to base number 347.4110 the numbers following 347.0 in 347.05–347.09, e.g., evidence 347.41106

.42	Civil procedure and courts of England
.420 1	*Courts

Add to base number 347.4201 the numbers following 347.01 in 347.012–347.017, e.g., general considerations 347.42012

For courts with specific kinds of jurisdiction, see 347.4202–347.4204

> 347.420 2–347.420 4 Courts with specific kinds of jurisdiction

Add to each subdivision identified by ‡ as instructed under 347.02–347.04, jurisdiction of County Court 347.420212

Class comprehensive works in 347.4201

*Add extended notation 026 as instructed under 342–347
‡Add as instructed under 347.02–347.04

>   347.420 2–347.420 3 Courts with general jurisdiction

           Class comprehensive works in 347.4201, procedure in specific levels of courts in 347.4205–347.4208

.420 2   Courts with original jurisdiction

.420 21   *‡County Court

.420 23   *‡Domestic Court of Magistrates Court

.420 25   *‡High Court of Justice

           Comprehensive works

           Class Family Division in 346.420150269

           For Chancery Division, see 347.42026; Queen's Bench Division, 347.42027

.420 26   *‡Chancery Division of the High Court of Justice

.420 27   *‡Queen's Bench Division of High Court of Justice

           For Divisional Court of Queen's Bench Division, see 345.42016

.420 29   *‡Supreme Court of Judicature

           For High Court of Justice, see 347.42025; Crown Court, 345.42014; Court of Appeal, 347.42032

.420 3   Courts with appellate jurisdiction

           Class here comprehensive works on appellate courts

           Class appellate courts devoted exclusively to criminal cases in 345.4201, appellate courts with specialized jurisdiction in 347.4204

.420 32   *‡Court of Appeal

           For Criminal Division, see 345.42018; Civil Division, 347.42035

.420 35   *‡Civil Division of Court of Appeal

.420 39   *‡House of Lords (Court of last resort)

           Criminal and civil jurisdiction

.420 4   Courts with specialized jurisdiction

           General aspects: powers, functions, jurisdiction, organization, judges, other officials; rules, procedure

           Example: Judicial Committee of the Privy Council

           Class courts dealing with a specific subject with the subject in law, using notation 0269 from the table under 342–347, e.g., Lands Tribunal 346.420430269

*Add extended notation 026 as instructed under 342–347

‡Add as instructed under 347.02–347.04

.420 5–.420 9   Procedure and arbitration

    Add to base number 347.420 the numbers following 347.0 in 347.05–347.09, e.g., evidence 347.4206

.73   Civil procedure and courts of the United States

    Federal procedure and courts; national and regional treatment of state and local procedure and courts

    For civil procedure and courts of specific states and localities, see 347.74–347.79

.731   *Courts

    Add to base number 347.731 the numbers following 347.01 in 347.012–347.017, e.g., judges 347.7314

    For specific court systems, see 347.732–347.734

> 347.732–347.734 Specific court systems

    Class comprehensive works in 347.731

.732   *Federal courts

    Add to base number 347.732 the numbers following 347 in 347.02–347.04, e.g., federal judges 347.732034

> 347.732 2–347.732 8 Federal courts with specific kinds of jurisdiction

    Class here procedure in specific courts

    Add to each subdivision identified by ‡ as instructed under 347.02–347.04, e.g., Supreme Court rules 347.73265

    Class comprehensive works in 347.732

> 347.732 2–347.732 6 Federal courts with general jurisdiction

    Class comprehensive works in 347.732, procedure in specific levels of courts in 347.735–347.738

.732 2   *‡District courts

    Courts of original jurisdiction

.732 4   *‡Courts of appeal

    For the Supreme Court, see 347.7326

.732 6   *‡Supreme Court

*Add extended notation 026 as instructed under 342–347
‡Add as instructed under 347.02–347.04

.732 8   Courts of specialized jurisdiction

General aspects: powers, functions, jurisdiction, organization, judges, other officials, rules, procedure

Example: United States Court of Customs and Patent Appeals

Class courts dealing with a specific subject with the subject in United States law, using notation 0269 from the table under 342–347, e.g., tax courts 343.73040269

.733   *State courts

Add to base number 347.733 the numbers following 347.732 in 347.7322–347.7328, e.g., state supreme courts 347.7336

Class courts of specific states in 347.74–347.79

.734   *Local courts

Class courts of specific localities in 347.74–347.79

.735–.738   Procedure

Class here procedure in specific levels of federal courts

Add to base number 347.73 the numbers following 347.0 in 347.05–347.08, e.g., rules of evidence 347.736

Class procedure in specific courts in 347.732–347.734

.739   *Arbitration, mediation, conciliation

.74–.79   Civil procedure and courts of specific states and localities of the United States

Add to base number 347 notation 74–79 from Table 2, e.g., civil procedure and courts of Pennsylvania 347.748, of Philadelphia 347.74811; then to the result add the numbers following 347 in 347.001–347.09, e.g., the Supreme Court of Pennsylvania 347.748035, courts of Philadelphia 347.7481101

Class civil procedure and courts of Hawaii in 347.969

348   Laws (Statutes), regulations, cases

Forms listed here are comprehensive in nature, covering the whole of the law of a specific jurisdiction or a major portion thereof

Class treatises on the whole of the law of a specific jurisdiction in 349; forms confined to a specific branch or topic with the branch or topic in law, using notation 026 from the table under 342–347, e.g., a digest of tax laws 343.0402638

(Option: Class here laws, regulations, cases covering specific subjects in law; prefer specific subject, using notation 026 from the table under 342–347)

.001–.002   Standard subdivisions

.003   Encyclopedias [*formerly* 348.06], dictionaries, concordances

.004   Codification

Class proposed codes in 348.023

*Add extended notation 026 as instructed under 342–347

| .005–.009 | Standard subdivisions |
| .01 | Preliminary materials |

Examples: bills, hearings, reports, executive messages, statements of witnesses, legislative histories, slip laws

Including statistical reports of bills passed or vetoed, reports on the status of bills

| .02 | Laws (Statutes) and regulations |

Including laws arranged in alphabetical order

> 348.022–348.024 Collections of laws

Class comprehensive works and collections in 348

| .022 | Statutes |

Contains compilations of laws in chronological order

Examples: statutes at large, revised statutes, session laws

(If the option under 348 is chosen, class here individual laws)

| .023 | Codes |

Contains compilations of statutes in classified order

Including compiled and consolidated statutes

| .024 | Selected laws |
| .025 | Administrative regulations |

> 348.026–348.028 Guides to laws and regulations

Class comprehensive works and guides in 348.026, guides to a specific collection of laws with the collection, e.g., a citator to the U.S. Code 348.7323

| .026 | Digests of laws and regulations |

Including summaries of changes

Class here comprehensive guides to laws and regulations

For citators to laws and regulations, see 348.027; checklists, tables, indexes of laws and regulations, 348.028

| .027 | Citators to laws and regulations |
| .028 | Checklists, tables, indexes of laws and regulations |

Class union lists of general legal material in 016.34; of legal materials on a specific subject with the subject, e.g., of criminal materials 016.345

.04   **Cases**

> Do not use for casebooks

> Class cases in a specific subject in law with the subject, using special subdivision 0264, e.g., censorship cases 344.05310264

> **348.041–348.043 Reports**

> Official and unofficial

> Reports of cases contain a relatively full treatment of each case as well as the ultimate decision

> Class comprehensive works in 348.04

.041   National reports

.042   Regional reports

.043   State and provincial reports

.044   Court decisions

> Texts of decisions with or without accompanying information

.045   Decisions (Rulings) of regulatory agencies

> **348.046–348.048 Guides to cases**

> Class here combined guides to laws, regulations, cases

> Class comprehensive works and guides in 348.046; guides to a specific set of court reports with the reports, e.g., a citator to U.S. Supreme Court reports 348.73413

> *For guides to laws and regulations, see 348.026–348.028*

.046   Digests of cases

> Class here comprehensive guides to cases

> *For citators to cases, see 348.047; checklists, tables, indexes of cases, 348.048*

.047   Citators to cases

.048   Checklists, tables, indexes of cases

.05   Advisory opinions of attorneys-general (ministers of justice)

[.06]   Encyclopedias

> Encyclopedias on law in general relocated to 340.03, on the forms legal materials may take to 348.003

.3–.9	**Specific jurisdictions and areas**

Class here general collections of repealed laws

Add to base number 348 notation 3–9 from Table 2, e.g., laws, regulations, cases of Australia 348.94, of New South Wales 348.944, of African states 348.6; then to the result add the numbers following 348 in 348.001–348.05, e.g., selected laws of Australia 348.94024, of New South Wales 348.944024, of African states 348.6024

Class the legislative procedure involved in enacting or repealing a law in 328.37; repealed laws on a specific subject with the subject in law, e.g., the repeal of a prohibition on the sale and consumption of alcohol 344.0541

A special development for the United States follows

.73	**Federal laws (statutes), regulations, cases of the United States**

Including national and regional treatment of state and local laws, regulations, cases

For laws, regulations, cases of specific states and localities, see 348.74–348.79

.730 3	Encyclopedias [*formerly* 348.736], dictionaries, concordances
.730 4	Codification

Class proposed codes in 348.7323

.731	**Preliminary materials**

Examples: bills, hearings, reports, executive messages, statements of witnesses, legislative histories, slip laws

.732	**Federal laws (statutes) and regulations**

>	348.732 2–348.732 5 Collections of federal laws and regulations

Class comprehensive works and collections in 348.732

.732 2	Federal statutes

(Option: If the option under 348 is chosen, class here individual laws)

.732 3	United States Code
.732 4	Selected Federal laws
.732 5	Federal administrative regulations

>	348.732 6–348.732 8 Guides to federal laws and regulations

Class comprehensive works and guides in 348.7326

.732 6	Digests of federal laws and regulations
	Including summaries of changes
	Class here comprehensive guides to federal laws and regulations

> *For citators to federal laws and regulations, see 348.7327; checklists, tables, indexes of federal laws and regulations, 348.7328*

.732 7	Citators to federal laws and regulations
.732 8	Checklists, tables, indexes of federal laws and regulations
.734	Federal cases
	Do not use for casebooks

> 348.734 1–348.734 2 Reports of federal cases

Official and unofficial

Class comprehensive works and reports in 348.734

.734 1	Federal court reports
.734 13	Supreme Court
.734 15	Lower Federal courts
.734 2	National reporter system
.734 22	Atlantic federal reporter system
.734 23	Northeastern federal reporter system
.734 24	Northwestern federal reporter system
.734 25	Southeastern federal reporter system
.734 26	Southwestern federal reporter system
.734 27	Southern federal reporter system
.734 28	Pacific federal reporter system
.734 4	Court decisions
.734 5	Decisions (Rulings) of regulatory agencies

> 348.734 6–348.734 8 Guides to federal cases

Class here combined guides to federal laws, regulations, cases

Class comprehensive works and guides to federal cases in 348.7346

For guides to federal laws and regulations, see 348.7326–348.7328

.734 6	Digests of federal cases

Class here comprehensive guides to federal cases

> *For citators to federal cases, see 348.7347; checklists, tables, indexes of federal cases, 348.7348*

.734 7	Citators to federal cases
.734 8	Checklists, tables, indexes of federal cases
.735	Advisory opinions of Attorney-General
[.736]	Encyclopedias

Relocated to 348.7303

.74–.79   Laws, regulations, cases of specific states and localities of the United States

Add to base number 348 notation 74–79 from Table 2, e.g., laws, regulations, cases of Pennsylvania 348.748, of Philadelphia 348.74811; then to the result add the numbers following 348 in 348.001–348.05, e.g., Pennsylvania statutes 348.748022, Philadelphia code of ordinances 348.74811023

Class laws, regulations, cases of Hawaii in 348.969

349   Law of specific jurisdictions and areas

Comprehensive works on the law of specific jurisdictions and areas in the modern world

Add to base number 349 notation 4–9 from Table 2, e.g., works on the ordinances of the City of Los Angeles 349.79494

Class specific branches of the law of specific jurisdictions in 342–347, original materials on the law of a specific jurisdiction in 348

(If Option A under 340 is chosen, class here comparative law and law without jurisdiction by adding to base number 349 the numbers following 34 in 342–348, e.g., comparative criminal procedure 349.505, criminal procedure of Australia 349.59405)

350   Public administration and military science

Class here the executive branch of government and its structure, description and administration of government organizations and agencies, comprehensive works on public administration of the three branches of government

Class comprehensive works on the structure and functions of government or of two or more branches of government in 320.4, the relation of executive branch to other branches in 320.404

> *For public administration of legislative branch, see 328.068; of judicial branch, 347.013*

> *See Manual at 350; 350.354; 350–354 vs. 320.4, 320.9; 350–354 vs. 658, T1—068; 361–365 vs. 350–354; 363 vs. 340, 350–354*

SUMMARY

350.000 1–.9   Standard subdivisions; specific aspects of public administration

351   Administration of central governments
.000 1–.000 9   Standard subdivisions
.001–.009   [Bureaucracy, chief executives, cabinets and councils of state, fundamentals of administration, special agencies]
.01–.09   [Specific departments and ministries of cabinet rank, intergovernmental administration]
.1   Personnel management
.2   Lists and directories of officials and employees
.3   Civil service examinations
.4   Government work force
.5   Pensions
.6   Civil service system (Merit system)
.7   Property and financial management and related topics; administration of public safety and related fields
.8   Administration of specific fields
.9   Malfunctioning of administration

352   Administration of local governments
.000 1–.000 9   [Standard subdivisions and fundamentals of administration]
.002–.009   General topics of local administration
.03–.09   Treatment by specific continents, countries, localities
.1   Financial and property management and related topics
.2   Police
.3   Fire protection and accident prevention
.4   Safeguarding public health
.5   Regulation and control of public buildings
.6   Environmental sanitation and related activities
.7   Public works and housing
.8   Licensing
.9   Miscellaneous fields

353   Administration of United States federal and state governments
.000 1–.000 9   Standard subdivisions
.001–.009   Government service, property and financial management and related topics, administration of specific fields, malfunctioning of administration
.01–.09   [Bureaucracy, presidents and vice-presidents, the cabinet, fundamentals of administration, special agencies]
.1   Department of State
.2   Department of the Treasury
.3   Department of the Interior
.4   Post Office Department (1829-1971)
.5   Department of Justice
.6   Department of Defense
.7   Department of the Navy
.8   Other departments
.9   State governments

354   Administration of specific central governments; international administration
.1   International administration
.3–.9   Specific central governments other than those of United States

355	Military science
.001–.009	Standard subdivisions
.02–.07	Basic considerations
.1	Military life and customs
.2	Military resources
.3	Organization and personnel of military forces
.4	Military operations
.5	Military training
.6	Military administration
.7	Military installations and land reservations
.8	Military equipment and supplies (Matériel)

356	Foot forces and warfare
.1	Infantry

357	Mounted forces and warfare
.04	General topics
.1	Horse cavalry
.2	Remount and training services
.5	Mechanized cavalry

358	Air and other specialized forces and warfare; engineering and related services
.1	Missile forces and warfare; army artillery and armored forces and warfare
.2	Army engineering and related services
.3	Chemical, biological, radiological forces and warfare
.4	Air forces and warfare
.8	Space forces and warfare

359	Sea (Naval) forces and warfare
.001–.009	Standard subdivisions
.03–.07	[Situation and policy, research and development of equipment and supplies]
.1–.2	Naval life and resources
.3	Organization and personnel of naval forces
.4–.7	Naval operations, training, administration, installations
.8	Naval equipment and supplies (Naval matériel)
.9	Specialized combat forces; engineering and related services

.000 1–.9	Standard subdivisions; specific aspects of public administration

Add to base number 350 the numbers following 351 in 351.0001–351.9, e.g., personnel management 350.1

See Manual at 350.0001–350.9 vs. 351

> ## 351–354 Administration of central and local governments

Class comprehensive works in 350

See Manual at 350–354; 350–354 vs. 320.4; 350–354 vs. 658, T1—068; 361–365 vs. 350–354; 363 vs. 340, 350–354

351   Administration of central governments

National and state or provincial governments

Class works dealing comprehensively with central and local governments in 350

For specific central governments, see 354

See Manual at 350–354; 350–354 vs. 320.4, 320.9; 350–354 vs. 658, T1—068; 350.0001–350.9 vs. 351; 361–365 vs. 350–354; 363 vs. 340, 350–354

SUMMARY

351.000 1–.000 9		**Standard subdivisions**
	.001–.009	**[Bureaucracy, chief executives, cabinets and councils of state, fundamentals of administration, special agencies]**
	.01–.09	**[Specific departments and ministries of cabinet rank, intergovernmental administration]**
	.1	**Personnel management**
	.2	**Lists and directories of officials and employees**
	.3	**Civil service examinations**
	.4	**Government work force**
	.5	**Pensions**
	.6	**Civil service system (Merit system)**
	.7	**Property and financial management and related topics; administration of public safety and related fields**
	.8	**Administration of specific fields**
	.9	**Malfunctioning of administration**

.000 1   Philosophy and theory

Including relation of public administration to social and political factors

[.000 11]   Systems

Do not use; class 351.0073

.000 2   Miscellany

.000 25   Directories of persons and organizations

Class directories of officials and employees in 351.2

.000 3   Dictionaries, encyclopedias, concordances

.000 5   Serial publications

Including official gazettes

Class serial administrative reports in 351.0006

.000 6   Administrative reports

Class administrative reports of cabinet-level departments and ministries in 351.01–351.08, of other departments and agencies in 351.1–351.8; administrative reports on a specific subject with the subject in public administration, using notation 06 from Table 1, e.g., annual administrative reports on property management 351.71306 (*not* 351.71305)

See Manual at 351.0006

.000 7	Education, research, related topics
[.000 76]	Review and exercise
	Relocated to 351.3
.000 8–.000 9	Standard subdivisions

SUMMARY

351.001	**Bureaucracy**
.003	**Chief executives**
.004	**Cabinets and councils of state**
.007	**Fundamentals of public administration**
.009	**Special agencies**

.001   Bureaucracy

Class specific aspect of bureaucracy with the aspect, e.g., reorganization 351.0073

.003   Chief executives

Class here relationship to citizens

Use of this number for general considerations of executive branch other than chief executives discontinued; class in 351

Relation of executive branch to fundamental instruments of government relocated to 342.06

See Manual at T1—092: Comprehensive biography: Public figures

.003 1   Kinds of chief executives

Including plural executives

Use of this number for comprehensive treatment of the chief executive discontinued; class in 351.003

Class specific aspects of chief executives regardless of kind in 351.0032–351.0036

.003 12   Monarchs and their representatives

Examples: governors-general of Canada, regents, viceroys

.003 13   Presidents, premiers and related kinds of chief executives

Examples: chancellors, prime ministers, governors

.003 16   Autocratic chief executives

Class a specific type of autocratic chief executive with the type, e.g., absolute monarchs 351.00312

.003 18   Deputy chief executives

Examples: vice-presidents, deputy prime ministers and chancellors, lieutenant governors

>   351.003 2–351.003 6 Specific aspects of the chief executive

       Class comprehensive works in 351.003

.003 2   Powers, functions, privileges of chief executive

.003 22   Powers

               Examples: judicial and legislative powers

.003 23   Leadership role

               Class relationship to legislature in 320.404

.003 28   Privileges

.003 4   Qualifications and term of office

               Method of selection of chief executive relocated to 321

               Class termination of tenure before expiration of term in 351.0036

.003 5   Executive messages, speeches, writings

               Collections, history, description, criticism

               Class speeches and messages on a specific subject with the subject, e.g., budget messages 351.72256

.003 52   Addresses to legislature

.003 54   Inaugural addresses

.003 6   Termination of tenure of chief executive before expiration of term

               Examples: abdication, impeachment, recall, resignation

               Class history of specific impeachments in 930–990

                 See also 324.68 for recall procedures, 328.3453 for impeachment power of legislatures, 342.062 for law of impeachment

[.003 7]   Relation to other branches of government

               Relocated to 320.404

.004   Cabinets and councils of state

               Class here comprehensive works on departments and ministries of cabinet rank

               Class works dealing comprehensively with structure, agencies, programs, services of central governments in 351; specific kinds of departments and ministries of cabinet rank in 351.01–351.08

.007	**Fundamentals of administration**
	Class here executive management
	Class staffing in 351.1, other aspects not provided for here in 351.7
.007 2	Planning and policy making
.007 22	Information and its use
	Including use of experts and consultants
	Class advisory and consultative bodies in 351.0093
.007 25	Decision making
.007 3	Organization
	As a process or technique
	Including centralization and decentralization, modernization, reorganization, systems analysis, work flow design
	Class description of the structure of the executive branch in 351
.007 4	Leadership (Direction)
	Class here executive development, management of executive personnel
.007 5	Control
	Day-to-day oversight of internal operations to ensure conformity to plan
	Including promotion of economy and efficiency
	Legislative control and oversight of executive branch relocated to 328.3456
	Class control of activities outside of government in 351.0091
	See also 351.102 for supervision of personnel
.007 6	Evaluation and reporting
	Including internal inspection
	See Manual at at 351.0006
.007 8	Management by objectives
	Including management for specific objectives not otherwise provided for, e.g., development administration
.009	**Special agencies**
	Examples: independent agencies, quasi-administrative bodies, special commissions
	Class special agencies concerned with a specific activity with the activity in public administration, e.g., agencies regulating railroads 351.875043
.009 1	Regulatory agencies and autonomous authorities
	Class here regulation, control, inspection of activities outside of government

.009 2	Government corporations (Public enterprises)

Class government corporations engaged in commerce, communications, transportation in 380, using notation 065 from table under 380, e.g., a government railroad corporation 385.065; those engaged in finance in 332.1–332.6, in real estate in 333.33, in insurance in 368, in other specific economic enterprises in 338.76

.009 3	Advisory, consultative, ad hoc fact-finding bodies

> **351.01–351.08 Specific departments and ministries of cabinet rank**

Class comprehensive works in 351.004; subordinate branches of specific departments or ministries with the branch, e.g., sports departments 351.858

.01	Foreign affairs departments
.02	Finance departments
.03	Home affairs (Interior) departments
.05	Justice departments
.06	Defense departments
.07–.08	Other departments

Add to base number 351.0 the numbers following 351 in 351.7–351.8, e.g., departments of labor 351.083

.09	Intergovernmental administration

Administration of agencies established cooperatively by two or more governments at the same level, of agencies established to deal with affairs of subordinate units

Class international administration in 354.1; intergovernmental administration of a specific kind of activity with the kind of activity, e.g., fiscal relations between levels 351.725

.091	Interstate and interprovincial relations
.092	Administrative relations of state or provincial governments with national governments
.093	Administrative relations of local governments with higher levels

See also 320.8 for governmental relations between local and higher levels of government, 352.0095 for administrative cooperation among local governments

> **351.1–351.6 Government service**

Class comprehensive works in 351.1; government service in administration of specific fields in 351.8

.1 Personnel management

Class here comprehensive works on government service

Class personnel management in a specific field of activity with the field, using notation 0683 from Table 1, e.g., personnel management in labor agencies 351.830683

For management of executive personnel, see 351.0074; lists and directories of officials and employees, 351.2; civil service examinations, 351.3; government work force, 351.4; pensions, 351.5; civil service system, 351.6

SUMMARY

351.100 1–.100 9	**Standard subdivisions**
.101–.104	**[Planning and policy, supervision, job classification, equal employment]**
.12	**Wage and salary administration**
.13	**Recruitment and selection of personnel**
.14	**Utilization of personnel**
.15	**Training**
.16	**Conditions of employment**
.17	**Employer-employee relationships**
.18	**Separation from service**

.100 1   Philosophy and theory

.100 2   Miscellany

[.100 25]   Directories of personnel

       Do not use; class in 351.2

.100 3–.100 9   Standard subdivisions

.101   Personnel planning and policy

     Including assessments of man- and womanpower needs

     Class planning and policy with respect to a specific aspect of public personnel management with the aspect, e.g., selection policies 351.132

.102   Supervision

     Including human relationships, utilization of psychology in personnel management

.103   Job classification, analysis, description

.104   Equal employment opportunity programs

     Class preferential hiring in 351.13243, equal employment opportunity programs for persons outside the government work force in 351.833

.12   Wage and salary administration

.123   Wages, salaries, benefits

     Including wage incentives

     See also 331.2041351 for economic aspects of wages, salaries, benefits of central government employees

.123 2	Wages and salaries
	Including adjustments, deductions
.123 4	Employee benefits
	Including life and health insurance
	Class in-kind services provided to employees in 351.16
	For pensions, see 351.5
	See also 351.8256 for administration of government insurance for nongovernment work force, 351.835 for administration of employee benefits of nongovernment work force
.125	Payroll administration
	Including methods of payment, e.g., composite checks
.13	Recruitment and selection of personnel
.131	Recruitment
.132	Selection
	Class here comprehensive works on selection and placement
	For placement, see 351.14
.132 2	Personal requirements
	Examples: age, physical characteristics, sex, aptitudes
	Class testing in 351.1325
[.132 202 87]	Testing and measurement
	Do not use; class in 351.1325
.132 3	Professional, occupational, educational requirements
[.132 302 87]	Testing and measurement
	Do not use; class in 351.1325
.132 4	Other requirements
.132 42	Loyalty and security considerations
	Including loyalty oaths
	Class security clearance in 351.1325
.132 43	Preferential hiring of specific classes of persons
.132 44	Bonding of employees
.132 5	Selection procedures
	Including forms, physical examinations, investigations, interviews, polygraph (lie detector) tests, security clearance
	Class here comprehensive works on tests and testing
	For civil service examinations, see 351.3

.14	Utilization of personnel

Including placement, promotion, demotion, transfer

.142	Performance rating (Evaluation)
.147	Motivation

Including discipline, interpersonal relations, promotion of creativity

Class here promotion of employee morale, productivity, efficiency

.15	Training

Including educational programs

.16	Conditions of employment

Including employee health services; economic services to employees, e.g., housing, transportation, food services, credit facilities, discounts; counseling

For wages, salaries, benefits, see 351.123

.161	Physical conditions

Examples: safety, ventilation, heating, lighting, noise, space requirements

.163	Days and hours of work
.164	Leaves of absence
.17	Employer-employee relationships

Class interpersonal relations in 351.147

.172	Employee participation in management
.173	Labor unions and other employee organizations

For collective bargaining, see 351.174

.174	Collective bargaining

Including drafting of labor agreements

.176	Grievances and appeals

Class grievances relating to a specific aspect of personnel administration with the aspect, e.g., grievances about hours of work 351.163

.18	Separation from service

Including resignation and dismissal for cause

Class pensions in 351.5

.182	Retirement
.184	Reduction in force (Layoff for retrenchment)

.2   Lists and directories of officials and employees

Including registers of personnel

Directories of public officials and employees of specific occupational categories relocated to the subject with use of notation 025 from Table 1, e.g., diplomats 327.2025 (*not* 351.892025)

Class lists and directories of specific agencies with the agency, e.g., of cabinet departments of labor 351.83025, of civil defense agencies 351.755025

[.208]   History and description with respect to kinds of persons

Do not use; class 351.26

[.22]   Elected officials

Relocated to 324.025

.23   Employees at specific levels of rank

.26   Employees belonging to disadvantaged groups

Class here lists and directories of specific kinds of persons, e.g., women

Class employees belonging to disadvantaged groups at specific levels of rank in 351.23

.3   Civil service examinations

Class here review and exercise [*formerly also* 351.00076]

Class examinations on a specific subject with the subject, using notation 076 from Table 1, e.g., on accounting 657.076

.4   Government work force

History, description, surveys of composition

Class a specific aspect of government work force with the aspect, e.g., agency relationships with employee unions 351.173

.5   Pensions

See also 331.2529 for economic aspects of government employee pensions

.6   Civil service system (Merit system)

Class civil service examinations in 351.3

.7   Property and financial management and related topics; administration of public safety and related fields

SUMMARY

351.71	**Property and records management and related topics**
.72	**Financial management**
.74	**Police**
.75	**Public safety**
.76	**Factors affecting public morals**
.77	**Safeguarding public health**
.78	**Fire and accident protection**

>   **351.71–351.72 Property and financial management and related topics**

Class comprehensive works in 351.7; property and financial management and related topics applied to personnel management in 351.1, to administration of specific fields in 351.8

.71   **Property and records management and related topics**

.711   **Contracts and contracting**

Class here comprehensive works on contracts and contracting

Class contracts and contracting for nonmilitary property in 351.712, for specific services in public administration with the service, e.g., for training 351.15; military contracts and contracting in 355.6211

.711 2   Award

Evaluation of contractor; solicitation, submission, evaluation of bids

.711 3   Performance and settlement

Including cost overruns, renegotiation, settlement of claims, recovery of costs and losses, payment

.711 8   Subcontracting

.712   **Procurement**

Class comprehensive works on contracts and contracting in 351.711, military procurement in 355.6212

See also 351.862 for construction of government buildings

.712 04   Special topics

.712 042   Sources of supply

.712 043   Specifications

.712 044   Cost and price determination

.712 045   Payment

.712 048   Specific objectives in procurement

Example: procurement in an area of surplus labor

.712 2   Purchase and rental of land

Class government purchase of land for natural resource conservation in 351.8232, for public works other than government buildings in 351.86

See also 333.1 for economic aspects of public ownership of land

.712 3   Purchase and rental of buildings

See also 351.862 for construction of government buildings

.712 4   Purchase and rental of equipment

Including government vehicles

.712 5	Purchase and manufacture of supplies
	Example: printing of stationery
.712 6	Procurement of services and utilities
	Class procurement of personnel services in 351.1
.713	Property management
.713 04	Special topics
.713 042	Physical inventory
.713 043	Utilization
.713 044	Maintenance
.713 045	Disposal
	By sale, rental, gift
.713 2	Land
	See also 333.7313 for public land management in the sense of land use
.713 3	Buildings
	Example: executive residences
.713 4	Equipment
	Including government vehicles
	Class here materials management
	Class management of supplies in 351.7135
.713 5	Supplies
.714	Records management
	Class here clerical services
.714 2	Communication
.714 4	Design of forms
.714 5	Security classification of documents
.714 6	Archives
	Class interdisciplinary works on archival administration in 025.1714

.72   Financial management

Including public debt management, administration of economic assistance

Financial management of a specific agency or activity relocated to the agency or activity in 351.003–351.9, e.g., of a forestry bureau 351.82338

Class interdisciplinary works on, and economic and public policy aspects of public finance in 336; cabinet level finance departments in 351.02; administration of money in 351.822, of financial institutions and transactions in 351.825; administration of economic assistance in a specific field in 351.8, using notation 045 from table under 351.8

See Manual at 336 vs. 351.72

SUMMARY

351.722	**Budgets and budgeting**
.723	**Accounting and auditing**
.724	**Tax administration**
.725	**Fiscal relations between governmental units**
.726	**Revenue administration**

.722   Budgets and budgeting

Class here budget systems

.722 2   Formulation and preparation of budgets

Class here executive budgets

.722 202 02   Rules, manuals, synopses, outlines, instructions for budget preparation

.722 204   Special topics

.722 204 2   Program-performance budgeting

.722 204 3   Zero-base budgeting

.722 21   Relation of budgeting to political process

.722 23   Priorities and objectives

.722 24   Budget requests from subordinate levels

.722 25   Budget estimates

Class completed budgets in 351.7225

.722 252   Of revenues

.722 253   Of expenditures

.722 253 2   New expenditures

Class specific budgetary items in 351.7222538

.722 253 4   Capital expenditures

Class specific budgetary items in 351.7222538

.722 253 6   Development expenditures

Class specific budgetary items in 351.7222538

.722 253 8	For specific budgetary items
	Example: supplies
.722 3	Adoption of budgets

Class here legislative budgets, enactment of budgets

Class completed budgets in 351.7225

See also 340 for bills to authorize and appropriate funds, e.g., bills for public education appropriations 344.071

.722 34	Authorization
.722 36	Appropriation
.722 4	Supplemental and deficiency budgeting

Including recision and deferral

Class supplemental and deficiency budgets in 351.72254

.722 43	Supplemental estimates
.722 48	Supplemental appropriation
.722 5	Budget documents

Class executive budgets in 351.7222, legislative budgets in 351.7223

.722 52	Budgets
.722 53	Digests of budgets (Budgets in brief)
.722 54	Supplemental and deficiency budgets
.722 55	Appendixes and reports
.722 56	Budget messages of executives
.723	**Accounting and auditing**

Planning, administration, use

Class accounting and auditing procedures in 657.835

.723 1	Accounting and accounts

Including financial statements, reports

.723 2	Auditing and audits

Including disclosure of fraud

Class use of audits to evaluate efficiency or utility of programs in 351.0076; evaluation of specific activities with the activity, e.g., of military procurement 355.6212

.723 202 02	Synopses and outlines

Manuals of government audit procedures relocated to 657.835045

.724   Tax administration

Including administration of poll taxes

Add to each subdivision identified by * as follows:
1   Assessment
2   Collection

Class interdisciplinary works on taxes in 336.2, tax law in 343.04

See Manual at 336.2 vs. 351.724, 343.04

.724 001–.724 009   Standard subdivisions

.724 2   *Real property taxes

Class here comprehensive works on administration of property taxes

For personal property taxes, see 351.7243

.724 3   *Personal property taxes

.724 4   *Income taxes

Class administration of social security taxes in 351.8256

.724 6   *Customs duties

.724 7   Other taxes

Examples: luxury, sales, use, value-added taxes

.724 71   *Excise taxes

.724 76   Estate, inheritance, gift taxes

Add as instructed under 351.724 for estate taxes; for inheritance taxes; for combined treatment of estate, inheritance, and gift taxes

.725   Fiscal relations between governmental units

Class here grants, aid, revenue sharing

Add to base number 351.725 the numbers following 351.09 in 351.091–351.093, e.g., grants by national governments to localities 351.7253

.726   Revenue administration

Examples: administration of revenue from government commercial undertakings, from fees and charges for government services, from lotteries

For tax administration, see 351.724

>   351.74–351.78 Administration of public safety and related fields

Class comprehensive works in 351.75

*Add as instructed under 351.724

.74   Police

        Including operative management of police agencies

        Class administration of traffic control in 351.87831

.75   Public safety

        Including censorship; control of information, of public gatherings, of explosives and firearms

          For police, see 351.74; safeguarding public health, 351.77; fire and accident protection, 351.78

          See also 323.445 for the right to information, 351.996 for the denial of the right to information in public administration

.754   Disaster and emergency planning and relief

          For civil defense, see 351.755

.755   Civil defense

.76   Factors affecting public morals

        Including gambling, prostitution

.761   Alcoholic beverages

          See also 351.8429 for administration of public services to alcoholics

.765   Drugs

          See also 351.8429 for administration of public services to addicts

.77   Safeguarding public health

        Class comprehensive works on administration of public health in 351.841, regulation and control of water supply in 351.871

.772   Environmental sanitation and comfort

        Examples: waste disposal, noise control

        Including disposal of dead

.773   Physical fitness programs

.774   Medical screening

.776   Control of disease

        Physical, mental, occupational

.778   Control of product hazards

        Including textiles, toys, household appliances

.778 2   Adulteration and contamination of food

        Including beverages, dairy products, food additives

.778 4   Medicines and drugs

.778 6   Cosmetics

.78	Fire and accident protection
.782	Fire protection and prevention
.783	Accident prevention

> Class administration of safety measures in a specific field of activity with the field, using notation 0289 from Table 1, e.g., safety administration in urban transportation 351.87840289

.8   Administration of specific fields

Including administration of charters, licenses, certification, registration

Aside from additions, changes, deletions, exceptions shown under specific entries, add to notation for each term identified by * as follows:

01–03	Standard subdivisions	
04	Special topics	
042		Information and research services
		Class comprehensive works in 351.819
043		Regulation and control
		Including inspection and rationing
		Class comprehensive works on regulation, control, inspection in 351.0091, on rationing in 351.829
		For control of prices, rates, charges, see 044
044		Control of prices, rates, charges
		Class comprehensive works in 351.820424
045		Economic assistance
		To producers and users
		Examples: grants-in-aid, loans
		Class comprehensive works in 351.72
046		Licensing
		Class here chartering, certification, registration
		Class comprehensive works in 351.8, occupational licensing in 351.8243046
05–09	Standard subdivisions	

Class cabinet-level departments in specific fields in 351.01–351.08, management of services in a specific field with the subject, e.g., of services to veterans 362.86

For public administration of public safety and related fields, see 351.74–351.78

SUMMARY

351.81	**Human relations, information, related programs**
.82	**Production, commerce, consumption**
.83	**Labor**
.84	**Social welfare and corrections**
.85	**Culture and religion**
.86	**Public works and housing**
.87	**Public utilities and transportation**
.88	**Justice**
.89	**Foreign affairs**

.81	Human relations, information, related programs
.811	Civil and human rights

Including elections, election campaigns

Class programs for achieving civil and human rights for specific groups of persons in 351.812–351.814

> 351.812–351.814 Programs for specific groups of persons

Class comprehensive works in 351.81, programs in a specific field of activity with the field, e.g., veterans' hospitals 351.841

.812	Programs for veterans
.813	Programs for women

Class programs for women veterans in 351.812

.814	Programs for racial, ethnic, national groups

Add to base number 351.814 notation 1–9 from Table 5, e.g., programs for Blacks 351.81496

Class programs for women of various racial, ethnic, national groups in 351.813, for veterans of various racial, ethnic, national groups in 351.812

.815	Population control and family planning
.816	Registration and certification of births and deaths
.817	Immigration and naturalization
.818	Regional and urban development
.819	Information and research services

Including public relations

Class here census taking, government publication programs

Class information and research services in a specific field of activity with the field in public administration using notation 042 from table under 351.8, e.g., agricultural information services 351.8233042; results of information and research services in a subject with the subject, e.g., demographic statistics 304.6021

See also 323.445 for the right to information, 351.75 for censorship, 351.996 for denial of the right to information in public administration

.82	Production, commerce, consumption

Class here economic development, promotion of productivity

SUMMARY

351.820 4	**Special topics**
.821	**Standards**
.822	**Issue and regulation of money**
.823	**Natural resources and primary industries**
.824	**Secondary industries**
.825	**Financial institutions and transactions**
.826	**Domestic commerce**
.827	**Foreign commerce**
.829	**Rationing**

.820 4   Special topics

.820 42   Economic information and research services; consumer protection; control of prices, rates, charges

.820 422   Economic information and research services

Including economic advisers

Class consumer information and research services in 351.820423

.820 423   Consumer protection

Class control of prices, rates, charges in 351.820424

.820 424   Control of prices, rates, charges

Class control of prices, rates, charges in a specific field with the subject in public administration, using notation 044 from table under 351.8, e.g., control of crop prices 351.82333044

.820 43   Regulation and control of the economy

.820 44   Promotion of equal economic opportunity

.820 48   *Small business

.821   Standards

Including weights and measures, metric conversion (metrication)

.822   Issue and regulation of money

Class administration of financial transactions in 351.825

.823   Natural resources and primary industries

Class public utilities, e.g., organizations supplying water, gas, electricity, in 351.87

.823 2   Natural resources and their conservation

Class administration of primary industries using natural resources in 351.8233–351.8238, of public works to develop and protect resources in 351.86

.823 21   Environmental protection

Class environmental sanitation in 351.772, pollution control in 351.82322, flood control in 351.82329

*Add as instructed under 351.8

.823 22	Pollution control

Class control of pollution by specific pollutants in 351.82323, control of pollution of specific natural resources in 351.82324–351.82328

.823 23	Control of pollution by specific pollutants

Examples: oils, pesticides, radioactive materials

Class control of pollution of specific resources by specific pollutants in 351.82324–351.82328

>   351.823 24–351.823 28 Specific natural resources and their conservation

Class here control of pollution of specific natural resources

Class comprehensive works in 351.8232

.823 24	Air (Atmosphere)

Including administration of weather control

> *See also 351.8555163 for administration of weather forecasting*

.823 25	Water

Surface and ground waters

Class here comprehensive works on marine resources

Class wetlands, shorelands, beaches in 351.82326; marine mineral resources in 351.82327; marine biological resources in 351.82328; construction of dams for water supply and conservation in 351.867

.823 26	Land and soil

Including wetlands, shorelands, beaches; reclamation, irrigation; parks

.823 27	Mineral (Geological) resources

Including metals

Class administration of mineral extractive industries in 351.8238

.823 28	Biological resources

Class administration of fishing and hunting industries in 351.8236

.823 29	Flood control

Class construction of dams for flood control in 351.867

>   351.823 3–351.823 8 Primary industries

Class comprehensive works in 351.823, control of prices in 351.826–351.827

.823 3	*Agriculture and forestry

Class here comprehensive works on public administration of agricultural industries

Class administration of soil conservation and irrigation in 351.82326, of agricultural processing industries other than dairy industries in 351.824, of agricultural trade in 351.8261

.823 33	*Plant crops
.823 36	*Animal husbandry
.823 37	*Dairy industry
.823 38	*Forestry
.823 6	Fishing and hunting

Class here comprehensive works on administration of fishing and hunting

Class administration of hunting and fishing for sport in 351.858

.823 62	*Fisheries
.823 8	*Extraction of mineral resources
.823 82	*Mines and mining
.823 88	*Extraction of oil and gas
.824	*Secondary industries

Including administration of patents, copyrights, trademarks

Class administration of housing in 351.865, of public utilities in 351.87

.824 2	*Manufacturing and construction

Class administration of public works in 351.86

.824 3	*Service and professional
.824 304 6	Licensing

Class here comprehensive works on occupational licensing and registration

Class licensing and registration of a specific occupation with the subject in public administration, e.g., of a manufacturing occupation 351.8242

.825	*Financial institutions and transactions

Class administration of institutions providing services to a specific industry with the administration of the industry, e.g., of institutions providing agricultural loans 351.8233045

.825 2	*Banks
.825 5	*Insurance companies

*Add as instructed under 351.8

.825 6	Government-sponsored insurance

.825 6   Government-sponsored insurance

Services provided to persons outside the government work force

Examples: health, life, old age and survivors, unemployment insurance

Class insurance provided to government employees in 351.1234; insurance of a specific activity with the activity in public administration, e.g., insurance of bank deposits 351.825045

.825 8   Securities and securities exchanges

.826   *Domestic commerce

Class here commodity exchanges, comprehensive works on commerce

For foreign commerce, see 351.827

.826 1   *Trade in products of agriculture

Class here marketing orders and regulations

Add to base number 351.8261 the numbers following 63 in 633–638, e.g., trade in milk 351.826171; then add further as instructed under 351.8, e.g., milk inspection 351.826171043

.826 2   *Trade in products of mineral extraction

Add to base number 351.8262 the numbers following 553 in 553.2–553.9, e.g., trade in coal 351.826224; then add further as instructed under 351.8, e.g., price control of coal 351.826224044

.826 3   Trade in products of other extractive industries

Fishing, whaling, hunting, trapping, culture of invertebrates and cold-blooded vertebrates

Class insect culture in 351.82618

.826 5   Trade in products of secondary industries and services

Use 351.82650001–351.82650009 for standard subdivisions

Add to base number 351.8265 notation 001–999, e.g., trade in lumber 351.8265674, domestic tourism 351.826591

.827   Foreign commerce

Including tourism by foreigners

.827 5   Imports

.827 6   Exports

.829   Rationing

Class rationing of a specific product or service with the subject in public administration, using notation 043 from table under 351.8, e.g., rationing natural gas 351.8723043

*Add as instructed under 351.8

.83   **Labor**

Unless other instructions are given, class complex subjects with aspects in two or more subdivisions of this schedule in the number coming last in the schedule, e.g., equal pay for women 351.837 (*not* 351.835)

Class social welfare services to laboring classes in 351.8485; labor in a specific occupation with the subject in public administration, e.g., farm workers 351.8233; a specific service to laboring classes not provided for here with the subject in public administration, e.g., control of prices 351.820424

.832   **Labor relations**

Including collective bargaining

Class labor relations of governments with their own employees in 351.17

.833   **Employment services**

Including equal employment opportunity programs

.834   **Employment security**

Example: tenure

.835   **Wages and hours**

Including regulation of pensions and fringe benefits

Class administration of fringe benefits for government employees in 351.1234, of pensions for government employees in 351.5, of government-sponsored insurance for nongovernment work force in 351.82568

.836   **Disadvantaged workers**

Examples: workers belonging to specific racial, ethnic, national groups; immigrants, handicapped workers

For women, see 351.837; workers of specific ages, 351.838

.837   **Women workers**

.838   **Workers of specific ages**

.838 2   Young workers

Through age thirty-five

.838 27   Through age twenty

.838 28   Aged twenty-one to thirty-five

.838 6   Older workers

.84   *Social welfare and corrections

Unless other instructions are given, observe the following table of precedence, e.g., mentally-ill handicapped children 351.842 (*not* 351.844, 351.847)

Services to the physically ill	351.841
Services to the mentally retarded	351.843
Services to the mentally ill	351.842
Services to the handicapped	351.844
Correctional administration	351.849
Services to old persons	351.846
Services to young people	351.847
Services to other groups	351.848
Services to the poor	351.845

.841   *Health services

Class here services to the physically ill

Class administration of government-sponsored health insurance in 351.8256; health services to the mentally ill in 351.842, to the mentally retarded in 351.843, to the handicapped in 351.844

.842   *Services to the mentally ill

.842 9   *Services to the addicted

.843   *Services to the mentally retarded

.844   *Services to the handicapped

.845   *Services to the poor

Class promotion of equal economic opportunity in 351.82044

.846   *Services old persons

.847   *Services to young people

Through age 20

Including day-care services

Class aid to families with dependent children (AFDC) in 351.8482

.848   Services to other groups

Observe the following table of precedence, e.g., services to families of laboring class members of minority groups 351.8484 (*not* 351.8482 or 351.8485)

To victims of crime	351.8488
To minority groups	351.8484
To laboring classes	351.8485
To families	351.8482

.848 2   *To families

Including aid to families with dependent children (AFDC)

Class family planning in 351.815, day-care services in 351.847

*Add as instructed under 351.8

.848 4	*To minority groups
	Class programs for achieving civil and human rights in 351.811
.848 5	*To laboring classes
	Class employment services in 351.833, services to impoverished laborers in 351.845
.848 8	*To victims of crime
.849	*Correctional administration
.849 2	*Preventive welfare work
.849 3	Parole and probation
.849 5	*Penal institutions
.85	*Culture and religion
	Including language, bilingual programs
	Class here cultural exchanges
	Class interdisciplinary works on language planning and policy in 306.449
.851	Education
	Class operational administration of public school systems in 371.2
	Use only for aspects of public administration not provided for in 379
.852	*Libraries
	Class operational administration of library systems in 025.1, public policy issues of library relationships with governments in 021.8
.853	*Museums
	Class museums devoted to a specific subject with the subject in 351.85, e.g., history museums 351.859
.854	*Humanities and arts
	Including architecture, music
.855	*Science
	Class here comprehensive works on public administration of science and technology
	Add to base number 351.855 the numbers following 5 in 510–590, e.g., weather forecasting 351.8555163
	For technology, see 351.856
	See Manual at 500 vs. 338.926, 351.855
.856	*Technology
	Class a specific technology with the subject in public administration, e.g., agricultural technology 351.8233

*Add as instructed under 351.8

.857   *Religion

.858   *Sports and recreation

> Including fishing and hunting
>
> Class regulation and control of betting and gambling on sporting events in 351.76, of parks in 351.82326, of park and recreational public works in 351.863

.859   *History and related activities

> Including archaeology, historic preservation, monuments and shrines, patriotic commemorations and celebrations

.86   *Public works and housing

> Construction, maintenance, use
>
> Including cemeteries
>
> Class public administration of urban development in 351.818, of architecture in 351.854, of historic preservation in 351.859

.862   *Public buildings

> Including buildings of specific agencies, e.g., courthouses
>
> Class procurement of public buildings in 351.7123; management of public buildings in 351.7133

.863   Park and recreational public works

.863 2   *Parks

> Including development of scenic areas
>
> Class recreational facilities in parks in 351.8635, public administration of parks in 351.82326

.863 5   *Recreational facilities

> Class public administration of recreation in 351.858

.864   *Highways and related public works

> Including tunnels

.864 2   *Highways and roads

.864 5   *Bridges

.865   *Housing

.867   *Dams

*Add as instructed under 351.8

.87   Public utilities and transportation

> Class environmental impact of utilities, conservation of energy-producing resources in 351.8232, extraction of energy-producing mineral resources in 351.8238

SUMMARY

351.870 01–.870 09	**Standard subdivisions**
.871	**Water supply**
.872	**Electric power and gas**
.873	**Postal communication**
.874	**Telecommunication**
.875	**Transportation Railroad transportation**
.876	**Inland water and ferry transportation**
.877	**Water, air, space transportation**
.878	**Ground transportation**

.870 01–.870 09   Standard subdivisions

.871   Water supply

> For agricultural, domestic, industrial use

> Use 351.871001–351.871009 for standard subdivisions

> Class construction of dams for water supply in 351.867, hydroelectric power in 351.8722

.871 04   Special topics

> Add to base number 351.87104 the numbers following 04 in notation 042–046 from table under 351.8, e.g., control of water supply 351.871043

.872   Electric power and gas

.872 2   Electric power

> Including hydroelectric, nuclear power

> Use 351.8722001–351.8722009 for standard subdivisions

.872 204   Special topics

> Add to base number 351.872204 the numbers following 04 in notation 042–046 from the add table under 351.8, e.g., control of electric power 351.8722043

.872 3   Gas

> Use 351.8723001–351.8723009 for standard subdivisions

.872 304   Special topics

> Add to base number 351.872304 the numbers following 04 in notation 042–046 from the add table under 351.8, e.g., control of gas 351.8723043

.873   Postal communication

> Class postal organization in 383.4

.874   *Telecommunication

Add to base number 351.874 the numbers following 384 in 384.1–384.8, e.g., radiobroadcasting 351.87454; then add further as instructed under 351.8, e.g., economic assistance to radiobroadcasting 351.87454045

.875   Transportation   Railroad transportation

Class here comprehensive works on public administration of mass transit

Class urban mass transit in 351.8784

For inland waterway and ferry transportation, see 351.876; water, air, space transportation, 351.877; ground transportation, 351.878

.875 001–.875 009   Standard subdivisions

As modified in table under 351.8, e.g., economic support of transportation 351.8750045

.875 01–.875 09   Standard subdivisions of railroad transportation

As modified in table under 351.8 e.g., chartering railroads 351.875046

.875 1–.875 7   Railroad transportation

Add to base number 351.875 the numbers following 385 in 385.1–385.7, e.g., railroad rates 351.87512

.876   *Inland waterway and ferry transportation

Add to base number 351.876 the numbers following 386 in 386.1–386.8, e.g., carriage of freight 351.876244

.877   *Water, air, space transportation

Add to base number 351.877 the numbers following 387 in 387.1–387.8, e.g., ports 351.8771

For inland waterway and ferry transportation, see 351.876

.878   *Ground transportation

For highways and related public works, see 351.864; railroad transportation, 351.875

.878 3   Vehicular transportation

Including transportation by means of air-cushion vehicles

.878 31   Traffic control

Examples: lighting, signs, signals, use by specific types of vehicles, vehicle weight

Including police patrols

.878 32   Vehicular services

Class here regulation and control of vehicle operations, of driver qualifications

Add to base number 351.87832 the numbers following 388.32 in 388.321–388.324, e.g., bus services 351.878322

*Add as instructed under 351.8

.878 34	Vehicles
	Ownership, registration, condition, licenses
	Class vehicles belonging to governments and their agencies in 351.7134
.878 4	Urban transportation
	Class here urban mass transit
	Add to base number 351.8784 the numbers following 388.4 in 388.41–388.47, e.g., urban bus systems 351.87841322; however, class administration of urban roads and streets in 351.8642
	See also 352.9184 for local government administration of urban transportation
.88	Justice
	Including administration of land claims
	Class administration of courts in 347.013, police administration in 351.74, civil rights administration in 351.811, correctional administration in 351.849
.89	Foreign affairs
	Including propaganda and information
	Class foreign affairs departments in 351.01, cultural exchanges in 351.85
.892	Embassies and legations
	Diplomatic lists relocated to 327.2025
.896	Voluntary service agencies
	Class unofficial voluntary service groups with the subject, e.g., peace movements 327.172
.898	Passports and visas
.9	**Malfunctioning of administration**
	Class malfunctioning of a specific agency with the agency, e.g., police abuses 351.74
	See also 342.06 for administrative law, 364.13 for aspects of malfunctioning considered as crime
.91	Grievances and claims against the state
	Including interdisciplinary works on ombudsmen
	Class legislators as ombudsmen in 328.3452
.99	Specific aspects of malfunctioning
.991	Abuse of powers
	For denial of political, civil, human rights, see 351.996
.992	Public inquiries and investigations
.993	Impeachment

.994	Corruption and venality
.995	Conflict of interest

> Class corruption and venality in 351.994

.996	Denial of political, civil, human rights

352   Administration of local governments

Unless other instructions are given, observe the following table of precedence, e.g., local cooperation in police administration 352.2 (*not* 352.0095)

Local administration of specific fields	352.2–.9
Government service	352.005
Financial and property management and related topics	352.1
Administration of kinds and levels of local government	352.007
Local intergovernmental cooperation	352.0095
Fundamentals of administration	352.00047
Municipal executives	352.008
Special districts and authorities (*except* 352.0095)	352.009
Malfunctioning of administration	352.002

Note exceptions to the foregoing table of precedence explained in Manual at 352.03–352.09 vs. 352.002–352.009

Class interdisciplinary works on local government in 320.8, local politics in 320

See Manual at 352

SUMMARY

352.000 1–.000 9	[Standard subdivisions and fundamentals of administration]
.002–.009	General topics of local administration
.03–.09	Treatment by specific continents, countries, localities
.1	Financial and property management and related topics
.2	Police
.3	Fire protection and accident prevention
.4	Safeguarding public health
.5	Regulation and control of public buildings
.6	Environmental sanitation and related activities
.7	Public works and housing
.8	Licensing
.9	Miscellaneous fields

.000 1	Philosophy and theory

> Including relation of public administration to social and political factors

[.000 11]	Systems

> Do not use; class in 352.000473

.000 2	Miscellany
.000 25	Directories of persons and organizations

> Class directories of officials and employees in 352.0052

.000 3	Dictionaries, encyclopedias, concordances
.000 4	Special topics
.000 47	Fundamentals of administration

Class here executive management

Add to base number 352.00047 the numbers following 351.007 in 351.0072–351.0078, e.g., reorganization 352.000473

.000 5	Serial publications

Class serial administrative reports in 352.0006

.000 6	Administrative reports

Class administrative reports of specific agencies in 352.1–352.9, administrative reports on a specific subject with the subject in public administration, e.g., reports on government reorganization 352.000473

See Manual at 351.0006

.000 7–.000 8	Standard subdivisions
.000 9	Historical, geographical, persons treatment

Class treatment by specific continents, countries, localities in 352.03–352.09 (*not* 352.00093–352.00099)

> ### 352.002–352.009 General topics of local administration

Class comprehensive works in 352, general topics relating to specific local governments in 352.03–352.09

See Manual at 352.03–352.09 vs. 352.002–352.009

.002	Malfunctioning of administration

Including denial of political, civil, human rights; grievances and claims against the government, ombudsmen, public inquiries and investigations

Class malfunctioning of a specific agency with the agency, e.g., police abuses 352.2

See also 342.06 for administrative law, 364.13 for aspects of malfunctioning considered as crime

.003	Municipal incorporation

Class interdisciplinary works in 320.85, legal aspects in 342.02

.005	Government service

Add to base number 352.005 the numbers following 351 in 351.1–351.6, e.g., personnel management 352.0051, lists of officials and employees 352.0052

Class management of executive personnel in 352.000474, programs for working persons outside the government work force in 352.943

.006   Annexation

> Class interdisciplinary works in 320.859, legal aspects in 342.0413

.007   Administration of kinds and levels of local government

> Class interdisciplinary works on forms, structure, and function of local government in 320.8

.007 2   Municipalities

> Class here urban municipalities

.007 22   Rural municipalities

.007 23   Towns and incorporated villages

.007 24   Cities

> Class metropolitan areas (conurbations) in 352.0094

.007 3   Intermediate levels

> Examples: counties, districts, departments, arrondissements, Landkreise; provinces in certain jurisdictions, e.g., Costa Rica

> *See Manual at 350–354: State and provincial administration*

.008   Municipal executives

> Examples: mayors, city managers, commissioners, chiefs of departments

> Including executive councils and departments

> Class here forms of municipal government

> Class interdisciplinary works on forms of municipal government in 320.8; chiefs of a specific department with the subject in public administration, e.g., water commissioners 352.61

.008 2   Mayor-council administration with weak mayor

.008 3   Mayor-council administration with strong mayor

.008 4   Council-manager administration

.008 5   Commission administration

.009   Special districts and authorities; local intergovernmental cooperation

> Including commissions, corporations

> Class school boards and districts in 379.153; other special districts and authorities controlling a specific field of activity with the activity in public administration, e.g., local transit authorities 352.9184

.009 2   Regulatory agencies and autonomous authorities

> Class here regulation, control, inspection of activities outside of government

.009 3   Service districts and authorities

> Urban and rural

.009 4   Metropolitan areas (Conurbations)

.009 5   Local intergovernmental cooperation

Including intermunicipal authorities

Class cooperation in a specific field of activity with the activity, e.g., police cooperation 352.2

.03–.09   Treatment by specific continents, countries, localities

Class here general topics relating to specific local governments

Add to base number 352.0 notation 3–9 from Table 2, e.g., local governments in Illinois 352.0773, government of Chicago 352.077311

Class general topics relating to local government in specific continents, countries, states, local areas (but not to specific local governments) in 352.002–352.009, e.g., government service in municipalities of Illinois 352.00509773, but government service in Chicago 352.077311

Class specific administrative activities, administration of specific fields of activity by specific continents, countries, states, local areas (including specific local areas) in 352.1–352.9, e.g., local transportation in municipalities of Illinois 352.918409773, in Chicago 352.91840977311

See Manual at 352.03–352.09 vs. 352.002–352.009

.1   **Financial and property management and related topics**

Examples: public debt management, administration of economic assistance

Class financial and property management and related topics applied to specific fields in 352.2–352.9

See also 352.5 for regulation and control of public buildings

---

>   352.12–352.14 Financial management

Class comprehensive works in 352.1, accounting and auditing in 352.17

.12   Budgets and budgeting

Add to base number 352.12 the numbers following 351.722 in 351.7222–351.7225, e.g., budget estimates 352.1225

.13   Tax administration

.134   Special assessments

.135   Specific kinds of taxes

Including sales taxes, income taxes

.135 2   Property taxes

.135 21   Assessment

.135 23   Collection

.14 Revenue administration

Examples: administration of revenue from government commercial undertakings, from fees and charges for government services, from lotteries

Class fiscal relations between local governmental units and higher levels in 351.725

For tax administration, see 352.13

.16 Property management and related topics

Add to base number 352.16 the numbers following 351.71 in 351.711–351.714, e.g., rental of equipment 352.1624

Class purchase and rental of land for public works other than government buildings in 352.7, utilization of government property for a specific purpose with the purpose, e.g., use of computers in government accounting 352.1710285

.17 Accounting and auditing

Planning, administration, use

Class accounting and auditing procedures in 657.835

.171 Accounting and accounts

Including financial statements, reports

.172 Auditing and audits

Including disclosure of fraud

Class use of audits to evaluate efficiency or utility of programs in 352.000476, evaluation of specific activities with the activity, e.g., of revenue administration 352.14

> **352.2–352.9 Local administration of specific fields**

Class comprehensive works in 352

See Manual at 352.2–352.9

> **352.2–352.4 Police, fire and accident protection, safeguarding public health**

Class comprehensive works in 352.935

.2 **Police**

Class traffic control in 352.91831

.3 **Fire protection and accident prevention**

Class administration of accident prevention measures in a specific field of activity with the activity in local public administration, using notation 0289 from Table 1, e.g., safety in construction of public buildings 352.50289

.4   **Safeguarding public health**

Including medical screening, control of diseases and product hazards

Class comprehensive works on administration of health services in 352.9441

For environmental sanitation and related activities, see 352.6

.5   **Regulation and control of public buildings**

Construction, maintenance, use, disposal

Class procurement of government buildings in 352.1623

.6   **Environmental sanitation and related activities**

.61   Water supply

Including saline water conversion, purification of water

Class hydroelectric power in 352.9122, water pollution in 352.942325

.62   Sewage disposal

.63   Waste and refuse collection and disposal

.7   **Public works and housing**

Construction, maintenance, use

Class urban development in 352.9418, architecture in 352.9454, historic preservation in 352.9459

For regulation and control of public buildings, see 352.5; environmental sanitation and related activities, 352.6

.72   Cemeteries

.73   Parks and recreational facilities

.732   Parks

Class recreational facilities in parks in 352.735

.735   Recreational facilities

Class public administration of recreation in 352.9458

.74   Streets, roads, highways, bridges, tunnels

.75   Housing

.8   **Licensing**

Class here certification, chartering, registration

Class licensing of a specific activity with the activity, e.g., licensing of hospitals 352.9441

.9   **Miscellaneous fields**

Limited to fields provided for below

SUMMARY

352.91	**Public utilities and transportation**
.92	**Construction**
.93	**Public health and related fields**
.94	**Economic, welfare, cultural activities**
.96	**Planning and zoning**
.98	**Justice**

.91   Public utilities and transportation

Add to base number 352.91 the numbers following 351.87 in 351.872–351.878, e.g., urban transportation 352.9184

Class procurement of government vehicles in 352.1624; management of government vehicles in 352.1634; environmental impact of utilities, conservation of energy-producing resources in 352.94232

For water supply, see 352.61

.92   Construction

Class here administration of permits, codes, inspections, standards

Class construction of a specific facility with the facility in public administration, e.g., housing 352.75

.922   Building construction

.923   Electrical installations

.926   Plumbing

.93   Public safety and related fields

.935   Public safety

Including censorship; control of information, of public gatherings, of explosives and firearms

For police, see 352.2; fire protection and accident prevention, 352.3; safeguarding public health, 352.4

See also 323.445 for the right to information, 352.002 for denial of the right to information in local administration

.935 4   Disaster and emergency planning and relief

For civil defense, see 352.9355

.935 5   Civil defense

.936   Factors affecting public morals

Including gambling, prostitution

.936 1   Alcoholic beverages

See also 352.94429 for services to alcoholics

.936 5   Drugs

See also 352.94429 for services to narcotics addicts

.94   Economic, welfare, cultural activities

.941   Human relations, information, related programs

Add to base number 352.941 the numbers following 351.81 in
351.811–351.819, e.g., urban development 352.9418

.942   Production, commerce, consumption

Including consumer protection

Class here economic development, promotion of productivity

.942 1   Standards

Example: weights and measures

.942 3   Primary industries and natural resources

Add to base number 352.9423 the numbers following 351.823 in
351.8232–351.8238, e.g., natural resources 352.94232, control of
water pollution 352.942325

Class public utilities, e.g., organizations supplying gas, electricity, in
352.91

.942 4   Secondary industries

Class solid waste control in 352.63, public utilities in 352.91

.942 42   Manufacturing and construction

Class public works in 352.7, regulation of construction in 352.92

.942 43   Service and professional

Including occupational licensing and registration

Class licensing and registration of occupations in a specific field
with the field in local administration, e.g., of a manufacturing
occupation 352.94242

.942 6   Trade and commerce

Including trade in agricultural products

.943–.945   Labor, social welfare and corrections, culture and religion

Add to base number 352.94 the numbers following 351.8 in
351.83–351.85, e.g., services to workers 352.943, sports and recreational
services 352.9458

Class relations of governments with their own employees in 352.0051,
recreational facilities in 352.735, control of betting and gambling on
sporting events in 352.936

.96   Planning and zoning

.961   Zoning

.962   Land subdivision

.98   Justice

Class police administration in 352.2, administration of courts in 347.013

353   Administration of United States federal and state governments

(Option: This number may be used to give local emphasis and shorter notation to central governments of a specific country other than United States; in that case, class central governments of United States in 354.73–354.79, 354.969)

Class administration of Confederate States of America in 354.75, of any jurisdiction before it became part of United States in 354, e.g., Texas Republic 354.764

See Manual at 353–354

SUMMARY

353.000 1–.000 9	Standard subdivisions
.001–.009	Government service, property and financial management and related topics, administration of specific fields, malfunctioning of administration
.01–.09	Federal bureaucracy, presidents and vice-presidents, the cabinet, fundamentals of administration, special agencies
.1	Department of State
.2	Department of the Treasury
.3	Department of the Interior
.4	Post Office Department (1829-1971)
.5	Department of Justice
.6	Department of Defense
.7	Department of the Navy
.8	Other departments
.9	State governments

.000 1–.000 8   Standard subdivisions

As modified under 351, e.g., administrative reports 353.0006

.000 9   Historical and persons treatment

Class treatment of state governments in 353.9

.001–.008   Government service, property and financial management and related topics, administration of specific fields

Add to base number 353.00 the numbers following 351 in 351.1–351.8, e.g., tax administration 353.00724

Class application of specific concepts covered here to specific federal departments of cabinet rank in 353.1–353.8

.009   Malfunctioning of administration

Add to base number 353.009 the numbers following 351.9 in 351.91–353.99, e.g., conflict of interest 353.00995

Class malfunctioning of a specific aspect of administration with the aspect, e.g., conflict of interest in tax administration in 353.00724

.01   Bureaucracy

Class a specific aspect of bureaucracy with the aspect, e.g., malfunctioning 353.009

.03–.09   **Presidents and vice-presidents, the cabinet, fundamentals of administration, special agencies**

> Add to base number 353.0 the numbers following 351.00 in 351.003–351.009, e.g., the cabinet 353.04, presidents 353.0313; however, method of selection of president relocated from 353.034 to 321.80420973
>
> Class application of concepts provided for here to government service, property and financial management and related topics, administration of specific fields in 353.001–353.008; to specific federal departments of cabinet rank in 353.1–353.8; to administrative relations between federal and state government in 353.9292

> **353.1–353.8 Specific federal departments of cabinet rank**

> Class comprehensive works in 353.04

.1   **Department of State**

.2   **Department of the Treasury**

.3   **Department of the Interior**

.4   **Post Office Department (1829–1971)**

> Class United States Postal Service in 353.00873

.5   **Department of Justice**

.6   **Department of Defense**

> Class administration of armed forces in 355.6
>
> *For Department of the Navy, see 353.7*

.62   Department of the Army

.63   Department of the Air Force

.7   **Department of the Navy**

.8   **Other departments**

.81   Department of Agriculture

.82   Department of Commerce

.83   Department of Labor

.84   Department of Health and Human Services, and Department of Education

> Class here the former Department of Health, Education, and Welfare

.842   Department of Health and Human Services

.844   Department of Education

.85   Department of Housing and Urban Development

.86   Department of Transportation

.87   Department of Energy

.9   State governments

.909   Historical, geographical, persons treatment

> Class specific state governments in 353.97–353.99 (*not* 353.9097–353.9099)

>   353.91–353.93 State governments in general

Class complex subjects with aspects in two or more subdivisions of this schedule according to the order of precedence that governs 351, e.g., reorganization of revenue agencies 353.93724 (corresponding to 351.724), not 353.9173 (corresponding to 351.0073)

Class comprehensive works in 353.9, governments of specific states in 353.97–353.99

.91   Bureaucracy, chief executives, cabinets and councils of state, fundamentals of administration, special agencies

Add to base number 353.91 the numbers following 351.00 in 351.001–351.009, e.g., governors 353.91313; however, methods of selection of governors relocated from 353.9134 to 321.80420973

Class specific executive departments at the council-of-state level in 353.921–353.928; special agencies concerned with specific activities with the subject in 353.92–353.93, e.g., taxation review boards 353.93724

.92   Specific departments at council-of-state level and intergovernmental administration

.921–.928   Specific executive departments at the council of state level

Add to base number 353.92 the numbers following 351.0 in 351.01–351.08, e.g., departments of labor 353.9283

.929   Intergovernmental administration

.929 1   Between states

Examples: interstate agreements, cooperation, disputes

.929 2   Between states and federal government

.929 3   Between states and local governments

.93   Government service, property and financial management and related topics, administration of specific fields, malfunctioning of administration

Add to base number 353.93 the numbers following 351 in 351.1–351.9, e.g., tax administration 353.93724

.97–.99   Specific states

> Add to base number 353.9 notation 7–9 from Table 2, e.g., administration of government of Hawaii 353.9969; then add further as follows:
>
> 0001–0009   Standard subdivisions
> > As modified under 351, e.g., administrative reports 0006
>
> 001–008   Government service, property and financial management and related topics, administration of specific fields
> > Add to base number 00 the numbers following 351 in 351.1–351.8, e.g., tax administration 00724
> > Class application of specific concepts covered here to specific departments at council-of-state level in 1–8
>
> 009   Malfunctioning of administration
> > Add to base number 009 the numbers following 351.9 in 351.91–351.99, e.g., conflict of interest 00995
> > Class malfunctioning of a specific aspect of administration with the aspect, e.g., conflict of interest in tax administration 00724
>
> 01   Bureaucracy
> > Class a specific aspect of bureaucracy with the aspect, e.g., malfunctioning 009
>
> 03–09   Chief executives, cabinets and councils of state, fundamentals of administration, special agencies
> > Add to base number 0 the numbers following 351.00 in 351.003–351.009, e.g., council of state 04, the governor 0313; however, methods of selection of governors relocated from 034 to 321.8042097–321.8042099
> > Class application of concepts covered here to government service, property and financial management and related topics, administration of specific fields in 001–008; to a specific department at council-of-state level in 1–8; to intergovernmental administration in 9
>
> 1–8   Specific departments at council-of-state level
> > Add to base number for the state the numbers following 351.0 in 351.01–351.08, e.g., department of labor 83
> > Class comprehensive works in 04
>
> 9   Intergovernmental administration
> > Class intergovernmental administration of government service, property and financial management and related topics, administration of specific fields in 001–008; of specific cabinet departments in 1–8
>
> 91   Between the state and other states
> > Examples: interstate agreements, cooperation, disputes
> 92   Between the state and the federal government
> 93   Between the state and local governments

> Class administration of the District of Columbia in 352.0753

354   Administration of specific central governments; international administration

> *For administration of United States federal and state governments, see 353*
>
> *See Manual at 353–354*

.1   International administration

Administration of public international agencies and organizations

Use 354.1001–354.1009 for standard subdivisions

.103   United Nations

Including the Secretariat

Class specific subordinate bodies and affiliated organizations dealing with specific subjects in 354.11–354.19

.104   Regional associations and organizations

Add to base number 354.104 the numbers following 341.24 in 341.242–341.249, e.g., Organization of American States 354.1045

Class specific subordinate bodies and affiliated organizations dealing with specific subjects in 354.11–354.19

.11–.19   International personnel service, property and financial management and related topics, administration of specific fields, malfunctioning of administration

Add to base number 354.1 the numbers following 351 in 351.1–351.9, e.g., World Health Organization 354.177

.3–.9   Specific central governments other than those of United States

(Option: To give local emphasis and shorter notation to central governments of a specific country other than United States, class central governments of the country in 353; in that case, class central governments of United States in 354.73–354.79, 354.969)

Add to base number 354 notation 3–9 from Table 2, e.g., administration of government of Germany 354.43; then add further as follows:

0001–0009	Standard subdivisions
	As modified under 351, e.g., administrative reports 0006
001–008	Government service, property and financial management and related topics, administration of specific fields
	Add to 00 the numbers following 351 in 351.1–351.8, e.g., tax administration 00724
	Class application of specific concepts covered here to specific departments and ministries of cabinet rank in 06
009	Malfunctioning of administration
	Add to base number 009 the numbers following 351.9 in 351.91–351.99, e.g., conflict of interest 00995
	Class malfunctioning of a specific aspect of administration with the aspect, e.g., conflict of interest in tax administration 00724
01	Bureaucracy
	Class a specific aspect of bureaucracy with the aspect, e.g., malfunctioning 009
03–04	Chief executives; cabinets and councils of state
	Add to 0 the numbers following 351.00 in 351.003–351.004, e.g., chief executives 03
	Class specific departments and ministries of cabinet rank in 06

(continued)

.3–.9   Specific central governments other than those of United States (continued)

06	Specific departments and ministries of cabinet rank
	Add to 06 the numbers following 351.0 in 351.01–351.08, e.g., a ministry of foreign affairs 061
	Class comprehensive works in 04
>07–09	Fundamentals of administration, intergovernmental administration, special agencies
	Class comprehensive works in base number for country; application of specific concepts covered here to government service, property and financial management and related topics, administration of specific fields in 001–008, to specific departments and ministries of cabinet rank in 06
07	Fundamentals of administration
	Add to 07 the numbers following 351.007 in 351.0072–351.0078, e.g., reorganization 073
08	Intergovernmental administration
	Add to 08 the numbers following 351.09 in 351.091–351.093, e.g., relation between national and state governments 082
09	Special agencies
	Examples: independent agencies, quasi-administrative bodies, special commissions
	Add to 09 the numbers following 351.009 in 351.0091–351.0093, e.g., regulatory agencies 091

355   Military science

Class here armed forces and services, ground forces and services

For specific kinds of military forces and warfare, see 356–359

See also 306.27 for sociological aspects of military institutions, 322.5 for relation of the state to military organizations, 343.01 for military, defense, and veterans' law

See Manual at 355 vs. 623

SUMMARY

355.001–.009	**Standard subdivisions**
.02–.07	**Basic considerations**
.1	**Military life and customs**
.2	**Military resources**
.3	**Organization and personnel of military forces**
.4	**Military operations**
.5	**Military training**
.6	**Military administration**
.7	**Military installations and land reservations**
.8	**Military equipment and supplies (Matériel)**

.001	Philosophy and theory
.002	Miscellany
[.002 8]	Auxiliary techniques and procedures; apparatus, equipment, materials
	Relocated to 355.8

.003–.005	Standard subdivisions
.006	Organizations
[.006 8]	Management

> Do not use; class in 355.6

.007	Education, research, related topics

> Class reserve training in 355.2232, in-service training in 355.5

.007 11	Military colleges and universities

> *See Manual at 355.00711*

.007 2	Research

> Class research and development of military equipment and supplies in 355.07

.008	History and description with respect to kinds of persons
.009	Historical, geographical, persons treatment

> Class historical and geographical treatment of military situation and policy in 355.033, of specific military establishments in 355.309; military aspects of the history of specific wars in 900

> *See Manual at 355.009 vs. 930–990*

> 355.02–355.07 Basic considerations

Class comprehensive works in 355

.02	War and warfare

> Class here conventional warfare, total war, warfare between states

> *See also 341.6 for law of war*

> *See Manual at 355.02 vs. 355.4*

.021	General topics
.021 3	Militarism

> Class here antimilitarism, interdisciplinary works on the military-industrial complex

> Class the relation of military organizations to the state in 322.5, promotion of peace in 327.172, economic aspects of the military-industrial complex in 338.47355

.021 5	Limited war

> Use of this number for total war discontinued; class in 355.02

.021 7	Nuclear warfare

Including comprehensive works on nuclear forces [*formerly* 358.39], issues of deterrence

Use of this number for conventional warfare discontinued; class in 355.02

Class specific nuclear forces and their warfare with the forces, e.g., nuclear missile forces and warfare 358.17

See also 327.174 for nuclear disarmament, 355.825119 for problems of verifying nuclear arms control treaty provisions

.021 8	Insurgent, revolutionary, resistance warfare

Class here civil war, guerrilla warfare

Use of this number for scope of war discontinued; class in 355.02

Class guerrilla tactics in 355.425

[.021 82]	Warfare between and among states

Number discontinued; class in 355.02

[.021 84]	Insurgent, revolutionary, resistance warfare

Number discontinued; class in 355.0218

[.022]	Sociological factors affecting warfare

Number discontinued; class in 355.02

[.023]	Economic factors affecting warfare

Number discontinued; class in 355.02

.027	Causes of war

Class causes of specific wars in 930–990

.027 2	Political and diplomatic causes
.027 3	Economic causes
.027 4	Social causes

See also 303.66 for sociology of war

.027 5	Psychological causes
.028	Aftermath of war

Examples: occupation, dislocation, reconstruction

Class aftermath of specific wars in 930–990

Class government of occupied territories in 355.49

.03   Military situation and policy

Including disarmament

Class interdisciplinary works on disarmament in 327.174; disarmament problems of specific kinds of weapons common to two or more forces in 355.82, of a force dedicated to use of a specific kind of weapon with the force, e.g., Strategic Arms Limitation Treaty verification problems 358.17182

[.030 9]   Historical, geographical, persons treatment

Do not use; class historical and geographical treatment in 355.033, persons treatment in 355.0092

>   355.031–355.032 Specific elements

Class comprehensive works in 355.03

.031   Mutual security pacts

Class here military alliances

.032   Military missions and assistance

Class here military attachés

.032 09   Historical, geographical, persons treatment

Class military missions and assistance to specific continents, countries, localities in 355.0323–355.0329

.032 3–.032 9   Military missions and assistance to specific continents, countries, localities

Add to base number 355.032 notation 3–9 from Table 2, e.g., military assistance to Vietnam 355.032597

Class comprehensive works on military assistance by specific regions and countries in 355.03209

.033   General history and description

Class general history and description of specific elements in 355.031–355.032

.033 001–.033 09   Historical and geographical treatment

Add to base number 355.0330 notation 01–9 from Table 2, e.g., military situation and policy in the 1930s 355.0330043, military situation of Brazil 355.033081

.033 01–.033 09   Geographical treatment

Add to base number 355.0330 notation 1–9 from Table 2, e.g., military situation and policy in Brazil 355.033081

.033 2	Military capability

Class here combat readiness

Add to base number 355.0332 notation 1–9 from Table 2, e.g., military capability of Sweden 355.0332485

Use of this number for military situation discontinued; class in 355.03

Class combat readiness of specific units in 355.3

.033 5	Military policy

Add to base number 355.0335 notation 1–9 from Table 2, e.g., military policy of Italy 355.033545

.07	Military research and development of equipment and supplies

See Manual at 355.07 and 355.8

.1   Military life and customs

[.100 1–.100 9]	Standard subdivisions of military life and postmilitary benefits

Numbers discontinued because no longer needed after the narrowing of the subject

.11	Service periods; promotion and demotion
.111	Length of service
.112	Promotion and demotion
.113	Inactive periods

Examples: leaves, furloughs, reserve status, status during captivity or internment

.114	Termination of service

Examples: resignation, retirement

Including reinstatement

[.115]	Veterans' rights and benefits

Relocated to 362.86

[.115 1]	Veterans' pensions

Relocated to 331.25291355

.12	Living conditions

Class here living conditions of dependents, comprehensive works on military housing

Class administration of military housing in 355.67, quarters for personnel at military installations in 355.71

.123	Morale and motivation

.129	Living conditions in specific situations

Class morale in specific situations in 355.123, life in military prisons and prison camps in 365.48

.129 2	In regular quarters

Including quarters during basic training

.129 3	During maneuvers, aboard ship, in transit
.129 4	In combat zones
.129 6	In prisoners-of-war camps
.13	Conduct and rewards

Class here discipline

See also 343.014 for law of discipline and conduct

.133	Regulation of conduct

Class rewards in 355.134

.133 2	Enforcement and punishments

Class offenses in 355.1334

.133 23	Enforcement

Example: criminal investigation

Including military police [*formerly also* 355.34]

.133 25	Punishments

Class military prisons in 365.48

.133 4	Offenses against military discipline

Including mutinies

Class interdisciplinary works on mutinies in 364.131

See also 364.138 for war crimes

.133 6	Etiquette

Class dress regulations, etiquette of uniforms in 355.14

.134	Rewards

Including citations, special privileges

See Manual at 355.134092

.134 2	Honorary insignia

Examples: badges, decorations, medals

Class here comprehensive works on insignia

Class comprehensive works on insignia and uniforms in 355.14

For insignia of rank, see 355.14

.134 9   Gifts and gun salutes

> Use of this number for other rewards discontinued; class in 355.134

.14   Uniforms

Including accessories, insignia of rank and service

Class here etiquette of uniforms, comprehensive works on insignia and uniforms

Class issue and use of uniforms in 355.81

> *For comprehensive works on insignia, honorary insignia, see 355.1342*
>
> *See Manual at 355.14 vs. 355.81; 355.1409*

.15   Colors and standards

.16   Celebrations and commemorations

.17   Ceremonies

Class ceremonies for a specific occasion with the occasion, e.g., gun salutes 355.1349

.2   **Military resources**

.21   Preparation, evaluation, preservation

Class preparation, evaluation, preservation of specific resources in 355.22–355.27

> 355.22–355.27 Specific resources

Class comprehensive works in 355.2

.22   Human resources

For civilian personnel, see 355.23

.223   Procurement and reserve training

Class here enlistment, recruitment

.223 2   Reserve training

Pre- and post service

.223 207 11   Schools and courses in higher education

Class here training in academic settings, e.g., Reserve Officers' Training Corps

.223 4   Qualifications for service

.223 6   Specific methods and procedures of procurement

Including registration, classification, examination, commissioning

Do not use standard subdivisions; class in 355.22301–355.22309

.223 62	Voluntary enlistment
	Class here the all-volunteer army
.223 63	Draft (Conscription)
	For universal training and service, see 355.225
.224	Conscientious objectors
	Class here draft resistance
	Class ethics of conscientious objection in 172.1, techniques for evading the draft in 355.22363
.225	Universal training and service
.23	Civilian personnel
.24	Raw materials
	Class here comprehensive works on nonhuman resources
	For industrial resources, see 355.26; transportation and communication facilities, 355.27
.242	Metals
.243	Nonmetallic minerals
.245	Agricultural products
.26	Industrial resources
	Including manufacturing war matériel [*formerly* 358.3]
.27	Transportation and communication facilities
.28	Mobilization
	Examples: requisition, commandeering
	Class mobilization of specific resources in 355.22–355.27
.29	Demobilization
	Class demobilization of specific resources in 355.22–355.27
.3	**Organization and personnel of military forces**
	Class here combat readiness of specific units
	Class comprehensive works on combat readiness in 355.0332
.309	Historical, geographical, persons treatment
	Class here military establishments of specific countries
.31	Kinds of military units
	Examples: armies, divisions, brigades, regiments, companies; military districts
	Class kinds of units limited to a specific service with the service, e.g., reserve units 355.37, armored units 358.183

.33   Personnel and their hierarchy

                 Class persons treatment of soldiers in 355.0092, promotion and demotion in
                 355.112

.330 4   Line and staff functions

.330 41   Line functions

                        Including leadership

.330 42   Staff functions

                        Class here general staffs, joint chiefs of staff

                        Class line functions of chiefs of staff in 355.33041

.331   General and flag officers

                 Above the rank of colonel (naval rank of captain)

.332   Commissioned and warrant officers

                 Use 355 for officers' manuals

                 For general and flag officers, see 355.331

.338   Enlisted personnel

                 Including noncommissioned officers

                 See also 331.8811355 for military unions

.34   Noncombat services

             Including social and financial services for soldiers, services for dependents,
             interdisciplinary works on civil activities of armed forces, propaganda

             Class here operations of noncombat services

             Military police relocated to 355.13323

             Class a specific noncombat service not provided for here with the subject,
             e.g., personnel administration 355.61; a specific civil activity of armed
             forces with the activity, e.g., public works of U.S. Army Corps of Engineers
             363.0973

.341   Supply issuing and related services

                 Examples: canteens, post exchanges [*both formerly also* 355.71], army
                 catering units, mess services

                 Administrative services relocated to 355.6

                 Class officers' and noncommissioned officers' clubs in 355.346

.342   Public information services

.343   Unconventional warfare services

                 Class interdisciplinary works on espionage and subversion in 327.12

.343 2	Intelligence
	Examples: cryptanalysis, mapping, weather services
	Class here military espionage
	Class counterintelligence in 355.3433
.343 3	Counterintelligence
	Including security classification services
.343 4	Psychological warfare
	Use of this number for propaganda discontinued; class in 355.34
.343 7	Subversion and sabotage
.345	Health services
	Example: ambulance services
	Including sanitary, veterinary services
	Class here medical services
.346	Recreational services
	Examples: library services, officers' and noncommissioned officers' (NCO) clubs
.347	Religious and counseling services
	Standard subdivisions are added regardless of religion
.348	Women's units
	Class women in armed forces in 355.0082; women as a military resource in 355.22082; a specific service performed by women with the service, using notation 082 from Table 1, e.g., women in intelligence services 355.3432082
.35	Combat units according to field of service
	Including mercenary troops, soldiers of fortune
.351	Units serving wholly within their own frontiers
	Class here frontier troops, active units called home guards
	Class reserve units called home guards in 355.37
.352	Expeditionary forces
	Class here expeditionary forces of colonies, forces of mother countries dedicated to service in colonies
.356	Allied and coalition forces
.357	International forces
	Troops serving under the command of international bodies
	Class interdisciplinary works on peaceful resolution of conflict in 327.17
	See also 341.58 for legal aspects of international forces

.359   Foreign legions

Units of national armies consisting primarily of foreign recruits

Class here auxiliaries (troops of foreign countries serving with a state's armies)

.37   Reserves

Class here home guards, home reserves, militia, national guards, military departments devoted to reserve or national guard affairs

Class training of reserves in 355.2232, active units called home guards in 355.351; reserve units of a specific kind of military force with the force, e.g., army engineer reserves 358.223

.4   Military operations

Class here attack and defense operations, strategy

See Manual at 355.02 vs. 355.4

.409   Historical and persons treatment

Class geographical treatment in 355.47

.41   Support operations

Examples: camouflage, deception, handling prisoners of war

Class support operations in a specific situation with the situation, e.g., logistics of siege warfare 355.44

.411   Logistics

Including troop movements

For troop support, see 355.415

.412   Encampment

.413   Reconnaissance

Class here patrolling

.415   Troop support

Operations for providing immediate necessities for the maintenance of troops

Use of this number for prisoner handling discontinued; class in 355.41

Class comprehensive works on operations for provisioning troops in 355.411; a specific aspect of troop support with the aspect, e.g., medical service 355.345

.42   Tactics

> Nuclear tactics relocated to 355.43
>
> Class tactics of siege warfare in 355.44, of defense of home territory in 355.45

.422   Specific tactics

> Examples: antiaircraft defenses, attacks and counterattacks, debarkation and landing, retreats, skirmishing; mobile (blitz), commando (hit-and-run), infiltration tactics
>
> Class specific tactics in specific conditions in 355.423–355.426

>   355.423–355.426 Tactics in specific conditions

> Class comprehensive works in 355.42

.423   Tactics in various kinds of terrain, climate, weather

.424   Use of animals

.425   Guerrilla tactics

> Class here tribal fighting
>
> Class guerrilla warfare in 355.0218

.426   Tactics in cities

> Examples: street fighting, house-to-house fighting
>
> Quelling riots relocated to 363.32

.43   Nuclear operations

> Nuclear tactics [*formerly* 355.42] and strategy
>
> Use 355.43001–355.43009 for standard subdivisions
>
> Use of this number for nonnuclear strategy discontinued; class in 355.4
>
> Class nuclear warfare in 355.0217
>
> *See Manual at 355.02 vs. 355.4*

[.430 5] Strategy of limited and total war

> Number discontinued; class in 355.4

[.430 7] Strategy of nuclear and conventional warfare

> Number discontinued; class conventional strategy in 355.4, nuclear strategy in 355.43

.44   Siege and trench warfare, blockades

> Class naval blockades in 359.44

.45   Defense of home territory

> Class a specific defensive fort or installation in 355.709

.46   Combined operations

Coordination of two or more kinds of military forces

Examples: amphibious operations

Class amphibious operations in which marines are main land component in 359.9646

.47   Military geography

Class here geographical treatment of military operations

Add to base number 355.47 notation 1–9 from Table 2, e.g., military geography of Russia 355.4747

.48   Technical analyses of military events

Including real and imaginary wars, campaigns, battles

Class here war gaming

See also 793.92 for recreational war games

.49   Occupation of conquered territory

Including military government

Class occupation as an aftermath of war in 355.028

.5   Military training

Of individuals and units

Use notation 09 from Table 1 for training in specific countries, e.g., military training in Switzerland 355.509494 (*not* 355.5070494)

For reserve training, see 355.2232; universal military training, 355.225

.52   Maneuvers

For maneuvers involving civil population, see 355.58

.54   Basic training

Including drills, survival training, tactical exercises

.544   Encampment and field training

Examples: setting up and dismantling camps, constructing temporary fortifications, running obstacle courses

.547   Small arms and bayonet practice

Class here manual of arms

If emphasis is on use by the infantry, class in 356.184

.548   Self-defense

Unarmed combat and combat with knife

If emphasis is on use by the infantry, class in 356.184

.55	Training of officers

Class here mid-career training that is an integral part of an officer's career development, even if conducted at armed forces schools with full academic accreditation

Class university type service academies in 355.00711, training through war games in 355.48

.56	Technical training
.58	Maneuvers involving civil population
.6	**Military administration**

Including military consultants

Class here administrative services [*formerly also* 355.341]

Class administration of functions not provided for here with the subject, e.g., administration of training 355.5

For organization of military forces, see 355.3

.61	Personnel administration

Civilian and military personnel

Class personnel and their hierarchy in 355.33

For wage and salary administration, see 355.64

.62	Supply and financial administration
.621	Supply administration

Class here comprehensive works on supply services

Class inspection in 355.63, administration of specific kinds of supplies in 355.8

For supply issuing and related services, see 355.341; supply depots and installations 355.75

.621 1	Contracts and contracting

Class here comprehensive works on military contracts and contracting

Class contracts and contracting for nonsupply items with the item, e.g., for housing 355.67

.621 2	Procurement

Class contracts and contracting in 355.6211

.621 3	Utilization and disposal
.622	Financial administration

Class here military budgets and budgeting

For wage and salary administration, see 355.64

.63	Inspection

.64   Wage and salary administration

.67   Housing administration

> Class administration of housing at military installations in 355.71, comprehensive works on military housing in 355.12

.69   Military mail; graves registration and burial services

> Use of this number for other administrative services discontinued; class in 355.6

.693   Military mail

.699   Graves registration and burial services

.7   Military installations and land reservations

> Class here military bases, forts, permanent camps, posts

.709   Historical, geographical, persons treatment

> Class here specific forts or systems of fortifications, installations having two or more functions
>
> Use notation for area of installation, not country maintaining it, e.g., United States bases in Panama Canal Zone 355.70972875

.71   Quarters for personnel

> Housing at military installations
>
> Example: barracks
>
> Including prisoner-of-war camps
>
> Canteens, post exchanges relocated to 355.341
>
> Class comprehensive works on military housing in 355.12, on administration of housing in 355.67

.72   Medical installations

> Class medical supply depots in 355.75, veterans' hospitals in 362.11, comprehensive works on medical services in 355.345

.73   Artillery installations

> Class army artillery installations in 358.127

.74   Engineering installations

> Class army engineering installations in 358.227

.75   Supply depots and installations

> Class comprehensive works on supply services in 355.621

.79   Land

.8   **Military equipment [*formerly also* 355.0028] and supplies (Matériel)**

General aspects: development, procurement, issue, operation, use, packing, shipping

Including auxiliary techniques and procedures [*formerly also* 355.0028]

Class here apparatus [*formerly also* 355.0028], research and development, administration of specific kinds of supplies and equipment

Class comprehensive works on research and development of equipment and supplies in 355.07, on supply administration in 355.621; mobilization of military resources in 355.28

See Manual at 355.07 and 355.8

[.807 2]   Research

Do not use; class in 355.07

.81   Clothing, food, camp equipment, office supplies

Use of this number for comprehensive works on equipment other than ordnance discontinued; class in 355.8

See Manual at 355.14 vs. 355.81

.82   Ordnance

Class here problems of arms limitation and of verifying arms-control treaty provisions for specific kinds of weapons common to two or more forces

For combat vehicles, see 355.83

See also 327.174 for negotiations directed towards arms control, 341.733 for legal aspects of arms control

See Manual at 355 vs. 623; 355.82

.821   Artillery

Class land artillery in 358.1282

For specific pieces of artillery, see 355.822; artillery projectiles, 355.82513

.822   Specific pieces of artillery

Class specific pieces of land artillery in 358.1282

.823–.826   Other specific kinds of weapons

Add to base number 355.82 the numbers following 623.4 in 623.43–623.46, e.g., nuclear weapons 355.825119, artillery projectiles 355.82513; however, class ordnance of forces dedicated to specific kinds of weapons in 356–359, e.g., of guided missile forces 358.17182

.83   Transportation equipment and supplies

Examples: fuel, support vehicles, trains

Including aircraft used outside air forces, ships used outside naval forces

Class here combat vehicles

Class comprehensive works on aircraft in 358.4183, on ships in 359.83

.85   Communication equipment

Class army communication equipment in 358.248

.88   Medical supplies

Class ambulances in 355.83

> ## 356–359 Specific kinds of military forces and warfare

Class here the history of specific military forces not limited to any one war, services and units dedicated to specific forces, countermeasures against specific forces

Aside from additions, changes, deletions, exceptions shown under specific entries, add to notation for each term identified by * as follows:

01–09	Standard subdivisions
	Notation from Table 1 as modified under 355.001–355.009, e.g., management 6 (*not* 068), management of artillery forces 358.126 (*not* 358.12068)
1	Military life and customs
14	Uniforms
3	Organization and personnel
	Class here units
309	Historical, geographical, persons treatment
	Class here units of specific countries regardless of size of unit
4	Operations
	Class here tactics
5	Training
6	Administration
7	Installations
8	Equipment and supplies (Matériel)
82	Weapons other than combat vehicles
83	Combat vehicles

Class comprehensive works in 355, a specific countermeasure with the force wielding it, e.g., coast artillery 358.16 (*not* 359)

See Manual at 355 vs. 623; 356–359

> ## 356–357 Land forces and warfare

Class comprehensive works in 355

For artillery, missile, armored forces and warfare, see 358.1; chemical, biological, radiological forces and warfare, 358.3

356   Foot forces and warfare

.1   Infantry

>   356.11–356.16 Specific kinds of infantry

> Class comprehensive works in 356.1

.11   *Motorized infantry

> Use of this number for regular troops discontinued; class in 356.1

.15   *Irregular troops

> Examples: self-organized infantry, guerrillas, brigand troops

.16   Troops having special combat functions

.162   Troops specializing in specific weapons

> Examples: bazookamen, grenadiers, machine gunners, sharpshooters (snipers)

.164   *Mountain and ski troops

.166   *Paratroops

.167   *Commandos and *rangers

.18   General topics of infantry

> Do not use standard subdivisions; class in 356.101–356.109

> Class general topics of specific kinds of infantry in 356.11–356.16

.181   Life and customs

.181 4   Uniforms

.183   Operations

> Class here tactics

.184   Training

.186   Equipment and supplies

.187   Installations

.189   Organization and personnel

> Class here units

.189 09   Historical, geographical, persons treatment

> Class here units of specific countries regardless of size of unit

*Add as instructed under 356–359

357   Mounted forces and warfare

.04   *General topics

> Do not use standard subdivisions; class in 357.01–03, 357.05–357.09

.043   Organization and personnel

> Class here comprehensive works on units that served as horse cavalry and mechanized or armored cavalry, e.g., the U.S. Third Cavalry Division 357.0430973
>
> Class a specific period of service of a unit which changed kinds of mounts with the kind of mount, e.g., the U.S. Third Cavalry Division as a horse unit 357.1830973

.1   **Horse cavalry**

> Class here dragoons, lancers
>
> *For remount and training services, see 357.2*
>
> *See also 358.12 for horse artillery*

.18   *General topics

> Do not use standard subdivisions; class in 357.101–357.109

.2   **Remount and training services**

.5   **Mechanized cavalry**

>   357.52–357.54 Specific kinds

> Class comprehensive works in 357.5, armored cavalry in 358.18

.52   *Bicycle

.53   *Motorcycle

.54   Large motor vehicle

> Examples: jeep and truck cavalry

.58   *General topics of mechanized cavalry

> Do not use standard subdivisions; class in 357.501–357.509
>
> Class generalities of specific kinds of mechanized cavalry in 357.52–357.54

358   Air and other specialized forces and warfare; engineering and related services

SUMMARY

358.1	Missile forces and warfare; army artillery and armored forces and warfare
.2	Army engineering and related services
.3	Chemical, biological, radiological forces and warfare
.4	Air forces and warfare
.8	Space forces and warfare

*Add as instructed under 356–359

.1   **Missile forces and warfare; army artillery and armored forces and warfare**

.12   *Army artillery

> Example: antitank artillery

> Class here field artillery

> *For antiaircraft artillery, see 358.13; coast artillery, 358.16*

.13   *Antiaircraft artillery

.16   *Coast artillery

.17   Guided missile forces and warfare

> Class here strategic missile forces and warfare, nuclear missile forces and warfare

> Class naval guided missile forces in 359.9817

> *For air guided missile forces, see 358.42*

.171   *General topics

> Do not use standard subdivisions; class in 358.1701–358.1709

.174   *Antimissile defense

> Class here Strategic Defense Initiative (SDI, star wars), surface-to-air missile forces

> Class a specific defense other than surface-to-air missiles with the defense, e.g., beam weapon forces 358.39, air-to-air missile forces 358.43

.175   Specific surface-to-surface missile forces

> Use of this number for comprehensive works on surface-to-surface missile forces discontinued; class in 358.17

.175 2   *Short range

> Class here tactical missile forces

.175 3   *Intermediate range

.175 4   *Long range

> Class here strategic land missile forces

.176   *Surface-to-underwater missile forces

.18   *Armored forces and warfare

> Class here tank forces and warfare, armored cavalry

*Add as instructed under 356–359

.2   Army engineering and related services

.22   *Engineering services

> Examples: construction of buildings and camouflage [*both formerly* 358.3], property maintenance

> Class here construction engineer services

> Class communications services in 358.24, transportation services in 358.25, civil works of army engineering services in 363

.23   *Demolition services

> Including bomb disposal units

.24   *Communications (Signals and signaling) forces

> Including military cryptography services

.25   *Transportation services

.3   Chemical, biological, radiological forces and warfare

> Regardless of service or force to which assigned

> Use of this number for other specialized forces and warfare discontinued; class in 358

> Manufacturing war matériel relocated to 355.26, construction of buildings and camouflage to 358.22

.34   *Chemical warfare

.38   *Biological warfare

.39   *Radiation and beam warfare

> Class here passive defense against nuclear radiation

> Nuclear forces relocated to 355.0217

.4   Air forces and warfare

> Naval air forces and warfare relocated to 359.94

.400 1–.400 9   Standard subdivisions

> As modified under 355.001–355.009, e.g., air forces management 358.416 (*not* 358.40068)

.403   Situation and policy

> Standard subdivisions may be used for situation, for policy

.407   Research and development of equipment and supplies

.41   General topics

> Do not use standard subdivisions; class in 358.4001–358.4009

> Class general topics of specific forces in 358.42–358.47

*Add as instructed under 356–359

.411–.413	Military life and customs, resources, organization and personnel

Add to base number 358.41 the numbers following 355 in 355.1–355.3, e.g., air force uniforms 358.4114

.414	Air operations

Including camouflage, deception, prisoner handling

Class here attack and defense, strategy

> *For bombing operations, see 358.42; pursuit and fighter operations, 358.43; reconnaissance operations, 358.45*

.414 09	Historical and persons treatment

Class geographical treatment in 358.4147

.414 1	Logistics

> *For transportation, see 358.44; communication, 358.46*

.414 12	Encampment
.414 15	Troop support

Use of this number for prisoner handling discontinued; class in 358.414

Class a specific aspect of troop support with the aspect, e.g., medical service 358.41345

.414 2	Tactics

Including close air support of combat

Class tactics of defense of home territory in 358.4145

[.414 3]	Strategy

Number discontinued; class in 358.414

.414 5	Defense of home territory
.414 7	Air operations geography

Add to base number 358.4147 notation 1–9 from Table 2, e.g., air operations geography of Canada 358.414771

.414 8	Technical analyses of air war events

Examples: analyses of real and imaginary air wars, campaigns, battles

.415–.418	Training, administration, installations, equipment and supplies

Add to base number 358.41 the numbers following 355 in 355.5–355.8, e.g., aircraft 358.4183; however, class a specific kind of aircraft with the force dedicated to its use in 358.42–358.47

See Manual at 358.4183

.418 2	Air ordnance

> 358.42–358.47 Specific forces

Class comprehensive works in 358.4; chemical, biological, radiological forces in 358.3

.42   *Bombing forces and operations

Including air-to-underwater guided missile forces

Class here strategic missions of air forces; air-to-surface guided missile forces; comprehensive works on air guided missile forces, on air nuclear forces

For air-to-air guided missile forces, air-to-air nuclear forces, see 358.43

.43   *Pursuit and fighter forces and operations

Including air-to-air guided missile forces, air-to-air nuclear forces, air artillery

Class here tactical missions of air forces

.44   *Transportation services

.45   *Reconnaissance forces and operations

Example: antisubmarine reconnaissance

.46   *Communications (Signals and signaling) services

.47   *Engineering services

.8   **Space forces and warfare**

See also 358.17 for missile forces when either launch or target is from or to the earth or its atmosphere

359   Sea (Naval) forces and warfare

SUMMARY

359.001–.009	**Standard subdivisions**
.03–.07	**[Situation and policy, research and development of equipment and supplies]**
.1–.2	**Naval life and resources**
.3	**Organization and personnel of naval forces**
.4–.7	**Naval operations, training, administration, installations**
.8	**Naval equipment and supplies (Naval matériel)**
.9	**Specialized combat forces; engineering and related services**

.001   Philosophy and theory

.002   Miscellany

[.002 8]   Auxiliary techniques and equipment; apparatus, equipment, materials

Relocated to 359.8

*Add as instructed under 356–359

.003–.009   Standard subdivisions

>As modified under 355.001–355.009, e.g., naval management 359.6 (*not* 359.0068)

.03   Situation and policy

>Standard subdivisions may be used for situation, for policy

.07   Research and development of equipment and supplies

.1–.2   Naval life and resources

>Add to base number 359 the numbers following 355 in 355.1–355.2, e.g., uniforms 359.14

.3   Organization and personnel of naval forces

.31   Naval units

>Examples: fleets, squadrons, flotillas, divisions
>
>Crews of ships relocated to 359.32
>
>Class noncombat services in 359.34, reserves in 359.37
>
>*For ships as naval units, see 359.32*

.32   Ships as naval units

>Class here crews of ships [*formerly also* 359.31]
>
>*See also 358.83 for ships as naval equipment*
>
>*See Manual at 359.32 vs. 359.83*

.322   Wind-driven ships as units

>Class here wind-driven ships of war

.325–.326   Specific kinds of powered ships as naval units

>Add to base number 359.32 the numbers following 623.82 in 623.825–623.826, e.g., cruisers 359.3253; however, aircraft carriers relocated from 359.3255 to 359.9435, submarines from 359.3257 to 359.933, military transport ships from 359.3264 to 359.9853, military supply ships from 359.3265 to 359.9853

.33–.37   Personnel, noncombat services, fields of combat service, reserves

>Add to base number 359.3 the numbers following 355.3 in 355.33–355.37, e.g., noncombat services 359.34

.4–.7   Naval operations, training, administration, installations

>Add to base number 359 the numbers following 355 in 355.4–355.7, e.g., naval installations 359.7

.8   **Naval equipment [*formerly also* 359.0028] and supplies (Naval matériel)**

General aspects: development, procurement, issue, operation, use, packing, shipping

Including auxiliary techniques and procedures [*formerly also* 359.00285]

Class here apparatus [*formerly also* 359.0028]; research and development, administration of specific kinds of supplies and equipment

Class comprehensive works on research and development of equipment and supplies in 359.07, on supply administration in 355.621; mobilization of naval resources in 359.28

See Manual at 355.07 and 355.8

[.807 2]   Research

Do not use; class in 359.07

.81   **Clothing, food, camp equipment, office supplies**

Use of this number for comprehensive works on equipment other than ordnance discontinued; class in 358.8

See Manual at 355.14 vs. 355.81

.82   **Ordnance**

Class here problems of arms limitation and of verification of arms-control treaty provisions

Add to base number 359.82 the numbers following 623.4 in 623.43–623.46, e.g., small arms 359.824; however, class ordnance on specific kinds of ships in 359.83, artillery in 359.981282, guided missiles in 359.981782

Class combat vehicles and craft in 359.83

.83   **Transportation equipment and supplies**

Examples: fuel, support vehicles

Class here comprehensive works on ships in the armed forces

Class ships as naval units in 359.32; ships used outside the naval forces with the force using them, e.g., coast guard ships 359.9783

See Manual at 359.32 vs. 359.83

.832   **Wind-driven ships as equipment**

Class here wind-driven ships of war

.835–.836   **Specific kinds of power-driven warships as equipment**

Add to base number 359.83 the numbers following 623.82 in 623.825–623.826, e.g., cruisers 359.8353; however, aircraft carriers relocated from 359.8355 to 359.94835, submarines from 359.8357 to 359.9383, military supply and transport ships from 359.836 to 359.98583

.85   **Communication equipment**

.88   **Medical supplies**

.9	**Specialized combat forces; engineering and related services**

Class chemical, biological, radiological forces in 358.3

.93	*Submarine forces and warfare
.933	Units

Class here submarines as units [*formerly* 359.3257]

See Manual at 359.32 vs. 359.83

.938	Equipment and supplies (Matériel)
.938 3	Submarines as equipment [*formerly* 359.8357]

See Manual at 359.32 vs. 359.83

.938 32	Conventionally powered
.938 34	Nuclear powered
.94	*Naval air forces and warfare [*formerly* 358.4]
.943	Units
.943 4	Aircraft units

Examples: flights, groups, squadrons, wings

.943 5	Aircraft carriers as units [*formerly* 359.3255]

See Manual at 359.32 vs. 359.83

.948	Equipment and supplies (Matériel)
.948 3	Combat vehicles

Class combat vehicles as units in 359.943

.948 34	Aircraft
.948 35	Aircraft carriers as equipment [*formerly* 359.8355]

See Manual at 359.32 vs. 359.83

.96	Marine forces

Add to base number 359.96 the numbers following 355 in 355.1–355.8, e.g., training 355.965

.97	*Coast guard

See Manual at 359.97

.98	Artillery and guided missile forces; engineering and related services
.981	Artillery and guided missile forces
.981 2	*Artillery services

Class artillery units aboard specific kinds of ships in 359.32; artillery ordnance aboard specific kinds of ships in 359.83

*Add as instructed under 356–359

.981 7	*Guided missile forces

Class guided missile units aboard specific kinds of ships in 359.32, guided missile ordnance aboard specific kinds of ships in 359.83

.982	*Engineering services

Military sealift commands relocated to 359.985

.983	*Communications (Signals and signaling) services
.984	Underwater demolition and reconnaissance services

Example: frogmen

.985	*Transportation services

Class here military sealift commands [*formerly* 359.982]

.985 3	Units

Including military transport ships as units [*formerly* 359.3264]

Class here military supply ships as units [*formerly* 359.3265]

See Manual at 359.32 vs. 359.83

.985 8	Supplies and equipment (Matériel)
.985 83	Military supply and transport ships as equipment [*formerly* 359.836]

See Manual at 359.32 vs. 359.83

360   Social problems and services; association

SUMMARY

361	Social problems and social welfare in general
362	Social welfare problems and services
363	Other social problems and services
364	Criminology
365	Penal and related institutions
366	Association
367	General clubs
368	Insurance
369	Miscellaneous kinds of associations

> ## 361–365 Social problems and services

Class here work and policy of government agencies that enforce the law in matters of social problems and services

Class comprehensive works in 361, insurance in 368; social services in armed forces in 355–359, in specific wars in 900; the internal administration of governmental agencies, including their administrative annual reports, in 350–354; the law itself, draft laws, enforcement by courts in 341–346

See Manual at 301 vs. 361–365; 361–365; 361–365 vs. 350–354

*Add as instructed under 356–359

361   Social problems and social welfare in general

Social welfare: social assistance, either free or paid for in part or in full by recipients, to enable individuals to cope with situations usually beyond their individual capacities to overcome

Class here comprehensive works on socioeconomic planning and development, on programs and services encompassing several branches of social sciences, on social problems and services

Class social problems considered purely as social phenomena in 301–307, community planning and development in 307, economic planning and development in 338.9, specific problems and services in 362–365, description of present or past social conditions in 930–990

See Manual at 361 vs. 362

SUMMARY

361.001–.008		**Standard subdivisions**
	.02–.06	**Specific kinds of assistance, counseling**
	.1	**Social problems**
	.2	**Social action**
	.3	**Social work**
	.4	**Group work**
	.6	**Government action**
	.7	**Private action**
	.8	**Community action**
	.9	**Historical, geographical, persons treatment**

.001–.008   Standard subdivisions

[.009]   Historical, geographical, persons treatment

Do not use; class in 361.9

>   361.02–361.06 Specific kinds of assistance, counseling

Class here general discussions covering various problems and client groups, and both governmental and private assistance

Class comprehensive works in 361, governmental assistance in 361.6, private assistance in 361.7, assistance with respect to a specific problem with the problem, e.g., free assistance to persons in late adulthood 362.6

.02   Free assistance

Class specific kinds of free assistance in 361.05–361.06

.04   Paid assistance

Assistance for which the recipient pays all or part of cost

Class specific kinds of paid assistance in 361.05–361.06

.05   Material assistance

Examples: financial aid; relief; direct provision of food, clothing, shelter; recreational activities and facilities; institutional care

.06 **Guidance and related services**

Services directed toward enabling individuals and groups to assist themselves

Example: citizens advice bureaus

Class social work in 361.3

.1 **Social problems**

History, description, appraisal of areas and kinds of social breakdown, of problems endemic to human society

Class specific problems in 362

See Manual at 361.1 vs. 362.042, 301

.2 **Social action**

Organization, role, description, history

Class here methods of social action [*formerly also* 362.0425]

Class change as a social phenomenon in 303.4

.23 **Protest and dissent**

See Manual at 361.23–361.24 vs. 322.44

.24 **Reform movements**

See Manual at 361.23–361.24 vs. 322.44

.25 **Action within established social framework**

Class here policy, planning, programs, proposals; citizen participation; comprehensive works on governmental and private action

Class governmental action in 361.6, private action in 361.7

For international action, see 361.26; social work, 361.3

.26 **International action**

Class public international action in 361.6, private international action in 361.77

See Manual at 361.6 and 361.7, 361.8

.3 **Social work**

.301 **Philosophy and theory**

Including policy

.32 **Practice of social work**

Class here casework

For group work, see 361.4

.320 8 Casework with respect to kinds of persons [*formerly also* 361.38]

.322 Interviewing

.323	Counseling

> Example: telephone counseling, e.g., hot lines

.37   Volunteer social work

> Class a specific aspect of volunteer social work with the subject, e.g., interviewing 361.322

[.38]   Casework with respect to kinds of persons

> Relocated to 361.3208

.4   Group work

> Class counseling in group work in 361.323

.6   Governmental action

> Class here intergovernmental assistance and planning, governmental international action, interdisciplinary works on government-sponsored socioeconomic planning and development

> Class public social work in 361.3, combined public and private community action in 361.8, management of public agencies regulating social welfare services in 351.84

> *See Manual at 361.6 and 361.7, 361.8*

.61   Social policy

> Class welfare reform in 361.68

.612   Goals, values, priorities

.613   Politics and social action

> Relation of proposed actions to political structures and values

> Class effect of social action on political structures and values in 320

.614   Welfare and human rights

> Including use of compulsory remedial action

> Class interdisciplinary works on human rights in 323

> *See Manual at 323.46 vs. 361.614*

.615   Relation of government and private sectors

> Class welfare state in 361.65

.65   Welfare state

> Class economics of welfare state in 330.126

.68   Welfare reform

.7   Private action

> Class private social work in 361.3, relation of government and private sectors in 361.615, combined governmental and private community action in 361.8

> *See Manual at 361.6 and 361.7, 361.8*

.706 81   Organization and financial management

Class here fund raising

.74   By individual philanthropists

Class an organization that controls the use of the money donated by a philanthropist with the organization, e.g., Rockefeller Foundation 361.7632

.75   By religious organizations

.76   By private organizations

Class religious organizations in 361.75, private international organizations in 361.77

.763   By nonprofit organizations

Including CARE [*formerly* 361.77]

.763 2   Foundations and charitable trusts

.763 4   Red cross national societies

Class here affiliated societies, e.g., Red Crescent

Class comprehensive works on the Red Cross in 361.77

.765   By business organizations

Class ways that management can deal with charitable donations in 658.153, programs of employers for employees in 658.38

.766   By labor unions

.77   By private international organizations

Organizations whose membership is international

Example: International Red Cross

Including comprehensive works on the Red Cross and affiliated societies such as the Red Crescent

Class Red Cross and affiliated societies of a specific nation in 361.7634

CARE relocated to 361.763

See also 361.76 for local organizations providing services worldwide

.8   Community action

Coordination of governmental and private action to promote the welfare of individuals in the community

Examples: community chests, united givers funds

Class community development in 307.14, governmental community action in 361.6, private community action in 361.7

See also 307.12 for planning for the community as a whole

See Manual at 361.6 and 361.7, 361.8

.9   Historical, geographical, persons treatment

Add to base number 361.9 notation 01–9 from Table 2, e.g., welfare work in Arizona 361.9791

Class historical, geographical, persons treatment of specific kinds of social action in 361.2–361.8

> ## 362–363 Specific social problems and services

Except for additions, changes, deletions, exceptions shown under specific entries, add to each subdivision identified by * as follows:

01	Philosophy and theory
02	Miscellany
[0218]	Standards
	Do not use; class in 62
[0289]	Safety measures
	Do not use; class in 363.1
03–05	Standard subdivisions
06	Organizations and management
0681	Organization and financial management
	Including managerial cost control
	Class social measures to hold down costs in 5
07–09	Standard subdivisions
>1–3	Characteristics of problem
	Class comprehensive works in 362–363, without adding from this table
1	Social causes
2	Incidence, extent, severity
3	Problems as they appear within or affect groups
	Example: co-workers
	Class here families [*formerly* 362.82]
	Use of this subdivision for comprehensive works on social effects discontinued; class in 362–363, without adding from this table
	Class family problems in 362.82
5	Social action
	Class here social measures to hold down costs
	Add to 5 the numbers following 361 in 361.2–361.8, e.g., international action 526, rationing 56; however, class counseling in 86
	Class specific forms of action in 6–8; governmental administration of rationing programs in 351.829

(continued)

>   **362–363 Specific social problems and services (continued)**

>6–8	Specific forms of action
	Class comprehensive works in 5
	Works containing topics from any two of these subdivisions are classed in 5
6	Control
	Elimination and reduction of hazards, of sources and causes of difficulty
	Class measures to protect against and to limit effects of problems in 7
62	Standards
63	Monitoring, surveillance, reporting
64	Inspection and testing
65	Investigation of specific incidents
66	Certification
7	Measures to prevent, protect against, limit effects of problems
	Class here preparedness
	Class measures that both control and prevent problems in 6
72	Protective measures
	Examples: design of environments, warning and guidance systems
[75]	Safety measures
	Relocated to 363.1
8	Remedial measures, services, forms of assistance
	Measures applicable primarily to individuals, even if in large groups
	Class remedial measures directed toward altering a social function, e.g., cost control, in 5; social work in 53
809	Historical, geographical, persons treatment
	Class here the area receiving assistance, e.g., relief to Italy provide by the United States 80945
	Class the area providing assistance in 8, without adding from Table 1, e.g., relief provided by the United States to many countries 8, not 80973
81	Rescue operations
82	Financial assistance
	Class social insurance in 368.4
83	Provision of food, shelter, household assistance, clothing, recreation
84	Employment services
	Including vocational rehabilitation, sheltered employment
85	Residential care
	Care within institutions existing for the purpose
86	Counseling and guidance
	Example: legal aid

Class comprehensive works in 361, discrimination in 305

For criminology, see 364

See Manual at 362–363; 364.1 vs. 362–363; 614.5 vs. 362–363

362   Social welfare problems and services

Class here social security

Unless other instructions are given, observe the following table of precedence, e.g., mentally ill women veterans 362.2 (*not* 362.86 or 362.83)

Physical illness	362.1
Mental and emotional illnesses and disturbances	362.2
Mental retardation	362.3
Problems of and services to people with physical disabilities	362.4
Victims of political oppression	362.87
Victims of crimes	362.88
Veterans	362.86
Problems of and services to persons in late adulthood	362.6
Problems of and services to young people	362.7
Laboring classes	362.85
Women	362.83
Members of racial, ethnic, national groups	362.84
Problems of and services to the poor	362.5
Families	362.82

To indicate the relation of a specific kind of problem to a specific kind of person, add notation 08 from Table 1 to the number for the problem, e.g., narcotic addiction among young adults 362.2930835

For social security as a form of social insurance, see 368.4

See Manual at 361 vs. 362; 364.1 vs. 362–363; 368.4 vs. 362

SUMMARY

362.04		**Special topics**
	.1	**Physical illness**
	.2	**Mental and emotional illnesses and disturbances**
	.3	**Mental retardation**
	.4	**Problems of and services to people with physical disabilities**
	.5	**Problems of and services to the poor**
	.6	**Problems of and services to persons in late adulthood**
	.7	**Problems of and services to young people**
	.8	**Problems of and services to other groups**
	.9	**Historical, geographical, persons treatment**

.04   Special topics

.042   Social problems

       See Manual at 361.1 vs. 362.042, 301

.042 2   Incidence, extent, severity

       Including social effects

.042 3   Social causes

.042 4   Prevention

.042 5   Social action

Including remedial measures

Methods of social action relocated to 361.2

Class prevention in 362.0424

[.08]   Social welfare problems and services with respect to kinds of persons

Do not use; class in 362.1–362.8

[.09]   Historical, geographical, persons treatment

Do not use; class in 362.9

>   **362.1–362.4 Problems of and services to sick and disabled people**

Class comprehensive works in 362.1; incidence of and public measures to prevent physical diseases in 614.4–614.5

See Manual at 362.1–362.4 vs. 610; 614.4–614.5 vs. 362.1–362.4

.1   **Physical illness**

Class here interdisciplinary works on illness and disability, on medical care and treatment, on medical missions, on public health

Class problems of and services to persons with a specific physical disability regardless of cause in 362.4; technology of medicine in 610; religious aspects of medical missions in 266; sociology of medicine, of health, of illness in 306.461

For mental and emotional illness, see 362.2; mental retardation, 362.3

.102 3   Services to physically ill persons as a profession, occupation, hobby

Class here comprehensive works on health occupations peripheral to the medical and paramedical professions

Class specific peripheral professions with the subject, e.g., medical social workers 362.10425, hospital secretaries 651.3741; works covering both the medical and peripheral occupations in 610

.104   Special topics

.104 2   Social aspects

Class preventive measures in 614.4–614.5

See Manual at 368.382 vs. 362.1042

.104 22   Social effects

Class incidence in 614.4

.104 25   Forms of assistance

Including services to indigent patients [*formerly* 362.19], medical social work, services of health maintenance organizations (HMOs), rural health services

Class accident and health insurance in 368.38, government-sponsored accident and health insurance in 368.42

.104 252	Financial assistance
.104 256	Counseling and guidance
.106 8	Management

Class here peer reviews

Class the results of peer reviews with the subject, e.g., the results of the evaluation of New York City hospitals 362.11097471

.108   Services to specific kinds of physically ill persons

Class services rendered by groups of persons to the physically ill in 362.1, physical illness among groups of persons in 616.008

.108 3   Services to young people

Class services to infants and children up to puberty in 362.19892

[.108 46]   Services to persons in late adulthood

Do not use; class 362.19897

> **362.11–362.19 Medical services**

Free and paid

Class comprehensive works in 362.1, medical treatment in 616

> **362.11–362.16 Services of specific kinds of institutions**

Class comprehensive works in 362.1, services of health maintenance organizations in 362.10425, specific kinds of services provided by a specific institution in 362.17, services by a specific institution to patients with specific conditions in 362.19

.11   Services of hospitals and related institutions

For clinics and related institutions, see 362.12; extended care facilities, 362.16

.12   Services of clinics and related institutions

Examples: health centers, dispensaries, outpatient departments of general hospitals

Class here ambulatory services, community health services

.14   Professional home care

Including visiting nurses' services, services of health visitors

See also 649.8 for home care by family members

.16 Services of extended care facilities

Services of institutions rendering medical care for patients requiring long-term or convalescent care

Example: services of convalescent homes

Including sanitoriums for persons suffering from chronic diseases

Class here life care communities, nursing and rest homes, services of extended care facilities for persons in late adulthood

[.160 846] Services of extended care facilities for persons in late adulthood

Do not use; class in 362.16

.17 Specific services

Unless other instructions are given, class complex subjects with aspects in two or more subdivisions of this number in the number coming last, e.g., diagnostic services by doctors 362.177 (*not* 362.172)

Class forms of assistance in 362.10425, emergency services in 362.18, specific kinds of services to patients with specific conditions in 362.19, technology of the services in 610, group practice in 610.65, preventive services in 614.44

See Manual at 362.17 vs. 610

.172 Services of doctors

Including referral and consulting services

.173 Services of nurses

Class visiting nurses' services in 362.14

.173 068 Management of services of nurses

Class here nonmedical aspects of ward management

.174 Intensive care

.175 Terminal care

Including hospices

Class here services to terminal patients [*formerly* 362.19]

.176 Nutritional services

Class here feeding of sick, comprehensive works on the provision of special diets for various classes of sick people

Class nutritional services applied to malnutrition disorders in 362.19639, nutritional programs for the population at large in 363.8

.177 Diagnostic and screening services

Example: radiology services

.178	Therapeutic services
.178 2	Pharmaceutical services

Class nutritional services in 362.176

.178 3   Tissue and organ banks

Example: eye banks

For blood and blood plasma banks, see 362.1784

.178 4   Blood and blood plasma banks

.178 6   Rehabilitation services

.18   Emergency services

.188   Ambulance services

.19   Services to patients with specific conditions

Class here living with a physical disease

Add to base number 362.19 the numbers following 61 in 616–618, e.g., maternity hospitals 362.1982, children's wards 362.19892, dental care 362.1976; however, class services to the mentally ill in 362.2. In adding to 362.19, the tables under 616.1–616.9, 617, or 618.1–618.8 are used only for the addition of notation from Table 1, e.g., periodicals on dental care 362.1976005, services to patients with congenital dental disorders 362.1976 (*not* 362.1976043)

Services to indigent patients relocated to 362.10425, terminal patients to 362.175

Class incidence of disease in 614.4, of specific diseases in 614.5

.2   Mental and emotional illnesses and disturbances

Class here mental handicaps that consist of mental retardation combined with mental illness

Class mental retardation in 362.3, life with a psychiatric disorder in 616.890092

See Manual at 614 vs. 362.1, 362.2

.204   Special topics

.204 2   Social aspects

.204 22   Incidence, extent, severity

Including social effects

.204 25   Prevention and forms of assistance

Class here psychiatric social work

.204 251   Emergency and rescue operations

Class here comprehensive works on emergency services [*formerly* 362.28], hot lines

.204 252   Financial assistance

.204 256   Counseling and guidance

>   362.21–362.24 Medical services

           Class comprehensive works in 362.2, medical treatment in 616.8, care for specific problems in 362.25–362.29

.21   Services of psychiatric hospitals and related institutions

           For services of psychiatric clinics, see 362.22; of sanitoriums and nursing homes, 362.23

.22   Community mental health services

           Class here services of psychiatric clinics

.223   Group homes

.23   Services of sanitoriums and nursing homes

.24   Professional home care

>   362.25–362.29 Specific problems

           Class comprehensive works in 362.2

.25   Neuroses

           Examples: anorexia nervosa, compulsive gambling, depression

.26   Psychoses

           Example: schizophrenia

.27   Disorders of personality and character

           Example: kleptomania

           For suicide, see 362.28; substance abuse, 362.29

.28   *Suicide

           Class here suicidal compulsions

           Comprehensive works on emergency services relocated to 362.204251

.288 1   Emergency and rescue services

           Class here hot lines

.29   Substance abuse

           Class here drug abuse; interdisciplinary works on substance abuse, addiction, habituation, intoxication

           Class subculture of substance abusers in 306.1, drug traffic in 363.45, drug use as a custom in 394.1, medical aspects of substance abuse in 616.86; abuse of substances associated with systems other than the nervous system in 362.19, e.g., food addiction 362.19639808

           Works on "drug abuse" in the sense of only narcotic abuse are classed in 362.293

*Add as instructed under 362–363

.291   Specific aspects of substance abuse

Add to base number 362.291 notation 1–8 from table under 362–363, e.g., prevention of substance abuse 362.2917; however, class control of drug traffic in 363.45

Notation from 362–363 is added for both specific aspects of two or more of the substances provided for in 362.292–362.298 and for a combination of substances provided for in 362.292–362.298 and in 362.299, e.g., counseling for alcohol and cocaine abuse, for narcotics and stimulant abuse 362.29186

Class specific aspects of a specific substance in 362.292–362.299

.292   *Alcohol

Class here interdisciplinary works on alcoholism

Class a specific aspect of alcoholism with the aspect, e.g., medical aspects 616.861

[.292 6]   Control of sale of alcoholic beverages

Do not use; class in 363.41

.292 7   Measures to prevent alcohol abuse and limit its effects[*formerly* 362.29286]

.292 8   Remedial measures, services, forms of assistance

.292 86   Counseling and guidance

Class here services of Alcoholics Anonymous

Measures to prevent alcohol abuse and limit its effects relocated to 362.2927

.293   *Narcotics

Opium and its derivatives and synthetic equivalents

Class here specific narcotics, e.g, heroin, morphine

Use of this number for comprehensive works on drug abuse discontinued; class in 362.29

Cocaine relocated to 362.298

.293 7   Measures to prevent narcotic abuse and limit its effects [*formerly* 362.29386]

.293 8   Remedial measures, services, forms of assistance

.293 86   Counseling and guidance

Measures to prevent narcotic abuse and limit its effects relocated to 362.2937

.294   *Hallucinogens and *psychedelics

Class here specific hallucinogens and psychedelics, e.g., LSD, mescaline, PCP

Class cannabis in 362.295

*Add as instructed under 362–363

.295   *Cannabis

>   Class here specific kinds of cannabis, e.g., hashish, marijuana

.296   *Tobacco

.298   *Cocaine [*formerly* 362.293]

>   Class here specific forms of cocaine, e.g., crack

.299   Other substances

>   Examples: analgesics, depressants, inhalants, sedatives, stimulants
>
>   Class here designer drugs (synthetic drugs of abuse), prescription drugs
>
>   Class alcohol in 362.292, designer hallucinogens in 362.294, cocaine in 362.298

.299 1   Specific aspects of more than one substance

>   Add to base number 362.2991 notation 1–8 from table under 362–363, e.g., prevention of abuse of uppers and downers 362.29717

.3   *Mental retardation

Class comprehensive works on treatment of mental retardation and mental illness in 362.2, on problems of and services to developmentally disabled people (those who have neurological diseases combined with mental retardation and whose problems exhibit themselves before age 18) in 362.1968

.36   Control of mental retardation

Including eugenic measures to reduce mental retardation

.4   Problems of and services to people with physical disabilities

Regardless of cause

Class here comprehensive works on problems of and services to people with disabilities, to people with mental and physical disabilities

Class problems of and services to people with mental disabilities in 362.3, comprehensive medical works in 617

.404   Special topics

>   Add to base number 362.404 notation 1–8 from table under 362–363, e.g., social work with people with physical disabilities 362.40453

.41   *Persons with impaired vision

Class here blind persons, blind-deaf persons

For deaf persons, see 362.42

.42   *Persons with impaired hearing

Class here deaf persons

Class comprehensive works on persons with linguistic and communication disabilities in 362.196855, blind-deaf persons in 362.41

See also 371.912 for teaching of the deaf

*Add as instructed under 362–363

.428 3   Direct relief

> Including provision of hearing aids [*formerly also* 362.63]

.43   *Persons with mobility impairment

> Subdivisions are added for services to persons with specific mobility impairments, e.g., residential care for paraplegics 362.4385

.5   ***Problems of and services to the poor**

> Class here services to homeless people

.51   Social causes

> Class economic causes in 339.46

.53   Social effects

> Class economic effects in 339.46

.57   Measures to prevent and limit effects of poverty

> Class economic measures to prevent poverty in 339, eugenic measures in 363.98

.58   Remedial measures, services, forms of assistance

> Class food stamp programs in 363.882, birth control as a remedy for poverty in 363.96, assistance to the poor under social security in 368.4

.582   Financial assistance

> Including guaranteed minimum income, negative income tax

> Class here supplementary social security for low income people

> Class aid to families with dependent children (AFDC) in 362.713

.583   Direct relief

> Class housing in 363.5, food programs in 363.8

.6   **Problems of and services to persons in late adulthood**

> Class here social gerontology

[.604]   Special topics

> Number and its subdivision for social gerontology discontinued; class in 362.6

.61   Residential (Institutional) care

> Class here services of homes, institutions providing complete care

> Class institutions providing residential care to medical patients in 362.16, housing in 363.5946

*Add as instructed under 362–363

.63   Direct relief

Including provision of financial aid, food, shelter, household assistance, clothing, recreation

Provision of hearing aids relocated to 362.4283

For residential care, see 362.61, employment services, 362.64

.64   Employment services

Including sheltered employment, vocational rehabilitation

.66   Counseling and guidance

.7   Problems of and services to young people

Through age 17

Class here children

[.704]   Special topics

Number and its subdivision for social aspects discontinued; class in 362.7

[.704 4]   Socially and economically handicapped, illegitimate, abandoned, abused and neglected children; orphans

Socially and economically handicapped children relocated to 362.7086; illegitimate children to 362.7086945; abandoned children, orphans to 362.73; abused and neglected children to 362.76

.708 3   Young people

Class here young men [*formerly* 362.792] and young women [*formerly* 362.793]

.708 6   Persons by social and economic characteristics

Class here socially and economically handicapped children [*formerly also* 362.7044]

[.708 692]   Maladjusted young people

Do not use; class in 362.74

.708 694 5   Illegitimate children [*formerly* 362.7044]

Class abandoned children, orphans in 362.73; abused and neglected children in 362.76

[.708 9]   Racial, ethnic, national groups

Do not use; class in 362.797

>   362.71–362.73 Specific kinds of services to young people

Class comprehensive works in 362.7, services to specific kinds of young people in 362.74–362.79

.71		Direct relief

Including recreational services

Protection for abused and neglected children relocated to 362.768

.712   Day care services

.713   Aid to families with dependent children (AFDC)

.73   Institutional and related services

Class here abandoned children, orphans [*both formerly* 362.7044]

.732   Institutional care

Examples: services of children's homes

Including houseparents

.733   Foster home care

Class here comprehensive works on foster home care and adoption

For adoption, see 362.734

.734   Adoption

Including confidentiality of adoption records

Class comprehensive works on the activities of adopted persons seeking their natural parents in 362.8298

>   362.74–362.79 Specific kinds of young people

Class comprehensive works in 362.7; abandoned children, orphans in 362.73

.74   Maladjusted young people

Including predelinquents, runaways

Class here specific services to maladjusted young people, halfway houses for young people who have not committed any crimes

Class mentally and emotionally ill young people in 362.2083, juvenile delinquents in 364.36, halfway houses for the transition from reform school to society in 365.42, families with missing children in 362.8297

.76   *Abused and neglected children [*formerly* 362.7044]

.768   Remedial measures, services, forms of assistance

Including protection for abused and neglected children [*formerly* 362.71]

.79   Classes of young people

Limited to classes listed below

Class maladjusted young people regardless of other characteristics in 362.74, specific services to specific classes of young people in 362.71–362.73

*Add as instructed under 362–363

[.792]	Young men
	Relocated to 362.7083
[.793]	Young women
	Relocated to 362.7083
[.795]	Children
	Use of this number discontinued; class in 362.7
.796	Young adults
	Ages 12 to 17
	Class city, rural, immigrant young adults in 362.799
.797	Young people of racial, ethnic, national groups

Add to base number 362.797 notation 03–99 from Table 5, e.g., young Afro-Americans 362.79796073

Class city and rural young people, immigrants of racial, ethnic, national groups in 362.799; young adults of racial, ethnic, national groups in 362.796

.799   City and rural youth, immigrants

Use of this number for miscellaneous classes discontinued; class in 362.7

.8   Problems of and services to other groups

.82   *Families

Specific problems not provided for here relocated to the specific problem, using 3 from table under 362–363, e.g., families with alcoholic members 362.2923

Family welfare when synonymous with general welfare is classed in 362

.828   Remedial measures, services, forms of assistance

Class services and forms of assistance for specific problems in 362.829, family planning programs in 363.96

.828 2   Financial assistance

Class aid to families with dependent children (AFDC) in 362.713

.828 3   Direct relief

Example: visiting housekeepers

Class day care in 362.712

.828 6   Counseling and guidance

Examples: premarital and marriage counseling

.829   Specific problems

Not provided for elsewhere

*Add as instructed under 362–363

.829 2	*Abuse within the family
	Class here parent, spouse abuse
	Class abused children in 362.76, abuse as a crime in 364.1555
.829 4	*Single-parent family
	Class here divorce
.829 5	*Parents in prison
.829 7	*Missing children
	Class here parental kidnapping
	Class runaway children in 362.74
.829 8	*Adoptees and biological parents
	Class adoption in 362.734; a specific aspect of children seeking their biological parents with the aspect, e.g., confidentiality of adoption records 362.734, genealogical searching 929.1
.83	*Women
	Class wife abuse in 362.8292, rape in 362.883
.839	Specific classes of women
.839 2	*Unmarried mothers
.84	Members of racial, ethnic, national groups
	Add to base number 362.84 notation 03–99 from Table 5, e.g., social services to Italians in the United States 362.8451073
.85	*Laboring classes
	Including migrant workers
.86	*Veterans
	Class here veterans' rights and benefits [*formerly also* 355.115]
.868	Remedial measures, services, forms of assistance
.868 2	Financial assistance
	Including financial assistance for education
	Class veterans' pensions in 331.2529
.87	*Victims of political oppression

*Add as instructed under 362–363

.88   Victims of crimes

Including crime prevention for the individual

Class here victimology

Class services to abused and neglected children in 362.76, services to abused family members in 362.8292, crime prevention for society as a whole in 364.4

.883   Rape

Including rape prevention for individuals

.9   **Historical, geographical, persons treatment**

Add to base number 362.9 notation 01–9 from Table 2, e.g., social welfare in France 362.944

Class historical, geographical, persons treatment of specific social problems in 362.1–362.8

363   Other social problems and services

Class here public works

Class communication facilities in 384, transportation facilities in 388

Standard subdivisions are added for comprehensive treatment of environmental and safety problems of society, e.g., assuring a safe and secure environment for Japan 363.0952

See Manual at 363; 363 vs. 340, 350–354; 364.1 vs. 362–363

SUMMARY

363.1	**Public safety programs**
.2	**Police services**
.3	**Other aspects of public safety**
.4	**Controversies related to public morals and customs**
.5	**Housing**
.6	**Public utilities and related services**
.7	**Environmental problems and services**
.8	**Food supply**
.9	**Population problems**

.1   Public safety programs

Class here safety measures [*formerly also* with the specific topic, using 75 from table under 362–363], interdisciplinary works on safety

Unless other instructions are given, observe the following table of precedence, e.g., use of hazardous materials in health care facilities 363.17 (*not* 363.15)

Hazardous materials	363.17
Hazards in sports and recreation	363.14
Transportation hazards	363.12
Hazardous machinery	363.18
Product hazards	363.19
Domestic hazards	363.13
Hazards in health care facilities	363.15
Occupational and industrial hazards	363.11

Class police services in 363.2, aspects of public safety not provided for here in 363.3; managerial response to safety requirements in 658.408, safety management in a specific industry with the industry, using notation 0684 from Table 1, e.g., safety management in petroleum industry 665.50684; a specific kind of remedial measure other than rescue operations with the measure, e.g., medical care for the injured 362.1; safety technology of a specific subject with the subject, using notation 0289 from Table 1, e.g., safety technology in hydraulic engineering 627.0289; comprehensive works on safety management in 658.408

See Manual at 363.1

SUMMARY

363.100 1–.105		**Standard subdivisions and general topics**
	.11	**Occupational and industrial hazards**
	.12	**Transportation hazards**
	.13	**Domestic hazards**
	.14	**Hazards in sports and recreation**
	.15	**Hazards in health care facilities**
	.17	**Hazardous materials**
	.18	**Hazardous machinery**
	.19	**Product hazards**

.100 1–.105   Standard subdivisions and general topics

Add to base number 363.10 notation 01–5 from table under 362–363, e.g., public action to promote safety 363.1056

.106   Public control of safety

.106 2   Standards

.106 3   Monitoring, surveillance, reporting

.106 4   Inspection and testing

.106 5	Investigation of specific incidents

Class here comprehensive works on safety investigation

Class technical or engineering aspects in 600, e.g., wreckage studies of automobile accidents 629.2826; accounts of specific incidents that affected general social life and history in 900, e.g., San Francisco earthquake 979.461051

See Manual at 363.1065; 363.34

.106 6	Certification
.107–.108	Prevention; remedial measures, services, forms of assistance

Add to base number 363.10 notation 7–8 from table under 362–363, e.g., alarm and warning systems 363.1072 [*formerly also* 384.7], counseling 363.1086

.11	*Occupational and industrial hazards
.119	Occupational and industrial hazards in specific industries and occupations

Add to base number 363.119 notation 001–999, e.g., hazards in coal mining 363.119622334; however, class hazards to transportation workers in 363.12, to domestic workers in 363.13, to professional athletes in 363.14, to workers in health care facilities in 363.15

.12	Transportation hazards

Class here accidents, fires resulting from accidents

Class transportation fires (e.g., fires caused by deficient electrical wiring in a railroad car) in 363.379

.120 01–.120 8	Standard subdivisions and general topics

Add to base number 363.120 notation 01–8 from table under 362–363, e.g., accident prevention 363.1207

.122	*Rail transportation
.123	*Water transportation

Class here water safety

Class safety in water sports in 363.14

.124	*Air and space transportation
.124 1	Causes of air and space accidents
.124 12	Natural factors

Examples: birds, clear-air turbulence (CAT)

.124 14	Operator failures
.124 16	Vehicle failures
.124 18	Failures of traffic control

Class traffic control as a preventive measure in 363.12472

*Add as instructed under 362–363

.124 65	Investigation of specific air and space accidents
	Class here general investigations of aircraft accidents
	Class wreckage studies in 629.13255
.124 9	Specific types of accidents and accidents in specific types of services
.124 92	Specific types of accidents
	Examples: midair collisions, takeoff accidents
.124 93	Accidents in specific types of services
	Examples: air-taxi services, helicopter services
	Class specific types of accidents in specific types of services in 363.12492
.125	*Highway and urban vehicular transportation
.125 1	Causes of accidents
	Examples: operator failures and disabilities, use of drugs, vehicle failures, highway and street conditions, weather conditions
.125 65	Investigation of specific vehicular and highway accidents
	Class here general investigations of automobile accidents
	Class wreckage studies in 629.2826
.125 9	Hazards in use of specific types of vehicles other than automobiles
	Examples: bicycles, motorcycles, trucks
.13	*Domestic hazards
.14	Hazards in *sports and *recreation
.15	*Hazards in health care facilities
.17	*Hazardous materials
	Manufacture, transportation, use
	Class here interdisciplinary works on hazardous materials, works on the control of such materials in their ordinary commercial setting (manufacture, sale, commercial and industrial use, disposal)
	Class hazardous materials as components of articles that become hazardous products in 363.19, as impurities in the water supply 363.61, as hazardous wastes in 363.728, as environmental pollutants in 363.738
	See Manual at 363.17; 363.176 vs. 604.7
.176 3	Monitoring, surveillance, reporting
	Class here studies on the applicability of both social and technical findings of environmental chemistry and additive toxicology to the monitoring of hazardous materials

*Add as instructed under 362–363

.179	Specific hazardous materials
	Example: corrosive materials
.179 1	Toxic chemicals
	Examples: asbestos, lead
	Class toxic agricultural chemicals in 363.1792
.179 2	*Agricultural chemicals
	Class here pesticides
.179 8	Explosives, fuels, related products

Class here safety considerations with respect to especially flammable materials, control of explosives as ordinary hazardous materials

Class control of use of explosives by potentially reckless or malign users in 363.33

See also 363.19 for products (e.g., sweaters, mattresses) that might constitute unsuspected fire hazards, 363.377 for measures to control accumulation of ordinary combustible materials

.179 9	*Radioactive materials

Class here nuclear accidents [*formerly also* 363.3497]

.18	*Hazardous machinery
.189	Specific kinds of hazardous machinery

Examples: electrical, x-ray equipment

.19	Product hazards

Adulteration, contamination, safety, adequacy, effectiveness of products offered for human consumption and use

Including household appliances, textiles, toys

Class here hazards due to containers and applicators that accompany products

.192	*Foods
.192 9	Specific foods

Examples: beverages, canned goods, dairy products, meats

.194	*Drugs and medicines
.196	*Cosmetics
.2	**Police services**

Class social service functions of police in 362, e.g., counseling of rape victims 362.883; police services in control of factors affecting public morals in 363.4

*Add as instructed under 362–363

SUMMARY

363.22	**Personnel**
.23	**Police functions**
.24	**Auxiliary services**
.25	**Detection of crime (Criminal investigation)**
.28	**Services of special kinds of security and law enforcement agencies**

[.206 8]   Management

> Do not use; class in 351.74

.22   Personnel

> Duties, functions, activities
>
> Class specific duties, functions, activities in 363.23–363.25

> 363.23–363.25 Specific aspects of police services

> Class comprehensive works in 363.2, specific aspects of services of special kinds of security and law enforcement agencies in 363.28

.23   Police functions

> Class here prevention of crime by police [*formerly also* 364.46], law enforcement
>
> *For detection of crime, see 363.25; control of violence and terrorism, 363.32*

.232   Patrol and surveillance

> Including pursuit and apprehension of lawbreakers, use of deadly force, undercover work
>
> *For highway patrol, see 363.2332*

.233   Enforcement of civil laws

> Example: enforcement of building codes, licensing laws and ordinances, sanitation laws

.233 2   Traffic control

> Including highway patrol
>
> Class comprehensive works on traffic control in 363.1256, investigation of traffic offenses in 363.25, wreckage studies in 629.2826

.233 6   Location of missing persons

.24   Auxiliary services

> Examples: communication services, photograph and fingerprint files, police records

.25   Detection of crime (Criminal investigation)

Class here forensic science (criminalistics); evidence, circumstantial evidence

For forensic medicine, see 614.1

See also 364.1 for criminal offenses

> 363.252–363.258 Specific techniques and kinds of evidence

Class comprehensive works in 363.25; comprehensive works on detection of a specific kind of offense in 362.259; detection of a specific offense in 364.1, e.g., detection of a murder in New York City 364.1523097471

> 363.252–363.256 Procurement and analysis of evidence

Class comprehensive works in 363.25, evidence used in identification of criminals not listed here in 363.258

.252   Procurement of evidence

Examples: electronic surveillance, search and seizure, use of informers and secret agents

For interrogation of witnesses, see 363.254

.254   Interrogation of witnesses

Including use of polygraph (lie detector)

.256   Analysis of evidence

Class here laboratories

Class files resulting from criminal investigations in 363.24

.256 2   Physical evidence

Examples: analysis of blood and hair, use of ballistics

.256 5   Documentary evidence

Including analysis of handwriting and typewriting

.258   Identification of criminals

Examples: artists' sketches, fingerprints, lineups, photographs, voice prints

Class files resulting from criminal investigations in 363.24

.259   Detection of specific types of offenses

Add to base number 363.259 the numbers following 364.1 in 364.13–364.18, e.g., investigation of murder 363.259523

Class specific techniques of investigation of specific types of offenses in 363.252–363.258; detection of a specific crime in 364.1, e.g., detection of a murder in New York City 364.1523097471

.28   Services of special kinds of security and law enforcement agencies

Example: park police

Class agencies to carry out specific police functions in 363.23, to investigate specific kinds of crime in 363.259, postal inspectors in 383.46

.282   Sheriffs and marshals

.283   Secret police

[.284]   Narcotics agents

Relocated to 363.45

.285   Border patrols

.286   Coast guards and harbor patrols

.287   Transportation security services

Class automobile traffic control in 363.2332

For harbor patrols, see 363.286

See also 363.379 for transportation fire hazards

.287 2   River security services

.287 4   Railway security services

.287 6   Air transportation security services

Examples: airport police, sky marshals

.289   Private detective and police services

Examples: body guards, campus police, store detectives

.3   Other aspects of public safety

See Manual at 363.1

.31   Censorship and control of information

Class here censorship and control of information as routine governmental functions

Class civil rights aspects in 323.445, legal aspects in 342.0853; censorship as an illicit governmental activity in 351.996

See Manual at 303.376 vs. 363.31, 791.4

.32   Control of violence and terrorism

Including quelling riots [*formerly also* 355.426], crowd control

.33   Control of explosives and firearms

Class here control of use by potentially reckless or malign users, comprehensive works on gun control

Class gun control as a civil rights issue in 323.43, control of explosives as ordinary hazardous materials in 363.1798

.34 *Disasters

Class a specific kind of remedial measure other than those applied immediately at the time and site of the disaster with the subject, e.g., medical care for the injured 362.1; disasters treated as historical events in 900

.348 Rescue and salvage operations

Forms of assistance applied immediately at the time and site of the disaster

Class here comprehensive works on disaster relief, rescue and salvage operations for disasters in general

Class a specific form of disaster relief not provided for here with the relief, e.g., long-range planning to replace housing lost due to a volcanic eruption 363.58; disaster relief, rescue and salvage operations for specific types of disasters with the type, using subdivision 81 from the table under 362–363, e.g., rescue operations for flood victims 363.349381; raising funds for mounting and carrying out the disaster relief in 363.34570681

.349 Specific kinds of disasters

Class epidemics, pandemics in 362.1; fires in 363.37

Specific kinds of disasters resulting from one of the hazards listed in 363.1 are classed with the hazard, e.g., shipwrecks 363.123, transportation accidents in 363.12, nuclear accidents 363.1799

.349 2 Disasters caused by weather conditions

Examples: hurricanes, snowstorms, tornadoes

For floods, see 363.3493

.349 3 *Floods

.349 36 Control of floods

Class technology of flood control in 627.4

.349 5 Earthquakes and volcanic eruptions

.349 7 Disasters induced by human activity

Examples: civil disorders, explosions, riots

Nuclear accidents relocated to 363.1799

For transportation accidents, see 363.119; war, 363.3498

.349 8 *War

For civil defense, see 363.35

See also 303.66 for sociology of war

[.349 87] Measures to prevent, protect against, limit effects of war

Do not use; class in 327.17

*Add as instructed under 362–363

.349 88	War relief

Class problems of war refugees when not treated directly in the context of the war in 362.87; war relief during a specific war with the war, e.g., relief work of Germany during World War I 940.477843

.35	Civil defense

Measures to defend civilian populations only against war

.37	*Fire hazards

Class fire fighting and fire safety technology in 628.92

.377	Fire prevention

Class here measures to control accumulation of ordinary combustible materials

Class safety considerations with respect to especially flammable materials in 363.1798, safety of products (e.g., sweaters, mattresses) that might constitute unsuspected fire hazards in 363.19

.378	Fire extinction and related services
.378 1	Rescue operations
.379	Fire hazards in specific situations

Examples: in transportation, in schools, in high-rise buildings

Including forest fires

.4	**Controversies related to public morals and customs**

Treated as social problems

Class censorship and control of information in 363.31; a controversy treated other than as a social issue with the aspect of the controversy, e.g., ethics of gambling 174.6 (*not* 363.42)

.41	Sale of alcoholic beverages

Class problems of and services to alcoholics in 362.292, sale of alcoholic beverages as an offense against revenue in 364.133, public drunkenness as an offense in 364.173

.42	Gambling

Class compulsive gambling in 362.25, gambling as a crime in 364.172

.44	Prostitution

Class prostitution as a crime in 364.1534

*Add as instructed under 362–363

| .45 | Drug traffic |

Class here narcotics agents [*formerly also* 363.284]

Class problems of and services to drug addicts in 362.29, illegal sale, possession, use of drugs in 364.177

See also 363.41 for sale of alcoholic beverages

| .46 | Abortion |

Class abortion as a crime in 364.185

| .47 | Obscenity and pornography |

Class obscenity and pornography as crimes in 364.174

| .48 | Pre- and extramarital relations |

Class pre- and extramarital relations as crimes in 364.153

For prostitution, see 363.44

| .49 | Homosexuality |

Class interdisciplinary works in 306.766, homosexuality as a crime in 364.1536

| .5 | ***Housing** |

Class here interdisciplinary works on housing, housing as a social problem

Class a specific aspect of housing with the subject, e.g., sociological aspects 307.336, economic aspects 333.338, provision of temporary housing (shelter) 361.05

See Manual at 307.336 vs. 307.34, 363.5; 363.5, 363.6, 363.8 vs. 338; 643.1 vs. 363.5

| [.508] | Housing of specific kinds of persons |

Do not use; class in 363.59

| .51 | Housing conditions |

Including discrimination in housing

Class housing allocation to relieve discrimination in 363.55

| [.52] | Incidence, extent, severity of housing problems |

Do not use; class in 363.51

| .55 | Social action with respect to housing |

Class here housing allocation to relieve discrimination

| .58 | Programs and services |

Do not use subdivisions of 8 from the table under 362–363

| .582 | Financial assistance |

Class here housing allowances, rental subsidies, subsidized housing

*Add as instructed under 362–363

.583 Programs and services for specific objectives

    Examples: home ownership, payment of energy bills, rehabilitation, resettlement, urban homesteading, weatherization

.585 Public operated housing

    Class here council housing

.59 Housing of specific classes of people

    Add to base number 363.59 the numbers following —08 in notation 081–089 from Table 1, e.g., housing for persons in late adulthood 363.5946; however, class extended medical care for older adults in 362.16, comprehensive works on homelessness in 362.5, institutional care for healthy older adults in 362.61, specific aspects of housing the poor or low-income housing in 363.51–363.58

[.590 8] Housing of specific kinds of persons

    Do not use; class in 363.59

.6 Public utilities and related services

    Class here problems of allocation among end users, measures to assure abundance of immediately available supplies and services

    Class communication in 384, transportation in 388

    See Manual at 363.5, 363.6, 363.8 vs. 338; 363.6 vs. 333.7

.61 Water supply

    Class here comprehensive works on water supply, on water-related public works, e.g., a study covering waterworks, treatment plants, canals, flood control, hydroelectric generation

    Class a specific topic with the subject, e.g., flood control 363.34936

    See Manual at 363.61

[.62] Electrical utilities

    Relocated to 333.7932

.63 Gas

.68 Park and recreation services

    Class here services maintained or proposed after land has been designated for parks, establishment and operation of recreational centers primarily serving the general public

    Class park policy and park development in 333.783; recreational centers in 790.068; a specific cultural institution maintained by park and recreation services with the institution, e.g., museums 069, theaters 792

.69   Historic preservation

Including identification and designation of historic buildings and areas

Class here public policies to protect and restore historic buildings and areas and to promote appreciation of them

Class technology of building restoration and preservation in 721.0288

.7   **Environmental problems and services**

Class here environmental protection; impact of wastes, of pollution, of actions to control waste and pollution

Class comprehensive works on the environment in 333.7; impacts on specific environments or resources with the impact, e.g., economic impact on Rome of a major new waste treatment facility 330.945632, impact of the same treatment plant on the waters of the Tiber River 333.916214094562; projected impacts with the program or development that is being studied, e.g., projected impact of proposed standards for water pollution 363.739462

See Manual at 363.7 vs. 333.72, 304.28

SUMMARY

363.700 1–.707 2	**Standard subdivisions and general topics**
.72	**Sanitation problems and services**
.73	**Pollution**
.74	**Noise**
.75	**Disposal of the dead**
.78	**Pest control**

.700 1–.707 2   Standard subdivisions and general topics

Add to base number 363.70 notation 01–72 from table under 362–363, e.g., international action to protect the environment 363.70526

.72   *Sanitation problems and services

Use of subdivisions 1–7 from table under 362–363 for specific wastes discontinued; class in 363.72

.728   Waste disposal

Class here industrial, municipal wastes; waste management

Unless other instructions are given, class complex subjects with aspects in two or more subdivisions of 363.728 in the one coming last, e.g., recycling scrap metal 363.7288 (*not* 363.7282)

Class dangerous wastes still in hands of processors or users in 363.17, pollution by waste disposal in 363.73, dangerous wastes which have escaped both safety and sanitary controls in 363.738

.728 2   Recycling

See Manual at 363.61

*Add as instructed under 362–363

.728 4	*Liquid wastes
	Examples: combined sewage, sewage sludge, urban water runoff
	Including dredging spoil, waste-water irrigation, water reuse planning
	Class here waste-water management
	See Manual at 363.61
.728 5	*Solid wastes
.728 7	*Hazardous wastes
.728 8	Specific kinds of wastes
	Examples: agricultural wastes, automobiles, beverage containers, garbage, household wastes, papers, pesticides, plastics, scrap metal
	For radioactive wastes, see 363.7289
	See Manual at 628.44042 vs. 363.7388, 628.445
.728 9	*Radioactive wastes
.729	Sanitation in specific environments
.729 1	Streets
.729 2	Recreational areas
	Example: swimming pools
.729 3	Public carriers
.729 4	Public toilets
.729 5	In work places
.729 6	In food service establishments
.729 7	In health facilities
	Including ambulances
.729 8	In residential buildings
	Other than private family dwellings
.729 9	In barbershops, beauty shops, laundries
.73	*Pollution

Class sanitation in 363.72, noise in 363.74, technology of pollution prevention in 628.5, management responsibilities and measures with respect to protection and preservation of the environment in 658.408

Works that discuss waste and sanitation problems as well as subdivisions of 363.73 are classed in 363.7

See Manual at 574.5222 vs. 574.24, 363.73

*Add as instructed under 362–363

.731	Sources of pollution

Examples: agriculture, industry, transportation, domestic and recreational activities

Class specific pollutants from specific sources in 363.738

.732	Incidence, extent, severity

Class incidence, extent, severity of pollution from specific sources in 363.731

.735	Social action

Class here remedial measures

.737	Measures to prevent, protect against, limit effects of pollution

Class waste disposal as a method of pollution prevention in 363.728

.738	Pollutants

Class here specific pollutants in specific environments [*formerly* 363.739], chemical pollutants

Do not use for remedial measures; class in 363.735

.738 2	Oil
.738 4	Toxic chemicals

Including lead emissions, pesticides

Use of this number for comprehensive works on chemical pollutants discontinued; class in 363.738

.738 6	*Acid precipitation
.738 7	Smoke, gas, fumes

Class lead emissions in 363.7384

.739	Pollution of specific environments

Specific pollutants in specific environments relocated to 363.738

.739 2	*Air pollution
.739 4	*Water pollution

Class here comprehensive works on water pollution

Class assurance of clean water supply in 363.61

See Manual at 363.61; 628.168 vs. 363.7394

.739 46	Control

Class here abatement programs [*formerly also* 628.1688]

.739 6	*Soil pollution

*Add as instructed under 362–363

.74   *Noise

.741   Sources of noise

Examples: forms of transportation, e.g., aircraft, automobile traffic; construction equipment, industry

Class effects of specific sources of noise in 363.742

.742   Incidence, extent, severity

Class incidence, extent, severity of noise from specific sources in 363.741

.75   Disposal of the dead

Social aspects and services

Class death customs in 393, technology of disposal of the dead in 614.6

.78   Pest control

Including dog pounds, removal of animal carcasses, rat and mosquito abatement programs

Class here interdisciplinary works on pest control

Class comprehensive works on the technology of pest control in 628.96, control of disease-carrying pests in 614.43, of agricultural pests in 632.9, of household pests in 648.7

.8   *Food supply

Class here hunger, famine; interdisciplinary works on food supply, on nutrition

Class economics of food supply in 338.19

Food stamp programs are classed in 363.882, food relief in 363.883

See also 362.19639 for problems of malnutrition, 614.5939 for prevention of malnutrition

See Manual at 363.5, 363.6, 363.8 vs. 338; 363.8 vs. 338.19; 613.2 vs. 641.3, 363.8; 614.5939 vs. 363.82

.856   Public action on food supply

Class here food rationing

.9   Population problems

Class here interdisciplinary works on population problems

Class interdisciplinary works on population in 304.6; works on specific manifestations of a population problem with the manifestation, e.g., pressure on food supply leading to famine 363.8, population growth as a cause of poverty 362.51

See Manual at 301 vs. 361–365; 304.66 vs. 363.9

.91   Population quantity [*formerly also* 304.664]

Overpopulation [*formerly also* 304.65] and underpopulation

Class remedial measures for overpopulation in 363.96

*Add as instructed under 362–363

.92   Population quality [*formerly also* 304.662]

Class here interdisciplinary works on eugenics

Class eugenic measures to control population in 363.98, to reduce crime in 364.4; application of eugenics to a specific social problem with the problem using subdivision 6 from table under 362–363, e.g., eugenic measures to reduce mental retardation 362.36; other specific aspects of eugenics with the aspect, e.g., civil rights 323.4

See also 613.94 for family planning techniques

.96   Birth control

Class here interdisciplinary works on birth control, on family planning programs

Class abortion in 363.46, family planning techniques in 613.94

For sterilization, see 363.97

See Manual at 304.66 vs. 363.9

.97   Sterilization

Including eugenic and involuntary sterilization

Class here voluntary sterilization

.98   Eugenic measures to control population

Class sterilization in 363.97

364   Criminology

Crime and its alleviation

Class here comprehensive works on criminology and criminal law, on criminal justice that includes criminology, police services, and criminal law

Class social services to victims of crimes and self-protection from criminals in 362.88

Unless other instructions are given, observe the following table of precedence, e.g., punishment of specific types of offenders 364.6 (*not* 364.3)

Penology	364.6
Discharged offenders	364.8
Offenders	364.3
Prevention of crime and delinquency	364.4
Causes of crime and delinquency	364.2
Criminal offenses	364.1
Historical, geographical, persons treatment of crime and its alleviation	364.9

For criminal law, see 345

SUMMARY

364.01–.09	**Standard subdivisions**
.1	**Criminal offenses**
.2	**Causes of crime and delinquency**
.3	**Offenders**
.4	**Prevention of crime and delinquency**
.6	**Penology**
.8	**Discharged offenders**
.9	**Historical, geographical, persons treatment of crime and its alleviation**

.019   Psychological principles

> Class criminal psychology of offenders in generalin 364.3, of specific offenses in 364.1

.04   Special topics

.042   Extent and incidence of crime

> Class criminal offenses in 364.1, offenders in 364.3

> Criminal offenses and offenders

[.08]   Treatment with respect to kinds of persons

> Do not use; class victimology in 362.88, victims of specific crimes in 364.1, offenders in 364.3

.09   Historical, geographical, persons treatment of criminology as a discipline

> Class historical, geographical, persons treatment of crime and its alleviation in 364.9

.1   **Criminal offenses**

> Class here conspiracy to and incitement to commit an offense, individuals identified with a specific offense or type of offense, investigation of specific crimes, crimes without victims, terrorism as a crime

> Class sociology of terrorism in 303.625, investigation of specific types of offenses in 363.259, crime as an event in history in 900

> *See Manual at 364.1 vs. 362–363*

SUMMARY

364.101–.109	**[Standard subdivisions, organized crime]**
.13	**Political and related offenses**
.14	**Offenses against public health, safety, order**
.15	**Offenses against persons**
.16	**Offenses against property**
.17	**Offenses against public morals**
.18	**Miscellaneous offenses**

.106	Organized crime

Class here Mafia

Class organizations dealing with criminal offenses in 364.06

[.106 092]	Persons treatment

Do not use; class organized crime figures not associated with a specific offense in 364.1092, those associated with a specific offense with the offense, e.g., hired killers 364.15230922

.106 6	Gangsterism

Engagement of organized groups in piracy, robbery, theft, hijacking

Class interdisciplinary works on and sociology of gangs in 302.34

.106 7	Racketeering

Engagement of organized groups in extortion from legitimate or illegitimate enterprises through intimidation and force

Including union racketeering

.106 8	Syndicated crime

Engagement of organized groups in furnishing illegal goods or services

.109 2	Persons treatment

Criminals are classed with the crime for which they are most noted unless they are discussed with relationship to a specific crime, e.g., a general biography of Jesse James, a bank robber, is classed in 364.1552092, but a study of Jesse James' killings is classed in 364.1523092

Class comprehensive works on offenders in 364.3

.13	Political and related offenses
.131	Political offenses

Examples: espionage, rebellion, seditious libel, subversion, treason

Sabotage relocated to 364.164

Class genocide in 364.151, assassination of heads of state and government in 364.1524, industrial sabotage in 364.164

For war crimes, see 364.138

.132	Offenses against proper government

For offenses against administration of justice, see 364.134

.132 2	Violation and denial of civil rights
.132 3	Corruption

Examples: graft, bribery of officials

.132 4	Electoral offenses

Examples: bribery of voters, fraudulent reporting of votes, illegal voting, violations of campaign finance laws

.133	Offenses against revenue
	Examples: bootlegging, counterfeiting, illicit distilling, smuggling, tax evasion
	See also 363.41 for sale of alcoholic beverages
.134	Offenses against administration of justice
	Examples: collusion, contempt of court, lynching, perjury, subornation of perjury
.135	International offenses
	Class a specific type of international offense with the subject, e.g., piracy 364.164
.136	Offenses against postal laws
.138	War crimes
	Class specific kinds of war crimes with the kind, e.g., genocide 364.151
	See also 341.69 for war crime trials
.14	Offenses against public health, safety, order
	Use 364.14001–364.14009 for standard subdivisions
.142	Against public health and safety
	Examples: adulteration of food and drugs, violations of product and building safety laws
.143	Against public order
	Examples: carrying concealed weapons, disorderly conduct, rioting, unlawful assembly
.147	Traffic offenses and misuse of communications facilities
	Class offenses against postal laws in 364.136
.148	Vagrancy
.15	Offenses against persons
.151	Genocide
.152	Homicide
	For lynching, see 364.134; genocide, 364.151
.152 2	Suicide
	Class assisting suicide in 364.1523
.152 3	Murder
	Including assisting suicide
	For assassination, see 364.1524
.152 4	Assassination

.152 5	Manslaughter
.153	Sex offenses

Examples: adultery, indecent exposure, seduction, statutory rape

Class rape in 364.1532, bigamy in 364.183

.153 2	Rape

Class social services aspects of rape in 362.883

See also 364.153 for statutory rape

.153 4	Prostitution

See also 363.44 for prostitution as a public morals issue

.153 6	Sexual deviations

Examples: incest, sodomy

.154	Kidnapping, abduction, taking and holding of hostages

Class parental kidnapping in 362.8297

.155	Other violent offenses against persons
.155 2	Robbery

Thefts including threat of violence or bodily harm, or actual occurrence of violence

Class here comprehensive works on hijacking

Class a specific type of hijacking with the type, e.g., taking hostages 364.154

.155 5	Assault and battery
.155 53	Spouse abuse

Class social services to battered wives, spouse abuse as a social problem in 362.8292

.155 54	Child abuse

Class child abuse as a social problem in 362.76

.156	Offenses against reputation and honor

Examples: defamation, libel, slander, invasion of privacy

Class seditious libel in 364.131

.16	Offenses against property
.162	Larceny (Theft)

Examples: burglary, embezzlement

Including fencing

Class robbery in 364.1552, fraud in 364.163

.163   Fraud

> Including forgery, imposture, e.g., literary forgery; welfare fraud, e.g., Medicare fraud

.164   Violent offenses against property

> Examples: sabotage [*formerly also* 364.131], arson, piracy, vandalism

> Class robbery, comprehensive works on hijacking in 364.1552

.165   Extortion and blackmail

.168   Business, financial, professional offenses

> Examples: criminal usury, unfair trade practices; violation of antitrust laws, of laws respecting securities and their exchange

> Class here computer, white-collar crime

> Class a specific type of computer crime not provided for here with the subject, e.g., tax evasion 364.133

> *For embezzlement, see 364.162; fraud, 364.163*

.17   Offenses against public morals

> *For sex offenses, see 364.153*

.172   Gambling

> *See also 363.42 for gambling as a public morals question*

.173   Public drunkenness

> *See also 363.41 for sale of alcoholic beverages*

.174   Obscenity and pornography

> *See also 363.47 for obscenity and pornography as a public morals question*

.177   Illegal sale, possession, use of drugs

> *See also 363.45 for drug traffic*

.18   Other offenses

> Example: illegal adoption

.183   Bigamy

.185   Criminal abortion

> Class abortion as a public morals question in 363.46

.187   Cruelty to animals

.188   Offenses against religion

> Offenses defined and penalized by the state

> Examples: blasphemy, heresy, sacrilege, witchcraft

> Class offenses against church law in 262.9

.2	**Causes of crime and delinquency**

Class here criminal anthropology

Class victimology in 362.88

.22   Influence of physical environment

Examples: climate, seasons, weather

.24   Influence of personal factors

Contains biological factors, e.g., effects of heredity, genetic defects, physical typology; psychological factors

.25   Influence of social factors

Including leisure and recreation

.253   Influence of family and peer groups

.254   Influence of communications media

Examples: books, motion pictures, radio, television

.256   Influence of social conflicts

Examples: class, race, religion, socioeconomic conditions

.3   **Offenders**

Class here criminal psychology

Class individuals chiefly identified with a specific offense or type of offense in 364.1; a specific aspect of the justice system for specific types of offenders with the aspect, e.g., determination of sentences for juvenile offenders 364.650835, offenders as prisoners in 365.6

[.308 1]   Men

Do not use; class in 364.373

[.308 2]   Women

Do not use; class in 364.374

[.308 3]   Young people

Do not use; class in 364.36

[.308 75]   Mentally ill and mentally handicapped persons

Do not use; class in 364.38

[.308 9]   Members of specific racial, ethnic, national groups

Do not use; class in 364.34

.34   Members of specific racial, ethnic, national groups

Add to base number 364.34 notation 03–9 from Table 5, e.g., Germans as offenders 364.3431

Class juvenile delinquents of specific racial, ethnic, national groups in 364.36, women in 364.374, mentally ill and mentally handicapped offenders in 364.38

.36   Juvenile delinquents

Including status offenders (juveniles who have broken laws pertaining only to their age group, e.g., curfew laws, drinking below legal age)

Class here comprehensive works on juvenile delinquency, juvenile delinquents, juvenile justice system

.37   Adult offenders

Class mentally ill and mentally handicapped adult offenders in 364.38

.373   Men

Works specifically emphasizing male sex

.374   Women

.38   Mentally ill and mentally handicapped offenders

Class mentally ill and mentally handicapped juvenile offenders in 364.36

.4   Prevention of crime and delinquency

What society does to prevent crime

Examples: curfew, eugenic measures

Class law enforcement in 363.23; penalties as a deterrent in 364.601; a specific aspect of prevention by a potential victim with the aspect, e.g., what the individual can do 362.88, household security 643.16, business intelligence and security 658.47

.404   Special topics

.404 5   Social action

Add to base number 364.4045 the numbers following 361 in 361.2–361.8, e.g., social policy 364.404561

.41   Identification of potential offenders

Including genetic screening

.43   Citizen participation

Class individual action in 362.88

.44	Welfare services

Examples: financial assistance, foster home care; recreational services, e.g., camps, playgrounds

Class preventive police work in 363.23

For counseling and guidance, see 364.48

[.46] Prevention of crime by police

Relocated to 363.23

.48 Counseling and guidance

.49 Environmental design

.6 Penology

Treatment and punishment of offenders

Class here welfare services to offenders, reform of penal system

Class welfare services to prisoners in 365.66, reform of penal institutions in 365.7

For institutions for correction of offenders, see 365; discharged offenders, 364.8

.601 Philosophy and theory

Class here punishment as retribution, deterrent, protection to society, reformation of offenders

.62 Parole and indeterminate sentence

Standard subdivisions are added for parole and indeterminate sentence, for parole alone

Class services to prisoners to prepare them for parole in 365.66

.63 Probation and suspended sentence

Standard subdivisions are added for probation and suspended sentence, for probation and parole, for probation alone

Including reprieve

Class here comprehensive works on probation and parole

For parole, see 364.62

.65 Determination of sentence

Including commutation of sentence, pardon, amnesty

Class a specific punishment with the subject, e.g., imprisonment 365, probation 364.63

.66 Capital punishment

.67 Corporal punishment

.68   Noninstitutional penalties

> Examples: community service, deportation, fines, loss of citizenship, loss of vote

> *For capital punishment, see 364.66; corporal punishment, 364.67*

.8   Discharged offenders

.9   Historical, geographical, persons treatment of crime and its alleviation

> Add to base number 364.9 notation 01–9 from Table 2, e.g., persons associated with crime and its alleviation 364.92

> Class victims in 362.88, police in 363.2, criminologists in 364.092, offenders associated with specific kinds of crime in 364.1, comprehensive works on offenders in 364.3, penologists in 364.6

365   Penal and related institutions

> Institutions for correction of offenders and for incarceration of other groups considered socially undesirable

> Class here imprisonment and detention

> Unless other instructions are given, class complex subjects with aspects in two or more subdivisions of this schedule in the number coming last in the schedule, e.g., maximum security prisons for women 365.43 (*not* 365.33)

> Class parole and indeterminate sentence in 364.62, probation and suspended sentence in 364.63

SUMMARY

365.3	**Kinds of penal institutions**
.4	**Institutions for specific classes of inmates**
.5	**Prison plant**
.6	**Inmates**
.7	**Reform of penal institutions**
.9	**Historical, geographical, persons treatment**

[.068 2]   Plant management

> Do not use; class in 365.5

[.09]   Historical, geographical, persons treatment

> Do not use; class in 365.9

.3   Kinds of penal institutions

> Class specific institutions in 365.93–365.99

.32   By level of government

> National, state or provincial, local

.33   By degree of security

> Maximum, medium, minimum

.34   By purpose or type of program

Examples: jails, penitentiaries, penal colonies, prerelease guidance centers, prison farms, reformatories, work camps

Concentration camps relocated to 365.45

Class penal colonies as a part of history of a place in 930–990, e.g., penal colony of Botany Bay as founding settlement of New South Wales 994.402

.4   Institutions for specific classes of inmates

Example: debtors' prisons

Class here personal narratives of inmates

Class comprehensive works on inmates in 365.6, specific institutions in 365.93–365.99

.42   For juveniles

Examples: borstals, reformatories; industrial, reform, training schools; halfway houses for the transition from reform school to society

.43   For adult women

.44   For adult men

Works specifically emphasizing inmates of the male sex

Class institutions in general, specific kinds of institutions for men in 365.3

.45   For political prisoners and related classes of persons

Class here concentration camps [*formerly* 365.34]

Class concentration camps associated with a specific war with the war, e.g., World War II concentration camps 940.5317

.46   For the criminally insane

.48   Military prisons and prison camps

Institutions whose inmates are military personnel

Class institutions for prisoners of war in 355.1296, military institutions for the insane in 365.46

.5   Prison plant

Grounds, buildings, equipment

Class prison architecture in 725.6

.6   Inmates

Former heading: Prison economy

Handling and treatment

Including reception and classification

Class here offenders as inmates; community-based corrections; social aspects of prison life, e.g., conjugal rights, drug abuse

Class institutions for specific classes of inmates, personal narratives of inmates in 365.4

.602 1   Tabulated and related materials

Class statistics of inmates when used to indicate general statistics of offenders in 364.3021

.609 2   Persons

Class personal narratives of inmates in 365.4, using notation 092 from Table 1

.64   Security, discipline, daily routine

Class here treatment of inmates

.641   Security

Including escapes, riots, disturbances

.643   Discipline

Rules, rights, privileges

Including furloughs

Class work furloughs in 365.65

For punishments, see 365.644

.644   Punishments for infractions of prison discipline

.646   Daily routine

Including hours, meals

Recreational services relocated to 365.66

For labor, see 365.65; services to prisoners, 365.66

.647   Release and discharge

Class work release in 365.65, services to prepare prisoners for release in 365.66

.65   Labor

Examples: chain gangs, contract system, lease system, work furloughs, work release

.66   Services to prisoners

Examples: recreational services [*formerly also* 365.646], counseling, education, group therapy, health services, prerelease programs, rehabilitation, religious services

Class prerelease institutions in 365.34

.7   **Reform of penal institutions**

Class reform of penal system, reform to eliminate prisons as form of punishment for certain types of crimes in 364.6

.9   **Historical, geographical, persons treatment**

Add to base number 365.9 notation 01–9 from Table 2, e.g., prison administrators 365.92; however, class inmates in 365.4092

Class specific aspects of penal institutions in specific times and places, of specific kinds of institutions in 365.3–365.7

366   Association

Organizations formed for fraternizing or for mutual assistance

Use 366.001–366.009 for standard subdivisions

Class associations dealing with a specific subject with the subject, using notation 06 from Table 1, e.g., mathematical associations 510.6

For general clubs, see 367; miscellaneous kinds of associations, 369

See also 200 for religious associations, 368.363 for fraternal insurance

.01–.09   Standard subdivisions of esoteric associations and societies

---

>   **366.1–366.5 Esoteric (Secret and semisecret) associations and societies**

Class comprehensive works in 366

For orders of knighthood, see 929.71

.1   **Freemasonry**

.12   Rituals

.16   Nobles of the Mystic Shrine (Shriners)

.17   Order of DeMolay

.18   Women in Freemasonry

Including Order of the Eastern Star, Job's Daughters, Order of the Rainbow

.2   **Knights of Pythias**

.3   **Independent Order of Odd Fellows**

.38   International Association of Rebekah Assemblies

Former heading: Daughters of Rebekah

.5   **Benevolent and Protective Order of Elks**

367   General clubs

Examples: social clubs, study clubs

Class here social clubs for specific types of people, e.g., social clubs for actors

Class clubs dealing with a specific subject with the subject, using notation 06 from Table 1, e.g., pinochle clubs 795.41606

[.09]   Historical, geographical, persons treatment

Do not use; class in 367.9

.9   **Historical, geographical, persons treatment**

Add to base number 367.9 notation 01–99 from Table 2, e.g., The Lamb (social club in New York City composed chiefly of actors, musicians, and playwrights) 367.97471

368   Insurance

Class here production economics of insurance industry [*formerly* 338]; comprehensive works on insurance industry, on risk

Class credit and loan functions of insurance companies in 332.38, risk management in 658.155

See also 658.153 for managerial decisions on choosing insurance

SUMMARY

368.001–.009	**Standard subdivisions**
.01–.09	**[Finance, specific forms of risk, sales groupings]**
.1	**Insurance against damage to and loss of property**
.2	**Insurance against damage to and loss of property in transit (Marine insurance, Transportation insurance)**
.3	**Insurance against death, old age, illness, injury**
.4	**Government-sponsored insurance**
.5	**Liability insurance**
.6	**Glass insurance**
.7	**Insurance against industrial casualties (accidents)**
.8	**Other casualty insurance**
.9	**Insurance by specific continents, countries, localities in modern world**

.001   Philosophy and theory

[.001 51]   Mathematical principles

Relocated to 368.01

.002–.005   Standard subdivisions

.006   Organizations and management

.006 5		Insurance companies

Class here interdisciplinary works on insurance companies

Add to base number 368.0065 notation 4–9 from Table 2, e.g., insurance companies of Texas 368.0065764

Class credit and loan functions of insurance companies in 332.38

.007–.008   Standard subdivisions

.009   Historical, geographical, persons treatment

Class treatment by specific continents, countries, localities in modern world in 368.9

.01   Finance

Expenses, profitability, reserves

Class here mathematical principles [*formerly* 368.00151], actuarial science

Class investments by insurance companies in 332.67154

.011   Rates and rate making

.012   Underwriting

Risk selection and estimation

.012 2   Reinsurance

.014   Claims

Including adjustment of claims, settlement of losses, fraudulent claims

Class fraudulent claims, insurance fraud as crimes in 364.163

[.015]   Finance

Number discontinued; class in 368.01

.016   Lapsation, persistence, termination

.019   Government policies with respect to insurance, insurance industry

---

>   368.06–368.08 Specific forms of risk

Class comprehensive works in 368

.06   Property risks

Risk of loss from impairment or destruction of property

Class risk of consequential loss in 368.08

.062   Risks to tangible property

.063   Risks to intangible property

.07   Personal risks

Risk of loss of income or augmented expenditure due to hazards to the person

.08	Other risks

Examples: liability risks, risk of consequential loss, risks due to the failure of others, statutory liability risks

.09	Conventional comprehensive sales groupings

Combinations of different lines of insurance, e.g., property-casualty, property-casualty-life and health

Class here all-risk, multiple-line coverage

Class one line of insurance with the line, e.g., homeowner's liability insurance 368.56

.092	Automobile insurance
.093	Aviation insurance

See also 368.24 for air transportation insurance as a branch of inland marine insurance

.096	Multi-peril real property insurance

Coverage of perils associated with land and whatever is growing on or affixed to it

Class here homeowner's insurance

> **368.1–368.8 Specific kinds of insurance**

Add to the notation for each term identified by * as follows:
001–005	Standard subdivisions
006	Organizations and management
0065	Insurance companies

Add to 0065 notation 4–9 from Table 2, e.g. insurance companies in Great Britain 06541
007–009	Standard subdivisions
01	General principles

Add to 01 the numbers following 368.01 in 368.011–368.019, e.g., underwriting 012

Class comprehensive works in 368

.1	***Insurance against damage to and loss of property**

Class property damage (liability) insurance with the specific type of liability insurance, e.g., property damage insurance as part of public liability 368.56

For transportation insurance, see 368.2; casualty insurance, 368.5–368.8

.11	***Fire insurance**

For extended coverage endorsement, see 368.129

See also 368.12 for allied fire insurance lines

*Add as instructed under 368.1–368.8

.12   *Allied fire insurance lines and extended coverage endorsement

               Perils and losses traditionally associated with fire insurance

               Including crop insurance

               See Manual at 368.12

.122   *Disaster insurance

               Against damage and loss from floods, earthquakes, storms

.125   *Riot and civil commotion insurance

.129   *Extended coverage endorsement

.14   *War risk insurance

               Class ocean marine war risk insurance in 368.22, war risk life insurance in 368.364

.2   *Insurance against damage to and loss of property in transit (Marine insurance, Transportation insurance)

               Including postal insurance

               Class here insurance against damage to and loss of instrumentalities of transportation

               Class a combination of transportation property insurance and transportation liability insurance in 368.09

.22   *Ocean marine insurance

               Over-the-sea transportation insurance

               Including ocean marine war risk insurance

.23   *Inland marine insurance

               Land or over-the-land (including over inland waterways) transportation insurance

               For air transportation insurance, see 368.24

.232   *Automobile insurance

               Including bus, truck insurance

               Class comprehensive works on all types of automobile insurance in 368.092

.233   *Railroad insurance

.24   *Air transportation insurance

               Class comprehensive works on all types of air transportation and aviation insurance in 368.093

*Add as instructed under 368.1–368.8

.3 ***Insurance against death, old age, illness, injury**

Class here comprehensive works on insurance for the aged, group insurance, industrial insurance, survivors' insurance

Class comprehensive works on insurance as a fringe benefit in 331.255, personnel administration of insurance in 658.3254

For government-sponsored insurance, see 368.4

.32 *Life insurance

Class here endowment insurance

For special fields of life insurance, see 368.36

.36 Special fields of life insurance

.362 *Industrial life insurance

.363 *Fraternal insurance

.364 *Life insurance for members of armed services

Examples: National Service Life Insurance, war risk life insurance

Including veterans' life insurance

.37 *Annuities

Class comprehensive works on pensions in 331.252, pensions as an element of personnel administration in 658.3253

.375 *Variable annuities

.38 *Accident and health insurance

.382 *Health insurance

Examples: Blue Cross, Blue Shield, health maintenance organizations (HMOs), reimbursement health insurance (insurance in which the insured first pays the bills)

Class here prepaid health insurance (insurance in which the insurer first pays the bills)

Class government-sponsored accident and health insurance in 368.42

See Manual at 368.382 vs. 362.1042

.382 2 *Medical and surgical

.382 3 *Dental

.382 7 *Hospital

.384 *Accident insurance

.386 · *Disability income insurance

See also 368.382 for disability insurance

*Add as instructed under 368.1–368.8

.4   *Government-sponsored insurance

> Class here social insurance, social security as a form of social insurance
>
> Class government-sponsored bank deposit insurance in 368.854
>
> *See Manual at 336.249 vs. 368.401, 368.4011; 368.4 vs. 362*

.400 68   Management

> Class personnel management of insurance for government employees in 351.1234

[.400 973]   Social security in the United States

> Do not use; class in 368.4300973

.41   *Workers' (Workmen's) compensation insurance

> Protection against losses incurred through disablements caused on the job
>
> Class here comprehensive works on workers' (workmen's) compensation insurance
>
> Class workers' (workmen's) compensation (employer liability insurance) in 368.56

.42   *Accident and health insurance

> *For workers' (workmen's) compensation insurance, see 368.41*
>
> *See also 362.1042520973 for United States' Medicaid financial benefits, 362.10973 for United States' Medicaid health services, 368.382 for comprehensive works on health insurance*

.424   *Maternity insurance

.426   *Accident and health insurance for the aged

> Class comprehensive works on accident and health insurance for the aged in 368.38200846

.43   *Old-age and survivors' insurance

> Class here social security (United States)
>
> Class supplementary social security for low income people in 362.582, comprehensive works on insurance for the aged in 368.300846
>
> *For accident and health insurance for the aged, see 368.426*
>
> *See Manual at 336.249 vs. 368.401, 368.4011*

.44   *Unemployment insurance

.48   *Insurance against crimes of violence

> Class comprehensive works on crime insurance in 368.82

>   368.5–368.8 Against casualties (Casualty insurance)

> Class comprehensive works in 368.5

*Add as instructed under 368.1–368.8

.5   *Liability insurance

Class here comprehensive works on casualty insurance

For glass insurance, see 368.6; insurance against industrial casualties, 368.7; other casualty insurance, 368.8

.56   Miscellaneous lines

Examples: contractual, elevator, employers', landlords', owners', tenants'; livestock liability; personal liability

Class here public liability insurance

.562   *Product liability insurance

.564   *Professional (Errors and omissions, Malpractice) liability insurance

.57   *Instrumentalities of transportation

.572   *Automobile

.576   *Aviation

.6   *Glass insurance

Examples: coverage on plate glass, windows, neon and fluorescent signs and lamps

.7   *Insurance against industrial casualties (accidents)

Examples: boiler and machinery, power plant, nuclear energy, power interruption insurance

.8   Other casualty insurance

.81   *Business insurance

.815   *Business interruption insurance

Including strike insurance

.82   *Burglary, robbery, theft insurance

Including extortion, kidnap and ransom insurance

Class here comprehensive works on crime insurance

.83   *Fidelity bonds

Guarantee against loss to employers because of dishonesty of employees

Class here comprehensive works on bonds

For surety bonds, see 368.84

.84   *Surety bonds

Guarantee against loss due to failure to perform an obligation or fulfill a contract

*Add as instructed under 368.1–368.8

.85	Guarantees

Class a specific guarantee not provided for here with the guarantee, e.g., surety bonds 368.84

.852	*Mortgage insurance
.853	*Investment guarantees
.854	*Bank deposit insurance

Class here government-sponsored bank deposit insurance

.87	*Credit insurance

Insurance of creditor against loss due to debtor's insolvency

.88	*Title insurance
.9	**Insurance by specific continents, countries, localities in modern world**

Add to base number 368.9 notation 4–9 from Table 2, e.g., insurance in South America 368.98

369 Miscellaneous kinds of associations

.1 Hereditary, military, patriotic societies of United States

Including state and local societies

(Option: To give local emphasis and a shorter number to hereditary, military, patriotic societies of a specific country, class them in this number; in that case, class hereditary, military, patriotic societies of United States in 369.273)

.11	General societies

Examples: military and naval orders, Medal of Honor Legion, Military Order of Foreign Wars of the United States, Veterans of Foreign Wars

.12	Colonial America societies

Examples: General Society of Colonial Wars, General Society of Mayflower Descendants, National Society of the Colonial Dames of America

.13	Revolutionary War societies

Examples: Society of the Cincinnati, Sons of the American Revolution

.135	Daughters of the American Revolution
.14	Societies commemorating events of 1789–1861
.15	Union Civil War societies

Example: Grand Army of the Republic

Including auxiliary Union societies [*formerly* 369.16]

Class here comprehensive works on societies of Civil War

For Confederate Civil War societies, see 369.17

*Add as instructed under 368.1–368.8

[.16]	Auxiliary Union societies of Civil War

Relocated to 369.15

.17	Confederate Civil War societies

Examples: United Confederate Veterans, United Daughters of the Confederacy

.18	Societies commemorating wars from 1898 to present
.181	Spanish-American War, 1898
.186	World Wars I and II and later wars
.186 1	American Legion
.186 2	American Veterans of World War II, Korea, and Vietnam (AMVETS)
.186 3	Disabled American Veterans
.2	**Hereditary, military, patriotic societies**

Class here nationality clubs

(Option: To give local emphasis and a shorter number to hereditary, military, patriotic societies of a specific country, use one of the following:

(Option A: Place them first by use of a letter or other symbol, e.g., hereditary, military, patriotic societies of France 369.F [preceding 369.1]

(Option B: Class them in 369.1; in that case, class hereditary, military, patriotic societies of United States in 369.273)

.209	Historical, geographical, persons treatment

Class treatment by specific continents, countries, localities in 369.23–369.29

.21	International
.23–.29	Specific continents, countries, localities

Add to base number 369.2 notation 3–9 from Table 2, e.g., patriotic societies of Italy 369.245; however, class hereditary, military, patriotic societies of United States in 369.1

Notation 09 from Table 1 is added to indicate nationality clubs not located with the nation of interest, e.g., Order Sons of Italy in America 369.23450973

Class clubs of ethnic groups not defined by specific country or locality in 369.3

.3	**Racial and ethnic clubs**

Add to base number 369.3 notation 03–9 from Table 5, e.g., B'nai B'rith 369.3924

Class clubs of ethnic groups defined by specific country or locality in 369.23–369.29

.4   **Young people's societies**

Class a specific aspect of young people's societies with the aspect, e.g., Boy Scout camps 796.5422

.42   **Boys'**

> *For Boy Scouts, see 369.43*

.43   **Boy Scouts**

> Including Cub Scouts, Explorers

.46   **Girls'**

> *For Camp Fire, inc., see 369.47; Explorers, 369.43*

.463   **Girl Scouts and Girl Guides**

.47   **Camp Fire, inc.**

> Former name: Camp Fire Girls

.5   **Service clubs**

Examples: Kiwanis International, Lions International, Rotary International, Zonta International

370   Education

Class education in a specific subject at the elementary level in 372.3–372.8, in special education in 371.9; at higher levels with the subject, using notation 07 from Table 1, e.g., the study of comparative religion 291.07

Unless other instructions are given, observe the following table of precedence, e.g., curriculums for women's colleges 376.8, (*not* 375.00082)

Special education	371.9
Education of women	376
Levels of education	372–374
Higher education	378
School organization and management (*except* 371.9)	371
Government regulation, control, support of education	379
Curriculums	375
Schools and religion	377

See Manual at 370

SUMMARY

370.1–.9   Standard subdivisions

371   School organization and management; special education
　.001–.009   Standard subdivisions
　.01–.04   [Public, private, community, experimental schools and school systems]
　.1   Teaching and teaching personnel
　.2   School administration and management
　.3   Methods of instruction and study
　.4   Guidance and counseling
　.5   School discipline
　.6   Physical plant
　.7   School health and safety
　.8   The student
　.9   Special education

372   Elementary education
　.01–.09   Standard subdivisions
　.1   Organization and management of elementary education; curriculums
　.2   Levels of elementary education
　.3   Science, technology, health
　.4   Reading
　.5   Creative and manual arts
　.6   Language and literature
　.7   Mathematics
　.8   Other studies
　.9   Historical, geographical, persons treatment of elementary education

373   Secondary education
　.01–.09   Standard subdivisions
　.1   Organization and management of secondary education; curriculum
　.2   Types and levels of secondary education
　.3–.9   Secondary education and schools by specific continents, countries, localities

374   Adult education
　.001–.008   Standard subdivisions
　.01   Adult education for specific objectives
　.1   General topics
　.2   Group education
　.4   Correspondence schools and instruction
　.8   Schools
　.9   Historical, geographical, persons treatment

375   Curriculums
　.000 1–.000 9   Standard subdivisions
　.001–.009   [General topics of curriculums]
　.01–.99   Curriculums and courses of study in specific subjects

376   Education of women
　.5   Convent education
　.6   Education of women by level
　.8   Colleges for women
　.9   Historical, geographical, persons treatment

377   Schools and religion
　.1   Religion and secular education
　.3   Monastic schools
　.6   Mission schools
　.8   Schools supported by Christian groups
　.9   Schools supported by other groups

378	Higher education
.001–.009	Standard subdivisions
.01–.05	[General topics of higher education]
.02	Financial management
.03	Alternative (Nontraditional) higher education
.04	Private colleges and universities
.05	Public colleges and universities
.1	Organization and management of institutions of higher education; curriculums
.2	Academic degrees
.3	Student finances
.4–.9	Higher education and institutions by specific continents, countries, localities in the modern world

379	Government regulation, control, support of education
.01–.09	Standard subdivisions
.1	Finance, supervision, control of public education
.2	Public education and the state
.3	Private education and the state
.4–.9	Government regulation, control, support of public education by specific continents, countries, localities in the modern world

.1 Philosophy, theories, general aspects

SUMMARY

370.11	Education for specific objectives
.12	Classification and other philosophical foundations
.15	Educational psychology
.19	Social aspects of education

.11 Education for specific objectives

Including basic education, basic skills education

Class here the value of education

Do not use for systems; class in 370.1

.112 Humanistic education (Liberal education)

.113 Vocational education (Career education)

Class vocational secondary schools in 373.246, adult vocational education in 374.013; schools for a specific subject with the subject, using notation 07 from Table 1, e.g., medical schools 610.711

See also 331.25922 for training undertaken by industry, 331.702 for choice of vocation, 371.425 for counseling in schools

.114 Moral, ethical, character education

Class education for social responsibility in 370.115; the moral, ethical, and character training of children in the home in 649.7

.115 Education for social responsibility

Including education for international understanding, democracy, social education

.116   Education for effective use of leisure

Including education for individual fulfillment

.118   Education for creativity

.12   Classification and other philosophical foundations

Examples: idealism, realism, pragmatism

[.13]   Scientific principles

Number discontinued; class in 370.1

.15   Educational psychology

Including the principles of behavior modification

Do not use for scientific principles; class in 370.1

Class behavior modification for classroom discipline in 371.1024, the psychology of a specific topic in education with the topic, using notation 019 from Table 1, e.g., the psychology of adult education 374.0019

See also 153 for intellectual and mental processes in general psychology

See Manual at 153.15 vs. 370.15

.151   Differential psychology

Educational psychology of specific ages and sexes

Class the specific aspects of the psychology of specific ages and specific sexes in 370.152–370.158

.152   Cognition

Class here intelligence

Class creativity in 370.157

.152 2   Memory

.152 3   Learning

.152 4   Reason

.153   Emotion and behavior

Relation of behavior patterns, feelings, emotions to learning, to the classroom situation

Including unconscious and subconscious processes, emotional disturbances, extroversion-introversion, personality

For motivation to learn, see 370.154

.154   Motivation to learn

.155   Psychomotor and sensory processes in learning

Including perception, motor skills, left-handedness

.156	**Psychology of learning specific subjects**

Add to base number 370.156 notation 001–999, e.g., the psychology of learning mathematics 370.15651

Class the psychology of learning specific subjects at a specific level with the level at which the subject is taught, using notation 019 from Table 1, e.g., the psychology of learning to read at the elementary level 372.4019

.157	**Imagination and creativity**

See also 370.152 for cognitive creativity

.158	**Psychological effects of education**

Example: effect of the school situation on students

.19	**Social aspects of education**

Class here educational sociology, educational anthropology, sociology applied to the solution of large-scale social problems in education

Do not use for psychological principles; class in 370.15

Class education for social responsibility in 370.115; the functional planning carried out by superintendents and principals in connection with the operations of a given school system in 371.207; governmental policy, planning, and control in 379

.192	**Cultural foundations of education**
.193	**School and society relations**
.193 1	Community-school relations
.193 12	Parent-teacher associations
.193 16	Industry-school relations
.193 4	Sociocultural factors affecting education

Class here comprehensive works on equal educational opportunity, on the sociology of the student

Class students in the school in 371.8; students' attitudes and behavior in 371.81; effects of a specific factor on a specific aspect of education with the subject, e.g., effect on school finance 379.11–379.13

.193 41	Economic and cultural situation of students

Including socioeconomic status, family background

Class here multicultural education, school attendance

Class the education of socially and culturally disadvantaged students in 371.967

.193 42	Racial and ethnic factors

> Including integration, busing of students to achieve integration
>
> Class here affirmative action in education
>
> Class affirmative action with respect to teachers in 331.133
>
> > *For segregation of racial and ethnic groups, see 370.19344*
> >
> > *See also 370.89 for the education of ethnic groups*

.193 44	Segregation of racial and ethnic groups
.193 45	Sex of students

> Including sexism in education
>
> *See also 376 for the education of women*

> 370.193 46–370.193 49 Political and locale factors

Class comprehensive works in 370.1934

.193 46	Rural environments
.193 48	Urban environments
.193 49	Political factors
.194	Fundamental education

> Preparation of educationally disadvantaged children and adults for participation in community life
>
> Class here community education
>
> *See also 371.967 for compensatory education, 374.012 for adult basic education*

.195	Comparative education

> *See Manual at 370.195 vs. 370.9*

.196	Intercultural education

> Programs to promote mutual understanding among nations and cultures through the exchange of instructional materials, techniques, students, teachers, technicians
>
> Class education within a country for international understanding in 370.115; international law of educational and cultural exchanges in 341.767, domestic law of educational and cultural exchanges in 344.08; public administration of exchange programs in 351.85
>
> *See also 370.19341 for multicultural education*

.196 2	Exchange of students
.196 3	Exchange of teachers

.196 5	Educational aid

Including the establishment of schools in other countries

Recipients of the aid are indicated by notation 09 from Table 1 followed by the area number of the recipient, e.g., German aid to North American schools 370.1965097

[.287]	Testing and measurement

Do not use; class in 371.26

[.68]	Management

Do not use; class in 371.2

.7	**Education, research, related topics**
.71	Professional education of teachers

Including training classes

Class here the study of how to teach, the teaching of teachers

Teachers' and faculty meetings relocated to 371.146

Do not use for schools and courses; class in 370.73

Class in-service training in 371.146

[.711]	Colleges and universities

Do not use; class in 370.73

.712	For specific grades or levels
.712 2	Kindergarten and primary

Including preschool education

.712 3	Secondary
.712 4	Tertiary (Higher)
.72	Teachers' centers, conferences, institutes, workshops

Do not use for research; class in 370.78

.73	Institutions of higher education

Class here teachers' colleges, education departments of universities

.732	Courses and programs
.732 6	For specific grades or levels
.732 62	Kindergarten and primary level

Including preschool education

.732 63	Secondary level
.732 64	Tertiary (Higher) level

.733	Practice teaching

Class here comprehensive works on practice teaching

Class practice teaching at the elementary level in 372.07, in a specific subject at the elementary level with the subject in 372.3–372.8, using notation 044 from the table under 372.3–372.8, e.g., practice teaching in arithmetic 372.72044; practice teaching in a specific subject at secondary and higher levels with the subject, using notation 0711–0715 from Table 1, e.g., practice teaching in United States history at the secondary level 973.0712

[.75]	Collecting objects

Do not use; class in 370.775

.76	Professional education of administrators

Do not use for review and exercise; class in 370.776

See also 658.007 for the study and teaching of general management

.77	Other aspects of education for education

Do not use for programmed texts; class in 370.777

.775	Collecting objects

Class museums, collections, exhibits in 370.74

.776	Review and exercise
.777	Programmed texts
.778	Use of apparatus and equipment

Class the use of apparatus and equipment in teaching in 371.3078

.78	Educational research

Add to base number 370.78 the numbers following —072 in notation 07201–0724 from Table 1, e.g., surveys 370.783

Do not use for apparatus and equipment; class in 370.778

[.82]	History and description with respect to women

Do not use; class in 376

371   School organization and management; special education

Class here schools and school systems, school policy

Class government regulation, control, support of education in 379; schools of specific levels in 372–374, 378

See also 370.19 for the social aspects of education

See Manual at 371.2 vs. 379

SUMMARY

371.001–.009		Standard subdivisions
.01–.04		[Public, private, community, experimental schools and school systems]
.1		Teaching and teaching personnel
.2		School administration and management
.3		Methods of instruction and study
.4		Guidance and counseling
.5		School discipline
.6		Physical plant
.7		School health and safety
.8		The student
.9		Special education

.001–.005	Standard subdivisions
.006	Organizations and management
[.006 8]	Management

> Do not use; class in 371.2

.007–.009	Standard subdivisions
.01	Public schools and school systems

Class public community schools in 371.03, public experimental schools in 371.04; public education and the state in 379.2; a specific kind or level of public school with the subject, e.g., public elementary schools 372.10421

.02	Private schools and school systems

Class here publicly supported private schools, schools not under the control of the government

Class private community schools in 371.03; private experimental schools in 371.04; private education and the state in 379.3; a specific kind or level of private school with the subject, e.g., private secondary schools 373.222

.03	Community schools
.04	Experimental schools

Including alternative education, free schools

> **371.1–371.8 Organization and management**

Class comprehensive works in 371; organization and management of special education in 371.9; at specific levels in 372–374, 378; government regulation, control, and supervision of schools in 379

For type of school, see 371.01–371.04

.1 Teaching and teaching personnel

Class here teaching personnel management

Use 371.1001–371.1009 for standard subdivisions

.102	Teaching

Class the evaluation of teachers in 371.144

For methods of instruction, see 371.3

.102 2	Communication in teaching
.102 3	Teacher-student relations
.102 4	Classroom management

Class here classroom discipline

[.102 8]	Open classroom approach to learning

Number discontinued; class in 371.102

.103	Teacher-parent relations

Class parent-teacher associations in 370.19312

.104	Relation of teachers to society

Example: public status of teachers

Class here comprehensive works on teacher relations, on academic freedom

For teacher-student relations, see 371.1023; teacher-parent relations, 371.103; relation of teachers to school administration and staff, 371.106

.106	Relation of teachers to school administration and staff
.11	Personal characteristics and qualifications of teachers

Class here discrimination because of sex, race, marital status

.12	Professional qualifications of teachers

The training and educational requirements of teachers in general and those for teachers of specific subjects are classed here, but the techniques and methods of teaching a specific subject are classed with the subject at the secondary and higher levels, using notation 071 from Table 1 for secondary and higher levels, and in 372.3–372.8 at the elementary level

Class legal aspects of the certification of teachers in 344.078, educational aspects of certification in 379.157

See also 370.71 for the professional education of teachers

.122	Training

Educational requirements, standards, criteria

Class schools and colleges, courses of study in 370.7, in-service training in 371.146, practice teaching in 370.733

.123	Participation in professional organizations and activities

.14	Organization of the teaching force in the school

.14   Organization of the teaching force in the school

Including tenure

Class performance contracting in 371.15

See also 331.2596 for the economic aspects of tenure

.141   Duties and responsibilities

.141 2   Staffing

Former heading: Teaching load

For team teaching, see 371.148

.141 22   Substitute teaching

.141 23   Differentiated staffing

Class the use of teachers' assistants (aides) in 371.14124

.141 24   Use of teachers' assistants (aides)

Including paraprofessionals, volunteers

.141 4   Nonteaching activities

.144   Evaluation of teachers

Class here accountability, probation

See also 371.15 for performance contracting, 379.154 for educational accountability

.146   In-service training

Including teachers' and faculty meetings [*formerly also* 370.71], staff handbooks

.148   Team teaching

.15   Performance contracting

See also 371.144 for teacher accountability

.2   School administration and management

For plant management, see 371.6

See Manual at 371.2 vs. 379

SUMMARY

371.200 1–.200 9	**Standard subdivisions**
.201–.209	**[General topics]**
.21	**Matriculation (Admission)**
.22	**Scholarships**
.23	**School year**
.24	**School day and week**
.25	**Grouping of students for instruction**
.26	**Educational tests and measurements**
.27	**School and classroom evaluation of student progress**
.28	**Promotion and failure**
.29	**Other topics**

.200 1–.200 5	Standard subdivisions
.200 6	Organizations and management
[.200 68]	Management of schools

Do not use; class in 371.2 and its subdivisions

.200 7	Education, research, related topics

Class professional education of school administrators in 370.76

.200 8–.200 9	Standard subdivisions
.201	Personnel management

Class personnel management of the teaching staff in 371.1, of nonacademic and staff personnel in 371.202

> 371.201 1–371.201 3 Executive personnel and their activities

Class comprehensive works in 371.201

.201 1	Superintendents
.201 2	Principals
.201 3	Supervisors
.202	Nonacademic and staff personnel
.202 2	School guidance counselors and related personnel

Examples: school psychologists, school social workers

.202 3	Support personnel

Examples: school business administrators, school secretaries

.204	Standards and accreditation of schools

Class professional qualifications of teachers in 371.12; state regulation, control, support of schools in 379

.206	Financial management

Including tuition in private schools

Class the financial administration of public schools in 379.11

See Manual at 658 and s.s. 068

.207	Executive management

Planning, organizing, directing, coordinating, reporting, decision making, leadership

Class here planning as a part of the educational function; planning carried out by superintendents, principals, and others in connection with the operations of a given school or school system

Class government planning in 379.154; planning with respect to a particular function with the function, e.g., planning for school health and safety 371.7

.208	Internal organization of schools

.208   Internal organization of schools

Including open plan schools

.209   School materials

Including purchasing, storage, inventory

.21   Matriculation (Admission)

.216   Admission procedures

For entrance requirements, see 371.217

.217   Entrance requirements

Class the use of tests for admission in 371.264

.218   Articulation

Class here comprehensive works on credits

Class credits in relation to promotion and failure in 371.28

.219   School enrollment

.219 09   Historical and persons treatment

Class geographical treatment in 371.2191–371.2199 (*not* 371.219091–371.219099)

.219 1–.219 9   Geographical treatment

Add to base number 371.219 notation 1–9 from Table 2, e.g., school enrollment in Communist countries 371.2191717

.22   Scholarships

Including fellowships, grants

Class here student aid, student loans

Class tuition in public schools in 379.13, in private schools in 371.206

.23   School year

Including school calendar

.232   Summer school

.236   All-year school

Including four-quarter staggered school year, extended school year

.24   School day and week

Including school attendance

.242   Schedules and scheduling

Individual, class, all-school

Including integrated day

.242 1	Class schedules and periods
	Including flexible modular scheduling
.242 2	Homeroom periods
.242 4	Activity periods

.244   Length of school day

.25   Grouping of students for instruction

.251   Class size

.252   Heterogeneous grouping

.254   Homogeneous grouping

     Including nongraded schools

.256   Open plan

.26   Educational tests and measurements

Testing in a specific subject or discipline at the secondary and tertiary levels is classed with the subject plus notation 076 from Table 1, e.g., testing in chemistry 540.76. In elementary education, testing is classed with the subject in 372.3–372.8, using notation 044 from the table under 372.3–372.8, e.g., testing in elementary physical education 372.86044

Class the use of educational tests and measurements in guidance in 371.42

For school and classroom evaluation of student progress, see 371.27

See also 153.93 for general intelligence tests in psychology

.260 13   Validity and reliability of tests

     Including race and sex bias in tests

.261   Test construction

Class evaluation of tests in 371.26013

See also 371.271 for test construction for the evaluation of student progress

.262   Standard examinations

Examinations conducted by authorities or organizations external to the individual school in order to determine general educational level and academic achievement

Class here organizations producing standard examinations

Class academic prognosis and placement in 371.264, achievement tests on a specific subject with the subject, using notation 076 from Table 1, e.g., on high school mathematics 510.76

.264	Academic prognosis and placement

Use of tests of academic achievement and general education for prediction of future academic achievement, for admission to educational institutions

Including vocational interest tests, educational quotient

Class comprehensive works on and the psychological aspects of aptitude tests in 153.94, achievement tests on a specific subject with the subject, using notation 076 from Table 1, e.g., on high school mathematics 510.76

.27	School and classroom evaluation of student progress
.271	Tests and examinations

Types, value, methods of construction

Including the construction of tests by teachers

.272	Marking systems

Methods used for recording and reporting achievement of students in school studies

.272 1	Grades and grading
.272 2	Reporting progress to parents
.28	Promotion and failure

Including accelerated promotion, grade repetition

.29	Other topics
.291	Student mobility
.291 2	School completion
.291 3	Dropouts (Early school leavers)

Class student failures in 371.28

.291 4	Transfers
.295	Truancy

Class here school attendance officers

Class truancy as a discipline problem in 371.58

.3	**Methods of instruction and study**

Class the methods used in teaching specific subjects at the elementary level in 372.3–372.8, using notation 044 from the table under 372.3–372.8; at higher levels with the subject, using notation 07 from Table 1, e.g., methods used in teaching economics 330.07

.302 8	Techniques and procedures

Including lessons plans and planning

Class apparatus, equipment, materials in 371.3078

.302 81	Techniques of study
[.302 813]	For parents
	Relocated to 649.68
.302 814	For teachers
.302 82	Classroom techniques
[.302 85]	Data processing　Computer applications
	Do not use; class in 371.334
.307 8	Teaching aids, materials, devices

Including curriculum laboratories, educational technology, instructional materials centers, school resource centers, educational games, educational toys

Class specific aids in 371.32–371.33, instructional materials center or school resource center combined with a collection of library materials for students in 027.8

See also 370.7 for educational innovations, 370.778 for the use of apparatus and equipment in teacher education

---

> 　**371.32–371.33 Specific teaching aids, materials, devices**

Methods, use, value

Class comprehensive works in 371.3078

.32	**Textbooks and primary print media**

Class here works about textbooks and primary print media in general

Class textbooks on a specific subject with the subject, e.g., textbooks on mathematics 510

.33	**Other teaching aids, materials, devices**

Former heading: Audio and visual materials for teaching

.331	**Administration**

Evaluation, planning for and coordination of use

Class the administration of specific aids in 371.333–371.335

.332	**Teaching methods**

Example: the use of drama

Class methods of teaching with specific aids in 371.333–371.335

.333	**Audio materials and devices**
.333 1	Radio
.333 2	Phonograph and phonograph records
.333 3	Tape recorder and recordings

.334		Computer

Class here electronic programmed learning [*formerly* 371.39442], teaching machines [*formerly* 371.39445], computer-assisted instruction (CAI)

Unless it is redundant, add to base number 371.334 the numbers following 00 in 004–006, e.g., the use of computer graphics in teaching 371.33466

.335   Visual and audiovisual materials and devices

> *See also 371.32 for textbooks and primary print media, 371.333 for audio materials and devices*

.335 2   Pictures

.335 22   Slides and filmstrips

.335 23   Motion pictures

.335 6   Bulletin boards

.335 8   Television

.335 82   Effectiveness

.335 84   Teaching methods

.335 87   Administration

> Scheduling, planning for use
>
> Including interinstitutional teaching

.335 89   Production of programs and specific programs

>   371.36–371.39 Specific methods of teaching

Class comprehensive works in 371.3

.36   Project (Unit) method

.37   Recitation and discussion methods

Example: class discussion, seminar

.38   Methods employed outside the classroom

Former heading: Laboratory method

Including field trips, outdoor education

.39   Other methods

.392   Montessori system

The Montessori method is usually confined to the elementary level in 372.1392. Discussions of advancing it to higher grades are classed with the appropriate level

.393	Methods based on behavior modification	
	Including behavioral outcomes approach	
.394	Individualized instruction	
	Including private tutoring	
.394 1	Open classroom methods	
.394 2	Honors work	
.394 3	Independent study plans	
.394 4	Auto-instructional methods	
.394 42	Programmed learning	
	Electronic programmed learning relocated to 371.334	
[.394 45]	Use of teaching machines	
	Relocated to 371.334	
.395	Group teaching	
	Examples: heterogeneous group teaching, homogeneous group teaching	
.396	Lecture method	
.397	Gaming and simulation	

.4   Guidance and counseling

.404   Special topics

.404 2   Management of guidance programs

.404 4   Guidance methods

.404 6   Role of teachers in guidance

[.406 8]   Management

Do not use; class in 371.4042

.42   Educational and vocational guidance

.422   Intellectual and educational guidance

.425   Vocational guidance

Class choice of vocation in 331.702, characteristics of a specific occupation with the subject, using notation 023 from Table 1, e.g., law as a profession 340.023

.46   Personal guidance

Assistance with social, emotional, personal problems

Example: the services of school social workers

Class student mental health in 371.71

.5	**School discipline**

Overseeing student conduct

For classroom discipline, see 371.1024

See also 371.782 for school programs to reduce violence

.51	General regulations for student conduct
.53	Incentives
.54	Punishments
.542	Corporal punishment
.543	Probation, suspension, expulsion
.58	Discipline problems

Examples: student violence, vandalism

See also 371.78 for the protection of students from criminal activity

.59	Student participation in the maintenance of discipline

Examples: monitorial and prefectorial systems, honor systems, student government

.6	**Physical plant**

Class here plant management

[.602 88]	Maintenance and repair

Do not use; class in 371.68

.61	Locations, sites, grounds
.62	Buildings

See also 727 for the architecture of buildings for educational purposes

---

>	371.621–371.625 Rooms and buildings for specific purposes

Class here furnishings, apparatus, equipment, supplies

Class comprehensive works in 371.62

.621	Instructional spaces

Examples: general-purpose classrooms, study rooms, auxiliary facilities

For instructional spaces for specific educational objectives, see 371.623

.623	Instructional spaces for specific educational objectives

For physical and health education facilities, see 371.624

.623 2	For experimental methods of instruction
.623 4	For instruction in specific subjects and types of subjects

.624	Physical and health education facilities
	Examples: gymnasiums, swimming pools
.625	Noninstructional facilities
	Facilities for student societies, student unions, dormitories, infirmaries, food services
.629	Design for noninstructional objectives
	Examples: for health and safety, for protection from vandalism
	Class health and safety in specific types of spaces in 371.621–371.625
.63	Furnishings
	Class furnishings for specific rooms and purposes in 371.621–371.625
.67	Apparatus, equipment, supplies
	Class apparatus, equipment, supplies for specific rooms and purposes in 371.621–371.625
.68	Renovation, repair, custodial management
.7	**School health and safety**
.71	Physical and mental welfare of students
	Including birth control programs, sexual hygiene programs
	Class here school social services
	See also 371.78 for protecting students from various forms of abuse and criminal activity
.712	Physical welfare of students
	Including services of school nurses
.713	Mental welfare of students
	Including the services of school psychologists
.716	Nutrition of students
	Examples: lunch and milk programs, nutrition programs for pregnant students
.77	Safety programs
	Class the safety of school personnel in 363.11937
	For safety from abuse and criminal activity, see 371.78
.774	Fire safety
.775	Safety in specific situations
.775 2	In traffic
.775 4	In athletics
.775 6	In laboratories, shops, kitchens

.78	Safety from criminal activity
.782	Programs to reduce violence
.784	Programs to eliminate drug traffic and use

> *See also 371.58 for drug abuse as a cause of discipline problems*

.786	Programs to reduce sexual abuse
.8	**The student**

General aspects: nonacademic life and welfare

.805	Serial publications

Class here student serials dealing with the school and its activities

Class student periodicals on general subjects in 051–059; school yearbooks for a specific school with the school, student serials on a specific subject with the subject, using notation 05 from Table 1, e.g., student literary periodicals 805

.806	Organizations and management

Class student organizations in 371.83

[.808]	History and description with respect to kinds of persons

Do not use; class in 371.82

.81	Attitudes and behavior

Including student protest, activism, unrest

Class school discipline in 371.5; guidance and counseling in 371.4

.82	Specific kinds of students

Add to base number 371.82 the numbers following —08 in —082–087 from Table 1, e.g., female students 371.822

Class specific aspects of specific kinds of students in 371.81, 371.83–371.89

.83	Student organizations

> *For student organizations in specific fields, see 371.84; Greek-letter societies, 371.85*

> *See also 371.855–371.856 for social societies*

.84	Student organizations in specific fields

Add to base number 371.84 notation 001–999, e.g., literary societies 371.848

> *For Greek-letter societies in specific fields, see 371.854*

.85	Greek-letter societies
.852	Honorary societies

Not in a specific subject field

.854	Societies in specific fields

Add to base number 371.854 notation 001–999, e.g., Greek-letter societies in the social sciences 371.8543

.855	Men's social societies and fraternities
.856	Women's social societies and sororities
.87	Housing and transportation of students
.871	Housing
.872	Transportation

See also 363.1259 for school bus accidents, 370.19342 for busing to achieve racial balance

.89	Activities

Examples: nonathletic competitions, intramural athletics, public entertainment activities, clubs

Class interschool competitions with the competition in 790

.897	School journalism

Class here photography

Class student serials in 371.805

.897 4	Producing newspapers
.897 5	Producing magazines
.897 6	Producing yearbooks
.9	**Special education**

Education employing special curriculums, methods, facilities for exceptional (atypical) students, i.e., students with physical, intellectual, mental, or social differences

Class here the organization and administration of special education, specific subjects, learning disabilities

Unless other instructions are given, observe the following table of precedence, e.g., language difficulties of deaf retarded students 371.92 (*not* 371.914, 371.912)

Gifted students	371.95
Retarded students and slow learners	371.92
Emotionally disturbed students	371.94
Students with physical handicaps	371.91
Socially and culturally disadvantaged students	371.967
Delinquent and problem students	371.93
Students belonging to the upper classes	371.962
Students exceptional because of racial, ethnic, national origin	371.97

Class government regulation, control, support of special education in 379

SUMMARY

371.901–.909	**Standard subdivisions**
.91	**Students with physical handicaps**
.92	**Retarded students and slow learners**
.93	**Delinquent and problem students**
.94	**Emotionally disturbed students**
.95	**Gifted students**
.96	**Students exceptional because of class distinction**
.97	**Students exceptional because of racial, ethnic, national origin**

[.902 8]   Auxiliary techniques and procedures; apparatus, equipment, materials

> Do not use; class auxiliary techniques and procedures in 371.9043;
> apparatus, equipment, materials in 371.9045

.904   General topics

.904 2   Management

> Add to base number 371.9042 the numbers following —068 in
> notation 0681–0688 from Table 1, e.g., financial management of
> special education 371.90421; however, class plant management in
> 371.9045

.904 3   Teaching methods

> Including use of behavior modification

.904 4   Specific subjects

> Add to base number 371.9044 the numbers following 372 in
> 372.3–372.8, e.g., mathematics 371.90447

.904 5   Facilities

> Buildings, rooms, furnishings, apparatus, equipment, supplies

.904 6   Special education in special schools versus special education in general
schools (Mainstreaming)

.904 7   Special education by level

.904 72   Infant and primary

.904 73   Secondary

.904 74   Tertiary (Higher)

.904 75   Adult

[.906 8]   Management

> Do not use; class in 371.9042

.91   Students with physical handicaps

Class here comprehensive works on disabled students

Unless other instructions are given, observe the following table of precedence, e.g., blind, motor-impaired students 371.916 (*not* 371.911)

Students with linguistic disorders	371.914
Motor-impaired students	371.916
Blind and partially sighted students	371.911
Deaf and hearing-impaired students	371.912

.911   *Blind and partially sighted students

Add to base number 371.911 the numbers following 371.904 in 371.9042–371.9046, e.g., teaching methods 371.9113

.912   *Deaf and hearing-impaired students

Class education of the deaf-blind in 371.911

.912 2–.912 6   General topics

Add to base number 371.912 the numbers following 371.904 in 371.9042–371.9046, e.g., teaching methods 371.9123

.912 7   Instruction in visual communication

Including lipreading, manual alphabet, sign language; instruction of the nondeaf in visual communication with the deaf

.914   Students with linguistic disorders

.914 2   Students with speaking disorders

Examples: aphasias, stuttering

.914 4   Students with reading disorders

Example: dyslexia

See also 372.43 for reading difficulties and failures

.916   Motor-impaired students

Class here brain-damaged students

Class students suffering a disorder because of brain damage with the disorder, e.g., speaking disorders brought on by brain damage 371.9142

.92   Retarded students and slow learners

Class here the developmentally disabled student, the mentally handicapped student

Class brain-damaged students in 371.916

.926   *Slow learners

Add to base number 371.926 the numbers following 371.904 in 371.9042–371.9046, e.g., teaching methods 371.9263

---

*Do not use notation 068 from Table 1; class management in 371.9112

.928   Mentally retarded students

.928 001–.928 005   Standard subdivisions

.928 006   Organizations

                           Class management in 371.92802

.928 007–.928 009   Standard subdivisions

.928 02–.928 06   General topics

                           Add to base number 371.9280 the numbers following 371.904 in
                           371.9042–371.9046, e.g., teaching methods 371.92803

.928 2   Educable retarded students

.928 3   Trainable retarded students

.928 4   Severely retarded students

.93   Delinquent and problem students

                        Examples: disruptive, hyperactive, maladjusted students

.94   Emotionally disturbed students

                        Examples: autistic students, mentally ill students

                        For delinquent and problem students, see 371.93

.95   Gifted students

.952   Identification

.953   Programs and curriculums

.956   Teaching methods and practices

                           Including motivation of gifted underachievers

.96   Students exceptional because of class distinction

.962   Upper classes

                           Royalty, nobility, gentry

.967   Socially and culturally disadvantaged students

                           Class here compensatory education, teacher corps

                           Class students socially disadvantaged because of racial, ethnic, national
                           origin in 371.97

[.967 2]   Urban and slum students

                           Number discontinued; class in 371.967

.967 5   Migrant students

.97   Students exceptional because of racial, ethnic, national origin

Class here bilingual education

Use 371.97001–371.97009 for standard subdivisions

Add to base number 371.97 notation 03–99 from Table 5, e.g., education of Jews in France 371.97924044

Class the study and teaching of languages at secondary and higher levels in 400

> ## 372–374 Levels of education

Class comprehensive works on education and works dealing comprehensively with elementary and secondary education in 370, on schools in 371

Works treating two sublevels of education that are not subdivisions of the same number are classed with the higher level, e.g., kindergarten and first grade 372.241 (*not* 372.218)

For higher education, see 378

372   Elementary education

Class here preschool education, comprehensive works on elementary schools

Class special education at the elementary level in 371.9

SUMMARY

372.01–.08	[Standard subdivisions, objectives, experimental schools]
.1	Organization and management of elementary education; curriculums
.2	Levels of elementary education
.3	Science, technology, health
.4	Reading
.5	Creative and manual arts
.6	Language and literature
.7	Mathematics
.8	Other studies
.9	Historical, geographical, persons treatment of elementary education

.01   Philosophy and theory

.011   Elementary education for specific objectives

Including evaluation of effects and effectiveness

Add to base number 372.011 the numbers following 370.11 in 370.112–370.118, e.g., character education 372.0114

[.013]   Value

Do not use; class in 372.011

[.068]   Management

Do not use; class in 372.12

.07	Education, research, related topics

Class professional education for elementary school teachers in 370.7122

[.071 1]	Schools and courses

Do not use; class in 370.73262

[.09]	Historical, geographical, persons treatment

Do not use; class in 372.9

.1 Organization and management of elementary education; curriculums

Class comprehensive works on specific levels in 372.2

.104	Special topics
.104 2	Kinds of schools
.104 21	Public schools

Class community public schools in 372.10423, public experimental schools in 372.10424

.104 22	Private schools

Class private community schools in 372.10423, private experimental schools in 372.10424

.104 23	Community schools
.104 24	Experimental schools

Class community schools in 372.10423

[.109]	Historical, geographical, persons treatment

Do not use; class in 372.9

.11–.18	Organization and management

Add to base number 372.1 the numbers following 371 in 371.1–371.8, e.g., elementary school day 372.124

Class kinds of schools in 372.1042

.19	Curriculums

Class here comprehensive works on elementary school subjects and courses of study

Add to base number 372.19 the numbers following 375.008 in 375.0082–375.0088, e.g., ethnic studies 372.194; however, curriculums in environmental studies relocated from 372.193 to 372.357043

Class curriculums in specific elementary school subjects in 372.3–372.8, using notation 043 from the add table under 372.3–372.8, e.g., a curriculum in mathematics 372.7043

.2 Levels of elementary education

Class organization, management, curriculums of a specific level in 372.1; specific schools in 372.93–372.99

.21	Preschool institutions

Class here headstart programs

Class comprehensive works on equal educational opportunity in 370.1934

.210 7   Education, research, related topics

Class professional education for preschool teachers in 370.7122

.216   Nursery schools

Including play-group movements

.218   Kindergartens

When not considered part of elementary grades

.218 07   Education, research, related topics

Class professional education for kindergarten teachers in 370.7122

.24   Specific levels of elementary school

Including elementary sections of all-age schools

Class postelementary, advanced elementary sections, upper sections of all-age schools in 373.23

.241   Lower level

Examples: primary grades (1–3), infant schools (United Kingdom)

.242   Upper level

Examples: intermediate grades (4–6), junior schools (United Kingdom)

> ### 372.3–372.8 Specific elementary school subjects

Add to the notation for each term identified by * as follows:
```
01–03    Standard subdivisions
04       Special topics
042          Place of subject in education
043          Curriculums
                Courses of study, content, emphasis
044          Teaching
                Methods, materials, aids, sources, testing
                Class textbooks on a specific subject with the subject, e.g.,
                an elementary textbook on music 780
[0442]       Works for parents
                Relocated to 649.68
(045)        Textbooks
                (Optional notation; prefer the specific subject, e.g.,
                elementary textbooks on arithmetic 513)
049          Specific levels of instruction
                Example: the subject for primary grades
                Class a specific aspect of instruction at a given level with
                the aspect, e.g., curriculums for primary grades 043
05–09    Standard subdivisions
```

Class comprehensive works in 372.19

.3	**Science, technology, health**
.35	*Science and technology
	Including computers, the metric system
.357	*Nature study
	Class here environmental studies
.357 043	Curriculums
	Class here curriculums in environmental studies [*formerly also* 372.193]
.358	*Technology [*formerly* 372.8]
	Including robotics
	For home economics, see 372.82; physical education, 372.86
.37	*Health and hygiene
	Class here diet, food, nutrition
.372	*Sex education
.4	**Reading**
.41	General topics
	Including reading comprehension
(.412)	Readers
	(Optional number; prefer specific language, using notation 86 from Table 4, e.g., English-language readers 428.6
	(If this number is used, class readers on a specific subject with the subject in elementary education, using notation 045 as shown under 372.3–372.8, e.g., science readers 372.35045)
.414	Readiness and methods of instruction
.414 2	Fostering and determining readiness
.414 4	Whole-word methods (Word recognition)
.414 5	Part methods
	Examples: phonic, alphabetic, structural analysis methods
	Including special teaching alphabets
.414 7	Individualized (Personalized) reading instruction
.43	Remedial reading
	Including reading difficulties, reading failure
	See also 371.9144 for reading disorders
.5	***Creative and manual arts**

*Add as instructed under 372.3–372.8

.52	*Drawing, painting, design
.53	*Modeling and sculpture
.54	*Sewing
.55	*Handicrafts

> Example: paper work (cutting, pasting, modeling, origami)
>
> *For sewing, see 372.54*

.6 ***Language and literature**

> Including listening
>
> *For reading, see 372.4*

.61	Grammar, usage, word study
.62	Expression
.622	Phonetics and speech

> Class phonetics in reading in 372.4145

.623	*Composition
.63	Spelling and handwriting
.632	*Spelling and orthography
.634	*Handwriting (Penmanship)
.64	*Literature (Belles-lettres)

> *See also 372.66 for drama and theater*

.642	*Storytelling
.65	*Foreign languages

> Add to base number 372.65 notation 1–9 from Table 6, e.g., English as a foreign language 372.6521; then add further as instructed under 372.3–372.8, e.g., testing students in English as a foreign language 372.6521044

.66	*Drama and theater

> Class here dance
>
> Class the use of drama and theater as a method of instruction in 372.1332, plays taught as literature in 372.64

.7 ***Mathematics**

.72	*Arithmetic

> Class here numeracy

[.73]	Modern mathematics

> Number discontinued; class in 372.7

*Add as instructed under 372.3–372.8

.8   **Other studies**

         Technology relocated to 372.358

.82   *Home economics

         Class here family life education

         For sewing, see 372.54

.83   *Social studies

         For history and geography, see 372.89

.832   *Civics (Citizenship)

.84   *Religion

.86   *Physical education

         Including movement education

         See also 372.66 for dance

.87   *Music

.872   Appreciation

.873   Performance

         Including reading music

.874   Composition

.89   History and geography

.890 1–.890 3   Standard subdivisions of history

.890 4   Special topics

.890 42–.890 44   Special subdivisions of history

         Add to base number 372.8904 the numbers following 04 in notation 042–044 from the table under 372.3–372.8, e.g., teaching history 372.89044

(.890 45)   Textbooks of general history

         (Optional number; prefer 909)

         (If this number is used, class history textbooks on specific continents, countries, localities in 372.893–372.899)

.890 49   Specific levels of instruction in history

.890 5–.890 9   Standard subdivisions of history

.891   Geography

.891 01–.891 03   Standard subdivisions of geography

.891 04   Special topics

*Add as instructed under 372.3–372.8

.891 042–.891 044   Special subdivisions of geography

> Add to base number 372.89104 the numbers following 04 in notation 042–044 from the table under 372.3–372.8, e.g., using maps in geography 372.891044

(.891 045)   Textbooks of general geography

> (Optional number; prefer 910

> (If this number is used, class geography textbooks on specific places in 372.8911–372.8919)

.891 049   Specific levels of instruction in geography

.891 05–.891 09   Standard subdivisions

(.891 1–.891 9)   Geography textbooks on specific places

> (Optional number; prefer 910.91, 913–919)

> Add to base number 372.891 notation 1–9 from Table 2, e.g., geography textbooks on Asia 372.8915

(.893–.899)   History textbooks on the ancient world, on specific continents, countries, localities

> (Optional number; prefer 930–990)

> Add to base number 372.89 notation 3–9 from Table 2, e.g., history textbooks on ancient Egypt 372.8932

> _For geography textbooks on specific places, see 372.8911–372.8919_

.9   **Historical, geographical, persons treatment of elementary education**

> Add to base number 372.9 notation 01–9 from Table 2, e.g., elementary education in Brazil 372.981

373   Secondary education

> Class special education at the secondary level in 371.9

SUMMARY

373.01–.09	[Standard subdivisions, objectives, experimental schools]
.1	Organization and management of secondary education; curriculums
.2	Types and levels of secondary education
.3–.9	Secondary education and schools by specific continents, countries, localities

.01   Philosophy and theory

.011   Secondary education for specific objectives

> Including evaluation of effects and effectiveness

> Add to base number 373.011 the numbers following 370.11 in 370.112–370.118, e.g., education for social responsibility 373.0115

> Do not use for systems; class 373.01

[.013]   Value

> Do not use; class in 373.011

.04	Special topics
.042	Experimental schools
[.068]	Management

Do not use; class in 373.12

.07	Education, research, related topics

Class professional education for secondary school teachers in 370.7123

[.071 1]	Schools and courses in higher education

Do not use; class in 370.73263

[.082]	History and description with respect to women

Do not use; class in 376.63

.09	Historical, geographical, persons treatment

Class treatment by specific continents, countries, localities in 373.3–373.9 (*not* 373.093–373.099)

.1 Organization and management of secondary education; curriculums

Class comprehensive works on specific types and levels in 373.2

.109	Historical, geographical, persons treatment

Class treatment by continent, country, locality in 373.3–373.9 (*not* 373.1093–373.1099)

.11–.18	Organization and management

Add to base number 373.1 the numbers following 371 in 371.1–371.8, e.g., professional qualifications of teachers 373.112

For experimental schools, see 373.042

.19	Curriculums

Add to base number 373.19 the numbers following 375.008 in 375.0082–375.0088, e.g., vocational education curriculums 373.196

Class courses of study in a specific subject with the subject, using notation 0712 from Table 1, e.g., mathematics curriculums 510.712; educational programs of secondary schools offering specific types of curriculums in 373.24–373.26

.2 Types and levels of secondary education

Class continuation schools in 374.8, organization and administration of a specific type or level in 373.11–373.18, specific schools in 373.3–373.9

.22	Public and private

Class curriculums in 373.19

.222 Private schools

Boarding and day schools regardless of level or type of curriculum

Examples: public schools (United Kingdom), military academies basically academic in nature, preparatory schools

For schools supported by religious groups, see 377.8–377.9

.224 Public schools

Class specific levels of public secondary schools in 373.23, public secondary schools offering specific types of curriculum in 373.24–373.26

.23 Levels of secondary schools

Class here upper sections of all-age schools

Use of this number for comprehensive works on all-age schools discontinued; class in 370

Class schools offering specific types of curriculum regardless of level in 373.24–373.26, curriculums of other schools regardless of level in 373.19, private schools regardless of level in 373.222

For the elementary sections of all-age schools, see 372.24

.236 Lower level

Examples: junior high schools, middle schools

Including advanced and postelementary classes of elementary schools, transition classes

.238 Upper level

Examples: senior high schools, sixth-form colleges (United Kingdom)

Including high school equivalency programs

> **373.24–373.26 Schools offering specific types of curriculum**

Class comprehensive works in 373.2, private schools regardless of type of curriculum in 373.222

.24 Academic and vocational schools

> **373.241–373.242 Academic schools**

Schools preparing for higher education

Class comprehensive works in 373.24

.241 Modern academic

Schools emphasizing sciences and modern languages

Examples: grammar schools (United Kingdom), gymnasiums, lycées

.242   Classical

Schools emphasizing Latin and Greek

.243   Military schools

Schools offering professional military education at secondary levels

Including naval schools

.246   Vocational schools

Schools that offer both a general education and a vocational program

Vocational schools concentrating in specific subjects relocated to the subject, with use of notation 0712 from Table 1, e.g., a secondary school of business and commerce 650.0712

Class comprehensiveworks on vocational education in 370.113, vocational training for adults in 374.013

See also 373.243 for military schools

.25   Comprehensive schools

Schools offering academic, vocational, general programs

Including bilateral schools (United Kingdom)

.26   General secondary schools

Schools offering nonvocational, general terminal education

Including secondary modern schools (United Kingdom)

.27   Apprenticeship training

Conducted as part of the educational system

Including apprenticeship centers

Class the economic aspects of apprenticeship training offered by industry in 331.25922, managerial aspects in 658.3124

.28   Work-study programs

Programs in which the student spends part of his day in school and part on a job, usually in the community

.3–.9   Secondary education and schools by specific continents, countries, localities

Add to base number 373 notation 3–9 from Table 2, e.g., secondary schools of Australia 373.94

374   Adult education

Education outside the regular sequence of schools and courses, offered to and pursued by individuals beyond school-leaving age

Class here continuing (nondegree) education, further education, lifelong education, permanent education, recurrent education

Class special education of adults in 371.9; the educational role of libraries in 021.24; programs leading to a degree, diploma, certificate with the program, e.g., high school equivalency programs 373.238, university extension work 378.1554; schools and courses on a specific subject with the subject, using notation 0715, e.g., a law course for adults 340.0715

> *See also 378.03 for alternative higher education*

.001–.008	Standard subdivisions
[.009]	Historical, geographical, persons treatment

> Do not use; class in 374.9

.01   Adult education for specific objectives

> Class here curriculums

.012   Adult basic education

> Including adult literacy programs, citizenship programs, remedial education

.013   Vocational and occupational education

> Schools and courses in specific subjects relocated to the subject, with use of notation 0715 from Table 1, e.g., a course on office management 651.30715

[.02]   Methods of instruction and study

> Relocated to 374.13

.1   General topics

> Add to base number 374.1 the numbers following 371 in 371.1–371.8, e.g., methods of instruction and study 374.13 [*formerly* 374.02]; however, class use of computers and electronic devices in 374.26, of mass media in 374.27

> Class schools in 374.8

.2   Group education, use of electronic and mass media, institutions and agencies

[.21]   Special-interest groups

> Relocated to 374.22

.22   Kinds of groups

> Examples: special-interest groups [*formerly* 374.21], discussion, reading, self-help, study groups

.26   Use of electronic media and devices

> Examples: television [*formerly* 374.27], computers, radio

.27   Use of mass media

> Television relocated to 374.26
>
> *For use of electronic media and devices, see 374.26*

.28   Community centers for adult education

.29   Institutions and agencies

> Including day-release courses (United Kingdom)
>
> *For community centers, see 374.28; schools, 374.8*
>
> *See also 020 for libraries and library services*

.4 Correspondence schools and courses

.409   Historical, geographical, persons treatment

> Class treatment by specific continents, countries, localities in the modern world in 374.44–374.49 (*not* 374.4094–374.4099)

.44–.49   Treatment by specific continents, countries, localities in the modern world

> Add to base number 374.4 notation 4–9 from Table 2, e.g., correspondence schools in Canada 374.471

.8 Schools

> Examples: continuation schools, folk high schools, night schools, proprietary vocational schools, vacation schools
>
> Class comprehensive works on institutions and agencies in 374.29
>
> *For correspondence schools, see 374.4*
>
> *See also 378.1554 for university extension departments*

.809   Historical, geographical, persons treatment

> Class treatment by specific continents, countries, localities in the modern world in 374.84–374.89 (*not* 374.8094–374.8099)

.84–.89   Treatment by specific continents, countries, localities in the modern world

> Add to base number 374.4 notation 4–9 from Table 2, e.g., schools in Canada 374.871

.9 Historical, geographical, persons treatment

> Add to base number 374.9 notation 01–99 from Table 2, e.g., adult education in the 20th century 374.904

375 Curriculums

Programs of study covering more than one level of education

Class here curriculums in demonstration schools having no specific level

Class curriculums at a specific level with the level, e.g., secondary 373.19

See Manual at 375

.000 1–.000 8	Standard subdivisions
.000 9	Historical periods

> Class regions; persons; treatment by specific continents, countries, localities in 375.009

.001	Planning, design, construction
.002	Required courses
.004	Elective courses
.006	Evaluation and revision
.008	Curriculums and courses of study directed toward specific objectives
.008 2	International studies
.008 3	Environmental studies
.008 4	Ethnic studies
.008 5	Consumer education
.008 6	Vocational education (Career education)
.008 8	Humanistic education (Liberal education)
.009	Geographical and persons treatment

> Add to base number 375.009 notation 1–9 from Table 2, e.g., curriculums in India 375.00954

.01–.03   Curriculums and courses in bibliography, library and information sciences, encyclopedias

> Add to base number 375 notation 010–039, e.g., curriculums in cataloging and classification 375.0253

.04   Curriculums and courses in knowledge, systems study, data processing, computer science

> Add to base number 375.04 the numbers following 00 in 001–006, e.g., curriculums in computer science 375.044

.05–.99   Curriculums and courses of study in other specific subjects

> Add to base number 375 notation 050–999, e.g., curriculums in history 375.9

> Class curriculums and courses of study in specific subjects at the elementary level in 372.3–372.8; at higher levels with the subject, using notation 071 from Table 1, e.g., curriculums in law 340.071

376   Education of women

Including coeducation versus separate education for women

See also 370.19345 for sexism in education

[.09]   Historical, geographical, persons treatment

Do not use; class in 376.9

.5   **Convent education**

.6   **Education of women by level**

Class the elementary education of girls in 372

.63   Secondary

Class specific schools in 373.3–373.9, specific topics in 373.1–373.2

.65   Higher

Class specific topics in 378.01–378.38

For colleges for women, see 376.8

.8   **Colleges for women**

Class specific colleges for women in 378.4–378.9

.9   **Historical, geographical, persons treatment**

Add to base number 376.9 notation 01–99 from Table 2, e.g., collected biographies of persons important in the education of women 376.922

377   Schools and religion

Class aspects of schools and religion not provided for below with the subject in education, e.g., a Catholic secondary school in New York City 373.7471 (*not* 377.82097471)

.1   **Religion and secular education**

Including released time

.14   Religious observances in public schools

Examples: morning assembly, prayer

.3   **Monastic schools**

.6   **Mission schools**

Schools operated by religious bodies as part of their missionary work

---

>   **377.8–377.9 Schools supported by religious groups**

Class comprehensive works in 377, schools for women supported by religious groups in 376, a specific school with its level, e.g., a specific secondary school in the appropriate subdivision of 373.3–373.9

For monastic schools, see 377.3; mission schools, 377.6

.8 **Schools supported by Christian groups**

Add to base number 377.8 the numbers following 28 in 281–289, e.g., Roman Catholic schools 377.82

.9 **Schools supported by other groups**

Add to base number 377.9 the numbers following 29 in 292–299, e.g., Islamic schools 377.97

378 Higher education

Class special education at higher levels in 371.9; institutions for higher education in a specific subject with the subject, using notation 0711 from Table 1, e.g., law schools 340.0711

SUMMARY

378.001–.009	Standard subdivisions
.01–.05	[General topics in higher education]
.1	Organization and management of institutions of higher education; curriculums
.2	Academic degrees
.3	Student finances
.4–.9	Higher education and institutions by specific continents, countries, localities in the modern world

.001 Philosophy and theory

[.001 3] Value

Do not use; class in 378.01

.002–.005 Standard subdivisions

.006 Organizations and management

[.006 8] Management

Do not use; class in 378.1

.007 Education, research, related topics

Class professional education of college and university teachers in 370.7124

[.007 11] Schools and courses in higher education

Do not use; class in 370.73264

.007 9 Competitions and awards

Do not use for financial support; class in 378.3

.008 History and description with respect to kinds of persons

[.008 2] Women

Do not use; class in 376.65

.009   Historical, geographical, persons treatment

       Class treatment by specific continents, countries, localities in the modern world in 378.4–378.9 (*not* 378.0094–378.0099)

.01   Higher education for specific objectives

       Including evaluation of effects and effectiveness

       Add to base number 378.01 the numbers following 370.11 in 370.112–370.118, e.g., professional education 378.013

.02   Financial management

       Including fees and tuition

       Class financial administration of publicly supported universities and colleges in 379.118

.03   Alternative (Nontraditional) higher education

       Examples: free universities, open universities, universities without walls; external degrees, independent study plans, learner-centered education, open learning

       Class ownership and control of alternative (nontraditional) institutions in 378.04–378.05, extension courses in 378.1554

       See also 374 for adult education

\>   378.04–378.05 Kinds of colleges and universities

       Class comprehensive works in 378; specific institutions in 378.4–378.9; colleges and universities on a specific subject with the subject, e.g., the U.S. Military Academy at West Point 355.0071173

.04   Private colleges and universities

       For schools supported by religious groups, see 377.8–377.9

.05   Public colleges and universities

.052   City, county, regional colleges and universities

.053   State, provincial colleges and universities

       Use of this number for comprehensive works on institutions controlled by central governments discontinued; class in 378.05

       For land-grant institutions, see 378.054

.054   Land-grant institutions

.055   National colleges and universities

.1   **Organization and management; curriculums**

       Class financial management in 378.02

SUMMARY

378.100 1–.100 9	**Standard subdivisions**	
	.101–.107	**[General topics]**
	.11	**Staff**
	.12	**Faculty**
	.14	**College year**
	.15	**Types and levels of institutions**
	.16	**Educational measurement and student placement**
	.17	**Methods of instruction and study**
	.18	**School discipline**
	.19	**Other aspects**

.100 1–.100 8   Standard subdivisions

.100 681   Higher education

.100 9   Historical, geographical, persons treatment

> Class treatment by specific continents, countries, localities in the modern world in 378.4–378.9 (*not* 378.10094–378.10099)

.101   Government

.101 1   Governing bodies

> Examples: boards, trustees, faculty senates and councils

.101 2   Policies and regulations

.103   Relations with the community

> Example: community service by institutions of higher education

.104   Cooperation among colleges and universities

> Class specific instances of cooperation with the subject, e.g., cooperation in computer networking 004.6

.105   Matriculation

> Including advanced placement

> Add to base number 378.105 the numbers following 371.21 in 371.216–371.219, e.g., entrance requirements 378.1057

.107   Aspects of administration

> Planning, organizing, directing, coordinating, reporting, decision making, leadership

> Including student participation in administration

.11   Staff

> Class here personnel administration

.111   Academic staff

> Examples: college and university presidents, deans of academic departments

> *For faculty, see 378.12*

.112	Nonacademic staff

Examples: deans of men and women, counselors

.12	Faculty
.121	Academic privileges, prerogatives, immunities, responsibilities

Including academic freedom

Class tenure in 378.122

.122	Organization

Examples: hierarchy, work load, tenure

.124	Personal and professional qualifications
.125	Teaching in colleges and universities

For methods of instruction and study, see 378.17

.14	College year

Including school calendar

.142	Summer school
.146	All year school
.15	Types and levels of institutions

Class specific institutions in 378.4–378.9, specific topics of organization and management regardless of type or level in 378.101–378.146, 378.16–378.19

.154	Lower-level institutions

Academic institutions not offering professional programs, generally not awarding advanced degrees

.154 2	Four-year colleges
.154 3	Two-year colleges

Including junior colleges

See also 378.052 for community colleges

.154 4	Evening colleges
.155	Universities

Institutions offering a wide range of academic and professional studies

.155 2	Undergraduate departments

Departments offering programs leading to lower degrees, e.g., bachelor's degrees

.155 3	Graduate departments and schools

Departments and schools offering programs leading to advanced degrees

Class here postdoctoral programs

.155 4	Extension departments

For evening colleges, see 378.1544

.16	Educational measurement and student placement
.166–.167	Educational tests, measurements, marking systems

Add to base number 378.16 the numbers following 371.2 in 371.26–371.27, e.g., the use of college entrance board examinations 378.1664

.168	Credit and credit systems

Including college level examination programs

.169	Student mobility

Including dropouts, transfer students

.17	Methods of instruction and study

Add to base number 378.17 the numbers following 371.3 in 371.3028–371.39, e.g., seminars 378.177

.18	School discipline

Add to base number 378.18 the numbers following 371.5 in 371.51–371.59, e.g., student government 378.189

.19	Other topics
.194	Guidance and counseling

Add to base number 378.194 the numbers following 371.4 in 371.42–371.46, e.g., educational guidance 378.19422

.196–.198	Physical plant, health and safety, the student

Add to base number 378.19 the numbers following 371 in 371.6–371.8, e.g., student unrest 378.1981

.199	Curriculums

Add to base number 378.199 the numbers following 375.008 in 375.0082–375.0088, e.g., vocational education 378.1996

Class courses of study in a specific subject with the subject, using notation 0711 from Table 1, e.g., mathematics curriculums 510.711

.2	**Academic degrees**
.24	Earned degrees
.241	Course, residence, subject requirements
.242	Thesis and dissertation requirements

Class preparation of theses in 808

.25	Honorary degrees
.28	Costumes and symbols

.3   **Student finances**

Class finances of students in a specific field with the field, using notation 071 from Table 1, e.g., in medical education 610.711

\>   378.33–378.36 Sources of income

Class comprehensive works in 378.3, veterans' education benefits in 362.8682

.33   Fellowships and grants

.34   Scholarships

.35   Educational exchanges

Financing of college study through grants for international study

Class comprehensive works on educational exchange in 370.196

.36   Loans and employment

.362   Loans

.365   Employment

.38   Costs and expenditures

.4–.9   **Higher education and institutions by specific continents, countries, localities in the modern world**

Class here directories

Add to base number 378 notation 4–9 from Table 2, e.g., higher education in Mexico 378.72

(Option: If it is desired to give local emphasis and a shorter number to a specific college or university, place it first by use of a letter or other symbol, e.g., University of South Africa 378.S [preceding 378.4])

Class a school, institute, or college of a university with the subject, using notation 071 from Table 1, e.g., Harvard Law School 340.07117444; alumni of a specific institution with the institution, faculty in 378.12, administrators in 378.11

379   Government regulation, control, support of education

Former heading: Education and the state

Not provided for in 370–378

Class the administration of education departments in 351.851, of cabinet level departments of education in 351.0851

See Manual at 371.2 vs. 379

SUMMARY

379.09	**Historical, geographical, persons treatment**
.1	**Finance, supervision, control of public education**
.2	**Public education and the state**
.3	**Private education and the state**
.4–.9	**Government regulation, control, support of public education by specific continents, countries, localities in the modern world**

.09   Historical, geographical, persons treatment

> Class treatment by specific continents, countries, localities in modern world in 379.4–379.9 (*not* 379.094–379.099)

.1   **Finance, supervision, control of public education**

>   379.11–379.13 Finance

> Class comprehensive works in 379.11

.11   Financial administration in public education

> General aspects: costs, expenditures, allocation and management of funds, budgets, budgeting, financial reports

> Class the financial administration of schools in a specific field with the field, using notation 071 from Table 1, e.g., costs for medical schools 610.711; sources of funds in 379.13

.112   Elementary education

.113   Secondary education

.114   Adult education

.118   Higher education

.119   Special education

.12   Assistance by central governments

> Class financial administration of schools and educational systems operated by central governments in 379.11, revenue sources in 379.13

.121   By national governments

.121 2   For elementary and secondary education

.121 4   For higher education

.121 5   For adult education

.121 6   For special education

.122   By state, provincial, regional governments

> Add to base number 379.122 the numbers following 379.121 in 379.1212–379.1216, e.g., support for adult education 379.1225

.123   By local governments

.13	Revenue sources

> Examples: bond issues, taxation, tuition in public schools, voucher system
>
> *See also 379.12 for assistance from higher governmental levels*

.15	Supervision and control

> **379.151–379.153 By governmental level**
>
> Class comprehensive works in 379.15, elements of supervision and control regardless of level in 379.154–379.158

.151	National
.152	State, regional, provincial
.153	Local
.153 1	School boards
.153 5	School districts

> Including centralization and consolidation

> **379.154– 379.158 Elements of supervision and control**
>
> Class comprehensive works in 379.15

.154	Policy, planning, related elements

> Including school evaluation, accountability
>
> Class evaluation of teachers in 371.144, accreditation and standards in 379.158

.155	Supervision and control of curriculum and courses of study
.155 2	Vocational education programs
.156	Supervision of educational materials

> Examples: library books, textbooks

.157	Supervision of teachers, administrators, their activities

> Class here supervision of personnel actions, such as certification, registration, tenure
>
> Class personnel management in 371.1

.158	School standards and accreditation

> Class here governmental commissions on higher education that operate in a supervisory capacity and play an important role in accreditation and development of school standards
>
> Class accreditation of schools teaching a specific subject with the subject, using notation 07 from Table 1, e.g., accreditation of library schools 020.711

.2   Public education and the state

> Class here educational policy

> Class religion in public education in 377.1; public regulation, control, support of private education in 379.3

> *For finance, supervision, control, see 379.1*

.201   Theory

> Aims, objectives, values; effect of political process on quantity and quality of education

.209   Historical, geographical, persons treatment

> Class treatment by specific continents, countries, localities in the modern world in 379.4–379.9 (*not* 379.2094–379.2099)

.23   Compulsory education

> Including school-leaving age

.24   Reduction of illiteracy

.3   Private education and the state

> Class here public regulation, control, support of private education

.32   Financial assistance

.322   Elementary and secondary education

.324   Higher education

.326   Adult education

.328   Special education

.34   Supervision and control

.342   Elementary and secondary education

.344   Higher education

.346   Adult education

.348   Special education

.4–.9   Government regulation, control, support of public education by specific continents, countries, localities in the modern world

> Add to base number 379 notation 4–9 from Table 2, e.g., government regulation of public education in the United States 379.73

380 Commerce, communications, transportation

Use 380.01–380.09 for standard subdivisions

Aside from additions, changes, deletions, exceptions shown under specific entries, add to notation for each term identified by * as follows:

06		Organization and management
065		Business organizations
		Examples: individual proprietorships, partnerships, companies, public and private corporations, combinations
		Add to 065 notation 3–9 from Table 2, e.g., business organizations of France 06544
068		Management
		Class here public and private policy, planning, programs, proposals
09		Historical and geographical treatment
		Class specific business organizations in 065

Class public regulation and control in 351.8

See Manual at 380

SUMMARY

380.1	**Commerce (Trade)**
381	**Internal commerce (Domestic trade)**
382	**International commerce (Foreign trade)**
383	**Postal communication**
384	**Communications Telecommunication**
385	**Railroad transportation**
386	**Inland waterway and ferry transportation**
387	**Water, air, space transportation**
388	**Transportation Ground transportation**
389	**Metrology and standardization**

.1 ***Commerce (Trade)**

Class here marketing, warehousing

Class interdisciplinary works on consumption in 339.47; supply and demand in 338.1–338.5; restrictive practices in business organizations engaged in commerce in 338.6–338.8

For domestic trade, see 381; foreign trade, 382; cooperative marketing, 334.6813801

See Manual at 380.1 and 381, 382; 380.1 vs. 658.8

*Add as instructed under 380

.102 9   Commercial miscellany

Class here interdisciplinary works on commercial miscellany

Class commercial miscellany respecting specific goods and services with the goods and services, using notation 029 from Table 1, e.g., buyers guides' for tools 621.900296

In most cases, notation 029 from Table 1 is not to be used with the subdivisions of 380.1, the major exception being 380.14500029

See Manual at 380.1 and 381, 382

[.102 97]   Evaluation and purchasing manuals

Do not use; class in 381.33

.13   Commercial policy

Class commercial policy with respect to specific commodities and services, to specific groups of commodities and services in 380.14

.14   Specific commodities and services and specific groups of commodities and services

.141   *Products of agriculture

[.141 029]   Commercial miscellany

Relocated to 630.209

.141 3–.141 8   Specific products

Add to base number 380.141 the numbers following 63 in 633–638, e.g., rice 380.141318

.142   *Products of mineral industries

[.142 029]   Commercial miscellany

Relocated to 553.029

.142 2–.142 9   Specific products

Add to base number 380.142 the numbers following 553 in 553.2–553.9, e.g., petroleum 380.142282

.143   *Products of other extractive industries

[.143 029]   Commercial miscellany

Relocated to 639.029

.143 1   *Products of culture of invertebrates and cold-blooded vertebrates

Class products of insect culture in 380.1418

[.143 102 9]   Commercial miscellany

Relocated to 639.029

.143 13–.143 17   Specific products

Add to base number 380.1431 the numbers following 639 in 639.3–639.7, e.g., oysters 380.143141

*Add as instructed under 380

.143 2–.143 9   Products of fishing, whaling, hunting, trapping

Add to base number 380.143 the numbers following 59 in 592–599, e.g., bearskins 380.143974446, comprehensive works on products of both finfishing and shellfishing industries 380.1437

.144   *Human beings (Slave trade)

.145   *Products of secondary industries and services

Use 380.1450001–380.1450009 for standard subdivisions

Add to base number 380.145 notation 001–999, e.g., clothing 380.145687

See Manual at 709.2 vs. 380.1457092

[.3]   **Communications**

Relocated to 384

[.5]   **Transportation**   KEEP HERE. 388 NOT SUITABLE FOR CHILDREN'S BOOKS.

Relocated to 388

>   **381–382 General internal and international commerce (Trade)**

Class here marketing

Class comprehensive works in 380.1; supply and demand in 338.1–338.5; restrictive practices in, business organizations engaged in commerce in 338.6–338.8

381   *Internal commerce (Domestic trade)

See Manual at 380.1, 381, 382

[.029 6]   Evaluation and purchasing manuals

Do not use; class in 381.33

.1   *Retail trade

Including exhibit and trade shows, telemarketing, telephone selling, television selling

Class consumer problems and their alleviation in 381.3; retail trade in specific commodities and services, in specific groups of commodities and services in 381.4

Telephone-order houses, telephone selling organizations class in 381.142

For consumer cooperatives, see 334.5

.12   *Chain stores

Class chain stores with a specific merchandising pattern in 381.14

*Add as instructed under 380

.13   *Franchise businesses

> Class franchise businesses with a specific merchandising pattern in 381.14

.14   Retail channels by merchandising pattern

.141   *Department stores

.142   *Mail-order and *telephone-order houses

> Including television selling organizations

.147   *Convenience stores

.148   *Supermarkets

.149   *Discount stores

.15   *Factory outlets

.17   *Auctions

.18   *Outdoor and street markets

> Including fairs

> Class outdoor and street markets for secondhand goods in 381.19

.19   *Outlets for secondhand goods

> *For auctions, see 381.17*

.192   *Flea markets

.195   Garage, yard, apartment sales

.2   *Wholesale trade

> Class wholesale trade in specific commodities and groups of commodities in 381.4

.3   Commercial policy

> Class here consumer problems and their alleviation, consumerism

> Class commercial policy with respect to specific kinds of domestic trade in 381.1–381.2, 381.5; with respect to specific commodities and services, to specific groups of commodities and services in 381.4

.32   Consumer movements

> Class specific activities of consumer movements in 381.33–381.34

*Add as instructed under 380

.33   Consumer information

             Provision of information to consumers by governments and private groups

             Including research, testing of products

             Class here comprehensive works on evaluation of commodities to be
             purchased [*formerly* 658.72], interdisciplinary evaluation and purchasing
             manuals

             Class evaluation and purchasing guides and consumer education for
             household and personal products and services in 640.73; evaluation and
             purchasing manuals for specific products or services with the subject with
             use of notation 0297 from Table 1, e.g., manual on evaluating tools
             621.900297

.34   Consumer protection

             Government and private action directed toward producers and sellers to
             promote product quality and safety, truth in advertising and labeling

             Class product hazards in 363.19

.4   **Specific commodities and services and specific groups of commodities
             and services**

             Class here works discussing consumption as a measure of the volume, value, or
             kind of trade in specific commodities

             Add to base number 381.4 the numbers following 380.14 in 380.141–380.145,
             e.g., domestic trade in rice 381.41318; however, commercial miscellany for
             products of agriculture relocated from 381.41029 to 630.209, commercial
             miscellany for products of mineral industries relocated from 381.42029 to
             553.029, commercial miscellany for products of other extractive industries
             relocated from 381.43029 to 639.029, commercial miscellany for products of
             culture of invertebrates and cold-blooded vertebrates relocated from
             381.431029 to 639.029

             Class interdisciplinary works on consumption of specific commodities and
             services in 339.48

.5   ***Interregional and interstate commerce**

             Commerce between parts of a single jurisdiction

             Class specific kinds of interregional and interstate commerce in 381.1–381.2;
             interregional and interstate commerce in specific commodities and services in
             specific groups of commodities and services in 381.4

382   ***International commerce (Foreign trade)**

             Class here trade between nations and their colonies, protectorates, trusts

             See Manual at 380.1 and 381, 382

*Add as instructed under 380

SUMMARY

382.01–.09	**Standard subdivisions**	
.1	**Generalities of international commerce**	
.3	**Commercial policy**	
.4	**Specific commodities and services and specific groups of commodities and services**	
.5	**Import trade**	
.6	**Export trade**	
.7	**Tariff policy**	
.9	**Trade agreements and their implementation**	

.01   Philosophy and theory

> Class theories in 382.104

.09   Historical, geographical, persons treatment

> Add to base number 382.09 notation 1–9 from Table 2, e.g., international trade of United Kingdom 382.0941; then, for trade between two countries, regions, areas, places, add 0† and again add notation 1–9 from Table 2, e.g., trade between United Kingdom and communist bloc 382.094101717

> Give priority in notation to the country, region, area, place emphasized. If emphasis is equal, give priority to the one coming first in the sequence of area notations
>> (Option: Give priority in notation to the country, region, area, place requiring local emphasis, e.g., libraries in United States class trade between United Kingdom and United States in 382.0973041)

.1   **Generalities of international commerce**

> *See also 337 for international economics*

.104   Theories

.104 2   Specialization and comparative advantage

> Advantages enjoyed by an area for engaging in certain kinds of production, e.g., climate; supply of capital, labor, land and other natural resources; transportation, access to markets

.104 4   Price determination in international markets

.17   Balance of payments

> Relation between payments and receipts resulting from all commercial and financial transactions carried on between the citizens and government of a country and the citizens and governments of all other countries

> Class here balance of trade

.173   Capital transactions

> Relation between receipts and payments on long- and short-term loans and credit

.174   Currency movements

> Including gold movements, relation of monetary conditions to world trade

†Use 00 for standard subdivisions; see instructions at beginning of Table 1

.3　　**Commercial policy**

> Class policy with respect to specific aspects and kinds of trade in 382.1, 382.5–382.9; with respect to specific commodities and services, to specific groups of commodities and services in 382.4; economic imperialism in 337

.4　　**Specific commodities and services and specific groups of commodities and services**

> Class here works discussing consumption as a measure of the volume, value, or kind of trade in specific commodities

> Add to base number 382.4 the numbers following 380.14 in 380.141–380.145, e.g., foreign trade in rice 382.41318; however, commercial miscellany for products of agriculture relocated from 382.41029 to 630.209, commercial miscellany for products of mineral industries relocated from 382.42029 to 553.029, commercial miscellany for products of other extractive industries relocated from 382.43029 to 639.029, commercial miscellany for products of culture of invertebrates and cold-blooded vertebrates relocated from 382.431029 to 639.029

> Class interdisciplinary works on consumption of specific commodities and services in 339.48

.5　　***Import trade**

> Class here nontariff barriers to trade

> Class import of specific products and services and specific groups of products and services in 382.4; the combined import and export trade of a country, the trade between two countries in 382.09; agreements on nontariff barriers to trade in 382.9

> *For tariff policy, see 382.7*

.52　　Import quotas

.53　　Embargoes on imports

.54　　Licensing of imports

.6　　***Export trade**

> Class export of specific products and services and specific groups of products and services in 382.4; the combined import and export trade of a country, the trade between two countries in 382.09

.61　　Nature and utilization of specific export market areas

.610 9　　　Historical, geographical, persons treatment

> > Class here the area to which goods are being exported

> > Class the area doing the exporting in 382.609

.63　　Export policy

> Including subsidies, services to exporters

> *For export controls and restrictions, see 382.64*

*Add as instructed under 380

.64   Export controls and restrictions

>   Including licensing, inspection

.7   Tariff policy

>   Example: drawbacks
>
>   Class here comprehensive works on trade barriers and restrictions
>
>   Class tax aspects of customs duties in 336.26, agreements on trade barriers in 382.9; tariff policies with respect to specific commodities and groups of commodities in 382.4
>
>   *For nontariff barriers to trade, see 382.5*

.71   Free trade (No tariff)

.72   Tariff for revenue (Fiscal tariff)

.73   Protective and prohibitive tariff

.75   Single and multiple column tariffs

.752   Single column tariffs

>   Single rates for each commodity

.753   Multiple column tariffs

>   Varying rates on the same commodity designed to favor certain countries of origin
>
>   Example: generalized system of preference (GSP)

.78   Exemptions

.782   Personal and institutional

>   Examples: commodities used for educational purposes, privileges for foreign-service personnel, for tourists

.788   On relief supplies

.9   Trade agreements and their implementation

>   Class here agreements on nontariff barriers to trade, on tariffs
>
>   Class trade agreements on other specific subjects in 382.1, 382.4–382.6; general economic cooperation and international arrangements for this purpose in 337; texts and discussions of treaties in 341.754

.909   Historical, geographical, persons treatment

>   Class multilateral agreements in 382.91, treatment by specific countries in 382.93–382.99

.91   Multilateral agreements and customs unions

>   Class bilateral agreements in 382.93–382.99
>
>   *For General Agreement on Tariffs and Trade, see 382.92*

.911	In areas, regions, places in general

Add to base number 382.911 the numbers following —1 in notation 11–19 from Table 2, e.g., Western Hemisphere 382.911812

.913	In ancient world

Add to base number 382.91 the numbers following —3 in notation 31–39 from Table 2, e.g., ancient Greece 382.9138

>   382.914–382.919 In modern world

Class comprehensive works in 382.91

.914	In Europe
.914 2	European Economic Community (European Common Market, EEC)
.914 3	European Free Trade Association (EFTA)
.914 7	Council for Mutual Economic Assistance (COMECON)

          Former heading: East European Economic Organization

.915–.919	In other continents and regions

Add to base number 382.91 notation 5–9 from Table 2, e.g., southeast Asia 382.9159

.92	General Agreement on Tariffs and Trade (GATT)
.93–.99	By specific countries

Add to base number 382.9 notation 3–9 from Table 2, e.g., trade agreements of United Kingdom 382.941; then, for bilateral agreements, add 0* and again add notation 3–9 from Table 2, e.g., agreements between United Kingdom and France 382.941044

Give priority in notation to the country emphasized. If emphasis is equal, give priority to the one coming first in the sequence of area notations (Option: Give priority in notation to the country requiring local emphasis, e.g., libraries in United States class agreements between United Kingdom and United States in 382.973041)

>   **383–388 Communications and transportation**

Class comprehensive works on communications and transportation, on transportation in 388, on communications in 384

See Manual at 383–388

383   Postal communication

Class comprehensive works on communications in 384

See also 769.56 for philately

See Manual at 383–388

*Use 00 for standard subdivisions; see instructions at beginning of Table 1

.06	Organizations and management
	Class postal organizations in 383.4
[.09]	Historical, geographical, persons treatment
	Do not use; class in 383.49

.1 Mail handling

.12 Classes of mail

Use 383.12001–383.12009 for standard subdivisions

Class a specific service for a specific class of mail with the service, e.g., special delivery of letters 383.183

> 383.120 2–383.120 5 Special classes

Class comprehensive works in 383.12

.120 2 Free mail

Example: franking privileges

.120 5 Nonmailable matter

Examples: fraudulent promotion and advertising, obscene and subversive material

.122 Letters, postcards, sealed material

Class here first-class mail

.123 Newspapers and periodicals

Class here second-class mail

.124 Printed material

Not provided for elsewhere

Examples: books, catalogs, circulars

Including bulk mailings

Class here third-class mail

.125 Parcels

Class here fourth-class mail

Class printed matter in 383.124

.14 Collection, transportation systems, delivery

> 383.141–383.144 Transportation systems

Class comprehensive works in 383.14

.141 Instantaneous facsimile transmission

.142	Sea mail
.143	Overland mail

.143 Overland mail

Examples: highway, railroad, inland waterway

Including star routes

.144 Air mail

Including mail carried through space

.145 Collection and delivery

Including postal zones, zip codes

Class star routes in 383.143, special delivery in 383.183, collection and delivery of mail within the military services in 355.69

.18 Other services

.182 Insurance and registry of mail

.183 Special delivery and special handling

.184 Collection of charges on delivery (COD)

.186 Dead letter services

.2 Economic aspects of postal service

Class economic aspects of mail handling in 383.1

.23 Rates and costs

Including use of postage stamps

.24 Efficiency of operation

Including use of mechanization and automation

.4 Postal organization

See Manual at 351.873 vs. 383.4

[.409] Historical, geographical, persons treatment

Do not use; class in 383.49

.41 International systems and conventions

.42 Post offices

.46 Internal services

Examples: dispatching and routing, postal inspection

.49 Historical, geographical, persons treatment of postal communication, of postal organizations and systems

Add to base number 383.49 notation 1–9 from Table 2, e.g., postal communication in Europe 383.494

384   *Communications [*formerly* 380.3]   Telecommunication

Examples: recordings, visual signaling

Class comprehensive works on communications and transportation in 388

For postal communication, see 383

See also 302.2 for sociology of communication

See Manual at 383–388

SUMMARY

384.04	**Special topics**
.1	**Telegraphy**
.3	**Computer communication**
.5	**Wireless communication**
.6	**Telephony**
.8	**Motion pictures**

.04   Special topics

.041   Economic aspects

Examples: competition, costs, efficiency, finance, income, market, rates, supply and demand

Including forms of ownership

Class economic aspects of facilities in 384.042, of services in 384.043

.042   Facilities

Examples: apparatus, stations

Class use of facilities in specific services in 384.043

.043   Services

>   **384.1–384.7 Telecommunication**

Class comprehensive works in 384

.1   ***Telegraphy**

Class here submarine cable telegraphy [*formerly* 384.4]

For radiotelegraphy, see 384.52

.102 8   Auxiliary techniques and procedures, materials

Class apparatus and equipment in 384.15

*Add as instructed under 380

.13   Economic aspects

             Examples: competition, costs, efficiency, finance, income, market, rates, supply and demand

             Including forms of ownership

             Economic aspects of activities and services relocated to 384.14, of facilities to 384.15

.14   *Activities and services

             Examples: Morse and other code telegraphy, printing telegraphy (teletype, telex, facsimile, stock tickers)

             Class here economic aspects of activities and services [*formerly* 384.13]

             Class comprehensive works on electronic mail in 384.34

             For postal facsimile transmission, see 383.141

.15   Facilities

             Examples: apparatus, stations

             Class here economic aspects of facilities [*formerly* 384.13]

             Class use of facilities in specific activities and services in 384.14

.3   *Computer communication

             Transfer of computer-based information by any of various media (e.g., coaxial cable or radio waves) from one computer to another or between computers and terminals

             Class here links between computers via telephone lines [*formerly* 384.648]; computer communications networks

             Class interdisciplinary works on computer communications in 004.6

             See Manual at 384.3 vs. 004.6

.302 85   Data processing   Computer applications

                     Class here computer science applied to economic and related aspects of providing computer communication to the public

.31   Economic aspects

             Examples: competition, costs, efficiency, finance, income, market, rates, supply and demand

             Class economic aspects of facilities in 384.32, of services in 384.33; economic aspects of production of computer communication hardware and software and comprehensive works on production and sale in 338.470046; sale of computer communication hardware and software in 380.1450046

.32   Facilities

             Class use of facilities in specific services in 384.33

*Add as instructed under 380

.33   Services

      Example: services of value-added networks

      For electronic mail, see 384.34; videotex, 384.35

.34   *Electronic mail

      Example: teletex

      Class here comprehensive works on electronic mail

      Class a specific kind of electronic mail with the kind, e.g., postal facsimile transmission 383.141, telex 384.14

      See Manual at 384.34 and 384.352

.35   *Videotex

.352   *Broadcast videotex (Teletext)

      See Manual at 384.34 and 384.352

.354   *Interactive videotex (Viewdata)

[.4]   **Submarine cable telegraphy**

      Relocated to 384.1

.5   ***Wireless communication**

SUMMARY

384.51	**Satellite communication**
.52	**Radiotelegraphy**
.53	**Radiotelephony**
.54	**Radiobroadcasting**
.55	**Television**

.51   *Satellite communication

      Class a specific form of satellite communication with the subject, e.g., television transmission by satellite 384.552

.52   *Radiotelegraphy

      Add to base number 384.52 the numbers following 384.1 in 384.13–384.15, e.g., apparatus 384.525

.53   *Radiotelephony

      Including ship-to-shore communication, citizens' band radio

      Class here portable telephones

      Add to base number 384.53 the numbers following 384.6 in 384.63–384.65, e.g., transmitting and receiving equipment 384.535

*Add as instructed under 380

.54   *Radiobroadcasting

Class here interdisciplinary works on radio- and television broadcasting, public aspects of amateur radio

Class techniques of producing radio programs in 791.44

For television broadcasting, see 384.55

See Manual at 384.54, 384.55, 384.8 vs. 791.4

.540 65   Business organizations (Stations [*formerly also* 384.5453] and networks [*formerly also* 384.5455])

Examples: public (noncommercial) networks and stations, network affiliates

Add to base number 384.54065 notation 3–9 from Table 2, e.g., NBC (National Broadcasting Company) 384.5406573

See Manual at 384.5453 and 384.5455 vs. 384.54065

.543   Economic aspects

Examples: competition, costs, efficiency, finance, income, market, rates, supply and demand

Including forms of ownership

Economic aspects of activities and services relocated to 384.544, of facilities to 384.545

.544   *Activities and services

Class here economic aspects of activities and services [*formerly* 384.543], public (noncommercial) broadcasting services

.544 2   Scheduling

Including sale of time

.544 3   Presentation of programs

General aspects: commercial, sustaining, noncommercial

Class the technique of producing programs in 791.44, a specific type of program with the subject, e.g., news broadcasts 070.19

.545   Facilities

Class here economic aspects of facilities [*formerly* 384.543]

Class use of facilities in specific activities and services in 384.544

.545 2   Broadcasting channels

Examples: clear, regional, local

Including allocation of frequencies [*formerly also* 621.38417]

*Add as instructed under 380

.545 3   Stations

Examples: AM, FM

Stations as business organizations relocated to 384.54065

See Manual at 384.5453 and 384.5455 vs. 384.54065

.545 5   Networks

Networks as business organizations relocated to 384.54065

See Manual at 384.5453 and 384.5455 vs. 384.54065

.545 6   Satellites

.55   Television

Including low power television (LPTV) stations (stations that rebroadcast the programs of full-service stations, originate programming that often includes pay television, and are usually limited in power to 10–1000 watts and a 10– to 15–mile broadcasting radius)

Unless other instructions are given, class complex subjects with aspects in two or more subdivisions of 384.55 in the one coming last, e.g., economic aspects of cable television and controlled transmission television 384.5561 (*not* 384.5551)

See Manual at 384.54, 384.55, 384.8 vs. 791.4

SUMMARY

384.550 65	**Business organizations (Stations and networks)**
.551	**Economic aspects**
.552	**Facilities and channels**
.553	**Activities and services**
.554	**General broadcasting (Free television)**
.555	**Pay television**
.556	**Controlled transmission television (Closed-circuit television)**
.558	**Video products**

.550 65   Business organizations (Stations and networks)

Contains network affiliates; nonaffiliated commercial, public (noncommercial), private television

Add to base number 384.55065 notation 3–9 from Table 2, e.g., NBC (National Broadcasting Company) 384.5506573

See Manual at 384.5522 and 384.5523 vs. 384.55065

>   384.551–384.553 Economic aspects, facilities and channels, activities and services

Class comprehensive works in 384.55

.551	Economic aspects

Examples: competition, costs, efficiency, finance, income, market, rates, ratings, supply and demand

Including forms of ownership

.552	Facilities and channels

Class here direct broadcast satellite (DBS) systems, satellites, satellite dishes

.552 1	Broadcasting channels

Contains clear, regional, local channels

Including allocation of frequencies

.552 2	Stations

Class stations as organizations in 384.55065

See Manual at 384.5522 and 384.5523 vs. 384.55065

.552 3	Networks

Class networks as organizations in 384.55065

See Manual at 384.5522 and 384.5523 vs. 384.55065

.553	*Activities and services
.553 1	Scheduling

Including sale of time

.553 2	Presentation of programs

General aspects: commercial, sustaining, noncommercial

Including local programming

.554	*General broadcasting (Free television)

Transmitting signals over the air for use by the general public

Including translator stations (low-power stations for transmitting the signals of television broadcast stations to areas where reception is unsatisfactory)

Class works combining both general broadcasting and cable television in 384.55

.554 3	Economic aspects

Economic aspects of activities and services relocated to 384.5544; of facilities and channels to 384.5545

*Add as instructed under 380

.554 4	*Activities and services

Class here economic aspects of activities and services [*formerly* 384.5543]

.554 42	Scheduling

Including sale of time

.554 43	Presentation of programs

General aspects: commercial, sustaining, noncommercial

Including local programming ·

.554 5	Facilities and channels

Class here economic aspects of facilities and channels [*formerly* 384.5543]; direct broadcast satellite (DBS) systems, satellites, satellite dishes

Class use of facilities and channels in specific activities and services in 384.5544

.554 52	Broadcasting channels

Contains clear, regional, local channels

Including allocation of frequencies

.554 53	Stations

Class stations as organizations in 384.554065

See Manual at 384.5522 and 384.5523 vs. 384.55065

.554 55	Networks

Class networks as organizations in 384.554065

See Manual at 384.5522 and 384.5523 vs. 384.55065

[.554 56]	Satellites

Use of this number discontinued; class in 384.5545

.554 6	*Community antenna television (CATV) systems [*formerly* 384.5556]

Systems that provide television reception to remote communities, using a tall antenna, usually limited to no more than 12 channels

Add to base number 384.5546 the numbers following 384.55 in 384.551–384.553, e.g., networks 384.554623

[.554 7]	Pay television

Relocated to 384.555

*Add as instructed under 380

.555   *Pay television [*formerly* 384.5547]

> Systems that receive and distribute signals to customers who pay for the service
>
> Class here cable television
>
> Closed-circuit television relocated to 384.556
>
> Class works combining general broadcasting and cable television in 384.55, use of cable television in closed-circuit television in 384.556
>
> Pay television in Canada is classed in 384.5554
>
> *See Manual at 384.555 and 384.5554*

.555 1–.555 3   Economic aspects, facilities and channels, activities and services

> Add to base number 384.555 the numbers following 384.55 in 384.551–384.553, e.g., networks 384.55523, viewer access in 384.5553

.555 4   *Premium (Subscription) television

> Systems that scramble signals that are decoded for a fee
>
> Examples: Cinemax, Home Box Office (HBO), Showtime, The Movie Channel (TMC)
>
> Class here pay-cable, pay television in Canada
>
> Add to base number 384.5554 the numbers following 384.55 in 384.551–384.553, e.g., rates 384.55541
>
> > *See also 384.55 for low power television (LPTV) stations*
> >
> > *See Manual at 384.555 and 384.5554*

[.555 6]   Cable television and community antenna television (CATV)

> Use of this number for cable television discontinued; class in 384.555
>
> Community antenna television (CATV) relocated to 384.5546

[.555 7]   Industrial uses

> Relocated to 384.556

.556   *Controlled transmission television (Closed-circuit television) [*formerly* 384.555]

> Systems where the signals are carried to a specific audience
>
> Example: theater television
>
> Class here industrial uses [*formerly* 384.5557], e.g., surveillance, monitoring of hazardous industrial processes
>
> Add to base number 384.556 the numbers following 384.55 in 384.551–384.553, e.g., rates 384.5561

*Add as instructed under 380

.558   *Video products

General aspects: use, control, regulation

Examples: video cassette recorders (VCR's), video disc players (VDP's), videotapes, laser optical disks (LOD's)

Class use, control, regulation of video products associated with a specific aspect of television communication with the aspect, e.g., use in cable television 384.555

See also 004.16 for home computers

.6   *Telephony

Class here comprehensive works on wire and cable communication

For telegraphy, see 384.1; radiotelephony, 384.53; cable television, 384.555

.63   Economic aspects

Examples: competition, costs, efficiency, finance, income, market, rates, supply and demand

Including forms of ownership

Economic aspects of activities and services relocated to 384.64, of facilities to 384.65

.64   *Activities and services

Examples: conference calls; emergency services; local, long-distance, overseas service

Class here economic aspects of activities and services [*formerly* 384.63]

[.642]   General communications

Number discontinued; class in 384.64

[.648]   Links between computers via telephone lines

Relocated to 384.3

.65   Facilities

Examples: stations, lines, switchboards, dialing systems, transmitting and receiving equipment

Class here economic aspects of facilities [*formerly* 384.63]

Class use of facilities in specific activities and services in 384.64

[.7]   Alarm and warning systems

Relocated to 363.1072

.8   *Motion pictures

Add to base number 384.8 the numbers following 384.1 in 384.13–384.15, e.g., activities 384.84

See Manual at 384.54, 384.55, 384.8 vs. 791.4

*Add as instructed under 380

[.9] **Visual signaling**

Number discontinued; class in 384

385 *Railroad transportation

Class here standard- and broad-gage railways

Class comprehensive works on transportation, on ground transportation in 388

For local rail transit systems, see 388.42

See Manual at 383–388; 629.046 vs. 388

SUMMARY

385.065	**Railroad companies**
.1	**Economic aspects**
.2	**Activities and services**
.3	**Facilities**
.5	**Narrow-gage and special-purpose railroads**
.6	**Inclined and mountain railroads**
.7	**Railroad combined with other transportation systems**

.065   Railroad companies

See also 385.5065 for narrow-gage and special-duty railroad companies, 385.6065 for inclined and mountain railroad companies

---

> **385.1–385.3 Specific aspects**

Class comprehensive works in 385, specific aspects of narrow-gage and special-duty railroads in 385.5, of inclined and mountain railroads in 385.6

.1   **Economic aspects**

Examples: competition, costs, efficiency, finance, income, market, rates and fares, supply and demand

Including forms of ownership

Economic aspects of activities and services relocated to 385.2, of facilities to 385.3

[.12]   Rates and fares

Use of this number discontinued; class in 385.1

.2   **Activities and services**

Class here economic aspects of activities and services *[formerly 385.1]*

.204   Special topics

.204 2   Basic activities

Examples: routing, scheduling, dispatching, traffic control

For operation of rolling stock, see 385.2044

.204 4   Operation of rolling stock

*Add as instructed under 380

>   385.22–385.24 Transportation activities and services

      Class comprehensive works in 385.2

.22   *Passenger services

      Examples: baggage, meal, sleeper services

.23   *Express transportation of goods

.24   *Freight services

      Class unitized cargo services in 385.72

      For express transportation of goods, see 385.23

.26   Activities and services of terminals and stations

      Examples: fueling, victualing

.262   Passenger services

      Examples: booking services, passenger amenities

.264   Freight services

      Examples: freight handling, warehousing, storage

.3   **Facilities**

      Class here economic aspects of facilities [*formerly* 385.1]

      Class use of facilities in specific activities and services in 385.2

.31   Stationary

.312   The way

      Contains tracks, roadway, bridges, tunnels, grade crossings

.314   Terminals and stations

      Examples: yards, roundhouses, train sheds, shop buildings

.316   Communication facilities

      Example: signals

.32–.34   Cars

      Add to base number 385.3 the numbers following 625.2 in 625.22–625.24, e.g., diners 385.33

      Class comprehensive works in 385.37

.36   Locomotives

      Add to base number 385.36 the numbers following 625.26 in 625.261–625.266, e.g., steam locomotives 385.361

*Add as instructed under 380

.37	Rolling stock

> For cars, see 385.32–385.34; locomotives, 385.36

.5   *Narrow-gage and special-purpose railroads

Including monorail railroads

Class here interurban railroads

Class special-purpose railroads located entirely within a metropolitan region in 388.42–388.46

> For inclined and mountain railroads, see 385.6

.52   *Narrow-gage railroads

Class narrow-gage industrial railroads in 385.54

.54   *Industrial railroads

Standard subdivisions are added without regard to the purpose of the railroad, e.g., lumber railroads in Georgia 385.5409758, mine railroads in Colorado 385.5409788

.6   *Inclined and mountain railroad systems

Examples: cable, funicular, rack

.7   Railroad combined with other transportation systems

.72   *Unitized cargo

Examples: piggyback (trucks, trailers, buses, private automobiles on flatcars)

> For container-ship operations, see 387.5442

.77   *Ship railroad systems

Rail transportation of vessels overland between bodies of water

386   *Inland waterway and ferry transportation

Class comprehensive works on water transportation in 387, on transportation in 388

> See Manual at 383–388; 629.046 vs. 388

SUMMARY

386.1	**Economic aspects**
.2	**Activities, services, facilities**
.3	**River transportation**
.4	**Canal transportation**
.5	**Lake transportation**
.6	**Ferry transportation**
.8	**Ports**

*Add as instructed under 380

.1   **Economic aspects**

Examples: competition, costs, efficiency, finance, income, market, rates and fares, supply and demand

Including forms of ownership

Economic aspects of facilities in general relocated to 386.2, of activities and services in general relocated to 386.24, of specific kinds of inland water and ferry transportation to 386.3–386.6

.2   **Activities, services, facilities**

Class here economic aspects of facilities [*formerly* 386.1]

Class activities, services, facilities of ports in 386.8; and, except for ships and ports, class activities and facilities of specific types of inland water systems in 386.3–386.6

.22   Ships

General aspects: rating, tonnage

Including air-cushion vehicles

Add to base number 386.22 the numbers following 623.82 in 623.821–623.829, e.g., tugboats 386.2232

Class use of ships in specific activities and services in 386.24

.24   Activities and services

Class here economic aspects of activities and services in general [*formerly* 386.1]

.240 4   Special topics

.240 42   Basic activities

Examples: routing, scheduling, dispatching, traffic control

For operation of ships, see 386.24044

.240 44   Operation of ships

.242   *Passenger services

Examples: baggage, meal, sleeping services

.244   *Freight services

>   **386.3–386.6 Specific kinds of inland water and ferry transportation**

General aspects: activities, services, facilities

Class here economic aspects of specific kinds of inland water and ferry transportation [*formerly* 386.1]

Class comprehensive works in 386, ships for specific kinds of inland water transportation in 386.22, ports for specific kinds of inland water transportation in 386.8

*Add as instructed under 380

>   **386.3–386.5 Specific kinds of waters**

Class comprehensive works in 386, ferry transportation on specific kinds of waters in 386.6

.3   ***River transportation**

Class here transportation by canalized rivers

Class combined river, lake, canal systems in 386.5

.32   The way

.35   Activities and services

Add to base number 386.35 the numbers following 386.24 in 386.2404–386.244, e.g., freight services 386.354

.4   ***Canal transportation**

Class canalized rivers in 386.3; combined river, lake, canal systems in 386.5

.404   Special topics

.404 2   Activities and services

Add to base number 386.4042 the numbers following 386.24 in 386.2404–386.244, e.g., freight services 386.40424

>   **386.42–386.48 Specific canals and kinds of canals**

Existing and proposed

Class comprehensive works in 386.4

.42   Interoceanic canals

For canals connecting specific oceans, see 386.43–386.45

>   **386.43–386.45 Canals connecting specific oceans**

Class comprehensive works in 386.42

.43   Canals connecting Indian and Atlantic Oceans

Class here Suez Canal

.44   Canals connecting Atlantic and Pacific Oceans

Class here Panama Canal

[.444]   Panama Canal

Number discontinued; class in 386.44

.445   Proposed Nicaragua Canal

.447   Proposed Tehuantepec Canal

*Add as instructed under 380

.45   Canals connecting Pacific and Indian Oceans

.46   Noninteroceanic canals

> Including canals connecting parts of one ocean
>
> *For kinds of noninteroceanic canals, see 386.47–386.48*

\>   386.47–386.48 Kinds of noninteroceanic canals

> Class here specific canals
>
> Class comprehensive works in 386.46

.47   *Ship canals

.48   *Small craft and barge canals

.5   ***Lake transportation**

> Class here transportation on combined river, lake, canal systems, e.g., Saint Lawrence Seaway

.52   The way

.54   Activities and services

> Add to base number 386.54 the numbers following 386.24 in 386.2404–386.244, e.g., passenger services 386.542

.6   ***Ferry transportation**

> Oceanic and inland

.8   ***Ports**

> Add to base number 386.8 the numbers following 387.1 in 387.12–387.16, e.g., freight terminals 386.853
>
> *See Manual at 386.8 vs. 387.1*

387   Water, air, space transportation

> Class here comprehensive works on water transportation
>
> Class comprehensive works on transportation in 388
>
> *For inland waterway and ferry transportation, see 386*
>
> *See Manual at 383–388; 629.046 vs. 388*

SUMMARY

387.001–.009	**Standard subdivisions of water transportation**
.1	**Ports**
.2	**Ships**
.5	**Ocean (Marine) transportation**
.7	**Air transportation**
.8	**Space transportation**

*Add as instructed under 380

.001–.009   Standard subdivisions of water transportation

> Notation from Table 1 as modified under 380, e.g., water transportation business organizations 387.0065

.1   Ports

> Activities, services, facilities
>
> Class inland ports in 386.8
>
> *See Manual at 386.8 vs. 387.1*

.109   Historical, geographical, persons treatment

> Class here specific ports

.12   Physiographic location of ports

> Examples: ports on natural bays, river mouths, tidal rivers, estuaries, roadsteads
>
> Class specific ports in 387.109, facilities of specific types of ports in 387.15, activities and services of specific types of ports in 387.16

.13   Free ports

> Class specific ports in 387.109, facilities of free ports in 387.15, activities and services of free ports in 387.16

.15   Port facilities

> Examples: docks, marinas, piers, quays
>
> Class here economic aspects of port facilities
>
> Class use of port facilities in specific activities and services in 387.16

.152   Passenger terminals

.153   Freight terminals

.155   Navigational aids

> Class here lighthouses regardless of location
>
> Class piloting in 387.166

.16   Activities and services

> Example: port maintenance
>
> Class here economic aspects of activities and services

.162   *Passenger services

> Example: booking services

.164   *Freight services

> Examples: freight handling, warehousing, storage, connection with land transportation

*Add as instructed under 380

.166	Operational services

        Examples: ship-to-shore communication, piloting, towing, tug services

.168	Auxiliary services

        Examples: fueling, victualing

.2   **Ships**

General aspects: rating, tonnage

Including air-cushion vehicles

Class here economic aspects of ships [*formerly* 387.51]

Class use of ships in specific activities and services in 387.54, in inland waterway transportation in 386.22

.204   General types

        Add to base number 387.204 the numbers following 623.820 in 623.8202–623.8205, e.g., sailing craft 387.2043

.21–.29   Specific types

        Add to base number 387.2 the numbers following 623.82 in 623.821–623.829, e.g., cargo ships 387.245

.5   ***Ocean (Marine) transportation**

Class seaports in 387.1

For ships, see 387.2

.51   Economic aspects

        Examples: competition, costs, efficiency, finance, income, market, rates and fares, supply and demand

        Including forms of ownership

        Economic aspects of ships relocated to 387.2, of routes and kinds of routes to 387.52, of activities and services to 387.54, of facilities to 387.58

.52   Routes and kinds of routes

        Class here economic aspects of routes and kinds of routes [*formerly* 387.51], specific routes

        Class use of facilities on routes and kinds of routes in 387.2, 387.58; activities and services on routes and kinds of routes in 387.54

.522   Intercoastal routes

.523   Auxiliary, irregular, tramp routes

.524   Coastwise routes

*Add as instructed under 380

.54	Activities and services

Class here economic aspects of activities and services [*formerly* 387.51]

Class activities and services of ports in 387.16

.540 4	Special topics
.540 42	Basic activities

Examples: routing, scheduling, dispatching, traffic control

For operation of ships, see 387.54044

.540 44	Operation of ships

Including life and activities of marine personnel at sea

.542	*Passenger services

Examples: baggage, meal, sleeping services

.544	*Freight services
.544 2	*Container-ship operations

Class carriage of specific kinds of cargo in container-ship operations in 387.5448

See also 385./2 for unitized cargo

.544 8	Carriage of specific kinds of cargo

Examples: dry cargo, fertilizer, petroleum

.55	*Salvage
.58	Facilities

Class here economic aspects of facilities [*formerly* 387.51]

Class facilities of ports in 387.15, ships in 387.2, use of facilities in specific activities and services in 387.54

.7	***Air transportation**
.71	Economic aspects

Examples: competition, costs, efficiency, finance, income, market, supply and demand

Economic aspects of routes and kinds of routes relocated to 387.72, of facilities to 387.73, of activities and services to 387.74

.712	Rates and fares
.72	Routes and kinds of routes

Examples: international, domestic trunk, limited range and local services

Including specific routes, helicopter routes to and from airports

Class here economic aspects of routes and kinds of routes [*formerly* 387.71]

Class use of facilities on routes and kinds of routes in 387.73, activities and services on routes and kinds of routes in 387.74

*Add as instructed under 380

.73   Facilities

Class here economic aspects of facilities [*formerly* 387.71]

.732–.733   Aircraft

Add to base number 387.73 the numbers following 629.133 in 629.1332–629.1333, e.g., helicopters 387.73352

Class use of aircraft in specific activities and services in 387.74

.736   Airports

Class here landing fields

.736 2   Facilities

Examples: terminal buildings, control towers, hangars, warehouses, runways

Including access to airports

Class use of facilities in specific activities and services in 387.7364

.736 4   Activities and services

Examples: booking, passenger services, fueling, victualing

.74   Activities and services

Class here economic aspects of activities and services [*formerly* 387.71]

Class activities and services of airports and landing fields in 387.7364

.740 4   Special topics

.740 42   Basic activities

Examples: routing, scheduling, dispatching, traffic control

Including airport noise and its alleviation

For operation of aircraft, see 387.74044

.740 44   Operation of aircraft

Class here operating personnel, flight crews

Class maintenance and maintenance personnel in 387.73

.742   *Passenger services

Examples: baggage, meal, sleeping services

.742 8   *Charter services

.744   *Freight services

Example: all-cargo plane services

See also 383.144 for air mail

.8   *Space transportation

*Add as instructed under 380

388 ***Transportation [*formerly* 380.5]** **Ground transportation**

Class here interdisciplinary works on transportation

Comprehensive works on the activities, services, and facilities of a system are classed in the number for the system, e.g., seaport activities, services, and facilities 387.1, not 387.15 nor 387.16

Class transportation safety and safety measures in 363.12, transportation security in 363.287, transportation technology in 629.04; services designed to facilitate the use of transportation by the handicapped in 362.40483, by the elderly in 362.63

> *For postal transportation, see 383.14; railroad transportation, 385; water, air, space transportation, 387*
>
> *See also 385.7 for railroad combined with other transportation systems*
>
> *See Manual at 383–388; 629.046 vs. 388*

SUMMARY

388.04		**Special topics**
.1		**Road and highways**
.3		**Vehicular transportation**
.4		**Local transportation**
.5		**Pipeline transportation**

.04   Special topics

.041   Activities and services

> Examples: routing, scheduling, dispatching, traffic control
>
> Class here economic aspects of activities and services [*formerly* 388.049]
>
> Class specific kinds of services in 388.042–388.044

.042   *Passenger services

> Examples: baggage, booking, meal, sleeping services
>
> Class here economic aspects of passenger services [*formerly* 388.049], mass transportation

.044   *Freight services

> Examples: handling, warehousing, storage
>
> Class here economic aspects of freight services [*formerly* 388.049]

.047   Comparative studies of kinds of transportation

> Class a comparative study of a specific kind of transportation with the subject, e.g., comparative study of local transportation 388.4

*Add as instructed under 380

.049 Economic aspects

> Examples: competition, costs, efficiency, finance, income, market, rates and fares, supply and demand
>
> Including forms of ownership
>
> Economic aspects of activities and services relocated to 388.041, of passenger services to 388.042, of freight services to 388.044

.1 *Roads and highways

> Class highway operation, services, use in 388.31
>
> *For urban roads and streets, see 388.411*

.11 Economic aspects

> Examples: supply and demand, efficiency, economic effects
>
> Class economic effects of highways on a specific aspect of economic activity with the subject, e.g., effect on business location 338.6042
>
> Economic aspects of kinds of roads and highways relocated to 388.12, of special highway and road features to 388.13

.112 Costs

.114 Finance

> Including user charges, tolls

.12 Kinds of roads and highways

> Examples: primary and secondary roads, bicycle paths, pedestrian paths
>
> Class here economic aspects of kinds of roads and highways [*formerly* 388.11]
>
> Class special features of kinds of roads and highways in 388.13

.122 Expressways

> Variant names: beltways, freeways, motorways, parkways, throughways, tollways, turnpikes

.13 Special highway and road features

> Examples: tunnels, access roads, intersections, grade separations
>
> Class here economic aspects of special highway and road features [*formerly* 388.11]
>
> Class signs and signals for traffic control in 388.3122

.132 Bridges

*Add as instructed under 380

.3   *Vehicular transportation

Class urban vehicular transportation in 388.41

SUMMARY

388.31	**Traffic flow and maintenance**
.32	**Vehicular services**
.33	**Terminals, stations, stops**
.34	**Vehicles**
.35	**Air-cushion vehicles**

.31   Traffic flow and maintenance

.312   Highway services   Traffic control

Examples: lighting, roadside park facilities, route markers, snow and ice removal

Class police services in traffic control in 363.2332

.312 2   Traffic control through signs and signals

.312 4   Driver information

Information supplied en route

Example: information on traffic patterns via commercial radio

.314   Highway use

See Manual at 388.314 and 388.41314

.314 2   Volume of traffic

Class peak hours in 388.3143

.314 3   Traffic patterns

Examples: patterns by origin, by destination

Including peak hours, use by specific kinds of vehicles

.314 4   Speed

.32   *Vehicular services

See also 388.34 for vehicles

.321   *Services of private passenger automobiles

Example: limousine services

.322   *Bus services

Class services of terminals, stations, stops in 388.33

.322 04   Special topics

.322 042   Basic services

Examples: routing, scheduling, dispatching, traffic control

For operation of vehicles, see 388.322044

.322 044   Operation of vehicles

*Add as instructed under 380

.322 1	Routes
	Intercity, trunk
	Class services offered on specific routes and kinds of routes in 388.3222
.322 2	Types of services
	Examples: passenger, charter, baggage, meal, small package and express services; sightseeing
.322 8	*Stagecoach services
	Class stagecoach routes in 388.3221, types of stagecoach services in 388.3222
.324	*Trucking services
	Class services of terminals in 388.33
.324 04	Special topics
.324 042	Basic services
	Examples: routing, scheduling, dispatching, traffic control
	For operation of vehicles, see 388.324044
.324 044	Operation of vehicles
.324 2	Routes
	Contains long-haul, line-haul, intercity
.324 3	Kinds of carriers
	Contains private, contract, common (for-hire) carriers
.33	Terminals, stations, stops
	General aspects: activities, services, facilities (e.g., vehicle sheds, docks, booking facilities)
.34	Vehicles
	Example: snowmobiles
	Class use of vehicles in specific services, vehicle operation in 388.32
	For air-cushion vehicles, see 388.35
.341	Carts, wagons, carriages, stagecoaches
	Including rickshaws, animal-drawn omnibuses
	Class here nonmotor land vehicles
	Class cycles in 388.347

*Add as instructed under 380

.342–.348   Gasoline-, oil-, man-powered vehicles

> Add to base number 388.34 the numbers following 629.22 in
> 629.222–629.228, e.g., buses 388.34233

> *For rickshaws, see 388.341*

.35   Air-cushion vehicles

> Class here comprehensive works on air-cushion vehicles

> Class air-cushion ships for inland waterways in 386.22, for ocean
> transportation in 387.2

.4   *Local transportation

> Class here urban and suburban transportation, rapid transit, mass transit,
> commuter services

> *See also 385.5 for interurban railways*

.404   Special topics

.404 2   Economic aspects

> Examples: competition, costs, efficiency, finance, income, market,
> rates and fares, supply and demand, costs, rates and fares

> Including forms of ownership

> Economic aspects of activities and services relocated to 388.413

>   388.41–388.46 Specific kinds

> Class comprehensive works in 388.4, terminals and parking facilities for
> specific kinds of transportation in 388.47

.41   Vehicular and pedestrian traffic

> General aspects: activities, services, facilities

> Example: moving street belts for pedestrian traffic

> Class vehicles in 388.34–388.35

.411   Urban roads and streets

> Examples: parkways, expressways, arterial and side streets, sidewalks,
> cycling paths (bikeways)

> Including intersections, traffic circles (roundabouts)

> Class operation, services, use of roads and streets in 388.4131

.413   Activities and services

> Class here economic aspects of activities and services [*formerly*
> 388.4042]

*Add as instructed under 380

.413 1	Traffic flow and maintenance
	Add to base number 388.4131 the numbers following 388.31 in 388.312–388.314, e.g., peak hours 388.413143
.413 2	Vehicular services
.413 21	*Services by private passenger automobiles
.413 212	*Car and van pools
.413 214	*Taxicabs and limousines
.413 22	*Bus services
	Example: animal-drawn omnibuses
.413 223	Trolleybuses
.413 24	*Trucking services
.42	*Local rail transit systems
	Example: guided-way systems
	Class rail terminals and stations in 388.472
	For elevated rail transit systems, see 388.44; surface rail transit systems, 388.46
.428	*Underground (Subway) systems
.44	*Elevated rail transit systems
	Example: elevated monorail systems
.46	*Surface rail transit systems
	Class here tramways
.47	Terminals, stations, parking facilities
.472	Rail terminals and stations
.473	Truck and bus stations and terminals
	Including bus stops
.474	Parking facilities and services
	Examples: on- and off-street parking facilities, facilities located above and below street level, perimeter parking
	Class here interdisciplinary works on parking
	Class a specific aspect of parking with the subject, e.g., city planning 711.73
.5	***Pipeline transportation**

>	388.55–388.57 By commodity
	Class comprehensive works in 388.5

*Add as instructed under 380

.55	*Oil (Petroleum)
.56	*Natural gas
.57	*Coal

389   Metrology and standardization

.1   Metrology

Social use of systems of measurement

Class interdisciplinary works on measurement in 530.8

[.109]   Historical, geographical, persons treatment

Do not use; class in 389.15

.15   Systems of measurement

Examples: metric system (système internationale, SI), imperial (British) system

Class adoption of metric system in 389.16, mathematical tables of conversion from one system to another in 530.81

.16   Adoption of metric system (système internationale, SI)

See also 658.4062 for management measures for coping with conversion to metric system

.17   Time systems and standards [*formerly* 529.75]

Examples: daylight savings, standard, universal, zone time

Including conversion tables

.6   Standardization

.62   Of quantity and size

For interchangeability

.63   Of quality

For performance

390   Customs, etiquette, folklore

Class here folkways

Use 390.001–390.009 for standard subdivisions

Class customs of military life in 355.1

See Manual at 390

*Add as instructed under 380

SUMMARY

390.01–.09   **Standard subdivisions of customs**
.1–.4   **Customs of specific economic, social, occupational classes**
391   **Costume and personal appearance**
392   **Customs of life cycle and domestic life**
393   **Death customs**
394   **General customs**
395   **Etiquette (Manners)**
398   **Folklore**
399   **Customs of war and diplomacy**

.01–.07   Standard subdivisions of customs

.08   History and description of customs with respect to kinds of persons

[.086]   Persons by social and economic characteristics

> Do not use; class customs of persons by economic status in 390.1, by social class in 390.2

.088   Religious groups

> Class customs with respect to occupational groups in 390.4

.09   Historical, geographical, persons treatment of customs

> **390.1–390.4 Customs of specific economic, social, occupational classes**

Class comprehensive works in 390

.1   **Customs of people by economic status**

Class customs of slaves and serfs in 390.25

.2   **Customs of people by social class**

.22   Royalty

.23   Nobility

.24   Common people

> Class customs of common people of specific economic statuses in 390.1, of specific occupations in 390.4

.25   Slaves and serfs

.4   **Customs of people by occupation**

> Add to base number 390.4 notation 09–99 from Table 7, e.g., customs of lawyers 390.4344; however, class customs of military personnel in 355.1, of diplomats in 399

[.5]   **Customs of people by level of education**

> Number discontinued; class in 390

> ### 391–394 Customs

Class comprehensive works in 390, customs of specific economic, social, occupational classes in 390.1–390.4

For customs of war and diplomacy, see 399

391   Costume and personal appearance

Class here interdisciplinary works on costume, clothing, fashion

Class costumes and clothing associated with a specific occasion with the occasion in 392–394; a specific aspect of costume and clothing with the aspect, e.g., military uniforms 355.14, stage costuming 792.026, clothing construction 646.4

For fashion design, see 746.92

See Manual at 391 vs. 646.3, 746.92

.001–.007	Standard subdivisions
.008	History and description with respect to kinds of persons
[.008 1–.008 4]	Sex and age groups
	Do not use; class in 391.1–391.3
[.008 6]	Persons by social and economic characteristics
	Do not use; class costumes of people by economic status in 391.01, by social class in 391.02
.008 8	Religious groups
	Class costumes with respect to occupational groups in 391.04
.009	Historical, geographical, persons treatment
.01–.04	Costumes of economic, social, occupational groups
	Add to base number 391.0 the numbers following 390 in 390.1–390.4, e.g., costumes of lawyers 391.04344; however, class military costume in 355.14
[.05]	Costumes of groups by level of education
	Number discontinued; class in 391

> #### 391.1–391.3 Costumes of specific ages and sexes

Class comprehensive works in 391; auxiliary garments and accessories for specific age and sex groups in 391.4; costumes of specific economic, social, occupational classes regardless of age or sex in 391.01–391.04

.1	**Costumes of men**
.2	**Costumes of women**
.3	**Costumes of children**
.4	**Auxiliary garments and accessories**

.41	Hand-, foot-, neckwear
	Examples: muffs, scarves
.412	Gloves and mittens
.413	Footwear
	Example: hosiery
	Class here shoes and boots
.42	Underwear and nightclothes
.43	Headwear
	Example: hats
.434	Masks
.44	Accessories
	Examples: canes, combs, eyeglasses, fans, flowers, parasols
	For jewelry, see 391.7
.45	Buttons
.5	**Hair styles**
	Including beards, wigs
.6	**Personal appearance**
	For hair styles, see 391.5
.62	Body contours
.63	Use of cosmetics and perfume
.64	Personal cleanliness and hygiene
	Example: bathing
.65	Tattooing and incision
.7	**Jewelry**
	Class here interdisciplinary works on jewelry
	Class interdisciplinary works on making jewelry in 739.27
[.8]	**Costumes for specific occasions**
	Relocated to specific occasion, e.g., wedding apparel 392.54

392   Customs of life cycle and domestic life

For death customs, see 393

.1	**Birth, puberty, majority**
.12	Birth customs
	Examples: couvade, infanticide, name giving, baptism

.13	Child-rearing customs

.14   Customs relating to attainment of puberty

            Example: initiation rites

.15   Customs relating to attainment of majority

            Example: debuts

.3   **Dwelling places and domestic arts**

.36   Dwelling places

            Class here heating, lighting, furnishings, sanitation

.360 01–.360 07   Standard subdivisions

.360 08   Dwelling places with respect to kinds of persons

[.360 086]   Persons by social and economic characteristics

            Do not use; class customs of persons by economic status in 392.3601, by social class in 392.3602

.360 088   Religious groups

            Class dwelling places with respect to occupational groups in 392.3604

.360 09   Historical, geographical, persons treatment

.360 1–.360 4   Of specific economic, social, occupational classes

            Add to base number 392.360 the numbers following 390 in 390.1–390.4, e.g., dwelling places of royalty 392.36022

[.360 5]   Of persons by level of education

            Number discontinued; class in 392.36

.37   Cooking

            See also 394.1 for eating and drinking customs

[.38]   Other domestic arts and sciences

            Number discontinued; class in 392.3

.4   **Courtship and betrothal**

            Examples: bride purchase, bundling, infant betrothal, matchmaking

.5   **Wedding and marriage**

            See also 395.22 for etiquette of weddings

.54   Apparel

.6   **Relations between sexes**

            Example: chaperonage

            For courtship and betrothal, see 392.4; wedding and marriage, 392.5

.9   **Treatment of old persons**

393   Death customs

.1   Burial

Including entombment

.2   Cremation

.3   Embalming

.4   Exposure

.9   Mourning

Examples: funerals, suttee, wakes

394   General customs

Examples: kissing, swearing

SUMMARY

394.1	Eating, drinking; using drugs
.2	Special occasions
.3	Recreational customs
.4	Official ceremonies and observances
.5	Pageants, processions, parades
.6	Fairs
.7	Customs of chivalry
.8	Dueling and suicide
.9	Cannibalism

.1   Eating, drinking; using drugs

Use situations, methods of use, prohibited uses

Class here food and meals

For cooking, see 392.37

.12   Eating and drinking

Class eating and drinking customs of a specific meal in 394.15, food taboos in 394.16

For drinking of alcoholic beverages, see 394.13

.13   Drinking of alcoholic beverages

.14   Use of drugs

Examples: marijuana, narcotics, tobacco

For alcoholic beverages, see 394.13

.15   Specific meals

Examples: breakfast, tea

.16   Food taboos

.2   Special occasions

Examples: anniversaries, birthdays, celebrations, fast days

For official ceremonies, see 394.4; pageants, processions, parades, 394.5

.25   Carnivals

Example: Mardi Gras

.26   Holidays

Class here festivals

The season associated with the holiday is classed with the holiday, e.g., the twelve days of Christmas is classed with Christmas in 394.268282

Class the technology or craft associated with holidays with the technology or craft, e.g., making fireworks 662.1, decorating Easter eggs 745.5944

[.260 9]   Historical, geographical, persons treatment

Do not use; class in 394.269

.268   Specific kinds of holidays

For Mardi Gras, see 394.25

.268 2   Religious holidays

See Manual at 394.2682 vs. 263.9, 290

.268 28   Christian holidays

Holidays of the church year

.268 282   Christmas

.268 283   Easter

.268 29   Other religious holidays

Add to base number 394.26829 the numbers following 29 in 292–299, e.g., religious holidays of Judaism 394.268296

.268 3   Seasonal holidays

Examples: Halloween, May Day, New Year, Thanksgiving

.268 4   Patriotic holidays

Class here independence days

Add to base number 394.2684 notation 3–9 from Table 2, e.g., Bastille Day 394.268444

.269   Historical, geographical, persons treatment

Add to base number 394.269 notation 01–9 from Table 2, e.g., holidays of Mexico 394.26972

Class historical, geographical, persons treatment of specific kinds of holidays in 394.268

.3 **Recreational customs**

> Examples: dances, games, toys
>
> Including gambling

.4 **Official ceremonies and observances**

> Examples: coronations, inaugurations, jubilees, state visits, triumphs
>
> *See also 355.17 for military ceremonies*

.5 **Pageants, processions, parades**

> Class pageants, processions, parades associated with a specific activity with the activity, e.g., Thanksgiving Day parades 394.2683
>
> *See Manual at 394.5 vs. 791.6*

.6 **Fairs**

.7 **Customs of chivalry**

.8 **Dueling and suicide**

.9 **Cannibalism**

395 Etiquette (Manners)

> Prescriptive and practical works on social behavior
>
> Unless other instructions are given, class complex subjects with aspects in two or more subdivisions of this schedule in the number coming last in the schedule, e.g., table manners for children 395.54 (*not* 395.122)
>
> Class customs in 391–394
>
> *For protocol of diplomacy, see 327.2*
>
> *See Manual at 395*

[.081–.084] **With respect to sex and age groups**

> Do not use; class in 395.1

.1 **For specific ages and sexes**

.12 For specific age groups

.122 Children

.123 Young adults

.123 2 Men

.123 3 Women

.126 Adults aged sixty-five and over

.14 For specific sexes

> Class etiquette for specific age groups regardless of sex in 395.12

.142 Male

.144		Female
.2		**For stages in life cycle**
.22		Engagements and weddings
.23		Funerals
.24		Occasions associated with birth, puberty, majority

Examples: christening, confirmation, bar mitzvah, debut

.3 **For social occasions**

Example: dances [*formerly also* 395.59]

Class here hospitality and entertainment

Class etiquette for stages in life cycle in 395.2, invitations in 395.4

.4 **Social correspondence**

Including invitations and announcements

Class here written and spoken styles and forms of address and greeting

.5 **In specific situations**

Examples: school, sports

.52 Business and office etiquette

.53 Public behavior

Examples: in church, at theater, in stores and shops

.54 Table manners

.59 Conversation

Class here telephone etiquette

Use of this number for school and sports discontinued; class in 395.5

Dances relocated to 395.3

[396] **[Unassigned]**

Most recently used in Edition 16

[397] **[Unassigned]**

Most recently used in Edition 16

398 **Folklore**

See also 291.13 for religious mythology, 800 for belles-lettres by identifiable authors, anonymous literary classics

See Manual at 398.2 vs. 291.13

SUMMARY

398.01–.09	Standard subdivisions
.2	Folk literature
.3	Natural and physical phenomena as subjects of folklore
.4	Paranatural and legendary phenomena as subjects of folklore
.5	Chapbooks
.6	Riddles
.8	Rhymes and rhyming games
.9	Proverbs

.01   Philosophy and theory

> Class here specific theories [*formerly* 398.1]

.04   Special topics

.042   Sociology and criticism

> Origin, role, function of folklore as a cultural and social phenomenon
>
> Including social role and function
>
> Class here comprehensive works on sociology and literary criticism
>
> Class purely literary criticism in 398.2, 398.5–398.9, sociology of specific subjects of folklore in 398.3–398.4, historical and geographical treatment of sociology of folklore in 398.09

.09   Historical, geographical, persons treatment of sociology of folklore

> Class historical, geographical, persons treatment of folk literature in 398.209

[.1]   **Theories of folklore**

> Relocated to 398.01

.2   **Folk literature**

> Folklore as literature
>
> Class here literary appraisal and criticism, interdisciplinary works on mythology
>
> Class religious mythology in 291.13
>
> *For minor forms of folk literature, see 398.5–398.9*
>
> *See Manual at 398.2; 398.2 vs. 291.13; 800 vs. 398.2*

.204   By language

> Add to base number 398.204 notation 1–9 from Table 6, e.g., folk tales from French-speaking areas of the world 398.20441; however, class tales of a specific language where that language predominates in 398.209, e.g., French folk tales from France 398.20944, from Quebec 398.209714

.21   Tales and lore of paranatural and legendary beings of human and semihuman form

> Examples: centaurs, fairies, giants, mermaids and mermen, ogres, vampires
>
> Class here fairy tales
>
> *See Manual at 398.21 vs. 398.22*

.22	Tales and lore of historical and quasi-historical persons and events

Examples: heroes, kings, witches

See Manual at 398.21 vs. 398.22

.23	Tales and lore of places and times
.232	Real places

Add to base number 398.232 notation 1–9 from Table 2, e.g., tales about India 398.23254

Class tales of real places at special times in 398.236

See also 398.209 for tales originating in specific places

.234	Legendary places

Example: Atlantis

.236	Special times

Examples: seasons, special days

.24	Tales and lore of plants and animals
.242	Plants

Real and legendary

.245	Animals

See Manual at 800 vs. 591, 636, 398.245

.245 2	Real

Add to base number 398.2452 the numbers following 59 in 592–599, e.g., cats 398.2452974428

.245 4	Legendary

Examples: dragons, phoenixes, unicorns, werewolves

.25	Ghost stories
.26	Tales and lore involving physical phenomena

Real and legendary

Examples: heavenly bodies, weather, fire, water, minerals

.27	Tales and lore of everyday human life

Examples: birth, love, marriage, death, occupations, recreation, dwellings, food

See Manual at 615.882

> **398.3–398.4 Sociology of specific subjects of folklore**

Origin, role, function of themes and subjects of folklore as cultural and social phenomena

Class comprehensive works in 398.042

.3   **Natural and physical phenomena as subjects of folklore**

.32   Places

.322   Physiographic regions

.329   Specific places

Add to base number 398.329 notation 3–9 from Table 2, e.g., London as a subject for folklore 398.329421

Class historical and political themes, historical events in specific places in 398.358

.33   Times

Examples: seasons; parts of day, e.g., darkness, dawn

Including holidays

.35   Humanity and human existence

.352   Persons

Examples: heroes, kings, witches

Including individual persons

See Manual at 398.352 vs. 398.45

.353   Human body, mind, personality, qualities, activities

Examples: chivalry, friendship, insanity, pride, sex, success

Including medical folklore

For love, see 398.354

See Manual at 615.882

.354   Life cycle

Examples: birth, love, marriage, death

.355   Social themes

Examples: commerce, crime, dwellings, environment, food, law, occupations, recreation, violence

.356   Technical themes

Examples: engineering, flight, ships

Scientific themes relocated to 398.36

For medical folklore, see 398.353

.357	Artistic and literary themes

        Examples: books, music, painting

.358	Historical and political themes

        Examples: nationalism, war

        Class here historical events in specific places

.36	Scientific themes [*formerly also* 398.356]

        Class here physical phenomena

.362	Heavenly bodies
.363	Weather
.364	Fire and water
.365	Minerals
.368	Plants

        Add to base number 398.368 the numbers following 58 in 582–589, e.g., flowers 398.368213

.369	Animals

        Add to base number 398.369 the numbers following 59 in 592–599, e.g., rabbits 398.3699322

.4	**Paranatural and legendary phenomena as subjects of folklore**

        Class here magic

        See also 133.43 for magic in occultism

.41	Folk beliefs

        Including superstitions

.42	Legendary places

        Example: Atlantis

.45	Legendary beings of human and semihuman form

        Examples: fairies, giants, ogres, vampires

        Class ghosts in 398.47

        See Manual at 398.352 vs. 398.45

.46	Legendary minerals, plants, animals
.465	Minerals

        Example: philosopher's stone

.468	Plants
.469	Animals

        Examples: dragons, phoenixes, unicorns, werewolves

.47   Ghosts

Including haunted places

> **398.5–398.9 Minor forms of folk literature**

Class here literary appraisal and criticism

Class comprehensive works in 398.2

.5   **Chapbooks**

.6   **Riddles**

Class here interdisciplinary works

Class riddles as parlor games in 793.735, as belles-lettres in 808.882

.8   **Rhymes and rhyming games**

Examples: jump rope rhymes, tongue twisters

Class here nursery rhymes

.84   Counting-out (Counting) rhymes

.87   Street cries and songs

.9   **Proverbs**

Class here folk aphorisms

Add to base number 398.9 notation 1–9 from Table 6, e.g., French proverbs 398.941

399   Customs of war and diplomacy

Examples: dances, peace pipe, treatment of captives, e.g., scalping

Class cannibalism in 394.9, protocol of diplomacy in 327.2, customs of military life in 355.1

400

400 Language

Class here interdisciplinary works on language and literature

(Option A: To give local emphasis or a shorter number to a specific language, class in 410, where full instructions appear

(Option B: To give local emphasis or a shorter number to a specific language, place before 420 through use of a letter or other symbol. Full instructions appear under 420–490)

Class the language of a specific discipline or subject with the discipline or subject, using notation 014 from Table 1, e.g., language of science 501.4

> *For rhetoric, see 808; literature, 800*

> *See Manual at T4—864 vs. T1—014; 400; 400 vs. 800; 400 vs. 900*

401 Philosophy and theory

.3 International languages

Class here universal languages; general discussions of international languages, e.g., diplomatic languages, lingua francas

Do not use for value; class in 401

Class artificial languages in 499.99; specific languages with the language in 420–490, e.g., Latin as a diplomatic language 470, Swahili as a lingua franca 496.392

.4 Language (Terminology) and communication

> *See also 410.14 for discursive treatment of terminology of linguistics, 410.3 for dictionaries of linguistics, 413 for general polyglot dictionaries*

.41 Semiotics

Former heading: Communication

Class here content analysis, discourse analysis

Class interdisciplinary works on semiotics in 302.2, pragmatics in 306.44

> *For semantics, see 401.43*

> *See also 121.68 for semiotics as a topic in philosophy*

[.42] Etymology

Do not use; class in 412

.43   Semantics [*formerly* 412]

> Class the history of word meanings in 412

>> *See also 121.68 for semantics as a topic in philosophy, 149.94 for general semantics as a philosophical school*

>> *See Manual at 401.43 vs. 412, 415, 306.44, 401.9*

[.48]   Abbreviations and symbols

> Do not use; class abbreviations and symbols as part of writing systems in 411, dictionaries of abbreviations and symbols in 413.1

.51   Mathematical principles

> Class here mathematical linguistics

.9   **Psycholinguistics**

> Sociolinguistics relocated to 306.44

> Class psychology of bilingualism in 404.2019

>> *See Manual at 401.43 vs. 412, 415, 306.44, 401.9*

.93   Language acquisition

>> *See also 418.007 for the study and teaching of language, 418.4019 for the psychology of reading*

>> *See Manual at 407, T1—07 vs. 410.7, 418.007, T4—8007, 401.93*

402   **Miscellany**

403   **Dictionaries, encyclopedias, concordances**

> Class here dictionaries, encyclopedias, concordances that treat comprehensively both language and literature

> Class dictionaries, encyclopedias, concordances of linguistics in 410.3, general polyglot dictionaries in 413

404   **Special topics**

.2   **Bilingualism**

> Specific instances of bilingualism are classed with the language dominant in the country in which the linguistic interaction occurs, e.g., a discussion of Spanish-English bilingualism in Los Angeles in 420.42610979494. If neither language is dominant, class with the one coming later in the schedules

>> *See also 306.446 for sociology of bilingualism*

405   **Serial publications**

406   **Organizations and management**

407   **Education, research, related topics**

> *See Manual at 407, T1—07 vs. 410.7, 418.007, T4—8007, 401.93*

408 Treatment of language with respect to kinds of persons

See also 306.44 for sociology of language

.9 Treatment of language with respect to specific racial, ethnic, national groups

Ethnolinguistics relocated to 306.44089

409 Geographical and persons treatment

Language history not limited by area relocated to 417.7

Class specific languages and groups of languages in 420–490

See also 410.9 for geographical and persons treatment of linguistics

410 Linguistics

Science and structure of spoken and written language

Class here descriptive, synchronic linguistics; comprehensive works on Indo-European languages

(Option A: To give local emphasis and a shorter number to a specific language, e.g., Russian, class it here and add to base number 41 as instructed under 420–490; in that case class linguistics in 400, its subdivisions in 401–409, standard subdivisions of language and of linguistics in 400.1–400.9. Option B is described under 420–490)

Class linguistics of specific languages in 420–490

For specific Indo-European languages, see 420–480

See Manual at 410; 411–418

.1–.9 Standard subdivisions of linguistics

Class standard subdivisions of language and languages in 401–409

411 Writing systems

Examples: alphabets, syllabaries, ideographs; braille

Including abbreviations, acronyms, capitalization, punctuation, spelling, transliteration

See also 652 for practical works on how to write by hand or machine, e.g., penmanship 652.1

.7 Paleography [*formerly* 417.7]

Study of ancient and medieval styles of writing

412 Etymology

Semantics other than the history of word meanings relocated to 401.43

Class comprehensive works on historical linguistics in 417.7; specific aspects of etymology with the aspect, e.g., phonetic development of words 414

See Manual at 401.43 vs. 412, 415, 306.44, 401.9

413 Dictionaries

Class here polyglot dictionaries

.028 Techniques, procedures, apparatus, equipment, materials

Class here lexicography

.1 Specialized dictionaries

Examples: dictionaries of abbreviations and acronyms; picture dictionaries

.2–.9 Polyglot dictionaries with entry words or definitions in only one language

Add to base number 413 notation 2–9 from Table 6, e.g., a dictionary with terms in English, French, and German, but with definitions only in English 413.21

414 Phonology

Class here phonetics

Class comprehensive works on phonology and morphology or syntax in 415

.6 Suprasegmental features

Vocal effects extending over more than one sound element

Examples: juncture (pauses), pitch, stress

Class here intonation

See Manual at 808.1 vs. 414.6

415 Structural systems (Grammar)

Historical and descriptive study of morphology and syntax

Including generative and transformational grammar

Class here comprehensive works on morphology, syntax, and phonology

For phonology, see 414

See also 418 for prescriptive grammar

See Manual at 401.43 vs. 412, 415, 306.44, 401.9

[416] [Unassigned]

Most recently used in Edition 18

417   Dialectology and historical (diachronic) linguistics

.2   Dialectology

Including the study of nongeographical language variations, e.g., slang and jargon

Class here the study of geographical language variations

.22   Pidgins and creoles

Standard subdivisions are added for either or both of the topics named in the heading

See Manual at T4—7

.7   Historical (Diachronic) linguistics

Study of the development of language over time

Class here language history not limited by area [*formerly also* 409], language change

Paleography relocated to 411.7

Class change in and the history of specific elements of language with the element, e.g., grammar 415

See also 409 for geographical treatment of language history, 410.9 for the history of linguistics

See Manual at 410

418   Standard usage (Prescriptive linguistics)   Applied linguistics

Including multilingual phrase books

Use 418.001–418.009 for standard subdivisions

Class dictionaries and lexicography in 413

See Manual at 407, T1—07 vs. 410.7, 418.007, T4—8007, 401.93

.02   Translation and interpretation

Standard subdivisions are added for either or both of the topics named in the heading, e.g., computerized translation 418.020285

.4   Reading

419   Structured verbal language other than spoken and written

Class here manual language for the deaf

Class nonlinguistic (nonstructured) communication in 302.222

> 420–490 Specific languages

Class here comprehensive works on specific languages and their literatures

(Option B: To give local emphasis and a shorter number to a specific language, place it first by use of a letter or other symbol, e.g., Arabic language 4A0 [preceding 420], for which the base number is 4A. Option A is described under 410)

Except for additions, changes, deletions, exceptions shown under specific entries, add to base number for each language identified by * notation 01–86 from Table 4, e.g., grammar of Yoruba 496.3335. The base number is the number given for the language unless the schedule specifies a different number

(Option: For any group of languages, add notation 04 to the base number and then add notation 01–86 from Table 4, e.g., grammar of Macro-Penutian languages 497.4045)

The numbers used in this schedule for individual languages do not necessarily correspond exactly with those in 810–890 or with the notation in Table 6. Use notation from Table 6 only when so instructed, e.g., at 494.1–494.3

Class comprehensive works in 410

> *For literatures of specific languages, see 810–890*

> *See Manual at 420–490*

> 420–480 Specific Indo-European languages

Class comprehensive works in 410

> *For East Indo-European and Celtic languages, see 491*

420 †English and Old English (Anglo-Saxon)

Base number for English: 42

Special interpretations of and exceptions to Table 4 for use with English appear below under 421–428

421 †Writing system and phonology of standard English

.52 Spelling (Orthography) and pronunciation

Including standard Canadian spelling and pronunciation

Class here description and analysis of the nature, history, and function of spelling and pronunciation of English

Class comprehensive works on writing systems for English in 421.1, specialized spelling and pronouncing dictionaries in 423.1, training in standard pronunciation in 428.1

> *For standard American (U.S.) spelling and pronunciation, see 421.54; standard British spelling and pronunciation, 421.55*

†Add to 42 as instructed under 420–490

.54	Standard American (U.S.) spelling and pronunciation
.55	Standard British spelling and pronunciation

422 †**Etymology of standard English**

423 †**Dictionaries of standard English**

[424] **[Unassigned]**

Most recently used in Edition 16

425 **Structural system (Grammar) of standard English**

[426] **[Unassigned]**

Most recently used in Edition 18

427 **Historical and geographical variations, modern nongeographical variations**

Use 427.001–427.009 for standard subdivisions

For Old English (Anglo-Saxon), see 429

.02 Middle English, 1100–1500

.09 Modern nongeographical variations

Examples: ephemera, slang

.1–.8 **Geographical variations in England**

Add to 427 the numbers following —42 in notation 421–428 from Table 2, e.g., dialects of London 427.1

Geographical variations in Scotland, Wales, and Ireland are classed in 427.9 plus the appropriate notation from Table 2, e.g., dialects of North Wales 427.94291

.9 **Geographical variations in other places**

Class here pidgins, creoles

Add to 427.9 notation 4–9 from Table 2, e.g., Tok Pisin 427.9953, dialects of Canada 427.971

428 †**Standard English usage (Prescriptive linguistics)** **Applied linguistics**

Class here Basic English

429 *****Old English (Anglo-Saxon)**

See also 427.02 for Middle English

430 **Germanic (Teutonic) languages** **German**

For English and Old English (Anglo-Saxon), see 420

*Add to base number as instructed under 420–490
†Add to 42 as instructed under 420–490

.01–.09   Standard subdivisions of Germanic (Teutonic) languages

---

> **430.1–438.6 Subdivisions of ‡German language**

Base number: 43

Class comprehensive works in 430

431   ‡Writing systems and phonology of standard German

432   ‡Etymology of standard German

433   ‡Dictionaries of standard German

[434]   [Unassigned]

Most recently used in Edition 16

435   Structural system (Grammar) of standard German

[436]   [Unassigned]

Most recently used in Edition 18

437   Historical and geographical variations, modern nongeographical variations

Use 437.001–437.009 for standard subdivisions

Class Old Low German in 439.1, Middle and Modern Low German in 439.4

.01   Old High German to 1100

.02   Middle High German and early New High German, 1100–1500

.09   Modern nongeographical variations

Examples: ephemera, slang

.1–.6   Geographical variations in Germany and Austria

Add to 437 the numbers following —43 in notation 431–436 from from Table 2, e.g., dialects of Bavaria 437.3

.9   Geographical variations in other places

Add to 437.9 notation 4–9 from Table 2, e.g., Yiddish 437.947

438   ‡Standard German usage (Prescriptive linguistics)   Applied linguistics

439   Other Germanic (Teutonic) languages

> **439.1–439.4 West Germanic languages**

Class comprehensive works in 439

‡Add to 43 as instructed under 420–490

.1   Old Low Germanic languages

> Examples: Old Frisian, Old Low Franconian, Old Low German, Old Saxon

---

> **439.2–439.4 Modern Low Germanic languages**

> Class comprehensive works in 439

.2   *Frisian

.3   Netherlandish languages

.31   *Dutch

> Class here Flemish [*formerly* 439.32]

[.32]   Flemish

> Relocated to 439.31

.36   *Afrikaans

.4   *Low German (Plattdeutsch)

.5   Scandinavian (North Germanic) languages

> *For specific Scandinavian languages, see 439.6–439.8*

> **439.6–439.8 Specific Scandinavian languages**

> Class comprehensive works in 439.5

.6   West Scandinavian languages   Old Norse (Old Icelandic)

.600 1–.600 9   Standard subdivisions of West Scandinavian languages

.601–.686   Subdivisions of *Old Norse (Old Icelandic)

> Base number: 439.6

.69   Modern West Scandinavian languages   Modern Icelandic

.690 01–.690 09   Standard subdivisions of modern West Scandinavian languages

.690 1–.698 6   Subdivisions of *Modern Icelandic

> Base number: 439.69

.699   *Faeroese

> **439.7–439.8 East Scandinavian languages**

> Class comprehensive works in 439.5

.7   *Swedish

.8   Danish and Norwegian

*Add to base number as instructed under 420–490

.81	*Danish

Class Dano-Norwegian in 439.82

.82	*Norwegian (Bokmal, Riksmal)

Class here Dano-Norwegian, comprehensive works on Norwegian

For New Norse, see 439.83

.83	*Norwegian (New Norse, Landsmal)

Class comprehensive works on Norwegian in 439.82

.9　East Germanic languages

Examples: Burgundian, Gothic, Vandalic

440　Romance languages　French

For Italian, Romanian, Rhaeto-Romanic, see 450; Spanish and Portuguese, 460

.01–.09　Standard subdivisions of Romance languages

> **440.1–448.6 Subdivisions of †French language**

Base number: 44

Class comprehensive works in 440

441　†Writing system and phonology of standard French

442　†Etymology of standard French

443　†Dictionaries of standard French

[444]　[Unassigned]

Most recently used in Edition 16

445　Structural system (Grammar) of standard French

[446]　[Unassigned]

Most recently used in Edition 18

447　Historical and geographical variations, modern nongeographical variations

Use 447.001–447.009 for standard subdivisions

.01	Old French to 1400
.02	Middle French, 1400–1600

*Add to base number as instructed under 420–490

†Add to 44 as instructed under 420–490

.09   Modern nongeographical variations

        Examples: ephemera, slang

.1–.8   **Geographical variations in France**

        Add to 447 the numbers following —44 in notation 441–448 from Table 2, e.g., dialects of southern France (Langue d'oc) 447.8

        Class dialects of southeastern France (Provençal) in 449

.9   **Geographical variations in other places**

        Class here pidgins, creoles

        Add to 447.9 notation 4–9 from Table 2, e.g., dialects of Quebec 447.9714, Haitian Creole 447.97294

448   **†Standard French usage (Prescriptive linguistics)   Applied linguistics**

449   ***Provençal and Catalan**

        Base number for Provençal: 449

.9   ***Catalan**

450   ‡Italian, Romanian, Rhaeto-Romanic languages

        Base number for Italian: 45

451   **‡Writing system and phonology of standard Italian**

452   **‡Etymology of standard Italian**

453   **‡Dictionaries of standard Italian**

[454]   **[Unassigned]**

        Most recently used in Edition 16

455   **Structural system (Grammar) of standard Italian**

[456]   **[Unassigned]**

        Most recently used in Edition 18

457   **Historical and geographical variations, modern nongeographical variations**

        Use 457.001–457.009 for standard subdivisions

.01   Old Italian to 1300

.02   Middle Italian, 1300–1600

*Add to base number as instructed under 420–490
†Add to 44 as instructed under 420–490
‡Add to 45 as instructed under 420–490

.09   Modern nongeographical variations

         Examples: ephemera, slang

.1–.7   Geographical variations in continental Italy

         Add to 457 the numbers following —45 in notation 451–457 from Table 2, e.g., dialects of Lombardy 457.2

.8   Geographical variations in Sicily

         Add to 457.8 the numbers following —458 in notation 4581–4582 from Table 2, e.g., dialects of Palermo 457.823

.9   Other geographical variations

.91–.94   In Sardinia

         Add to 457.9 the numbers following —459 in notation 4591–4594 from Table 2, e.g., dialects of Cagliari 457.91

.95   In Corsica

.99   In other places

         Add to 457.99 notation 4–9 from Table 2, e.g., dialects in Ticino Canton of Switzerland 457.9949478

458   ‡Standard Italian usage (Prescriptive linguistics)   Applied linguistics

459   *Romanian and Rhaeto-Romanic

         Base number for Romanian: 459

.9   Rhaeto-Romanic languages

         Examples: Friulian, Ladin, Romansh

460   Spanish and Portuguese languages

.01–.09   Standard subdivisions for comprehensive works on Spanish and Portuguese

---

>   **460.1–468.6 Subdivisions of †Spanish language**

         Base number: 46

         Class comprehensive works in 460

461   †Writing system and phonology of standard Spanish

462   †Etymology of standard Spanish

463   †Dictionaries of standard Spanish

*Add to base number as instructed under 420–490
†Add to 46 as instructed under 420–490
‡Add to 45 as instructed under 420–490

[464] **[Unassigned]**

> Most recently used in Edition 16

465 **Structural system (Grammar) of standard Spanish**

[466] **[Unassigned]**

> Most recently used in Edition 18

467 **Historical and geographical variations, modern nongeographical variations**

> Use 467.001–467.009 for standard subdivisions

.01 Old Spanish to 1100

.02 Middle Spanish, 1100–1600

.09 Modern nongeographical variations

> Examples: ephemera, slang

.1–.8 **Geographical variations in Spain**

> Add to 467 the numbers following —46 in notation 461–468 from Table 2, e.g., dialects of Andalusia 467.8

.9 **Geographical variations in other places**

> Class here pidgins, creoles

> Add to 467.9 notation 4–9 from Table 2, e.g., Judeo-Spanish (Ladino) 467.9496, Papiamento 467.972986, Latin American dialects 467.98

468 **†Standard Spanish usage (Prescriptive linguistics)   Applied linguistics**

469 ***Portuguese**

.7 **Historical and geographical variations, modern nongeographical variations**

> Use 469.7001–469.7009 for standard subdivisions

.701 Old Portuguese to 1100

.702 Middle Portuguese, 1100–1600

.709 Modern nongeographical variations

> Examples: ephemera, slang

.71–.76 Geographical variations in continental Portugal

> Add to 469.7 the numbers following —469 in notation 4691–4696 from Table 2, e.g., dialects of Lisbon 469.7425

.78 Geographical variations in Madeira

*Add to base number as instructed under 420–490

†Add to 46 as instructed under 420–490

.79	Other geographical variations

Class here pidgins, creoles

.791	In Azores

.794	In Spain

Class here comprehensive works on Galician (Gallegan)

Class Galician dialects in Portugal in 469.71–469.72

.798	In Brazil

Add to 469.798 the numbers following —81 in notation 811–817 from Table 2, e.g., dialects of São Paulo 469.79861

.799	In other places

Add to 469.799 notation 4–9 from Table 2, e.g., dialects of Guinea-Bissau 469.7996657

See also 467.972986 for Papiamento

470 Italic languages   Latin

Class comprehensive works on Latin and Greek in 480

For Romance languages, see 440

See Manual at 470

.01–.09	Standard subdivisions of Italic languages

> **470.1–478.6 Subdivisions of ‡Latin language**

Base number: 47

Class comprehensive works in 470

471	**‡Writing system and phonology of classical Latin**
472	**‡Etymology of classical Latin**
473	**‡Dictionaries of classical Latin**
[474]	**[Unassigned]**

Most recently used in Edition 16

475	**Structural system (Grammar) of classical Latin**
[476]	**[Unassigned]**

Most recently used in Edition 18

477	**Old (Preclassical), Postclassical, Vulgar Latin**

‡Add to 47 as instructed under 420–490

478 ‡**Classical Latin usage (Prescriptive linguistics)** **Applied linguistics**

> Class here classical-revival Latin usage of medieval or modern times

479 **Other Italic languages**

.4–.9 **Specific languages**

> Add to 479 the numbers following —79 in notation 794–799 from Table 6, e.g., Umbrian 479.9

480 Hellenic languages   Classical Greek

> Classical Greek: the Greek that flourished between 750 and 350 B.C.
>
> Class here comprehensive works on classical languages
>
> *For Latin, see 470*

.01–.09 Standard subdivisions of classical languages

.1–.9 **Standard subdivisions of Hellenic languages, of classical Greek**

> **481–488 Subdivisions of †classical, preclassical, postclassical Greek**
>
> Base number: 48
>
> Dialects of classical Greek are classed in the numbers for classical Greek (480.1–485, 488)
>
> Special interpretations of and exceptions to Table 4 for use with Greek appear below
>
> Class comprehensive works in 480

481 †**Writing systems and phonology of classical Greek**

.1 **Writing systems**

> Class here paleography of classical Greek [*formerly* 481.7], comprehensive works on Greek paleography
>
> Class paleography of preclassical and postclassical Greek in 487.1

[.7] **Paleography**

> Paleography of classical Greek relocated to 481.1; of preclassical Greek, Minoan Linear B to 487.1

482 †**Etymology of classical Greek**

483 †**Dictionaries of classical Greek**

†Add to 48 as instructed under 420–490
‡Add to 47 as instructed under 420–490

[484]   [Unassigned]

Most recently used in Edition 16

485   Structural system (Grammar) of classical Greek

[486]   [Unassigned]

Most recently used in Edition 18

487   Preclassical and postclassical Greek

.1   Preclassical Greek

Including paleography of preclassical Greek, Minoan Linear B [*both formerly* 481.7]

See also 492.6 for Minoan Linear A

.3   Postclassical Greek

Including Byzantine Greek

For Koine, see 487.4

.4   Koine (Hellenistic Greek)

Class here Biblical Greek

488   †Classical Greek usage (Prescriptive linguistics)   Applied linguistics

489   Other Hellenic languages

.3   *Modern Greek

Examples: Demotic, Katharevusa

490   Other languages

SUMMARY

491	East Indo-European and Celtic languages
492	Afro-Asiatic (Hamito-Semitic) languages Semitic languages
493	Non-Semitic Afro-Asiatic languages
494	Ural-Altaic, Paleosiberian, Dravidian languages
495	Sino-Tibetan and other languages of East and Southeast Asia
496	African languages
497	North American native languages
498	South American native languages
499	Nonaustronesian languages of Oceania, Austronesian languages, miscellaneous languages

*Add to base number as instructed under 420–490

†Add to 48 as instructed under 420–490

491   East Indo-European and Celtic languages

SUMMARY

491.1	**Indo-Iranian (Aryan) languages**	
.2	**Sanskrit**	
.3	**Middle Indic languages (Secondary Prakrits)**	
.4	**Modern Indic languages (Tertiary Prakrits)**	
.5	**Iranian languages**	
.6	**Celtic languages**	
.7	**East Slavic languages**	**Russian**
.8	**Slavic languages**	
.9	**Baltic and other Indo-European languages**	

.1   **Indo-Iranian (Aryan) languages**

> *For Indic (Indo-Aryan) languages, see 491.2–491.4; Iranian languages, 491.5*

\>   **491.2–491.4 Indic (Indo-Aryan) languages**

Class comprehensive works in 491.1

.2   ***Sanskrit**

Including Vedic (Old Indic)

.3   **Middle Indic languages (Secondary Prakrits)**

Class here comprehensive works on Prakrit languages

Class tertiary Prakrits in 491.4

.37   *Pali

.4   **Modern Indic languages (Tertiary Prakrits)**

.41   *Sindhi and Lahnda

           Base number for Sindhi: 491.41

.419   *Lahnda

.42   *Panjabi

.43   Western Hindi languages   Hindi

.430 01–.430 09   Standard subdivisions of Western Hindi languages

.430 1–.438 6   Subdivisions of *Hindi

           Base number: 491.43

.439   *Urdu

.44   *Bengali

           Class Assamese in 491.451

*Add to base number as instructed under 420–490

.45	Assamese, Bihari, Oriya
.451	*Assamese
.454	*Bihari
.454 7	Historical and geographical variations, modern nongeographical variations

Examples: Bhojpuri, Magahi, Maithili

.46	*Marathi
.467	Historical and geographical variations, modern nongeographical variations

Example: Konkani

.47	*Gujarati and Rajasthani

Base number for Gujarati: 491.47

.479	*Rajasthani
.479 7	Historical and geographical variations, modern nongeographical variations

Examples: Jaipuri, Marwari

.48	Sinhalese-Maldivian languages *Sinhalese
.487	Historical and geographical variations, modern nongeographical variations

Example: Divehi (Maldivian)

.49	Other Indic (Indo-Aryan) languages

Examples: Eastern Hindi, Nepali, Pahari

Including Awadhi, Bagheli, Chattisgarhi

See also 495.49 for Himalayan languages, e.g., Newari

.499	Dardic (Pisacha) languages

Examples: Kashmiri, Khowar, Kohistani, Shina

Including Nuristani (Kafiri), Romany (Gypsy)

.5	**Iranian languages**
.51	*Old Persian

Class here ancient West Iranian languages

See also 491.52 for Avestan language

.52	*Avestan

Class here ancient East Iranian languages

.53	Middle Iranian languages

Examples: Khotanese (Saka), Pahlavi (Middle Persian), Sogdian

*Add to base number as instructed under 420–490

.55	*Modern Persian (Farsi)

Class Tajik in 491.59

.59	Other modern Iranian languages

Examples: Baluchi, Kurdish, Ossetic, Tajik, Yaghnobi

.593	Pamir (Galcha) languages *Pashto (Afghan)

.6   Celtic languages

Example: Gaulish

.62	*Irish Gaelic
.63	*Scottish Gaelic
.64	*Manx
.66	*Welsh (Cymric)
.67	*Cornish
.68	*Breton

.7   East Slavic languages   Russian

.700 1–.700 9	Standard subdivisions of East Slavic languages
.701–.786	Subdivisions of *Russian

Base number: 491.7

.77	Historical and geographical variations, modern nongeographical variations

Use 491.77001–491.77009 for standard subdivisions

.770 1	Old Russian to 1550
.770 2	Middle Russian, 1550–1750
.770 9	Modern nongeographical variations

Examples: ephemera, slang

.774–.779	Geographical variations

Add to 491.77 notation 4–9 from Table 2, e.g., dialects of Far Eastern Siberia 491.77577

.79	*Ukrainian and Belorussian

Base number for Ukrainian: 491.79

.799	*Belorussian

*Add to base number as instructed under 420–490

.8   **Slavic languages**

Example: Common Slavic

Class here comprehensive works on Balto-Slavic languages

For East Slavic languages, see 491.7; Baltic languages, 491.9

.81   South Slavic languages   Bulgarian

For Serbo-Croatian, see 491.82; Slovenian, 491.84

.810 01–.810 09   Standard subdivisions of South Slavic languages

.810 1–.818 6   Subdivisions of *Bulgarian

Base number: 491.81

.817   Historical and geographical variations, modern nongeographical variations

Use 491.817001–491.817009 for standard subdivisions

.817 01   Old Bulgarian (Church Slavonic)

.819   *Macedonian

.82   *Serbo-Croatian

.84   *Slovenian

.85   West Slavic languages   Polish

Example: Kashubian

For Czech, see 491.86; Slovak, 491.87; Wendish, 491.88; Polabian, 491.89

.850 01–.850 09   Standard subdivisions of West Slavic languages

.850 1–.858 6   Subdivisions of *Polish

Base number: 491.85

.857   Historical and geographical variations, modern nongeographical variations

Use of this number for Kashubian discontinued; class in 491.85

.86   *Czech

For Moravian dialects, see 491.87

.87   *Slovak

Including Moravian dialects

.88   *Wendish (Sorbian, Lusatian)

.89   *Polabian

*Add to base number as instructed under 420–490

.9   **Baltic and other Indo-European languages**

> \>   491.91–491.93 Baltic languages

          Class comprehensive works in 491.9

.91   Old Prussian

.92   *Lithuanian

.93   *Latvian (Lettish)

.99   Other Indo-European languages

.991   *Albanian

.992   *Armenian

.993–.998   Other

          Add to 491.99 the numbers following —9199 in notation 91993–91998 from Table 6, e.g., Tocharian language 491.994

          Base number for *Hittite: 491.998

492   Afro-Asiatic (Hamito-Semitic) languages   Semitic languages

          For non-Semitic Afro-Asiatic languages, see 493

.1   **East Semitic languages   Akkadian (Assyro-Babylonian)**

          Including Assyrian, Babylonian, Chaldean dialects of Akkadian

          See also 492.2 for Aramaic, 499.95 for Sumerian

> \>   492.2–492.9 West Semitic languages

          Class comprehensive works in 492

> \>   492.2–492.6 Northwest Semitic languages

          Class comprehensive works in 492

.2   **Aramaic languages**

          For Eastern Aramaic languages, see 492.3

.29   Western Aramaic languages

          Former heading: Biblical Aramaic (Chaldee) and Samaritan

.3   **Eastern Aramaic languages   *Syriac**

*Add to base number as instructed under 420–490

.4   ***Hebrew**

.47   Historical and geographical variations, modern nongeographical variations

        Ammonite, Moabite languages relocated to 492.6

.6   **Canaanite-Phoenician languages**

        Examples: Ammonite, Moabite [*both formerly* 492.47], Eblaite, Punic, Ugaritic, the language of Minoan Linear A

        Class here comprehensive works on Canaanitic languages

          For Hebrew, see 492.4

          See also 487.1 for Minoan Linear B, 499.95 for Sumerian

---

>   **492.7–492.9 Southwest Semitic languages**

        Class comprehensive works in 492

.7   **North Arabic languages**   ***Arabic**

        Base number for Arabic: 492.7

          See also 492.9 for South Arabic languages

.77   Historical and geographical variations, modern nongeographical variations

        Example: Maltese

.8   **Ethiopic languages**

        Examples: Geez, Gurage, Harari, Tigre, Tigrinya

.87   *Amharic

.877   Nonstandard Amharic

        Example: Argobba dialect

.9   **South Arabic languages**

        Examples: Mahri, Qarawi, Shkhauri, Sokotri

          See also 492.7 for North Arabic languages

493   Non-Semitic Afro-Asiatic languages

        Former heading: Hamitic and Chad languages

        Add to 493 the numbers following —93 in notation 931–937 from Table 6, e.g., Oromo (Galla) 493.5

        Base number for *Coptic: 493.2

        Base number for *Hausa: 493.72

*Add to base number as instructed under 420–490

494   Ural-Altaic, Paleosiberian (Hyperborean), Dravidian languages

Add to base number 494 the numbers following —94 in —941–948 from Table 6, e.g., Mongolian 494.2

Base number for *Turkish (Osmanli): 494.35

Base number for *Azerbaijani: 494.361

Base number for *Hungarian (Magyar): 494.511

Base number for *Finnish (Suomi): 494.541

Base number for *Estonian: 494.545

Base number for *Lapp: 494.55

Base number for *Tamil: 494.811

Base number for *Malayalam: 494.812

Base number for *Kannada (Kanarese): 494.814

Base number for *Gondi: 494.823

Base number for *Khond (Kandh): 494.824

Base number for *Telugu: 494.827

Base number for *Brahui: 494.83

Class Japanese in 495.6, Korean in 495.7

See also 497.1 for Inuit-Aleut languages

495   Languages of East and Southeast Asia   Sino-Tibetan languages

Examples: Karen, Miao (Hmong), Yao

Here are classed South Asian languages closely related to the languages of East and Southeast Asia

For Malay languages, see 499.2

.1   *Chinese

Base number for Mandarin (Putonghua) (standard written Chinese): 495.1

.17   Historical and geographical variations, modern nongeographical variations

Examples: Amoy, Cantonese, Foochow, Hakka, Pekingese (Beijing), Swatow, Wu dialects

*Add to base number as instructed under 420–490

.4   **Tibeto-Burman languages**   **Tibetan**

> Including the Bodo-Naga-Kachin, Kuki-Chin, Loloish groups
>
> *For Burmese, see 495.8*

.400 1–.400 9   Standard subdivisions of Tibeto-Burman languages

.401–.486   Subdivisions of *Tibetan

> Base number: 495.4

.49   Himalayan (Gyarung-Mishmi) languages

> Example: Newari
>
> *See also 491.49 for Nepali*

.6   ***Japanese**

.7   ***Korean**

.8   ***Burmese**

.9   **Miscellaneous languages of Southeast Asia; Munda languages**

> Limited to the languages provided for below

.91   Thai (Tai) languages   Thai (Siamese)

.910 01–.910 09   Standard subdivisions of Thai (Tai) languages

.910 1–.918 6   Subdivisions of *Thai (Siamese)

> Base number: 495.91

.919   Other Thai (Tai) languages

> Examples: Ahom, Khamti, Lao, Shan
>
> Use of this number for Karen discontinued; class in 495
>
> *For Annam-Muong languages, see 495.92*

.92–.95   Annam-Muong, Mon-Khmer, Munda languages

> Add to 495.9 the numbers following —959 in notation 9592–9595 from Table 6, e.g., Wa 495.93
>
> Base number for *Vietnamese (Annamese): 495.922
>
> Base number for *Khmer (Cambodian): 495.932

*Add to base number as instructed under 420–490

496   African languages

> Add to 496 the numbers following —96 in notation 961–969 from Table 6, e.g., Bambara 496.34
>
> Base number for *Wolof: 496.3214
>
> Base number for *Fulani (Fulah): 496.322
>
> Base number for *Ibo (Igbo): 496.332
>
> Base number for *Yoruba: 496.333
>
> Base number for *Ewe: 496.3374
>
> Base number for *Akan: 496.3385
>
> Base number for *Bemba: 496.3915
>
> Base number for *Nyanja: 496.3918
>
> Base number for *Swahili: 496.392
>
> Base number for *Kongo: 496.3931
>
> Base number for *Ruanda: 496.39461
>
> Base number for *Rundi: 496.39465
>
> Base number for *Kikuyu: 496.3954
>
> Base number for *Ganda (Luganda): 496.3957
>
> Base number for *Lingala: 496.39686
>
> Base number for *Shona: 496.3975
>
> Base number for *Northern Sotho: 496.39771
>
> Base number for *Southern Sotho: 496.39772
>
> Base number for *Tswana: 496.39775
>
> Base number for *Xhosa: 496.3985
>
> Base number for *Zulu: 496.3986

> *For Ethiopic languages, see 492.8; non-Semitic Afro-Asiatic languages, 493*

497   North American native languages

> Class here comprehensive works on North and South American native languages
>
> Add to 497 the numbers following —97 in notation 971–979 from Table 6, e.g., Macro-Penutian languages 497.4

> *For South American native languages, see 498*

498   South American native languages

> Add to 498 the numbers following —98 in notation 982–984 from Table 6, e.g., Andean-Equatorial languages 498.3
>
> Base number for *Quechua: 498.323

*Add to base number as instructed under 420–490

499   Nonaustronesian languages of Oceania, Austronesian languages, miscellaneous languages

Use of this number for other languages discontinued; class in 490

Add to 499 the numbers following —99 in notation 991–999 from Table 6, e.g., Etruscan 499.94

Base number for *Tagalog (Filipino): 499.211

Base number for *Indonesian (Bahasa Indonesia): 499.221

Base number for *Javanese: 499.222

Base number for *Malay (Bahasa Malaysia): 499.28

Base number for *Malagasy: 499.3

Base number for *Basque: 499.92

Base number for *Sumerian: 499.95

Base number for *Esperanto: 499.992

Base number for *Interlingua: 499.993

*Add to base number as instructed under 420–490

500

500 Natural sciences and mathematics

Natural sciences: sciences that deal with matter and energy, or with objects and processes observable in nature

Class here interdisciplinary works on natural and applied sciences

Class scientific principles of a discipline or subject with the discipline or subject, using notation 015 from Table 1, e.g., scientific principles of photography 770.15

Natural history is classed in 508

> *For applied sciences, see 600*

> *See Manual at 500 vs. 001; 500 vs. 338.926, 351.855; 500 vs. 600*

.2 Physical sciences

> *For astronomy and allied sciences, see 520; physics, 530; chemistry and allied sciences, 540; earth sciences worlds, 550*

> *See Manual at 530 vs. 500.2*

.5 Space sciences

Class astronomy in 520; earth sciences in other worlds in 550; space sciences aspects of other subjects with the subject, e.g., chemical reactions in space in 541.390919

.8 History and description with respect to kinds of persons [*formerly* 509]

Add to base number 500.8 the numbers following 08 in —081–089 from Table 1, e.g., women as scientists 500.82

501 Philosophy and theory

Class scientific method as a general research technique in 001.42, scientific method applied in the natural sciences in 507.2

502 Miscellany

.8 Auxiliary techniques and procedures; apparatus, equipment, materials

.82 Microscopy

Class here interdisciplinary works on microscopy

Class manufacture of microscopes in 681.413

.822 Simple microscopes

.823 Compound microscopes

.824	Ultramicroscopes
.825	Electron microscopes

503   Dictionaries, encyclopedias, concordances

[504]   [Unassigned]

Most recently used in Edition 16

505   Serial publications

506   Organizations and management

507   Education, research, related topics

.2   **Research**

> See also 001.4 for research covering science in general
>
> See Manual at 500 vs. 001

.8   **Use of apparatus and equipment in study and teaching**

> Class here science fair projects, science projects in schools

508   Natural history

> Class here description and surveys of phenomena in nature
>
> Do not use for history and description of natural sciences and mathematics with respect to groups of persons; class in 500.8
>
> Class natural history of organisms in 574
>
> See Manual at 508 vs. 574, 910, 304.2

.09   Historical and persons treatment

> Class geographical treatment in 508.3–508.9

.3   **Treatment by areas, regions, places in general; by specific continents, countries, localities in the ancient world**

> Add to base number 508.3 notation 1 or 3 from Table 2, e.g., natural history of the sea 508.3162, of ancient Greece 508.338

.4–.9   **Treatment by specific continents, countries, localities in the modern world**

> Add to base number 508 notation 4–9 from Table 2, e.g., natural history of Brazil 508.81

509   Historical, geographical, persons treatment

> History and description with respect to kinds of persons relocated to 500.8
>
> Class historical, geographical, persons treatment of natural phenomena in 508

510 Mathematics

Class here finite mathematics

See Manual at 003, T1—011 vs. 510, T1—0151; 005.1 vs. 510; 510; 510, T1—0151 vs. 004–006, T1—0285

SUMMARY

510.1	Philosophy and theory
511	General principles
512	Algebra and number theory
513	Arithmetic
514	Topology
515	Analysis
516	Geometry
519	Probabilities and applied mathematics

.1   **Philosophy and theory**

Including metamathematics

Class mathematical logic in 511.3

511 General principles

Class topics found here applied to a specific branch of mathematics with the branch, e.g., arithmetic approximation 513.24

.2   **Mathematical systems**

.22   Inductive and intuitive mathematics

.24   Deductive mathematics

.3   **Mathematical (Symbolic) logic**

Including automata theory [*formerly also* 001.535], infinite-state machines [*formerly also* 621.3819594], Turing machines [*formerly also* 621.381952, 621.381954], sequential machines [*formerly also* 629.891], formal languages, machine theory; completeness theorem, continuum hypothesis, decidability, Godel's theorem

Class here logic operators; axioms, postulates, proof, hypotheses; predicate calculus, propositional calculus

Class proof for inductive and intuitive mathematics in 511.22

.32   Sets

For point sets, see 511.33

.322   Set theory

Class here transfinite numbers [*formerly* 512.7]

.324   Algebra of sets (Boolean algebra)

.33   Relations, lattices, ordered systems and structures

Examples: equations, functions, mappings, point sets, transformations

.35		Recursion theory

Including recursive functions

.4 **Approximations and expansions**

.42 Methods

Examples: curve fitting, interpolation, splines

.43 Error analysis

.5 **Theory and construction of graphs**

Including nomography, trees

.6 **Combinatorial analysis**

Including combinatorial configurations and designs

Class graph theory in 511.5

.62 Enumeration

.64 Permutations and combinations

.65 Choice

See also 519.3 for decision making in game theory

.66 Maxima and minima

.8 **Mathematical models (Mathematical simulation)**

Including algorithms

512 Algebra and number theory

Including numerical algebra

Class here universal algebra, modern algebra (abstract algebra combined with number theory)

Use 512.001–512.009 for standard subdivisions

Foundations of algebra is classed in 512.9

SUMMARY

512.02	**Abstract algebra**
.1	**Algebra combined with other branches of mathematics**
.2	**Groups and group theory**
.3	**Fields**
.4	**Rings, integral domains, ideals**
.5	**Linear, multilinear, multidimensional algebras**
.7	**Number theory**
.9	**Foundations of algebra**

.02 Abstract algebra

For subdivisions of abstract algebra, see 512.2–512.5

.1   **Algebra combined with other branches of mathematics**

> *For arithmetic and algebra, see 513.12*
>
> *See Manual at 510: Combination of topics*

.12   Algebra and Euclidean geometry

.13   Algebra and trigonometry

.14   Algebra and analytic geometry

.15   Algebra and calculus

>   **512.2–512.5 Subdivisions of abstract algebra**

> Class comprehensive works in 512.02

.2   **Groups and group theory**

> Class here cosets, semigroups, subgroups; partitions; cyclic, permutation, Abelian (commutative) groups; Brauer groups
>
> *For topological and related algebras and groups, see 512.55; algebraic topology, 514.2*

[.22]   Group theory

> Number discontinued; class in 512.2

.24   Algebras based on group properties

> Examples: Jordan algebra [*formerly* 512.53], commutative, associative, nonassociative, flexible, free algebras
>
> Class algebras defined by dimension in 512.53, topological algebras in 512.55

.3   **Fields**

> Class here field theory, Galois theory
>
> Class linear algebra in 512.5, number theory in 512.7

[.32]   Field theory

> Number discontinued; class in 512.3

[.33]   Abstract algebraic geometry

> Relocated to 516.35

.4   **Rings, integral domains, ideals**

> Including subrings, extension theory
>
> Class here modules [*formerly* 512.522], radical theory [*formerly* 512.94]
>
> *For fields, see 512.3*

.5   **Linear, multilinear, multidimensional algebras**

Including Cayley algebra, quaternions

Class here vector algebra, linear algebra combined with analytic geometry

Standard subdivisions are added for combined linear, multilinear, multidimensional algebras, for linear algebra alone

Geometry of numbers relocated to 512.75

Class foundations of algebra in 512.9, analysis combined with linear algebra in 515.14

> *See Manual at 510: Combination of topics*

.52   Vector spaces

Class bilinear forms in 512.944, topological vector spaces in 515.73

[.522]   Modules

Relocated to 512.4

[.523]   Vector spaces

Number discontinued; class in 512.52

.53   Algebras defined by dimension of space and other geometric algebras

Jordan algebra relocated to 512.24

.55   Topological and related algebras and groups

Examples: homological algebra, categories, morphisms, functors; toposes; Banach, Frechet, Hopf, Lie, operator (e.g., C*, Von Neumann, W*), reductive, Stein, uniform algebras and their groups

Including algebraic K-theory

> *For differential and difference algebras, see 512.56; factor algebras, 512.57*

.56   Differential and difference algebras

.57   Factor algebras

Examples: Clifford, exterior, spinor, tensor algebras

.7   **Number theory**

Class here lattices

Transfinite numbers relocated to 511.322

> *For the theory of equations, see 512.94*

.72   Elementary number theory

Including combinations, congruence, continued fractions, Diophantine equations, divisibility, Fibonacci numbers, natural numbers, operations, power residues, prime numbers, quadratic residues, representations, residues, roots, sequences of integers, sieves, transformations

Geometry of rational numbers relocated to 512.75

.73	Analytic number theory

Including additive properties, Diophantine approximations, distribution theory of prime numbers, functions, modular forms, multiplicative properties, number theoretic functions, partitions, Riemannian hypothesis, transcendental numbers

.74	Algebraic number theory

Including algebraic function theory, class groups, class numbers, discriminants, factorization, field extension, fields, ideals, p-adic numbers, quadratic forms, reciprocity, rings, unit theory

.75	Geometry of numbers [*formerly* 512.5]

Class here the geometry of rational numbers [*formerly* 512.72]

.76	Probabilistic number theory
.9	**Foundations of algebra**

Class algebra combined with other branches of mathematics in 512.1

.900 1–.900 9	Standard subdivisions
[.904]	Elementary, intermediate, advanced algebras

Numbers discontinued; class in 512.9

.92	Algebraic operations

Class here addition, subtraction, multiplication, division

.922	Exponents and logarithms
.923	Root extraction

Including factoring

.924	Approximation, ratio, proportion
.925	Combinations, permutations, distributions
.93	Simple algebraic and geometric progressions
.94	Theory of equations

Radical theory relocated to 512.4

.942	Specific types and systems of equations

Examples: binomial, polynomial, quadratic, cubic, quartic, mixed

.943	Determinants and matrices
.943 2	Determinants

Class determinants of matrices in 512.9434

.943 4	Matrices

Including eigenvalues and eigenvectors

.944	Theory of forms and algebraic invariant theory

.96   Algebra of non-equation functions

     Example: rational functions

     For inequalities, see 512.97

     See also 512.944 for quantics

.97   Inequalities

513   Arithmetic

     Including numeracy

.1   Arithmetic combined with other branches of mathematics

     See Manual at 510: Combination of topics

.12   Arthmetic and algebra

.122   Separate treatment

.123   Combined treatment

.13   Arithmetic and geometry

.132   Separate treatment

.133   Combined treatment

.14   Arithmetic, algebra, geometry

.142   Separate treatment

.143   Combined treatment

.2   Arithmetic operations

     Decimal (base 10) system relocated to 513.55

.21   Basic operations

.211   Addition

     Including counting

.212   Subtraction

.213   Multiplication

.214   Division

.22   Exponents and logarithms

.23   Root extraction

     Examples: factoring; square root, cube root

.24   Approximation, ratio, proportion

     Including percentage

.25   Combinations, permutations, distributions

.26   Fractions

.4	**Arithmetic and geometric progressions**
.5	**Numeration systems**

Examples: base 3, 5, 20 systems

.52 Binary (Base 2) system

.54 Octal (Base 8) system

.55 Decimal (Base 10) system [*formerly* 513.2]

.56 Duodecimal (Base 12) system

.57 Sexadecimal (Hexadecimal, Base 16) system

.6 **Nonweighted systems**

Example: modular arithmetic

.9 **Rapid calculations, shortcuts, ready reckoners**

Former heading: Special purpose arithmetics

This number should not be confused with the idea of arithmetic formulas 513.0212. Class here hints on the methods of solving arithmetic problems rapidly, e.g., when adding nines add an equal number of tens and then subtract one for each nine added; mental arithmetic

[.92] Rapid calculations and shortcuts

Number discontinued; class in 513.9

[.93] Business arithmetic

Relocated to 650.01513

514 Topology

Class here analysis situs, homogeneous spaces, homeomorphisms, mappings

Class topology combined with analysis in 515.13

For topological vector spaces, see 515.73

.2 **Algebraic topology**

See also 512.55 for topological algebras

.22 Combinatorial topology

.223 Combinatorial elements

Examples: simplexes, complexes, nets, topological manifolds

.224 Structures and spaces

Examples: sheaves, fiber bundles (fiber spaces), knots, links, braids, path spaces

.23 Homology and cohomology theories

Including K-theory

See also 512.55 for topological groups

.24	Homotopy theory
	Including retracts
.3	**Topology of spaces**
	Class here manifold topology, metric topology
.32	Systems and spaces
	Use 514.32001–514.32009 for standard subdivisions
.320 2	Uniform spaces
.320 3	Derived spaces
.322	Point set topology (General topology)
.323	Proximity topology
.7	**Analytic topology**
.72	Differential topology
	Including foliations
.74	Global analysis
	See also 515 for global analysis in analysis

515 Analysis

Including comprehensive works on global analysis

Class here calculus, comprehensive works on the theory of functions

Class probabilities in 519.2, the theory of a specific function or group of functions with the subject, e.g., analysis of continued fractions 512.72

SUMMARY

515.1	**Analysis and calculus combined with other branches of mathematics**
.2	**General aspects**
.3	**Differential calculus and equations**
.4	**Integral calculus and equations**
.5	**Special functions**
.6	**Other analytic methods**
.7	**Functional analysis**
.8	**Functions of real variables**
.9	**Functions of complex variables**

.1	**Analysis and calculus combined with other branches of mathematics**
	For algebra and calculus, see 512.15
	See Manual at 510: Combination of topics
.13	Analysis and topology
.14	Analysis and linear algebra
.15	Calculus and analytic geometry
.16	Calculus and trigonometry

.2	**General aspects**

Class a specific application with the subject, e.g., the expansion of functions of real variables 515.8234

.22	Properties of functions
.222	Continuity, dimension, limit
.223	Uniformity and multiformity

Including Riemann surfaces, analytic spaces (generalization of Riemann surfaces to n-dimensional spaces)

Class here uniform and multiform functions

.23	Operations on functions

For differentiation, see 515.33; integration, 515.43

.232	Determination of functions
.234	Expansion of functions
.235	Evaluation of functions

Real- , complex- , vector-valued functions relocated to 515.7

.24	Sequences and series

Class here infinite processes

.243	Series

Including summability

Class here infinite series

Class number theory of continued fractions in 512.72

.243 2	Power series
.243 3	Fourier and harmonic analysis

Class abstract harmonic analysis in 515.785, Fourier transforms in 515.723

.25	Equations and functions
.252	By degree

Examples: linear, nonlinear, quadratic equations

.253	By property

Examples: homogeneous, indeterminate, reciprocal equations

.254	By origin

Example: conditional equations

.26	Inequalities

.3   **Differential calculus and equations**

Class differential topology in 514.72, differential operators in 515.7242, differential geometry in 516.36

.33   Differential calculus

Including ordinary, partial, total differentiations; total and directional derivatives, mean value theorems, differentials

Class numerical differentiation in 515.623, vector differentiation in 515.63, probability differentiation in 519.2

.35   Differential equations

Class here the Cauchy problem; orders, degrees; comprehensive works on boundary-value problems; bifurcation, perturbation, stability theories

Class boundary-value problems of finite differences in 515.62

.352   Ordinary differential equations

Class here dynamical systems

.353   Partial differential equations

Examples: elliptic, hyperbolic, parabolic equations

.354   Linear differential equations

Class linear ordinary differential equations in 515.352, linear partial differential equations in 515.353

.355   Nonlinear differential equations

Class nonlinear ordinary differential equations in 515.352, nonlinear partial differential equations in 515.353

.36   Differential inequalities

.37   Differential forms

.38   Mixed equations

Examples: integro-differential, difference-differential equations

.4   **Integral calculus and equations**

Class special functions in 515.5, integral transforms in 515.723, integral geometry in 516.362

.42   Theory of measure and integration

Including ergodic theory

For functionals, see 515.74

.43	Integral calculus

Including integration, summation, arc length, cubature, quadrature; Cauchy, definite, Denjoy, Green, Haar, improper, Lebesgue, line, Poisson, Poisson-Stieltjes, proper, Riemann, Stokes', surface integrals

Class vector integration in 515.63, numerical integration in 515.624, probability integration in 519.2

.45	Integral equations
.46	Integral inequalities
.5	**Special functions**
.52	Eulerian integrals

Examples: gamma, beta functions

.53	Harmonic functions

Examples: Bessel, Hankel, Laplace, Legendre, Neumann functions

.54	Mathieu functions
.55	Orthogonal polynomials

Examples: Chebyshev, Hermite, hypergeometric, Jacobi, Lagrange, Laguerre, Legendre polynomials

.56	Zeta function

Class the application of the Riemann zeta function with respect to prime number theory in 512.73

.6	**Other analytic methods**

For functional analysis, see 515.7

.62	Calculus of finite differences

Class here boundary-value problems when either limit has a numerical value

.623	Numerical differentiation
.624	Numerical integration
.625	Difference equations

Class difference-differential equations in 515.38

.63	Vector, tensor, spinor analysis

Including vector and tensor calculus

Class algebraic vector analysis in 512.52, geometric vector analysis in 516.182

.64	Calculus of variations

Including control theory

See also 629.8312 for control theory

.7   **Functional analysis**

Class here comprehensive works on real- , complex- , vector-valued functions [*all formerly* 515.235]; abstract potential theory

Class the theory of measure and integration in 515.42, potential theory in 515.9

For topological algebras, see 512.55; functions of real variables, 515.8; functions of complex variables, 515.9

.72   Operational calculus

Class a specific application with the subject, e.g., differential operators in topological vector spaces 515.73

.722   Spectral and representation theories

.722 2   Spectral theory

.722 3   Representation theory

Including forms

Generalized functions relocated to 515.782

Class abstract harmonic analysis in 515.785

.723   Transforms (Integral operators)

Examples: Fourier, Hilbert, Laplace, Legendre, Z transforms

.724   Operator theory

For integral operators, see 515.723

.724 2   Differential operators

Example: elliptic operators

.724 6   Linear operators

Class linear integral operators in 515.723, linear differential operators in 515.7242

.724 8   Nonlinear operators

Class nonlinear integral operators in 515.723, nonlinear differential operators in 515.7242

.73   Topological vector spaces

Examples: spaces of continuous functions; spaces of measurable functions, e.g., L^p spaces, Orlicz spaces; spaces of analytic functions; Hermitian (unitary) and Riesz spaces

Including mappings between spaces

Class here linear topological spaces

For functionals, see 515.74

.732   Banach spaces

Class here normed linear spaces

For Hilbert spaces, see 515.733

.733	Hilbert spaces

Class here inner product spaces

.74	Functionals
.78	Special topics
.782	Distribution theory

Including duality, distribution spaces, Sobolev spaces

Class here generalized functions [*formerly* 515.7223]

.783	Abstract measure theory
.784	Valuation theory
.785	Abstract harmonic analysis

Including Fourier analysis on groups

.8	**Functions of real variables**

Class the combined treatment of the functions of real and complex variables in 515.9

.82	General aspects

Add to base number 515.82 the numbers following 515.2 in 515.22–515.26, e.g., the expansion of functions 515.8234

Class a specific application with the subject, e.g., the expansion of functions of several real variables 515.84

.83	Functions of one real variable
.84	Functions of several real variables
.88	Specific types of real variable functions

Example: real variable analytic functions

.9	**Functions of complex variables**

Class here the classical theory of functions, conformal mapping, automorphic functions, potential theory

.92	General aspects

Add to base number 515.92 the numbers following 515.2 in 515.22–515.26, e.g., expansion of functions 515.9234

Class a specific application with the subject, e.g., expansion of functions of several complex variables 515.94

.93	Functions of one complex variable
.94	Functions of several complex variables
.98	Specific types of complex variable functions

Examples: entire, pseudonanalytic functions

.982   Meromorphic functions

.983   Elliptic functions

> Class special elliptic functions in 515.5

.984   Theta function

516   Geometry

Use 516.001–516.009 for standard subdivisions

Class here geometry combined with topology

Class algebra combined with geometry in 512.1, arithmetic combined with geometry in 513.13, analysis combined with geometry in 515.1, geometric probability in 519.2

For topology, see 514

SUMMARY

516.02–.08	[Classical and modern geometry; planes, solids, manifolds, convex sets]
.1	General aspects
.2	Euclidean geometry
.3	Analytic geometries
.4	Affine geometry
.5	Projective geometry
.6	Abstract descriptive geometry
.9	Non-Euclidean geometries

.02   Classical geometry

.04   Modern geometry

.05   Planes

.06   Solids

.07   Manifolds

.08   Convex sets

.1   General aspects

Class here metric geometry, transformations, automorphisms

Class general aspects applied to a specific geometry with the geometry, e.g., angles in Euclidean geometry, 516.215

.12   Incidence geometry

.13   Combinatorial and constructive geometry

.15   Geometric configurations, measures, shapes

Examples: angles, circles, conic sections, cubes, curves, polyhedrons, spheres, spirals, squares, surfaces; pattern, shapes, sizes, space

Class a specific configuration, measure, shape with the subject, e.g., measuring the sphere in solid geometry 516.23

Including mensuration

.16	Coordinate systems

> Examples: Cartesian, curvilinear, homogeneous systems

.17	Geometry of inequalities
.18	Nonpoint base geometries
.182	Vector geometry
.183	Line geometry
.184	Circle geometry
.185	Modular geometry
.186	Geometries over algebras, groups, rings

.2 Euclidean geometry

> Including the imbedding of Euclidean spaces in other geometries
>
> Class here congruences, similarity, metric geometry
>
> Use 516.2001–516.2009 for standard subdivisions
>
> Class a specific type of Euclidean geometry with the subject, e.g., Euclidean analytic geometry 516.3

.204	Famous problems

> Contains trisecting an angle, squaring the circle, doubling the cube

.21	General aspects

> Add to base number 516.21 the numbers following 516.1 in 516.12–516.18, e.g., angles 516.215
>
> Class a specific application with the subject, e.g., angles in plane geometry 516.22

.22	Plane geometry

> Including the Pythagorean theorem

.23	Solid geometry
.24	Trigonometry
.242	Plane trigonometry
.244	Spherical trigonometry

.3 Analytic geometries

> Class linear algebra combined with analytic geometry in 512.5, analytic affine geometry in 516.4, analytic projective geometry in 516.5

.32	Plane analytic geometry
.33	Solid analytic geometry
.34	Analytic trigonometry

> Plane and spherical

.35   Algebraic geometry

Geometries based on linear algebra

Examples: enumerative geometry, lattice point geometry

Class here abstract algebraic geometry [*formerly* 512.33], birational and conformal transformations, intersections, connections, dual geometries; bilinear and sesquilinear forms; polytopes; complex multiplication

.352   Curves and surfaces on projective and affine planes

Class here the theory of curves

.353   Algebraic varieties of higher dimensions

.36   Differential and integral geometry

Class here surfaces, curves, differentiable manifolds

Use 516.36001–516.36009 for standard subdivisions

For metric differential geometries, see 516.37

[.360 2]   Classical differential geometry

Relocated to 516.363

[.360 4]   Modern differential geometry

Relocated to 516.362

.362   Integral geometry (Global differential geometry)

Including arc length, curvature, evolutes, fiber spaces (fiber bundles), geodesics, involutes, tangent space at a point; analytic, convex, developable, minimal, ruled surfaces; analytic, asymptotic, minimal curves

Class here modern differential geometry [*formerly* 516.3604]

.363   Local and intrinsic differential geometry

Curvature and torsion

Class here classical differential geometry [*formerly* 516.3602]

.37   Metric differential geometries

.372   Euclidean geometry

.373   Riemannian geometry [*formerly also* 516.92]

Example: Sasakian

Einstein geometry relocated to 516.374

.374   Minkowski geometry [*formerly* 516.93]

Example: Einstein geometry [*formerly* 516.373]

.375   Finsler geometry

.376   Cartan geometry

[.377]	Kawaguchi geometry

Number discontinued; class in 516.37

.4 **Affine geometry**

Class affine differential geometry in 516.36

.5 **Projective geometry**

Class projective differential geometry in 516.36

.6 **Abstract descriptive geometry**

See also 604.2015166 for descriptive geometry in technical drawing

.9 **Non-Euclidean geometries**

Examples: Bolyai, Gauss, hyperbolic, inversive, Lobachevski geometries

Including imbeddings of non-Euclidean spaces in other geometries

Class a specific type of non-Euclidean geometry with the subject, e.g., non-Euclidean analytic geometries in 516.3

[.92]	Riemannian geometry

Relocated to 516.373

[.93]	Minkowski geometry

Relocated to 516.374

[517] **[Unassigned]**

Most recently used in Edition 17

[518] **[Unassigned]**

Most recently used in Edition 15

519 **Probabilities and applied mathematics**

Class a specific application with the subject, e.g., game theory in gambling 795.01

SUMMARY

519.2	Probabilities
.3	Game theory
.4	Applied numerical analysis
.5	Statistical mathematics
.7	Programming
.8	Special topics

.2 **Probabilities**

Class here random (stochastic) processes, probability calculus, conditional probabilities, independent and dependent trials, geometric probability, games of chance

Class probabilities applied to statistical mathematics in 519.5

.23 Probabilistic processes

.232	Stationary processes
	Including time series
.233	Markov processes
	Including Markov chains
.234	Branching processes
.24	Probability distribution
	Class here descriptive probabilities
.26	Probabilities over rings, algebras, other algebraic structures
.28	Special topics
.282	Random walks
	Class here the Monte Carlo method
.287	Expectation and prediction
	Examples: martingales, Markov risk; reliability, renewal, estimation theories

.3   Game theory

Class here mathematical optimization

Class control theory in 515.64, games of chance in 519.2

See also 511.65 for choice and decision making in combinatorial analysis

.4   Applied numerical analysis

Coding theory relocated to 003.54, computer mathematics to 004.0151

.5   Statistical mathematics

Class here numerical data, parametric and nonparametric methods

See Manual at 519.5, T1—015195 vs. 001.422, T1—072

.52	Theory of sampling
.53	Descriptive statistics, multivariate analysis, analysis of variance and covariance
	Including cluster analysis
.532	Frequency distributions
.533	Measures of central tendency
	Contains median, mean, mode
.534	Measures of deviation
	Example: standard deviation

.535	Multivariate analysis

> *For regression analysis, see 519.536; correlation (association) analysis, 519.537*

[.535 2]	Analysis of variance and covariance

> Relocated to 519.538

.535 4	Factor analysis
.536	Regression analysis
.537	Correlation (Association) analysis
.538	Analysis of variance and covariance [*both formerly* 519.5352]
.54	Statistical inference

> Including expectation, nonparametric statistics, prediction, sequential analysis

.542	Decision theory

> Including Bayesian statistical decision theory

.544	Estimation theory
.55	Time-series analysis
.56	Hypothesis testing

> Example: chi-square test

.7	**Programming**

> Use 519.7001–519.7009 for standard subdivisions

.702	Single-stage programming
.703	Multistage programming

> Including dynamic programming

.72	Linear programming
.76	Nonlinear programming

> Examples: convex and quadratic programming
>
> Class integer programming in 519.77

.77	Integer programming
.8	**Special topics**
.82	Queuing

> Including congestion, order

.83	Inventory and storage
.84	Success runs
.85	Epidemics and fluctuations
.86	Quality control and other statistical adjustments

520   Astronomy and allied sciences

See Manual at 520 vs. 523.1

SUMMARY

520.1–.9   **Standard subdivisions**
521   **Celestial mechanics**
522   **Techniques, procedures, apparatus, equipment, materials**
523   **Specific celestial bodies and phenomena**
525   **Earth (Astronomical geography)**
526   **Mathematical geography**
527   **Celestial navigation**
528   **Ephemerides**
529   **Chronology**

.1   Philosophy and theory

Class here theoretical astronomy [*formerly* 521.5]

[.153]   Physical principles

Do not use; class in 523.01

[.154]   Chemical principles

Do not use; class in 523.02

[.28]   Auxiliary techniques and procedures; apparatus, equipment, materials

Do not use; class in 522

>   521–525 Astronomy

Class comprehensive works in 520

For geodetic and positional astronomy, see 526.6

521   Celestial mechanics

Including equilibrium, problems of three and *n* bodies

Class here motion

Class applications to specific celestial bodies, kinds of bodies, phenomena in 523

.1   Gravitation

Use of this number for celestial mechanics discontinued; class in 521

.3   Orbits

Including apogee and perigee, Kepler's laws

.4   Perturbations

[.5]   **Theoretical astronomy**

Comprehensive works relocated to 520.1, theoretical astronomy of specific celestial bodies, kinds of bodies, other phenomena to 523

[.6]   **Theory of satellites**

Relocated to 523.9801

[.62]   Of moon (Lunar theory)

Relocated to 523.301

[.7]   **Theory of meteoroids and comets**

Theory of meteoroids [*formerly* 521.75] relocated to 523.5101, of comets [*formerly* 521.76] to 523.601

[.8]   **Theory of eclipses, transits, occultations**

Relocated to 523.9901

.9   **Precession and nutation**

Class corrections of precession and nutation in 522.9

522   Techniques, procedures, apparatus, equipment, materials

Class here practical astronomy; computations

[.028]   Auxiliary techniques and procedures; apparatus, equipment, materials

Do not use; class general works in 522, specific auxiliary techniques and procedures in 522.8

\>   **522.1–522.6 Practical astronomy**

Class comprehensive works in 522, applications to specific celestial bodies, kinds of bodies, phenomena in 523

For corrections, see 522.9

.1   **Observatories**

.109   Historical and persons treatment

Geographical treatment relocated to 522.19

.19   Geographical treatment [*formerly also* 522.109]

Add to base number 522.19 notation 1–9 from Table 2, e.g., observatories in China 522.1951

.2   **Astronomical instruments   Telescopes**

Class use of astronomical instruments in nonoptical astronomy in 522.68

For meridional instruments, see 522.3; extrameridional instruments, 522.4; auxiliary instruments, 522.5

.209	Historical, geographical, persons treatment

Class here specific movable nonspace telescopes [*formerly* 522.29]

.29	Fixed location and space telescopes

Add to base number 522.29 notation 1–9 from Table 2, e.g., space telescopes 522.2919

Specific movable nonspace telescopes relocated to 522.209

.3	**Meridional instruments**

For zenith telescopes, see 522.4

.4	**Extrameridional instruments**

Examples: astrolabes, quadrants, reflecting circles, sextants, zenith and equatorial telescopes

.5	**Auxiliary instruments**

Examples: chronographs, chronometers, micrometers, personal equation machines, sidereal clocks

Coronagraphs, heliographs, heliostats relocated to 523.7028

Class use of auxiliary instruments in special methods of observation in 522.6

.6	**Special methods of observation**
.62	Photometry
.622	Photographic photometry
.623	Photoelectric photometry
.63	Photography

For photographic photometry, see 522.622

.65	Polarimetry
.67	Spectroscopy
.68	Nonoptical astronomy
.682	Radio astronomy
.684	Radar astronomy
.686	Particle methods of observation
.686 2	Gamma-ray astronomy
.686 3	X-ray astronomy
.7	**Spherical astronomy**

Including celestial sphere and coordinates, meridians, variation of compass

.8	**Specific auxiliary techniques and procedures**

Add to base number 522.8 the numbers following 028 in notation 0285–0289 from Table 1, e.g., data processing 522.85

.9 **Corrections**

Of aberration, astronomical refraction, nutation, parallax, precession; of instrumental errors; of personal equation

523 **Specific celestial bodies and phenomena**

Including zodiac

Class here theoretical astronomy of specific celestial bodies, kinds of bodies, other phenomena [*formerly* 521.5]

Do not use standard subdivisions; class in 520.1–520.9

Use of this number for comprehensive works on descriptive astronomy discontinued; class in 520

Class phenomena of celestial bodies directly comparable to terrestrial phenomena in 550, e.g., volcanic activity on Mars 551.21099923

SUMMARY

523.01–.02		[Astrophysics and cosmochemistry]
	.1	The universe; space, galaxies, quasars
	.2	Solar system
	.3	Moon
	.4	Planets
	.5	Meteoroids, solar wind, zodiacal light
	.6	Comets
	.7	Sun
	.8	Stars
	.9	Satellites and rings; eclipses, transits, occultations

.01 Astrophysics

For celestial mechanics, see 521

.013 Heat

Add to base number 523.013 the numbers following 536 in 536.1–536.7, e.g., heat transfer 523.0132

.015 Light and paraphotic phenomena

Add to base number 523.015 the numbers following 535 in 535.01–535.84, e.g., ultraviolet radiation 523.015014

.018 Electricity and magnetism

Add to base number 523.018 the numbers following 53 in 537–538, e.g., magnetism 523.0188

.019 Molecular, atomic, nuclear physics

Add to base number 523.019 the numbers following 539 in 539.1–539.7, e.g., cosmic rays 523.0197223

.02 Cosmochemistry

.1	**The universe; space, galaxies, quasars**

Class here cosmology

See also 523.8875 for black holes

See Manual at 520 vs. 523.1

.101	Philosophy and related topics

Use of this number for cosmological theories discontinued; class in 523.1

.11	Space, galaxies, quasars
.111	Space
.112	Galaxies

For Milky Way, see 523.113

See Manual at 523.8 vs. 523.112

.112 5	Intergalactic and interstellar matter

Class here cosmic dust

.113	Milky Way
.113 5	Interstellar matter

Examples: diffuse and planetary nebulas, H I and H II regions

.115	Quasars

Quasi-stellar sources or objects

.12	Cosmogony

For expanding universe theories, see 523.18

.18	Expanding universe theories
.19	End of the universe theories
.2	**Solar system**

For specific parts, see 523.3–523.7

> **523.3–523.7 Specific parts of solar system**

Class comprehensive works in 523.2

.3	**Moon**
.301	Theory [*formerly* 521.62] and philosophy
.302	Miscellany
.302 12	Tables [*formerly* 523.39], formulas, specifications
.302 22	Charts, photographs [*both formerly* 523.39], pictures, other related illustrations

.302 87	Testing and measurement
	Class here spectroscopy [*formerly* 523.37]
.31	Constants and dimensions
	Examples: size, mass, parallax
.32	Optical, thermal, electromagnetic, radioactive phenomena
	Examples: brightness, phases
.33	Orbit and motions
	Examples: librations
	Including sidereal month
[.37]	Spectroscopy
	Relocated to 523.30287
.38	Eclipses
[.39]	Charts, photographs, tables
	Tables relocated to 523.30212, charts and photographs to 523.30222

.4   **Planets**

Class here comprehensive works on planets, satellites, rings

Add to notation for each number identified by * the numbers following 523.3 in 523.31–523.33, e.g., orbit of Mars 523.433

For earth, see 525; satellites and rings, 523.98; transits, occultations, 523.99

.402 12	Tables [*formerly* 523.49], formulas, specifications
.402 22	Charts, photographs [*both formerly* 523.49], pictures, other related illustrations
.41	*Mercury
.42	*Venus
.43	*Mars
.44	Asteroids (Planetoids)
.45	*Jupiter
.46	*Saturn
.47	*Uranus
.48	Trans-uranian planets
.481	*Neptune
.482	*Pluto

*Add as instructed under 523.4

[.49]   Charts, photographs, tables

> Tables relocated to 523.40212, charts and photographs to 523.40222

.5   Meteoroids, solar wind, zodiacal light

> Class here interplanetary matter, comprehensive works on meteoroids and asteroids
>
> *For asteroids, see 523.44*

.51   Meteoroids

> Variant names: meteors, meteorites
>
> *For meteoric showers and radiant points, see 523.53*

.510 1   Theory [*formerly* 521.75] and philosophy

.510 2   Miscellany

.510 287   Testing and measurement

> Class here spectroscopy [*formerly* 523.57]

.53   Meteoric showers and radiant points

[.57]   Spectroscopy

> Relocated to 523.510287

.58   Solar wind

.59   Zodiacal light

> Including counterglow (gegenschein)

.6   Comets

.601   Theory [*formerly* 521.76] and philosophy

.602   Miscellany

.602 12   Tables [*formerly* 523.69], formulas, specifications

.602 22   Charts, photographs [*both formerly* 523.69], pictures, other related illustrations

.602 8   Auxiliary techniques and procedures; apparatus, equipment, materials

.602 87   Testing and measurement

> Class here spectroscopy [*formerly* 523.67]

.63   Motion and orbits

> Class motion and orbits of specific comets in 523.64

.64   Specific comets

.642   Halley's comet

.66   Physical phenomena and constitution

> Class physical phenomena and constitution of specific comets in 523.64

[.67]	Spectroscopy
	Relocated to 523.60287
[.69]	Charts, photographs, tables
	Tables relocated to 523.60212, charts and photographs to 523.60222

.7   Sun

.702 12	Tables, formulas, specifications

    See also 525.38 for tables of the sun indicating orbit and motions of the earth.

.702 22	Charts, photographs [*both formerly* 523.79], pictures, other related illustrations
.702 8	Auxiliary techniques and procedures; apparatus, equipment, materials

    Examples: coronagraphs, heliographs, heliostats [*all formerly* 522.5]

.702 87	Testing and measurement

    Class here spectroscopy [*formerly* 523.77]

.71	Constants and dimensions

    Examples: size, mass, parallax

.72	Optical, thermal, electromagnetic, radioactive phenomena

    See also 523.59 for zodiacal light

.73	Motions

    Example: rotation

    Including apparent motion

.74	Photosphere

    Including faculae, solar granulation, sunspots

.75	Chromosphere and corona

    Including solar flares and prominences

    See also 523.58 for solar wind

.76	Internal constitution
[.77]	Spectroscopy
	Relocated to 523.70287
.78	Eclipses
[.79]	Charts and photographs
	Relocated to 523.70222

.8   **Stars**

> Class here comprehensive works on stars and galaxies

> > *For galaxies, see 523.112; sun, see 523.7*

> > *See also 523.115 for quasars*

> > *See Manual at 523.8 vs. 523.112*

SUMMARY

523.801–.809	**Standard subdivision**
.81	**Constants and dimensions**
.82	**Optical thermal, electromagnetic, radioactive phenomena**
.83	**Motions**
.84	**Aggregations and variable stars**
.85	**Clusters**
.86	**Physical constitution**
.87	**Spectral types**
.88	**Kinds of stars characteristic of stages of stellar evolution**

.802 12   Tables [*formerly* 523.89], formulas, specifications

> Class here star catalogs [*formerly* 523.8908]

.802 22   Charts, photographs [*both formerly* 523.89], pictures, other related illustrations

.802 23   Maps and related forms, plans, diagrams

> Class here observers' atlases of constellations [*formerly* 523.8903]

[.802 87]   Testing and measurement

> Relocated to 523.87

>   523.81–523.83 Properties and phenomena

> Class comprehensive works in 523.8; properties of a specific kind or aggregation of star with the subject, e.g., of supernovae 523.8446, of spectral types 523.87

> *For physical constitution, see 523.86*

.81   Constants and dimensions

> Examples: size, mass, parallax

.82   Optical, thermal, electromagnetic, radioactive phenomena

.822   Magnitudes

.83   Motions

> Including velocity

.84   Aggregations and variable stars

> *For clusters, see 523.85*

> *See also 523.112 for galaxies*

| .841 | Binary and multiple stars |

Example: visual binaries

For spectroscopic binaries, see 523.842; astrometric binaries, 523.843; eclipsing binaries, 523.8444

.842	Spectroscopic binaries
.843	Astrometric binaries
.844	Variable stars
.844 2	Intrinsic variables

For eruptive variables, see 523.8446

| .844 25 | Pulsating variables |

Example: RR Lyrae variables (cluster-type variables)

Class here Cepheids

For long-period and semi-regular variables, see 523.84426; pulsars, 523.8874

.844 26	Long-period and semi-regular variables
.844 4	Eclipsing binaries (Extrinsic variables)
.844 6	Eruptive variables

Examples: flare stars, novas, recurrent novas, supernovas

.85	Clusters
.852	Open and moving clusters
.855	Globular clusters
.86	Physical constitution

Class physical constitution of a specific kind and aggregation of star with the subject, e.g., of neutron stars 523.8874

| .87 | Spectral types |

Class here testing and measurement [*formerly also* 523.80287], spectroscopy

Class spectral types representative of specific stages in the evolution of stars in 523.88, e.g., R, N, or S types considered as giant stars; spectroscopy of a specific kind or aggregation of star with the subject, e.g., of neutron stars 523.88740287

| .88 | Kinds of stars characteristic of stages of stellar evolution |

Examples: giant (R, N, or S spectral type), main sequence, red dwarf, Wolf-Rayet stars

Including star formation

Class here stellar evolution

For intrinsic variables, see 523.8442

.887	Terminal stages

.887 Terminal stages

Including white dwarf stars

.887 4 Neutron stars

Class here pulsars

.887 5 Black holes

[.89] Charts, photographs, tables

Tables relocated to 523.80212, charts and photographs to 523.80222

[.890 3] Observers' atlases of constellations

Relocated to 523.80223

[.890 8] Star catalogs

Relocated to 523.80212

.9 Satellites and rings; eclipses, transits, occultations

.91 Transits of Mercury

.92 Transits of Venus

Examples: transits of 1761, 1769, 1874 [*all formerly* 523.96]; transit of 1882 [*formerly* 523.97]

[.96] Venus transits of 1761, 1769, 1874

Relocated to 523.92

[.97] Venus transit of 1882

Relocated to 523.92

.98 Satellites and rings

For the moon, see 523.3

.980 1 Philosophy and theory

Class here theory of satellites [*formerly* 521.6]

.983–.988 Of specific planets

Add to base number 523.98 the numbers following 523.4 in 523.43–523.48, e.g., satellites of Mars 523.983, orbits of Martian satellites 523.9833

.99 Eclipses, transits, occultations

Class eclipses of a specific celestial body with the body, e.g., of the moon 523.38

For transits of Mercury, see 523.91; of Venus, 523.92

.990 1 Philosophy and theory

Class here theory of eclipses, transits, occultations [*all formerly* 521.8]

[524]   [Unassigned]

Most recently used in Edition 14

525   Earth (Astronomical geography)

.1   Constants and dimensions

Examples: size, shape, parallax

Class determination of size and shape in 526.1

.2   Optical, thermal, radioactive properties

.3   Orbit and motions

.35   Rotation

.36   Foucault's pendulum

.38   Tables of the sun

.5   Seasons and zones

[.6]   Tides

Relocated to 551.4708

.7   Astronomical twilight

526   Mathematical geography

Class here cartography (map making)

Class map making for a specific purpose with the purpose, e.g., military map making 623.71

For astronomical geography, see 525

See also 912.014 for map reading

.022 1   Drafting illustrations

Class here map drawing [*formerly* 526.86]

.1   Geodesy

For geodetic surveying, see 526.3; geodetic and positional astronomy, 526.6; gravity determinations, 526.7

.3   Geodetic surveying

Surveying in which the curvature of the earth is considered

.31   Reconnaissance (Preliminary surveys)

.32   Bench marks

Add to base number 526.32 notation 1–9 from Table 2, e. g., bench marks in California 526.32794

.33   Triangulation, traversing, trilateration

Including base lines, nets

.36	**Leveling**

Example: spirit leveling

For bench marks, see 526.32; barometric leveling, 526.37; trigonometric leveling, 526.38

.37	**Barometric leveling**
.38	**Trigonometric leveling (Geodetic refraction)**
.6	**Geodetic and positional astronomy**

Class here geodetic coordinates

.61	**Latitude**

See also 527.1 for determination of latitude in navigation

.62	**Longitude**

See also 527.2 for determination of longitude in navigation

.63	**Azimuth**
.64	**Geographic position**

Including effect of irregularities of the earth's surface on determining position

.7	**Gravity determinations (Physical geodesy)**
.8	**Map projections**

Class map reading in 912.014

.82	**Conformal (Orthomorphic) projections**
.85	**Equal-area (Equivalent) projections**
[.86]	**Map drawing**

Relocated to 526.0221

.9	**Surveying**

Class here plane surveying (surveying in which curvature of the earth is disregarded)

Class engineering surveys in 622–629

For geodetic surveying, see 526.3

See also 333.08 for chartered surveyors (United Kingdom)

.92	**Boundary surveying**

Class here making land surveys

.98	**Topographic surveying**
.981	**Contour surveying**

.982	Photogrammetry
	Class here aerial and space surveying
[.982 3]	Aerial and space surveying
	Number discontinued; class in 526.982
.982 5	Ground (Terrestrial) photogrammetry
.99	Hydrographic surveying

527   Celestial navigation

Class celestial navigation of specific craft with the subject, e.g., of nautical craft 623.69

.1	**Determination of latitude**
.2	**Determination of longitude**
.3	**Fixes**
	Examples: Sumner's and line-of-position methods
.5	**Direction and course**
.53	Rhumb line course
.55	Great circle course

528   Ephemerides

Variant names: astronomical, nautical almanacs

Class tables of specific celestial bodies in 523

.1–.8	**In specific countries**
	Add to base number 528 the numbers following 06 in 061–068, e.g., ephemerides of England 528.2
.9	**Ephemeris making**

529   Chronology

.1	**Days**
	Examples: sidereal and solar days
	Including apparent and mean time, equation of time, causes of inequality
.2	**Intervals of time**
	Examples: years, months, weeks
	For days, see 529.1
	See also 523.33 for sidereal month as a topic in lunar astronomy, 525.5 for seasons
.3	**Calendars**
	For Western calendars, see 529.4; calendar reform 529.5

.32   Calendars of specific religions and traditions

Add to base number 529.32 the numbers following 29 in 292–299, e.g., Jewish calendar 529.326; however, class Julian calendar in 529.42

For Christian calendars, see 529.4

.4   **Western calendars**

Class here Christian calendars

.42   Julian calendar

.43   Gregorian calendar

.44   Christian church calendar

Including determination of movable feasts and fast days

.5   **Calendar reform**

.7   **Horology**

Finding and measuring time

[.75]   Time systems and standards

Relocated to 389.17

[.78]   Instruments for measuring time

Relocated to 681.11

530   Physics

Class here matter and antimatter, energy, comprehensive works on classical and quantum mechanics

Class physical chemistry in 541.3; general physics of specific elements, compounds, mixtures in 546

Use 530.12 for treatment of energy in quantum mechanics, 531.6 for treatment in classical mechanics

See also 523.01 for astrophysics

See Manual at 530 vs. 500.2; 530 vs. 540; 621 vs. 530

SUMMARY

530.01–.09	**Standard subdivisions**
.1–.8	**[Theories, states of matter, instrumentation, testing and measurement]**
531	**Classical mechanics Solid mechanics**
532	**Fluid mechanics Liquid mechanics**
533	**Gas mechanics**
534	**Sound and related vibrations**
535	**Light and paraphotic phenomena**
536	**Heat**
537	**Electricity and electronics**
538	**Magnetism**
539	**Modern physics**

SUMMARY

530.01–.09   **Standard subdivisions**
    .1   **Theories and mathematical physics**
    .4   **States of matter**
    .7   **Instrumentation**
    .8   **Testing and measurement**

.01   Philosophy and theory

Class theories in 530.1

[.015 1]   Mathematical physics

Do not use; class in 530.15

.02   Miscellany

.028   Auxiliary techniques and procedures; apparatus, equipment, materials

Class instrumentation in 530.7

[.028 7]   Testing and measurement

Relocated to 530.8

.03–.09   Standard subdivisions

.1   Theories and mathematical physics

Class applications to specific states of matter in 530.4

.11   Relativity theory

Including fourth dimension, space and time, mass-energy equivalence ($E=mc^2$)

Class relativistic quantum mechanics in 530.12, relativistic statistical mechanics in 530.13, relativistic field theories in 530.14

.12   Quantum mechanics (Quantum theory)

General aspects: relativistic and nonrelativistic

Class quantum mechanics of specific states of matter in 530.4

For quantum statistics, see 530.133; quantum kinetic theories, 530.136; quantum field theory, 530.143; quantum electronics, 537.5; quantum electrodynamics, 537.67

See Manual at 530.12 vs. 531; 530.475 vs. 531.16, 530.12

.122   Matrix mechanics (Heisenberg representation)

.124		Wave mechanics

Waves considered as a fundamental property of matter

Variant name: Schrödinger wave mechanics

Including Schrödinger wave equation

See also 530.141 for waves in electromagnetic theory, 531.1133 for waves observable in the matter of classical physics

.13	Statistical mechanics

General aspects: relativistic and nonrelativistic

.132	Classical statistical mechanics (Boltzmann statistics)
.133	Quantum statistics (Quantum statistical mechanics)
.133 2	Bose-Einstein statistics
.133 4	Fermi-Dirac statistics
.136	Kinetic theories

General aspects: quantum and combined quantum-classical

Class classical kinetic theory in 531.113

.138	Transport theory
.14	Field and wave theories

Theories accounting for fundamental particles and interactions

General aspects: quantum and classical, relativistic and nonrelativistic

Example: theory of continuum physics

Including problem of few bodies

For wave mechanics, see 530.124

.141	Electromagnetic theory

Electromagnetic fields and waves considered in terms of the fundamental structure of matter

Including Maxwell's equations

Class electromagnetic spectrum and waves in 539.2

See also 537.1 for theories of electricity, 538.01 for theories of magnetism

.142	Unified field theory

Including supergravity

.143	Quantum field theory
.143 5	Gauge fields
.144	Problem of many bodies

.15   Mathematical physics

Add to base number 530.15 the numbers following 51 in 511–519, e.g., statistics 530.1595

Class mathematical description of physical phenomena according to a specific theory with the theory in 530.1, e.g., statistical mechanics 530.13 (*not* 530.1595)

.16   Measurement theory

.4   States of matter

Class here quantum mechanics of specific states of matter; sound, light, heat, electricity, magnetism as properties of a specific state of matter

Unless other instructions are given, class complex subjects with aspects in two or more subdivisions of this schedule in the one coming last, e.g., tunneling in thin films 530.4175 (*not* 530.416)

Class forms of energy studied as forms with the form, e.g., heat 536

For superconductivity and superconductors, see 537.623

.41   Solid-state physics

Class here physics of condensed matter

For liquid-state physics, see 530.42; crystallography, 548

See Manual at 530.41 vs. 548

.411   Structure

Examples: electron arrangement, lattice dynamics

.412   Properties

Examples: elastic, electrical, magnetic, optical, thermal, thermoluminescent, thermophysical

.413   Kinds

Examples: amorphous, crystalline and noncrystalline, metallic and nonmetallic, ordered and disordered, organic, porous solids; polymers; solid particles

For dielectric matter, see 537.24; semiconductors, 537.622; crystals, 548

.414   Phase changes (Phase transformations)

Between different phases of condensed matter, between solid and gas phases

.415   Diffusion and mass transport phenomena

Variant name: mass transfer

Class here transport phenomena in solids [*formerly also* 531.7]

.416 Responsive behavior and energy phenomena

Examples: phonons [*formerly* 539.7217], bombardment, collisions, emission, excitation, excited states, exitons, field effects, internal friction, ion implantation, Jahn-Teller effect, Josephson effect, oscillation, radiation damage, relaxation, scattering, sputtering, tunneling, vibrations

Class responsive behavior and energy phenomena in semiconductors in 537.622

See Manual at 530.416 vs. 539.75

.417 Surface physics

Including interface with other states of matter

Class surface physics of semiconductors in 537.622

.417 5 Thin films

.42 Liquid-state physics

Including superfluidity

Class here fluid-state physics

.424 Phase changes (Phase transformations)

Between different fluid phases

Including critical points

.425 Diffusion and mass transport phenomena

Example: Brownian motion in liquids, osmosis

Class here transport phenomena of fluids [*formerly also* 532.057], of liquids [*formerly also* 532.7]

.427 Surface physics

Examples: surface tension, capillarity

Including drops

Class here surface phenomena of liquids [*formerly also* 532.6], interface with gases

Class interface with solids in 530.417

.427 5 Thin films

Class here bubbles

.429 Liquid crystals [*formerly* 548.9]

Example: liquid polymers

.43　　　Gaseous-state physics

Including absorption and adsorption [*formerly also* 533.1], transport phenomena [*formerly also* 533.13], transport phenomena of air [*formerly also* 533.63], ionization of gases

Class interface with solids in 530.417, with liquids in 530.427; plasma physics in 530.44

See also 537.532 for ionization of gases in electronics

.44　　　Plasma physics

Physics of ionized gases

Add to base number 530.44 the numbers following 530.41 in 530.412–530.416, e.g., optical properties of plasmas 530.442, phase changes between plasmas and other states of matter 530.444

.47　　　Generalities of states of matter

Class generalities of specific states of matter in 530.41–530.44

.474　　　Phase changes (Phase transformations)[*formerly also* 536.401]

Including critical phenomena, e.g., critical points [*formerly also* 536.443]; phase diagrams, phase equilibria, phase stability, phase transitions, triple points

Class phase changes between different phases of condensed matter (between solids and gases) in 530.414; between fluid phases in 530.424, between plasmas and other states of matter in 530.444

See Manual at 536.4 vs. 530.474

.475　　　Diffusion and mass transport phenomena [*formerly also* 531.1137]

Variant name: mass transfer

Class here Brownian motion [*formerly* 531.163], comprehensive works on transport phenomena

For heat transfer, see 536.2

See Manual at 530.475 vs. 531.16, 530.12

.7　　　**Instrumentation**

For measurement, control, recording

.8　　　**Testing and measurement [*formerly also* 530.0287]**

Including dimensional analysis

Class here interdisciplinary works on measurement, on mensuration

Class instrumentation for measurement in 530.7; measurement in a specific subject with the subject using notation 0287 from Table 1, e.g., psychological measurement 150.287

For measurement theory, see 530.16

See also 516.15 for geometric mensuration

.81 Physical units, dimensions, constants

Class here systems of measurement, conversion tables between systems

Class horology in 529.7

For social use of systems of measurement, see 389.1

.812 Metric system (Système internationale, SI)

.813 British system

Variant names: English, Imperial system

Class here United States customary units

531 Classical mechanics Solid mechanics

Variant names for classical mechanics: mechanics, continuum mechanics

For fluid mechanics, see 532

See Manual at 530.12 vs. 531

SUMMARY

531.01–.09		**Standard subdivisions**
	.1	**Dynamics, statics, particle mechanics**
	.2	**Solid statics**
	.3	**Solid dynamics (Solid kinetics and kinematics)**
	.4	**Friction and viscosity of solids**
	.5	**Mass and gravity of solids; projectiles**
	.6	**Energy**

.015 195 Statistical mathematics

Class classical statistical mechanics in 530.132

.021 2 Tables, formulas, specifications

Class here tables for solid mechanics [*formerly* 531.9]

.076 Review and exercise

Class here review and exercise for solid mechanics [*formerly* 531.9]

.1 Dynamics, statics, particle mechanics

Including pressure, mechanics of points

Do not use standard subdivisions; class in 531.01–531.09

.11	Dynamics

        Examples: flow, rheology

        Class particle dynamics in 531.163

        For solid dynamics, see 531.3

.112	Kinematics (Pure motion, Abstract motion)

        Examples: linear and relative motion, velocity, acceleration, vector quantities

        Including search for a moving target

.113	Kinetics

        Examples: effects of centrifugal and centripetal forces

.113 3	Waves

        Waves observable in the matter of classical physics

        Example: shock waves

        See also 530.124 for waves considered as a fundamental property of matter

.113 4	Friction and viscosity
[.113 7]	Diffusion and mass transport phenomena

        Relocated to 530.475

.12	Statics

        Example: graphic statics

        Including inertia

        Class particle statics in 531.162

        For solid statics, see 531.2

.14	Mass and gravity

        Examples: specific gravity, terrestrial gravity

        Including density

        For gravitation in celestial mechanics, see 521.1

        See also 526.7 for terrestrial gravity determinations, 539.754 for fundamental gravitational interactions

.16	Particle mechanics

        Class mechanics of molecular, atomic, and subatomic particles in 530.12

        See Manual at 530.475 vs. 531.16, 530.12

.162	Statics
.163	Dynamics

        Including torque

        Brownian motion relocated to 530.475

> **531.2–531.5 Mechanics of solids**

    Class here mechanics of rigid bodies

    Class comprehensive works in 531

.2   **Solid statics**

    Example: graphic statics

    Including inertia

.3   **Solid dynamics (Solid kinetics and kinematics)**

    Examples: flow, torque

    For friction and viscosity, see 531.4; ballistics, 531.55

.31   Trajectories

.32   Vibrations

    Class here oscillations

[.322]   Oscillations

    Number discontinued; class in 531.32

.324   Pendulum motion

.33   Waves

    Example: shock waves

.34   Gyrodynamics

.35   Centrifugal and centripetal forces

.38   Deformation and stresses

    Examples: plasticity (plastic or permanent deformation); bending, compressive, shearing, tensile, torsional stresses

    Including yield point

.381   Elastic constants

    Examples: bulk modulus, shear modulus (modulus of rigidity), Young's modulus; Poisson's ratio

    Class application to elastic deformation in 531.382, to permanent deformation in 531.38

.382   Elastic deformation

    Variant names: elasticity, temporary deformation

    Including elastic limit, coefficient of restitution

    Class here Hooke's law

    Class elastic vibrations in 531.32

[.382 2]	Stresses
	Number discontinued; class in 531.38
[.382 3]	Temporary deformation (Elasticity)
	Number discontinued; class in 531.382
[.382 5]	Permanent deformation (Plasticity)
	Number discontinued; class in 531.38

.4   Friction and viscosity of solids

.5   Mass and gravity of solids; projectiles

   Including laws of falling bodies

.54   Density and specific gravity

.55   Projectiles

   Class here ballistics

   For trajectories, see 531.31

[.552–.555]   In air and space

   Number discontinued; class in 531.55

.6   Energy

   Including momentum, work

.62   Conservation of energy

   Including law of conservation of mass-energy

[.64]   Types of energy

   Number discontinued; class in 531.6

.68   Transformation

   Change in form of energy

   Class a specific transformation with the resultant form, e.g., of light to heat 536

[.7]   Transport phenomena in solids

   Relocated to 530.415

[.8]   Principles of simple machines

   Relocated to 621.811

[.9]   Tables, review, exercise for solid mechanics

   Tables relocated to 531.0212, review and exercise to 531.076

532   Fluid mechanics   Liquid mechanics

   Variant names for liquid mechanics: hydraulics, hydromechanics

   For gas mechanics, see 533

SUMMARY

532.001–.009   **Standard subdivisions**
    .02–.05   **Generalities of fluid mechanics**
     .2   **Hydrostatics**
     .4   **Mass, density, specific gravity of liquids**
     .5   **Hydrostatics (Kinetics and kinematics of liquids)**

.001   Philosophy and theory

.002   Miscellany

.002 12   Tables, formulas, specifications

                Class here tables for hydromechanics [*formerly* 532.9]

.003–.006   Standard subdivisions

.007   Education, research, related topics

.007 6   Review and exercise

                Class here review and exercise for hydrodynamics [*formerly* 532.9]

.008–.009   Standard subdivisions

>   532.02–532.05 Generalities of fluid mechanics

          Class comprehensive works in 532

.02   Statics

          Examples: buoyancy, transmission of pressure

          Including inertia

           For hydrostatics, see 532.2

.04   Mass, density, specific gravity

           For mass, density, specific gravity of liquids, see 532.4

.05   Dynamics (Kinetics and kinematics)

          Examples: centrifugal and centripetal forces, vibrations

           For hydrodynamics, see 532.5

.051   Flow

           For types of flow, see 532.052; flow properties, 532.053

.052   Types of flow

          Examples: rotational, steady, streamline, uniform

          Class properties of specific types of flow in 532.053

.052 5   Laminar flow

.052 6   Transitional flow

.052 7   Turbulent flow

.053	Flow properties
.053 2	Velocity
.053 3	Viscosity and friction
.053 5	Elasticity and compressibility
[.057]	Transport phenomena of fluids

Relocated to 530.425

.059	Waves, vortex motions, cavitation
.059 3	Waves

Example: shock waves

.059 5	Vortex motions and cavitation
[.1]	**Liquid mechanics**

Number discontinued; class in 532

> **532.2–532.5 Liquid mechanics**

Class comprehensive works in 532

.2	**Hydrostatics**

Variant name: liquid statics

Examples: buoyancy, inertia, transmission of pressure

.4	**Mass, density, specific gravity of liquids**
.5	**Hydrodynamics (Kinetics and kinematics of liquids)**

Examples: centrifugal and centripetal forces

.51	Flow

Examples: rotational, steady, streamline, uniform flow

For flow variations, see 532.52–532.56; flow velocity, 532.57; flow viscosity, friction, elasticity, compressibility, 532.58

.510 1	Philosophy and theory

Class here theories [*formerly also* 532.511]

[.511]	General principles and theories

Use of this number for general principles discontinued; class in 532.51

Theories relocated to 532.5101

.515	Laminar
.516	Transitional
.517	Turbulent

> 532.52–532.56 Flow variations

Class comprehensive works in 532.51

.52 Flow through openings

.53 Flow over and around obstacles

.54 Flow through open and closed channels

.55 Flow through bends and irregular enclosures

.56 Flow when pressure is variable

Including flow over and around submerged bodies, multiphase flow

.57 Flow velocity

.58 Flow viscosity, friction, elasticity, compressibility

Examples: viscous, elastic flow

See also 536.413 for expansion and contraction of liquids as a result of heating and cooling

.59 Waves, vortex motions, cavitation

.593 Waves

Example: shock waves

.595 Vortex motions and cavitation

[.6] **Surface phenomena of liquids**

Relocated to 530.427

[.7] **Transport phenomena of liquids**

Relocated to 530.425

[.9] **Tables, review, exercise for hydromechanics**

Tables relocated to 532.00212, review and exercise to 532.0076

533   Gas mechanics

SUMMARY

533.01–.09	**Standard subdivisions**
.1	**Statics; mass, density, specific gravity**
.2	**Dynamics (Kinetics and kinematics)**
.5	**Vacuums**
.6	**Aeromechanics**
.7	**Kinetic theory of gases**

.021 2   Tables [*formerly* 533.9], formulas, specifications

.076   Review and exercise [*formerly* 533.9]

.1 **Statics; mass, density, specific gravity**

Absorption and adsorption relocated to 530.43

For vacuums, see 533.5

.12 Statics

Examples: buoyancy, transmission of pressure

Including inertia

For aerostatics, see 533.61

[.13] Transport phenomena

Relocated to 530.43

.15 Mass, density, specific gravity

For mass, density, specific gravity of air, see 533.6

.2 **Dynamics (Kinetics and kinematics)**

For aerodynamics, see 533.62; kinetic theory of gases, 533.7

.21 Flow

Examples: rotational, steady, streamline, uniform

Class flow at specific speeds in 533.27

For viscous, elastic, compressible flow, see 533.28

.215 Laminar flow

.216 Transitional flow

.217 Turbulent flow

.27 Velocity

.273 Subsonic flow

.274 Transonic flow

.275 Supersonic flow

For hypersonic flow, see 533.276

.276 Hypersonic flow

.28 Viscosity, elasticity, compressibility

Examples: viscous, elastic, compressible flow

Including friction

See also 536.412 for expansion and contraction of gases resulting from heating and cooling

.29 Waves, vortex motions, cavitation

.293 Waves

Example: shock waves

.295	Vortex motions and cavitation

.5 Vacuums

Vacuum technology relocated to 621.55

.6 Aeromechanics

Including mass, density, specific gravity of air

For vacuums, see 533.5

.61 Aerostatics

Example: buoyancy

.62 Aerodynamics

[.621–.629] Specific topics

Numbers discontinued; class in 533.62

[.63] Transport phenomena

Relocated to 530.43

.7 Kinetic theory of gases

[.9] Tables, review, exercise

Tables relocated to 533.0212, review and exercise to 533.076

534 Sound and related vibrations

Class sound and related vibrations as properties of states of matter in 530.4

.021 2 Tables [*formerly* 534.9], formulas, specifications

.028 7 Measurement [*formerly also* 534.42] and testing

.076 Review and exercise [*formerly* 534.9]

\> **534.1–534.4 Sound**

Class comprehensive works in 534

.1 Generation of sound

.2 Transmission of sound

Use 534.2001–534.2009 for standard subdivisions

.202 Velocity

[.203] Directionality

Number discontinued; class in 534.2

.204 Reflection (Echoes)

[.205] Refraction

Number discontinued; class in 534.2

[.206]	Diffraction
	Number discontinued; class in 534.2
[.207]	Polarization
	Number discontinued; class in 534.2
.208	Absorption (Damping)
.22	Transmission in solids
.23	Transmission in liquids
.24	Transmission in gases
.3	**Characteristics of sound**
.32	Frequency and pitch
	Including Doppler effect
[.33]	Intensity and loudness
	Number discontinued; class in 534.3
[.34]	Amplitude and timbre
	Number discontinued; class in 534.3
[.35]	Irregular and discordant frequencies
	Number discontinued; class in 534.3
[.4]	**Measurements, analysis, synthesis of sound**
	Analysis and synthesis relocated to 620.21
[.42]	Measurement techniques
	Relocated to 534.0287
.5	**Vibrations related to sound**
	Class here vibrations that can not be heard by the human ear
.52	Subsonic vibrations
.55	Ultrasonic vibrations
[.9]	**Tables, review, exercise**
	Tables relocated to 534.0212, review and exercise to 534.076

535 Light and paraphotic phenomena

Class here optics

Class light and paraphotic phenomena as properties of states of matter in 530.4

See also 537.56 for electron and ion optics

SUMMARY

535.01–.09	**Spectral regions and standard subdivisions**
.1	**Theories**
.2	**Physical optics**
.3	**Transmission, absorption, emission of light**
.4	**Dispersion, interference, diffraction of light**
.5	**Beams**
.6	**Color**
.8	**Special developments**

.01   Spectral regions; philosophy and theory

.010 1–.010 9   Standard subdivisions of spectral regions

.012   Infrared region

> Class heat radiation in 536.33

.013   Visible region

> Class comprehensive works on visible light in 535

.014   Ultraviolet region

.019   Philosophy and theory of light and paraphotic phenomena

> Add to base number 535.019 the numbers following —01 in —011–019 from Table 1, e.g., abbreviations and symbols in optics 535.01948
>
> Class theories in 535.1

.02   Miscellany

.021 2   Tables [*formerly* 535.9], formulas, specifications

.028   Auxiliary techniques and procedures; apparatus, equipment, materials

> Class spectroscopy in 535.84

.076   Review and exercise [*formerly* 535.9]

.1   **Theories**

> *See also 539.7217 for photons*

.12   Corpuscular theory

.13   Mechanical wave theory

.14   Electromagnetic theory

.15   Quantum theory

> **535.2–535.6 Specific elements of light**
>
> Class comprehensive works in 535, light spectroscopy in 535.843

.2	**Physical optics**

Examples: coherent optics, nonlinear optics

For dispersion, interference, diffraction, see 535.4; beams, 535.5

.22	Intensity of light
.220 287	Testing and measurement

Class here photometry

.24	Velocity of light
.3	**Transmission, absorption, emission of light**
.32	Geometrical optics
.322	Rectilinear propagation
.323	Reflection
.324	Refraction
.326	Absorption
[.33]	Optical instruments

Relocated to 681.4

.35	Luminescence

Examples: fluorescence, phosphorescence

.4	**Dispersion, interference, diffraction of light**

Including holography

Class here interdisciplinary works on prisms

Comprehensive works on dispersion, interference, diffraction of light (535.4) and beams (535.5) are classed in 535.2

.5	**Beams**
.52	Polarization
.523	Plane polarization
.524	Rotary polarization
[.58]	Amplification

Use of this number for amplification discontinued; class in 535.5

Lasers relocated to 621.366

.6	**Color**
.8	**Special developments**

.84	Optical and paraphotic spectroscopy

Class here comprehensive works on spectroscopy in physics

Class interdisciplinary works on spectroscopy in 543.0858; each kind of spectroscopy in physics other than optical and paraphotic with the kind, e.g., radiofrequency spectroscopy 537.534; a specific application with the application, e.g., Raman qualitative analysis 544.64

.842	Infrared spectroscopy
.843	Light (Chromatic) spectroscopy
.844	Ultraviolet spectroscopy
.845	Vacuum ultraviolet spectroscopy
.846	Raman spectroscopy

Including Raman effect

[.89]	Fiber optics

Relocated to 621.3692

[.9]	**Tables, review, exercise**

Tables relocated to 535.0212, review and exercise to 535.076

536   Heat

Class heat as a property of states of matter in 530.4

SUMMARY

536.01–.09	**Standard subdivisions**
.1	**Theories**
.2	**Heat transfer (transmission)**
.3	**Radiation and related phenomena**
.4	**Effects of heat on matter**
.5	**Temperature**
.6	**Heat capacity and specific heats**
.7	**Thermodynamics**

.01	Philosophy and theory

Class theories in 536.1

.02	Miscellany
.021 2	Tables [*formerly* 536.9], formulas, specifications
.076	Review and exercise [*formerly* 536.9]
.1	**Theories**

.2   **Heat transfer (transmission)**

Use 536.2001–536.2009 for standard subdivisions

For radiation and related phenomena, see 536.3

.201   Material properties

Class specific heats in 536.6

.201 2   Conductivity

.201 4   Diffusivity

.23   Conduction

Class here heat transfer in solids

Class conduction in fluids in 536.25

.25   Convection

Class here heat transfer in fluids

.3   **Radiation and related phenomena**

.31   Reflection

.32   Refraction

.33   Radiation

.34   Absorption

.4   **Effects of heat on matter**

Use 536.4001–536.4009 for standard subdivisions

See Manual at 536.4 vs. 530.474

[.401]   Change of state (Phase changes)

Use of this number for comprehensive works on fusion and solidification (536.42) and vaporization and condensation (536.44) discontinued; class in 536.4

Phase changes (phase transformations) relocated to 530.474

.41   Expansion and contraction

Including coefficients of expansion

Class here pressure-volume-temperature relationships

Class pressure-volume-temperature relationships and coefficients of expansion in fusion and solidification in 536.42, in vaporization and condensation in 536.44

.412   Of gases

For liquefaction of gases at low temperatures, see 536.56

.413   Of liquids

.414   Of solids

.42   Fusion and solidification (Melting and freezing)

Including freezing and melting points, latent heat of fusion

Comprehensive works on fusion and solidification (536.42) and vaporization and condensation (536.44) are classed in 536.4

.44   Vaporization and condensation

Including liquefaction of gases at normal temperatures [*formerly also* 536.56], boiling points, dew points, heat of vaporization

For liquefaction of gases at low temperatures, see 536.56

[.443]   Liquid-to-gas and gas-to-liquid transformations

Use of this number for liquid-to-gas and gas-to-liquid transformations discontinued; class in 536.44

Critical points relocated to 530.474

.445   Sublimation

.45   Incandescence

.5   **Temperature**

Class here absolute temperature

.502 87   Testing and measurement

Class here thermometry

For measurement of normal-range temperatures, see 536.51; of high temperatures, 536.52; of low temperatures, 536.54

\>   536.51–536.54 Measurement

Class comprehensive works in 536.50287

.51   Measurement of normal-range temperatures

Including liquid-in-glass thermometry

For electrical resistance thermometry, see 536.53

.52   Measurement of high temperatures (Pyrometry)

Including pyrometers, thermocouples

.53   Electrical resistance thermometry

.54   Measurement of low temperatures (Cryometry)

.56   Cryogenics and low temperatures

Including liquefaction of gases at low temperatures, properties of matter at low temperatures

Class a specific property of matter at low temperature with the subject, e.g., conduction of electricity at low temperatures 537.62

Use of this number for absolute temperature discontinued; class in 536.5

Liquefaction of gases at normal temperatures relocated to 536.44

.560 287   Testing

Class measurement in 536.54

.57   High temperatures

Including plasma temperatures, properties of matter at high temperature

Class a specific property of matter at high temperature with the property, e.g., conduction of electricity 537.62

.570 287   Testing

Class measurement in 536.52

.6   **Heat capacity and specific heats**

Class here calorimetry

Class heats of transformation in fusion and solidification in 536.42, in vaporization and condensation in 536.44

[.62]   Calorimeters

Relocated to 681.2

.63   Of solids and liquids

.65   Of gases

.7   **Thermodynamics**

.701   Philosophy and theory

Class theories in 536.71

.71   Theories

Examples: laws of thermodynamics, Joule's law, Maxwell's thermodynamic formulas

Including Carnot cycle

.73   Entropy

[.9]   **Tables, review, exercise**

Tables relocated to 536.0212, review and exercise to 536.076

537   Electricity and electronics

Class here electromagnetism

Class electrical and electronic properties of specific states of matter in 530.4

For magnetism, see 538

See also 530.141 for electromagnetic theory of matter

SUMMARY

537.01–.09	**Standard subdivisions**
.1	**Theories**
.2	**Electrostatics**
.5	**Electronics**
.6	**Electrodynamics (Electric currents) and thermoelectricity**

.01   Philosophy and theory

> Class theories in 537.1

.02   Miscellany

.021 2   Tables [*formerly* 537.9], formulas, specifications

.076   Review and exercise [*formerly* 537.9]

.1   Theories

.12   Microwave and waveguide theories

.123   Microwave theory

.125   Wave-guide theory

.14   Corpuscular theory

.2   Electrostatics

.21   Electric charge and potential

> Including triboelectricity

[.23]   Static generators

> Relocated to 621.313

.24   Dielectrics

> Examples: electrocapillarity, electrostriction

> Including electrets

[.242]   Capacitors (Condensers)

> Relocated to 621.315

.243   Dipole moments

| .244 | Pyroelectricity, piezoelectricity, ferroelectricity |

See also 548.85 for electrical properties of crystals

.244 2	Pyroelectricity
.244 6	Piezoelectricity
.244 8	Ferroelectricity
[.245]	Electrocapillarity

Number discontinued; class in 537.24

| [.246] | Electrostriction |

Number discontinued; class in 537.24

.5 **Electronics**

Including exploding wire phenomena

Class here quantum electronics

For semiconductors, see 537.622

| .52 | Disruptive discharges |

Examples: electric arcs, coronas

Class discharge through rarified gases and vacuums in 537.53

| .53 | Discharge through rarefied gases and vacuums |
| .532 | Ionization of gases |

Including electron ballistics

| .533 | Thermionic emission |
| .534 | Radio wave and microwave electronics |

Class here spectroscopy

Circuitry, tubes, waveguides relocated to the subject in technology, e.g., radio wave circuitry 621.38412

| .534 2 | Long waves |

Waves with frequency ranges between 10^0 and 10^6 cycles per second

| .534 3 | Short waves |

Waves with frequency ranges between 10^7 and 10^8 cycles per second

| .534 4 | Microwaves and ultra-high-frequency waves |

Waves with frequency ranges between 10^9 and 10^{12} cycles per second

Masers relocated to 621.381336

See also 537.123 for microwave theory of electricity

| .535 | X-ray and gamma-ray electronics |

Electronics with wave frequencies over 10^{17} cycles per second

.535 2	Spectroscopy	

Including Mössbauer spectroscopy and effect

Class a specific application with the subject, e.g., qualitative analysis 544.66

[.535 3]   Circuitry

Relocated to 621.381

[.535 5]   Tubes

Relocated to 621.381

.54   Photoelectric phenomena

Examples: photoconductivity, photoemissivity, photovoltaism

.56   Electron and ion optics

.6   Electrodynamics (Electric currents) and thermoelectricity

.61   Direct currents

Circuitry relocated to 621.3192

.62   Conduction and resistance

Class here conductivity and resistivity

For dielectrics, see 537.24

.622   Semiconductivity and semiconductors

Class here the solid-state physics of semiconductors

.622 1   Structure of semiconductors

Class structure of specific kinds of semiconductors in 537.6223

.622 3   Kinds of semiconductors

Class transport phenomena of specific kinds in 537.6225, interactions in and specific properties of specific kinds in 537.6226

.622 5   Transport phenomena in semiconductors

.622 6   Interactions in and specific properties of semiconductors

Examples: effects of beams and electromagnetic fields, Hall effects; adsorption, instabilities, resistivity, tunneling

.623   Superconductivity and superconductors

Class here the solid-state physics of superconductors

Add to base number 537.623 the numbers following 537.622 in 537.6221–537.5226, e.g., ternary superconductors 537.6233

.624   Thermal effects of currents

[.63]   Alternating currents and circuitry

Alternating currents relocated to 621.31, circuitry to 621.3192

.65	Thermoelectricity
.67	Quantum electrodynamics
[.9]	**Tables, review, exercise**

Tables relocated to 537.0212, review and exercise to 537.076

538 Magnetism

Class magnetism as a property of states of matter in 530.4

SUMMARY

538.01–.09	**Standard subdivisions**
.3	**Magnetic properties and phenomena**
.4	**Magnetic substances and their characteristic phenomena**
.6	**Magnetohydrodynamics**
.7	**Geomagnetism and allied phenomena**

.021 2	Tables [*formerly* 538.9], formulas, specifications
.076	Review and exercise [*formerly* 538.9]
[.2]	**Magnets and magnetic induction**

Natural magnets and magnetic induction relocated to 538.4, artificial magnets and magnetic induction to 621.34

.3 Magnetic properties and phenomena

Examples: permeability [*formerly* 538.4]; hysteresis; magnetic attraction, flux, moment, potential, relaxation, reluctance, repulsion, susceptibility; magnetization, magnetostriction, piezomagnetism, pyromagnetism

Class specific magnetic substances and their characteristic phenomena in 538.4

.36	Magnetic resonance

Examples: ferromagnetic, ferrimagnetic, antiferromagnetic, diamagnetic resonance

.362	Nuclear magnetic resonance (NMR)

Examples: nuclear quadrupole resonance (NQR), electron-nuclear double resonance (ENDOR)

.364	Paramagnetic resonance

Variant names: electron magnetic resonance, electron paramagnetic resonance (EPR), electron spin resonance

.4 Magnetic substances and their characteristic phenomena

Class here natural magnets and magnetic induction [*formerly also* 538.2]

Permeability relocated to 538.3

Class comprehensive works on specific magnetic phenomena in 538.3

For magnetic resonance, see 538.36

.42	Diamagnetic substances and diamagnetism

.43	Paramagnetic substances and paramagnetism
.44	Ferromagnetic substances and ferromagnetism
.45	Ferrimagnetic substances and ferrimagnetism
.6	**Magnetohydrodynamics**
.7	**Geomagnetism and allied phenomena**
.72	Magnetic fields of the solid earth

        Including paleomagnetism

        Class transient magnetism of the solid earth in 538.74

          For magnetic surveys, see 538.78

.74	Transient magnetism

        For auroras, see 538.768; magnetic observations at permanent stations, 538.79

.742	Diurnal variations
[.743]	Other periodic variations

        Number discontinued; class in 538.74

.744	Magnetic storms and pulsations
.746	Sunspot effects
.748	Earth currents
.76	Magnetosphere, ionosphere, auroras
.766	Magnetosphere

        Including Van Allen radiation belts

        Class transient magnetism of the magnetosphere in 538.74

.767	Ionosphere

        Class here atmospheric ionization

.767 2	D region
.767 3	E region

        Variant name: Kennelly-Heaviside layers

        Contains E and sporadic E layers

.767 4	F region

        Variant name: Appleton layers

        Contains F_1 and F_2 layers

.768	Auroras

.78	Magnetic surveys

Add to base number 538.78 notation 1–9 from Table 2, e.g., surveys of Ireland 538.78415

.79	Magnetic observations at permanent stations

Add to base number 538.79 notation 1–9 from Table 2, e.g., observations from stations in Russia 538.7947

[.9]	**Tables, review, exercise**

Tables relocated to 538.0212, review and exercise to 538.076

539   Modern physics

Class here quantum physics, chemical physics

Class the modern physics of electricity in 537, of magnetism in 538; the use of modern physics in explaining sound and related vibrations in 534, light and paraphotic phenomena in 535, heat in 536

For quantum mechanics, see 530.12; states of matter, 530.4

See Manual at 530 vs. 500.2

SUMMARY

539.01–.09	Standard subdivisions
.1	Structure of matter
.2	Radiations (Radiant energy)
.6	Molecular physics
.7	Atomic and nuclear physics

.01	Philosophy and theory

Class theories in 530.1

[.015 1]	Mathematical principles

Do not use; class in 530.15

.02	Miscellany
.021 2	Tables [*formerly* 539.9], formulas, specifications
.076	Review and exercise [*formerly* 539.9]

.1	**Structure of matter**

Class structure of condensed states of matter in 530.411

For nuclear structure, see 539.74

.12	Molecular structure

Use 539.12 only for studies of molecular structure without reference to chemical characteristics. Prefer 541.22 if there is discussion of chemical phenomena

.14	Atomic structure

.2   **Radiations (Radiant energy)**

Class here the electromagnetic spectrum, electromagnetic waves and radiations

Class a specific kind of radiation with the subject, e.g., ultraviolet radiation 535.014, ionizing radiation 539.722

.6   **Molecular physics**

Atom-atom and molecule-molecule relationships

Including molecular and vibrational spectra

For molecular structure, see 539.12

.602 87   Testing and measurement

Class here comprehensive works on mass spectrometry in physics

Class interdisciplinary works on mass spectrometry in 543.0873; spectrometry of nonmolecular masses with the subject using notation 0287 from Table 2, e.g., atomic spectrometry 539.70287

.7   **Atomic and nuclear physics**

For atomic structure, see 539.14

SUMMARY

539.72	**Particle physics; ionizing radiations**
.73	**Particle acceleration**
.74	**Nuclear structure**
.75	**Nuclear reactions and interactions**
.76	**High-energy physics**
.77	**Detection and measurement of particles and radioactivity**

.72   Particle physics; ionizing radiations

Particle physics: the study of kinds of particles and of particle characteristics considered individually

Class here antiparticles, relativistic particles

Class field theories covering fundamental particles in 530.14, reactions and interactions between two or more different kinds of particles in 539.75

For particle acceleration, see 539.73; detection and measurement of particles and radioactivity, 539.77

[.720 287]   Testing and measurement

Do not use; class in 539.77

.721	Specific kinds of subatomic particles

Examples: bosons and fermions

Including Regge poles

Do not use standard subdivisions; class in 539.7201–539.7209

Use of this number for antiparticles and relativistic particles discontinued; class in 539.72

Class subatomic particles considered as cosmic rays in 539.7223

.721 1	Leptons

For neutrinos and antineutrinos, see 539.7215; photons, 539.7217

.721 12	Electrons

Including beta particles

Class positrons in 539.7214

See also 537.5 for electronics

.721 14	Muons (Mu-mesons)
.721 2	Nucleons

Examples: protons, antiprotons

Class protons considered as cosmic rays in 539.7223

For neutrons and antineutrons, see 539.7213

.721 3	Neutrons and antineutrons
.721 4	Positrons
.721 5	Neutrinos and antineutrinos
.721 6	Hadrons

Class here strange particles and strangeness

.721 62	Mesons

Examples: pions (pi-mesons), kaons (K-mesons)

For mu-mesons, see 539.72114

.721 64	Baryons

Including hyperons

For nucleons, see 539.7212

.721 67	Quarks

Including quantum flavor

See also 539.7548 for quantum chromodynamics

.721 7	Photons
	Phonons relocated to 530.416
	See also 539.756 for photonuclear reactions
.722	Ionizing radiations
	Wave and particle radiations
	Class a specific kind of ionizing radiation not provided for here with the subject, e.g., alpha particles 539.7232
	See also 537.532 for ionization of gases by electron discharge
.722 2	X and gamma rays
	Including bremsstrahlung (secondary X rays), gamma particles
	See also 537.535 for x-ray and gamma-ray electronics
.722 3	Cosmic rays
	Class here any particle considered as a cosmic ray or secondary cosmic ray
.723	Nuclei and atoms considered as particles
.723 2	Nuclei
	Including deuterons, alpha particles
	Class nuclear structure in 539.74, component particles of the nucleus in 539.7212
.723 4	Heavy ions
.725	Particle characteristics
	Examples: mass, size; charge, energy levels, symmetry, supersymmetry; motion, velocity, orbits, spin, angular momentum
	Class supergravity in 530.142; characteristics of specific particles with the particle, e.g., orbits of electrons 539.72112, strangeness of strange particles 539.7216
	For magnetic properties, see 538.3
.73	Particle acceleration
	Including bombardment [*formerly also* 539.754], particle beams
.732	In high-voltage accelerators
	Examples: voltage multipliers, Van de Graaff electrostatic generators
.733	In resonance accelerators
	Examples: cyclotrons, linear accelerators
.734	In induction accelerators
	Example: betatrons

.735	In synchronous accelerators

> Examples: synchro-cyclotrons and synchrotrons (betatron-synchrotrons)

.737	Acceleration of specific particles

> Add to base number 539.737 the numbers following 539.721 in 539.7211–539.7217, e.g., electron acceleration 539.73712

> Class acceleration of specific particles in specific accelerators in 539.732–539.735

.74	Nuclear structure

> Class here isotope and nuclide structure, nuclear models

.742	Liquid-drop model
.743	Shell model
.744	Interpretation through spectroscopy
.75	Nuclear reactions and interactions

> Reactions and interactions between two or more different kinds of particles

> Examples: annihilation, capture, coupling, creation

> Class here reaction cross sections

>> *For ionizations of gases, see 537.532; reactions emitting high energy, 539.76*

>> *See Manual at 530.416 vs. 539.75*

.752	Natural radioactivity

> Including half-life periods

> Class here decay schemes, element and nucleus disintegration, radioisotopes, radioelements, radionuclides; comprehensive works on radioactivity

>> *For artificial radioactivity, see 539.753*

[.752 028 7]	Testing and measurement

> Do not use; class 539.77

.752 2	Alpha decay
.752 3	Beta decay
.752 4	Gamma decay
.753	Artificial radioactivity

> Including radioactive fallout

>> *See also 363.738 for pollution from radioactive fallout*

[.753 028 7]	Testing and measurement

> Do not use; class 539.77

.754		Fundamental interactions

Example: gravitational interaction

Use of this number for annihilation, capture, coupling, creation discontinued; class in 539.75

Bombardment relocated to 539.73, collision to 539.757, scattering to 539.758

Class field theories covering fundamental interactions in 530.14

See also 531.14 for gravity

.754 4   Weak interaction

For beta decay, see 539.7523

.754 6   Electromagnetic interaction

.754 8   Strong interaction

Including quantum chromodynamics

.756   Photonuclear reactions

.757   Collision [*formerly* 539.754]

.758   Scattering [*formerly* 539.754]

.76   High-energy physics

Class here reactions emitting high energy

Class high-energy levels of particles in 539.725

.761   Chain reactions

.762   Nuclear fission

.764   Nuclear fusion (Thermonuclear reaction)

.77   Detection and measurement of particles and radioactivity

Class here monitoring, dosimetry

.772   In ionization chambers

.773   In proportional counters

.774   In Geiger-Müller counters

.775   In scintillation counters

.776   In crystal conduction counters

.777   In Wilson cloud chambers

.778   Through photographic means

[.9]   **Tables, review, exercise**

Tables relocated to 539.0212, review and exercise to 539.076

540   Chemistry and allied sciences

Class cosmochemistry in 523.02

See Manual at 530 vs. 540

SUMMARY

540.1–.9	**Standard subdivisions**
541	**Physical and theoretical chemistry**
542	**Techniques, procedures, apparatus, equipment, materials**
543	**Analytical chemistry**
544	**Qualitative analysis**
545	**Quantitative analysis**
546	**Inorganic chemistry**
547	**Organic chemistry**
548	**Crystallography**
549	**Mineralogy**

.1   Philosophy and theory

Class theoretical chemistry in 541.2

.11   Ancient and medieval theories

.112   Alchemy

Including philosopher's stone

.118   Phlogiston theory

[.28]   Auxiliary techniques and procedures; apparatus, equipment, materials

Do not use; class in 542

.72   Research

Class laboratories in 542.1

> ## 541–547 Chemistry

Class comprehensive works in 540

> ## 541–545 General topics in chemistry

Inorganic and combined inorganic-organic

Class comprehensive works in 540, general topics of specific inorganic chemicals and groups of chemicals in 546, general topics in organic chemistry in 547

541   Physical and theoretical chemistry

Class physical and theoretical chemistry of specific elements, compounds, mixtures, groupings in 546; physical and theoretical topics of crystals in 548

See Manual at 546 vs. 541

SUMMARY

541.04   **[States of matter]**
     .2   **Theoretical chemistry**
     .3   **Physical chemistry**
     .7   **Optical activity**

.04   Special topics

.042   States of matter

> Add to base number 541.042 the numbers following 530.4 in 530.41–530.44, e.g., solid-state chemistry 541.0421

.2   **Theoretical chemistry**

> Class chemical crystallography in 548.3

.22   Molecular structure

> *For quantum chemistry, see 541.28*
>
> *See also 539.12 for physics of molecular structure*

.221   Structural formulas

.222   Molecular weights

.223   Stereochemistry

.224   Molecular bonds and valences, radicals

> Class here comprehensive works on bonds and bondings
>
> Class bond distances in 541.223
>
> *For atomic bonds, see 541.244*

.224 2   Coordination chemistry

> Including coordination numbers, ligands, molecular complexes
>
> *For chelates, see 541.2253*

.225   Structural variations

.225 2   Isomers

> Class here tautomerism

.225 3   Chelates

.225 4   Polymers

> Class comprehensive works on polymers in 547.7

.226   Intermolecular forces

.24   Atomic structure

> Class here periodicity, periodic law [*both formerly* 541.901]
>
> Class periodic table in 546.8
>
> *For quantum chemistry, see 541.28; radiochemistry, 541.38*

.242	Atomic constants
	Atomic weights, numbers, mass
.243	Spatial atomic arrangements
.244	Atomic bonds
	Homopolar and heteropolar bonds
.246	Interatomic forces
.26	Stoichiometry
.28	Quantum chemistry
	Including molecular and atomic orbitals, magnetic resonance spectroscopy

.3   **Physical chemistry**

> Class chemical physics in 539

> *For optical activity, see 541.7*

SUMMARY

541.33	**Surface chemistry (Surface phenomena)**	
.34	**Solution chemistry**	
.35	**Photochemistry and chemiluminescence**	
.36	**Thermochemistry and thermodynamics**	
.37	**Electro- and magnetochemistry**	
.38	**Radiochemistry (Nuclear chemistry)**	
.39	**Chemical reactions and synthesis**	

.33	Surface chemistry (Surface phenomena) [*formerly* 541.3453]
	Examples: absorption, adhesion, adsorption, bubbles, capillarity, chemisorption, cohesion, interfacial tension, surface tension
.34	Solution chemistry
	For electrolytic solutions, see 541.372
.341	Properties of solutions
.341 3	Mechanical properties
.341 4	Optical properties
.341 5	Colligative properties
	Examples: freezing-point depression, boiling-point elevation, vapor-pressure lowering, osmotic pressure
.341 6	Thermal properties
.342	Solutions by type of solvent
	Class here solubility
.342 2	Aqueous solutions
.342 3	Nonaqueous solutions

.345	Colloid chemistry

               Liesegang rings relocated to 541.3485

.345 1	Specific types of colloids

               Use of this number for comprehensive works on colloids discontinued; class in 541.345

.345 13	Matter dispersed in solids

               Examples: gels, solid foams

.345 14	Hydrosols

               Examples: emulsions, foams, froths, lathers

               Class solid foams in 541.34513

.345 15	Aerosols

               Examples: fogs, smokes, mists

[.345 3]	Surface chemistry (Surface phenomena)

               Relocated to 541.33

.348	Solution components
.348 2	Solvents
.348 3	Solutes
.348 5	Precipitates

               Including Liesegang rings [*formerly* 541.345]

.35	Photochemistry and chemiluminescence
.351	Energy transformations
.353	Photochemical reactions due to specific radiations
.353 2	Infrared radiations
.353 3	Visible light
.353 4	Ultraviolet radiations
.36	Thermochemistry and thermodynamics

>	541.361–541.368 Thermochemistry

               Class comprehensive works in 541.36

.361	Combustion

               Including heat liberated during combustion [*formerly* 541.362], explosion, flame, ignition

.362	Exothermic and endothermic reactions
	Including latent heats
	Heat liberated during combustion relocated to 541.361
	For combustion, see 541.361
.363	Change of state (Phase transformations)
	Including Gibb's phase rule, triple points
.364	Thermal dissociation
.368	Reactions under temperature extremes
.368 6	Low temperatures
	Reactions below -100° C
.368 7	High temperatures
	Class here pyrometry
.369	Thermodynamics
.37	Electro- and magnetochemistry

>   541.372–541.377 Electrochemistry

Class comprehensive works in 541.37

.372	Electrolytic solutions
	Including electrodialysis, electrophoresis, electrolyte conductivity
	Class here ions
	For non-electrical properties, see 541.374
.372 2	Ionization (Electrolytic dissociation)
.372 3	Ion exchange and ionic equilibriums
.372 4	Electrodes and electrode phenomena
.372 8	Hydrogen-ion concentration
	Class here pH value
.374	Non-electrical properties of electrolytic solutions
	Add to base number 541.374 the numbers following 541.341 in 541.3413–541.3416, e.g., optical properties 541.3744
.377	Semiconductors
.378	Magnetochemistry
.38	Radiochemistry (Nuclear chemistry)
.382	Radiolysis
	Class here radiation chemistry

.388	Isotopes
.388 4	Radioisotopes
.39	Chemical reactions and synthesis

Class thermochemistry of reactions in 541.36

.392	Chemical equilibriums

Including law of mass action, Le Chatelier's principle

.393	Specific reactions

Examples: addition, condensation, hydrolysis, oxidation, polymerization, reduction, substitution; chain, heterogeneous, homogeneous, irreversible, reversible reactions

Class comprehensive works on polymerization in 547.28

.394	Reaction kinetics

Class kinetics of specific reactions in 541.393

For catalysis, see 541.395

.395	Catalysis
.7	**Optical activity**

Examples: mutarotation, racemization

Class here optical rotation

[.9]	**Other topics**

Number discontinued; class in 541

[.901]	Periodicity and periodic law

Relocated to 541.24

542 Techniques, procedures, apparatus, equipment, materials

Class a specific application with the application, e.g., apparatus for study of solutions 541.34028

.1	**Laboratories**

Class specific types of laboratory apparatus in 542.2–542.8

> ## 542.2–542.8 Specific techniques, procedures, apparatus, equipment

Class comprehensive works in 542

.2	**Receptacles and accessory equipment**

Examples: crucibles, test tubes, tubing

Class receptacles and accessory equipment for testing and measuring in 542.3, for distilling in 542.4; gas apparatus in 542.7

.3   **Testing and measuring**

Class gas measuring apparatus in 542.7, analytical chemistry in 543

.4   **Heating and distilling**

.5   **Blowpipes**

.6   **Filtering and dialyzing**

.7   **Gas production, processing, measuring**

.8   **Auxiliary techniques and procedures, electrical and electronic equipment**

Add to base number 542.8 the numbers following —028 in notation 0285–0289 from Table 1, e.g., digital computers 542.85416; however, class testing and measurement in 542.3

543   Analytical chemistry

Use 543.001–543.009 for standard subdivisions

Class analytical chemistry of specific elements, compounds, mixtures, groupings in 546, using notation 6 from table under 546

For qualitative analysis, see 544; quantitative analysis, 545

See Manual at 544–545 vs. 543

.01   Reagents

.02   Sample preparation

.07   Instrumentation

.08   Specific methods

Examples: gas analysis

SUMMARY

543.081	**Micro and semimicro methods**
.083	**Mechanical methods**
.085	**Optical methods**
.086	**Thermal methods**
.087	**Electromagnetic methods**
.088	**Radiochemical analysis**
.089	**Chromatographic analysis**

.081   Micro and semimicro methods

.081 2   Microscopical analysis

.081 3   Microchemical analysis

Reactions performed with small quantities, e.g., micrograms and microliters, and using small apparatus

.081 32   Systematic analysis

.081 34   Spot tests

.081 5	Semimicroanalysis
	Small-scale adaptations of existing macro methods
.083	Mechanical methods
	Example: gravimetric analysis
.085	Optical methods
.085 2	Photometric analysis
	Examples: colorimetric, fluorophotometric, nephelometric, turbidimetric methods
.085 3	Refractometric and interferometric analysis
.085 6	Polarimetric (Polariscopic) analysis
.085 8	Spectrochemical (Spectroscopic) analysis
	Class here interdisciplinary works on spectroscopy
	Class spectroscopy in physics in 535.84; spectroscopic interpretation of chemical structure in 541.2; each kind of spectroscopic analysis not provided for here with the kind, e.g., mass spectrographic methods 543.0873
.085 82	Microwave analysis
.085 83	Infrared analysis
.085 84	Visible light analysis
	Including Raman spectroscopy
.085 85	Ultraviolet analysis
.085 86	X-ray and gamma-ray analysis
	Including Mössbauer analysis
.086	Thermal methods
	Examples: blowpipe analysis, combustion analysis, thermometric titrimetry
.087	Electromagnetic methods
.087 1	Electrical methods
	For polarographic methods, see 543.0872; coulometric methods, 543.0874
.087 11	Conductometric methods
.087 12	Potentiometric methods
.087 2	Polarographic methods
.087 3	Mass spectrographic methods
.087 4	Coulometric methods
	Including electrodeposition methods

.087 7	Magnetic methods

Including nuclear magnetic resonance methods

For mass spectrographic methods, see 543.0873

.088	Radiochemical analysis
.088 2	Activation (Radioactivation) analysis
.088 4	Tracer techniques
.089	Chromatographic analysis
.089 2	Separation by specific types of interaction

Examples: adsorption, molecular sieve, partition

Class specific types of interaction applied to liquid chromatography in 543.0894, to gas chromatography in 543.0896

For ion-exchange separations, see 543.0893

.089 3	Ion-exchange separations

Class application to liquid chromatography in 543.0894, to gas chromatography in 543.0896

.089 4	Liquid chromatography

Example: column chromatography

For paper and thin-layer chromatography, see 543.0895

.089 5	Paper and thin-layer chromatography
.089 52	Paper chromatography
.089 56	Thin-layer chromatography
.089 6	Gas chromatography

544 Qualitative analysis

Use 544.001–544.009 for standard subdivisions

Class qualitative analysis of specific elements, compounds, mixtures, groupings in 546, using notation 64 from table under 546

See Manual at 544–545 vs. 543

.01	Reagents
.02	Sample preparations
.07	Instrumentation
.1	**Systematic separations**

Including decomposition analysis

.12	Cation separation and identification
.13	Anion separation and identification

.2   **Thermal methods**

Examples: pyrolysis, combustion

For blowpipe analysis, see 544.3

.3   **Blowpipe analysis**

.4   **Gas analysis**

.5   **Diffusion analysis**

Including ultrafiltration methods (dialysis)

.6   **Spectrochemical (Spectroscopic) analysis**

Add to base number 544.6 the numbers following 543.0858 in 543.08582–543.08586, e.g., microwave analysis 544.62

.8   **Micro and semimicro methods**

Add to base number 544.8 the numbers following 543.081 in 543.0812–543.0815, e.g., microscopical analysis 544.82

.9   **Other methods**

.92   Chromatographic analysis

Add to base number 544.92 the numbers following 543.089 in 543.0892–543.0896, e.g., paper chromatography 544.9252

.93   Mechanical methods

Example: gravimetric analysis

.94   Biochemical methods

Including identification by means of microorganisms

.95   Optical methods

For spectrochemical analysis, see 544.6

.952   Photometric analysis

Examples: colorimetric, fluorophotometric, nephelometric, turbidimetric methods

.953   Refractometric and interferometric analysis

.956   Polarimetric (Polariscopic) analysis

For spectrochemical analysis, see 544.6

.97   Electromagnetic methods

Add to base number 544.97 the numbers following 543.087 in 543.0871–543.0877, e.g., coulometric methods 544.974

.98   Radiochemical methods

.982   Activation (Radioactivation) analysis

.984   Tracer techniques

545 Quantitative analysis

Use 545.001–545.009 for standard subdivisions

Class quantitative analysis of specific elements, compounds, mixtures, groupings in 546, using notation 65 from table under 546

See Manual at 544–545 vs. 543

.01 Reagents

.02 Sample preparation

.07 Instrumentation

.08 Mechanical methods

.1 Gravimetric analysis

Including gravimetric analysis of precipitates

For thermogravimetric methods, see 545.4

.2 Volumetric analysis

.22 Neutralization methods

Acidimetry and alkalimetry

.23 Oxidation-reduction methods

Example: iodometry

.24 Precipitation methods

.3 Electromagnetic methods

Add to base number 545.3 the numbers following 543.087 in 543.0871–543.0877, e.g., electrodeposition 545.34

.4 Thermal methods

Class here thermogravimetric methods

.42 Pyrolysis and combustion

.43 Blowpipe analysis

.46 Volatilization

.7 Gas analysis

.8 Other methods

.81 Optical methods

For spectroscopic analysis, see 545.83

.812 Photometric analysis

.813 Refractometric and interferometric analysis

.816 Polarimetric (Polariscopic) analysis

.82 Radiochemical methods

.822	Activation analysis (Radioactivation analysis)
.824	Tracer techniques
.83	Spectrochemical (Spectroscopic) analysis

> Add to base number 545.83 the numbers following 543.0858 in 543.08582–543.08586, e.g., microwave analysis 545.832

.84	Micro and semimicro methods

> Add to base number 545.84 the numbers following 543.081 in 543.0812–543.0815, e.g., semimicro quantitative analysis 545.845

.89	Chromatographic analysis

> Add to base number 545.89 the numbers following 543.089 in 543.0892–543.0896, e.g., gas chromatography 545.896

546   Inorganic chemistry

Class here physical and theoretical chemistry, analytical chemistry, physics of specific elements, compounds, mixtures, groupings; comprehensive works on inorganic and organic chemistry of specific elements, compounds, mixtures, groupings

Specific compounds are classed with the first element named, except that for acids, hydrogen is disregarded

Add to each subdivision identified by * as follows:

>1–3	The element, compounds, mixtures
	Class comprehensive works in base number; theoretical, physical, analytical chemistry of the element, compounds, mixtures in 4–6
1	The element
2	Compounds
	Names of compounds usually end in -ide or one of the suffixes listed in 22 and 24 below
22	Acids and bases
	Names of acids usually end in -ic or -ous
24	Salts
	Names of salts frequently end in -ate or -ite
25	Complex compounds
3	Molecular and colloidal mixtures
	Class here alloys
4	Theoretical chemistry
	Add to 4 the numbers following 541.2 in 541.22–541.28, e.g., molecular structure 42
5	Physical chemistry
	Add to 5 the numbers following 541.3 in 541.33–541.39, e.g., radiochemistry 58
6	Analytical chemistry
64	Qualitative
65	Quantitative

Class general topics of chemistry applied to inorganic chemistry as a whole in 541–545; organic chemistry of specific elements, compounds, mixtures, groupings in 547

See Manual at 546 vs. 541; 546 vs. 549

SUMMARY

546.2	**Hydrogen and its compounds**
.3	**Metals, their compounds and mixtures**
.4	**Group 3B**
.5	**Groups 4B, 5B, 6B, 7B**
.6	**Groups 8, 1B, 2B, 3A, 4A**
.7	**Groups 5A, 6A, 7A, O**
.8	**Periodic table**

.2   **Hydrogen and its compounds**

.21   The element

.212   Deuterium

.213   Tritium

\>   546.22–546.24 Compounds

        Class comprehensive works in 546.2

        For bases, see 546.32

.22   Water

        Including deuterium oxide (heavy water)

.224   Theoretical chemistry

        Add to base number 546.224 the numbers following 541.2 in 541.22–541.28, e.g., quantum chemistry 546.2248

.225   Physical chemistry

        Add to base number 546.225 the numbers following 541.3 in 541.33–541.39, e.g., thermochemistry 546.2256

.226   Analytical chemistry

.24   Acids

        Class a specific acid with its distinguishing element, e.g., hydrochloric acid 546.73222

.25   Theoretical chemistry

        Add to base number 546.25 the numbers following 541.2 in 541.22–541.28, e.g., molecular bonds 546.2524

.26   Physical chemistry

        Add to base number 546.26 the numbers following 541.3 in 541.33–541.39, e.g., thermochemistry 546.266

.3   **Metals, their compounds and mixtures**

        Class specific metals and their compounds and mixtures of groups other than 1A and 2A in 546.4–546.7, physical and chemical metallurgy in 669.9

.31   Metallic elements

>   546.32–546.34 Compounds

        Class comprehensive works in 546.3

.32   Bases

        Class specific bases with the metallic or metal-like radical, e.g., ammonium hydroxide 546.71122

.34   Salts

.342   Simple salts

        Examples: acidulous, alkaline, amphoteric, binary, neutral salts

.343   Double salts

        Salts formed by union of two simple salts

        For complex salts, see 546.345

.345   Complex salts

        Double salts that do not form their component salts on solution

[.37]   Alloys

        Number discontinued; class in 546.3

>   546.38–546.39 Alkali and alkaline earth metals

        Class comprehensive works in 546.38

.38   Alkali metals (Group 1A)

.381   *Lithium

.382   *Sodium

.383   *Potassium

.384   *Rubidium

.385   *Cesium

.386   *Francium

.39   Alkaline-earth metals (Group 2A)

.391   *Beryllium

.392   *Magnesium

.393   *Calcium

.394   *Strontium

.395   *Barium

.396   *Radium

*Add as instructed under 546

.4   **Group 3B**

Use 546.4001–546.4009 for standard subdivisions

.401   *Scandium

.403   *Yttrium

.41   Rare earth elements (Lanthanide series)

.411   *Lanthanum

.412   *Cerium

.413   Praseodymium and neodymium

.414   *Promethium

.415   Samarium and europium

.416   Gadolinium and terbium

.417   Dysprosium and holmium

.418   Erbium and thulium

.419   Ytterbium and lutetium

.42   Actinide series

> For uranium, see 546.431; transuranium elements, 546.44

.421   *Actinium

.422   *Thorium

.424   *Protactinium

.43   Uranium, neptunium, plutonium

.431   *Uranium

.432   *Neptunium

.434   *Plutonium

.44   Transuranium elements

> For neptunium, see 546.432; plutonium, 546.434; rutherfordium, 546.51; hahnium, 546.52

.440 01–.440 09   Standard subdivisions

.441   Americium

.442   Curium

.444   Berkelium

.448   Californium

*Add as instructed under 546

.449		Other
		Contains einsteinium, fermium, lawrencium, mendelevium, nobelium
.5		**Groups 4B, 5B, 6B, 7B**
.51		Titanium group (Group 4B)
		Contains rutherfordium
.512		*Titanium
.513		*Zirconium
.514		*Hafnium
.52		Vanadium group (Group 5B)
		Contains hahnium
.522		*Vanadium
.524		*Niobium (Columbium)
.526		*Tantalum
.53		Chromium group (Group 6B)
.532		*Chromium
.534		*Molybdenum
.536		*Tungsten
.54		Manganese group (Group 7B)
.541		*Manganese
.543		*Technetium
.545		*Rhenium
.6		**Groups 8, 1B, 2B, 3A, 4A**
		Class here comprehensive works on transition metals
		For group 3B, see 546.4; groups 4B, 5B, 6B, 7B, 546.5

> 546.62–546.64 Group 8

         Class comprehensive works in 546.6

.62		Iron, cobalt, nickel
.621		*Iron
.623		*Cobalt
.625		*Nickel

*Add as instructed under 546

.63	Platinum metals	

For osmium, iridium, platinum, see 546.64

.632	*Ruthenium
.634	*Rhodium
.636	*Palladium
.64	Osmium, iridium, platinum
.641	*Osmium
.643	*Iridium
.645	*Platinum

Class comprehensive works on platinum metals in 546.63

.65	Group 1B
.652	*Copper
.654	*Silver
.656	*Gold
.66	Group 2B
.661	*Zinc
.662	*Cadmium
.663	*Mercury
.67	Group 3A
.671	*Boron
.673	*Aluminum
.675	*Gallium
.677	*Indium
.678	*Thallium
.68	Group 4A
.681	*Carbon
.681 2	Carbon compounds

Use this number for carbon oxides, carbonates, metal carbonyls, carbon halides when treated as inorganic compounds by the author; class other carbon compounds in 547

.683	*Silicon
.684	*Germanium
.686	*Tin

*Add as instructed under 546

.688	*Lead
.7	**Groups 5A, 6A, 7A, O**
	Class here nonmetals
	Class a specific nonmetalic element not provided for here with the element, e.g., silicon 546.683
.71	Group 5A
.711	*Nitrogen
.712	*Phosphorus
.715	*Arsenic
.716	*Antimony
.718	*Bismuth
.72	Group 6A
.721	*Oxygen
.723	*Sulfur
.724	*Selenium
.726	*Tellurium
.728	*Polonium
.73	Halogens (Group 7A)
.731	*Fluorine
.732	*Chlorine
.733	*Bromine
.734	*Iodine
.735	*Astatine
.75	Noble gases (Group 0)
	Variant names: inert, rare gases
.751	*Helium
.752	*Neon
.753	*Argon
.754	*Krypton
.755	*Xenon
.756	*Radon

*Add as instructed under 546

.8   **Periodic table**

Class specific elements, groups, series in 546.2–546.7

[.81–.87]   Specific periods

Numbers discontinued; class in 546.8

547   Organic chemistry

Class here biochemicals when not considered in their biological context

Add to notation for each term identified by * as follows:
    04   Special topics
    044   Theoretical chemistry
                        Add to 044 the numbers following 541.2 in 541.22–541.28,
                        e.g., molecular structure 0442
    045   Physical chemistry
                        Add to 045 the numbers following 541.3 in 541.34–541.39,
                        e.g., radiochemistry 0458
    046   Analytical chemistry
    0464   Qualitative
    0465   Quantitative

Class interdisciplinary works on biochemicals in 574.192

For biochemistry, see 574.192

SUMMARY

547.001–.009	**Standard subdivisions**
.01–.08	**Kinds of compounds identified by component elements**
.1	**Physical and theoretical chemistry**
.2	**Synthesis and named reactions**
.3	**Analytical chemistry**
.4	**Aliphatic compounds**
.5	**Cyclic compounds**
.6	**Aromatic compounds**
.7	**Macromolecular and related compounds**
.8	**Other organic substances**

.001   Philosophy and theory

Class theoretical organic chemistry in 547.12

.002–.009   Standard subdivisions

>   547.01–547.08 Kinds of compounds identified by component elements

Unless other instructions are given, class compounds with components in two
or more subdivisions of this schedule in the number coming last in the schedule,
e.g., sulfonamides 547.067 (*not* 547.042)

Class comprehensive works in 547, reactions identified by a component element
in 547.2, kinds of compounds identified by structure and function in
547.4–547.8

.01   *Hydrocarbons

*Add as instructed under 547

.02	*Halocarbons
.03	*Oxy and hydroxy compounds
.031	*Alcohols
.035	*Ethers
.036	*Aldehydes and *ketones
.037	*Acids
.038	*Esters
.04	*Nitrogen compounds
.041	*Nitro and nitroso compounds
.042	*Amines and *amides
.043	*Azo compounds
.044	*Nitriles and *isonitriles
.05	*Organometallic compounds

Add to base number 547.05 the numbers following 546 in 546.38–546.72, e.g., organozinc compounds 547.05661; then add as instructed under 547, e.g., analytical chemistry of organozinc compounds 547.05661046; however, class phosphorus compounds in 547.07, silicon compounds in 547.08

.06	*Sulfur compounds
.061	*Sulfites (Thioethers)
.063	*Hydrosulfites (Thioalcohols)
.064	*Thioacids
.065	Oxy derivatives of thioethers

Examples: sulfones, sulfoxides, thioaldehydes, thioketones

.066	*Sulfinic acids
.067	*Sulfonic acids
.07	*Phosphorus compounds
.071	*Phosphonium compounds, *phosphines
.073	*Phosphoalcohols
.074	*Phosphoacids
.075	*Phosphoaldehydes, *phosphoketones
.076	*Phosphinic acids
.077	*Phosphonic acids

*Add as instructed under 547

.08   *Silicon compounds

.1   **Physical and theoretical chemistry**

Add to base number 547.1 the numbers following 541 in 541.2–541.7, e.g., specific reactions 547.1393; however, class synthesis (e.g., addition, condensation, hydrolysis, oxidation, polymerization, reduction) and name reactions in 547.2

Class physical and theoretical chemistry of specific compounds and groups of compounds in 547.01–547.08, 547.4–547.8

.2   **Synthesis and name reactions**

Class here reactions identified by a component element

Class comprehensive works on chain, reversible, irreversible, homogeneous, heterogeneous reactions in 547.1393; synthesis and name reactions involving a specific compound and group of compounds in 547.01–547.08, 547.4–547.8

.21   Alkylation, acylation, aromatization

Examples: Friedel-Crafts, Würtz-Fittig reactions

.22   Halogen and hydroxy addition and substitution

.223   Halogenation

.225   Hydrolysis and saponification

.23   Oxidation and reduction

Examples: hydrogenation, dehydrogenation, peroxidation, quinonization

.24   Esterification

.25   Amination and diazotization

.26   Nitration and nitrosation

.27   Sulfonation

.28   Polymerization and condensation

Examples: copolymerization, addition and condensation polymerization

.29   Fermentation

.3   **Analytical chemistry**

Use 547.3001–547.3009 for standard subdivisions

.301–.308   General topics and methods

Add to base number 547.30 the numbers following 543.0 in 543.01–543.08, e.g., reagents 547.301

.34   Qualitative chemistry

Use 547.34001–547.34009 for standard subdivisions

Add to base number 547.34 the numbers following 544 in 544.01–544.98, e.g., qualitative organic diffusion analysis 547.345

*Add as instructed under 547

.35   Quantitative chemistry

Use 547.35001–547.35009 for standard subdivisions

Add to base number 547.35 the numbers following 545 in 545.01–545.89, e.g., volumetric analysis 547.352

> **547.4–547.8 Kinds of compounds identified by structure and function**

Class comprehensive works in 547

.4   ***Aliphatic compounds**

Observe order of precedence in note under 547.01–547.08

Class macromolecular compounds in 547.7

.41   *Hydrocarbons

.411   *Paraffins (Alkanes)

.412   *Olefins (Alkenes)

.413   *Acetylenes (Alkynes)

.42–.48   Other compounds

Add to base number 547.4 the numbers following 547.0 in 547.02–547.08, e.g., carboxylic acids 547.437

For proteins, see 547.75

.5   ***Cyclic compounds**

Class here alicyclic compounds

For aromatic compounds, see 547.6

> 547.51–547.58 Alicyclic compounds

Observe order of precedence in note under 547.01–547.08

Class comprehensive works in 547.5

.51   *Alicyclic hydrocarbons

.511   *Cycloparaffins

.512   *Cycloolefins

.513   *Cycloacetylenes

.52–.58   Other alicyclic compounds

Add to base number 547.5 the numbers following 547.0 in 547.02–547.08, e.g., alicyclic acids 547.537

---

*Add as instructed under 547

.59	*Heterocyclic compounds
.592	*With hetero oxygen atoms
	Examples: furans, oxazoles, pyrans
.593	*With hetero nitrogen atoms
	Examples: chlorophylls, diazines, imidazoles, porphyrins, pyrazoles, pyridines, pyrroles
.594	*With hetero sulfur atoms
	Examples: thiazoles, thiophenes
.595	With two or more different hetero atoms
	Examples: oxazines, oxdiazines, oxdiazoles
.596	*With fused hetero rings
	Examples: purines, quinolines
.6	***Aromatic compounds**
	Observe order of precedence in note under 547.01–547.08
.61	*Hydrocarbons
.611	*Benzenes
.613	*Polyphenyl hydrocarbons
	Including diphenyl hydrocarbons
.615	*Fused hydrocarbons
	Including naphthalenes
	For anthracenes, see 547.616
.616	*Anthracenes
.62	*Halogenated compounds
.63	*Oxy and *hydroxy compounds
.631	*Alcohols
	Class phenols in 547.632
.632	*Phenols
	Including monohydric hydroxy aromatics
.633	*Polyhydroxy aromatics
	Examples: dihydroxy and trihydroxy aromatics, catechols, hydroquinones, resorcinols
.635	*Ethers
.636	*Aldehydes and *ketones
.637	*Acids

*Add as instructed under 547

.638	*Esters
.64–.68	Other aromatic compounds

> Add to base number 547.6 the numbers following 547.0 in 547.04–547.08, e.g., aromatic amines 547.642

.7   ***Macromolecular and related compounds**

> Class here macromolecular biochemicals when not considered in their biological context, polymers

> Class interdisciplinary works on macromolecular biochemicals in 574.192, comprehensive works on high polymers in 547.84, polymerization as a reaction in 547.28; fossil substances in 547.82, dyes and pigments in 547.86

.71	Terpenes and essential oils

> Including camphors

.72	*Alkaloids

> *See also 615.7 for pharmacodynamics of alkaloids*

.73	*Steroids and hormones
.731	*Sterols

> Examples: cholesterol, ergosterol

.734	*Hormones

> Class here steroid hormones

.734 2	*Auxins

> Including gibberellins

.734 3	*Sex hormones
.734 5	Nonsteroid hormones

> Examples: adrenalin, cortin, insulin, oxytocin, thyroxine, vasopressin

.737	*Bile acids (Cholic acids)
.74	*Vitamins
.75	*Proteins

> Class here amino acids

> Class protein hormones in 547.7345

>   547.752–547.756 By structure

> Class comprehensive works in 547.75

.752	Simple proteins

> Examples: albumins, globulins, histones

*Add as instructed under 547

.753	Scleroproteins	

Examples: collagen, keratin

.754   Conjugated proteins

Examples: chromoproteins, hemoglobins, lipoproteins, nucleoproteins, phosphoproteins

.756   Derived proteins

Examples: peptides, peptones

.758   *Enzymes

Class here coenzymes

.76   *Antibiotics

.77   *Lipids

For steroids, see 547.73

.78   *Carbohydrates

Class here saccharides

.781   *Sugars

.781 3   *Monosaccharides

Examples: fructose, glucose (dextrose), ribose

.781 5   *Oligosaccharides

Examples: lactose, maltose, sucrose

.782   *Polysaccharides

Examples: cellulose, chitin, dextrans, glycogen, pectins, starches

Class conjugated carbohydrates in 547.783

.783   *Conjugated carbohydrates

Contains gums [*formerly* 547.8434], glycosides

Examples of glycosides: saponins, tannins

Class glycoside pigments in 547.869

.79   *Nucleic acids

.8   Other organic substances

.82   *Fossil substances

Including coal tar

Class a specific compound derived from a fossil substance with the compound, e.g., synthetic rubber 678.72

For petroleum, see 547.83

.83   *Petroleum

*Add as instructed under 547

.84   *High polymers

Class high polymers of a specific chemical group with the group, e.g., polysaccharides 547.782

.842   *Elastomers

.842 5   *Latexes

Synthetic latexes relocated to 678.71

.842 6   *Rubber

[.842 7]   Synthetic polymers

Relocated to 668.9

.843   *Flexible polymers

[.843 2]   Plastics

Relocated to 668.4

.843 4   *Resins

Gums relocated to 547.783

[.85]   Man-made fibers

Relocated to 677.4

.86   *Dyes and pigments

[.862–.867]   Specific dyes

Numbers discontinued; class in 547.86

.869   *Pigments

548   Crystallography

Class comprehensive works on solid state physics in 530.41, crystallographic mineralogy in 549.18

See Manual at 530.41 vs. 548; 548 vs. 549

[.1]   **Geometrical crystallography**

Relocated to 548.81

.3   **Chemical crystallography**

Relationship between structure and bondings

Including isomorphism, polymorphism, pseudomorphism

.5   **Crystallization and crystal growth**

.7   **Mathematical crystallography**

Measurement and calculation of angles

*Add as instructed under 547

.8   Physical and structural crystallography

.81   Structural crystallography

              Class here geometrical crystallography [*formerly* 548.1], crystal lattices

              Structural crystallography of specific substances relocated to the substance, e.g., of silicates 549.6

                   For diffraction methods, see 548.83

.810 151   Mathematical principles

                        Class mathematical crystallography (measurement and calculation of angles) in 548.7

.83   Diffraction crystallography

              Including crystallograms

              Class optical methods of crystal study in 548.9

              _____

>   548.84–548.86 Physical properties of crystals

              Class comprehensive works in 548.8

                   For optical properties, see 548.9

.84   Mechanical properties

.842   Stresses, deformation, strength properties

                   Examples: elasticity, plasticity; dislocation, fracture, hardness

.843   Cleavage and cohesion

.845   Density and specific gravity

.85   Electrical, electronic, magnetic properties

                   Examples: conductivity, semiconductivity, dielectricity, piezoelectricity, pyroelectricity

.86   Thermal properties

                   Example: fusibility

.9   Optical crystallography

              Optical properties of crystals and optical methods of crystal study

              Liquid crystals relocated to 530.429

549   Mineralogy

              Occurrence, description, classification, identification of naturally occurring minerals

              Class crystallography in 548, economic geology in 553

                   See Manual at 546 vs. 549; 548 vs. 549; 552 vs. 549

SUMMARY

549.09   **Geographical, historical, persons treatment**
.1   **Determinative mineralogy**
.2   **Native elements**
.3   **Sulfides, sulfosalts, related minerals**
.4   **Halides**
.5   **Oxides**
.6   **Silicates**
.7   **Other minerals**
.9   **Geographical treatment of minerals**

.09   Geographical, historical, persons treatment

>   Class geographical distribution of minerals in 549.9

.1   Determinative mineralogy

>   Class determinative mineralogy of specific minerals in 549.2–549.7

>   *See Manual at 549.1*

.11   Minerals in specific kinds of formations

.112   In meteorites

>   Class here mineralogy and petrology of meteorites

.113   In placers

.114   In rocks

>   Add to base number 549.114 the numbers following 552 in 552.1–552.5, e.g., determinative mineralogy in metamorphic rocks 549.1144

.116   In pegmatite dikes

.119   In veins and lodes

.12   Physical mineralogy

.121   Mechanical properties

>   Examples: cleavage, fracture, hardness

.125   Optical properties

>   Examples: color, fluorescence, iridescence, luminescence, luster, refractivity, streak

.127   Electrical, electronic, magnetic properties

>   Examples: pyroelectricity, piezoelectricity

.13   Chemical mineralogy

.131   Composition, properties, reactivity

.133   Analysis

.18   Crystallographic mineralogy

>   Study of crystalline structure and properties of minerals

> **549.2–549.7 Specific minerals**

> Class comprehensive works in 549

.2 **Native elements**

Use 549.7 for mineral compounds of specific elements not provided for elsewhere in 549.3–549.7

.23 Metals

Native metals only

Class interdisciplinary works on physico-chemical characteristics of metals in 669.9

.25 Semimetals

Examples: antimony, arsenic, bismuth, selenium, tellurium

.27 Nonmetals

Examples: carbon, iodine, silicon

.3 **Sulfides, sulfosalts, related minerals**

Class sulfates in 549.75

.32 Sulfides, selenides, tellurides, antimonides, arsenides

Examples: argentite, bismuthinite, calaverite, chalcocite, cinnabar, galena, greenockite, molybdenite, niccolite, pyrite, smaltite (skutterudite), sphalerite, stannite, stibnite

.35 Sulfosalts (Double sulfides)

Examples: bournonite, enargite, jamesonite, polybasite, proustite, pyrargyrite, stephanite, tetrahedrite

.4 **Halides**

Examples: atacamite, carnallite, cerargyrite, cryolite, fluorite (fluorspar), halite, sylvite

.5 **Oxides**

.52 Simple and multiple oxides

.522 Cuprite, ice, zincite

.523 Hematite group

Examples: corundum, ilmenite

.524 Rutile group

Examples: cassiterite, pyrolusite

.525 Goethite group

Example: diaspore

.526   Spinel group

Examples: chromite, franklinite, gahnite, magnetite

.528   Other groups

Examples: chrysoberyl, columbite, pitchblende, uraninite

.53   Hydroxides

Examples: bauxite, brucite, limonite, manganite, psilomelane

.6   Silicates

.62   Nesosilicates

Examples: andalusite, chondrodite, cyanite, dumortierite, garnet, kyanite, olivine, phenacite, sillimanite, sphene, staurolite, topaz, willemite, zircon

.63   Sorosilicates

Examples: epidote, hemimorphite, idocrase, lawsonite, prehnite

.64   Cyclosilicates

Examples: axinite, beryl, chrysocolla, cordierite, tourmaline

.66   Inosilicates

Examples: amphiboles, pectolite, pyroxenes, rhodonite, spodumene, wollastonite

.67   Phyllosilicates

Examples: glauconite [*formerly* 552.5], apophyllite, chlorite, garnierite, kaolinite, mica, pyrophyllite, sepiolite, serpentine, talc

.68   Tectosilicates

Examples: feldspar, lazurite, leucite, opal, quartz, scapolite, zeolite

.7   Other minerals

.72   Phosphates, vanadates, arsenates

Examples: apatite, erythrite, lazulite, monazite, scorodite, triphylite, turquoise, vanadinite, vivianite

.73   Nitrates and borates

.732   Nitrates

Examples: niter (saltpeter), soda niter (Chile saltpeter)

.735   Borates

Examples: boracite, borax, colemanite, kernite, ulexite

.74   Tungstates and molybdates

Examples: scheelite, wolframite, wulfenite

.75	Sulfates and chromates
.752	Chromates and anhydrous sulfates

Examples: anglesite, anhydrite, barite, celestite, crocoite, glauberite

.755	Hydrous and basic sulfates

Examples: alunite, antlerite, chalcanthite, epsomite, gypsum, polyhalite

.78	Carbonates
.782	Calcite group

Examples: dolomite, magnesite, rhodochrosite, siderite, smithsonite

.785	Aragonite group

Examples: azurite, cerussite, malachite, strontianite, witherite

.9   Geographical treatment of minerals

Add to base number 549.9 notation 1–9 from Table 2, e.g., minerals of Greenland 549.9982

550   Earth sciences

Class here geophysics; phenomena of celestial bodies directly comparable to terrestrial phenomena, e.g., volcanic activity on Mars 551.21099923

Use 550 and its standard subdivisions for works that deal comprehensively with geology, hydrology, and meteorology; for works about geology that deal with all earth sciences. Use 551 and its standard subdivisions for works on geology in the sense limited to properties and phenomena of the solid earth

See Manual at 550 vs. 910; 559.9

SUMMARY

550.1–.9	**Standard subdivisions**
551	**Geology, hydrology, meteorology**
552	**Petrology**
553	**Economic geology**
554	**Earth sciences of Europe**
555	**Earth sciences of Asia**
556	**Earth sciences of Africa**
557	**Earth sciences of North America**
558	**Earth sciences of South America**
559	**Earth sciences of other parts of world and of extraterrestrial worlds**

[.154]	Chemical principles

Relocated to 551.9

.9   Historical, geographical, persons treatment

Class treatment by continent, country, locality in modern world, extraterrestrial worlds in 554–559 (*not* 550.94–550.99)

551   Geology, hydrology, meteorology

Geology: science that deals with properties and phenomena of the solid earth (lithosphere)

Use 550 and its standard subdivisions for works that deal comprehensively with geology, hydrology, and meteorology; for works about geology that deal with all earth sciences. Use 551 and its standard subdivisions for works on geology in the limited sense

For astronomical geography, see 525; geodesy, 526.1; petrology, 552; economic geology, 553; physical geography, 910.02

SUMMARY

551.01–.09	[Standard subdivisions of geology of the solid earth]
.1	Gross structure and properties of the earth
.2	Volcanoes, earthquakes, thermal waters and gases
.3	Surface and exogenous processes and their agents
.4	Geomorphology and hydrosphere
.5	Meteorology
.6	Climatology and weather
.7	Historical geology
.8	Structural geology
.9	Geochemistry

.01   Philosophy and theory of geology

[.015 4]   Chemical principles

Relocated to 551.9

.02–.08   Standard subdivisions of geology

.09   Historical, geographical, persons treatment of geology

Class submarine geology in 551.4608 (*not* 551.09162–551.09168); geology by continent, country, locality in modern world, extraterrestrial worlds in 554–559 (*not* 551.094–551.099)

.1   Gross structure and properties of the earth

For geomagnetism, see 538.7

.11   Interior

For properties, see 551.12

.112   Core

.115   Gutenberg discontinuity

.116   Mantle

.119   Mohorovicic discontinuity

.12   Properties of interior

Examples: heat, isostasy, temperature ranges

.13   Crust

        Including magma

        Class structural geology of crust in 551.8

        For properties, see 551.14

.136   Plate tectonics (Continental drift)

        Including sea-floor spreading

        Class comprehensive works on tectonics in 551.8

.14   Properties of crust

        Examples: elasticity, heat, temperature ranges, thermal conductivity

        Deformation relocated to 551.8

.2   Volcanoes, earthquakes, thermal waters and gases

        See also 363.3495 for volcanic and earthquake disasters

.21   Volcanoes

        Including comprehensive works on craters [*formerly* 551.44], paleovolcanism

        Class volcanic products and rocks in 552.2

        For meteorite craters, see 551.397

.22   Earthquakes

        Class here seismology

        Class seismic sea waves in 551.47024

.220 287   Testing and measurement

        Class here seismography

.23   Thermal waters [*formerly also* 551.49] and gases

        Class here surface manifestations, e.g., fumaroles, hot springs

.3   Surface and exogenous processes and their agents

        Class here sedimentology as description of surface processes

        Use 551.3001–551.3009 for standard subdivisions

        Class comprehensive works on sedimentology in 552.5

        See Manual at 551.302–551.307 vs. 551.35

.302   Erosion and weathering

        Standard subdivisions are added for erosion and weathering, for erosion alone

        Class role of weathering in soil formation in 551.305

.303	Transporting and depositing of materials

Class here sedimentation

.304	Transported materials (Sediments)
.305	Soil formation

Class here soil formation by water [*formerly* 551.355], role of weathering in soil formation

Comprehensive works on land forms relocated to 551.41, on specific land forms to 551.42–551.45

.307	Mass movement (Mass wasting)

Examples: avalanches, creep, mud flows, rockfalls

Including subsidence

Class here work of water in mass movement [*formerly* 551.353], landslides, slope failure

See also 363.349 for disasters resulting from avalanches and other mass movements

.31	Geological work of ice Glaciology

Class here interdisciplinary works on ice

Class a specific aspect of ice with the aspect, e.g., ice manufacture 621.58

For ice in water and other forms of ice, see 551.34; geological work of frost, 551.38

.312	Glaciers

Nourishment, advances, recessions, oscillations

For icebergs, shelf ice, growlers, see 551.342

.313	Glacial action

Including work of glaciers in erosion, soil formation, weathering

.314	Material transported by glaciers

Class here glacial drift and till, moraines regarded as materials

Class glacial drift and till, moraines regarded as land forms in 551.315

.315	Land forms created by glaciers

Examples: cirques, drumlins, kames, kettles, roches moutonnées

Class here glacial drift and till, moraines regarded as land forms

.34	Ice in water and other forms of ice

For snow, see 551.5784

.342	Ice in the sea

Examples: icebergs, shelf ice, growlers

For sea ice, see 551.343

.343   Sea ice (Frozen seawater)

.344   Anchor and frazil ice

.345   Lake and river ice

> Class here ice cover
>
> *For anchor and frazil ice, see 551.344*

.35   Geologic work of water

> Work of precipitation, of surface and subsurface waters
>
> *For geologic work of marine waters, see 551.36*
>
> *See Manual at 551.302–551.307 vs. 551.35*

.352   Erosion and weathering

> Standard subdivisions are used for erosion and weathering, for erosion alone
>
> Class role of weathering in soil formation in 551.305

.353   Transporting and depositing materials

> Class here sedimentation in water
>
> Work of water in mass movement relocated to 551.307

.354   Transported materials (Sediments)

.355   Land forms created by water

> Soil formation by water relocated to 551.305, specific land forms created by water relocated to 551.42–551.45

.36   Geologic work of marine waters

> Examples: wave action, beach erosion
>
> Class specific land forms created by marine waters in 551.42–551.45

.37   Geologic work of wind

.372   Erosion

> Class here weathering

.373   Transportation and depositing of materials

.374   Transported materials

.375   Land forms created by wind

> Class here dunes

.38   Geologic work of frost

> Class here periglacial processes

.382   Fragmentation of rocks

.383   Nivation

Class here work of frost in erosion, soil formation, weathering

For fragmentation of rocks, see 551.382

.384   Permafrost

.39   Geologic work of other agents

Examples: gravity, temperature changes

.397   Meteorites

Class here meteorite craters [*formerly also* 551.44]

.4   Geomorphology and hydrosphere

SUMMARY

551.41	**Geomorphology**
.42	**Islands**
.43	**Elevations**
.44	**Depressions and openings**
.45	**Plane and coastal regions**
.46	**Hydrosphere Oceanography**
.47	**Dynamic oceanography**
.48	**Hydrology**
.49	**Ground waters (Subsurface waters)**

.41   Geomorphology

Creation and modification of topographic land forms by erosional and depositional processes

Class here comprehensive works on land forms [*formerly also* 551.305], geomorphology of continents

For specific land forms, see 551.42–551.45; submarine geomorphology, 551.46084

See also 551.136 for continental drift

.415   Arid-land geomorphology

Class here desert geomorphology

>   551.42–551.45 Specific land forms [*formerly also* 551.305]

Class here specific land formations created by water [*formerly also* 551.355], comprehensive works on specific kinds of topographical features, on present and past examples of specific land forms

Class comprehensive works in 551.41; land forms created by plutonic action in 551.2, e.g., volcanic mountains 551.21; land forms created primarily by exogenous agents other than water or living organisms in 551.3, e.g., glacial moraines 551.315; land forms created by tectonic deformations in 551.8, e.g., rift valleys 551.87

.42	Islands
.423	Barrier islands
.424	Reefs

Including atolls

.43	Elevations

For orogeny, see 551.82

.432	Mountains
.434	Plateaus
.436	Hills

Including slopes

.44	Depressions and openings

Example: ravines

Comprehensive works on craters relocated to 551.21, meteorite craters to 551.397

.442	Valleys

Including canyons, gorges, river beds

For rift valleys, see 551.87

.447	Caves

Including karst formations, sink holes

.45	Plane and coastal regions
.453	Plane regions

Class here pampas, plains, prairies, steppes, tundras

.456	Deltas
.457	Coastal regions

Example: beaches

For deltas, see 551.456; shorelines, 551.458

.458	Shorelines

Marine and lake

Class here changes in sea and lake levels

.46	Hydrosphere	Oceanography

> Class here hydrography, marine science, oceans and seas
>
> Use 551.46001–551.46009 for standard subdivisions
>
> Class interdisciplinary works on water in 553.7, ice in 551.31, geologic work of water in 551.35
>
> > *For dynamic oceanography, see 551.47; hydrology, 551.48; marine biology, 574.92*
> >
> > *See also 620.4162 for oceanographic engineering*
> >
> > *See Manual at 551.46 vs. 574.92*

.460 1   Composition and properties of seawater

> Examples: color, density, salinity, temperature, transparency
>
> Class effect of ocean and sea temperature on atmosphere in 551.5246

.460 7   Deep-sea surveys and explorations

.460 8   Submarine geology

.460 809   Historical, geographical, persons treatment

.460 809 01–.460 809 05   Historical treatment

> > Add to base number 551.460809 the numbers following —09 in notation 0901–0905 from Table 1 e.g., study of submarine geology in 19th century 551.460809034

.460 809 2   Persons treatment

.460 809 3–.460 809 8   Geographical treatment

> > Add to base number 551.460809 the numbers following —16 in notation 163–168 from Table 2, e.g., submarine geology of Arctic Ocean 551.46080932

.460 83   Composition of ocean floor, deposits, sediments

> > Add to base number 551.46083 the numbers following —16 in notation 163–168 from Table 2, e.g., marine sediments of Mediterranean Sea 551.4608338

.460 84   Submarine geomorphology

> Class here topography of ocean floor
>
> > Add to base number 551.46084 the numbers following —16 in notation 163–168 from Table 2, e.g., geomorphology of Pacific Ocean floor 551.460844

.460 9   Special saltwater forms

> Examples: coastal pools, estuaries, inland seas, salt lakes, saltwater lagoons
>
> Class specific coastal pools, estuaries, saltwater lagoons in 551.461–551.469

\>   551.461–551.469 Specific oceans and seas

> Class comprehensive works in 551.46, submarine geology of specific oceanic bodies in 551.4608

.461   Atlantic Ocean

> *For Mediterranean Sea, see 551.462; Gulf of Mexico, 551.4634; Caribbean Sea, 551.4635; south Atlantic Ocean, 551.464*

.461 1   North Atlantic

> *For northeast and northwest Atlantic, see 551.4613–551.4614; Arctic Ocean (North Polar Sea), 551.468*

.461 3–.461 4   Northeast and northwest Atlantic

> Add to base number 551.461 the numbers following —163 in notation 1633–1634 from Table 2, e.g., Chesapeake Bay 551.46147

.462   Mediterranean Sea

> Add to base number 551.462 the numbers following —1638 in notation 16381–16389 from Table 2, e.g., Black Sea 551.4629

.463   Caribbean Sea and Gulf of Mexico

> Add to base number 551.463 the numbers following —1636 in notation 16364–16365 from Table 2, e.g., Gulf of Darien 551.4635

.464   South Atlantic Ocean

> Add to base number 551.464 the numbers following —163 in notation 1636–1637 from Table 2, e.g., Sargasso Sea 551.46462; however, class Caribbean Sea and Gulf of Mexico in 551.463

> Class Atlantic sector of Antarctic waters in 551.4693

.465   Pacific Ocean

> Add to base number 551.465 the numbers following —164 in notation 1644–1649 from Table 2, e.g., South China Sea 551.46572

> Class Pacific sector of Antarctic waters in 551.4694

> *For east Pacific Ocean, see 551.466*

.466   East Pacific Ocean

> Add to base number 551.466 the numbers following —164 in notation 1641, or —1643 from Table 2, e.g., San Francisco Bay 551.46632

.467   Indian Ocean

> Add to base number 551.467 the numbers following —165 in notation 1652–1657 from Table 2, e.g., Red Sea 551.46733

> Class Indian Ocean sector of Antarctic waters in 551.4695

.468	Arctic Ocean (North Polar Sea)

Add to base number 551.468 the numbers following —1632 in notation 16324–16327 from Table 2, e.g., Hudson Bay 551.4687

.469   Antarctic waters

Add to base number 551.469 the numbers following —167 in notation 1673–1675 from Table 2, e.g., Drake Passage 551.4693

.47   Dynamic oceanography

Use 551.47001–551.47009 for standard subdivisions

.470 1   Ocean currents

Class specific ocean currents in 551.471–551.479

.470 2   Waves

Class here gravity, internal, surface waves

.470 22   Wind waves

Including storm surges, swell

Use of this number for comprehensive works on ocean waves discontinued; class in 551.4702

.470 23   Seiches

In bays, gulfs, inland seas

Class seiches in freshwater lakes in 551.482

.470 24   Seismic sea waves

Variant names: tidal waves, tsunami

.470 8   Tides [*formerly also* 525.6] and tidal currents

See also 551.36 for geological work of tides

.471–.479   Specific ocean currents

Add to base number 551.47 the numbers following 551.46 in 551.461–551.469, e.g., Gulf Stream 551.4711

Class comprehensive works in 551.4701, waves in 551.4702, tides and tidal currents in 551.4708

.48   Hydrology

Class here hydrological cycle, limnology, water balance

Class water resources, interdisciplinary works on water in 553.7

For fumaroles, see 551.23; ground waters, 551.49; hydrometeorology, 551.57

.482   Lakes, ponds, freshwater lagoons

Class inland seas and salt lakes in 551.4609

.483   Rivers and streams

For waterfalls, see 551.484; floods, 551.489

.484   Waterfalls

.488   Runoff

.489   Floods

.49   Groundwater (Subsurface waters)

Class here aquifers

Thermal waters relocated to 551.23

.492   Water table

.498   Surface manifestations

Examples: springs, wells

.5   Meteorology

Class forecasting and forecasts of specific phenomena in 551.64, forecasts of specific phenomena in specific areas in 551.65, micrometeorology in 551.66

For climatology and weather, see 551.6

See Manual at 551.6 vs. 551.5

SUMMARY

551.51	**Composition, regions, mechanics of atmosphere**
.52	**Thermodynamics, temperatures, radiations**
.54	**Atmospheric pressure**
.55	**Atmospheric disturbances and formations**
.56	**Atmospheric electricity and optics**
.57	**Hydrometeorology**

[.501 12]   Forecasting and forecasts

Do not use; class in 551.63

.51   Composition, regions, mechanics of atmosphere

.511   Composition

Class here chemistry, photochemistry of atmosphere

.511 2   Gases

.511 3   Aerosols and dust

Class dust storms in 551.559, electricity of aerosols and dust 551.564

>   551.513–551.514 Regions

Class comprehensive works in 551.51; a specific aspect with the subject, e.g., upper-atmosphere pressures 551.547

.513   Troposphere

.514	Upper atmosphere
	Including magnetosphere, mesosphere
.514 2	Stratosphere
.514 5	Ionosphere
.515	Mechanics
.515 1	Kinematics
.515 2	Statics
.515 3	Dynamics

For circulation, see 551.517

.517	Circulation

For wind systems, see 551.518; atmospheric disturbances and formations, 551.55

.518	Wind systems

Class atmospheric disturbances and formations in 551.55

> 551.518 3–551.518 5 Systems in troposphere

Class comprehensive works in 551.518

.518 3	Planetary (General) systems

Examples: doldrums, horse latitudes, polar easterlies, trade winds, westerlies

Including jet streams

.518 4	Continental systems (Monsoons)
.518 5	Local systems

Examples: coast (land and sea), drainage (slope), mountain and valley winds

.518 7	Systems in upper atmosphere
.52	Thermodynamics, temperatures, radiations
.522	Thermodynamics

Class thermodynamics of microclimatology in 551.66

.523	Earth temperatures affecting atmosphere
.524	Water temperatures affecting atmosphere
.524 6	Oceans and seas

Add to base number 551.5246 the numbers following —16 in notation 163–167 from Table 2, e.g., temperatures of Indian Ocean 551.52465

.524 8	Lakes and rivers

.525	Temperatures
	Class here air temperatures
	For earth temperatures affecting atmosphere, see 551.523; water temperatures affecting atmosphere, 551.524
.525 09	Historical, geographical, persons treatment
	Class geographic distribution at earth's surface in 551.5252
.525 2	Geographic distribution at earth's surface
	Including urban heat islands
.525 3	Variations over time at earth's surface
	Examples: diurnal and annual variations, maximums, minimums, frosts
	Class comprehensive work on frost in 551.38
.525 4	Vertical distribution in troposphere
.525 7	Upper-atmosphere temperatures
.527	Radiations
	Absorption, emission, reflection, scattering, transmission
	Class optical phenomena in 551.565
.527 1	Solar radiations
.527 2	Terrestrial radiations
	For radiations originating in atmosphere, see 551.5273
.527 3	Radiations originating in atmosphere
.527 6	Cosmic and corpuscular radiations
.54	Atmospheric pressure
.540 9	Historical, geographical, persons treatment
	Class geographical distribution at earth's surface in 551.542
.542	Geographical distribution at earth's surface
.543	Variations over time at earth's surface
	Class variations in a specific area in 551.54209
.547	Upper-atmosphere pressures
.55	Atmospheric disturbances and formations
	Class here storms
	Class precipitation from storms in 551.577
	See also 363.3492 for storms as disasters
.551	Formations
.551 2	Air masses and fronts

.551 3		Cyclones

          See also 551.552 for hurricanes, 551.553 for tornadoes (both sometimes called cyclones)

.551 4		Anticyclones

>   551.552–551.559 Disturbances

     Class comprehensive works in 551.55

.552   Hurricanes

         Variant names: typhoons, cyclones (India), baguios, willy-willies

.553   Tornadoes

         Variant names: cyclones (Midwest United States), twisters

         Including waterspouts

.554   Thermal convective storms

         Examples: hailstorms, thunderstorms

         For tornadoes, see 551.553

.555   Snowstorms

         Example: blizzards

.557   Upper-atmosphere storms

.559   Other storms

         Examples: dust, ice storms

.56   Atmospheric electricity and optics

         Class magnetic phenomena in 538.7

.561   Electricity in stable atmosphere

         Including charge potential gradient, conductivity, ionization

.563   Atmospheric electricity

         For electricity in stable atmosphere, see 551.561; electricity of aerosols and dust, 551.564

.563 2   Lightning

         For ball lightning, see 551.5634

.563 3   Saint Elmo's fire

.563 4   Ball lightning

.564   Electricity of aerosols and dust

         Examples: electricity of snow, ice crystals, water droplets

.565	Atmospheric optics

Class here optical phenomena produced by refraction, e.g., mirages, scintillation, distortion of celestial bodies

For optical phenomena produced by absorption and scattering, see 551.566; optical phenomena produced by condensation products, see 551.567

.566	Optical phenomena produced by absorption and scattering

Examples: sky color, twilight, night skies

.567	Optical phenomena produced by condensation products

Examples: cloud colors, halos, rainbows

.568	Visibility
.57	Hydrometeorology
.571	Humidity
.571 09	Historical, geographical, persons treatment

Class geographical treatment in troposphere in 551.5712

.571 2	Geographical distribution in troposphere
.571 3	Variations over time in troposphere
.571 4	Vertical distribution in troposphere
.571 7	In upper atmosphere
.572	Evaporation and evapotranspiration
.574	Condensation of moisture
.574 1	Condensation processes

Examples: nucleation, formation of cloud particles

Class formation of fogs and mists in 551.575, of clouds in 551.576

.574 4	Condensations on earth's surface

Examples: dew, glaze, hoarfrost, rime

Class comprehensive work on frost in 551.38

.574 7	Condensations on objects in upper atmosphere

Examples: formation of hailstones

Class comprehensive works on hail in 551.5787

.575	Fogs and mists
.576	Clouds

.577 **Precipitation**

Class here liquid precipitation, rain, rainfall [*all formerly* 551.5781]

Class geologic work of precipitation in 551.35

For frozen precipitation, see 551.578

.577 09 Historical and persons treatment

Class geographical treatment in 551.5772

.577 1 Properties

Examples: composition, structure, temperature

.577 2 Geographical distribution

Add to base number 551.5772 notation 1–9 from Table 2, e.g., rainfall in Nigeria 551.5772669

Class distribution of variations over time in 551.5773

.577 3 Variations over time

Examples: droughts, maximums, minimums

See also 551.489 for floods

.577 5 Factors affecting precipitation

Examples: bodies of water, cities, topography, vegetation

.578 **Frozen precipitation**

[.578 1] Liquid precipitation, rain, rainfall

Relocated to 551.577

.578 4 Snow

.578 409 Historical and persons treatment

Class geographical treatment in 551.57842

.578 41–.578 43 Properties, geographical distribution, variations over time

Add to base number 551.5784 the numbers following 551.577 in 551.5771–551.5773, e.g., variations in snow and snowfall over time 551.57843

.578 46 Snow cover

For snow surveys, see 551.579

.578 461 Duration

.578 464 Ablation

.578 465 Firnification

.578 466 Stratification

.578 47	Snow formations

Examples: drifts, cornices

For avalanches, see 551.57848

.578 48	Avalanches
.578 7	Hail and graupel

Class here comprehensive works on hail

Class formation of hail in 551.5747

.579	Snow surveys

Add to base number 551.579 notation 1–9 from Table 2, e.g., snow surveys in Nevada 551.579793

.6	**Climatology and weather**

See Manual at 551.6 vs. 551.5

[.601 12]	Forecasting and forecasts

Do not use; class in 551.63

.609	Historical, geographical, persons treatment

Class geographical treatment of weather in 551.65, of climate in 551.69

.62	Weather belts and general types of climate

Class climate of specific areas in 551.69

.63	Weather forecasting and forecasts, reporting and reports

For forecasting and forecasts of specific phenomena, see 551.64

.630 9	Historical and persons treatment

Class geographical treatment in 551.65

.631	Historic methods of forecasting

Class here weather lore

.632	Reporting and reports

Class reports of specific weather phenomena in 551.5, reports of specific areas in 551.65

For instrumentation in reporting, see 551.635

.633	Statistical forecasting
.634	Numerical forecasting
.635	Instrumentation in reporting and forecasting
.635 2	Radiosondes
.635 3	Radar
.635 4	Weather satellites

.636	Short- and long-range forecasts

Class a specific aspect of short- and long-range forecasts with the aspect, e.g., satellites in long-range forecasts 551.6354

.636 2	Short-range

Forecasts for a maximum of three days

.636 5	Long-range

Forecasts more than three days in advance

.64	Forecasting and forecasts of specific phenomena

Class here methods of forecasting specific phenomena for specific areas

Add to base number 551.64 the numbers following 551.5 in 551.51–551.57, e.g., hurricane warnings 551.6452

Class forecasts of specific phenomena for specific areas in 551.65

See also 551.4890112 for flood forecasting and forecasts

.65	Weather forecasts and reports for specific areas

Class here forecasts of specific phenomena for specific areas

Add to base number 551.65 notation 1–9 from Table 2, e.g., forecasts for South Africa 551.6568

.66	Microclimatology

Climatology of small areas

Including water-atmosphere interactions

Class here earth-atmosphere interactions, micrometeorology, thermodynamics of microclimatology

Class specific topics in microclimatology other than thermodynamics in 551.5

.68	Artificial modification and control of weather

Add to base number 551.68 the numbers following 551.5 in 551.51–551.57, e.g., cloud seeding 551.6876

.69	Geographical treatment of climate

Class here paleoclimatology of specific areas

Add to base number 551.69 notation 1–9 from Table 2, e.g., climate of Australia 551.6994

Class general types of climate in 551.62, microclimatology of specific areas in 551.66

.7   **Historical geology**

Class here paleogeography, stratigraphy

Class history of a specific kind of geological phenomena with the kind of phenomena, e.g., history of Jurassic volcanism in Pacific Northwest 551.2109795, Devonian reefs 551.424, paleozoic orogeny 551.82

> *For paleontology, see 560*
>
> *See Manual at 551.7; 551.7 vs. 560*

.700 1–.700 8   Standard subdivisions

.700 9   Historical, geographical, persons treatment

> Class comprehensive works on historical geology of specific continents, countries, localities of modern world and of extraterrestrial worlds in 554–559; historic geology of specific continents, countries, localities during a specific period in 551.71–551.79

.701   Geologic time and age measurements

.71   Precambrian eras

> Variant name: Cryptozoic eon

.712   Archean era

> Variant names: Archeozoic, Lower Precambrian era

.715   Proterozoic era

> Variant names: Algonkian, Upper Precambrian eras

.72   Paleozoic era

> *For Ordovician and Silurian periods, see 551.73; Devonian period, 551.74; Carboniferous and Permian periods, 551.75*

.723   Cambrian period

.73   Ordovician and Silurian periods

.731   Ordovician period

> Former name: Lower Silurian epoch

.732   Silurian period

> Former name: Upper Silurian epoch

.74   Devonian period

.75   Carboniferous and Permian periods

>   551.751–551.752 Carboniferous periods
>
> Class comprehensive works in 551.75

.751   Mississippian (Lower Carboniferous) period

.752	Pennsylvanian (Upper Carboniferous) period
.756	Permian period
.76	Mesozoic era

> *For Cretaceous period, see 551.77*

.762	Triassic period
.766	Jurassic period
.77	Cretaceous period
.78	Cenozoic era Tertiary period

> *For Quaternary period, see 551.79*

.782	Paleogene period

> *For Paleocene epoch, see 551.783; Eocene epoch, 551.784; Oligocene epoch, 551.785*

.783	Paleocene epoch
.784	Eocene epoch
.785	Oligocene epoch
.786	Neogene (Neocene) period

> Class Quaternary period in 551.79

> *For Miocene epoch, see 551.787; Pliocene epoch, 551.788*

.787	Miocene epoch
.788	Pliocene epoch
.79	Quaternary period
.792	Pleistocene epoch (Ice age)
.793	Recent (Postglacial) epoch
.8	**Structural geology**

> Class here deformation [*formerly also* 551.14], diastrophism, epeirogeny, tectonics

> Class geomorphology in 551.41

> *For plate tectonics, see 551.136*

.81	Stratifications

> Class stratifications in specific areas in 554–559; of specific periods, of specific periods in specific areas in 551.7

.82	Orogeny

> Class here lateral compression of earth's crust, specific orogenies

> Class comprehensive works on elevations (e.g., mountains, plateaus, hills) in 551.43; a specific aspect of orogeny with the aspect, e.g., volcanism 551.21

.84   Joints and cleavages

.85   Dips, outcrops, strikes

.86   Synclines and antisynclines

.87   Faults, folds, dislocations

         Including nappes, rift valleys

.88   Intrusions

         Examples: bosses, dikes, laccoliths, necks, sills, veins

         Class volcanoes in 551.21

.9   **Geochemistry**

         Class here chemical principles of earth sciences [*formerly also* 550.154], of geology [*formerly also* 551.0154]

         Class chemistry of hydrosphere in 551.46, of atmosphere in 551.511; geochemistry of minerals in 549.13, of rocks in 552.06, of useful geological materials in 553.1

         For organic geochemistry, see 553.2

552   Petrology

         Class here petrography, lithology, rocks

         Class structural geology in 551.8, petrology of geologic materials of economic utility other than structural and sculptural stone in 553

         For mineralogy, see 549

         See Manual at 552 vs. 549

.001–.008   Standard subdivisions

.009   Historical, geographical, persons treatment

         Class geographical distribution of rocks in 552.09

.03   Petrogenesis

         Class here diagenesis

.06   Properties, composition, analysis, structure of rocks

         Class comprehensive works on geochemistry in 551.9

.09   Geographical distribution of rocks

         Add to base number 552.09 notation 1–9 from Table 2, e.g., rocks of Sahara Desert 552.0966

         Class rocks studied in their stratigraphic setting in 554–559

>   **552.1–552.5 Specific kinds of rocks**

         Class comprehensive works in 552

.1	**Igneous rocks**

For *volcanic products and rocks, see 552.2; plutonic rocks, 552.3*

.2	**Volcanic products and rocks**

Examples: volatiles; andesite, felsites, obsidian, rhyolite

.22	Lavas
.23	Pyroclastic rocks

Examples: pumice, tuff, volcanic ashes

.26	Basalts
.3	**Plutonic rocks**

Examples: diorites, dolerites, gabbros, granites, norites, peridotites, porphyries, syenites

.4	**Metamorphic rocks**

Examples: gneisses, marbles, quartzites, schists, serpentines, slates

.5	**Sedimentary rocks**

Examples: gypsum, sandstones, shales, tufa

Including clay, diatomaceous earth, sand, silt, soil

Class here comprehensive works on sedimentology

Glauconite relocated to 549.67

Class sedimentology as description of surface processes in 551.3

.58	Carbonate rocks

Examples: chalk, dolomites, limestones, oolites, serpentinites

.8	**Microscopic petrology**

Study of rocks in thin sections and fragments

553 Economic geology

Quantitative occurrence and distribution of geological materials of economic utility

Class here interdisciplinary works on nonmetallic materials

Class interdisciplinary works on metals in 669; economic aspects other than reserves of geological materials in 333.7; other specific aspects of nonmetallic materials with the aspect, e.g., prospecting 622.18

See Manual at 333.8 vs. 338.2, 553; 553

.029	Commercial miscellany [*formerly also* 380.142029, 381.42029, 382.42029]

SUMMARY

553.1	**Formation and structure of deposits**
.2	**Carbonaceous materials**
.3	**Iron**
.4	**Metals and semimetals**
.5	**Structural and sculptural stone**
.6	**Other economic materials**
.7	**Water**
.8	**Gems**
.9	**Inorganic gases**

.1   Formation and structure of deposits

Class formation and structure of deposits of specific materials in 553.2–553.9

.13   Placers

.14   Stratified layers and beds

.16   Pegmatite dikes

.19   Veins and lodes

>   **553.2–553.9 Specific materials**

Class comprehensive works in 553

.2   Carbonaceous materials

Class here fossil fuels, organic geochemistry

For diamonds, see 553.82

>   553.21–553.25 Coal

Class comprehensive works in 553.24

.21   Peat and peat coal

.22   Lignite, brown coal, jet

.23   Cannel coal

Bituminous shale relocated to 553.283

.24   Bituminous and semibituminous coal

Class here comprehensive works on coal

For peat and peat coal, see 553.21; lignite, brown coal, jet, 553.22; cannel coal, 553.23; anthracite and graphitic anthracite coal, 553.25

.25   Anthracite and graphitic anthracite coal

.26   Graphite

Variant names: black lead, plumbago

See also 553.25 for graphitic anthracite coal

.27   Solid and semisolid bitumens

> Examples: asphalt (pitch), asphaltite, ozokerite, pitch

> Class liquid bitumens in 553.282, rocks and sands impregnated with solid or semisolid bitumens in 553.283

.28   Oil, oil shales, tar sands, natural gas

> Class here petroleum geology

> Use 553.28 for petroleum in the broad sense covering oil and gas, 553.282 for petroleum in the narrow sense limited to oil

.282   Oil

> Oil shale relocated to 553.283

.283   Oil shale [*formerly* 553.282] and tar sands

> Variant names for oil shale: bituminous shale [*formerly* 553.23], black shale; for tar sands: bituminous sands, oil sands

.285   Natural gas

.29   Fossil gums and resins

> Example: amber

.3   Iron

.4   Metals and semimetals

> *For iron, see 553.3*

.41   Gold

.42   Precious metals

> *For gold, see 553.41*

.421   Silver

.422   Platinum

.43   Copper

.44   Lead

.45   Zinc, tin, mercury

.452   Zinc

.453   Tin

.454   Mercury

.46   Metals used in ferroalloys

> *For nickel and cobalt, see 553.48*

.462   Titanium, vanadium, manganese

.462 3   Titanium

.462 6	Vanadium
.462 9	Manganese
.464	Chromium, molybdenum, tungsten
.464 3	Chromium
.464 6	Molybdenum
.464 9	Tungsten
.465	Zirconium and tantalum
.47	Antimony, arsenic, bismuth
.48	Cobalt and nickel
.483	Cobalt
.485	Nickel
.49	Other metals
.492	Light metals
.492 3	Beryllium
.492 6	Aluminum
.492 9	Magnesium
.493	Fissionable metals

Contains radium, thorium

.493 2	Uranium
.494	Rare-earth metals

Class here lanthanide series

.494 2	Scandium
.494 3	Cerium group

Contains cerium, europium, lanthanum, neodymium, praseodymium, promethium, samarium

.494 7	Yttrium group

Contains yttrium, dysprosium, erbium, gadolinium, holmium, lutetium, terbium, thulium, ytterbium

.495	Platinum group

Contains iridium, osmium, palladium, rhodium, ruthenium

For platinum, see 553.422

.499	Miscellaneous rare metals

Contains barium, cadmium, calcium, cesium, gallium, germanium, hafnium, indium, lithium, niobium, potassium, rhenium, rubidium, selenium, sodium, strontium, tellurium, thallium

.5   **Structural and sculptural stone**

> Class petrology of structural and sculptural stone in 552, semiprecious sculptural stone in 553.87

.51   Marbles and limestones

.512   Marbles

> *For verd antique and onyx marbles, see 553.55*

.516   Limestones

> Including dolomites, travertines

.52   Granites and syenites

.53   Sandstones

> Examples: bluestones, flagstones

.54   Slates

.55   Serpentines, soapstones, and their variants

> Including verd antique and onyx marbles
>
> Onyx relocated to 553.87

.6   **Other economic materials [*formerly* 553.9]**

> Example: diatomaceous earths
>
> Class here earthy materials, industrial minerals
>
> Soils relocated to 631.4

.61   Clays

> Examples: bentonite, diaspore clay, kaolin
>
> Including fuller's earth
>
> Class here comprehensive works on ceramic materials
>
> Class specific nonclay ceramic material with the material, e.g., glass sands 553.622
>
> *For fireclays, see 553.67*

.62   Sands and gravels

> Class here aggregates

.622   Sands

> Including glass sands

.626   Gravels

.63   Salts

> *For niter, soda niter, see 553.64; mineral waters, 553.73*

.632   Rock salt (Sodium chloride)

.633	Borates

Example: borax

.635	Gypsum

Including alabaster

.636	Potash salts

Class here potassium compounds

.64	Nitrates and phosphates

Examples: apatites, niter (saltpeter), soda niter (Chile saltpeter)

Class here mineral fertilizers

.65	Abrasive materials

Examples: carbonado, corundum, emery, flint, garnet, industrial diamonds, pumice

Class comprehensive works on diamonds in 553.82

For sands, see 553.622

.66	Pigment materials and sulfur
.662	Pigment materials

Examples: barite (heavy spar), ochers, rutile, sienna, umber

.668	Sulfur
.67	Refractory materials

Examples: alumina, fire clays, zirconia

For soapstones, see 553.55

.672	Asbestos
.674	Mica
.676	Talc
.678	Vermiculite
.68	Cementing materials

Examples: calcites, cements, chalks, limes, marls

For gypsum, see 553.635

.7	**Water**

Including ice

Thermal waters relocated to 333.88

Class interdisciplinary works on ice in 551.31

See Manual at 363.1

.72	Saline waters

| .73 | Mineral waters |

.73   Mineral waters

For saline waters, see 553.72

.78   Surface waters

.79   Groundwaters (Subsurface waters)

.8   Gems

>   553.82–553.86 Precious stones

Class comprehensive works in 553.8

.82   Diamonds

Class here comprehensive works on diamonds

For industrial diamonds, see 553.65

.84   Rubies and sapphires

.86   Emeralds

.87   Semiprecious stones

Examples: onyx [*formerly also* 553.55], amethysts, garnets, jade, opals, tanzanite

.9   Inorganic gases

Other economic materials relocated to 553.6

.92   Hydrogen

.93   Nitrogen

.94   Oxygen

.95   Chlorine and fluorine

.97   Noble gases

Variant name: inert, rare gases

Contains argon, helium, krypton, neon, radon, xenon

> ### 554–559 Earth sciences by continent, country, locality in modern world; extraterrestrial worlds

> Class here geology and geological surveys by continent, country, locality in modern world; extraterrestrial worlds

> Add to base number 55 notation 4–9 from Table 2, e.g., geology of Japan 555.2, of moon 559.91

> Class comprehensive works on earth sciences in 550, on geology in 551; geological surveys of specific areas emphasizing materials of economic importance in 553; a specific geological topic (other than historic geology taken as a whole) in a specific area with the topic, e.g., geomorphology of Japan 551.410952, Permian geology in Japan 551.7560952

554   *Earth sciences of Europe

555   *Earth sciences of Asia

556   *Earth sciences of Africa

557   *Earth sciences of North America

558   *Earth sciences of South America

559   *Earth sciences of other parts of world and of extraterrestrial worlds

> *See Manual at 559.9*

560   Paleontology   Paleozoology

> Use 560 for any organism of uncertain status as plant or animal, e.g., acritarchs; and for animals of unknown taxonomic position. However, class conodonts in 562.2

> Class the analysis of paleontological evidence to determine geological time and age in 551.701 or with the specific age in 551.71–551.79

> *See Manual at 551.7 vs. 560; 560 vs. 575*

SUMMARY

560.1–.9	Standard subdivisions, stratigraphic paleontology, paleoecology
561	Paleobotany
562	Fossil invertebrates
563	Fossil Protozoa, Parazoa, Coelenterata, Echinodermata, related phyla
564	Fossil Mollusca and Molluscoidea
565	Other fossil invertebrates
566	Fossil Vertebrata (Fossil Craniata)
567	Fossil cold-blooded vertebrates Fossil Pisces (Fossil fishes)
568	Fossil Aves (Fossil birds)
569	Fossil Mammalia

*Add as instructed under 554–559

.1	**Philosophy and theory; stratigraphic paleontology**
.17	Stratigraphic paleontology, paleobotany, paleozoology

     Class specific fossils or groups of fossils in 561–569

.171	Archeozoic and Proterozoic (Precambrian) paleontology
.172	Paleozoic paleontology
.172 3	Cambrian period
.172 4	Ordovician period
.172 5	Silurian period
.172 6	Devonian period
.172 7	Mississippian period

     Class here Carboniferous periods

     For Pennsylvanian period, see 560.1728

.172 8	Pennsylvanian period
.172 9	Permian period
.176	Mesozoic paleontology
.176 2	Triassic period
.176 4	Jurassic period
.176 6	Cretaceous period
.178	Cenozoic paleontology

     Contains paleontology of Tertiary and Quaternary periods

.4	**Special topics**
.45	Paleoecology Zoological paleoecology
.9	**Historical, geographical, persons treatment of paleontology, of paleozoology, of fossils**

     Class stratigraphic paleontology and paleozoology in 560.17

.901–.905	Historical periods
.909–.999	Geographical treatment

     Add to base number 560.9 the numbers following 574.9 in 574.909–574.999, e.g., cave fossils 560.90944

     Use 560.9 for persons treatment

561   Paleobotany

     Use 561 for plantlike fossils of uncertain taxonomic position; however class fernlike fossils of uncertain taxonomic position in 561.597

     Class stratigraphic paleobotany in 560.17

SUMMARY

561.01–.09   **Standard subdivisions**
     .1   **General topics**
     .2   **Fossil Spermatophyta**
     .3   **Fossil Dicotyledones**
     .4   **Fossil Monocotyledones**
     .5   **Fossil Gymnospermae and fernlike fossils of uncertain taxonomic position**
     .6   **Fossil Cryptogamia**
     .7   **Fossil Pteridophyta**
     .8   **Fossil Bryophyta**
     .9   **Fossil Thallobionta (Thallophyta) and Prokaryotae**

.09   Historical, geographical, persons treatment

>   Class geographical treatment of fossil plants in 561.19

.1   **General topics**

>   Including botanical paleoecology

>   Class general topics of specific plants and groups of plants in 561.2–561.9

.13   Fossil pollen and spores

>   Class here paleopalynology

.14   Fossil fruit and seeds

.19   Geographical treatment of fossil plants

>   Add to base number 561.19 the numbers following 574.9 in
>   574.909–574.999, e.g., freshwater fossil plants 561.1929

>   **561.2–561.9 Specific plants and groups of plants**

>   Class comprehensive works in 561

.2   **Fossil Spermatophyta**

>   *For Angiospermae, see 561.3–561.4; Gymnospermae, 561.5*

.21   Trees and petrified wood

>   Class specific trees in 561.3–561.5

>   **561.3–561.4 Fossil Angiospermae**

>   Class comprehensive works in 561.2

.3   **Fossil Dicotyledones**

.4   **Fossil Monocotyledones**

.45   Pamales

>   Contains Arecaceae (palms)

.49   Graminales

Class here grasses

.5   Fossil Gymnospermae and fernlike fossils of uncertain taxonomic position

.51   Gneticae

.52   Coniferales (Conifers) and Taxales (yews)

Examples: Araucariaceae, Cephalotaxaceae, Cupressaceae, Pinaceae, Podocarpaceae, Taxodiaceae

.55   Cordaitales

Contains Cordaiteae, Pityeae (Callixylon), Poroxyleae

.57   Ginkgoales

.59   Cycadales, Cycadeoidales, Pteridospermae, fernlike fossils of uncertain taxonomic position

.591   Cycadales (True cycads)

.592   Cycadeoidales (Bennettitales)

Contains Cycadeoidaceae, Williamsoniaceae

.595   Pteridospermae (Seed ferns)

Contains Calamopityaceae, Lyginopteridaceae, Medullosaceae

.597   Fernlike fossils of uncertain taxonomic position

Examples: Alethopteris, Alliopteris, Archaeopteris, Callipteris, Cyclopteris, Glossopteris, Linopteris, Mariopteris, Megalopteris, Neuropteris, Odontopteris, Pecopteris, Rhacopteris, Sphenopteris, Taeniopteris

.6   Fossil Cryptogamia

For Pteridophyta, see 561.7; Bryophyta, 561.8; Thallophyta, 561.9

.7   Fossil Pteridophyta

Class fernlike fossils of uncertain taxonomic position in 561.597

.71   Isoetales

.72   Sphenopsida

Contains Calamitales, Equisetales, Hyeniales, Pseudoborniales, Sphenophyllales

.73   Polypodiorsida (Filicineae)

Examples: Coenopteridales, Filicales, Marattiales, Ophioglossales

.74   Psilopsida

Examples: Psilophytales, Psilotales

.79   Lycopsida (Club mosses)

Contains Lepidodendrales, Lycopodiales, Pleuromeiales, Protolepidodendrales, Selaginellales

For Isoetales, see 561.71

.8   **Fossil Bryophyta**

.9   **Fossil Thallobionta (Thallophyta) and Prokaryotae**

.92   Fungi

.93   Algae

> ## 562–569 Specific animals and groups of animals

Class here taxonomic paleozoology

Class comprehensive works in 560

562   Fossil invertebrates

Including animal plankton and neuston

For fossil Protozoa and other simple fossil animals, see 563; fossil Mollusca and molluscoidea, 564; other fossil invertebrates, 565

.2   **Conodonts**

563   Fossil Protozoa, Parazoa, Coelenterata, Echinodermata, related phyla

SUMMARY

563.1	Protozoa	Plasmodroma
.4	Parazoa	Porifera (Sponges)
.5	Coelenterata (Cnidaria)	
.6	Anthozoa	
.7	Hydrozoa and related orders	
.8	Ctenophorae	
.9	Echinodermata, Linguatula, Hemichordata	

.1   **Protozoa**   **Plasmodroma**

.12   Foraminifera

.14   Radiolaria

.17   Ciliophora (Ciliata)

.18   Mastigophora

.4   **Parazoa**   **Porifera (Sponges)**

Contains Calcispongiae (Calcarea), Demospongiae, Hyalospongiae (Hexactinellida)

.47   Archaeocyatha

Cambrian fossils with characteristics of sponges and corals

.5   Coelenterata (Cnidaria)

For Anthozoa, see 563.6; Hydrozoa and related orders, 563.7

.6   Anthozoa

Class here corals

For Archaeocyatha, see 563.47

.7   Hydrozoa and related orders

.71   Hydrozoa

Contains Graptolitoidea, Hydroida, Milleporina, Siphonophora, Stylasterina

.73   Scyphozoa

Examples: Conulariida, Protomedusae

.78   Stromatoporoidea

.8   Ctenophora

.9   Echinodermata, Linguatula, Hemichordata

>   563.91–563.97 Echinodermata

Class comprehensive works in 563.9

.91   Crinoidea

Contains Adunata, Articulata, Camerata, Inadunata

.92   Blastoidea

.93   Asteroidea (Starfish)

Examples: Forcipulatida, Phanerozonida, Spinulosida

.94   Ophiuroidea

Examples: Ophiurida, Phrynophiurida, Stenurida

.95   Echinoidea

Contains Euechinoidea, Perischoechinoidea

.96   Holothurioidea

Example: Arthrochirotida

.97   Cystoidea

.99   Linguatula and Enteropneusta

.992   Linguatula (Pentastomida)

.993   Hemichordata

Contains Enteropneusta, Planctosphaeroidea

For Pterobranchia, see 564.7

564   Fossil Mollusca and Molluscoidea

Example: Apolacophora

> **564.1–564.5 Mollusca (Mollusks)**

Class comprehensive works in 564

.1   Bivalvia and Amphineura

.11   Bivalvia (Pelecypoda)

Examples: Mytiloida, Unionidae

Class here Lamellibranchia

.19   Amphineura (Polyplacophora)

Use of this number for Aplacophora discontinued; class in 564

.2   Scaphopoda

.3   Gastropoda

.32   Streptoneura (Prosobranchia)

Contains Archeogastropoda, Mesogastropoda, Neogastropoda

.35   Pteropoda and Sacoglossa

.36   Acoelea

Contains Notaspidea, Nudibranchia

.37   Tectibranchia (Anapsidea)

.38   Pulmonata

Contains Basommatophora, Stylommatophora, Systellommatophora

.5   Cephalopoda

.52   Nautiloidea

.53   Ammonitoidea

.55   Vampyromorpha

.56   Octopoda

.58   Decapoda

.6   Molluscoidea

For Bryozoa, see 564.7; Brachiopoda, 564.8; Entoprocta, Phoronidea, 565.1

.7   **Bryozoa and Pterobranchia**

.8   **Brachiopoda (Lamp shells)**

565   Other fossil invertebrates

SUMMARY

565.1   Worms and related animals
.2   Arthropoda
.3   Crustacea, Chelicerata, Trilobita
.4   Arachnida
.5   Onychophora
.6   Progoneata
.7   Insecta

.1   **Worms and related animals**

Contains Acanthocephala, Annelida, Aschelminthes, Chaetognatha, Entoprocta, Gastrotricha, Gephyrea, Nemertea (Rhynchocoela), Phoronidea, Platyhelminthes, Tardigrada

.2   **Arthropoda**

For Crustacea, Chelicerata, Trilobita, see 565.3; Progoneata, 565.6

.3   **Crustacea, Chelicerata, Trilobita**

.31   Branchiura, Cephalocarida, Mystacocarida

.32   Branchiopoda

Contains Anostraca, Cladocera, Conchostraca, Lipostraca, Notostraca

.33   Ostracoda

Contains Cladocopa, Myodocopa, Platycopa, Podocopa

.34   Copepoda

Contains Arguloida, Calanoida, Caligoida, Cyclopoida, Harpacticoida, Lernaeopodoida, Monstrilloida, Notodelphyoida

.35   Cirripedia (Barnacles)

Contains Acrothoracica, Ascothoracica, Rhizocephala, Thoracica

.36   Phyllocarida

Contains Archaeostraca, Hymenostraca, Leptostraca

.37   Eumalacostraca

Examples: Amphipoda, Isopoda, Pancarida (Thermosbaenacea), Syncarida, Tanaidacea

Class here Malacostraca, Peracarida

For Phyllocarida, see 565.36; Cumacea, Eucarida, Hoplocarida, Mysidacea, 565.38

.38	Cumacea, Eucarida, Hoplocarida, Mysidacea

Examples: Decapoda, Euphausiacea, Stomatopoda

.39	Chelicerata and Trilobita

For Arachnida, see 565.4

.391	Eurypterida and Synxiphosura
.392	Xiphosura (Horseshoe crabs)
.393	Trilobita
.394	Pycnogonida
.4	**Arachnida**

Contains Acari, Araneida (Araneae), Palpigradi, Pedipalpi, Phalangida (Opilionea), Pseudoscorpiones, Ricinulei, Scorpiones, Solifugae

.49	Architarbi
.5	**Onychophora**

Class here Oncopods (Pararthropoda)

For Linguatula (Pentastomida), see 563.992; Tardigrada, 565.1

.6	**Progoneata**

Class here Myriapoda

For Insecta, see 565.7

.61	Diplopoda (Millipedes)
.62	Chilopoda (Centipedes)

Class here Opisthogoneata

.63	Symphyla
.64	Pauropoda
.7	**Insecta**

Class here Hexapoda, Pterygota

.71	Apterygota

Contains Collembola, Diplura (Entotrophi), Protura, Thysanura

.72	Orthoptera and related orders

Contains Blatteria (cockroaches), Dermaptera, Mantodea, Phasmatodea

.73	Thysanoptera and miscellaneous orders

Contains Embioptera, Ephemeroptera (Plecoptera), Isoptera, Odonata, Plecoptera, Psocoptera (Corrodentia), Zoraptera

.74	Mecoptera, Neuroptera, Strepsiptera, Trichoptera

.75   Apterous insects (Anoplura and Mallophaga), Hemiptera (Heteroptera), Homoptera

.76   Coleoptera (Beetles)

Class here Polyphaga

.77   Diptera and Siphonaptera

.78   Lepidoptera

.79   Hymenoptera

566   Fossil Vertebrata (Fossil Craniata)

Examples: Cephalochordata, Urochordata (Tunicata)

Class here Chordata

For fossil cold-blooded vertebrates, see 567; fossil Aves, 568; fossil Mammalia, 569

567   Fossil cold-blooded vertebrates   Fossil Pisces (Fossil fishes)

.2   **Agnatha, Acanthodii, Placodermi**

Example: Cyclostomata

.3   **Chondrichthyes**

Contains Bradyodonti, Cladoselachii, Holocephali, Pleuracanthodii, Rajiformes (Batoidea), Squaliformes (sharks)

.4   **Chondrostei, Holostei, Sarcopterygii**

Examples: Acipenseriformes, Amiiformes, Crossopterygii, Dipnoi, Palaeonisciformes, Pholidophoriformes, Polypteriformes, Pycnodontiformes, Semionotiformes

Class here Ganoidei

Class comprehensive works on Actinopterygii in 567.5

.5   **Teleostei**

Contains Acanthopterygii, Clupeomorpha, Elopomorpha, Leptolepidimorpha, Ostariophysi, Osteoglossiomorpha, Paracanthopterygii, Protacanthopterygii, Scopelomorpha

Class here Actinopterygii, Osteichthyes

For Chondrostei, Holostei, see 567.4

.6   **Amphibia**

Contains Caudata (Urodela), Labyrinthodontia, Lepospondyli

For Gymnophiona, see 567.7; Anura, 567.8

.7   **Gymnophiona (Apoda, Caecilians)**

.8   **Anura (Salentia)**

Examples: Bufonoidea, Discoglossidea, Lepiopelmatidae, Pelobatoidea, Pipoidea, Proanura, Ranoidea

.9   **Reptilia**

Class here Diapsida

.91   Dinosaurs

Use 567.91 for dinosaurs in the broad sense, covering many or all extinct reptiles; use 567.97 for dinosaurs in the narrow sense, restricted to Ornithischia and Saurischia

.92   Anapsida

Contains Cotylosauria, Testudines (Chelonia)

For Mesosauria, see 567.93

.93   Euryapsida, Synapsida; Mesosauria

Contains Araeoscelidia (Thalattosauria), Ichthyosauria, Placodontia, Sauropterygia; Pelycosauria Therapsidia (Thermomorpha)

.94   Lepidosauria

Contains Eosuchia, Squamata

Use of this number for Diapsida discontinued; class in 567.9

For Sauria, see 567.95; Serpentes, 567.96

.945   Rhynchocephalia

.95   Sauria

.96   Serpentes

.97   Archosauria

Contains Ornithischia, Pterosauria (pterodactyls), Saurischia, Thecodontia

Use 567.97 for dinosaurs in the narrow sense, restricted to Ornithischia and Saurischia; use 567.91 for dinosaurs in the broad sense, covering many or all extinct reptiles

For Crocodilia, see 567.98

.98   Crocodilia

568   **Fossil Aves (Fossil birds)**

Class here Neornithes

.2   **Archaeornithes, Hesperornithiformes, Ichthyornithiformes**

.22   Archaeornithes

.23   Hesperornithiformes and Ichthyornithiformes

.3   **Charadriiformes, Ciconiiformes, Diatrymiformes, Gruiformes**

.4   **Anseriformes and other water birds**

Examples: Gaviiformes, Pelecaniformes, Podicipediformes (Colymbiformes), Procellariiformes, Sphenisciformes

.5   **Palaeognathae**

Class here ratites

Contains Aepyornithiformes, Apterygiformes, Caenagnathiformes, Casuariiformes, Dinornithiformes, Rheiformes, Struthioniformes, Tinamiformes

.6   **Galliformes and Columbiformes**

.7   **Psittaciformes, Piciformes, Trogoniformes, Cuculiformes, Coliiformes**

.8   **Passeriformes, Coraciiformes, Apodiformes**

.9   **Falconiformes, Strigiformes, Caprimulgiformes**

569   **Fossil Mammalia**

.1   **Monotremata, Allotheria, Pantotheria**

.12   Monotremata

Class here Prototheria

.17   Allotheria

Contains Multituberculata, Triconodonta

.18   Pantotheria

Example: Symmetrodonta

.2   **Marsupialia**

.3   **Unguiculata**

For Chiroptera, see 569.4; Primates, 569.8

.31   Edentata and Pholidota

Class here Palaeanodonta

.32   Glires

.322   Lagomorpha

.323   Rodentia

.33   Insectivora

.34   Dermoptera

.35   Tillodontia

.36   Taeniodontia

.4   **Chiroptera (Bats)**

Contains Megachiroptera, Microchiroptera

.5   Cetacea and Sirenia

Contains Archaeoceti, Desmostyliformes, Mysticeti, Odontoceti, Trichechiformes

Class here marine mammals, whales

For Pinnipedia, see 569.74

.6   Paenungulata

Contains Dinocerata, Embrithopoda, Hyracoidea, Pantodonta, Proboscidea, Pyrotheria

For Sirenia, see 569.5

.7   Ferungulata and Protungulata

For Paenungulata, see 569.6

.72   Perissodactyla

Contains Ceratomorpha, Hippomorpha

.73   Artiodactyla

Contains Ruminantia, Suiformes, Tylopoda

.74   Carnivora .

Contains Credonta, Fissipeda, Pinnipedia

.75   Protungulata

Contains Astrapotheria, Condylarthra, Litopterna, Notoungulata, Tubulidentata

.8   Primates

Contains Anthropoidea, Prosimii

For Hominidae, see 569.9

.9   Hominidae (Humankind and forebears)

Use 573.3 for any remains assigned to the genus *Homo* by any reputable authority, 569.9 for remains clearly of a different genus

For prehistoric man, see 573.3

570   Life sciences

Use 570 by itself only for works including substantial treatment of paleontology; use 574 for general biology

For paleontology, see 560

SUMMARY

572	Human races
573	Physical anthropology
574	Biology
575	Evolution and genetics
576	Microbiology
577	General nature of life
578	Microscopy in biology
579	Collection and preservation of biological specimens

[571]   [Unassigned]

Most recently used in Edition 16

572   Human races

Class here physical ethnology

Ethnology, cultural ethnology, ethnography relocated to 305.8

.09   Historical, geographical, persons treatment

Class origins of races in 572.2, geographical distribution of races in 572.9

.2   Origins and physical characteristics of races

Class origins and physical characteristics of specific races in 572.8, of extinct races in 573.3

For causes of physical differences, see 572.3

See also 573 for nonracial physical characteristics

.3   Causes of physical differences

.8   Specific races

Add to base number 572.8 notation 03–9 from Table 5, e.g., Celtic race 572.8916

Class extinct races in 573.3

.9   Geographical distribution of races

Add to base number 572.9 notation 1–9 from Table 2, e.g., races of Asia 572.95

Class specific races in a specific place in 572.8

573   Physical anthropology

Class here human biological ecology

Class comprehensive works on human ecology in 304.2; on Hominidae, on living humankind in 599.9

For human races, see 572

.2   Evolution and genetics of humankind

Add to base number 573.2 the numbers following 575 in 575.1–575.2, e.g., mutations 573.2292

See Manual at 573.2

.3   Prehistoric humankind

Examples: Cro-Magnon, Heidelberg, Java, Neanderthal, Peking, Rhodesian man

Including Piltdown man hoax [*formerly also* 001.95], Pithecanthropus (*Homo*) erectus

Class here extinct races, fossils assigned to genus *Homo*

Class comprehensive works on fossil Hominidae in 569.9, progenitors of contemporary races in 572.2

.4   Environmental effects on physique

.5   Pigmentation

.6   Anthropometry

Add to base number 573.6 the numbers following 611 in 611.1–611.9, e.g., comparative studies of bones 573.671; however, class craniology in 573.7

For abnormal dimensions and physique, see 573.8

See Manual at 573.6 vs. 611

.7   Craniology

.8   Abnormal dimensions and physique

Examples: dwarfs, midgets, giants

Class pathological aspects of abnormal dimensions in 616.043

574   Biology

Studies of a particular process or system associated with a specific kind of plant or animal are classed with the kind, not with the process, e.g., genetics of peas 583.322 (*not* 575.1 or 581.15)

Class microscopy in biology regardless of kind of organism in 578, collection and preservation of biological specimens regardless of kind of organism in 579

For evolution, see 575; microbiology, 576; botanical sciences, 580; zoological sciences, 590

See Manual at 508 vs. 574, 910, 304.2

SUMMARY

574.01–.09	**Standard subdivisions**
.1	**Physiology**
.2	**Pathology**
.3	**Development and maturation**
.4	**Anatomy and morphology**
.5	**Ecology**
.6	**Economic biology**
.8	**Tissue, cellular, molecular biology**
.9	**Geographical treatment of organisms**

.01   Philosophy and theory

> Class general nature of life in 577

.015 195   Statistical mathematics

> Class here biometrics, biostatistics [*both formerly* 574.072]
>
> *See Manual at 519.5, T1—015195 vs. 001.422, T1—072*

.072   Research

> Biometrics and biostatistics relocated to 574.015195

.072 4   Experimental biology

> Including tissue and organ culture

.075   Museum activities and services

> Class collection and preservation of biological specimens in 579

.09   Historical, geographical, persons treatment

> Class geographical treatment of organisms in 574.9

.1   **Physiology**

> Including physiology of integument
>
> Class here comprehensive works on anatomy, morphology, physiology

> *For pathological physiology, see 574.21; development and maturation, 574.3; anatomy and morphology, 574.4; tissue biology, 574.82; cell physiology and pathology, 574.876; genetics, 575.1*

SUMMARY

574.104	**[Regional physiology]**
.11	**Circulation**
.12	**Respiration**
.13	**Nutrition and metabolism**
.14	**Secretion and excretion**
.16	**Reproduction**
.17	**Histogenesis**
.18	**Movements and control processes**
.19	**Biophysics and biochemistry**

.104   Special topics

.104 2   Regional physiology

.11	Circulation
.113	Circulatory fluids
.116	Circulatory organs
.12	Respiration
.121	Aerobic respiration
.124	Intercellular respiration
.128	Anaerobic respiration
.13	Nutrition and metabolism
.132	Ingestion and digestion
.133	Metabolism

        Anabolism and catabolism

        Class metabolism of specific chemicals in 574.192

        Including assimilation and food storage

.14	Secretion and excretion
.16	Reproduction
.162	Parthenogenesis

        Class here asexual reproduction

           For vegetative reproduction, see 574.165

.163	Alternation of generations (Metagenesis)
.165	Vegetative reproduction
.166	Sexual reproduction

           For alternation of generations, see 574.163

.166 2	Conjugation
.166 7	Hermaphroditism
.17	Histogenesis

        Class cell differentiation in 574.87612

.18	Movements and control processes

        Class here locomotion

.188	Control processes

        Including homeostasis, physiological balance, response to stimuli

        Class control of a specific function with the subject, e.g., control of respiration 574.12

.188 2	Biological rhythms and chronobiology

.19 Biophysics and biochemistry

Class physics and chemistry of a specific process or part of living organisms with the process or part, e.g., physics of respiration 574.12, chemistry of nuclei 574.8732

SUMMARY

574.191	**Biophysics**
.192	**Biochemistry**

.191 Biophysics

Physical phenomena in organisms, effects of physical agents on organisms

.191 2 Physical phenomena in organisms

.191 21 Bioenergetics

.191 25 Bioluminescence

.191 27 Bioelectricity (Electrophysiology)

> 574.191 3–574.191 7 Effects of external forces

Class comprehensive works in 574.191, pathological effects in 574.24

.191 3 Effects of mechanical forces

.191 32 Gravitational forces

.191 34 Acceleration and deceleration

.191 35 Pressure

[.191 36] Impact

Number discontinued; class in 574.1913

.191 4 Effects of sound and related vibrations

.191 42 Subsonic vibrations

.191 43 Sound

.191 45 Ultrasonic vibrations

.191 5 Effects of radiations (Radiobiology)

.191 51 Radio waves and microwaves

.191 52 Infrared radiation

.191 53 Visible light

.191 54 Ultraviolet radiation

.191 55 X rays

.191 56	Particle radiations

Examples: beta, gamma, neutron radiations

Class cosmic rays in 574.19157

.191 57	Cosmic rays
.191 6	Effects of thermal forces (Thermobiology)
.191 62	High temperatures
.191 65	Low temperatures

For cryogenic temperatures, see 574.19167

.191 67	Cryogenic temperatures (Cryobiology)
.191 7	Effects of electricity and magnetism
.191 9	Extraterrestrial biophysics

Class here bioastronautics

Add to base number 574.1919 the numbers following 574.191 in 574.1913–574.1917, e.g., gravitational forces 574.191932

.192	Biochemistry

Class here interdisciplinary works on biochemicals, on macromolecular biochemicals

Class biochemicals not considered in their biological context in 547, macromolecular biochemicals not considered in their biochemical context in 547.7, industrial biochemistry in 660.63

.192 01	Philosophy and theory

Class theoretical biochemistry in 574.19282

.192 028	Auxiliary techniques and procedures; apparatus, equipment, materials

Class analytical biochemistry in 574.19285

>   574.192 1–574.192 7 Constituents of living matter

Class comprehensive works in 574.192

For biosynthesis, see 574.1929

.192 1	Fluids, pigments, inorganic constituents
.192 12	Fluids

Example: water

.192 14	Inorganic constituents

Examples: minerals

Class inorganic fluids in 574.19212, inorganic pigments in 574.19218

.192 18	Pigments

.192 4	Organic compounds

Add to base number 574.1924 the numbers following 547.7 in 547.72–547.78, e.g., phospholipids 574.19247; however, class enzymes in 574.1925, vitamins in 574.1926, hormones in 574.1927

Class organic fluids in 574.19212, organic pigments in 574.19218

.192 5	Enzymes

Examples: hydrolases, transferases

Class here coenzymes, cofactors

.192 53	Lipolytic enzymes

Examples: esterases, lipases, phosphatases

.192 54	Saccharolytic enzymes

Examples: carbohydrases, amylases, cellulases, maltases, emulsins

.192 56	Proteolytic enzymes

Example: proteases

.192 58	Oxidoreductases

Oxidizing and reducing enzymes

Examples: catalases, dehydrogenases, oxidases, zymases

.192 6	Vitamins
.192 7	Hormones
.192 8	Physical, theoretical, analytical biochemistry

Class physical, theoretical, analytical biochemistry of specific constituents in 574.1921–574.1927

.192 82	Theoretical biochemistry
.192 83	Physical biochemistry

For biosynthesis, see 574.1929

.192 85	Analytical biochemistry
.192 9	Biosynthesis
.192 93	Lipids
.192 94	Carbohydrates
.192 96	Proteins
.192 97	Pigments

.2 **Pathology**

Class here pathogenicity, degeneration, death

For histopathology, see 574.828; cytopathology, 574.8765

.21 Pathological physiology

Class here comprehensive works on pathological physiology, anatomy, morphology

Add to base number 574.21 the numbers following 574.1 in 574.11–574.19, e.g., nutritional diseases 574.213

For pathological anatomy and morphology, see 574.22

.22 Pathological anatomy and morphology

Class here teratology

Add to base number 574.22 the numbers following 574.4 in 574.41–574.47, e.g., deformities of circulatory organs 574.221

.23 Diseases induced by living organisms

Class diseases of specific systems and organs in 574.21

.232 Diseases due to parasitic plants

.232 2 Bacterial diseases

.232 6 Fungal diseases

.233 Diseases due to parasitic animals

.234 Viral and rickettsial diseases

.24 Diseases and injuries caused by physical and chemical factors

Examples: weather, radiations, pollution

Class diseases and injuries of specific systems and organs in 574.21

See Manual at 574.5222 vs. 574.24, 363.73

.29 Immunity

Class here autoimmunity, immunology, immunogenetics, cell-mediated immunity

See Manual at 591.29 vs. 616.079

.292 Antigens

.293 Antibodies

.295 Immune reactions

Examples: agglutination, complement fixation, neutralization, precipitation

.3 **Development and maturation**

For histogenesis, see 574.17

.31 Growth and regeneration

.32	Gametogenesis

Including haploid cells, germ cells, sex cells

Class here meiosis

.33	Embryology
.332	Embryological anatomy

Including morphogenesis

.333	Embryological physiology

Class here comprehensive works on embryological physiology and anatomy

For anatomy, see 574.332

.334	Developmental stages
.36	Sex differentiation

For gametogenesis, see 574.32

.37	Aging and longevity
.372	Aging
.374	Longevity

Including rejuvenation

.4	**Anatomy and morphology**

For pathological anatomy, see 574.22; embryological anatomy, 574.332

.41	Circulatory organs
.42	Respiratory organs
.43	Nutritive and metabolic organs
.44	Secretory and excretory organs
.46	Reproductive organs
.47	Motor organs and integument
.5	**Ecology**

Class here adaptations, behavior, biomes, ecosystems, ecological succession

For human behavior, see 150

SUMMARY

574.509 1	Treatment by areas, regions, places in general
.52	Specific relationships and kinds of environments
.53	Nutritive adaptations
.54	Adaptations to weather, climate, seasons
.56	Reproductive adaptations
.57	Protective adaptations

| .509 1 | Treatment by areas, regions, places in general |
| | Class ecology of specific kinds of environments in 574.526 |

.52 **Specific relationships and kinds of environments**

Including migration

Class specific adaptations to specific relationships and kinds of environments in 574.53–574.57

SUMMARY

574.522	**Specific interrelations of organisms and environment**
.524	**Synecology**
.526	**Specific kinds of environments**
.529	**Rare and endangered species**

.522 **Specific interrelations of organisms and environment**

Use of this number for comprehensive works on interrelations of organisms and environment discontinued; class in 574.5

Class interrelations of organisms and specific kinds of environments in 574.526

.522 2 Effects of specific aspects of environment on organisms

Examples: effects of climate, fire, geochemistry, pollution

Including bioclimatology, biogeochemistry

See Manual at 574.5222 vs. 574.24, 363.73

.522 3 Effects of organisms on environment

.524 Synecology

Class synecology in specific kinds of environments in 547.526

.524 6 Groups

.524 7 Communities

Including competition, ecological niches

For symbiosis, see 574.52482, predation 574.53

.524 8 Populations

.524 82 Symbiosis

Including commensalism, mutualism, consortism

For parasitism, see 574.5249

.524 9 Parasitism

.526 Specific kinds of environments

See Manual at 574.526 vs. 574.909–574.92

.526 2 Zonal environments

.526 21	Arctic environments
	Including glacial environments
	Class a specific arctic environment with the environment, e.g., tundras 574.52644
.526 23	Tropical environments
	Class a specific tropical environment with the environment, e.g., tropical swamps 574.526325
.526 3	Aquatic environments
.526 32	Freshwater environments
	Class here limnology
.526 322	Lakes, ponds, freshwater lagoons
.526 323	Rivers and streams
.526 325	Wetlands environments
	Bogs, marshes, swamps
	Class here comprehensive works on wetlands
	For saltwater wetlands, see 574.52636
.526 36	Saltwater environments
	Examples: salt lakes, saltwater lagoons, saltwater wetlands
	Class here marine ecology
.526 365	Estuaries
.526 367	Reefs
.526 38	Seashores
.526 4	Land environments
	Examples: cultivated areas, heaths, moors, mountains
	Class wetlands in 574.526325, seashores in 574.52638
	For alkaline, arid, semiarid environments, see 574.5265; island environments, 574.5267; urban environments, 574.5268
.526 404	Soil
.526 42	Forests, jungles, woodlands
	Standard subdivisions are added for forests, jungles, woodlands, for forests alone, for jungles alone, or for woodlands alone
.526 43	Grasslands, meadows, prairies
	Standard subdivisions may be used for grasslands, meadows, prairies, for grasslands alone, for meadows alone, or for prairies alone
.526 44	Tundras

.526 5	Alkaline, arid, semiarid environments
	Including dunes, rocks, salt flats
.526 52	Arid and semiarid environments
	Example: chaparrals
	Class here deserts
.526 7	Island environments
.526 8	Urban environments
.529	Rare and endangered species
	Including recently extinct species

> 574.53–574.57 Specific adaptations

Class comprehensive works in 574.5

.53	Nutritive adaptations
	Including food chains, predation
.54	Adaptations to weather, climate, seasons
.542	Weather and climate
	Examples: acclimatization, temperature adaptations
.543	Seasonal changes
.56	Reproductive adaptations
.57	Protective adaptations
.6	**Economic biology**
.61	Beneficial organisms
	See Manual at 580–590 vs. 630, 641.3
.65	Deleterious organisms
.8	**Tissue, cellular, molecular biology**

Class here tissue and cellular physiology and pathology of specific processes and structures

SUMMARY

574.82	**Tissue biology**
.87	**Cytology (Cell biology)**
.88	**Molecular biology**

.82	Tissue biology
.821	Histophysiology

For histogenesis, see 574.17

.821 2	Histochemistry	
.824	Histology	
.828	Histopathology	
.87	Cytology (Cell biology)	

> Including colonies
>
> Class here comparative cytology
>
> Class genetics in 575.1

.872　　　　　Cell structure

> *For specific components of cell anatomy, see 574.873–574.875*

> 　　574.873–574.875 Specific components of cell anatomy and physiology

> Class comprehensive works in 574.87

.873　　　　　Protoplasm

> Class here ultrastructure

.873 2　　　　Nucleus

> Including nucleolus, linin network, nuclear membrane, nuclear envelope, nucleoplasm

.873 22　　　Chromosomes

> Including nucleosomes
>
> Class here cytogenetics, physiological genetics, chromatin, genes
>
> *For nucleic acids, see 574.87328*

.873 223　　　Transcription and translation

> Use of this number for comprehensive works on cytogenetics discontinued; class in 574.87322
>
> Class errors of transcription and resulting variations in 575.2

.873 224　　　Biochemical genetics

.873 28　　　Nucleic acids

> Including nucleoproteins, nucleosides, nucleases
>
> Class here molecular genetics, nucleotides

.873 282　　　Deoxyribonucleic acid (DNA)

.873 283　　　Ribonucleic acid (RNA)

.873 3　　　Plastids

.873 4		Cytoplasm

Including blepharoplasts, centrosomes, cytoskeleton, endoplasmic reticulum, Golgi apparatus, microtubules, microfilaments, microtrabeculae, ribosomes

Class here comprehensive works on organelles

> *For plastids, see 574.8733; vacuoles and vesicles, 574.874; membranes, 574.875*

.873 42		Mitochondria
.874		Vacuoles and vesicles

Examples: lysosomes, peroxisomes, aleurone grains

.875		Cell membrane and cell wall

Class here biological transport

.876		Cell physiology and pathology

> *For specific components of cell physiology, see 574.873–574.875*

.876 04		Special topics
.876 041		Cell biophysics
.876 042		Cytochemistry
.876 1		Nutrition, metabolism, development

Including growth, regeneration

.876 12		Cell differentiation
.876 2		Cell division

Class here cytokinesis

.876 22		Amitosis
.876 23		Mitosis

Including chromatids, centromeres, kinetochores

Class here cell cycle

.876 4		Respiration, excretion, movement

Including cilia, flagella, basal body

.876 5		Cytopathology

Including degeneration and death

[.878]		Comparative cytology

Number discontinued; class in 574.87

.88	Molecular biology	

Class molecular biology of a specific process or part of the living organism with the process or part, e.g., molecular genetics of the nucleus 574.8732

.9 **Geographical treatment of organisms**

See Manual at 508 vs. 574, 910, 304.2

.909 Treatment by areas, regions, places in general

Add to base number 574.909 the numbers following —1 in notation 11–19 from Table 2, e.g., desert biology 574.90954; however, class insular biology in 574.91, hydrographic biology in 574.92

See Manual at 574.526 vs. 574.909–574.92

.91 Island biology

Add to base number 574.91 the numbers following notation 3–9 from Table 2, e.g., biology of the Hawaiian Islands 574.91969

See Manual at 574.526 vs. 574.909–574.92

.92 Aquatic biology   Marine biology

Class comprehensive works on marine and freshwater biology of specific continents, countries, localities in 574.93–574.99

Class here plankton, neuston

See Manual at 551.46 vs. 574.92; 574.526 vs. 574.909–574.92

.921–.928 Marine biology

Add to base number 574.92 the numbers following 551.46 in 551.461–551.468, e.g., Mediterranean Sea life 574.922; however, class Antarctic waters of Atlantic Ocean in 574.924, of Pacific Ocean in 574.9258, of Indian Ocean in 574.927; comprehensive works on Antarctic waters in 574.924

Class marine biology of specific continents, countries, localities in 574.93–574.99

.929 Freshwater biology (Limnetic biology)

Add to base number 574.929 the numbers following notation 3–9 from Table 2, e.g., aquatic biology of New York lakes 574.929747

.93–.99 Treatment by specific continents, countries, localities, extraterrestrial worlds

Class here comprehensive works on marine and freshwater biology of specific continents, countries, localities; marine biology of specific continents, countries, localities

Add to base number 574.9 notation 3–9 from Table 2, e.g., astrobiology 574.999

Class freshwater biology of specific continents, countries, localities in 574.929

575   Evolution and genetics

Class evolution of a specific process or structure with the process or structure, e.g., evolution of biorhythms 574.1882

> For evolution of humankind, see 573.2; of plants, 581.38; of animals, 591.38

> See Manual at 231.765 vs. 213, 575; 560 vs. 575; 573.2

.001   Philosophy

                   Class theory in 575.01

.002–.009   Standard subdivisions

.01   Theory

.016   Modern theories

.016 2   Darwinian and neo-Darwinian theories

                   Theories on natural selection and survival of the fittest

.016 3   Orthogenesis

.016 5   Mutation theories

.016 6   Lamarckian and neo-Lamarckian theories

                   Theories on inheritance of acquired characteristics, on hereditary effects of use and disuse of organs

.1   Genetics

Class here heredity

Class genetics of humankind in 573.21

> For cytogenetics, see 574.87322; molecular genetics, 574.87328; variation, 575.2; genetics of plants, 581.15; of animals, 591.15

.107 24   Experimental genetics

                   Including cloning, gene splicing, recombinant DNA

                   Class here genetic engineering

                   Class comprehensive works on experimental and industrial genetic engineering at 660.65

.11   Laws of genetics

                   Examples: laws of Galton, Weismann

                   Class here Mendel's laws

.12   Genetic makeup

                   Including genotypes, phenotypes

.13   Factors affecting heredity and variation

                   Including random assortment, recombination

.131	Environmental factors (Mutagens) [*formerly also* 575.22]

Examples: chemicals, radiations

.132	Outbreeding

Including hybrids

.133	Inbreeding
.134	Species interfertility
.137	Atavism
.15	Population genetics

Class a specific aspect with the subject, e.g., inbreeding 575.133

.2 Variation

Including alleles, nondisjunctions, polyploidy, transductions, transformations, transposons (jumping genes)

[.22]	Environmental factors affecting heredity and variation

Relocated to 575.131

[.28]	Variations

Number discontinued; class in 575.2

.29	Abrupt deviations

Including aneuploidy, crossing over, inversions, translocations

.292	Mutations

Inheritable abrupt deviations

[.293]	Sports

Number discontinued; class in 575.29

> **575.5–575.9 Specific topics in evolution**

Class comprehensive works in 575, theories in 575.01, role of genetics in evolution in 575.1

.5 Evolution through sexual selection

.7 Evolutionary cycles

Periodic proliferation and wide-spread extinction of species

.9 Origin and evolution of sexes

576   Microbiology

For fungi, see 589.2; algae, 589.3; bacteria, 589.9; Protozoa, 593.1

.09	Historical, geographical, persons treatment

Class geographical treatment of microbes in 576.19

.1   **Processes, parts, distribution**

> Class processes, parts, distribution of rickettsias and viruses in 576.6

.11   Physiology

> Add to base number 576.11 the numbers following 574.1 in 574.11–574.19, e.g., anaerobic respiration 576.1128
>
> *For genetics, see 576.139*

.13   Development, maturation, genetics

.131–.137   Specific phases

> Add to base number 576.13 the numbers following 574.3 in 574.31–574.37, e.g., microbial growth 576.131

.138   Evolution

.139   Genetics

.14   Anatomy and morphology

.15   Ecology

.16   Economic microbiology

.162   Beneficial microorganisms

> Class beneficial food microorganisms in 576.163

.163   Food microbiology

> Microorganisms occurring in food

.165   Deleterious microorganisms

> Toxic, pathogenic, obnoxious
>
> Class deleterious food microorganisms in 576.163

.19   Geographical treatment of microbes

> Add to base number 576.19 the numbers following 574.9 in 574.909–574.999, e.g., freshwater microorganisms 576.1929

.6   **Rickettsias and viruses**

.62   Rickettsias

> *For Chlamydiales, see 589.93*

.64   Viruses

> Class here virology
>
> Interferons relocated to 591.295

.648   Types of viruses

.648 2   Bacterial viruses (Bacteriophages)

.648 3   Plant viruses

Example: tobacco mosaic virus

Including viroids

Class bacterial viruses in 576.6482

.648 4   Animal viruses

Including prions

Examples: adenoviruses, bunyaviruses, coronaviruses, herpesviruses, myxoviruses, papovaviruses, paramyxoviruses, picornaviruses, poxviruses, retroviruses, rhabdoviruses, togaviruses

577   General nature of life

Origin and beginnings of life, conditions needed for life, differences between living and nonliving substances

578   Microscopy in biology

.4   Use of microscopes

Including photomicrography

Add to base number 578.4 the numbers following 502.82 in 502.822–502.825, e.g., use of electron microscopes 578.45

.6   Slide preparation

Including fixation, staining; microtomy

For slide preparation of plant tissues, see 578.8; of animal tissues, 578.9

.8   Slide preparation of plant tissues

.9   Slide preparation of animal tissues

579   Collection and preservation of biological specimens

.1   Preparing skeletons

.2   Preserving total specimens

Embalming, mummification, pickling

For taxidermy, see 579.4

.4   Taxidermy

.6   Techniques of collecting and transporting

580   Botanical sciences

Use 580 by itself only for works involving substantial treatment of paleobotany; use 581 for general botany

For paleobotany, see 561

See Manual at 580–590; 580–590 vs. 630, 641.3

SUMMARY

580.74	Museums, collections, exhibits
581	Botany
582	Spermatophyta (Seed-bearing plants)
583	Dicotyledones
584	Monocotyledones
585	Gymnospermae (Pinophyta)
586	Cryptogamia (Seedless plants)
587	Pteridophyta (Vascular cryptogams)
588	Bryophyta
589	Thallobionta (Thallophyta) and Prokaryotae

.74   Museums, collections, exhibits

Class here herbariums and botanical gardens limited to vascular plants, to spermatophytes, to angiosperms, to dicotyledons

Do not add as instructed under —074 in Table 1

Class herbariums and botanical gardens limited to groups other than those listed above with the specific group, e.g., nonornamental gardens of gymnosperms 585.074

.742   Herbariums

Collections of dried plants

Add to base number 580.742 notation 1 or 3–9 from Table 2, e.g., herbariums of Australia 580.74294

.744   Botanical gardens

Add to base number 580.744 notation 1 or 3–9 from Table 2, e.g., botanical gardens of Germany 580.74443

581   Botany

Studies of a particular process or system associated with a specific plant or group of plants are classed with the plant or group, not with the process or system, e.g., genetics of peas 583.322, not 581.15.

Class microscopy regardless of kind of plant in 578, collection and preservation of botanical specimens regardless of kind of plant in 579

For specific plants and groups of plants, see 582–589

See Manual at 581

SUMMARY

581.01–.09	Standard subdivisions
.1	Physiology of plants
.2	Pathology of plants
.3	Development and maturation of plants
.4	Anatomy and morphology of plants
.5	Ecology of plants
.6	Economic botany
.8	Tissue, cellular, molecular botany
.9	Geographical treatment of plants

.072	Research
.072 4	Experimental botany

> Including tissue and organ culture, use of specific plants and groups of plants to study general botany

.074	Museums, collections, exhibits

> Class herbariums in 580.742, botanical gardens in 580.744

.075	Museum activities and services

> Class collection and preservation of botanical specimens regardless of kind of plant in 579

.09	Historical, geographical, persons treatment

> Class geographical treatment of plants in 581.9

.1 **Physiology of plants**

Class here physiology of agricultural plants; comprehensive works on anatomy, morphology, physiology

Class microphysiology in 581.8

For pathological physiology, see 581.21; development and maturation, 581.3; anatomy and morphology, 581.4

SUMMARY

581.104	**[Regional physiology]**
.11	**Circulation**
.12	**Respiration and transpiration**
.13	**Nutrition and metabolism**
.14	**Secretion and excretion**
.15	**Genetics**
.16	**Reproduction (Propagation)**
.17	**Histogenesis**
.18	**Movements and control processes**
.19	**Biophysics and biochemistry**

.104	Special topics
.104 2	Regional physiology
.104 25	Stems
.104 27	Leaves and fronds
.104 28	Roots
.11	Circulation
.113	Circulatory fluids
.116	Organs of circulation
.12	Respiration and transpiration
.121	Aerobic respiration

.124	Intercellular respiration
.128	Anaerobic respiration
.129	Transpiration
.13	Nutrition and metabolism
.132	Ingestion and digestion
.133	Metabolism

        Anabolism and catabolism

        Including assimilation

        Class nitrogen fixation in 589.90133

.133 4	Food synthesis
.133 42	Photosynthesis

        Class chloroplasts in 581.8733

.133 43	Chemosynthesis
.133 45	Protein synthesis
.133 46	Lipid synthesis
.133 5	Mineral metabolism
.133 54	Macronutrient elements

        Examples: calcium, iron, magnesium, phosphorus, potassium, sodium salts, sulfur

.133 56	Micronutrient elements (Trace elements)

        Examples: aluminum, boron, copper, manganese, molybdenum, selenium, silicon, zinc

.133 8	Food storage
.14	Secretion and excretion

        For transpiration, see 581.129

.15	Genetics

        Class physiological genetics in 581.87322

.152	Environmental factors in heredity and variation
.158	Variations

        Example: hybrids

        For abrupt variations, see 581.159

.159	Abrupt variations

.159 2	Mutations
	Inheritable abrupt artificial and natural deviations
	Including effects of radiation (radiogenetics)
[.159 3]	Sports
	Number discontinued; class in 581.159
.16	Reproduction (Propagation)

> Add to base number 581.16 the numbers following 574.16 in 574.162–574.166, e.g., vegetative reproduction 581.165

.17	Histogenesis
.18	Movements and control processes

> Class here response to stimuli

.182	Dehiscence

> Former heading: hydration movements

.183	Growth movements
.183 2	Tropisms
.183 3	Nastic movements
.184	Turgor movements
.185	Nutation and circumnutation

> Example: twining

.188	Control processes

> Including physiological balance

> Class control of a specific function with the function, e.g., control of respiration 581.12

.188 2	Biological rhythms
.19	Biophysics and biochemistry

> Add to base number 581.19 the numbers following 574.19 in 574.191–574.192, e.g., enzymes 581.1925

> Class physics and chemistry of a specific process or part of plants with the process or part, e.g., chemistry of metabolism 581.133

.2	**Pathology of plants**

> Class here pathogenicity, degeneration, death, galls; agricultural plants used as models of pathological processes

> Class histopathology in 581.828, cell pathology in 581.8765, pathology of agricultural plants in 632

.21	Pathological physiology

> Add to base number 581.21 the numbers following 581 in 581.11–581.19, e.g., pathophysiology of metabolism 581.2133

.22   Pathological anatomy

Class here teratology

Add to base number 581.22 the numbers following 581.4 in 581.41–581.49, e.g., pathological anatomy of roots 581.2298

.23–.29   Causes and immunity

Add to base number 581.2 the numbers following 574.2 in 574.23–574.29, e.g., disease resistance 581.29

.3   Development and maturation of plants

For histogenesis, see 581.17

.31–.37   Sex and specific stages

Add to base number 581.3 the numbers following 574.3 in 574.31–574.37, e.g., growth 581.31

.38   Evolution

Class genetics in 581.15

.4   Anatomy and morphology of plants

Class here anatomy and morphology of agricultural plants

Class comprehensive works on anatomy, morphology, physiology in 581.1; anatomical embryology in 581.332; microanatomy in 581.8

For pathological anatomy, see 581.22

See Manual at 581

.41   Circulatory organs

Examples: cambium, phloem, vascular bundles, xylem

.42   Respiratory organs

Examples: guard cells, intercellular systems, lenticels, stomata

.43   Nutritive and metabolic organs

For leaves and fronds, see 581.497

.44   Secretory and excretory organs

For lenticels and stomata, see 581.42

.46   Reproductive organs

Class reproductive organs of seed plants in 582.046, of flowering plants in 582.130446

.47   Integumentary and motor organs (Epidermis)

Including tentacles, thorns

.49	Regional anatomy

Class comprehensive works on regional anatomy and physiology in 581.1042

.495	Stems
.497	Leaves and fronds
.498	Roots
.5	**Ecology of plants**

Class here plant adaptations, behavior

Add to base number 581.5 the numbers following 574.5 in 574.52–574.57, e.g., communities 581.5247

Class botanical paleoecology in 561.1

.6	**Economic botany**

See Manual at 580–590 vs. 630, 641.3

.61	Beneficial plants

For edible and medicinal plants, see 581.63; plants of industrial and technological value, 581.64

.63	Edible and medicinal plants

Class here herbs

.632	Edible plants
.634	Medicinal plants
.64	Plants of industrial and technological value
.65	Deleterious plants

For allergenic plants, see 581.67; poisonous plants, 581.69

.652	Weeds
.67	Allergenic plants
.69	Poisonous plants
.8	**Tissue, cellular, molecular botany**

Add to base number 581.8 the numbers following 574.8 in 574.82–574.88, e.g., physiological genetics 581.87322

For histogenesis, see 581.17

.9	**Geographical treatment of plants**

Add to base number 581.9 the numbers following 574.9 in 574.909–574.999, e.g., desert plants 581.90954

> 582–589 Specific plants and groups of plants

Add to each subdivision identified by * as follows:
04   Processes and parts
            Add to base number 04 the numbers following 581 in
            581.1–581.8, e.g., genetics 0415
075   Museum activities and services
            Class collection and preservation of botanical specimens in
            579
09   Historical, geographical, persons treatment
091   Treatment by areas, regions, places in general
0916   Air and water
            Class hydrographic botany of specific continents,
            countries, localities in 093–099
093–099   Treatment by specific continents, countries, localities

Class comprehensive works in 581

582   Spermatophyta (Seed-bearing plants)

For Angiospermae, see 583–584; Gymnospermae, 585

.001–.006   Standard subdivisions

.007   Education, research, related topics

.007 4   Museums, collections, exhibits

            Class herbariums and botanical gardens covering Spermatophyta
            taken as a whole in 580.74

.008   History and description with respect to kinds of persons

.009   Historical, geographical, persons treatment of the study of
            Spermatophyta

            Class geographical treatment of Spermatophyta in 582.09

> 582.01–582.09 Processes, parts, distribution

            Class comprehensive works in 582

.01–.03   Physiology, pathology, development, maturation

            Add to base number 582.0 the numbers following 581 in 581.1–581.3, e.g.,
            reproduction 582.016

.04   Anatomy and morphology

            Class comprehensive works on anatomy, morphology, physiology in 582.01;
            pathological anatomy in 582.022; anatomical embryology in 582.0332;
            microanatomy in 582.08

.041–.044	Circulatory, respiratory, nutritive, metabolic, secretory, excretory organs

> Add to base number 582.04 the numbers following 581.4 in 581.41–581.44, e.g., respiratory organs 582.042

.046	Reproductive organs

> Class reproductive organs of flowering plants in 582.130446

.046 3	Seed-producing organs

> Flowers and their parts relocated to 582.1304463

.046 4	Fruit
.046 7	Seeds
.047–.049	Motor and integumentary organs; regional anatomy

> Add to base number 582.04 the numbers following 581.4 in 581.47–581.49, e.g., stems 582.0495

.05–.08	Ecology; economic, tissue, cellular, molecular botany

> Add to base number 582.0 the numbers following 581 in 581.5–581.8, e.g., ecology 582.05

.09	Geographical treatment

> Add to base number 582.09 the numbers following 574.9 in 574.909–574.999, e.g., desert spermatophyta 582.090954

.1	**Nontaxonomic groupings**

> *See Manual at 582.1 vs. 635.9*

.12	*Herbaceous plants

> *For herbaceous flowering plants, see 582.13; herbaceous shrubs and vines, 582.14*

.13	*Herbaceous flowering plants

> Class here wild flowers, comprehensive works on Angiospermae (flowering plants)

> Class woody flowering plants in 582.15

> *For Dicotyledones, see 583; Monocotyledones, 584*

.130 446	Reproductive organs
.130 446 3	Flowers and their parts [*formerly also* 582.0463]

> Including ovaries, pistils, pollen, stamens

.130 74	Museums, exhibits, collections

> Class herbariums and botanical gardens covering Angiospermae (flowering plants) taken as a whole in 580.74

.14	*Herbaceous shrubs and vines

*Add as instructed under 582–589

.15   *Woody plants

> *For trees, see 582.16; woody shrubs, 582.17; woody vines, 582.18*

.16   Trees

Class here dendrology

.160 01–.160 08   Standard subdivisions

.160 09   Historical, geographical, persons treatment of dendrology

> Class geographical treatment of trees in 582.1609

.160 1–.160 8   Processes and parts

> Add to base number 582.160 the numbers following 581 in 581.1–581.8, e.g., ecology 582.1605

> Class comprehensive works on ecology of forest, jungle, woodland environments in 574.52642

.160 9   Geographical treatment

> Add to base number 582.1609 the numbers following 574.9 in 574.909–574.999, e.g., desert trees 582.16090954

.17   *Woody shrubs

Class here comprehensive works on shrubs

> *For herbaceous shrubs, see 582.14*

.18   *Woody vines

Class here comprehensive works on vines

> *For herbaceous vines, see 582.14*

> ## 583–584 Angiospermae (Flowering plants)

Class comprehensive works in 582.13

See Manual at 583–584

583   *Dicotyledones

SUMMARY

583.1	**Primitive orders**
.2	**Discifloral plants**
.3	**Leguminales, Rosales, Saxifragales, Hamamelidales, Cunoniales**
.4	**Myrtales, Lythrales, Loasales, Passiflorales, Cucurbitales, Cactales, Umbellales**
.5	**Rubiales, Valerianales, Bignoniales, Asterales, Campanales, Goodeniales**
.6	**Ericales, Primulales, Myrsinales, Ebenales, Styracales, Araliales**
.7	**Apocynales, Loganiales, Gentianales, Polemoniales, Boraginales, Solanales**
.8	**Personales, Lamiales, Verbenales, Plantaginales**
.9	**Apetalae**

*Add as instructed under 582–589

.1   Primitive orders

SUMMARY

583.11   **Ranales, Dilleniales, Magnoliales, Annonales, Berberidales**
.12   **Sarraceniales, Rhoeadales, Cruciales, Resedales**
.13   **Capparidales, Violales, Bixales**
.14   **Pittosporales and Polygalales**
.15   **Caryophyllales and Tamaricales**
.16   **Guttiferales, Theales, Ochnales**
.17   **Malvales**
.19   **Tiliales**

.11   Ranales, Dilleniales, Magnoliales, Annonales, Berberidales

.111   *Ranales

Contains Cabombaceae, Ceratophyllaceae (hornwort family), Helleboraceae, Nymphaeaceae (water-lily family), Paeoniaceae, Podophyllaceae, Ranunculaceae (buttercup family)

Common names: aconite, anemone, Christmas rose, clematis, columbine, larkspur, locoweeds, monkshood, peony, wolfsbane

Class comprehensive works on lilies in 584.324

.112   *Dilleniales

Contains Dilleniaceae, Crossosomataceae

For Connaraceae, see 583.28; Brunelliaceae, 583.397

.114   *Magnoliales

Contains Magnoliaceae (magnolia family), Cercidiphyllaceae, Himantandraceae, Illiciaceae, Lactoridaceae, Schisandraceae, Trochodendraceae, Winteraceae (winter's bark family)

Common names: cucumber tree, katsura tree, sweet bay, tulip tree, umbrella tree, yellow poplar

For Canellaceae, see 583.138

.115   *Annonales

Contains *Annonaceae (custard-apple family), Eupomatiaceae

Common names: cherimoya, papaw

.117   *Berberidales

Contains Berberidaceae (barberry family), Circaeasteraceae, Lardizabalaceae, Menispermaceae, Nandinaceae, Sargentodoxaceae

Common name: mayapple

.12   Sarraceniales, Rhoeadales, Cruciales, Resedales

*Add as instructed under 582–589

.121   *Sarraceniales

Contains Sarraceniaceae (New World-pitcher-plant family), Droseraceae (sundew family)

Common name: flytraps

Including comprehensive works on pitcher plants

Class here comprehensive works on insectivorous plants

Class pitcher plants of milkweed family in 583.72

> *For Byblidaceae, see 583.141; Cephalotaceae, 583.38; Lentibulariaceae, 583.81; Nepenthaceae, 583.922*

.122   *Rhoeadales

Contains Fumariaceae (fumitory family), Papaveraceae (poppy family)

Common names: bleeding heart, bloodroot, celandine, Dutchman's breeches

.123   *Cruciales

Contains Brassicaceae (Cruciferae, mustard family)

Common names: bok choy, broccoli, Brussels sprouts, cabbage, candytuft, cauliflower, cresses, horseradish, kale, kohlrabi, radishes, rape, rutabaga, shepherd's purse, stocks, sweet alyssum, turnip, wallflower, watercress

.124   *Resedales

Contains Resedaceae (mignonette family)

.13   Capparidales, Violales, Bixales

.131   *Capparidales

Contains Capparidaceae (caper family), Moringaceae, Tovariaceae

Common name: spiderflower

.135   *Violales

Contains Violaceae (violet family)

Common name: pansy

> *See also 583.81 for African, flame violets*

.138   *Bixales

Contains Bixaceae (annatto family), Achatocarpaceae, Canellaceae (wild cinnamon family), Cistaceae, Cochlospermaceae, Flacourtiaceae, Hoplestigmataceae, Samydaceae

Common name: buttercup tree

> *For Lacistemataceae, see 583.925*

.14   Pittosporales and Polygalales

*Add as instructed under 582–589

.141   *Pittosporales

              Contains Pittosporaceae (hedge laurel family), Byblidaceae,
              Stegnospermaceae, Tremandraceae, Vivianiaceae

              Class comprehensive works on laurels in 583.931

.143   *Polygalales

              Contains Polygalaceae (milkwort family), Krameriaceae, Trigoniaceae,
              Vochysiaceae (San Juan family)

              Common name: canaigre

.15   Caryophyllales and Tamaricales

.152   *Caryophyllales

              Contains Caryophyllaceae (pink family), Aizoaceae (Ficoidaceae),
              Elatinaceae (waterwort family), Molluginaceae, Portulacaceae (purslane
              family)

              Common names: baby's breath, campion, carnation, chickweed, dusty
              miller

.158   *Tamaricales

              Contains Tamaricaceae (tamarisk family), Fouquieriaceae (ocotillo
              family), Frankeniaceae

              Common name: candlewood

.16   Guttiferales, Theales, Ochnales

.163   *Guttiferales

              Contains Guttiferae (balsam fig family), Clusiaceae, Eucryphiaceae,
              Hypericaceae (Saint-John's-wort family), Quiinaceae

              Common names: garcinia, mammee apples, mangosteen

.166   *Theales

              Contains Theaceae (tea family), Actinidiaceae, Bonnetiaceae,
              Caryocaraceae, Chlaenaceae, Marcgraviaceae, Medusagynaceae,
              Pellicieraceae, Pentaphylacaceae, Saurauiaceae, Tetrameristaceae

              Common names: camellia, Stewartia

.167   *Ochnales

              Contains Ochnaceae (red ironwood family), Ancistrocladaceae,
              Dipterocarpaceae, Sarcolaenaceae, Sphaerosepalaceae, Strasburgeriaceae

.17   *Malvales

          Contains Malvaceae (mallow family)

          Common names: American hemp, cotton, hibiscus, hollyhock,
          marshmallow, okra, rose of Sharon

          Class comprehensive works on hemps in 583.962

*Add as instructed under 582–589

.19   *Tiliales

> Contains Tiliaceae (linden family), Bombacaceae (silk-cotton tree family), Dirachmaceae, Gonystylaceae, Peridiscaceae, Scytopetalaceae, Sterculiaceae (cacao family)
>
> Common names: balsa, baobab, basswood, jute

.2   *Discifloral plants

.21   Malpighiales and Geraniales

.214   *Malpighiales

> Contains Malpighiaceae, Balanitaceae, Ctenolphonaceae, Erythroxylaceae (coca family), Huaceae, Humiriaceae, Irvingiaceae, Ixonanthaceae, Ledocarpaceae, Lepidobotryaceae, Linaceae (flax family), Zygophyllaceae (lignum vitae family)
>
> Common names: creosote bush, wild mango

.216   *Geraniales

> Contains Geraniaceae (geranium family), Balsaminaceae (balsam family), Limnanthaceae (false-mermaid family), Oxalidaceae (wood-sorrel family), Tropaeolaceae (nasturtium family)
>
> Common names: impatiens, Indian cress, jewelweed, shamrocks, touch-me-nots
>
> *See also 583.917 for sorrel*

.24   *Rutales

> Contains Rutaceae (rue family), Averrhoaceae, Burseraceae (torchwood family), Simaroubaceae (ailanthus family)
>
> Common names: citrus fruits, frankincense, grapefruit, hop tree, incense tree, kumquat, lemons, limes, myrrh, orange jessamine, oranges, prickly ash
>
> Including comprehensive works on balms
>
> Class specific balms with the kind of plant, e.g. balms of the mint family 583.87
>
> *See also 583.74 for jasmines*

.25   *Meliales

> Contains Meliaceae (mahogany family)
>
> Common name: chinaberry

.26   *Olacales

> Contains Olacaceae, Aptandraceae, Dipentodontaceae, Medusandraceae, Octoknemaceae, Opiliaceae

.27   Celastrales and Rhamnales

*Add as instructed under 582–589

.271   *Celastrales

> Contains Celastraceae (staff-tree family), Aextoxicaceae, Aquifoliaceae (holly family), Capusiaceae, Cardiopteridaceae, Cneoraceae, Corynocarpaceae, Cyrillaceae, Empetraceae (crowberry family), Erythropalaceae, Goupiaceae, Hippocrateaceae, Icacinaceae, Koeberliniaceae, Pandaceae, Pentadiplandraceae, Salvadoraceae, Stackhousiaceae
>
> Common names: kat, maté
>
> *For Scyphostegiaceae, see 583.962*

.279   *Rhamnales

> Contains Rhamnaceae (buckthorn family), Elaeagnaceae (oleaster family), Heteropyxidaceae, Vitaceae (grape family)
>
> Common names: Boston ivy, buffalo berry, Christ's thorn, jujube, Virginia creeper
>
> Class comprehensive works on ivies in 583.687

.28   *Sapindales

> Contains Sapindaceae (soapberry family), Aceraceae (maple family), Akaniaceae, Anacardiaceae (cashew family), Connaraceae, Didiereaceae, Hippocastanaceae (buckeye family), Melianthaceae (honey-bush family), Podoaceae, Sabiaceae, Staphyleaceae (bladdernut family)
>
> Common names: akee, box elder, horse chestnut, lacquer tree, mango, pistachio, poison ivy, poison oak, poison sumac, smoke tree, Spanish plum, sumac, varnish tree
>
> Class comprehensive works on ivies in 583.687
>
> *For Julianaceae, see 583.973*
>
> *See also 583.372 for drupaceous plums*

.29   *Coriariales

> Contains Coriariaceae

.3   Leguminales, Rosales, Saxifragales, Hamamelidales, Cunoniales

.32   *Leguminales

.321   *Mimosaceae (Mimosa family)

> Common names: acacia, mesquite, sensitive plants, silk tree

.322   *Fabaceae (Papilionaceae, Pea family)

> Common names: alfalfa, beans, beggar's-lice, bluebonnet, carob, chick-peas, clover, cowpeas, groundnut, indigo, kudzu, lentils, lespedeza, locust, lupine, peanuts, scotch broom, soybeans, sweet peas, tamarind, vetch, wisteria

.323   *Caesalpiniaceae (Senna family)

> Common names: honey locust, redbud

*Add as instructed under 582–589

.37   *Rosales

Contains Dichapetalaceae

.372   *Rosaceae (Rose family)

Common names: almonds, apples, apricots, blackberry, boysenberry,
bridal wreath, cane fruit, cherry, chokeberry, cinquefoil, crab apples,
dewberry, drupaceous fruit, hawthorn, Juneberry, loquat, medlar,
peaches, pear, plum, pomaceous fruit, quince, raspberry, Rubus,
shadbush, strawberries

See also 583.28 for Spanish plums, 583.374 for strawberry shrubs

.373   *Chailletiaceae

.374   *Calycanthaceae (strawberry-shrub family)

Common name: sweet shrub

.38   *Saxifragales

Contains Saxifragaceae (saxifrage family), Adoxaceae, Cephalotaceae
(Australian pitcher-plant family), Crassulaceae, Donatiaceae,
Eremosynaceae, Francoaceae, Parnassiaceae, Vahliaceae

Common names: coralbell, jade plant, pickaback plant, Ribes, umbrella
plant

Class comprehensive works on pitcher plants in 583.121

.39   Hamamelidales and Cunoniales

.394   *Hamamelidales

Contains Hamamelidaceae (witch-hazel family), Bruniaceae, Buxaceae,
Daphniphyllaceae, Eucommiaceae, Myrothamnaceae, Platanaceae
(sycamore family), Stachyuraceae, Tetracentraceae

Common names: Allegheny spurge, boxwood, buttonball, ironwood,
plane tree, platanus, sweet gum

.397   *Cunoniales

Contains Cunoniaceae, Baueraceae, Brunelliaceae, Escalloniaceae,
Greyiaceae, Grossulariaceae (gooseberry family), Hydrangeaceae,
Philadelphaceae, Pterostemonaceae

Common names: apple blossom, currants, mock oranges

For Crypteroniaceae, Oliniaceae, see 583.44

.4   **Myrtales, Lythrales, Loasales, Passiflorales, Cucurbitales, Cactales,
Umbellales**

*Add as instructed under 582–589

.42   *Myrtales

> Contains Myrtaceae (myrtle family), Combretaceae (myrobalan family), Lecythidaceae (Brazil-nut family), Melastomataceae (meadow-beauty family), Rhizophoraceae (mangrove family)
>
> Common names: allspice, bayberry, clove, eucalyptus, guava, pimentos, Rangoon creeper, rose apples
>
> Including comprehensive works on myrtles
>
> Class running myrtles in 583.72, California myrtle in 583.931, bog and wax myrtles in 583.974
>
>> *For Punicaceae, Sonneratiaceae, see 583.44*
>>
>> *See also 583.372 for apples, 583.974 for bayberries of Myricaceae family*

.44   *Lythrales

> Contains Lythraceae (loosestrife family), Callitrichaceae, Crypteroniaceae, Haloragidaceae (mare's-tail family), Oliniaceae, Onagraceae (evening-primrose family), Punicaceae (pomegranate family), Sonneratiaceae, Trapaceae (Hydrocaryaceae)
>
> Common names: cigar flower, clarkia, crape myrtle, fireweed, fuchsia, gunnera, henna, water chestnut
>
> Class comprehensive works on myrtles in 583.42

.45   Loasales and Passiflorales

.453   *Loasales

> Contains Loasaceae, Turneraceae

.456   *Passiflorales

> Contains Passifloraceae (passionflower family), Achariaceae, Malesherbiaceae
>
> Common names: granadilla, maypop

.46   *Cucurbitales

> Contains Cucurbitaceae (gourd family), Begoniaceae (begonia family), Caricaceae (papaya family), Datiscaceae (false-hemp family)
>
> Common names: cantaloupe, cucumber, gherkins, luffa, melons, pepo, pumpkin, squash

.47   *Cactales

> Contains Cactaceae (cactus family)
>
> Common names: cholla, peyote

*Add as instructed under 582–589

.48   *Umbellales

        Contains Apiaceae (Umbelliferae, carrot family)

        Common names: anise, caraway, celery, chervil, coriander, cumin, dill, fennel, parsley, parsnip, poison hemlock, Queen Anne's lace

.5   Rubiales, Valerianales, Bignoniales, Asterales, Campanales, Goodeniales

.52   *Rubiales

        Contains Rubiaceae (madder family), Caprifoliaceae (honeysuckle family), Dialypetalanthaceae

        Common names: buttonbush, coffee, elder, fever tree, gardenia, partridgeberry, quinine, snowball

.53   *Valerianales

        Contains Valerianaceae, Calyceraceae, Dipsacaceae (teasel family)

.54   *Bignoniales

        Contains Bignoniaceae (catalpa family), Cobaeaceae, Martyniaceae (unicorn-plant family), Pedaliaceae (pedalium family)

        Common names: calabash tree, sesame, trumpet creeper

.55   *Asterales

        Contains Asteraceae (Compositae)

        Common names: artichoke, aster, black-eyed Susan, chamomile, chicory, chrysanthemum, cornflower, cosmos, cudweed, dahlia, daisy, dandelion, edelweiss, endive, everlasting, fleabane, goldenrod, ironweed, Jerusalem artichoke, lettuce, marigold, ragweed, safflower, sagebrush, sunflower, thistle, wormwood, zinnia

.57   *Campanales

        Contains Campanulaceae (bellflower family), Lobeliaceae

        Common names: bluebell, harebell, Indian tobacco, ladybell

         See also 583.77 for bluebells of the forget-me-not family

.58   *Goodeniales

        Contains Goodeniaceae, Brunoniaceae, Stylidiaceae

.6   Ericales, Primulales, Myrsinales, Ebenales, Styracales, Araliales

*Add as instructed under 582–589

.62   *Ericales

> Contains Ericaceae (heath family), Clethraceae (white-alder family), Diapensiaceae (flowering-moss family), Epacridaceae, Lennoaceae (sand-food family), Monotropaceae (Indian-pipe family), Pyrolaceae, Vacciniaceae
>
> Common names: azalea, blueberry, briar pipe, cranberry, galax, heather, huckleberry, laurel, mayflower, mountain laurel, rhododendron, sourwood, wintergreen
>
> Class comprehensive works on laurels in 583.931

.67   Primulales and Myrsinales

.672   *Primulales

> Contains Primulaceae (primrose family), Plumbaginaceae (leadwort family)
>
> Common names: cowslip, cyclamen, statice

.677   *Myrsinales

> Contains Myrsinaceae (marlberry family), Aegicerataceae, Theophrastaceae

.68   Ebenales, Styracales, Araliales

.685   *Ebenales

> Contains Ebenaceae (ebony family), Sapotaceae (sapodilla family), Sarcospermataceae
>
> Common names: chicle, gutta-percha, persimmon, star apples
>
> Class comprehensive works on plants producing rubber in 583.95

.686   *Styracales

> Contains Styracaceae (storax family), Diclidantheraceae, Lissocarpaceae, Symplocaceae (sweetleaf family)
>
> Common name: silver bell

.687   *Araliales

> Contains Araliaceae (ginseng family), Alangiaceae, Cornaceae (dogwood family), Nyssaceae (tupelo family)
>
> Common names: gum tree, wild sarsaparilla
>
> Including comprehensive works on ivies
>
> Class sweet gum in 583.394; ivies not belonging to the Araliaceae family with the family, e.g., poison ivies 583.28
>
> > *For Caprifoliaceae, see 583.52; Garryaceae, 583.982*
> >
> > *See also 584.323 for sarsaparillas of cat brier family*

.7   **Apocynales, Loganiales, Gentianales, Polemoniales, Boraginales, Solanales**

*Add as instructed under 582–589

.72 ***Apocynales**

Contains Apocynaceae (dogbane family), Asclepiadaceae (milkweed family), Periplocaceae, Plocospermaceae

Common names: frangipani, hoya, Indian hemp, oleander, periwinkle, pitcher plant, rauwolfia, running myrtle, stephanotis

Class comprehensive works on pitcher plants in 583.121, on myrtles in 583.42, on hemps in 583.962

.74 ***Loganiales**

Contains Loganiaceae, Antoniaceae, Buddleiaceae, Oleaceae (olive family), Potaliaceae, Spigeliaceae, Strychnaceae

Common names: ash tree, jasmine, lilacs, privet

See also 583.24 for orange jessamines

.75 ***Gentianales**

Contains Gentianaceae (buck-bean family), Menyanthaceae

Common names: carnation pinks, gentian, Indian sarsaparilla

See also 584.323 for sarsaparillas of cat brier family

.76 ***Polemoniales**

Contains Polemoniaceae (phlox family), Cuscutaceae (dodder family), Hydrophyllaceae (waterleaf family)

Common names: baby blue-eyes, Jacob's ladder, sweet William

.77 ***Boraginales**

Contains Boraginaceae (forget-me-not family)

Common names: bluebells, borage, comfrey, heliotrope, honeywort, hound's-tongue

See also 583.57 for bluebells of bellflower family

.79 ***Solanales**

Contains Solanaceae (nightshade family), Convolvulaceae (morning-glory family), Nolanaceae

Common names: aubergine, belladonna, cayenne peppers, chili, eggplant, henbane, jimsonweed, love apples, mandrake, paprika, petunias, potato, sweet peppers, sweet potato (yams), tobacco, tomato

Including comprehensive works on peppers

For Piperaceae (pepper family), see 583.925

See also 584.27 for yams of Dioscoreaceae family

.8 **Personales, Lamiales, Verbenales, Plantaginales**

*Add as instructed under 582–589

.81   *Personales

Contains Acanthaceae (acanthus family), Columelliaceae, Gesneriaceae, Lentibulariaceae (bladderwort family), Orobanchaceae (broomrape family), Scrophulariaceae (snapdragon family)

Common names: African violets, flame violets, foxglove, gloxinia

Class comprehensive works on violets in 583.135

.87   *Lamiales

Contains Labiatae (mint family), Globulariaceae (globe-daisy family), Myoporaceae, Selaginaceae

Common names: basil, bee balm, catnip, Chinese artichoke, dead nettles, ground ivy, horehound, hyssop, lavender, marjoram, peppermint, rosemarie, sage, thyme

Class comprehensive works on balms in 583.24, on ivies in 583.687, on nettles in 583.962

.88   *Verbenales

Contains Verbenaceae (vervain family), Chloanthaceae, Ehretiaceae, Phrymaceae (lopseed family), Stilbeaceae

Common names: black mangrove, teak, verbena

See also 583.42 for mangroves of Rhizophoraceae family

.89   *Plantaginales

Contains Plantaginaceae (plantain family)

.9   *Apetalae

SUMMARY

583.91	**Chenopodiales and Polygonales**
.92	**Podostemales, Aristolochiales, Piperales**
.93	**Laurales, Proteales, Thymelaeales**
.94	**Santalales**
.95	**Euphorbiales**
.96	**Balanopsidales and Urticales**
.97	**Leitneriales, Juglandales, Myricales, Casuarinales, Fagales**
.98	**Salicales and Garryales**

.91   Chenopodiales and Polygonales

.913   *Chenopodiales

Contains Chenopodiaceae (goosefoot family), Agdestidaceae, Amaranthaceae (amaranth family), Barbeuiaceae, Basellaceae, Batidaceae, Cynocrambaceae (dog-cabbage family), Gyrostemonaceae, Petiveriaceae, Phytolaccaceae (pokeweed family)

Common names: beets, chard, cockscomb, glasswort, lamb's quarters, pigweed, spinach, Swiss chard, tumbleweed

*Add as instructed under 582–589

.917   *Polygonales

        Contains Polygonaceae (buckwheat family), Illecebraceae

        Common names: coral vine, dock, rhubarb, smartweed, sorrel

        See also 583.216 for wood sorrels

.92   Podostemales, Aristolochiales, Piperales

.921   *Podostemales

        Contains Podostemaceae (riverweed family), Hydrostachyaceae

.922   *Aristolochiales

        Contains Aristolochiaceae (birthwort family), Cytinaceae, Hydnoraceae, Nepenthaceae (Old World-pitcher-plant family)

        Class comprehensive works on pitcher plants in 583.121

.925   *Piperales

        Contains Piperaceae (pepper family), Chloranthaceae, Lacistemataceae, Saururaceae (lizard's-tail family)

        Common name: peperomia

        Class comprehensive works on peppers in 583.79

.93   Laurales, Proteales, Thymelaeales

.931   *Laurales

        Contains Lauraceae (laurel family), Austrobaileyaceae, Gomortegaceae, Hernandiaceae, Monimiaceae, Myristicaceae (nutmeg family), Trimeniaceae

        Common names: avocado, bay leaf, bay tree, California myrtle, cassia, cinnamon, mace, sassafras, spicebush

        Including comprehensive works on laurels

        Class comprehensive works on myrtles in 583.42

        For hedge laurels, see 583.141; laurels of Ericaceae family, see 583.62; spurge laurels, 583.933

.932   *Proteales

        Contains Proteaceae (honeyflower family)

        Common name: macadamia nuts

.933   *Thymelaeales

        Contains Thymelaeaceae, Aquilariaceae, Geissolomataceae, Nyctaginaceae (four-o'clock family), Penaeaceae

        Common names: bougainvillea, daphne, mezereon, spurge laurel

        Class comprehensive works on laurels in 583.931

        For Gonystylaceae, see 583.19

*Add as instructed under 582–589

.94   *Santalales

Contains Santalaceae (sandalwood family), Balanophoraceae, Grubbiaceae, Loranthaceae (mistletoe family), Myzondendraceae

Common name: cynomorium

.95   *Euphorbiales

Contains Euphorbiaceae (spurge family)

Common names: cassava, castor-oil plant, copperleaf, croton, crown of thorn, hevea, manchineel, mercury, poinsettia, rubber tree, snow-on-the-mountain, tallow tree, tapioca, tung tree

Including comprehensive works on plants producing rubber

Class chicles and gutta-perchas in 583.685, rubber plants of mulberry family in 583.962

See also 583.394 for Allegheny spurges

.96   Balanopsidales and Urticales

.961   *Balanopsidales

Contains Balanopsidaceae

.962   *Urticales

Contains Urticaceae (nettle family), Barbeyaceae, Cannabiaceae (hemp family), Moraceae (mulberry family), Scyphostegiaceae, Ulmaceae (elm family)

Common names: artillery plant, banyan, breadfruit, figs, hackberry, hop, India-rubber tree, marijuana, Osage oranges, ramie, rubber plant, upas tree

Including comprehensive works on hemps, nettles

Class comprehensive works on plants producing rubber in 583.95, American hemp (genus Sida) in 583.17, Indian hemp (genus Apocynum) in 583.72, Manila hemp in 584.21, sisal hemps in 584.43, nettles of mint family in 583.87

For Eucommiaceae, see 583.394

.97   Leitneriales, Juglandales, Myricales, Casuarinales, Fagales

.972   *Leitneriales

Contains Leitneriaceae (corkwood family)

.973   *Juglandales

Contains Juglandaceae (walnut family), Julianaceae, Picrodendraceae, Rhoipteleaceae

Common names: butternut, hickory, pecan

*Add as instructed under 582–589

.974	*Myricales

Contains Myricaceae (bayberry family)

Common names: bog myrtle, wax myrtle

Class comprehensive works on myrtle, bayberry of myrtle family in 583.42

.975	*Casuarinales

Contains Casuarinaceae (beefwood family)

.976	*Fagales

Contains Fagaceae (oak family), Betulaceae (birch family), Corylaceae

Common names: alder, beech, chestnut, chinquapin, filberts, hazels, hornbeam

.98	Salicales and Garryales
.981	*Salicales

Contains Salicaceae (willow family)

Common names: aspen, cottonwood, poplar

.982	*Garryales

Contains Garryaceae (feverbush family)

584 *Monocotyledones

SUMMARY

584.1	Burmanniales and Orchidales
.2	Zingiberales, Bromeliales, Iridales, Amaryllidales, Dioscoreales, Haemodorales
.3	Liliales, Xyridales, Commelinales
.4	Alstroemeriales, Agavales, Juncales
.5	Palmales
.6	Pandanales, Typhales, Cyclanthales, Arales
.7	Triuridales, Alismatales, Najadales, Butomales, Potamogetonales, Aponogetonales, Juncaginales
.8	Eriocaulales and Cyperales
.9	Graminales

.1	Burmanniales and Orchidales
.13	*Burmanniales

Contains Burmanniaceae, Corsiaceae, Thismiaceae

.15	*Orchidales

Contains Orchidaceae (orchid family)

Common names: cattleya, cymbidium, lady's slipper, vanilla

.2	Zingiberales, Bromeliales, Iridales, Amaryllidales, Dioscoreales, Haemodorales

*Add as instructed under 582–589

.21   *Zingiberales

Contains Zingiberaceae (ginger family), Cannaceae (canna family), Lowiaceae, Marantaceae (arrowroot family), Musaceae (banana family), Strelitziaceae

Common names: abaca, cardamom, ginger lily, Manila hemp, prayer plant, turmeric, zebra plant

Class comprehensive works on hemps in 583.962

.22   *Bromeliales

Contains Bromeliaceae (pineapple family)

Common name: Spanish moss

.24   *Iridales

Contains Iridaceae (iris family)

Common name: crocus, freesia, gladiolus, saffron, tigerflower; blackberry, sword lily

Class comprehensive works on lilies in 584.324

.25   *Amaryllidales

Contains *Amaryllidaceae (amaryllis family)

Common names: daffodil, jonquil, narcissus, snowdrop, snowflake; atamasco, Guernsey, lent, Peruvian, spider lily

Class comprehensive works on lilies in 584.324

.27   *Dioscoreales

Contains Dioscoreaceae (yam family), Roxburghiaceae, Stenomeridaceae, Trichopodaceae

See also 583.79 for sweet potatoes (yams)

.29   *Haemodorales

Contains Haemodoraceae (bloodwort family), Apostasiaceae, Hypoxidaceae, Philydraceae, Taccaceae, Velloziaceae (tree lily family)

Class comprehensive works on lilies in 584.324

.3   Liliales, Xyridales, Commelinales

.32   *Liliales

Contains Pontederiaceae, Ruscaceae, Tecophilaeaceae

.323   *Smilacaceae (Cat brier)

Common names: carrion flower, greenbrier, sarsaparilla

See also 583.687 for wild sarsaparilla of ginseng family, 583.75 for Indian sarsaparilla

*Add as instructed under 582–589

.324   *Liliaceae (Lily family)

> Common names: aloe, asparagus, bluebells, chive, garlic, hyacinth, leek, lilies of the valley, onion, shallots, star-of-Bethlehem, tulips
>
> Class here comprehensive works on lilies
>
> Class lilies not belonging to the Liliaceae family with the family, e.g., water lilies in 583.111, lent lily 584.25
>
> > See also 583.57 for bluebells of bellflower family, 583.77 for bluebells of forget-me-not family

.325   *Trilliaceae (Trillium family)

.36   *Xyridales

> Contains Xyridaceae (yellow-eyed grass family), Rapateaceae

.38   *Commelinales

> Contains Commelinaceae (spiderwort family), Cartonemataceae, Flagellariaceae, Mayacaceae
>
> Common names: boat lily, wandering Jew
>
> Class comprehensive works on lilies in 584.324

.4   Alstroemeriales, Agavales, Juncales

.42   *Alstroemeriales

> Contains Alstroemeriaceae, Petermanniaceae, Philesiaceae
>
> Common name: box lily
>
> Class comprehensive works on lilies in 583.324

.43   *Agavales

> Contains Agavaceae, Xanthorrhoeaceae
>
> Common names: aloe, century plant, dracaena, sansevieria, sisal hemp, snake plant, tequila, yucca
>
> Class comprehensive works on hemps in 583.962

.45   *Juncales

> Contains Juncaceae (rush family), Centrolepidaceae, Restionaceae, Thurniaceae
>
> Class here comprehensive works on rushes
>
> Class rushes of cattail family in 584.613, of sedge family in 584.84

.5   *Palmales

> Contains Arecaceae (Palmae, palm family)
>
> Common names: betel nut, coconut, dates, palmetto, raffia, rattan

.6   Pandanales, Typhales, Cyclanthales, Arales

*Add as instructed under 582–589

| .61 | Pandanales and Typhales |
| .611 | *Pandanales |

Contains Pandanaceae (hala family)

> 584.612–584.613 Typhales

Class comprehensive works in 584.61

| .612 | *Sparganiaceae (Bur-reed family) |
| .613 | *Typhaceae (Cattail family) |

Common names: bulrush

Class comprehensive works on bulrushes in 584.84

| .62 | *Cyclanthales |

Contains Cyclanthaceae (Panama-hat-palm family)

Common name: jipijapa

| .64 | *Arales |

Contains Araceae (arum family), Lemnaceae (duckweed family)

Common names: caladium, calla lily, Chinese evergreen, dieffenbachia, dumb cane, elephant's ears, jack-in-the-pulpit, monstera, philodendron, pothos, skunk cabbage, taro, watermeal

Class comprehensive works on lilies in 584.324

See also 583.123 for cruciferous cabbages

.7   Triuridales, Alismatales, Najadales, Butomales, Potamogetonales, Aponogetonales, Juncaginales

| .71 | *Triuridales |

Contains Triuridaceae

| .72 | Alismatales and Najadales |
| .721 | *Alismatales |

Contains Alismataceae (water-plantain family), Petrosaviaceae, Scheuchzeriaceae

Common names: arrowhead

| .722 | *Najadales |

Contains Najadaceae (naiad family), Zanichelliaceae

| .73 | *Butomales |

Contains Butomaceae (water-poppy family), Hydrocharitaceae (frogbit family)

Common name: turtle grass

*Add as instructed under 582–589

.74 Potamogetonales, Aponogetonales, Juncaginales

.742 *Potamogetonales

Contains Potamogetonaceae (pondweed family), Ruppiaceae (widgeon-grass family)

.743 *Aponogetonales

Contains Aponogetonaceae (lattice-plant family), Zosteraceae (eelgrass family)

.744 *Juncaginales

Contains Juncaginaceae (arrow-grass family), Lilaeaceae, Posidoniaceae

.8 Eriocaulales and Cyperales

.81 *Eriocaulales

Contains Eriocaulaceae (pipewort family)

.84 *Cyperales

Contains Cyperaceae (sedge family)

Common names: Chinese water chestnut, cotton grass, papyrus, umbrella plant; beak, club, spike rush

Including comprehensive works on bulrushes

Class comprehensive works on rushes in 584.45, bulrushes of cattail family in 584.613

.9 *Graminales

Common name: *grasses, reeds

Class here Gramineae (Poaceae)

Class comprehensive works on ecology of grasslands, meadows, prairies in 574.52643

For Cyperaceae, see 584.84

.92 *Panicoideae

Contains Paniceae (millet tribe), Andropogoneae (sugar-cane tribe), Maydeae (maize tribe)

Common names: citronella grass, corn, crabgrass, durra, milo, panic grass, proso, shallu, sorghum, Sudan grass, thatching grass

*Add as instructed under 582–589

.93　　　　*Pooideae

> Contains Agrosteae, Anomochloeae, Arundineae, Arundinelleae, Aveneae (oat tribe), Bambuseae (bamboo tribe), Chlorideae (gama-grass tribe), Eragrosteae, Festuceae (fescue tribe), Hordeeae (barley tribe), Leptureae, Lygeeae, Nardeae, Olyreae, Oryzeae (rice tribe), Pappophoreae, Parianeae, Phalarideae (canary-grass tribe), Phareae, Sporoboleae, Stipeae, Streptochaeteae, Thysanolaeneae, Zoysieae
>
> Common names: bent grass, bluegrass, bromegrass, cocksfoot, fiorin, fodder grass, lawn grass, orchard grass, pampas grass, pasture grass, rye, timothy, wheat

585　　*Gymnospermae (Pinophyta)

> Common name: naked-seed plants

.1　　*Gneticae

> Contains Gnetales, Ephedrales, Welwitschiales
>
> Common names: ephedra, Gnetum, Mormon tea, tumboa plant

.2　　*Coniferales (*Conifers) and Taxales (yews)

> Coniferales contains Araucariaceae, Cephalotaxaceae, Cupressaceae (cypress family), Pinaceae (pine family), Podocarpaceae, Taxodiaceae (bald-cypress family)
>
> Common names: arborvitae, cedar, firs, hemlock, juniper, larch, piñon, redwoods, sequoias, spruce, tamarack

.7　　*Ginkgoales

> Contains *Ginkgoaceae
>
> Common names: *ginkgo, *maidenhair tree

.9　　*Cycadales (Cycads)

> Contains Cycadaceae
>
> Common name: sago palm

586　　Cryptogamia (Seedless plants)

> *For Pteridophyta, see 587; Bryophyta, 588; Thallophyta, 589*

.001–.008　　Standard subdivisions

.009　　Historical, geographical, persons treatment of the study of Cryptogamia

> Class geographical treatment of Cryptogamia in 586.09

.01–.08　　Processes and parts

> Add to base number 586.0 the numbers following 581 in 581.1–581.8, e.g., anatomy 586.04

*Add as instructed under 582–589

.09   Geographical treatment

> Add to base number 586.09 the numbers following 574.9 in 574.909–574.999, e.g., tropical Cryptogamia 586.09093

587   *Pteridophyta (Vascular cryptogams)

.1   ***Isoetales (Quillworts)**

.2   ***Sphenopsida**

> Contains Equisetales (horsetail family)

.3   ***Polypodiorsida (Filicineae)**

> Class here ferns

.31   *Polypodiales (Filicales), Marsileales, Saviniales

> Examples of *Polypodiales: Polypodiaceae, Aspleniaceae, Cyatheaceae, Gleicheniaceae, Osmundaceae, Schizaeaceae
>
> Common names: bracken, brake; maidenhair, royal, staghorn fern

.33   *Eusporangiated ferns

> Contains Marattiales, Ophioglossales
>
> Common names: adder's tongue, giant, grape, rattlesnake fern; moonwort

.4   ***Psilopsida**

> Contains Psilotales
>
> Common name: whisk fern

.9   ***Lycopsida (Club mosses)**

> Contains Lycopodiales, Selaginellales
>
> Common names: resurrection plant, spike moss
>
> *For Isoetales, see 587.1*

588   *Bryophyta

.1   ***Sphagnales**

> Contains Sphagnaceae (peat moss, bog moss)

.2   ***Musci (True mosses)**

> Contains Andreaeales (black mosses), Bryales (common mosses)
>
> *For Sphagnales, see 588.1*

.3   **Anthocerotae and Hepaticae**

.32   *Anthocerotae (Hornworts)

*Add as instructed under 582–589

.33   *Hepaticae (Liverworts)

> Contains Jungermanniaceae (scale mosses), Marchantiaceae (great liverworts), Ricciaceae
>
> Class Anthocerotae in 588.32

589   *Thallobionta (Thallophyta) and Prokaryotae

Class comprehensive works on microorganisms in 576

SUMMARY

589.1	**Lichens**
.2	**Fungi**
.3	**Algae**
.4	**Specific types of algae**
.9	**Prokaryotae Bacteria**

> ## 589.1–589.4 Thallobionta (Thallophyta)

Class comprehensive works in 589

.1   ***Lichens**

.2   ***Fungi**

> Class here mycology
>
> *For lichens, see 589.1*

> ## 589.22–589.25 Eumycophyta (True fungi)

Class comprehensive works in 589.2

.22   *Basidiomycetes

.221   *Homobasidiomycetidae

> Contains Exobasidiales, Hymenogastrales (false tubers), Lycoperdales (puffballs), Nidulariales (bird's-nest fungi), Phallales (stinkhorns), Sclerodermatales
>
> *For Agaricales and Polyporales, see 589.222*

.222   *Agaricales (Gill fungi) and Polyporales

> Examples of *Agaricales: Agaricaceae, Boletaceae (boletes), Hydnaceae (spine fungi), Thelephoraceae (leather fungi)
>
> Common name: toadstools
>
> Class here comprehensive works on mushrooms
>
> Class mushrooms of orders other than Agaricales with the order, e.g., morels 589.23

*Add as instructed under 582–589

| [.222 3] | Agaricaceae |

[.222 3] Agaricaceae

Number discontinued; class in 589.222

.222 5 *Polyporales

Common names: bracket, club, coral, pore, shelf fungi

.225 *Heterobasidiomycetidae

Contains *Uredinales (rusts), Tremellales (jelly fungi)

For Ustilaginales, see 589.227

.227 *Ustilaginales (Smuts)

.23 *Ascomycetes

Examples: Clavicipitales, Helotiales, Laboulbeniales, Microascales, Pezizales, Pleosporales, Tuberales (truffles), Xylariales

Common names: cup, sac, saddle fungi; Aspergillus, ergot, morel, Neurospora, penicillium, powdery mildew

.233 *Saccharomycetaceae (Sporogenous yeasts)

Class here comprehensive works on yeasts

For Cryptococcales (asporogenous yeasts), see 589.24

.24 *Fungi Imperfecti (Deuteromycetes)

Contains Cryptococcales (asporogenous yeasts), Melanconiales, Moniliales, Mycelia Sterilia, Sphaeropsidales

Class Penicillium in 589.23

.25 *Other fungi

Classes formerly known as Phycomycetes

Class here Mastigomycotina, comprehensive works on molds and mildews

Class ascomycete molds and mildew in 589.23, slime molds in 589.29

.251 *Oomycetes

Former name: Biflagellates

Contains Lagenidiales, Leptomitales

For Peronosporales, see 589.252; Saprolegniales, 589.256

.252 *Peronosporales (Downy mildews)

.256 *Saprolegniales

.258 Chytridiomycetes, Hyphochytridiomycetes, Plasmodiophoromycetes, Trichomycetes, Zygomycetes

Former heading: Uniflagellates and nonflagellates

Common name: bread molds, Rhizopus

*Add as instructed under 582–589

.29   *Myxomycophyta (Slime molds)

> Variant names: Myxomycetes, Myxomycota, Myxomycotina
>
> Examples: Physarales, Stemonitales, Trichiales
>
> Class Class Mycetozoa (Myxomycophyta considered as animals) in 593.115

.3   **Algae**

> Class here algology, phycology
>
> *For specific types of algae, see 589.4; lichens, 589.1*

.309   Historical, geographical, persons treatment of phycology

> Class geographical treatment of algae in 589.39

.31–.38   Processes and parts

> Add to base number 589.3 the numbers following 581 in 581.1–581.8, e.g., industrial algae 589.364

.39   Geographical treatment

> Add to base number 589.39 the numbers following 574.9 in 574.909–574.999, e.g., tropical algae 589.39093

.4   **Specific types of algae**

> Including Chloromonadophyta, Cryptophyta
>
> Class here phytoneuston, phytoplankton

.41   *Rhodophyta (Red algae)

> Contains Bangiales, Bonnemaisoniales, Ceramiales, Compsopogonales, Cryptonemiales, Gelidiales, Gigartinales, Goniotrichales, Nemalionales, Porphyridiales, Rhodochaetales, Rhodymeniales
>
> Common names: amanoris, red seaweed

.43   *Pyrrophyta (Dinoflagellates)

> Contains Dinocapsales, Dinococcales, Dinophysidales, Dinotrichales, Gymnodiniales, Peridiniales, Prorocentrales, Rhizodiniales
>
> Common name: red tide
>
> Class Dinoflagellida (Dinoflagellates considered as animals) in 593.18

.44   *Euglenophyta (Euglenoids)

> Contains Euglenales, Euglenamorphales, Eutreptiales, Heteronematales, Rhabdomonadales, Sphenomonadales
>
> Class Euglenida (Euglenophyta considered as animals) in 593.18

*Add as instructed under 582–589

.45   *Phaeophyta (Brown algae)

Contains Ascoseirales, Chordariales, Cutleriales, Desmarestiales, Dictyosiphonales, Dictyotales, Durvilleales, Ectocarpales, Fucales, Laminariales, Sphacelariales, Sporochnales, Tilopteridales

Common names: kelps, rockweeds, sargassum

Including algin, comprehensive works on seaweeds

For red seaweeds, see 589.41

.46   *Cyanophyta (Blue-green algae)

Variant name: cyanobacteria

Contains Chamaesiphonales, Chroococcales, Nostocales, Pleurocapsales, Stigonematales

Class comprehensive works on Prokaryotae in 589.9

.47   *Chlorophyta (Green algae)

Contains Chaetophorales, Charales, Chlorococcales, Cladophorales, Conjugales, Dasycladales, Derbesiales, Dichotomosiphonales, Halosphaerales, Oedongoniales, Pyramimonadales, Siphonales, Siphonocladales, Ulotrichales, Volvocales

Common names: Acetabularia, chlamydomonas, Codium, desmids, Eudorina, sea lettuce, spirogyra, stonewort, water net

.48   *Chrysophyta (Golden algae)

.481   *Bacillariophyceae (Diatoms)

Contains Centrales, Pennales

.486   *Xanthophyceae (Yellow-green algae)

Contains Chloramoebales, Heterogloeales, Mischococcales, Rhizochloridales, Tribonematales, Vaucheriales

Common name: water felt

.487   *Chrysophyceae and Haptophyceae

Contains Chrysocapsales, Chrysomonadales, Chrysosphaerales, Chrysotrichales, Isochrysidales, Prymnesiales, Rhizochrysidales

.9   Prokaryotae   Bacteria

Class here bacteriology, Monera, Schizomycetes, Schizophyta

Examples: Archaeobacteria (methane-producing bacteria); phototrophic (green and purple), sheathed, spiral and curved bacteria; Mycoplasmatales (Mollicutes)

For rickettsias and viruses, see 576.6; Cyanophyta, 589.46

.900 1–.900 8   Standard subdivisions

.900 9   Historical, geographical, persons treatment of prokaryotology, of bacteriology

Class geographical treatment of Prokaryotae, of bacteria in 589.909

*Add as instructed under 582–589

.901–.908 Processes and parts

Add to base number 589.90 the numbers following 581 in 581.1–581.8, e.g. anaerobic respiration 589.90128

.909 Geographical treatment

Add to base number 589.909 the numbers following 574.9 in 574.909–574.999, e.g., tropical bacteria 589.909093

.92 *Actinomycetales (Cornyform bacteria)

Examples: Actinomycetaceae, Frankiaceae, Mycobacteriaceae, Nocardiaceae, Streptomycetaceae, thermophylic bacteria

.93 *Chlamydiales

Class here Chlamydia

.94 *Budding and appendaged bacteria

Examples: Caulobacter, Gallionella, Hyphomicrobium, Nevskia, Pasteuria, Prothecomicrobia

.95 *Eubacteriales

Contains endospore forming rods and cocci, gram-negative aerobic rods and cocci, gram-negative anaerobic bacteria, gram negative anaerobic cocci, gram-negative cocci and coccobacilli, gram-negative facultatively anaerobic rods, gram-positive cocci, gram positive asporogenous rod-shaped bacteria

Examples: Acetobacteriaceae, Azotobacteriaceae, Bacillaceae, Bacteriaceae, Enterobacteriaceae, Halobacteriaceae, Lactobacteriaceae, Micrococcaceae, Neisseriaceae, Nitrobacteriaceae, Pseudomonadaceae, Rhizobiaceae, Streptococcaceae, Vibrionaceae

Common genera: Brucella, Clostridium, Erwinia, Escherichia, Gluconobacter, Klebsiella, Legionella, Listeria, Pasteurella, Proteus, Salmonella, Serritia, Shigella, Yersinia, Zoogloea

.96 *Gram-negative chemolithotrophic bacteria, gliding bacteria

Former heading: Thiobacteriales

Examples: Achromatiaceae, Beggiatoaceae, sulfur bacteria

For Nitrobacteriaceae, see 589.95; Myxobacterales, 589.98

.98 *Myxobacterales

Contains Archangiaceae, Cystobacteriaceae, Myxococcaceae, Polyangiaceae

Class comprehensive works on gliding bacteria in 589.96

.99 *Spirochaetales

Contains Spirochaetaceae

Common genera: Borrelia, Leptospira, Treponema

*Add as instructed under 582–589

590   Zoological sciences

Use 590 by itself only for works including substantial treatment of paleozoology. Use 591 for general zoology

For paleozoology, see 560

See Manual at 580–590; 580–590 vs. 630, 641.3; 800 vs. 591, 636, 398.245

SUMMARY

590.74	**Museums, collections, exhibits**
591	**Zoology**
592	**Invertebrates**
593	**Protozoa, Parazoa, Coelenterata, Echinodermata, related phyla**
594	**Mollusca and Molluscoidea**
595	**Other invertebrates**
596	**Vertebrata (Craniata, Vertebrates)**
597	**Cold-blooded vertebrates** **Pisces (Fishes)**
598	**Aves (Birds)**
599	**Mammalia (Mammals)**

.74   Museums, collections, exhibits

.742   Museums

Add to base number 590.742 notation 1 or 3–9 from Table 2, e.g., museums of Australia 590.74294

.744   Zoological gardens

Class here general zoos, zoos limited to vertebrates, to land vertebrates, to mammals

Add to base number 590.744 notation 1 or 3–9 from Table 2, e.g., zoos of Germany 590.74443

Class zoos limited to other groups of animals with the group, e.g., insect zoos 595.70074, aquariums for marine vertebrates in Spain 596.09207446

591   Zoology

Class microscopy regardless of kind of animal in 578, collection and preservation of zoological specimens regardless of kind of animal in 579

For specific animals and groups of animals, see 592–599

See Manual at 591; 591 vs. 610; 800 vs. 591, 636, 398.245

SUMMARY

591.01–.09	**[Standard subdivisions, rare and endangered animals]**
.1	**Physiology of animals**
.2	**Pathology of animals**
.3	**Development and maturation of animals**
.4	**Anatomy and morphology of animals**
.5	**Ecology of animals**
.6	**Economic zoology**
.8	**Tissue, cellular, molecular zoology**
.9	**Geographical treatment of animals**

.04	Special topics
[.042]	Rare and endangered animals
	Relocated to 591.529
.072	Research
.072 4	Experimental zoology
	Including tissue and organ culture, use of specific animals and groups of animals to study general zoology
.074	Museums, collections, exhibits
	Class zoological gardens in 590.744
.075	Museum activities and services
	Class collection and preservation of zoological specimens regardless of kind of animal in 579
.09	Historical, geographical, persons treatment
	Class geographical treatment of animals in 591.9

.1   **Physiology of animals**

Class here comprehensive works on physiology and anatomy

Class microphysiology in 591.8; physiology and anatomy of domesticated animals in 636.0891−636.0892

For pathological physiology, see 591.21; development and maturation, 591.3; anatomy, 591.4

See Manual at 612.1−612.8

.104	Special topics
.104 2	Regional physiology
	Examples: physiology of legs, of abdomens
.11−.13	Circulation, respiration, nutrition, metabolism
	Add to base number 591.1 the numbers following 574.1 in 574.11−574.13, e.g., circulatory fluids 591.113; however, class role of circulatory fluids and their components in immunity in 591.29
.14	Secretion and excretion
.142	Endocrine secretion
.143	Exocrine secretion
.149	Excretion
.15	Genetics
	Add to base number 591.15 the numbers following 581.15 in 581.152−581.159, e.g., mutations 591.1592
	Class physiological genetics in 591.87322

.16	Reproduction

Add to base number 591.16 the numbers following 574.16 in 574.162–574.166, e.g., parthenogenesis 591.162

.17	Histogenesis

Formation and differentiation of tissues

.18	Movements, senses, control processes
.182	Response to external stimuli

Class here sensory functions, physiology of sense organs

.182 3	To light
.182 5	To sound and related vibrations
.182 6	To chemical stimuli

Including olfaction and gustation

.182 7	To touch

Including irritability

.185	Motor system and integument
.185 2	Motor system

Contains muscles, connective tissue, skeletal system

Including locomotion, biomechanics

.185 8	Integument
.188	Control processes

Including nervous system, physiological balance

Class control of a specific organ or function with the subject, e.g., control of muscles 591.1852

.188 2	Biological rhythms
.19	Biophysics and biochemistry

Add to base number 591.19 the numbers following 574.19 in 574.191–574.192, e.g., radiobiology 591.1915

Class physics and chemistry of a specific process or part of animals with the process or part, e.g., sensory biophysics 591.182

.2	**Pathology of animals**

Class here pathogenicity, degeneration, death

Class histopathology in 591.828, cell pathology in 591.8765, pathology of agricultural animals in 636.089607

.21	Pathological physiology

Add to base number 591.21 the numbers following 591.1 in 591.11–591.19, e.g., pathological physiology of excretion 591.2149

.22   Pathological anatomy

Class here teratology

Add to base number 591.22 the numbers following 591.4 in 591.41–591.49, e.g., pathological anatomy of excretory organs 591.224

.23–.29   Causes of diseases and immunity

Add to base number 591.2 the numbers following 574.2 in 574.23–574.29, e.g., interferons 591.295 [*formerly* 576.64]

See Manual at 591.29 vs. 616.079

.3   Development and maturation of animals

For histogenesis, see 591.17

See Manual at 612.1–612.8

.31–.37   Sex and specific stages

Add to base number 591.3 the numbers following 574.3 in 574.31–574.37, e.g., sex 591.36

.38   Evolution

Class genetics in 591.15

.39   Young of animals

.4   Anatomy and morphology of animals

Class comprehensive works on anatomy, morphology, physiology in 591.1, anatomical embryology in 591.332, microanatomy in 591.8, anatomy of domesticated animals in 636.0891

For pathological anatomy, see 591.22

See Manual at 612.1–612.8

.41   Circulatory organs

.42   Respiratory organs

.43   Nutritive and metabolic organs

.44   Secretory and excretory organs

.46   Reproductive organs

.47   Muscular, skeletal, integumentary organs; connective tissues

.471   Skeletal organs

.48   Nervous system and sense organs

.49   Regional and topographical anatomy

Examples: anatomy of legs, of abdomens

.5   Ecology of animals

Class here adaptations

.51   Habits and behavior patterns (Ethology)

> Class specific habits or behavior patterns in 591.52–591.59
>
> *See Manual at 156 vs. 302–307*

.52   Specific relationships and kinds of environments

> Class animal paleoecology in 560.45; specific adaptations to specific relationships and kinds of environments in 591.53–591.59

.522–.524   Interrelations of organisms and environment, and of species to species

> Add to base number 591.52 the numbers following 574.52 in 574.522–574.524, e.g., animal populations 591.5248

.525   Migrations

.526   Specific kinds of environments

> Add to base number 591.526 the numbers following 574.526 in 574.5262–574.5268, e.g., urban environments 591.5268

.529   Rare and endangered animals [*formerly* 591.042]

> Including animals that have recently become extinct

>   591.53–591.59 Specific adaptations

Class comprehensive works in 591.5

.53   Nutritive adaptations

> Including food chains, predation

.54   Adaptations to weather, climate, seasons

.542   Weather and climate

> Examples: acclimation, temperature adaptations

.543   Seasonal changes

> Example: hibernation

.56   Reproductive and related adaptations

.562   Courtship

.564   Habitations

> Examples: burrows, nests

.566   Territoriality

.57   Protective adaptations

.572   Camouflage

.59   Communication and production of sound

.6　　　　**Economic zoology**

> See Manual at 580–590 vs. 630, 641.3

.61　　　Beneficial animals

.65　　　Deleterious animals

> *For poisonous animals, see 591.69*

.69　　　Poisonous animals

.8　　　**Tissue, cellular, molecular zoology**

> Add to base number 591.8 the numbers following 574.8 in 574.82–574.88, e.g., physiological genetics 591.87322

> *For histogenesis, see 591.17*

.9　　　**Geographical treatment of animals**

> Add to base number 591.9 the numbers following 574.9 in 574.909–574.999, e.g., marine zoology 591.92

> ## 592–599 Specific animals and groups of animals

> Aside from additions, changes, deletions, exceptions shown under specific entries, add to notation for each term identified by * as follows:
>
> 04　　　　　Processes and parts
> 　　　　　　　Add to base number 04 the numbers following 591 in 591.1–591.8, e.g., genetics 0415
> 　　　　　　　Do not add notation from 591.1–591.8 when redundant, e.g., sexual reproduction of carnivores 599.740416 (*not* 599.7404166)
>
> 075　　　　Museum activities and services
> 　　　　　　　Class collection and preservation of zoological specimens in 579
>
> 09　　　　　Historical, geographical, persons treatment
> 091　　　　Treatment by areas, regions, places in general
> 0916
>
> 　　　　　　　Class hydrographic zoology of specific continents, countries, localities in 093–099
> 093–099　Treatment by specific continents, countries, localities
>
> Class comprehensive works in 591
>
> *See Manual notes under subdivisions of 574; under 591 and subdivisions*

592　Invertebrates

> *For Protozoa, Parazoa, Coelenterata, Echinodermata, related phyla, see 593; Mollusca and Molluscoidea, 594; other invertebrates, 595*

.001–.008　　Standard subdivisions

.009	Historical, geographical, persons treatment of the study of invertebrates

Class geographical treatment of invertebrates in 592.09

.01–.08	Processes and parts

Add to base number 592.0 the numbers following 591 in 591.1–591.8, e.g., poisonous invertebrates 592.069

.09	Geographical treatment

Add to base number 592.09 the numbers following 574.9 in 574.909–574.999, e.g., desert invertebrates 592.090954

593 Protozoa, Parazoa, Coelenterata, Echinodermata, related phyla

SUMMARY

593.1	Protozoa Plasmodroma
.4	Parazoa Porifera (Sponges)
.5	Coelenterata (Cnidaria)
.6	Anthozoa
.7	Hydrozoa and Scyphozoa
.8	Ctenophora (Comb jellies)
.9	Echinodermata, Linguatula, Hemichordata

.1	*Protozoa *Plasmodroma
.11	*Sarcodina

Class here Rhizopodea

For Foraminifera, see 593.12; Actinopoda, 593.13

.113	*Proteomyxida
.115	*Mycetozoa

Contains Acrasida, Eumycetozoida, Plasmodiophorida

Class here Mycetozoia

Class Class Myxomycophyta (Mycetozoa considered as plants) in 589.29

.117	*Amoebida
.118	*Testacea (Arcellinida)
.12	*Foraminifera
.13	*Actinopoda

For Radiolaria, see 593.14

.132	*Heliozoa
.14	*Radiolaria

*Add as instructed under 592–599

.17   *Ciliophora (Ciliates)

Contains Holotricia, Peritrichia, Spirotrichia

[.172]   Ciliata

Number discontinued; class in 591.17

.175   *Suctoria

>   593.18–593.19 Plasmodroma

Class comprehensive works in 593.1

For Sarcodina, see 593.11

.18   *Mastigophora

Examples: Chloromonadida, Chrysomonadida, Cryptomonadida, Dinoflagellida, Euglenida, Hypermastigida, Rhizomastigida, Trichomonadida

Class Dinoflagellates (Dinoflagellida considered as plants) in 589.43, Euglenophyta (Euglenida considered as plants) in 589.44

.19   *Sporozoa and *Cnidospora

Examples: Coccidia, Toxoplasmea

.4   *Parazoa   *Porifera (Sponges)

.42   *Calcispongiae (Calcarea)

Contains Calcaronea, Calcinea

.44   *Hyalospongiae (Hexactinellida)

Common name: glass sponges

.46   *Demospongiae

Examples: Haplosclerida, Spongillidae

.5   *Coelenterata (Cnidaria)

For Anthozoa, see 593.6; Hydrozoa and Scyphozoa, 593.7

.6   *Anthozoa

Contains Alcyonaria, Zoantharia (Hexacorallia)

Common names: corals, sea anemones, sea fans, sea pens

.7   Hydrozoa and Scyphozoa

Class here jellyfish, medusas

.71   *Hydrozoa

Contains Chondrophora, Hydroida, Milleporina, Pteromedusae, Siphonophora, Stylasterina, Trachylina

Common names: hydras, hydroids, Portuguese man-of-war

*Add as instructed under 592–599

.73   *Scyphozoa

    Contains Coronatae, Cubomedusae, Rhizostomeae, Semaeostomeae, Stauromedusae (Lucernariida)

.8   *Ctenophora (Comb jellies)

    Contains Nuda, Tentaculata

    Example: sea walnuts

.9   *Echinodermata, Linguatula, Hemichordata

\>   593.91–593.96 Echinodermata

    Class comprehensive works in 593.9

    See also 595.185 for Echinodera

.91   *Crinoidea (Sea lilies)

    Examples: Adunata, Articulata

.93   *Asteroidea (Starfish)

    Examples: Forcipulatida, Phanerozonida, Spinulosida

.94   *Ophiuroidea

    Examples: Ophiurida, Phrynophiurida

    Common names: basket star, brittle star

.95   *Echinoidea

    Contains Euechinoidea, Perischoechinoidea

    Common names: sand dollar, sea urchin

.96   *Holothurioidea (Sea cucumbers)

    Examples: Apodida, Aspidochirotida, Dendrochirotida, Elasipodida, Molpadiida

.99   Linguatula and Hemichordata

.992   *Linguatula (Pentastomida)

.993   *Hemichordata

    Contains Enteropneusta, Planctosphaeroidea

    For Pterobranchia, see 594.73

*Add as instructed under 592–599

594   Mollusca and Molluscoidea

Examples: Aplacophora, Monoplacophora

.001–.008   Standard subdivisions of Mollusca

.009   Historical, geographical, persons treatment of the study of Mollusca

> Class geographic treatment of Mollusca in 594.09

.01–.08   Processes and parts of Mollusca

> Add to base number 594.0 the numbers following 591 in 591.1–591.8, e.g., shells 594.0471

.09   Geographical treatment of Mollusca

> Add to base number 594.09 the numbers following 574.9 in 574.909–574.999, e.g., tropical mollusks 594.09093

>   **594.1–594.5 Mollusca (Mollusks)**

Class comprehensive works in 594

.1   **Bivalvia and Amphineura**

.11   *Bivalvia (Lamellibranchia, Pelecypoda)

> Examples: Mytiloida, Unionidae
>
> Common names: clams, mussels, oysters, shipworms

.19   *Amphineura (Polyplacophora, Chitons)

> Use of this number for Aplacophora discontinued; class in 594

.2   ***Scaphopoda (Toothshells)**

.3   ***Gastropoda**

> Common names: limpet, slugs, snails

.32   *Streptoneura (Prosobranchia)

> Examples: Archeogastropoda, Mesogastropoda, Neogastropoda
>
> Common names: cowries, whelks

.34   *Opisthobranchia

> *For Pteropoda and Sacoglossa, see 594.35; Acoelea, 594.36; Tectibranchia, 594.37*

.35   *Pteropoda and *Sacoglossa

.36   *Acoelea

> Examples: Notaspidea, Nudibranchia (sea slugs)

.37   *Tectibranchia (Anaspidea)

*Add as instructed under 592–599

.38	*Pulmonata

        Contains: Basommatophora, Stylommatophora, Systellommatophora

.5   ***Cephalopoda**

        Including Coleoidea

.52	*Nautiloidea
.55	*Vampyromorpha
.56	*Octopoda (Octopuses)
.58	*Decapoda

        Contains Sepioidea, Teuthoidea

        Common names: cuttlefish, squid

.6   ***Molluscoidea**

        For Bryozoa, see 594.7; Brachiopoda, 594.8; Phoronidea, 595.17; Entoprocta, 595.188

.7   ***Bryozoa and Pterobranchia**

        Including Cyclostomata, Stenolaemata

>   594.71–594.72 Bryozoa (Ectoprocta, Polyzoa)

        Common names: moss animal, sea mat

        Class comprehensive works in 594.7

.71	*Gymnolaemata

        Contains *Cheilostomata, Ctenostomata

        Use of this number for Cyclostomata discontinued; class in 594.7

.72	*Phylactolaemata
.73	*Pterobranchia

.8   ***Brachiopoda (Lamp shells)**

595   Other invertebrates

SUMMARY

595.1	Worms and related animals
.2	Arthropoda
.3	Crustacea and Chelicerata
.4	Arachnida
.5	Onychophora
.6	Progoneata
.7	Insecta (Insects)

*Add as instructed under 592–599

.1	***Worms and related animals**
	Class here helminthology
.12	*Platyhelminthes and Nemertea

>	595.121–595.123 Platyhelminthes (Flatworms)
	Class comprehensive works in 595.12
.121	*Cestoda (Tapeworms)
	Contains Cestodaria, Eucestoda
.122	*Trematoda (Flukes) and Monogenea
	Trematoda contains Aspidogastrea, Digenea
.123	*Turbellaria
	Contains Acoela, Alloeocoela, Polycladida, Rhabdocoela, Tricladida (Planaria)
.124	*Nemertea (Rhynchocoela)
	Contains Anopla, Enopla
.13	*Acanthocephala
	Contains Archiacanthocephala, Eoacanthocephala, Palaeacanthocephala
	Common name: spiny-headed worm
.14	*Annelida (Segmented worms)
.142	*Archiannelida
.145	*Hirudinea (Leeches)
	Contains Acanthobdellida, Gnathobdellida, Pharyngobdellida, Rhynchobdellida
.146	*Oligochaeta
	Contains Opisthopora (Earthworms), Pleisiopora, Prosopora
.147	*Polychaeta
	Contains Errantia, Sedentaria
	For Archiannelida, see 595.142; Myzostomida, 595.148
.148	*Myzostomida
.17	Echiurida, Phoronidea, Priapulida, Sipunculida
	Class here Gephyrea
.18	*Aschelminthes and other groups

*Add as instructed under 592–599

>   595.181–595.185 Aschelminthes

            Class comprehensive works in 595.18

.181   *Rotifera

.182   *Nematoda (Roundworms)

.183   *Gastrotricha

.184   *Nematomorpha (Horsehair worms)

            Class here Gordioida

.185   *Kinorhyncha (Echinodera)

            See also 593.9 for Echinodermata

.186   *Chaetognatha (Arrowworms)

.187   *Tardigrada (Water bears)

.188   *Entoprocta

.2   ***Arthropoda**

            For Crustacea and Chelicerata, see 595.3; Progoneata, 595.6

.3   ***Crustacea and Chelicerata**

>   595.31–595.38 Crustacea

            Class comprehensive works in 595.3

.31   *Branchiura (Fish lice), Cephalocarida, Mystacocarida

.32   *Branchiopoda

            Contains Anostraca, Cladocera, Conchostraca, Notostraca

            Common names: clam, fairy, tadpole shrimp; water flea

.33   *Ostracoda (Seed shrimp)

            Contains Cladocopa, Myodocopa, Platycopa, Podocopa

.34   *Copepoda (Cyclops)

            Contains Arguloida, Calanoida, Caligoida, Cyclopoida, Harpacticoida, Lernaeopodoida, Monstrilloida, Notodelphyoida

.35   *Cirripedia (Barnacles)

            Contains Acrothoracica, Ascothoracica, Rhizocephala, Thoracica

.36   *Leptostraca

            Example: Nebaliacea

            Class Malacostraca in 595.37

*Add as instructed under 592–599

.37   *Eumalacostraca

Class here Malacostraca, Pericarida

For Leptostraca, see 595.36; Cumacea, Hoplocarida, Mysidacea, Decapoda, 595.38

.371   *Amphipoda

Contains Caprellidea, Gammaridea, Hyperiidea, Ingolfiellidea

Common names: sand flea, sand hopper, whale lice

.372   *Isopoda

Contains Anthuridea, Asellota, Epicaridea, Flabellifera, Gnathidea, Oniscoidea (sow bug, wood lice), Phreatoicidea, Valvifera

.373   *Pancarida (Thermosbaenacea)

.374   *Tanaidacea

.379   *Syncarida

Contains Anaspidacea, Bathynellacea, Stygocaridacea

.38   Cumacea, Hoplocarida, Mysidacea, Decapoda

.381   *Cumacea

.382   *Hoplocarida (Mantis shrimp)

Class here Stomatopoda

.383   *Mysidacea (Opossum shrimp)

.384   *Decapoda

Class here Eucarida, Reptantia

For Euphausiacea, see 595.385

.384 1   *Macrura (Lobster and crayfish)

.384 2   *Brachyura (Crabs)

.384 3   *Natantia (Shrimp and prawn)

.384 4   *Anomura (Hermit crab and king crab)

.385   *Euphausiacea

.39   *Chelicerata

For Arachnida, see 595.4

.392   *Xiphosura (Horseshoe crab)

.394   *Pycnogonida (Sea spiders)

.4   ***Arachnida**

.41   *Ricinulei

*Add as instructed under 592–599

.42	*Acari (Mites and ticks)

Contains Acariformes, Opilioacariformes, Parasitiformes

.43	*Phalangida (Opilionea)

Common names: daddy longlegs, harvestman

.44	*Araneida (Araneae)

Common name: spiders

.45	Palpigradi and Pedipalpi
.452	*Palpigradi
.453	*Pedipalpi
.453 2	*Uropygi (Whip scorpions)
.453 6	*Amblypygi (Tailless whip scorpions)
.46	*Scorpiones (Scorpions)
.47	*Pseudoscorpiones (False scorpions)
.48	*Solifugae (Weasel spiders and sun spiders)
.5	***Onychophora**

Class here Oncopods (Pararthropoda)

.6	***Progoneata**

Class here Myriapoda

For Insecta, see 595.7

.61	*Diplopoda (Millipedes)
.62	*Chilopoda (Centipedes)

Class here Opisthogoneata

.63	*Symphyla
.64	*Pauropoda

*Add as instructed under 592–599

.7 Insecta (Insects)

Class here entomology, Hexapoda, Pterygota

SUMMARY

595.700 1–.700 9	**Standard subdivisions**
.701–.709	**[Processes and parts, geographical treatment of Insecta]**
.71	**Apterygota**
.72	**Orthoptera and related orders**
.73	**Thysanoptera and miscellaneous orders**
.74	**Mecoptera, Trichoptera, Strepsiptera, Neuroptera**
.75	**Apterous insects, Homoptera, Hemiptera**
.76	**Coleoptera (Beetles)**
.77	**Diptera and Siphonaptera**
.78	**Lepidoptera**
.79	**Hymenoptera**

.700 1–.700 8	Standard subdivisions
.700 9	Historical, geographical, persons treatment of entomology

Class geographical treatment of Insecta in 595.709

.701–.708	Processes and parts

Add to base number 595.70 the numbers following 591 in 591.1–591.8, e.g., morphology 595.704

.709	Geographical treatment of Insecta

Add to base number 595.709 the numbers following 574.9 in 574.909–574.999, e.g., desert insects 595.7090954

.71	*Apterygota
.712	*Protura
.713	*Thysanura (Bristletails)
.714	*Diplura (Entotrophi)
.715	*Collembola (Springtails)
.72	Orthoptera and related orders
.721	*Dermaptera (Earwigs)
.722	*Blattaria (Cockroaches)
.724	*Phasmatodea

Common names: leaf insect, stick insect, walkingstick

.725	*Mantodea (Mantises)
.726	*Orthoptera

Common names: crickets, grasshoppers, katydids, locusts

.73	Thysanoptera and miscellaneous orders
.731	*Thysanoptera (Thrips)

*Add as instructed under 592–599

.732	*Psocoptera (Corrodentia)
	Common name: book lice
.733	*Odonata
	Common names: damselfly, dragonfly
.734	*Ephemeroptera (Mayfly)
.735	*Plecoptera (Stone flies)
.736	*Isoptera (Termites)
.737	*Embioptera
.738	*Zoraptera
.74	Mecoptera, Trichoptera, Strepsiptera, Neuroptera
.742	*Megaloptera
	Common name: dobsonflies
.744	*Mecoptera (Scorpion flies)
.745	*Trichoptera (Caddis flies)
.746	*Strepsiptera
.747	*Neuroptera
	Common names: ant lions, lacewings, snake flies
	For Megaloptera, see 595.742
.75	*Apterous insects, Homoptera, Hemiptera
.751	*Apterous insects (Lice)
.751 2	*Anoplura (True lice, Sucking lice)
.751 4	*Mallophaga (Bird lice, Biting lice)
.752	*Homoptera
	Examples: Aleyrodoidea, Cercopoidea, Coccoidea, Fulgoroidea, Membracoidea
	Common names: aphids, cicadas, leaf hoppers, scale insects, whiteflies
.754	*Hemiptera (True bugs)
	Variant name: Heteroptera
	Examples: Aradoidea, Cimicoidea, Coreoidea, Dipsocoroidea, Gerroidea, Helotrephoidea, Lygaeoidea, Reduvioidea, Tingoidea
	Class here comprehensive works on Hemiptera and Homoptera
	For Homoptera, see 595.752

*Add as instructed under 592–599

| .76 | *Coleoptera (Beetles) |
| | Class here Polyphaga |

.76   *Coleoptera (Beetles)

Class here Polyphaga

Not all beetle taxa are provided for below; use 595.76 for those not listed

Class Strepsiptera in 595.746

.762   *Adephaga

Examples: Caraboidea, Gyrinoidea, Rhysodoidea

Common names: ground, tiger, true water, whirligig beetle

.764   Miscellaneous Polyphaga

Only those named below

Use of this number for comprehensive works on Polyphaga discontinued; class in 595.76

.764 1   *Hydrophiloidea

.764 2   *Staphylinoidea

Common names: burying, carrion beetles

.764 3   *Cucujoidea

Class Colydioidea (consisting of families now usually considered part of Cucujoidea) in 595.769

.764 4   *Cantharoidea

Common names: fireflies, glowworms, soldier beetle

.764 5   *Dryopoidea

.764 6   Dascilloidea and Histeroidea

.764 7   *Tenebrionoidea

.764 8   *Chrysomeloidea and Cerambycoidea

Common name: leaf, wood-boring beetle

.764 9   *Scarabaeoidea

Common names: dung, June, stag beetle; rose chafers

.765   *Elateroidea

Common names: wireworms, click beetle

.767   *Meloidea and Mordelloidea

Common names: blister, tumbling flower beetle

.768   *Curculionoidea (Snout beetles)

Common name: bark beetle

Class here Curculionidae (weevils)

*Add as instructed under 592–599

.769   *Colydioidea

         Examples: Colydiidae (cylindrical bark beetles), Coccinellidae (ladybugs)

         Now usually considered part of Cucujoidea (595.7643)

.77   *Diptera and Siphonaptera

.771   *Orthorrhapha

         Examples: Bombyliidae, Chironomidae, Culicidae, Psychodidae, Sciaridae, Simuliidae, Stratiomyidae, Tabanidae

         Common names: gnats, midges, mosquitoes; bee, black, crane, dance, deer, hairy, horse, humpbacked, long-legged, March, moth, mydas, robber, snipe, soldier, stiletto, wood-boring flies

.774   *Cyclorrhapha

         Examples: Agromyzidae, Chyromyiidae, Drosophilidae, Ephydridae, Glossinidae, Muscidae, Sciomyzidae, Tachinidae

         Common names: bee lice; aphid, bat, bat tick, blow, bot, dung, flesh, fruit, house, leaf, miner, louse, rust, seashore, shore, skipper, spiny-legged, stable, stalk-eyed, sun, tachina, tsetse, vinegar, warble, wasp flies

.775   *Siphonaptera (Fleas)

.78   *Lepidoptera

.781   *Moths

         Examples: Bombycoidea, Geometroidea, Noctuoidea, Pyralididoidea, Tineoidea, Tortricoidea

.784   *Hesperiodea (Skippers)

.789   *Papilionoidea (Butterflies)

.79   *Hymenoptera

         Class here Apocrita, wasps

         Examples: Chalcidoidea, Ichneumonoidea, Symphyta (Sawflies)

.796   *Formicidea (Ants)

.798   *Scolioidea, Spehecoidea, Vespoidea

         Including true wasps

.799   *Apoidea (Bees)

596   Vertebrata (Craniata, Vertebrates)

         Class here Chordata

         For cold-blooded vertebrates, see 597; Aves, 598; Mammalia, 599

.001–.006   Standard subdivisions

*Add as instructed under 592–599

.007	Education, research, related topics
.007 4	Museums, collections, exhibits

Class vertebrate zoological gardens in 590.744

.008	History and description with respect to kinds of persons
.009	Historical, geographical, persons treatment of the study of Vertebrata

Class geographical treatment of Vertebrata in 596.09

.01–.08   Processes and parts

Add to base number 596.0 the numbers following 591 in 591.1–591.8, e.g., comparative anatomy 596.04

.09   Geographical treatment of Vertebrata

Add to base number 596.09 the numbers following 574.9 in 574.909–574.999, e.g., desert vertebrates 596.090954

.2   ***Urochordata (Tunicata)**

Contains Ascidiacea (sea squirts), Larvacea, Thaliacea

.4   ***Cephalochordata (Lancelets)**

597   Cold-blooded vertebrates   Pisces (Fishes)

Class here ichthyology

SUMMARY

597.001–.009	Standard subdivisions
.01–.09	[Processes and parts, geographical treatment of Pisces]
.2	Agnatha (Cyclostomata)
.3	Chondrichthyes (Cartilaginous fishes)
.4	Chondrostei, Holostei, Sarcopterygii
.5	Teleostei (Fully-boned fishes)
.6	Amphibia
.7	Gymnophiona (Apoda, Caecilians)
.8	Anura (Salientia)
.9	Reptilia

.001–.008   Standard subdivisions of cold-blooded vertebrates, of Pisces, of ichthyology

.009   Historical, geographical, persons treatment of cold-blooded vertebrates, of ichthyology

Class geographical treatment of Pisces in 597.09

.01–.08   Processes and parts of Pisces

Add to base number 597.0 the numbers following 591 in 591.1–591.8, e.g., biological rhythms 597.01882

.09   Geographical treatment of Pisces

.092   Hydrographic zoology of Pisces   Marine Pisces

*Add as instructed under 592–599

.092 1–.092 8   Marine Pisces

> Add to base number 597.092 the numbers following 551.46 in 551.461–551.468, e.g., fish of Indian Ocean 597.0927; however, class Antarctic waters of Atlantic Ocean in 597.0924, of Pacific Ocean in 597.09258, of Indian Ocean in 597.0927; comprehensive works on Antarctic waters in 597.0924

> Class marine Pisces of specific continents, countries, localities in 597.093–597.099

.092 9   Fresh-water Pisces

> Add to base number 597.0929 notation 1 or 3–9 from Table 2, e.g., fresh-water fish of New Hampshire 597.0929742

.093–.099   Treatment by specific continents, countries, localities

> Class here comprehensive works on marine and fresh-water Pisces of specific continents, countries, localities; marine Pisces of specific continents, countries, localities

> Add to base number 597.09 notation 3–9 from Table 2, e.g., fish of Brazil 597.0981

> Class fresh-water Pisces of specific continents, countries, localities in 597.0929

.2   *Agnatha (Cyclostomata)

> Common names: hagfish, lampreys

>   597.3–597.5 Pisces (Fishes)

> Class comprehensive works in 597

.3   *Chondrichthyes (Cartilaginous fishes)

>   597.31–597.35 Elasmobranchii

> Class comprehensive works in 597.3

.31   *Squaliformes (Sharks)

.35   *Rajiformes (Batoidea)

> Common names: guitarfish, rays, sawfish, skates, torpedoes

.38   *Holocephali (Chimeras)

.4   Chondrostei, Holostei, Sarcopterygii

> Class here Ganoidei

>   597.41–597.44 Ganoidei

> Class comprehensive works in 597.4

*Add as instructed under 592–599

.41   *Amiiformes (Bowfins, river dogfishes)

Class here Holostei (bony ganoids)

For Semionotiformes, see 597.47

.42   *Polypteriformes

Common names: birchir, reedfish

.44   *Acipenseriformes (Cartilaginous ganoids)

Class here Chondrostei

Common names: paddlefishes, spoonbill, sturgeon

.46   *Crossopterygii (Lobe-finned fishes)

Class here coelacanths

.47   *Semionotiformes (Gars)

Class here Lepisosteidae

.48   *Dipnoi (Lungfishes)

Contains Ceratodiformes, Lepidosireniformes

Class here Sarcopterygii (fleshy-finned fishes)

For Crossopterygii, see 597.46

.5   ***Teleostei (Fully-boned fishes)**

Class here Actinopterygii, Osteichthyes

For Chondrostei, Holostei, Sarcopterygii, see 597.4

.51   *Elopomorpha

Former heading: Apodes (Morays and true eels)

Contains Anguilliformes (Eels), Elopiformes, Notacanthiformes

.52   *Ostariophysi

Contains Cypriniformes, Siluriformes

Common names: barbel, carp, catfish, characin, chub, electric eel, goldfish, loach, minnow, piranha, suckers, tetras

For mudminnow, topminnow, see 597.53

*Add as instructed under 592–599

.53   Atheriniformes (Cyprinodontes and Synentognathi), Esocoidei
             (Haplomi), Gasterosteiformes (Thoracostei), *Paracanthopterygii

             Former heading: Mesichthyes

             Paracanthopterygii contains Batrachoidiformes, Gadiformes,
             Gobiesociformes, Lophiiformes, Percopsiformes, Polymixiformes

             Common names: anglerfish, clingfish, cod, cusk, flying fish, frogfish,
             grenadier, haddock, halfbeak, hake, killifish, mudminnow, needlefish, pike,
             pipefish, pirate perch, pollack, seahorses, silversides, stickleback, toadfish,
             topminnow, whiting

             Scopelomorpha (Iniomi) relocated to 597.55

.55   Scopelomorpha (Iniomi) [*formerly* 597.53], Clupeiformes (Isospondyli),
             Gonorynchiformes, Mormyriformes, Osteoglossiformes, Salmoniformes

             Common names: anchovy, arapaima, butterfly fish, grayling, herring, knife
             fish, lantern fish, lizard fish, mooneyes, salmon, sardines, smelts, tarpon,
             trout, whitefish

             For Esocoidei (pikes and mudminnows), see 597.53

.58   *Acanthopterygii   Perciformes

             Contains Beryciformes, Channiformes, Dactylopteriformes, Lampriformes,
             Pegasiformes, Pleuronectiformes, Scorpaeniformes, Synbranchiformes,
             Tetraodontiformes, Zeiformes

             Common names: albacore, angelfish, archerfish, barracuda, bass, blenny,
             bluefish, boarfish, bonito, bream, butterfish, cichlid, crappie, croaker,
             damselfish, darter, dory, dragonfish, drum, fingerfish, flatfish, flounder,
             goby, gourami, grouper, grunt, gunnel, gurnard, halfmoon, halibut, jack,
             jawfish, John Dory, leaf fish, mackerel, marlin, moonfish, mudskipper,
             mullet, parrot fish, perch, pilot fish, pomfret, pompano, porgy, puffer,
             redfish, remora, rockfish, sailfish, sand eel, sand lance, scad, scat, scorpion
             fish, sculpin, Siamese fighting fish, snakehead, snapper, snook, sole,
             squirrelfish, stonefish, sunfish, sweep, swordfish, triggerfish, tuna, turbot,
             walleye, weever, wrasse, yellowtail fish

             For Atheriniformes, Gasterosteiformes, see 597.53

.6   ***Amphibia**

             Class here herpetology, land vertebrates, Tetrapoda

             *For Gymnophiona, see 597.7; Anura, 597.8; Reptilia, 597.9; Aves, 598;
             Mammalia, 599*

.607 4   Museums, collections, exhibits

                Class zoological gardens in 590.744

.65   *Caudata (Urodela)

             Contains Amblystomoidea, Cryptobranchoidea, Salamandroidea, Sirenoidea

             Common names: mud puppies, newts, salamanders

.7   ***Gymnophiona (Apoda, Caecilians)**

*Add as instructed under 592–599

.8　　　***Anura (Salientia)***

Class here comprehensive works on frogs and toads

.83　　　*Leiopelmatidae

Former heading: Amphicocoela

.84　　　*Discoglossoidea and Pipoidea

Former heading: Opisthocoela

Including Pipidae

For Leiopelmatidae, see 597.83

.85　　　*Pelobatoidea

Former heading: Anomocoela

.87　　　*Bufonoidea

Former heading: Procoela

Examples: Brachycephalidae, Bufonidae (toads), Centrolendae (leaf frogs), Dendrobatidae (poison frogs), Hylidae (tree frogs), Leptodactylidae

.89　　　*Ranoidea

Former heading: Diplasiocoela

Contains Hyperoliidae, Ranidae (True frogs), Rhacophoridae

.9　　　***Reptilia***

.92　　　*Testudines (Chelonia)

Contains Cryptodira, Pleurodira

Common names: tortoises, turtles

.94　　　*Lepidosauria

Class here Squamata

For Sauria, see 597.95; Serpentes, 597.96

.945　　　*Rhynchocephalia (Tuataras)

.95　　　*Sauria

Common name: lizards

.96　　　*Serpentes (Snakes)

.98　　　*Crocodilia

Common names: alligators, crocodiles

*Add as instructed under 592–599

598   Aves (Birds)

Class here ornithology

Class comprehensive works on warm-blooded vertebrates in 599

SUMMARY

598.01–.09	**[Standard subdivisions, rare and endangered birds]**
.2	**Processes and parts, geographical treatment**
.3	**Gruiformes, Charadriiformes, Ciconiiformes**
.4	**Anseriformes and other water birds**
.5	**Palaeognathae**
.6	**Galliformes and Columbiformes**
.7	**Psittaciformes, Piciformes, Trogoniformes, Cuculiformes, Coliiformes**
.8	**Passeriformes, Coraciiformes, Apodiformes**
.9	**Falconiformes, Strigiformes, Caprimulgiformes**

.04   Special topics

.042   Rare and endangered birds

Including birds that have recently become extinct

.072   Research

.072 3   Descriptive research

.072 32   Birdbanding and census taking

.072 34   Bird watching

Add to base number 598.07234 notation 1 or 3–9 from Table 2, e.g., bird watching in East Africa 598.07234676

.09   Historical, geographical, persons treatment of ornithology

Class geographical treatment of Aves in 598.29

.2   Processes and parts, geographical treatment

.21–.28   Processes and parts

Add to base number 598.2 the numbers following 591 in 591.1–591.8, e.g., birdsong 598.259; however, class rare and endangered birds in 598.042

.29   Geographical treatment of Aves

.291   Treatment by areas, regions, places in general

Add to base number 598.291 the numbers following —1 in notation 11–18 from Table 2, e.g., forest birds 598.29152; however, class land birds in 598.2922, water birds in 598.2924, shore birds in 598.33

.292   Special groupings

Class treatment of special groupings by specific continents, countries, localities in 598.293–598.299

.292 2   Land birds

Class specific land birds in 598.5–598.9

.292 4   Water birds

Class specific water birds in 598.3–598.4

.293–.299 Treatment by specific continents, countries, localities

> Add to base number 598.29 notation 3–9 from Table 2, e.g., birds of Mexico 598.2972

> **598.3–598.4 Water birds**

Class comprehensive works in 598.2924

.3 Gruiformes, Charadriiformes, Ciconiiformes

.31 *Gruiformes

Contains Cariamae, Eurypygae, Grues, Heliornithes, Mesitornithides, Otides, Rhynocheti, Turnices

Common names: bustards, coots, cranes, gallinules, limpkins, rails, trumpeters

.33 *Charadriiformes

Examples: Alcidae, Charadriidae, Recurvirostridae, Scolopacidae

Common names: auks, avocets, curlews, jacanas, murres, oyster catchers, phalaropes, plovers, puffins, sandpipers, snipe, stilts, turnstones, woodcock

Class here Charadrii (shore birds)

.338 *Laridae

Common names: gulls, skimmers, terns

.34 *Ciconiiformes

Contains Ardeae, Balaenicipites, Ciconiae, Phoenicopteri

Common names: bitterns, egrets, flamingos, herons, ibises, spoonbills, storks

.4 Anseriformes and other water birds

.41 *Anseriformes

Contains Anatidae (waterfowl), Anhimidae

Common names: ducks, geese, mergansers, screamers, swans

.42 *Procellariiformes

Contains Diomedeidae, Hydrobatidae, Pelecanoididae, Procellaridae

Common names: albatrosses, fulmars, petrels, shearwaters

.43 *Pelecaniformes

Contains Fregatae, Odontopteryges, Pelecani, Phaëthontes

Common names: boobies, cormorants, darters, frigate birds, gannets, pelicans, snakebirds, tropic birds

.44 Sphenisciformes, Gaviiformes, Podicipediformes

*Add as instructed under 592–599

.441	*Sphenisciformes (Penguins)
.442	*Gaviiformes (Loons)
.443	*Podicipediformes (Colymbiformes)

Common name: grebes

> **598.5–598.9 Land birds**

Class comprehensive works in 598.2922

.5	***Palaeognathae**

Class here ratites

.51	*Struthioniformes (Ostriches)
.52	*Rheiformes (Rheas)
.53	*Casuariiformes (Cassowaries and emus)
.54	*Apterygiformes (Kiwis)
.55	*Tinamiformes (Tinamous)
.6	**Galliformes and Columbiformes**
.61	*Galliformes *Galli

For Opisthocomi, see 598.64

.612	*Megapodiidae

Common name: brush turkey

.614	*Cracidae

Common names: chachalacas, curassows, guans

.616	*Tetraonidae (Grouse)

Including prairie chickens

.617	*Phasianidae

Common names: domestic chickens, partridges, peafowl, pheasants, quail

.618	*Numididae (Guinea fowl)
.619	*Meleagrididae (Turkeys)
.64	*Opisthocomi (Hoatzins)
.65	*Columbiformes

Contains Columbae, Pterocletes

Common names: dodos, doves, pigeons, sand grouse, solitaries

.7	**Psittaciformes, Piciformes, Trogoniformes, Cuculiformes, Coliiformes**

*Add as instructed under 592–599

.71	*Psittaciformes

Common names: budgerigars, cockatoos, lories, macaws, parakeets, parrots

.72	*Piciformes

Contains Galbulae, *Pici

Common names: barbets, honey guides, jacamars, piculets, puffbirds, toucans, woodpeckers

.73	*Trogoniformes
.74	*Cuculiformes

Contains Cuculi, Musophagi

Common names: anis, cuckoos, plantain eaters, roadrunners, touracos

For Opisthocomi (Hoatzins), see 598.64

.75	*Coliiformes
.8	***Passeriformes, Coraciiformes, Apodiformes**

Examples: bell magpies, cuckoo shrikes, magpie larks, pepper shrikes, plush-capped finches, shrike-vireos, swallow tanagers, vanga shrikes, wattled crows, wood shrikes, wood swallows

---

>	598.81–598.88 Passeriformes (Passerine, Perching birds)

Class comprehensive works in 598.8

Use 598.8 for Oscines (Songbirds)

See Manual at 598.81–598.88

.81	Tyrannidae, Alaudidae, Hirundinidae
.811	*Tyrannidae (Tyrant flycatchers)
.812	*Alaudidae (Larks)

Use 598.8 for magpie larks

.813	*Hirundinidae

Common names: martins, swallows

Use 598.8 for wood swallows

.82	Sittidae, Certhiidae, Paridae
.822	*Sittidae (Nuthatches)
.823	*Certhiidae (Creepers)
.824	*Paridae (Titmice)

Including chickadees

.83	Cinclidae, Troglodytidae, Chamaeidae

*Add as instructed under 592–599

.832	*Cinclidae (Dippers and water ouzels)
.833	*Troglodytidae (Wrens)
.834	*Chamaeidae (Wren-tits)
.84	Mimidae, Turdidae, Sylviidae
.841	*Mimidae

Common names: catbirds, mockingbirds, thrashers

.842	*Turdidae (Thrushes)

Common names: cochoas, forktails, robins (American)

.843	*Sylviidae (Old World warblers)
.85	Bombycillidae, Ptilogonatidae, Motacillidae
.852	*Bombycillidae (Waxwings)
.853	*Ptilogonatidae (Silky flycatchers)
.854	*Motacillidae (Pipits and wagtails)
.86	Laniidae, Sturnidae, Corvudae, Paradisaeidae
.862	*Laniidae (Shrikes)

Use 598.8 for cuckoo shrikes, pepper shrikes, shrike-vireos, vanga shrikes, wood shrikes

.863	*Sturnidae (Starlings)
.864	*Corvidae

Common names: crows, jays, magpies, ravens, rooks

Use 598.8 for bell magpies, magpie larks, wattled crows

.865	*Paradisaeidae (Birds of paradise)
.87	Vireonidae, Parulidae, Ploceidae
.871	*Vireonidae (Vireos)

Use 598.8 for shrike-vireos

.872	*Parulidae (Wood warblers)
.873	*Ploceidae (Weaverbirds and weaver finches)

Including sparrows of the genus Passer, e.g., English sparrows, house sparrows

.88	Icteridae, Thraupidae, Fringillidae
.881	*Icteridae

Common names: blackbirds (American), cowbirds, meadowlarks, orioles, troupials

*Add as instructed under 592–599

| .882 | *Thraupidae (Tanagers) |

Use 598.8 for swallow tanagers

| .883 | *Fringillidae (Finches) |

Common names: buntings, canaries, cardinals, grosbeaks, sparrows

Use 598.8 for plush-capped finches, 598.873 for Passer sparrows

| .89 | Coraciiformes and Apodiformes |
| .892 | *Coraciiformes |

Examples: Alcedine, Bucerotidae, Corcaciidae, Meropidae

Common names: bee eaters, hoopoes, hornbills, kingfishers, motmots, rollers, todies

| .899 | *Apodiformes |

Contains Apodi (swifts), Trochili (hummingbirds)

.9   **Falconiformes, Strigiformes, Caprimulgiformes**

| .91 | *Falconiformes (Birds of prey) |
| .912 | *Cathartidae (New World vultures) |

Common names: condors; black, king, turkey vultures

| .915 | *Sagittariidae (Secretary birds) |
| .916 | *Accipitridae |

Common names: buteos, common or true buzzards, eagles, harriers, hawks, kites, Old World vultures

.917	*Pandionidae (Ospreys)
.918	*Falconidae (Falcons)
.97	*Strigiformes (Owls)
.99	*Caprimulgiformes

Contains Caprimulgi, Steatornithes

Common names: frogmouths, oilbirds, potoos

599   Mammalia (Mammals)

Class here warm-blooded vertebrates

For Aves, see 598

See Manual at 591; 591 vs. 610

*Add as instructed under 592–599

SUMMARY

599.001–.009   [Standard subdivisions, rare and endangered mammals]
        .01–.09   [Processes and parts, geographical treatment]
        .1   Monotremata
        .2   Marsupialia
        .3   Unguiculata
        .4   Chiroptera (Bats)
        .5   Cetacea and Sirenia
        .6   Paenungulata
        .7   Ferungulata and Tubulidentata
        .8   Primates
        .9   Hominidae (Humankind)

.001–.003   Standard subdivisions

.004   Special topics

.004 2   Rare and endangered mammals

Including mammals that have recently become extinct

.005–.006   Standard subdivisions

.007   Education, research, related topics

.007 4   Museums, collections, exhibits (AQUARIUMS – 639-34)

Class mammalian zoological gardens in 590.744

.008   History and description with respect to kinds of persons

.009   Historical, geographical, persons treatment of the study of Mammalia

Class geographical treatment of Mammalia in 599.09

.01–.08   Processes and parts

Add to base number 599.0 the numbers following 591 in 591.1–591.8, e.g., physiology of nervous system 599.0188; however, class rare and endangered mammals in 599.0042

See Manual at 599.03

.09   Geographical treatment of mammals

Add to base number 599.09 the numbers following 574.9 in 574.909–574.999, e.g., desert mammals 599.090954; however, class marine mammals in 599.5

.1   *Monotremata

Common names: platypuses, spiny anteaters (echidnas)

Class here Prototheria

.2   *Marsupialia

Contains Diprotodontia, Marsupicarnivora, Paucituberculata, Permelina

Common names: bandicoots, kangaroos, koalas, opossum rats, opossums, phalangers, Tasmanian devils, Tasmanian wolves, wallabies, wombats

*Add as instructed under 592–599

.3 ***Unguiculata**

For Chiroptera, see 599.4; Primates, 599.8

.31   *Edentata and *Pholidota

Common names: anteaters, armadillos, pangolins, sloths

.32   *Glires

.322   *Lagomorpha

Common names: hares, rabbits, pikas

.323   *Rodentia (Rodents)

.323 2   *Sciuromorpha

Common names: beavers, chipmunks, kangaroo mice, kangaroo rats, marmots, pocket gophers, pocket mice, prairie dogs, sewellels, springhaas, squirrels, woodchucks

.323 3   *Myomorpha

Common names: hamsters, dormice, gerbils, jerboas, lemmings, mice, muskrats, rats, voles

.323 4   *Hystricomorpha

Common names: agoutis, capybaras, cavies, chinchillas, coypus, guinea pigs, gundis, hutias, mole rats, nutria, pacas, porcupines, rock rats, spiny rats

Class here Caviomorpha

.33   *Insectivora

Common names: desmans, hedgehogs, moles, shrews, solenodons, tenrecs

.34   *Dermoptera (Flying lemurs)

.4 ***Chiroptera (Bats)**

Contains Megachiroptera, Microchiroptera

.5 ***Cetacea and Sirenia**

Class here marine mammals, whales

For Pinnipedia, see 599.745

.51   *Mysticeti (Baleen whales)

Common names: finbacks, rorquals; blue, gray, humpback, right whales

.53   *Odontoceti (Toothed whales)

Common names: belugas, cowfish, dolphins, narwhals, porpoises; beaked, killer, pilot, sperm, white whales

.55   *Sirenia (Sea cows)

Common names: dugongs, manatees

*Add as instructed under 592–599

.6 *Paenungulata

> *For Sirenia, see 599.55*

.61   *Proboscidea (Elephants)

.62   *Hyracoidea

> Common names: conies, dassies, hyraxes

.7 Ferungulata and Tubulidentata

> *For Paenungulata, see 599.6*

.72   *Perissodactyla

.725   *Equidae

> Common names: asses, horses, zebras

.727   *Tapiridae (Tapirs)

.728   *Rhinocerotidae (Rhinoceroses)

.73   *Artiodactyla

.734   *Suiformes

> Common names: boars, hippopotamuses, peccaries, pigs, swine, warthogs

.735   *Ruminantia (Ruminants)

.735 5   *Traguloidea (Chevrotains)

.735 7   *Cervoidea and *Giraffoidea

> Common names: caribou, deer, elk, moose, reindeer, wapiti; giraffes, okapis

.735 8   *Bovoidea

> Common names: antelopes, bison, buffaloes, cattle, duikers, elands, gazelles, goats, hartebeests, kudus, musk oxen, oryx, oxen, sheep, wildebeests, yaks, zebus

.736   *Tylopoda

> Common names: alpacas, camels, guanacos, llamas, vicuñas

.74   *Carnivora

.744   *Fissipeda (Land carnivores)

.744 2   *Feloidea

.744 22   *Viverridae

> Common names: civets, fossa, genets, linsangs, mongooses

.744 26   *Protelinae (Aardwolves)

*Add as instructed under 592–599

.744 27		*Hyaenidae (Hyenas)
		For Protelinae, see 599.74426
.744 28		*Felidae (Cats)
		Common names: cheetahs, leopards, lions, ocelots
.744 4		*Canoidea
.744 42		*Canidae
		Common names: coyotes, dingoes, dogs, foxes, jackals, wolves
.744 43		*Procyonidae
		Common names: bassarisks, coatis, kinkajous, pandas, raccoons
.744 46		*Ursidae (Bears)
.744 47		*Mustelidae
		Common names: badgers, ferrets, martens, minks, otters, polecats, sables, skunks, weasels, wolverines
.745		*Pinnipedia (Marine carnivores)
		For specific families, see 599.746–599.748

> 599.746–599.748 Specific families of marine carnivores

Class comprehensive works in 599.745

.746		*Otariidae (Eared seals)
		Common names: fur seals, sea bears, sea lions
.747		*Odobenidae (Walruses)
.748		*Phocidae (Earless seals)
		Common names: elephant seals, true seals
.75		*Tubulidentata (Aardvarks)
.8		***Primates**
.81		*Prosimii
		Examples: Lemuridae, Lorisidae, Tarsiidae
		Common names: aye-ayes, bush babies, galagos, indrises, lemurs, lorises, sifakas, tarsiers, tree shrews
.82		Cebidae (New World monkeys), Callithricidae, Cercopithecidae (Old World monkeys)
		Common names: baboons, marmosets, monkeys, tamarins

*Add as instructed under 592–599

.88   *Pongidae (Apes)

> Class here comprehensive works on Hominoidea
>
> *For Hominidae, see 599.9*

.882   *Hylobatinae

> Common names: gibbons, siamangs

.884   *Ponginae (Great apes)

.884 2   *Pongo (Orangutans)

.884 4   *Pan (Chimpanzees)

.884 6   *Gorilla

.9   Hominidae (Humankind)

> Use this number only for works treating both physical anthropology and at least one of the medical sciences (anatomy, physiology, medicine)
>
> *For physical anthropology, see 573; medicine, 610*

*Add as instructed under 592–599

The 20th edition of the Dewey Decimal Classification was designed by Lisa Hanifan of Albany, New York. Edition 20 is the first edition to be generated from an online database. Database design, technical support, and programming for this edition were provided by John J. Finni and Cora M. Arsenault from Inforonics, Inc., of Littleton, Massachusetts. Composition was done in Times Roman and Helvetica on a Linotronic L100 under the supervision of Inforonics, Inc. The book was printed and bound by Hamilton Printing Company of Rensselaer, New York.